W9-ADF-759

POEMS, POETS, POETRY

*An Introduction
and Anthology*

POEMS, POETS, POETRY

An Introduction and Anthology

Helen Vendler

HARVARD UNIVERSITY

Bedford Books *of* St. Martin's Press
Boston

FOR BEDFORD BOOKS

PRESIDENT AND PUBLISHER: Charles H. Christensen
GENERAL MANAGER AND ASSOCIATE PUBLISHER: Joan E. Feinberg
MANAGING EDITOR: Elizabeth M. Schaaf
DEVELOPMENTAL EDITOR: Stephen A. Scipione
EDITORIAL ASSISTANTS: Laura Arcari, Mark Reimold
PRODUCTION EDITOR: Ann Sweeney
PRODUCTION ASSISTANTS: Bill McKenna, Stasia Zomkowski, Ellen Thibault
COPYEDITOR: Maria Ascher
TEXT DESIGN: Anna George
COVER DESIGN: Sara Eisenman

Library of Congress Catalog Card Number: 95–80802

Copyright © 1997 by Bedford Books
A Division of St. Martin's Press, Inc.

All rights reserved. No part of this book may be reproduced, stored in a retrieval system, or transmitted by any form or by any means, electronic, mechanical, photocopying, recording, or otherwise, except as may be expressly permitted by the applicable copyright statutes or in writing by the Publisher.

Manufactured in the United States of America.

1 0 9 8 7
f e d c b a

For information, write: Bedford Books,
75 Arlington Street, Boston, MA 02116   (617–426–7440)

ISBN: 0–312–08537–0

Acknowledgments

Sherman Alexie, "Evolution" and "Reservation Love Song" reprinted from *The Business of Fancydancing* © 1992 by Sherman Alexie, by permission of Hanging Loose Press. "On the Amtrak from Boston to New York City" reprinted from *First Indian on the Moon* © 1993 by Sherman Alexie, by permission of Hanging Loose Press.

Elizabeth Alexander, "Nineteen" and "Ode" from *The Venus Hottentot,* by Elizabeth Alexander. Used by permission of the University Press of Virginia.

Paul Gunn Allen, "Zen Americana" reprinted from *Coyote's Daylight Trip.* Albuquerque: La Confluencia Press, © 1978. Reprinted by permission of the author.

Acknowledgments and copyrights are continued at the back of the book on pages 620–27, which constitute an extension of the copyright page. It is a violation of the law to reproduce these selections by any means whatsoever without the written permission of the copyright holder.

Preface: About This Book

This book offers ways to read and understand poems with the pleasure they deserve. Its nine chapters in Part I approach the poem from various directions, in the conviction that any artwork invites consideration from different perspectives. Chapter 1, "The Poem as Life," uses several short poems to show how a poetic utterance springs from a life-moment — sometimes a private one (falling in love), sometimes a public one (the decline of an aristocracy). Chapter 2, "The Poem as Arranged Life," considers the same poems that appear in Chapter 1, but this time treats them as arrangements, rather than as utterances; it asks why the poem takes the imaginative shape it does, and how its elements have been ordered. In Chapter 3, "Poems as Pleasure," aspects of poetry that give pleasure are mentioned and illustrated: formal aspects such as rhythm and rhyme, of course, but also construction and images; thematic aspects such as poignancy and wisdom, too, but in addition to these an individual personal language proper to each poet. Chapter 4, "Describing Poems," and Chapter 5, "The Play of Language," suggest some useful ways of describing poems — by the class of poems they belong to, by the little plots they act out through grammar and syntax, by the speech acts they engage in, by the agents they choose to do the work of the poem, and so on.

Chapter 6, "Constructing a Self," moves on to the psychological world of the poem. Since each poem is a fictive speech by an imagined speaker, how does the author make that speaker convincing? How is a credible self constructed on the page? The more abstract lyric self of Chapter 6 — ungendered, of no specified age or race, of no determined country — is contrasted, in Chapter 7, "Poetry and Social Identity," with the lyric self which is socially marked, as we encounter a speaker making clear her sex, or his race, or his age, or her sexual orientation. Our sense of the purpose and the audience of a poem depends to a great extent on how the self of the speaker is defined. Chapter 8, "History and Regionality," takes up the topics of time and space — the two great axes on which all literature turns — as they apply to lyric poetry. And finally, in Chapter 9, "Attitudes, Values, Judgments," the largest questions we can put to a literary work — questions about its attitudes, values, and judgments — are raised and discussed with respect to some crucial examples, old and new.

Each of these chapters takes up several poems by way of illustration, and each is followed by a section called "Reading Other Poems" that introduces a small group of poems which can be usefully read in the light of that chapter. These are usually short poems, and range from the canonical to the recent. The anthology of Part II that follows these nine chapters is intended to provide a wide sampling — more than 250 poems — from the literature of lyric, including some poems longer and more complex than those cited in the chapters. Arranged alphabetically by author, the anthology includes poems by more than a hundred poets, many of them represented in significant depth so as to suggest the range of an individual poet's work. Finally, my appendices on prosody, grammar, speech-acts, rhetorical devices, and lyric subgenres exist to provide further illustration of points taken up substantively but not exhaustively in individual chapters. They can help consolidate and extend — when assigned as home reading — the demonstrations given in class. I have also prepared a brief instructor's manual in which I discuss some of the issues of teaching poetry and suggest exercises that have, over the years, helped my students understand and appreciate poetry. The manual also comments on most of the poems in Part I that are not discussed in the text's nine chapters.

Acknowledgments

I'd like to thank all the reviewers who helped improve this book by their detailed and incisive suggestions, among them Charles Altieri, University of California, Berkeley; Paul Fry, Yale University; Vincent B. Leitch, Purdue University; Jeredith Merrin, Ohio State University; Robert Phillips, University of Houston; David Sofield, Amherst College;

Susan Schweik, University of California, Berkeley; and George Stade, Columbia University. I am grateful to Charles Christensen, Joan Feinberg, and Stephen Scipione at Bedford Books for their interest in this project, for their intuition about the shape it might take, and for their alert editorial guidance. I would also like to thank Elizabeth Schaaf, Ann Sweeney, Laura Arcari, Mark Reimold, Alanya Harter, Maria Ascher, Bill McKenna, and Stasia Zomkowski. I was assisted throughout by my graduate assistant, Nick Halpern, now of North Carolina State University, and by my administrative assistant, Susan Welby. Finally, I want to express my warmest gratitude to Sylvan Barnet, who first suggested I write such a book, who had faith in its completion, and who selflessly read, as a friend, every word. His detailed comments were invaluable; and his patient counsel, in the ups and downs of revision, was appreciated more than he will ever know and more than I can ever say.

About Poets
and Poetry

Poets possess two talents: one is imagination, the other is a mastery of language. Many people, writers and nonwriters alike, see the world imaginatively: to accompany such people to a party or an exhibition or a play is to see the event more keenly and more vividly than one might have done alone. The world takes on more color; things are seen from a new slant; events are freshly interpreted and highlighted; a vivacity of response is summoned up. With one sort of imaginative person, everything is seen more darkly: the guests at the party seem trivial, grotesque; the exhibition is tragic; the play is an emblem of despair. In the company of an imaginative person of a different sort, we see the world, as the cliché has it, through rose-colored glasses: people seem better, the world kinder, the cause for optimism stronger. In short, imaginative people have the gift of making others see the world as they see it. And as the poet Wallace Stevens put it, "Things seen are things as seen."

While many imaginative people are content to let their sense of the world, conveyed through conversation, vanish as they speak, writers feel compelled to set down their perceptions in writing. Writers often see the imagination, as Stevens saw it, as a "third planet." Just as a given scene looks one way in sunlight, another way in moonlight, so it looks yet a third way in the light of the imagination. "There's a certain slant of light," says Emily Dickinson; "In this blue light, I can take you there," promises Jorie Graham in "San Sepolcro." That is the implicit invitation offered by all writers: that you will see things in a new light, the light of their construction of the world.

We read imaginative works — whether epic, fiction, drama, or poetry — in order to gain a wider sense of the real. Our hunger to know the world, born with us and eager in childhood, finds one of its chief satisfactions in learning about the responses of others. Of course we are pleased to learn that others share our views, but we are also keenly interested to find out that others see the real differently from ourselves. This is partly a matter of temperament (say, mournful versus humorous), partly a matter of experience (male versus female, young versus old), partly an accidental matter of what happens in a writer's historical epoch (war versus peace). Some forms of literature (we can call them the social genres), such as epic, fiction, and drama, make us look at the wide panorama of a social group — a nation, a village, a family. Though all of the social genres used to be written in poetry (Milton, Chaucer, Shakespeare), nowadays the social world is usually observed through prose. We know one America through the eyes of Herman Melville, another through Edith Wharton, yet another through Ralph Ellison. Each of them induces us to live for a while in the light of a fresh imagining of the United States. And in addition to an imaginative view of America, each of these writers has a mastery of language — Melville's encyclopedic and torrential language of whaling. Wharton's fastidious language of social difference, and Ellison's brooding and intense intellectual language of the "invisible man."

But besides the narrative and dramatic social genres, there exists the large body of poetry we call lyric. Lyric is the genre of private life: it is what we say to ourselves when we are alone. Thee may be an addressee in lyric (God, or a beloved), but the addressee is always absent. (The dramatic monologue, a form Browning made famous, has a silent addressee on stage, but this is the exception to the rule of the absent addressee.) In a way, imagination is at its most unfettered in lyric because the writer need not give a recognizable portrait of society, as the novelist or dramatist must. Because the lyric represents a moment of inner meditation, it is relatively short, and always exists in a particular place — "here" — and a particular time — "now." It may speak about the there and then, but it speaks about them from the here and now. It lets us into the innermost chamber of another person's mind, and makes us privy to what he or she would say in complete secrecy and safety, with none to overhear.

The diary is the nearest prose equivalent to the lyric, but a diary is seen by a reader as the words of another person, whereas a lyric is meant to be spoken by its reader as if the reader were the one uttering the words. A lyric poem is a script for performance by its reader. It is, then, the most intimate of genres, constructing a twinship between writer and reader. And it is the most universal of genres, because it presumes that that reader resembles the writer enough to step into the writer's shoes and speak the lines the writer has written as though they were the reader's own:

> Two roads diverged in a yellow wood,
> And sorry I could not travel both
> And be one traveler, long I stood
> And looked down one as far as I could
> To where it bent in the undergrowth.
>
> —ROBERT FROST, "The Road Not Taken"

To read these lines is to be transformed into the hesitating speaker. We do not listen to him; we become him.

Sometimes, of course, the speaker is more narrowly specified, as a certain type of person or even as an individual. Yet even when there is a clear disparity of personal character — as when I, a twentieth-century white American woman, am reading Blake's lyric spoken by a little black boy in eighteenth-century England — the lyric poet expects that I will put myself into the subject-position of the little black boy, and make the boy's words my own. Though some theorists have suggested that we "overhear" the speaker of lyric (making lyric into a kind of monodrama of which we are the audience), it is more often true that I do not, as a disinterested spectator, overhear the lyric speaker: rather, the words of the speaker become my own words. This imaginative transformation of self is what is offered to us by the lyric.

Because lyric is a short form (unlike the epic or the verse-tale), it must be more concise than narrative or drama. Every word has to count. So does every gap. In fact, lyric depends on gaps, and depends even more on the reader to fill in the gaps. It is suggestive rather than exhaustive. As the poet W. B. Yeats said in a 1925 letter, referring to *Hamlet* (but perhaps with his own writing of lyric in mind), "Tell a little & he is Hamlet; tell all & he is nothing. Nothing has life except the incomplete." In the following pages, suggestions are made on how to go about exploring a lyric, in order to fill in its gaps and make the most of its hints, so that the course of its emotions can be understood in their full subtlety.

Even though lyric sometimes makes greater demands on us than do the more explicit genres, a poem always (if it is successful) attracts us enough to make us willing to bear with it while we try to understand it

better. A poem, said Coleridge, can communicate while it is still im-
perfectly understood. It can communicate because it exhibits a mastery
of language, in addition to an imaginative sense of the world. We are
drawn in by words used in unusual and compelling ways — ways that
appeal to the senses of sight and hearing and bodily tension, as well as to
the mind. We are also drawn in by the architecture of the poem — the
manner in which its parts are arranged, so as to make a structure that
reflects emotional intensity. We are drawn in by its volatility and its
surprising resources of strategy. And finally, we are drawn in because
every poem enters into a continuing conversation with its culture —
querying it, amplifying it, rebelling against it, subverting it, aestheticiz-
ing it, enhancing it. Robert Frost, in "The Gift Outright," says that
when the English came to the American continent, they found a land
"still unstoried, artless, unenhanced." Our present anthropological
awareness means that no twentieth-century poet could think of the
America of the Puritans as "unstoried" or "artless": the various and
widespread Native American cultures had already covered the American
continent with stories and with arts. The aim of every artist, then and
now, is to contribute those stories, that art, and enhancement that will
endow both place and time with significance.

Lyric has recently undergone, in the United States, many signifi-
cant changes. Twentieth-century America is a far more heterogeneous
country than pre-twentieth-century England, and contemporary Amer-
ican lyric naturally reflects its own culture and epoch. The availability of
translations means that an American poet is now almost as likely to be
influenced by a Polish or South American poet — Czeslaw Milosz or
Pablo Neruda — as by an English or American poet. Lyric speakers are
more ready to define themselves sexually, ethnically, or racially; yet lyric
still hopes for the reader's willingness to place himself or herself in the
writer's subject-position. Because the dominant influence on a medium
is always the medium itself as it has existed through time, the dominant
influence on English-language verse is still English as it has been used by
preceding poets. That is why one is unlikely to read contemporary
poetry well without having read the poetry of England from which it
descends. The selections here are all in English (lyric poetry being no-
toriously untranslatable) and are divided between poems that have stood
up well over time, and other, more recent poems which, while they may
reflect some long-continuing concerns in American life (racism, war,
religious faith) also take on new modes, in both content (Adrienne
Rich's feminism, W. S. Merwin's ecological concern) and style (the
reticence of Elizabeth Bishop, the dream-idiom of John Berryman, the
"snapshots" of Robert Lowell).

Like all arts, lyric is meant to give pleasure — imaginative, linguistic, intellectual, and moral. If one hasn't enjoyed a poem and been moved by it, one hasn't really experienced it as an artwork. There are moments in life when one poem suits and another doesn't. The poems in this book will not invariably please everybody, because each of us brings a unique life-experience, and a different expectation of art, to the page. Nonetheless, many of these poems have won and kept readers because in them readers have found the most moving revelation of all — that of their own inner life, enacted in words adequate to both sorrow and joy. The rule of thumb for the encounter with any art is to dwell on what moves you or gives you pleasure, and skip over, for the time being, what leaves you cold. But if you remember that someone, somewhere, has been fiercely attracted by each of these poems, you may be willing to give the ones you first neglect a second chance. Often, a door that has been shut can open marvelously at the second knock.

Contents

3.   Poems as Pleasure   67

6.   Constructing a Self   *171*

9.   Attitudes, Values, Judgments   *283*

Part II
Anthology   *309*

Appendices   *593*

POEMS, POETS, POETRY

*An Introduction
and Anthology*

I

POEMS, POETS, POETRY
An Introduction

1

The Poem as Life

Poems have their origins in life, especially in the formal or informal ceremonies that occur at crucial moments or phases in a single private life — birth, adolescence, marriage, death — or at public moments when we collectively commemorate a war, a religious feast, a holiday. Equally, poems show life lived in a spatial environment, whether immediate (one's house, one's region) or cosmic (the world, the galaxy); they also show seasonal or ritual moments of time. The first questions to ask of any poem are *What piece of life, private or public, is it concerned with?* and *Where and when is this life being lived?*

Of course, cliché haunts all the well-known and well-worn occasions of life. In the occasions of private life shown us by greeting cards or popular magazines, babies are "lovable," brides are "beautiful," fiftieth wedding anniversaries are "happy"; in the public life, cliché tells us that young men should fight in war, that cities are thriving communities, and that Americans should take pride in their country's history. We are also accustomed to clichés of time and space, often hearing, for example, that the springtime of life leads only to the narrow space of the grave. As we trace some of these crucial aspects of life through poems, the first thing to notice is how the poet manages to avoid cliché — how he or she brings originality to the moment. We look in this chapter at a sample of several poems, the first group representing events in private life, the second group chiefly taking up moments in public life, and the third group expressing some place in space or some moment in the natural seasons of Time. In Chapter 2 we will look again at the same poems, to see how they are not only representations of life but also works of art.

The Private Life

"Write a poem about a birth," says the culture to the poet; and what the poet writes (speaking in the person of a newborn baby) may shock the reader:

WILLIAM BLAKE
Infant Sorrow

My mother groaned, my father wept —
Into the dangerous world I leapt,
Helpless, naked, piping loud,
Like a fiend hid in a cloud.

Struggling in my father's hands,
Striving against my swaddling bands,
Bound and weary, I thought best
To sulk upon my mother's breast.

Precisely because our culture does not usually say that a baby resembles "a fiend hid in a cloud," we find the poem arresting. It makes us stop and think. Now let us look at the next phase of life, childhood.

The child's first day of school is an event marked by conventional behavior (new clothes, an apple for the teacher, says the cliché). Louise Glück has written a poem about how a mother feels seeing her child go off into the power of a new authority, who may or may not be kind to the child:

LOUISE GLÜCK
The School Children

The children go forward with their little satchels.
And all morning the mothers have labored
to gather the late apples, red and gold,
like words of another language.

And on the other shore
are those who wait behind great desks
to receive these offerings.

How orderly they are — the nails
on which the children hang
their overcoats of blue or yellow wool.

And the teachers shall instruct them in silence
and the mothers shall scour the orchards for a way out,
drawing to themselves the gray limbs of the fruit trees
bearing so little ammunition.

The new clothes and the apples for the teacher are here, but they have
been made strangely sinister. Once again, the reader is made to stop and
think. What is so disturbing about this poem?

Next, the child comes to the apparently quiet period between
infancy and puberty, a period psychologists call "latency" because sex-
uality seems dormant. At this time, intense same-sex friendships form;
the child is never seen without his or her "best friend," so much so that
Eddie and Bill become a single noun: "Have you seen EddieandBill?"
But gradually hormones change Eddie and Bill into adolescents, and the
pagan god of sex (whom E. E. Cummings here identifies with goat-
footed Pan, the god of all) makes his appearance. We know that in
heterosexual development the twosomes "eddieandbill" and "betty-
andisbel," so inseparable, will soon, with real anguish and yet with
painful anticipation of sexual joy, split up, leave their childish games,
and re-form into the new twosomes "eddieandbetty" and "billandis-
bel":

E. E. CUMMINGS
in Just-

spring   when the world is mud-
luscious the little
lame balloonman

whistles   far   and wee

and eddieandbill come
running from marbles and
piracies and it's
spring

when the world is puddle-wonderful

the queer
old balloonman whistles
far   and   wee
and bettyandisbel come dancing

from hop-scotch and jump-rope and
it's
spring
and

    the
        goat-footed
balloonMan   whistles
far
and
wee

The reader senses something threatening and seductive in the balloon-
man, and knows that this is not a simple poem about spring hop-scotch
and jump-rope. Also, the typographic arrangement is puzzling. What is
Cummings up to?

The young man or woman will experiment with love, and will dis-
cover that there is something inherent in many relationships which makes
them dissolve. As adolescents take their first step into adult emotional re-
lations, they learn what it is to be troubled in love, even forsaken. This
is a love poem by Walt Whitman to a male lover who has deserted him,
but it soon turns into a poem for everyone who has been deserted:

WALT WHITMAN
Hours Continuing Long

Hours continuing long, sore and heavy hearted,
Hours of the dusk, when I withdraw to a lonesome and unfre-
    quented spot, seating myself, leaning my face in my hands;
Hours sleepless, deep in the night, when I go forth, speeding
    swiftly the country roads, or through the city streets, or
    pacing miles and miles, stifling plaintive cries;
Hours discouraged, distracted — for the one I cannot content
    myself without, soon I saw him content himself without
    me;
Hours when I am forgotten (O weeks and months are passing,
    but I believe I am never to forget!)
Sullen and suffering hours! (I am ashamed — but it is use-
    less — I am what I am;)
Hours of my torment — I wonder if other men ever have the
    like, out of the like feelings?
Is there even one other like me — distracted — his friend, his
    lover, lost to him?
Is he too as I am now? Does he still rise in the morning, de-

jected, thinking who is lost to him? and at night, awaking,
     think who is lost?
Does he too harbor his friendship silent and endless? harbor his
     anguish and passion?
Does some stray reminder, or the casual mention of a name,
     bring the fit back upon him, taciturn and deprest?
Does he see himself reflected in me? In these hours, does he see
     the face of his hours reflected?

The phases of life succeed one another, and we could go on to give
examples of poems about parenting, maturity, loss, and old age. Poems,
in short, trace the general and special phases of life down to its end in
death, and, in religious poems, even to the afterlife. Each of these phases
can provoke many different responses — joy, bitterness, bravery, sto-
icism. Here, for instance, is a seventeenth-century poem about the last
phase of life by a writer who, to his grief, has grown too dim of sight to
read or write; but he will never be too old, he says, to think and perceive
and praise God. With the last power of his failing eyesight, he "indites,"
or writes, the final poem in his manuscript book: a poem of thanksgiv-
ing. He is able to do so because its subject — the praise of God — turns
him into pure soul unencumbered by body:

EDMUND WALLER
Of the Last Verses in the Book

When we for age could neither read nor write,
The subject made us able to indite;
The soul, with nobler resolutions decked,
The body stooping, does herself erect.
No mortal parts are requisite to raise
Her that, unbodied, can her Maker praise.
     The seas are quiet when the winds give o'er;
So calm are we when passions are no more!
For then we know how vain it was to boast
Of fleeting things, so certain to be lost.
Clouds of affection from our younger eyes
Conceal that emptiness which age descries.
     The soul's dark cottage, battered and decayed,
Lets in new light through chinks that time has made;
Stronger by weakness, wiser men become,
As they draw near to their eternal home.
Leaving the old, both worlds at once they view,
That stand upon the threshold of the new.

This poem of the very last phase of life shows the poet leaving the earthly world and standing upon the threshold of heaven. Though many of the thoughts Waller expresses are conventional religious ones, he succeeds in making them fresh.

These poems of the private life are all meant to be said by anyone, by everyone. We will come later, in a chapter about place and history, to poems that are more personally specific than these — poems that could be said only by a person belonging to a particular subgroup in society.

The Public Life

Some public poems commemorate communal celebration — Thanksgiving or the Fourth of July or Christmas. (What can a poet do to write a new kind of Christmas poem? Well, he can stage his poem a day early and write "The Night before Christmas," as Clement Moore did.) Public poems often concern crucial single public events. Here is Michael Harper's poem joining two events in the history of American blacks — the blowing-up of an Alabama church in which four young black girls were killed, and an imagined episode in the slave trade at the time of the American Revolution (the phrase "middle passage," in line 4, refers to the route that slave ships once took from Africa to the South):

MICHAEL HARPER
American History

For John Callahan
Those four black girls blown up
in that Alabama church
remind me of five hundred
middle passage blacks,
in a net, under water
in Charleston harbor
so *redcoats* wouldn't find them.
Can't find what you can't see
can you?

"History" rarely ends with a question mark, but Harper's cynical question replicates the cynicism of the slave dealers.

Other public poems are written about the state of common life, shared by some population in a certain time and place. We might tend to think of such poems as written about violent wrongs such as genocide or slavery, but Charles Simic's "Old Couple" is about the plight of a hidden group of victims — the urban poor in old age, for whom all possible scenarios — eviction, murder, illness, death from malnutrition — are equally frightening:

CHARLES SIMIC
Old Couple

They're waiting to be murdered,
Or evicted. Soon
They expect to have nothing to eat.
As far as I know, they never go out.

A vicious pain's coming, they think.
It will start in the head
And spread down to the bowels.
They'll be carried off on stretchers, howling.

In the meantime, they watch the street
From their fifth floor window.
It has rained, and now it looks
Like it's going to snow a little.

I see him get up to lower the shades.
If their window stays dark,
I know that his hand has reached hers
Just as she was about to turn on the lights.

Who is the watcher here? Does he share the life of the old couple, and if so, how?

Of course, the private life and the public life are not separate issues, and there are many poems in which the two are mirror-images of each other. In Robert Lowell's "Skunk Hour," the decline of the inhabitants of the Maine town where the speaker lives mirrors his own decline into voyeurism and madness. Besides the public life and the private life, "Skunk Hour" invokes the life of nature, which has a sturdy strength (pictured in the dauntless invading "mother skunk and her column of kittens") lacking in the public and private spheres:

ROBERT LOWELL
Skunk Hour

For Elizabeth Bishop
Nautilus Island's hermit
heiress still lives through winter in her Spartan cottage;

her sheep still graze above the sea.
Her son's a bishop. Her farmer
is first selectman in our village;
she's in her dotage.

Thirsting for
the hierarchic privacy
of Queen Victoria's century,
she buys up all
the eyesores facing her shore,
and lets them fall.

The season's ill —
we've lost our summer millionaire,
who seemed to leap from an L. L. Bean
catalogue. His nine-knot yawl
was auctioned off to lobstermen.
A red fox stain covers Blue Hill.

And now our fairy
decorator brightens his shop for fall;
his fishnet's filled with orange cork,
orange, his cobbler's bench and awl;
there is no money in his work,
he'd rather marry.

One dark night,
my Tudor Ford climbed the hill's skull;
I watched for love-cars. Lights turned down,
they lay together, hull to hull,
where the graveyard shelves on the town. . . .
My mind's not right.

A car radio bleats,
"Love, O careless Love. . . ." I hear
my ill-spirit sob in each blood cell,
as if my hand were at its throat. . . .
I myself am hell;
nobody's here —

only skunks, that search
in the moonlight for a bite to eat.
They march on their soles up Main Street:
white stripes, moonstruck eyes' red fire
under the chalk-dry and spar spire
of the Trinitarian Church.

I stand on top
of our back steps and breathe the rich air —
a mother skunk with her column of kittens swills the garbage pail.
She jabs her wedge-head in a cup
of sour cream, drops her ostrich tail,
and will not scare.

What relations are implied here between the town's public life and the speaker's private life, between his private life and the life of nature?

Nature and Time

The poem-as-life notices, besides the inevitable themes of public and private life, two other great intertwined subjects — nature (the earth, the sun, the moon, the stars, animals, plants) and time, with its seasons and months. Because nature and time are such ancient resources for poetry, perhaps the hardest achievement is to write an original poem about, say, spring. An anonymous thirteenth-century poet began our spring poetry, as he heard the cuckoo (the herald of spring) and saw all of nature come to life. At that time, there was only one word, "summer," for the new season after winter; the word "spring" was a later invention.

Sumer is icumen in,	
Lhude° sing, cuccu!	*loud*
Groweth sed and bloweth med°	*meadow*
And springth the wude nu.	
Sing, cuccu!	
Awe° bleteth after lomb,	*ewe*
Lhouth° after calve cu,°	*loweth / cow*
Bulluc sterteth,° bucke verteth° —	*leaps / breaks wind*
Murie sing, cuccu!	
Cuccu, cuccu.	
Wel singes thu, cuccu.	
Ne swik° thu never nu!	*stop*

The spring songs of the Middle Ages generated a whole series of seasonal poems.

A contemporary poet, Dave Smith, writes his spring poem in an auto junkyard, using a pun on the word "spring" to make new sap rise even in rusty steel:

DAVE SMITH
The Spring Poem

> *Every poet should write a Spring poem.*
> — LOUISE GLÜCK

Yes, but we must be sure of verities
such as proper heat and adequate form.
That's what poets are for, is my theory.
This then is a Spring poem. A car warms
its rusting hulk in a meadow; weeds slog
up its flanks in martial weather. April
or late March is our month. There is a fog
of spunky mildew and sweaty tufts spill
from the damp rump of a back seat. A spring
thrusts one gleaming tip out, a brilliant tooth
uncoiling from Winter's tension, a ring
of insects along, working out the Truth.
Each year this car, melting around that spring,
hears nails trench from boards and every squeak sing.

We feel that the rusting car warms into new life partly because it has
been used by courting couples who have lent their presence to the
phrases Smith uses for the back seat — its "damp rump," its "spunky
mildew and sweaty tufts." When even a metal spring puts out new
shoots, when even nails spring free from the boards they have been
hammered into, we know that spring is irresistible.

The seasons have become a constant resource for poets describing
stages of human life, so that in reading poems as life we can't fail to think
of Keats's sonnet on the human seasons, which sets out the great analogy
between nature and ourselves:

JOHN KEATS
The Human Seasons

Four seasons fill the measure of the year;
    Four seasons are there in the mind of man.
He hath his lusty spring, when fancy clear
    Takes in all beauty with an easy span:
He hath his summer, when luxuriously
    He chews the honied cud of fair spring thoughts,
Till, in his soul dissolv'd, they come to be
    Part of himself. He hath his autumn ports

And havens of repose, when his tired wings
    Are folded up, and he content to look
On mists in idleness: to let fair things
    Pass by unheeded as a threshold brook.
He hath his winter too of pale misfeature,
Or else he would forget his mortal nature.

A poet can choose any one of the "human seasons" and find its counterpart in the natural world.

    When poets describe Time, they tend to employ many of the images of passing time that have entered cultural memory — such motifs as the waves of the sea, the progress of the sun from dawn to dusk, the fall of great men, the tragedy of early death, Time the Grim Reaper, and so on. Here, using such time-honored resources, is Shakespeare on Time. In his first model of how we imagine Time (lines 1–4), the moments of our life are seen as waves of the sea, all alike; in his second model (lines 5–8), the moments of our life are like the dramatic rise and eclipse of a sun, or the rise and fall of a tragic hero; and in his third model (lines 9–12), we scarcely have time to live before Death scythes us down, one after the other.

WILLIAM SHAKESPEARE
Sonnet 60

Like as the waves make toward the pebbled shore,	
So do our minutes hasten to their end,	
Each changing place with that which goes before,	
In sequent° toil all forwards do contend.	*repetitive*
Nativity,° once in the main° of light,	*birth / sea*
Crawls to maturity, wherewith being crowned,	
Crooked eclipses 'gainst his glory fight,	
And Time that gave doth now his gift confound.	
Time doth transfix the flourish° set on youth,	*beauty*
And delves the parallels° in beauty's brow,	*furrows*
Feeds on the rarities of nature's truth,	
And nothing stands but for his scythe to mow.	
And yet to times in hope my verse shall stand,	
Praising thy worth, despite his cruel hand.	

What does Shakespeare set against Time in the couplet?

In Brief: The Poem as Life

The first thing to notice about *any* poem is what piece of life (a disappointment in love, the death of a parent, an absence from a friend, a crisis of personal confidence, a moment of fear) the poem is about. Lyric poems spring from moments of disequilibrium: something has happened to disturb the status quo. Hope has come to rebuke despair; love has come to thaw coldness; envy has come to upset happiness; shame has come to interfere with self-esteem. If you can't find the piece of life that the poem is about, read the poem again, speaking it aloud in your own voice. It helps to ask, "Under what circumstances would I find myself saying these words?" The poem is *written for you to say*. You are the speaker of every lyric poem you read. That is what a lyric poem is: it is a speech made for you to utter. (We will come later to poems spoken to a silent listener by a defined character — not you, but for instance a madman or a Renaissance duke — poems that we call dramatic monologues.)

Once you have made a plausible hypothesis about what piece of life the poem is about, you can go on to see how the poem, though *about* life, is *not* life. This is the subject of our next chapter, which returns to these poems.

Reading Other Poems

Think about the following poems as utterances coming out of a particular life-situation. Try to make deductions from each one. What has recently happened to the speaker? What aspect of his or her life has the speaker been thinking about? Is this a private life-situation (a family death, for instance) or a public situation (a religious massacre, a war memorial)? What stage of life has the speaker reached? How much does the speaker tell you about his or her feelings? You might ask, too, whether these are the feelings and the remarks you might expect to find expressed in this situation (comparing them with what people might normally say or feel).

How do Thomas Wyatt's feelings change as he reacts to having been jilted? Do John Milton's remarks about revenge surprise you? What feelings arise in Ben Jonson when his beloved first son dies? What does John Keats most regret when he thinks he will die while he is still young (as he did)? Why do you suppose Emily Dickinson represented herself as a boy in the poem about coming across a snake? Can you describe the feeling at the close of Dickinson's poem in different words?

Are Dylan Thomas's words the usual ones addressed by a son to a dying father?

"Theme for English B" and "Those Winter Sundays" are by black writers: one takes up the tension between a black student and his white teacher in a Freshman English class; the other doesn't mention race at all. When do you think a life-situation might lead to the mention of race, and when not? Jonson's poem expresses the feelings of a father for his son; can you compare it to Robert Hayden's poem expressing the feelings of a son for his father? How do these compare with the feelings expressed by Sylvia Plath when she thinks about her relation to her father? And with Rita Dove's recollection of her childhood evenings with her father in "Flash Cards"?

Both Milton and Yusef Komunyakaa look at large social issues: in Milton's case, the massacre of a large number of Protestant "heretics" by Catholic forces in northern Italy; in Komunyakaa's case, the residue of the Vietnam War as represented by the Vietnam War Memorial in Washington. In what way do the tones adopted by these two poets differ? How do you think a poet decides how "loudly" to speak when he or she speaks of public issues?

SIR THOMAS WYATT
They Flee From Me

They flee from me, that sometime did me seek,
With naked foot stalking in my chamber.
I have seen them, gentle, tame, and meek,
That now are wild, and do not remember
That sometime they put themselves in danger
To take bread at my hand; and now they range,
Busily seeking with a continual change.

Thanked be Fortune it hath been otherwise,
Twenty times better; but once in special,
In thin array, after a pleasant guise,
When her loose gown from her shoulders did fall,
And she me caught in her arms long and small,°   *slender*
And therewith all sweetly did me kiss
And softly said, "Dear heart, how like you this?"

It was no dream, I lay broad waking.
But all is turned, thorough my gentleness,
Into a strange fashion of forsaking;
And I have leave to go, of her goodness,

And she also to use newfangleness.
But since that I so kindly am served,
I fain would know what she hath deserved.

JOHN MILTON
On the Late Massacre in Piedmont[1]

Avenge, O Lord, thy slaughtered saints, whose bones
    Lie scattered on the Alpine mountains cold,
    Even them who kept thy truth so pure of old
    When all our fathers worshiped stocks° and stones,   *idols*
Forget not: in thy book record their groans
    Who were thy sheep and in their ancient fold
    Slain by the bloody Piedmontese that rolled
    Mother with infant down the rocks. Their moans
The vales redoubled to the hills, and they
    To Heaven. Their martyred blood and ashes sow
    O'er all th' Italian fields where still doth sway
The triple tyrant,[2] that from these may grow
    A hundredfold, who having learnt thy way
    Early may fly the Babylonian woe.[3]

BEN JONSON
On My First Son

Farewell, thou child of my right hand,[4] and joy;
My sin was too much hope of thee, loved boy:
Seven years thou'wert lent to me, and I thee pay,
Exacted by thy fate, on the just day.
O could I lose all father now! for why
Will man lament the state he should envy,
To have so soon 'scaped world's and flesh's rage,
And, if no other misery, yet age?
Rest in soft peace, and asked, say, "Here doth lie

---

[1] The Vaudois, or Waldenses, a Protestant people living in the northwestern part of Italy, were subjected in 1655 to a bloody persecution because they refused to accept Catholicism.

[2] The pope, as claiming authority on earth and in heaven and hell.

[3] Protestants frequently identified the Roman Catholic church with Babylon.

[4] A literal translation of the Hebrew "Benjamin," the boy's name. Jonson's son was born in 1596 and died of the plague in 1603.

Ben Jonson his best piece of poetry."
For whose sake henceforth all his vows be such
As what he loves may never like too much.

JOHN KEATS
When I Have Fears

When I have fears that I may cease to be
    Before my pen has gleaned my teeming brain,
Before high-pilèd books, in charact'ry,°   *written letters*
    Hold like rich garners the full-ripened grain;
When I behold, upon the night's starred face,
    Huge cloudy symbols of a high romance,
And think that I may never live to trace
    Their shadows, with the magic hand of chance;
And when I feel, fair creature of an hour,
    That I shall never look upon thee more,
Never have relish in the faery power
    Of unreflecting love! — then on the shore
Of the wide world I stand alone, and think
Till Love and Fame to nothingness do sink.

EMILY DICKINSON
A narrow Fellow in the Grass

A narrow Fellow in the Grass
Occasionally rides —
You may have met Him — did you not
His notice sudden is —

The Grass divides as with a Comb —
A spotted shaft is seen —
And then it closes at your feet
And opens further on —

He likes a Boggy Acre
A Floor too cool for Corn —
Yet when a Boy, and Barefoot —
I more than once at Noon

Have passed, I thought, a Whip lash
Unbraiding in the Sun
When stooping to secure it
It wrinkled, and was gone —

Several of Nature's People
I know, and they know me —
I feel for them a transport
Of cordiality —

But never met this Fellow
Attended, or alone
Without a tighter breathing
And Zero at the Bone —

LANGSTON HUGHES
Theme for English B

The instructor said,

> *Go home and write*
> *a page tonight.*
> *And let that page come out of you —*
> *Then, it will be true.*

I wonder if it's that simple?
I am twenty-two, colored, born in Winston-Salem.
I went to school there, then Durham, then here
to this college on the hill above Harlem.
I am the only colored student in my class.
The steps from the hill lead down into Harlem,
through a park, then I cross St. Nicholas,
Eighth Avenue, Seventh, and I come to the Y,
the Harlem Branch Y, where I take the elevator
up to my room, sit down, and write this page:

It's not easy to know what is true for you or me
at twenty-two, my age. But I guess I'm what
I feel and see and hear, Harlem, I hear you:
hear you, hear me — we two — you, me, talk on this page.
(I hear New York, too.) Me — who?
Well, I like to eat, sleep, drink, and be in love.
I like to work, read, learn, and understand life.
I like a pipe for a Christmas present,
or records — Bessie,[1] bop, or Bach.
I guess being colored doesn't make me *not* like
the same things other folks like who are other races.

---

[1] Bessie Smith (1898?–1937), African American blues singer.

So will my page be colored that I write?
Being me, it will not be white.
But it will be
a part of you, instructor.
You are white —
yet a part of me, as I am a part of you.
That's American.
Sometimes perhaps you don't want to be a part of me.
Nor do I often want to be a part of you.
But we are, that's true!
As I learn from you,
I guess you learn from me —
although you're older — and white —
and somewhat more free.

This is my page for English B.

ROBERT HAYDEN
Those Winter Sundays

Sundays too my father got up early
and put his clothes on in the blueblack cold,
then with cracked hands that ached
from labor in the weekday weather made
banked fires blaze. No one ever thanked him.

I'd wake and hear the cold splintering, breaking.
When the rooms were warm, he'd call,
and slowly I would rise and dress,
fearing the chronic angers of that house,

Speaking indifferently to him,
who had driven out the cold
and polished my good shoes as well.
What did I know, what did I know
of love's austere and lonely offices?

DYLAN THOMAS
Do Not Go Gentle into That Good Night

Do not go gentle into that good night,
Old age should burn and rave at close of day;
Rage, rage against the dying of the light.

Though wise men at their end know dark is right,
Because their words had forked no lightning they
Do not go gentle into that good night.

Good men, the last wave by, crying how bright
Their frail deeds might have danced in a green bay,
Rage, rage against the dying of the light.

Wild men who caught and sang the sun in flight,
And learn, too late, they grieved it on its way,
Do not go gentle into that good night.

Grave men, near death, who see with blinding sight
Blind eyes could blaze like meteors and be gay,
Rage, rage against the dying of the light.

And you, my father, there on the sad height,
Curse, bless, me now with your fierce tears, I pray.
Do not go gentle into that good night.
Rage, rage against the dying of the light.

SYLVIA PLATH
Daddy

You do not do, you do not do
Any more, black shoe
In which I have lived like a foot
For thirty years, poor and white,
Barely daring to breathe or Achoo.

Daddy, I have had to kill you.
You died before I had time —
Marble-heavy, a bag full of God,
Ghastly statue with one gray toe[1]
Big as a Frisco seal

And a head in the freakish Atlantic
Where it pours bean green over blue
In the waters off beautiful Nauset.
I used to pray to recover you.
Ach, du.[2]

---

[1] Otto Plath's diabetes caused a gangrenous toe, which led to the septicemia that killed him.

[2] German: "Ah, you." The second-person familiar form (*du*) is used for intimates.

In the German tongue, in the Polish town
Scraped flat by the roller
Of wars, wars, wars.
But the name of the town is common.
My Polack[3] friend

Says there are a dozen or two.
So I never could tell where you
Put your foot, your root,
I never could talk to you.
The tongue stuck in my jaw.

It stuck in a barb wire snare.
Ich, ich, ich, ich,[4]
I could hardly speak.
I thought every German was you.
And the language obscene

An engine, an engine
Chuffing me off like a Jew.
A Jew to Dachau, Auschwitz, Belsen.[5]
I began to talk like a Jew.
I think I may well be a Jew.

The snows of the Tyrol,[6] the clear beer of Vienna[7]
Are not very pure or true.
With my gypsy ancestress and my weird luck
And my Taroc pack and my Taroc pack[8]
I may be a bit of a Jew.

I have always been scared of *you*,
With your Luftwaffe,[9] your gobbledygoo.
And your neat moustache
And your Aryan[10] eye, bright blue.
Panzer-man, panzer-man,[11] O You —

---

[3] Derogatory slang for "Polish."

[4] German: "I,I,I,I."

[5] Nazi concentration camps.

[6] Alpine region of Austria.

[7] Capital of Austria. Plath's mother was of Austrian descent; Austria was annexed by the Nazis.

[8] Pack of cards used in fortune telling.

[9] The Nazi air force.

[10] Word used by Nazis to characterize those of "pure" or unadulterated German stock.

[11] Man resembling a German armored tank.

Not God but a swastika[12]
So black no sky could squeak through.
Every woman adores a Fascist,
The boot in the face, the brute
Brute heart of a brute like you.

You stand at the blackboard, daddy,[13]
In the picture I have of you,
A cleft in your chin instead of your foot
But no less a devil for that, no not
Any less the black man who

Bit my pretty red heart in two.
I was ten when they buried you.
At twenty I tried to die
And get back, back, back to you.
I thought even the bones would do.

But they pulled me out of the sack,
And they stuck me together with glue,
And then I knew what to do.
I made a model of you,
A man in black with a Meinkampf[14] look

And a love of the rack and the screw.[15]
And I said I do, I do.
So daddy, I'm finally through.
The black telephone's off at the root,
The voices just can't worm through.

If I've killed one man, I've killed two —
The vampire who said he was you
And drank my blood for a year,
Seven years, if you want to know.
Daddy, you can lie back now.

There's a stake in your fat black heart[16]
And the villagers never liked you.

---

[12] Symbol of the Nazi party.

[13] Otto Plath was a professor of entomology at Boston University.

[14] German: "My struggle," the title of Hitler's manifesto.

[15] Rack, screw: instruments of torture.

[16] Traditionally, a vampire was buried at a crossroads with a stake through his heart.

They are dancing and stamping on you.
They always *knew* it was you.
Daddy, daddy, you bastard, I'm through.

RITA DOVE
Flash Cards

In math I was the whiz kid, keeper
of oranges and apples. *What you don't understand,*
master, my father said; the faster
I answered, the faster they came.

I could see one bud on the teacher's geranium,
one clear bee sputtering at the wet pane.
The tulip trees always dragged after heavy rain
so I tucked my head as my boots slapped home.

My father put up his feet after work
and relaxed with a highball and *The Life of Lincoln*.
After supper we drilled and I climbed the dark

before sleep, before a thin voice hissed
numbers as I spun on a wheel. I had to guess.
Ten, I kept saying, *I'm only ten.*

YUSEF KOMUNYAKAA
Facing It

My black face fades,
hiding inside the black granite.
I said I wouldn't,
dammit: No tears.
I'm stone. I'm flesh.
My clouded reflection eyes me
like a bird of prey, the profile of night
slanted against morning. I turn
this way — the stone lets me go.
I turn that way — I'm inside
the Vietnam Veterans Memorial
again, depending on the light
to make a difference.
I go down the 58,022 names,

half-expecting to find
my own in letters like smoke.
I touch the name Andrew Johnson;
I see the booby trap's white flash.
Names shimmer on a woman's blouse
but when she walks away
the names stay on the wall.
Brushstrokes flash, a red bird's
wings cutting across my stare.
The sky. A plane in the sky.
A white vet's image floats
closer to me, then his pale eyes
look through mine. I'm a window.
He's lost his right arm
inside the stone. In the black mirror
a woman's trying to erase names:
No, she's brushing a boy's hair.

2

The Poem as Arranged Life

The preceding chapter, "The Poem as Life," suggested that poems originate in crucial moments of private life (for instance, marriage) or public life (for instance, a revolutionary era), and that they are set in recognizable places (in a junkyard, for example) or times (in spring). But to speak of the poem "as life" is not to say that it is simply a transcription of what has occurred. Life itself is a continuation of successive moments in one stream. Art interrupts the stream and constructs one segment or level of the stream for processing. In a single act, it describes, analyzes, and confers form on that segment. The form it confers by its ways of organizing the poem makes visible the contour of that life-moment as the poet perceives it. The poet discovers the emotional import of that life-moment by subjecting it to analysis; the analysis then determines how the moment is described, and the invented organizational form that replicates it. These are remarks that will become clear when we look at particular poems, so let us go back to our poems-as-life to see how they are *arranged* life — that is, in what way they are formal constructions of life. What organizational patterns have the poets chosen?

The Private Life

Blake's baby, first of all. For Blake, every moment in life could be seen in either of two ways — innocently or with experience. The innocent way of seeing a baby is what we might call both a cliché and a truth: a baby *is* beautiful, guileless, smiling, appealing, the joy of its mother's days. In an earlier poem, "Infant Joy," Blake shows us what the innocent mother, in her fantasy, would like the baby to say to her as he tells her how to name him (stanza 1), and what she would then say to him (stanza 2):

WILLIAM BLAKE
Infant Joy

"I have no name,
I am but two days old."
"What shall I call thee?"
"I happy am,
Joy is my name."
"Sweet joy befall thee!"

"Pretty joy!
Sweet joy but two days old,
Sweet joy I call thee;
Thou dost smile,
I sing the while —
Sweet joy befall thee!"

But a baby is also the bundle of tension that will generate its future sorrows, as Blake asserts in "Infant Sorrow," the companion-poem to "Infant Joy." If you think back, he suggests, to how awful it was to be a baby when you were one, then you will see infancy from the point of view of "experience" rather than the maternal doting "innocence." You will remember how dangerous the world seemed to you when you were small, how helpless you felt, how little power you had over your environment and your belongings, how often you cried in frustration, how fiendish your unsatisfied shrieks must have seemed to your parents, how you must have longed to wrest personal control of your physical self from your parents' attentions. This remarkable sympathetic description of *babyhood from the point of view of the rebellious and unhappy baby* was Blake's originating insight; he then had to arrange his intuition of the baby's rage into an analytic and poetic shape.

WILLIAM BLAKE
Infant Sorrow

My mother groaned, my father wept —
Into the dangerous world I leapt,

Helpless, naked, piping loud,
Like a fiend hid in a cloud.

Struggling in my father's hands,
Striving against my swaddling bands,
Bound and weary, I thought best
To sulk upon my mother's breast.

Blake analyzes the baby into two aspects, its physical body and its
mental operations; he gives a stanza to each aspect. The main verb of the
first stanza is the physical word "leapt"; the main verb of the second
stanza is the mental word "thought." First the baby leaps into the world;
then he thinks about his condition and decides what attitude to take
toward it (he finally decides to sulk, after fruitlessly struggling and striv-
ing).

If the *division into the physical and the mental* is the most basic analytic
move of the poem (causing it to divide itself into two stanzas), what
other shapes does Blake confer on his piece of life? We notice that the
baby's mother and father are present in each of the stanzas: by repeating
the shape "parents/baby, parents/baby," Blake shows us that the baby
does not exist alone but lives always in dependency on his parents. First,
they preside at his birth, while his mother groans in labor and his father
weeps in sympathy. Next, they literally enclose him, as they occupy the
first and last line of the second stanza; the baby is held in his father's
hands in the first line and supported on his mother's breast in the last.
This *environmental* "parents/baby, parents/baby" shape is superimposed
on the first shape ("baby/body, baby/mind") that we perceived. Just as
the first shape made concrete — physically represented — Blake's ana-
lytic separation of the baby into body and mind, the second shape shows
Blake's perception of the baby's total physical and moral impotence. He
must continue to live (stanza 2) in the power of his parents who gave
him existence (stanza 1), and it will be a long time before he will be old
enough to have the independence he furiously craves.

Blake confers a third analytic shape on the poem with all the
adjectives that the baby uses about himself: "helpless," "naked," "pip-
ing," "like a fiend hid," "struggling," "striving," "bound," and
"weary." These are all realistic except "like a fiend hid." The realistic
adjectives tell us how much any infant already knows about his intol-
erable condition; but the adjectival comparison, "[I am] like a fiend hid
in a cloud," tells us that the baby can summon up a very strange analogy.
We conclude (as would Blake, a Christian), that the baby has come into
this life from a previous supernatural existence where he knew angels
and devils. The baby (to his dismay) realizes that in this horrible new

struggling embodied state he is more like the fiends he remembers than like the angels he resembled in heaven. The adjectival division of the baby's *self-awareness* into an *"earthly"* one (conscious of being naked, struggling, etc.) and a *"supernatural"* one (recalling fiends — and presumably their counterpart angels — known to his former life) reflects the baby's rage and self-division.

The fourth analytic shape Blake confers on his picture of the baby's state is a grammatical one — a contrast between present participial adjectives and non"-ing" adjectives. We see in this shape Blake's *contrast between doing and feeling* — between the baby's participial adjectives of action ("piping," "struggling," "striving") and his other adjectives of feeling ("helpless," "naked," "like a fiend," "bound," "weary"). The present participles show us what the baby can *do* (he can pipe, he can struggle, he can strive); the other adjectives tell us how he *feels* — his sufferings and his self-estimation as a fiend. We can understand his struggling and striving; but the unusual word "piping" tells us that in Blake's view the baby is not screaming or shrieking — he is making a song. "Piping" is a musical word, and it represents the beginning of language (or at least vocal expression) in the baby. He is full of sorrow, but he is also expressing his sorrow vocally.

There are other verbal effects we could mention: for instance, the fact that the baby is shown actively "leaping" into the world, rather than passively "being born"; that the successively weaker participial line-beginnings — "Struggling," "Striving," "Bound" — enact (act out, give us in miniature) the baby's eventual resignation into his sulky state; that the little couplets (pairs of rhyming lines) demonstrate Blake's decision to use the simplest sort of rhyme for the baby's speech; that the space between the stanzas represents the transition from being born to living. But as we look back on the task the poet set himself — "Find a shape for saying how life seems to the baby as he's born and just afterward" — we see that the poem has had to find several shapes for just that. To the extent that the poem exhibits analytic shapes, it has been removed from the stream of undifferentiated moments of existence and brought into the formal world of art. A poem that at first looks like a description ("Helpless, naked, piping loud; / Like a fiend hid in a cloud") is in fact an analysis of aspects of the baby's condition, arranged in ways (such as division into physical and mental, parents in each stanza, recall of heavenly preexistence, a contrast between acting and feeling) that show how the baby perceives life.

To sum up: by "analytic shape" I mean any meaningful patterning in the poem that "acts out" one of the insights the poet has had about the experience treated by the poem. It is as though in this poem Blake, with a poet's instinct, thought, "How shall I show that the baby is a mind as well as a body?" and decided, "I'll make a two-stanza poem, with the main *verb* in the first stanza a body-word, and the main *verb* in the second stanza a mind-word" (Shape 1). Then he thought, "How will I show the baby's dependence on its parents?" and decided, "I'll put the *nouns* "mother" and "father" in each stanza to show that the baby is always dependent on his parents" (Shape 2). Then, "How will I show the baby's previous supernatural life? By having him, amid all his *realistic* self-adjectives, include one *supernatural* adjectival comparison alluding to that previous life" (Shape 3). Then, "How can I show what the baby is feeling as well as what the baby is doing? I'll give him *present-participial adjectives* of doing *and non-"ing" adjectives* of feeling" (Shape 4). These decisions organize the poem, giving it structures that are dynamic ones, constantly overlapping and interlocking, making up the overall organization of the poem.

Of course, such patterns occur in lightning-quick ways to the trained mind of the poet. A composer does not say, "I think this is the point for a diminished seventh," or "Perhaps it would be effective to follow eighth-note triplets with a dotted quarter note." No, the composer "hears the music" and writes it down; it is only later that analysts demonstrate the patterns that make the music seem intended, not chaotic. A poet, too, "hears the poem," writes it down, and then further refines its visible patterns. Naturally, when a given pattern precedes the composition of the poem ("I want to write a sonnet"), much will be dictated by the preexistent formal requirements; but even then, the swift internal processes of composition organize the temporal, spatial, grammatical, and syntactic shapes of the poem more by instinct than by conscious plan. One could say that artists are people who think naturally in highly patterned ways.

As this summary shows, it is up to the reader to notice patterns such as those Blake uses. "How is it that the main action of the baby is a body-action in stanza 1 and a mind-action in stanza 2? What does this tell me about the baby's condition?" Or, "How is it that among all these realistic adjectives suiting the baby's state I find this one weird one — 'like a fiend hid in a cloud'? How does the newborn baby know about fiends hiding in clouds? What does this tell me about the baby's mind?"

A pattern shows that the poet has analyzed, and then replicated in language, some aspect of the content of the poem. We can therefore call a pattern an analytic shape. (In well-written poems, most of the larger perceived patterns will be analytically meaningful.) Much is explained to us about the baby by the patterns we have seen. The *main-verb pattern* tells us that the baby is composed of mind and body, which do separate things. The *noun-repeat pattern* ("mother," "father") tells us of the baby's dependency. The *realistic/supernatural adjectival pattern* of contrast tells us of the baby's memory of a past state. The *present-participial adjectives /other adjectives pattern* shows us the baby doing and the baby feeling. These few patterns remind us that there can be shapes of:

1. simple meaning-contrast (the antonyms "leapt" and "thought");
2. word-repetition ("mother," "father");
3. series, whether similar or broken ("like a fiend" breaks the realistic series and therefore stands out);
4. grammatical contrast (here, present-participial adjectives versus other adjectives, showing us actions versus feelings).

To discern the patterns in any poem, you may have to notice, then, such things as contrasts of meaning, repetitions of words, items in series, and grammatical emphases. Then, having seen such patterns, you can begin to ask yourself if they show you something about the situation in the poem that makes sense of the experience depicted.

We can ask, now, how does Louise Glück give formal shape to the first day of school?

As we've seen, Glück takes her cast of characters and their props from our conventional picture of the first day of school: there are children with their new primary-color clothes ("overcoats of blue or yellow wool"), their first book-bags or lunch-boxes ("their little satchels"), and their apples (from their family's orchard) for the teachers. The teachers "wait behind . . . desks." The mothers are left behind as the children "go forward" to school. So far, so ordinary. No one would be surprised to be told these details about the first day of school. But Glück gives us more, and more sinister, details:

LOUISE GLÜCK
The School Children

The children go forward with their little satchels.
And all morning the mothers have labored
to gather the late apples, red and gold,
like words of another language.

And on the other shore
are those who wait behind great desks
to receive these offerings.

How orderly they are — the nails
on which the children hang
their overcoats of blue or yellow wool.

And the teachers shall instruct them in silence
and the mothers shall scour the orchards for a way out,
drawing to themselves the gray limbs of the fruit trees
bearing so little ammunition.

We perceive poetic shape mostly through *oddness*. There are several oddnesses here. The apples are said to be "like words of another language." The school is said to be "on the other shore" of some unspecified body of water. The teachers' (ordinary) desks are said to be "great" desks — and the teachers wait, like gods, to receive "offerings." The only detail given about the school itself is that it has an orderly row of nails serving as coat hooks. The limbs of the fruit trees in the orchards which the mothers "scour" for "a way out" are "gray," and the apples are seen, at the end of the poem, as "ammunition." These are the oddnesses any account of the shapes of the poem would have to make sense of.

We also perceive shape through the *division into stanzas* — here, four of them, with their appropriate dramatis personae, or cast of characters. Stanza 1 is for the *children,* the *mothers,* and the *apples;* stanza 2 is for the *teachers* and the *apples;* stanza 3 is for the *nails;* and stanza 4 is for the *teachers* (doing one thing at school) and the *mothers* (doing another thing in the orchards with apples). Why is this the way the characters come on the stage? Why do the nails have a stanza to themselves? Why isn't the word "apples" mentioned in the last stanza?

We perceive shape through *series:* the apples, which were "words from another language" in stanza 1, and "these offerings" in stanza 2, are "ammunition" in stanza 4. The apples are the only image that changes, and they become more pathetic as the poem goes on.

At this point, we can say that the first basic shape that the poem confers on the opening of school is a *spatial* one. There is a terrible and dangerous separation of teacher-territory from mother-territory: they lie on opposite shores of a watery divide. The two regions speak different languages, and the apples are the only words in the teacher-language that can bridge the gap. The two regions are also in conflict; but the teachers have nails and the mothers have only apples — as propitiatory offerings, as ammunition against the teacher's power. The mothers' desperate work ("all morning the mothers have labored"; "the mothers shall scour the orchards") to protect the children is bound to fail — they have "so little ammunition" from the already-withering fruit trees (next year's apples will be of no use, since the children will be wholly socialized into their public school-selves by then). The day will come when the children will have to go to school without an apple to offer to those mysterious strangers, the teachers, who speak another language, who wait behind their monumental "great desks." What will happen then?

The *spatial* shape of the great divide into two territories is matched by the *temporal* shape of the poem. By "temporal shape" I mean what happens to the poem as it progresses in time. Here, as the poem advances from stanza 1 to stanza 2 to stanza 3, the gaze of the narrator narrows from the home group (mothers and children) to the people behind the "great desks" to the sinister single objects "orderly . . . nails." Then the gaze of the narrator broadens again, to the children firmly in the power of the teacher (who will quell their native language and reduce them to the silence and orderliness of socialization) and the mothers, on the other shore, who will wildly seek a way, by scouring the orchards for apples (which they now think of solely as "ammunition") to fight the trap that is closing on their children.

These two axes, Space and Time, are often used to organize poems. In Glück's poem, the first represents the analysis of the life-event into different regions (home and school), and the second represents the analysis of the life-event into successive temporal stages (here, from the child's point of view — leaving home, seeing the teacher behind the "great desk," divesting yourself of your new coat and leaving an effigy of yourself hanging on a nail, and being "instructed in silence" by the teacher). The last stanza of the poem, unlike all the rest (which are written in the present tense) is written in the future tense: the teachers "shall instruct" the children; the mothers "shall scour" the orchards. This is a prophetic future tense (otherwise the phrases would read "will instruct" and "will scour"). The future tense represents a prediction from the main present-tense account in the poem, but it is a logical conjecture from the very first words, "The children go forward."

The purpose of Glück's two main shapes, one of space and one of time, is to make the transition from home to school sinister. We imagine primary-school children walking to a school close by, but we learn (in the shape of the two regions) that the school is on "another shore." We imagine a cordial relation between home and school, but the temporal plot shows us an alienation between them ("another language") so that the mothers must try propitiation ("offerings") and then open conflict ("ammunition") to save the children. These two sinister shapes of widening space and future loss "act out," most of all, the mothers' sense that their children are far off, in the power of alien beings, in danger, and essentially without hope of rescue. This reinterpretation of the conventionally cheerful view of the first day of school forces us to rethink our previous notion: Is not the first day of school really more like Glück's idea of it than like the conventionally happy version? The artist's distrust of group "order" and "silence" lies behind this critique of early education.

The shape that E. E. Cummings puts on life is simpler. He separates the two sexes, and shows us what age they are by their games (marbles and piracies for the boys, hop-scotch and jump-rope for the girls). He makes the children same-sex Siamese twins, so to speak — eddieandbill and bettyandisbel. He troubles their same-sex play by an apparently insignificant figure of pleasure, a balloonman:

E. E. CUMMINGS
in Just-

spring   when the world is mud-
luscious the little
lame balloonman

whistles   far   and wee

and eddieandbill come
running from marbles and
piracies and it's
spring

when the world is puddle-wonderful

the queer
old balloonman whistles
far   and   wee
and bettyandisbel come dancing

from hop-scotch and jump-rope and
it's
spring
and

    the
        goat-footed
balloonMan   whistles
far
and
wee

The balloonman enters three times with his seductive whistle. We are left to imagine its ultimate sexual effect on the preadolescent children — but the effect is not in doubt because he draws the couples away from their same-sex childhood play, forecasting their regrouping into sexual couples. In the triple appearance of the balloonman, we find him characterized by different adjectives — "little lame," "queer old," and "goat-footed." He also acquires an honorific capital "M" in his last appearance, where we see the goat-feet which proclaim him a nature-spirit, even a god — therefore he is a balloonMan. (In ancient Greece the god of nature was the goat-footed Pan.) We call the phrase repeating the return of the balloonman a *refrain*:

> The little lame balloonman whistles far and wee
> The queer old balloonman whistles far and wee
> The goat-footed balloonMan whistles far and wee

We notice that other things in the poem also come round thrice:

> in Just- / spring   when the world is mud- / luscious
> it's / spring / when the world is puddle-wonderful
> it's / spring

We can now see that the "plot" of the poem is:

1. Spring, balloonman, boys together;

2. Spring, balloonman, girls together;

3. Spring, balloonMan, ——— ?

When we ask ourselves: What does Cummings imply about the completion of the poem? What is the missing plot element? We answer: "girl with boy, boy with girl."

To his Siamese-twin trick, and his triple balloonman refrain, and his triple appearance of spring, and the "missing" sexual conclusion to his plot, Cummings adds yet another element of shape — his typographic arrangement of these things. The "horizontal" whistling — "whistles   far   and wee" — looks as though it is happening within the space we move in. But the "vertical" whistle —

> > whistles
> far
> and
> wee

makes it seem as though the balloonman is gradually, like a Pied Piper, receding in space, taking the newly sexual couples off with him. Typographically speaking, too, the important word "spring" always comes first in the lines in which it appears.

There is an odd stop, inserted at the line-break, between the adjectives characterizing the balloonman at first: "little — [Is he lame? Yes, maybe.] / lame balloonman"; "queer — [Does he walk that way because he's old, not lame? Yes, maybe.] / old balloonman." And then the puzzle is resolved: he's not lame; he's not old; he walks oddly because he is "goat-footed." And there's no more hesitation: he's a god — he's the balloonMan.

If we were talking about the life-moment Cummings has selected, we would say it is the spring of life — the moment when childhood ends, same-sex friendships break up, adolescents hear the alluring call of sexuality, and sexual couples first form. That is a summary of the poem, but it has not explained the shapes Cummings has invented to act out the life-moment. Only an examination of form — in Cummings, typographic as well as verbal form — shows us how the poem *enacts* (represents by several formal shapes) the moment it has chosen, and makes us see the *processes* of that moment, how it gradually unfolds in time, with both pathos and joy.

We have said that Whitman's "Hours Continuing Long" is a poem of forsaken love; its first line tells us that its special subject is how *long* the hours seem to the one forsaken. How does the poem act out the length of the hours?

WALT WHITMAN
Hours Continuing Long

Hours continuing long, sore and heavy hearted,
Hours of the dusk, when I withdraw to a lonesome and unfre-
    quented spot, seating myself, leaning my face in my hands;
Hours sleepless, deep in the night, when I go forth, speeding
    swiftly the country roads, or through the city streets, or pac-
    ing miles and miles, stifling plaintive cries;
Hours discouraged, distracted — for the one I cannot content my-
    self without, soon I saw him content himself without me;
Hours when I am forgotten (O weeks and months are passing, but
    I believe I am never to forget!)
Sullen and suffering hours! (I am ashamed — but it is useless — I
    am what I am;)
Hours of my torment — I wonder if other men ever have the like,
    out of the like feelings?
Is there even one other like me — distracted — his friend, his
    lover, lost to him?
Is he too as I am now? Does he still rise in the morning, dejected,
    thinking who is lost to him? and at night, awaking, think
    who is lost?
Does he too harbor his friendship silent and endless? harbor his
    anguish and passion?

Does some stray reminder, or the casual mention of a name, bring
    the fit back upon him, taciturn and deprest?
Does he see himself reflected in me? In these hours, does he see the
    face of his hours reflected?

Certainly the successive long weary lines beginning with the word
"Hours" — there are six of these, five in a row, then an interruption
("Sullen and suffering hours!"), then another one — act out the theme
of the poem. We will have to account for the interruption, but for the
moment we can say that the first seven lines of the poem make us see and
feel, by a series of statements exhaustedly resembling one another, the
inertia of the weary hours.

Then the poem makes its major change of shape, turning from one
grammatical form (*statements*) to a different one (*questions*). We see now
that it is basically a *two-part* poem, the parts distinguished by this central
grammatical turn. Do the two parts differ in anything besides grammat-
ical form? Part I is solely about the speaker; but Part II wonders whether
there are "other men" like the speaker, or even "one other like me."

Before the poem began, there was of course "one other like" the
speaker — his lover. The speaker was one of two; now he is alone; he
would like to be one of at least two again. The usual hope might be to
find another lover, but that is a path that this poem does not, cannot,
take, since the speaker is still too much in love to imagine finding a new
lover. No — the speaker will imagine that there is another person as
dejected as he is himself, a brother in suffering, who will be his twin in
endurance. This is a replacement strategy: the lost lover is "replaced" by
the imagined twin-in-grief.

What causes this evolution in the poem? Can we explain what
motivates the transition from solitary grief to the imagining of a fellow
sufferer? It may come from a wish to replace the lost lover; but the poem
suggests another motivation, too. Let us look at the two-line central
turning-point of the poem, beginning with the line that does not open
with "Hours" and continuing into the line where statements turn to
questions:

Sullen and suffering hours! (I am ashamed — but it is useless — I
    am what I am;)
Hours of my torment — I wonder if other men ever have the like,
    out of the like feelings?

We can see that the first movement out of the self toward society is one
of unexplained shame: "If others could see me, they would rebuke me;
and yes, I am ashamed — but it is useless — I am what I am." We do not

know, and will never know, whether the poet is ashamed of his homo-sexuality (he suppressed this poem from his collection *Leaves of Grass*) or of his sullen dejection (Whitman strongly wished to appear a positive poet of democratic strength). Eventually the poet surmises that some group of men might not recoil from him, because they themselves have had similar feelings. At least there may be one such man — and the poem then does a reprise in the third person ("Does he too harbor his friendship silent and endless?") of what the speaker had previously said of himself in the first person ("I withdraw to a lonesome and unfre-quented spot," etc.).

This shape — doing something once, then doing it again differ-ently — is one we have already seen in Cummings' poem, where we saw spring come three times and heard the balloonman whistle three times. Here, love is expressed in the first person, via statements, and then in the third person, via questions; this shape tells us that what seemed at first shamefully personal may perhaps be shared by others, perhaps by everyone. It is like hearing a melody twice, the first time in the major key, the second time in the minor. Art thrives on such variations.

Waller's poem, though it is written in nine five-beat couplets, is separated by paragraph indentations (rather than by the conventional white space) into three stanzas of six lines each, suggesting to us that it has a three-part shape. (*Stanza* is an Italian word meaning a room or a stopping place. A stanza in a poem is, so to speak, one room in the house that is the poem as a whole.)

EDMUND WALLER
Of the Last Verses in the Book

When we for age could neither read nor write,
The subject made us able to indite;
The soul, with nobler resolutions decked,
The body stooping, does herself erect.
No mortal parts are requisite to raise
Her that, unbodied, can her Maker praise.

The seas are quiet when the winds give o'er;
So calm are we when passions are no more!
For then we know how vain it was to boast
Of fleeting things, so certain to be lost.
Clouds of affection from our younger eyes
Conceal that emptiness which age descries.

The soul's dark cottage, battered and decayed,

Lets in new light through chinks that time has made;
Stronger by weakness, wiser men become,
As they draw near to their eternal home.
Leaving the old, both worlds at once they view,
That stand upon the threshold of the new.

As we scan the poem for pattern, we notice that the poem mentions *aspects of seeing* in each of its three parts, and seems in each stanza to redefine old age in terms of seeing. We can write out a thematic statement for each stanza:

1. The poet in old age finds his sight dimming, so that he is losing the capacity to read and write: "We for age could *neither read nor write.*" And nonetheless he does write, if only this last poem, because of the urgency of oncoming death: "The subject made us able to indite." The poet's topic — how to praise God even in the face of impending death — raises the soul to new efforts. It writes *without its eyes:* "No mortal parts are requisite to raise" the soul to its written prayer.

2. The poet finds that old age *sees the world more keenly* than youth did: in youth, clouds of emotion made us think the world full of good things, but age descries the world's true emptiness. This is an improvement on the approaching physical blindness of stanza 1.

3. The poet finds something even better to say. The internal spiritual vision of the old writer not only descries the emptiness of the world; it can also view, with "new light," the "eternal home" to which the old draw near:

   Leaving the old, *both* worlds at once they view,
   That stand upon the threshold of the new.

This brave expanding shape — "I am going blind"; "No, I see better than I did when my eyes were clouded by youth's desires"; "I find that by my new light of wisdom, I can see not just earth, but my eternal home" — is one of increasing praise of God for true enlightenment, even in physical blindness. Insight grows as sight fails.

If this three-part shape is the basic crescendo-shape of the poem, what other subordinate shapes can we see? First of all, there are many ways in which one can refer to the self:

We could neither read nor write

The soul erects *herself* as *the body* stoops

She [*the soul*] praises her Maker

We (like seas after winds) are calm after the storm of passion; *we* know the vanity of earthly things; what *our* younger *eyes* missed

Age [the allegorical quality] descries

The soul's dark cottage [*the body*] lets in new light

Men become wiser as *they* draw near heaven

They who, leaving the old world, stand on the threshold of the new world, view both worlds at once

Sometimes the self is a generalized "we" (which we nonetheless, because of the past tense of "made," interpret as a single person; if the lines read "When we for age can neither read nor write / The subject *makes* us able to indite," we would see the remark as applying to all of us). The poet refers to himself as "we" perhaps to introduce his double nature: he is composed of an erect soul and a stooping body. The soul can act alone, can indite without the eyes.

The next "we" is the truly generalized "we," speaking of all men: "We all are calm after the storm of passion." This is the present tense of objective description, the scientific present tense — ("All men are mortal," "Hope springs eternal," "All is fair in love and war"). Another universal generalization is set forth under the allegorical word "Age," meaning "Old People." "Age sees more than Youth" would be the "normal" way of putting the case, but Waller mixes his references, third-person singular and first-person plural: "*Age* descries more than *our* younger eyes."

Next, soul and body return, but now in the graphic metaphor of "The soul's dark cottage, battered and decayed," with its "chinks" made by time. At this moment, the author is at the greatest point of objectivity about his own body, looking at it from the outside, so to speak, and seeing how battered and decayed it is, how its walls have chinks of ruin in them. Yet at the very same moment, he sees what it is like inside, filled with "new light" coming through those very chinks. The sign of his objectivity is the search for and discovery of this visual metaphor (the body as a decaying cottage) to represent himself, outside and inside, to himself and his reader.

Next, he returns to a generalization about all *men* (meaning men and women) — how *they* (third-person plural) become wiser as they grow older, and stronger, paradoxically, by weakness. Finally, in the last generalization, he takes a subset of old men — the dying, those on the threshold of departure. *They* (third-person plural again, but this time, because it refers to the subset of which he is the only present member, more like the initial plural "we" which we interpreted as the singular) see eternity as well as time. This panoramic vision attained by the dying — as they view both worlds at once — is the prize claimed by the poet for himself, though he modestly puts it in terms of all the dying.

The constantly changing names by which the poet refers to himself — singular ("we," "Age," "the soul's dark cottage"); dual ("body," "soul"); and plural ("we," "men," "they that stand upon the threshold") — provide what anthropologists call a "thick description" of the person speaking, enabling us to see the many headings under which the poet classifies himself. A poem that said "I" all the way through would seem much poorer, and would not visibly represent, by a pattern of different naming, the coming separation of the body and soul that so much in the poem reflects.

There are other shapes in the poem. Perhaps the most notable one appears in the contrast between the couplets that are said freely, without pauses, and those that are more complex in their pauses. The things that are said freely, without stops, tend to be truisms of a sort:

> The seas are quiet when the winds give o'er;
> So calm are we when passions are no more!
>
> . . . . .
>
> Clouds of affection from our younger eyes
> Conceal that emptiness which age descries.

These couplets are epigrammatic (by which we mean that they say something in a short, pointed, conclusive, "wrapped-up" way).

Other couplets, by their pauses, emphasize conflicts, tensions, and divided views:

> The soul, with nobler resolutions decked,
> The body stooping, does herself erect.
>
> . . . . .
>
> Stronger by weakness, wiser men become,
> As they draw near to their eternal home.
> Leaving the old, both worlds at once they view,
> That stand upon the threshold of the new.

The sentences themselves, in their use or deletion of pauses, act out the alternation in the poem between truisms about old age and the gradual discoveries the speaker himself is making.

The Public Life

As we turn from the private to the public life, we come to this very brief poem by Michael Harper — which nonetheless has the comprehensive title "American History." It consists of two parts. The first is a personal statement ("Those girls remind me of five hundred blacks"), and the second is the sardonic quip following it, spoken by someone who seems to be giving us a knowing wink: "Can't find what you can't see / can you?"

MICHAEL HARPER
American History

For John Callahan

Those four black girls blown up
in that Alabama church
remind me of five hundred
middle passage blacks,
in a net, under water
in Charleston harbor
so *redcoats* wouldn't find them.
Can't find what you can't see
can you?

The "invisibility" of blacks in American culture has been a persistent theme of black authors; Ralph Ellison called his famous autobiographical novel *Invisible Man*. A few blacks more or less, in racist contexts, would scarcely be noticed. The furor caused by the death of four young black girls when a bomb exploded in a black church was one of the signs of the rising civil rights movement; yet those who placed the bomb didn't care how many blacks they killed. Harper's anecdote of American ship-captains drowning slaves so they would not be stolen, as items of value, by British troops suggests the perennial "invisibility" of blacks throughout American history, from the very beginning. The wry quip at the end of the poem makes even more horrible the "success" of hiding — by murder — the valuable slaves to keep them from the redcoats.

By calling his poem "American History" Harper suggests that the episodes he recounts represent, better than textbooks bearing that name, the real narrative of American events. The real American history remains to be written, the poem implies. So we must see, between these two markers — the invisibility of drowned blacks in the Revolution, the invisibility of bombed blacks in the twentieth century — a whole silent procession of comparable incidents, decade by decade, from the seventeenth century till today. In this way, by evoking the shape "normally" belonging to the title "American History" (a long textbook full of patriotic self-glorification), Harper makes us see his little shape as one that could be extended into a very big one.

We come to another marginalized group in public life, Charles Simic's aged poor:

CHARLES SIMIC
Old Couple

They're waiting to be murdered,
Or evicted. Soon
They expect to have nothing to eat.
As far as I know, they never go out.

A vicious pain's coming, they think.
It will start in the head
And spread down to the bowels.
They'll be carried off on stretchers, howling.

In the meantime, they watch the street
From their fifth floor window.
It has rained, and now it looks
Like it's going to snow a little.

I see him get up to lower the shades.
If their window stays dark,
I know that his hand has reached hers
Just as she was about to turn on the lights.

If we quickly sum up the subject of each of the four stanzas of Simic's "Old Couple," we might come up with something like this:

1. Three possible futures for the old couple — murdered, evicted, starved;

2. Another possible future — terminal illness;

3. The present interim before one of these horrors happens;

4. The suppositions of the speaker watching them.

A quick summary of this sort at least shows that the horrors die down, by stanza 3, to the brief and fragile peace of the interim moment at the end; this decline in horror is one overall shape of the poem. But it leaves out the presence of the person watching the old couple. It is this person who speaks the poem, and we identify him, since this is not a dramatic monologue, with the author of the poem. He knows, in stanza 1, what the old people are thinking. He comments on their behavior ("As far as I know, they never go out"). He watches them compulsively ("I see him get up to lower the shades"). He even invents what they do when he cannot observe them ("I know that his hand has reached hers").

If the shape of the old people's lives is a downhill dread of continual terror, what is the shape of the watcher's life? The poet asks us to imagine the passing days of a watcher in a nearby building. At some point in the past, he noticed the old couple across the way; perhaps at that point they were still going out for walks or to the store. That seems to have stopped. But when they were still visible in the neighborhood, the watcher noted their mutual devotion, which causes him now to imagine the old man reaching for his wife's hand. The watcher is so conscious of the few things the old couple can look at that he has reduced his own consciousness to the tenuousness of theirs: "It has rained, and now it looks / Like it's going to snow a little" — an observation of no real importance, except to people who have nothing else but the weather to observe (but it also suggests worsening weather, one more threat). The old couple have become so real to the watcher that he has absorbed their terrors into his own mind. He knows that one of these days he will either see them taken out on stretchers, howling in pain, or see their possessions on the sidewalk as they are evicted with no place to go, or he will hear that they have been murdered, or that someone has found them dead of malnutrition in their apartment. There are simply no other possible futures to imagine for them; the watcher knows this.

As soon as we see the watcher/speaker as the principal consciousness in the poem, we read the work as a protest-poem against the conditions of modern urban life. The neglect by society of its most helpless members means that anyone in a modern city becomes necessarily a watcher of cases like this. Nobody can be free of horror and guilt, as the probable future seeps from the victims to their neighbors.

The two interlocking shapes — the heading-for-disaster life-shape of the old couple, the ongoing and speculative life-shape of the watcher — make up the figure of the poem. Spatially, we are given two rooms — the implied room of the watcher, the room of the old couple across the street; temporally, we are presented with the several envisaged plots of the old couple meeting their end, each plot as terrifying as the other. The plots exhaust all possibilities. The old couple have no one to rescue them —

they will end in a public hospital ward for the indigent, in a shelter for the homeless, out on the street after being evicted, in the morgue after being murdered, or in their bed, starved.

Many poems have two or more interlocking shapes. We have seen such shapes in "Infant Sorrow" (the baby as mind and body; the baby as dependent on parents; the baby as part human, part supernatural; the baby as a doing creature and a feeling creature), and again in "Old Couple" (the successive shapes of the couple's envisaged horrifying futures; the watcher's steady-state speculative shape). When several over-lapping and interlocking shapes are present at once in a poem, it be-comes potentially more interesting — because more complex, as life is — than poems that have only one shape. The ideal poem would have a temporal shape, a spatial shape, a rhythmic shape, a phonetic shape, a grammatical shape, a syntactic shape, and so on — each one beautifully worked out, each one graphically presenting in formal terms an aspect of the emotional and intellectual import of the poem. One way we dis-tinguish more accomplished poems from less accomplished ones is the control of the artist over a number of shapes at once. Other things being equal, the more shapes that are being controlled, the more pleasure one derives from the poem because more of its inner life has been thought through, analyzed, and made visible in form by its creator.

The manuscript drafts of Robert Lowell's "Skunk Hour" show that it originally began in the way that a traditional lyric might — "One dark night," etc. The present stanza 5 was the beginning of the poem:

ROBERT LOWELL
Skunk Hour

For Elizabeth Bishop

Nautilus Island's hermit
heiress still lives through winter in her Spartan cottage;
her sheep still graze above the sea.
Her son's a bishop. Her farmer
is first selectman in our village;
she's in her dotage.

Thirsting for
the hierarchic privacy
of Queen Victoria's century,
she buys up all
the eyesores facing her shore,
and lets them fall.

The season's ill —
we've lost our summer millionaire,
who seemed to leap from an L. L. Bean
catalogue. His nine-knot yawl
was auctioned off to lobstermen.
A red fox stain covers Blue Hill.

And now our fairy
decorator brightens his shop for fall;
his fishnet's filled with orange cork,
orange, his cobbler's bench and awl;
there is no money in his work,
he'd rather marry.

One dark night,
my Tudor Ford climbed the hill's skull;
I watched for love-cars. Lights turned down,
they lay together, hull to hull,
where the graveyard shelves on the town. . . .
My mind's not right.

A car radio bleats,
"Love, O careless Love. . . ." I hear
my ill-spirit sob in each blood cell,
as if my hand were at its throat. . . .
I myself am hell;
nobody's here —

only skunks, that search
in the moonlight for a bite to eat.
They march on their soles up Main Street;
white stripes, moonstruck eyes' red fire
under the chalk-dry and spar spire
of the Trinitarian Church.

I stand on top
of our back steps and breathe the rich air —
a mother skunk with her column of kittens swills the garbage pail.
She jabs her wedge-head in a cup
of sour cream, drops her ostrich tail,
and will not scare.

Lowell brackets his "lyric center" — stanzas 5 and 6 — with a set of "characters" fore and a set of animals aft. This three-part shape is instantly visible:

1. Grotesque inhabitants of my Maine town;

2. Myself;

3. A mother skunk and her kittens taking over the town.

Each of the three parts has an inner shape of its own. In the first part, the native "hermit heiress" owns two stanzas, while the lesser summer millionaire and "fairy decorator," transients both, own only one stanza each. (The manuscript suggests that all of these are figures for the poet himself. Whereas the final version says "There is no money in his work, / he'd rather marry" about the "fairy decorator," in the draft the poet says this about himself: "There is no money in this work, / I'd rather marry"). Lowell inherited his house in Castine, Maine, from his aunt who lived there, but he only went there summers, like the "summer millionaire." No longer living in one of the roles proper to his Brahmin lineage — hermit, or bishop, or landowner — the speaker has declined into the unvirile role of an artist, comparable to that of the man whom the town contemptuously terms the "fairy decorator."

After presenting these disguised figures for himself in the first part of the poem, the speaker shows us himself in the second part as a voyeur, aware of his own madness as he spies on lovers in cars. The gradually intensifying shape of this middle part is one of mortified self-watching: "My Tudor Ford climbed the hill's skull," not "I drove up the hill." And it is one of psychological self-judging: "My mind's not right." And it is one of medical self-diagnosis: "I hear / my ill-spirit sob in each blood cell." Finally, it is one of ethical self-damnation: "I myself am hell." After the disengaged tone of detached social commentary which dominates the first part of the poem describing Castine, these damning first-person sentences chill the blood.

Then come the skunks. Nature takes over from the decadent culture of Castine. The skunks invade the town. The mother is the general; her offspring are her military "column." We are watching the barbarians (disciplined, vital, fiery-eyed) take over Rome (declining, degenerate, chalk-dry). The vivid verbs used of the skunks energize the exhaustions and distresses of the poem: the skunks *search,* and *march;* the mother skunk *swills* the garbage pail, *jabs* her head into the cup, *drops* her tail, *will not* scare. The speaker is (almost) glad to resign his inherited world to the skunks; certainly he is in no shape to govern it, or even to live in it, any more. It is a poem of total abdication from rule by the originally ruling, now depleted, Brahmin class. It was Lowell's revenge on his own heritage, which he always regarded with mixed admiration and contempt. And it shows his heritage gradually disappearing back into nature, as all cultures eventually do.

Nature and Time

Almost the whole appeal of the little medieval spring song we saw as our first example of nature poetry comes from its rhythm. Here I have marked the "silent *e*'s," which were pronounced ("uh") in the Middle Ages, so that the original rhythm can be heard:

> Sumer is icumen in,
> > Lhudè sing, cuccu!
> Groweth sed and bloweth med
> > And springth the wudè nu.
> > > Sing, cuccu!

> Awè bleteth after lomb,
> > Lhouth after calvè cu,
> Bulluc sterteth, buckè verteth —
> > Murie sing, cuccu!
> > > Cuccu, cuccu.
> Wel singès thu, cuccu.
> Ne swik thu never nu!

At first, as we expect in a simple ballad quatrain (a four-line stanza with alternating four-beat and three-beat lines), a four-beat line ("SUmer IS iCUMen IN") is here followed by a three-beat line ("LHUde SING, cuCU!") and another four-beat line is followed by a three-beat line, all of them about the renewing of vegetation. But to our surprise an unexpected three-beat echo-line is added as a fifth line — "Sing, cuccu!"

Then the poem starts up again. Naturally, we expect another 4 / 3 / 4 / 3 pattern, and we find it, yet this second quatrain is not about vegetation but about the renewing of animal life (ewe and lamb, cow and calf, bullock and buck). We might even expect another echo-line, and we receive it — "Cuccu, cuccu." But this is followed by another surprise — two more three-beat lines, a little congratulation to the harbinger of spring: "Wel singes thu, cuccu. / Ne swik thu never nu!" The lilt of the whole makes us recognize it as a song, even though we find it in printed form.

Besides its rhythmic shape, then, this little two-stanza poem has exhibited a logical shape, separating the vegetative springing of seed and mead and wood (stanza 1) from the animal springing of bullocks (stanza 2), and it has also made a pleasing alternation between description ("Sumer is icumen in") and direct address ("Sing, cuccu!"). It has even displayed another shape: in both stanzas some verbs precede their nouns ("Groweth sed," "Lhouth after calve cu") and some do not ("Sumer is icumen in," "Bulluc sterteth"). These changes make for unpredictability, and therefore pleasure, since we derive pleasure in poems, just as in life, not only from pattern but from the interruption of pattern. If everything were unpredictable we would have chaos, but what we usually find in a good poem is the unpredictable within an overarching purposiveness.

Dave Smith's poem on spring uses one of the oldest European lyric forms, that of the sonnet, *cdcd*. Smith's sonnet is a hybrid one, with a Shakespearean rhyming *abab* octave and a Petrarchan sestet, *efefee*:

DAVE SMITH
The Spring Poem

> *Every poet should write a Spring poem.*
> — LOUISE GLÜCK

Yes, but we must be sure of verities
such as proper heat and adequate form.
That's what poets are for, is my theory.
This then is a Spring poem. A car warms
its rusting hulk in a meadow; weeds slog
up its flanks in martial weather. April
or late March is our month. There is a fog
of spunky mildew and sweaty tufts spill
from the damp rump of a back seat. A spring
thrusts one gleaming tip out, a brilliant tooth
uncoiling from Winter's tension, a ring
of insects along, working out the Truth.
Each year this car, melting around that spring,
hears nails trench from boards and every squeak sing.

Although Smith, in homage to Shakespeare's spring sonnets ("From you have I been absent in the spring," etc.), has given his spring sonnet a Shakespearean octave, he has not divided his sonnet neatly, in terms of thought-units, into three quatrains and a couplet, as Shakespeare usually did. Instead, Smith's poem begins as a reply to the remark by Louise Glück, couching its reply in stern theoretical language about proper and adequate verities. It then announces its own existence: "This then is a Spring poem."

The rest of the poem is description: an actual present-tense description of the rusting car, followed (in the closing couplet) by a habitual-present-tense description of what happens "each year," reassuring us that the previous present-tense process has happened before and happens, in fact, every year. But there is one odd moment in the description of weeds, fog, mildew, tufts, back-seat spring, nails, and boards. It is the phrase about the insects who gather on the metal spring: they are "working out the Truth." The word "truth" is the Anglo-Saxon form of the Latinate word "verity" (used earlier in line 1 in the plural, "verities"), so we know that the insects are experiencing "proper heat and adequate form" and are stand-ins for the poet seeking his verities. As the metal tooth of the spring uncoils, so the weeds and the rest of nature are uncoiling from winter tension, and the poet has to follow along that uncoiling motion, tracing the path of truth as the insects trace the new path afforded them by the newly sprung spring.

From the end of line 4 through line 12, each line spills over into the next one as the scene uncoils before us. Nothing is end-stopped, everything is growing and expanding. (Poems usually indicate a pause at the end of a line either by a break in thought or by the use of a comma, a period, or some other mark of punctuation; when lines "run over," we are to infer an ongoing rush of thought or feeling.) The last two lines of Smith's poem, though, because they tell us what happens "every year" instead of what is happening "now," are a neat couplet; they represent not discovery but summary. Smith has given us first the theory of the spring poem, then the spring poem in action, and finally the spring poem in habitual summary, showing us his three responses to Glück's demand — "I know the theory, I know the thing itself, and I know it happens every year." He also shows us that he is aware Shakespeare did it first, while refusing, as a Modernist, to follow the Renaissance neatness of the four Shakespearean separate thought-units, one for each quatrain, one for the couplet.

Keats's sonnet on the human seasons is written in imitation of Shakespeare, meaning that it has four quatrains and a couplet. Spring happens in quatrain 1, summer in 2, autumn in 3, and winter in the couplet; we can see Keats's orderly arrangement at work. Since not only this procession of the four seasons but also its analogy to human life (from spring-youth to winter-old age) are all predictable once the subject is decided upon, how will Keats make his (known in advance) process aesthetically interesting?

JOHN KEATS
The Human Seasons

Four seasons fill the measure of the year;
   Four seasons are there in the mind of man.

He hath his lusty spring, when fancy clear
    Takes in all beauty with an easy span:
He hath his summer, when luxuriously
    He chews the honied cud of fair spring thoughts,
Till, in his soul dissolv'd, they come to be
    Part of himself. He hath his autumn ports
And havens of repose, when his tired wings
    Are folded up, and he content to look
On mists in idleness: to let fair things
    Pass by unheeded as a threshold brook.
He hath his winter too of pale misfeature,
Or else he would forget his mortal nature.

First of all, Keats doesn't speak of the seasons of the human *body* — doesn't say, "Man has his spring of youth, his summer of maturity, his autumn of decline, and his winter of death." That cliché was too well known. He decides to put the seasons inside man's *mind*. Does the mind, like the body, have seasons? And if so, what are they like (since the mind, in the ordinary sense, does not grow old)? Briefly put, what Keats says is that in youth the mind finds an easy pleasure in spanning the whole world, absorbing everything beautiful. In mental summer, man reconsiders the "fair thoughts" of his spring, redigesting them till they dissolve in his soul and become totally internalized, part of himself. During his mental autumn, he rests, folds his wings, and doesn't try to see everything — he is "content to look on mists in idleness." At this stage, he allows fair things to "pass by unheeded," as a cottager might fail to notice the brook that flows by beyond his threshold. What does the man look on in winter? Not "all beauty," not "fair things," not even "mists" — rather, he looks on "pale misfeature." Why must he look on the diseased and the deformed? Because otherwise, he would "forget his mortal nature." He would forget that he too must grow pale and die, if he looked only on the beautiful or the misty.

This is a brief summary of a complex poem, but it is enough to show the rapid progress of the Keatsian seasonal sketches — the winged fancy of spring, the cud chewing of summer during the pondering of beauty in the soul, the ports and havens for man's autumn migration, the folding of his tired wings among the mists of uncertainty, the threshold brook passing by unheeded outside the house of (as Keats called himself) the "spiritual cottager." Keats's poems often lead us along by a succession of such descriptions. Without the unexpectedness of all these lightly drawn images, the procession of the seasons might be too predictable. And Keats lets each of the first three seasons slip into the next almost imperceptibly, imitating the way of nature. Only winter is unmistakably set apart in the couplet, as misfeature replaces feature.

In Chapter 1, we looked at Shakespeare's three models of life in Sonnet 60: the steady-state model of successive waves in which each moment of life resembles its predecessor and its successor; the rise-and-eclipse-of-the-sun model that sketches a catastrophic view of life; and the third, worst, model, in which we do not even have time to grow before we are scythed down. This structure in itself would have seemed sufficient to many poets. In fact, it would have seemed too much. Often, poems offer only one model of whatever they are discussing. But Shakespeare found it irresistible, very often, to let each of his quatrains set up a model *different* from those set up by the others. The intellectual tension thereby generated — "Is life a steady-state procession? Or a single long climb and fall? Or nothing but successive and premature annihilations?" — involves the reader strongly in the progress of the poem:

WILLIAM SHAKESPEARE
Sonnet 60

Like as the waves make toward the pebbled shore,
So do our minutes hasten to their end,
Each changing place with that which goes before,
In sequent toil all forwards do contend.
Nativity, once in the main of light,
Crawls to maturity, wherewith being crowned,
Crooked eclipses 'gainst his glory fight,
And Time that gave doth now his gift confound.
Time doth transfix the flourish set on youth,
And delves the parallels in beauty's brow,
Feeds on the rarities of nature's truth,
And nothing stands but for his scythe to mow.
And yet to times in hope my verse shall stand,
Praising thy worth, despite his cruel hand.

Each of Shakespeare's three models of Time is a mini-poem in itself. The first model displays itself in balanced ceremonious full uninterrupted lines, like successive waves, making its analogy calmly, as a sermon might:

Metaphor	Like as the waves . . . shore,
Literal truth	So do our minutes . . . end,
Elaboration	Each changing . . . before,
	In sequent toil . . . contend.

The next model is far more troubled, and its pace is charted by its governing words in *cr*: *"crawls," "crowned," "crooked."*

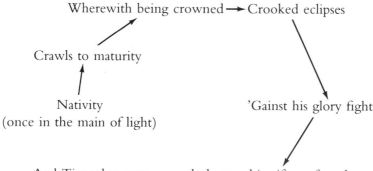

Wherewith being crowned → Crooked eclipses

Crawls to maturity

Nativity
(once in the main of light)   'Gainst his glory fight

And Time that gave ←── doth now his gift confound.

We see nativity crawl up to crowning, then crookedness fight it to death. Time gives on the left, takes away on the right. This is what we think of as the tragic model embedded in those of Shakespeare's plays that show the rise and fall of a character like Macbeth or Othello. It is completely different from Shakespeare's steady-state model in quatrain 1.

Shakespeare's third model consists neither of steady-state waves nor of rising and eclipsed sun. It shows us a drastic speed-up in his rate of extinction. It took three lines for the sun to be extinguished; now the deaths occur at the rate of one per line for two lines, and then several per line:

> Time doth transfix the flourish set on youth,
> And delves the parallels in beauty's brow,
> Feeds on the rarities of nature's truth,
> And nothing stands but for his scythe to mow.

These destructions take place with appalling rapidity, but, what is worse, the way they are related by the syntax of the clauses puts death before lived life. Transfixing precedes flourishing, wrinkles (delved "parallels") precede the appearance of the beautiful brow, devouring precedes the growing of the rare items in nature's garden. Finally, life itself is seen to exist for scything, and for that alone: "*Nothing* stands but *for* his scythe to mow." The poet Gerard Manley Hopkins was later to say bitterly, remembering this line, that man was born *for* death: "It is the blight man was *born for.*"

Shakespeare's three mini-poems, three incompatible models of life, have now been sketched in his sonnet. They are all about Time, and how nothing stands. The couplet, in revenge, shifts from "Time" to "times," and makes them "times in hope" — that is, the envisaged future. The couplet also shifts from "nothing stands" to something standing. In future times ("times in hope"), when the organic world has died, the inorganic world of art, which the scythe cannot mow down, will stand:

> And yet to *times* in hope my verse shall *stand,*
> Praising your worth, despite his cruel hand.

This boast might seem to vanquish Time, if the poem did not end with the hand of Time itself, characterized by an adjective — "cruel" — which opens with the same *cr-* of doom which we remember from the tragic series "crawls," "crowned," "crooked." "Cruel" comes from the Latin *cruor,* "blood" — and Time's bloody hand is set over against the "hand," or handwriting, that creates verse praising worth. It is something of a standoff — but even that is a victory for the rarities of art's truth. After the three competing models of natural life, each more destructive than the last, Shakespeare has closed his sonnet with a model of the endurance — not forever, but at least to "times in hope" — of his verse.

    This second look at our original poems suggests that one can't fully understand a poem until one sees the various shapes into which meaning has been arranged. We have seen steady-state shapes, and shapes of increase and decrease; shapes of contrast and alternation; shapes of series, both internally consistent and inconsistent; shapes of pointed metrical emphasis, of space and time. There is no lack of shapes for poets to imitate — every human action conducted over time offers such a shape, of success or failure, of stasis or catastrophe, of contest or conciliation. The dynamism of such shapes gives dynamism to poetry.

In Brief: The Poem as Arranged Life

    We have seen, by taking a second look at the poems introduced in Chapter 1, how each of these poems is not only an utterance springing from a life-situation, but also a construction, an arrangement. The elements that can enter into the arranging of a poem are very various. The author can be arranging a sound-pattern while arranging a list of parallel elements, and also, simultaneously, advancing the plot through a series of changes in tense or mood. Or the author can be setting up a stanza form at the same time as a logical form: the stanza form may tell us that the poem is a ballad, while the construction may tell us that the poem is built on a logical contrast between "then" and "now." A poem may say "the same thing" three times ("I am growing old"), but each time may use a different model for aging and thus convey a different emphasis. Tones of voice can be varied, from protest to resignation, while another element is held constant (say, the tense of the verbs). By learning to look at each level of organization — phonetic, grammatical, syntactic, psychological, temporal, spatial, and so on — you learn to see the work the author is doing to make the poem both interesting on many levels and coherent in its arrangements. We will be looking at all of these levels in greater detail in subsequent chapters.

Reading Other Poems

The following poems have strong and visible structures. Think first about the life-situation out of which each emerges, and then begin to explore the way in which the life-situation has been imagined and arranged. "Lord Randal," for instance, is structured by the stages of its narrative, as are George Herbert's "Love," John Keats's "La Belle Dame sans Merci," Emily Dickinson's "Because I could not stop for death," and Louise Erdrich's "Windigo." Does each of these poems begin at the outset of its narrative, or do some begin in the middle? Keats's poem begins at the end of the story. Why would a writer decide to begin at the end? How many people speak in "La Belle Dame"?

Given that every plot has a beginning and an end, the writer has the most free play in composing the middle. At the beginning of Herbert's poem, the sinful soul has arrived, after death, at the gate of heaven; at the end of the poem, the soul sits down and participates in the heavenly banquet. What happens in the middle? How many stages are there between beginning and end? John Donne's poem doesn't reach the beginning of its story about a husband's departure on a journey — "I must go" — until it has traversed a long comparison of the way virtuous men die and the way virtuous spouses part. How does Donne end his plot? What are the stages through which Silko takes us through her tale of supernatural abduction?

Shakespeare, Robert Herrick, and Robert Frost, on the other hand, use contrastive structures to explore two different states: Shakespeare contrasts depression and elation; Herrick presents a woman clothed and the same woman naked; Frost contrasts the life lived and the life unlived. Rather than contrast, Walt Whitman uses analogy: He explains his own actions through those of a spider. How does the structure of each of these poems reinforce the contrast or the comparison? What is the imaginative spin put on each poem by the images chosen?

Wordsworth writes a poem about experiencing life and then remembering it, recounting how he sees a host of daffodils and later finds them flashing on the inner screen of memory. However, he gives life three stanzas and memory only one. Can you speculate why? Yet memory has the "last word," which is, in a poem, a place of dominance. Can you think of other ways of arranging this material (say, putting memory first, or giving equal time to life and memory, or alternating from life to memory several times)? How would each of these change the effect of the poem?

Thomas Hardy's poem about the collision of an iceberg and the Titanic begins in the present, with the sunken ship. Where does it end? Where else could it have begun or ended?

The most tightly structured of all these poems is probably "Tichborne's Elegy." Each of its three stanzas is constructed on roughly the same plan, but with variations. Can you describe the basic plan and specify how it varies in each stanza? Try rearranging the stanzas. Would it be the same poem if you interchanged stanzas 1 and 3? Can you see how the tenses change in the poem?

ANONYMOUS
Lord Randal

1

"O where ha' you been, Lord Randal, my son?
And where ha' you been, my handsome young man?"
"I ha' been at the greenwood; mother, mak my bed soon,
For I'm wearied wi' huntin', and fain wad lie down."

2

"And wha met ye there, Lord Randal, my son?
And wha met you there, my handsome young man?"
"O I met wi' my true-love; mother, mak my bed soon,
For I'm wearied wi' huntin', and fain wad lie down."

3

"And what did she give you, Lord Randal, my son?
And what did she give you, my handsome young man?"
"Eels fried in a pan; mother, mak my bed soon,
For I'm wearied wi' huntin', and fain wad lie down."

4

"And wha gat your leavin's, Lord Randal, my son?
And wha gat your leavin's, my handsome young man?"
"My hawks and my hounds; mother, mak my bed soon,
For I'm wearied wi' huntin', and fain wad lie down."

5

"And what becam of them, Lord Randal, my son?
And what becam of them, my handsome young man?"
"They stretched their legs out and died; mother, mak my bed
    soon,
For I'm wearied wi' huntin', and fain wad lie down."

6

"O I fear you are poisoned, Lord Randal, my son!
I fear you are poisoned, my handsome young man!"
"O yes, I am poisoned; mother, mak my bed soon,
For I'm sick at the heart, and I fain wad lie down."

7

"What d' ye leave to your mother, Lord Randal, my son?
What d' ye leave to your mother, my handsome young man?"
"Four and twenty milk kye°; mother, mak my bed soon,   *cattle*
For I'm sick at the heart, and I fain wad lie down."

8

"What d' ye leave to your sister, Lord Randal, my son?
What d' ye leave to your sister, my handsome young man?"
"My gold and my silver; mother, mak my bed soon,
For I'm sick at the heart, and I fain wad lie down."

9

"What d' ye leave to your brother, Lord Randal, my son?
What d' ye leave to your brother, my handsome young man?"
"My houses and my lands; mother, mak my bed soon,
For I'm sick at the heart, and I fain wad lie down."

10

"What d' ye leave to your true-love, Lord Randal, my son?
What d' ye leave to your true-love, my handsome young man?"
"I leave her hell and fire; mother, mak my bed soon,
For I'm sick at the heart, and I fain wad lie down."

WILLIAM SHAKESPEARE

Sonnet 29

When, in disgrace° with fortune and men's eyes,   *disfavor*
I all alone beweep my outcast state,
And trouble deaf heaven with my bootless° cries,   *futile*
And look upon myself, and curse my fate,

Wishing me like to one more rich in hope,
Featured like him, like him with friends possessed,
Desiring this man's art and that man's scope,
With what I most enjoy contented least;
Yet in these thoughts myself almost despising,
Haply I think on thee — and then my state,
Like to the lark at break of day arising
From sullen earth, sings hymns at heaven's gate;
For thy sweet love remembered such wealth brings
That then I scorn to change my state with kings.

CHIDIOCK TICHBORNE
Tichborne's Elegy

Written with his own hand in the Tower before his execution

My prime of youth is but a frost of cares,
My feast of joy is but a dish of pain,
My crop of corn is but a field of tares,
And all my good is but vain hope of gain;
The day is past, and yet I saw no sun,
And now I live, and now my life is done.

My tale was heard and yet it was not told,
My fruit is fallen and yet my leaves are green,
My youth is spent and yet I am not old,
I saw the world and yet I was not seen;
My thread is cut and yet it is not spun,
And now I live, and now my life is done.

I sought my death and found it in my womb,
I looked for life and saw it was a shade,
I trod the earth and knew it was my tomb,
And now I die, and now I was but made;
My glass° is full, and now my glass is run,   *hourglass*
And now I live, and now my life is done.

JOHN DONNE
A Valediction: Forbidding Mourning

As virtuous men pass mildly away,
 And whisper to their souls to go,
Whilst some of their sad friends do say
  The breath goes now, and some say, No;

So let us melt, and make no noise,
    No tear-floods, nor sigh-tempests move,
'Twere profanation of our joys
    To tell the laity our love.

Moving of th' earth brings harms and fears,
    Men reckon what it did and meant;
But trepidation of the spheres,
    Though greater far, is innocent.

Dull sublunary° lovers' love   *earthly*
    (Whose soul is sense) cannot admit
Absence, because it doth remove
    Those things which elemented it.

But we by a love so much refined
    That our selves know not what it is,
Inter-assurèd of the mind,
    Care less, eyes, lips, and hands to miss.

Our two souls therefore, which are one,
    Though I must go, endure not yet
A breach, but an expansion,
    Like gold to airy thinness beat.

If they be two, they are two so
    As stiff twin compasses are two;
Thy soul, the fixed foot, makes no show
    To move, but doth, if th' other do.

And though it in the center sit,
    Yet when the other far doth roam,
It leans and hearkens after it,
    And grows erect, as that comes home.

Such wilt thou be to me, who must
    Like th' other foot, obliquely run;
Thy firmness makes my circle just,
    And makes me end where I begun.

ROBERT HERRICK
Upon Julia's Clothes

Whenas in silks my Julia goes,
Then, then, methinks, how sweetly flows
That liquefaction of her clothes.

Next, when I cast mine eyes, and see
That brave vibration, each way free,
O, how that glittering taketh me!

GEORGE HERBERT
Love (III)

Love bade me welcome: yet my soul drew back,
      Guilty of dust and sin.
But quick-eyed Love, observing me grow slack
      From my first entrance in,
Drew nearer to me, sweetly questioning
      If I lacked anything.

"A guest," I answered, "worthy to be here":
      Love said, "You shall be he."
"I, the unkind, ungrateful? Ah, my dear,
      I cannot look on thee."
Love took my hand, and smiling did reply,
      "Who made the eyes but I?"

"Truth, Lord; but I have marred them; let my shame
      Go where it doth deserve."
"And know you not," says Love, "who bore the blame?"
      "My dear, then I will serve."
"You must sit down," says Love, "and taste my meat."
      So I did sit and eat.

WILLIAM WORDSWORTH
I Wandered Lonely As a Cloud

I wandered lonely as a cloud
That floats on high o'er vales and hills,
When all at once I saw a crowd,
A host, of golden daffodils;
Beside the lake, beneath the trees,
Fluttering and dancing in the breeze.

Continuous as the stars that shine
And twinkle on the milky way,
They stretched in never-ending line
Along the margin of a bay:
Ten thousand saw I at a glance,
Tossing their heads in sprightly dance.

The waves beside them danced; but they
Outdid the sparkling waves in glee;
A poet could not but be gay,
In such a jocund company;
I gazed — and gazed — but little thought
What wealth the show to me had brought:

For oft, when on my couch I lie
In vacant or in pensive mood,
They flash upon that inward eye
Which is the bliss of solitude;
And then my heart with pleasure fills,
And dances with the daffodils.

JOHN KEATS
La Belle Dame sans Merci[1]

O what can ail thee, Knight at arms,
    Alone and palely loitering?
The sedge has withered from the Lake
    And no birds sing!

O what can ail thee, Knight at arms,
    So haggard, and so woebegone?
The squirrel's granary is full
    And the harvest's done.

I see a lily on thy brow
    With anguish moist and fever dew,
And on thy cheeks a fading rose
    Fast withereth too.

"I met a Lady in the Meads,°   *meadows*
    Full beautiful, a faery's child,
Her hair was long, her foot was light
    And her eyes were wild.

"I made a Garland for her head,
    And bracelets too, and fragrant Zone;°   *belt*
She looked at me as she did love
    And made sweet moan.

---

[1] The beautiful lady without mercy.

"I set her on my pacing steed
  And nothing else saw all day long,
For sidelong would she bend and sing
  A faery's song.

"She found me roots of relish sweet,
  And honey wild, and manna dew,
And sure in language strange she said
  'I love thee true.'

"She took me to her elfin grot
  And there she wept and sighed full sore,
And there I shut her wild wild eyes
  With kisses four.

"And there she lullèd me asleep,
  And there I dreamed, Ah Woe betide!
The latest° dream I ever dreamt   *last*
  On the cold hill side.

"I saw pale Kings, and Princes too,
  Pale warriors, death-pale were they all;
They cried, 'La belle dame sans merci
  Hath thee in thrall!'

"I saw their starved lips in the gloam
  With horrid warning gapèd wide,
And I awoke, and found me here
  On the cold hill's side.

"And this is why I sojourn here,
  Alone and palely loitering;
Though the sedge is withered from the Lake
  And no birds sing."

WALT WHITMAN

A Noiseless Patient Spider

A noiseless patient spider,
I mark'd where on a little promontory it stood isolated,
Mark'd how to explore the vacant vast surrounding,
It launch'd forth filament, filament, filament, out of itself,
Ever unreeling them, ever tirelessly speeding them.

And you O my soul where you stand,
Surrounded, detached, in measureless oceans of space,
Ceaselessly musing, venturing, throwing, seeking the spheres to
    connect them,
Till the bridge you will need be form'd, till the ductile anchor
    hold,
Till the gossamer thread you fling catch somewhere, O my soul.

EMILY DICKINSON
Because I could not stop for Death —

Because I could not stop for Death —
He kindly stopped for me —
The Carriage held but just Ourselves —
And Immortality.

We slowly drove — He knew no haste
And I had put away
My labor and my leisure too,
For His Civility —

We passed the School, where Children strove
At Recess — in the Ring —
We passed the Fields of Gazing Grain —
We passed the Setting Sun —

Or rather — He passed Us —
The Dews drew quivering and chill —
For only Gossamer, my Gown —
My Tippet° — only Tulle —   *shoulder cape*

We paused before a House that seemed
A Swelling of the Ground —
The Roof was scarcely visible —
The Cornice — in the Ground —

Since then — 'tis Centuries — and yet
Feels shorter than the Day
I first surmised the Horses' Heads
Were toward Eternity —

THOMAS HARDY

The Convergence of the Twain

Lines on the loss of the Titanic

1

In a solitude of the sea
Deep from human vanity,
And the Pride of Life that planned her, stilly couches she.

2

Steel chambers, late the pyres
Of her salamandrine fires,
Cold currents thrid,° and turn to rhythmic tidal lyres.   *thread*

3

Over the mirrors meant
To glass the opulent
The sea-worm crawls — grotesque, slimed, dumb, indifferent.

4

Jewels in joy designed
To ravish the sensuous mind
Lie lightless, all their sparkles bleared and black and blind.

5

Dim moon-eyed fishes near
Gaze at the gilded gear
And query: "What does this vaingloriousness down here?"

6

Well: while was fashioning
This creature of cleaving wing,
The Immanent Will that stirs and urges everything

7

Prepared a sinister mate
For her — so gaily great —
A Shape of Ice, for the time far and dissociate.

8

And as the smart ship grew
In stature, grace, and hue,
In shadowy silent distance grew the Iceberg too.

9

Alien they seemed to be:
No mortal eye could see
The intimate welding of their later history,

10

Or sign that they were bent
By paths coincident
On being anon twin halves of one august event,

11

Till the Spinner of the Years
Said "Now!" And each one hears,
And consummation comes, and jars two hemispheres.

ROBERT FROST
The Road Not Taken

Two roads diverged in a yellow wood,
And sorry I could not travel both
And be one traveler, long I stood
And looked down one as far as I could
To where it bent in the undergrowth;

Then took the other, as just as fair,
And having perhaps the better claim,
Because it was grassy and wanted wear;
Though as for that, the passing there
Had worn them really about the same,

And both that morning equally lay
In leaves no step had trodden black.
Oh, I kept the first for another day!
Yet knowing how way leads on to way,
I doubted if I should ever come back.

I shall be telling this with a sigh
Somewhere ages and ages hence:
Two roads diverged in a wood, and I —
I took the one less traveled by,
And that has made all the difference.

LOUISE ERDRICH

Windigo

> *The Windigo is a flesh-eating, wintry demon with a man buried deep inside of
> it. In some Chippewa stories, a young girl vanquishes this monster by forcing
> boiling lard down its throat, thereby releasing the human at the core of ice.*

You knew I was coming for you, little one,
when the kettle jumped into the fire.
Towels flapped on the hooks,
and the dog crept off, groaning,
to the deepest part of the woods.
In the hackles of dry brush a thin laughter started up,
Mother scolded the food warm and smooth in the pot
and called you to eat.
But I spoke in the cold trees:
New one, I have come for you, child hide and lie still.

The sumac pushed sour red cones through the air.
Copper burned in the raw wood.
You saw me drag toward you.
Oh touch me, I murmured, and licked the soles of your feet.
You dug your hands into my pale, melting fur.

I stole you off, a huge thing in my bristling armor.
Steam rolled from my wintry arms, each leaf shivered
from the bushes we passed
until they stood, naked, spread like the cleaned spines of fish.

Then your warm hands hummed over and shoveled themselves full
of the ice and the snow. I would darken and spill
all night running, until at last morning broke the cold earth
and I carried you home,
a river shaking in the sun.

3

Poems as Pleasure

Every artwork exists to evoke pleasures that are easier to feel than to describe. Music, for instance, gives rhythmic pleasure and melodic pleasure and harmonic pleasure, in different proportions in different pieces. Some paintings afford the pleasure of recognizable representation; some (purely abstract or nonobjective) do not. Sketches in black-and-white and sketches in color both give pleasure, but of different kinds. We can say in general that all artworks appeal to our (apparently inborn) love of patterning, whether the rhythmic and melodic patterning we hear in music, or the visual patterning we see in a painting or a quilt, or the patterning of volume that we see in architecture, from a cathedral to a cottage. Pattern and rhythm are very closely connected, so closely that people talk of the rhythm of repetition in the successive vaults of a church nave, or the rhythm of repeated curves in a painting.

Since the base of all organic life is repetition (repeated motion in growth and form), and since human life, by its heartbeat and breathing, is innately rhythmic, we can suppose that there is a biological basis for our recognition of, and apparently instinctive pleasure in, repetition. Besides our almost unconscious biological patterns of breathing and sleeping, we enjoy simple repetitive patterned body motions — rocking a baby, swimming, riding a bicycle. Babies learn by patterned repetition, and the pleasure of learning and recognizing new and old patterns is probably the source of our deepest pleasure in art. Most of the true and wise things said in artworks have also been said (in less-patterned and unrhythmic ways) in philosophy and letters and newspaper editorials and conversation, where they also may strike us as true and wise, but not as art. In distinguishing literary artworks from other verbal pieces of truth or wisdom, we tend to be moved by the more intense patterning of the artwork.

The excess of patterning, beyond what is necessary to convey paraphrasable meaning, gives the work what we sometimes call "literariness." Just as a painting can use its elements of pattern — line (bold or delicate), color (moody or cheerful), and visual allusions (such as posing a figure in a gesture known to us from Greek sculpture) — to "say" more than merely "Here is a young woman naked," or "Here is a house in a field," so poems too convey their effects through their manner as much as through their matter. In using pattern in excess of what is strictly necessary for prose meaning, the poet reveals an intent to make art as well as to represent being. The representational urge of most poets is very strong, and every serious poet has something serious to say. Yet though a poet such as Yeats often says "the same thing" in his essays, letters, and speeches — works which we would not tend to call art — as he has said in a poem, we feel a great difference in the manner of the saying. What, then, are the pleasures we find in poems that we cannot find in a prose paraphrase of the same poem or in an essay advocating the same ideas?

Rhythm

The first and most elementary pleasure in all poetry is rhythm. Poetry is far more visibly rhythmic than most prose, and its rhythms are recurrent. Even in free verse, where lines are of unpredictably different lengths and may not rhyme, we often hear the same rhythms recurring. T. S. Eliot's character J. Alfred Prufrock, for instance, both wants to encounter experience (especially sexual experience) and wants to run away from it. His "theme rhythm," as a fellow teacher once pointed out to me, is a little initial skip (˘˘´) in which *two* unstressed syllables are followed by one stressed syllable: "Let us GO." But the little excited skip can't be kept up — each time Prufrock uses it, it dies out into the "ordinary" rhythm of one unstressed syllable followed by one stressed syllable (˘´). "Let us GO, then, YOU and I." And the subsequent lines continue to begin with a skip and die out into a walk, off and on, throughout the poem, right down to the line that is the third from the end, which is the last time we hear the skip:

> We have LINGered in the chambers of the sea
> By sea-girls wreathed in seaweed red and brown
> Till human voices wake us, and we drown.

Good free verse always matches its rhythms to the emotional content of its utterance — in Prufrock's words, "As if a magic lantern threw the nerves in patterns on a screen."

But free verse, though it is a major form in contemporary poetry, is a relatively recent invention. Most poetry in most languages, historically speaking, has had a regular rhythm (though much of it has not had rhyme). English verse began in Anglo-Saxon poetry with no rhyme but a strong four-beat rhythm, and that four-beat rhythm is still very natural to us. In Anglo-Saxon poetic rules, at least three of the four stressed words in a line had to begin with the same consonant-sound ("cat" and "king," even though they begin with different consonants, begin with the same consonant-sound). A modern poet writing in four-beat lines reminds us, by his matching stressed consonant-sounds and words (see those italicized below) that he knows the old forms. Here is the beginning of Wallace Stevens's "A Postcard from the Volcano," in which the dead (like the dead buried in Pompeii by the eruption of Mount Vesuvius) speak to the generations following them who are excavating their buried city:

> Children picking up our bones
> Will *never know* that these *were once*
> As quick° as foxes on the hill;   *fast, alive*
>
> And that in autumn, when the grapes
> Made *sharp* air *sharper* by their smell
> These had a *being, breathing* frost;
>
> And least *will* guess that *with* our bones
> We *left much more, left what* still is
> The *look* of things, *left what we* felt
>
> At *what we* saw.

After the conquest of England by the French in 1066, Anglo-Saxon forms of poetry gave way to newer forms that counted by syllables instead of solely by stress. Gradually, a stable set of possible English rhythms evolved and were given names borrowed from Greek meters (iambic, trochaic, and so on; see appendix "On Prosody" in this volume). A number of rhymed stanza-forms (such as the sonnet and the villanelle) were adapted from European models. Poets can always invent new rhythms and new stanza-forms (as Gerard Manley Hopkins did in the second half of the nineteenth century, and as the free-verse poets did in the twentieth century). They can also revive or adapt older forms (Wallace Stevens, for instance, made the pentameter three-line stanza of Dante his favorite form, though he did not use Dante's rhymes). The more you read, the more you tend to notice the rhythms poets write in, and how the stanzas rhyme.

Rhythm itself is a distinct pleasure. Here are some samples of things people have liked:

Nursery rhythms, strong and emphatic:

> Ding, dong, bell,
> Pussy's in the well.
> Who threw her in?
> Little Johnny Thin.
> Who pulled her out?
> Little Tommy Stout.

The insistent hypnotic rhythms (ONE-two-three-four) of Edgar Allan Poe's four-beat lines in "The Raven":

> Once upon a midnight dreary, while I pondered weak and weary,
> Over many a quaint and curious volume of forgotten lore,
> As I nodded, nearly napping, suddenly I heard a tapping,
> As of someone gently rapping, rapping at my chamber door.

The excited and syncopated five-beat rhythms of Hopkins's "The Starlight Night":

> Look at the stars! look, look up at the skies!
>> O look at all the fire-folk sitting in the air!
>> The bright boroughs, the circle-citadels there!
> Down in dim woods the diamond-delves! the elves'-eyes!

The complex four-beat rhythms of Algernon Charles Swinburne's "When the Hounds of Spring," where dactyls (ONE-two-three) and trochees (ONE-two) predominate:

> And PAN by NOON and BACCHus by NIGHT,
>> FLEETer of FOOT than the FLEET-foot KID,
> FOLLows with DANCing and FILLS with deLIGHT
>> The MAEnad AND the BASSarid;°   *Bacchus's devotees*
> And SOFT as LIPS that LAUGH and HIDE,
> The LAUGHing LEAVES of the TREES diVIDE,
> And SCREEN from SEEing and LEAVE in SIGHT
>> The GOD purSUing, the MAIDen HID.

When rhythms become too insistent, they seem like parodies of themselves. For "Hiawatha," Henry Wadsworth Longfellow picked up the four-beat trochaic rhythm (ONE-two) of the Scandinavian epics, but because it is not, in its unrhymed form, a native narrative rhythm in

English, it becomes tedious, as in this description of Hiawatha making a picture of the earth:

> For the earth he drew a straight line,
> For the sky a bow above it;
> White the space between for day-time,
> Filled with little stars for night-time;
> On the left a point for sunrise,
> On the right a point for sunset,
> On the top a point for noon-tide.

Such a repetitive rhythm was bound to give rise to parodies. George A. Strong's runs, in part:

> Of the skin he made him mittens,
> Made them with the fur side inside,
> Made them with the skin side outside.

Most English verse is made up of rhythms less insistent than those I have been illustrating. The usual English rhythms are one-TWO (iambic) or ONE-two (trochaic), and the usual English line has three or four or five stresses. In most verse, the pleasures of rhythm come from the tension between the basic metrical scheme of the line (one-TWO, one-TWO, one-TWO, one-TWO, one-TWO, as if you were to say, five times, "Untie, untie, untie, untie, untie") and the actual spoken intonation of the line. The underlying scheme of *all* of Shakespeare's dramatic poetry is "Untie untie untie untie untie," but what we actually find is an enormously flexible spoken line:

> Tomorrow, and tomorrow, and tomorrow,
> Creeps in this petty pace from day to day,
> To the last syllable of recorded time.

We hear the undersong of the *metrical scheme* as a child might mechanically recite it, as if to a metronome:

> ToMORRow, AND toMORRow, AND toMORRow,
> Creeps IN this PETTy PACE from DAY to DAY,
> To THE last SYLLable OF reCORDed TIME.

And we also sense the oversong of the *natural intonation of the words* as they would be ordinarily spoken:

> ToMORRow, and toMORRow, and toMORRow,
> CREEPS IN this PETTy PACE from DAY to DAY,
> To the LAST SYLLable of reCORDed TIME.

A good actor makes an amalgam of metrical scheme and natural into-nation, so that the audience hears a *rhythm* that keeps both the undersong of five beats and the oversong of urgent speech. One of the hardest things to do in poetry is to write hundreds of lines obeying the same *scheme* (as Milton does with his unrhymed five-beat lines in *Paradise Lost*) while varying the *rhythm*, so that the reader's ear does not tire. Of course, composers do the same. Every measure of a musical piece in 4/4 time has four beats to the measure, but not every measure is composed of four quarter-notes. There are eighth-notes, sixteenth-notes, half-notes, whole notes, held notes, notes with trills on them, and so on.

Knowing the musical weight, so to speak, of every possible syllable in the language is the gift of great poets. Some syllables are heavy, some light; some long, some short; some open, some closed; some nasal, some mellow; some sharp, some sweet. Keats, in his poem "If by dull rhymes," advises himself and other poets to care at least as much for syllabic wealth as King Midas cared for his gold, and not to repeat lifeless and worn-out strategies:

> Let us inspect the lyre, and weigh the stress
> Of every chord, and see what may be gained
> By ear industrious, and attention meet;
> Misers of sound and syllable, no less
> Than Midas of his coinage, let us be
> Jealous of dead leaves in the bay wreath crown.

Rhythms should be recurrent but not boring, hearable but not predict-able.

Rhyme

We seem to be born liking sounds that match. Children make up games with simple counting rhymes. "One, two, button my shoe" still lives, though no one wears high-button shoes any more. Rhyme makes for conclusiveness and the sense of an ending. Once you accept the principle of rhyme, you can do many various things with it.

Rhythmically speaking, the simplest rhymes are monosyllables — *day, say*. You get a different effect from disyllables — *reason, treason*. The effect often becomes comic once you get trisyllables — *temptation, rela-tion*. You can combine words having different numbers of syllables — *lover, discover*.

Graphically speaking, the simplest rhymes are those that are spelled the same — *day, say*. You get a different effect, even with monosyllables, when they are spelled differently — *day, weigh*. When you have three monosyllables, all with different spelling, the sense of poetic invention is even stronger — *day, weigh, fey*. Though amateur poets tend to rhyme monosyllables spelled the same way, poets interested in technical invention tend to investigate all the possibilities of more complicated polysyllabic and differently spelled rhyming words.

Grammatically speaking, the simplest rhymes are those in which both words are the same part of speech — say, two verbs (*weigh, neigh*) or two nouns (*cat, hat*). As soon as you have two words that are matched by rhyme but that don't match in other ways — say, a noun and a verb (*day, weigh*) — you feel a slight shock of difference.

Semantically speaking, the most satisfactory rhymes are ones in which the two rhyming words have some meaning-relation to each other. The meaning-relation may be one of sameness (*high/sky*) or difference (*island/highland*).

Some poets care a great deal more about making their rhymes meaningful than others do. Comic poets especially like to make points by ridiculous rhymes: here is Lord Byron on the young Don Juan's classical education, which Juan's mother (Donna Inez) must countenance but which she finds shocking. We can imagine how Byron amused himself rhyming "goddesses," "bodices," and "Odysseys":

> His classic studies made a little puzzle,
>> Because of filthy loves of gods and goddesses,
> Who in the earlier ages raised a bustle,
>> But never put on pantaloons or bodices;
> His reverend tutors had at times a tussle,
>> And for their Aeneids, Iliads, and Odysseys,
> Were forced to make an odd sort of apology,
> For Donna Inez dreaded the Mythology.

To make end-rhymes, one must have at least two lines, explaining why Keats thought of a kiss as a rhyme (and perhaps of a rhyme as a kiss of language). Arranging lines (usually rhyming lines, but not necessarily so) in a perceptible shape makes a stanza. One of the well-known stanza forms in English is a stanza of six five-beat lines rhyming *ababcc*. That is, the first and third lines rhyme on one sound — here designated *a*; the second and fourth lines rhyme on a different sound, *b*; and the fifth and sixth lines rhyme on yet another sound, *c*. Though this can be used in a long poem (it is in fact called the "Venus and Adonis stanza" because Shakespeare used it in his narrative poem of that name), it is also used by Ben Jonson in his one-stanza satiric poem on a lustful glutton allegorically named "Gut":

BEN JONSON
On Gut

Gut eats all day and lechers all the night;
So all his meat he tasteth over twice;
And, striving so to double his delight,
He makes himself a thoroughfare of vice.
Thus in his belly can he change a sin:
Lust it comes out, that gluttony went in.

Most poems written in stanza-form, unlike "On Gut," consist of more than one stanza. Stanzas have names (see appendix "On Prosody"), and poems using the same stanza forms belong to a recognizable family. Yeats may use a stanza-form associated with Geoffrey Chaucer; Keats may use the sonnet-form we associate with Shakespeare. As we read the later poet, we are reminded of the earlier one (and as we read the earlier one, we sometimes think forward to how a later poet will write in this stanza-form). Poets make certain stanza-forms their own. Dante wrote the whole of the *Divine Comedy* in three-line pentameter stanzas with interlaced rhyme, and ever since, anyone writing in this form or one of its modern adaptations — from Percy Bysshe Shelley in the nineteenth century through Wallace Stevens and Seamus Heaney in the twentieth century — evokes Dante.

Some stanzaic forms undergo interesting changes over time. Early narrative ballads were written in a stanza rhyming *abxb*, meaning that only the second and fourth lines rhymed. Usually the first line had four beats, the second three, the third four, and the fourth three (which we represent as 4/3/4/3). The early ballads were primarily stories in verse: the important feature in them was a plot of love, mystery, or adventure that moved incrementally on, often to disaster. Characterization and emotional reaction and description were kept to a minimum. Here is a representative ballad stanza, clearly interested in setting up a story:

There lived a wife at Usher's Well,
    And a wealthy wife was she;
She had three stout and stalwart sons,
    And sent them o'er the sea.

In the nineteenth century, William Wordsworth, though he was still interested in telling stories, was more concerned with the inner states and emotional responses accompanying events than in the events themselves. He invented what he called "lyrical ballads"; they were still written in the ballad stanza, and were allied to storytelling, but their emphasis was "lyrical" — that is, emotional and private rather than factual and plot-governed. Here is the ending of one of Wordsworth's lyrical ballads:

> She lived unknown, and few could know
>> When Lucy ceased to be;
> But she is in her grave, and, oh,
>> The difference to me!

Both "The Wife of Usher's Well" and Wordsworth's poem have the same stanzaic arrangement — four beats, three beats, four beats, three beats — with the second and fourth lines rhyming (and in Wordsworth's poem the first and third lines rhyming as well). Whenever we see this 4/3/4/3 rhyming stanza turn up, we are reminded that it goes back to our earliest folk poetry. When later poets want to write in an archaic way, they often use this stanza (see Samuel Taylor Coleridge's "Rime of the Ancient Mariner" and Keats's "La Belle Dame sans Merci").

The ballad stanza is four lines long, and so is called a quatrain, as are all stanzas of four lines. But there are other kinds of rhymes that a quatrain can use besides *abxb* or *abab*. It can use *aabb*, as in "Infant Sorrow":

> My mother groaned, my father wept.
> Into the dangerous world I leapt,
> Helpless, naked, piping loud;
> Like a fiend hid in a cloud.

Or a quatrain can rhyme *abba*, a form that Alfred, Lord Tennyson used in his long elegy "In Memoriam":

> Ring out, wild bells, to the wild sky,
>> The flying cloud, the frosty light:
>> The year is dying in the night;
> Ring out, wild bells, and let him die.

Several different variables combine to make stanzas: the length of the stanza (here, in our examples, four lines); the stress-length of the individual lines (4/3/4/3 in the ballads, 4/4/4/4 in Blake's and Tennyson's poems); the arrangement of the rhymes (whether *abab*, *aabb*, or *abba*); and the combination of stressed and unstressed syllables. Poets experiment with all these variables to make the different kinds of stanzas named below (which are described at fuller length in the appendix "On Prosody"):

Two lines: couplet

Three lines: tercet

Four lines: quatrain

Five lines: cinquain

Six lines: sixain or sestet

Seven lines: rime royal (rhyming *ababbcc*)

Eight lines: ottava rima (rhyming *abababcc*)

Nine lines: Spenserian stanza (rhyming *ababbcbcc*)

Fourteen lines: sonnet

By and large, the longer stanzas listed above are written in five-beat widths. But almost any combination of width (number of beats per line) and length (number of lines) and rhyme has been tried by someone. The important thing is to notice what the poet has been up to in the way of metrical form — rhymes, line-width, and stanza-shape — and to recall, if you can, other poems that have the same stanzaic shape as the one you are reading. One of the pleasures offered by poetry is a technical cousinship among poems, recognizable if you are used to registering the stanzaic shapes they take.

Structure

The structures of a poem are the intellectual or logical shapes into which its thoughts are dynamically organized. Any overarching structure can have many substructures. We saw, in "Infant Sorrow," a general structure in which the first stanza shows us the physical baby, the second the baby as thinker. Within that general structure we saw others — the presence of the parents in each stanza, the decline from *struggling* to *striving* to *bound*, and so on. Perhaps the greatest pleasure given by poetry is the sense that dynamic structure and thought are so intimately connected that each gives coherence to the other. We sometimes express this by saying that the structure of the poem *enacts* (acts out, dramatizes) by way of a dynamic evolution of form what the poem *says* by way of assertion.

How does one come to perceive the structure by which the poem conveys its assertions? As we saw in Chapter 2, it takes something like X-ray vision, by which you look for patterns. Patterns occur at many levels in poetry, just as they do in the physical universe: one can look for patterns in subatomic behavior, in atomic behavior, in molecular behavior, and so on, all the way up to the patterns of the planets and the stars. If you think of a poem as a small universe, you can begin looking at the smallest patterns (the binding-together of certain words by rhyme or by similar initial sounds) or at the largest patterns (the number of sentences and their relations to each other as a dynamic pattern of thinking). One level of investigation may not yield much: the poem you are looking at may not rhyme, and there may be only a relatively small number of alliterating words (words beginning with the same consonant-sound). At this point, you would probably give up looking for inter-esting sound-patterns, and move on to sentence-relations. Or, on another level, the poem may not have many descriptive phrases repre-senting people or a landscape — it may be mostly statement (say, of philosophical truths). At this point, you would stop looking for a pattern of descriptive images, and perhaps move on to patterns of diction. Or, on another level, that of plot, nothing much may seem to happen. Do not be discouraged; if the energy of the poem is not in plot, it may be in its grammatical play; if it is not in grammatical play, it may be in images; if it is not in images, it may be in rhythm.

What, for instance, could we find to say about this poem, called simply "Poem," by William Carlos Williams?

WILLIAM CARLOS WILLIAMS
Poem

As the cat
climbed over
the top of

the jamcloset
first the right
forefoot

carefully
then the hind
stepped down

into the pit of
the empty
flowerpot

There certainly isn't much that is philosophical or intellectual here. In fact, if the four stanzas were written out as the one sentence they are, it wouldn't seem like a poem at all: "As the cat climbed over the top of the jamcloset, first the right forefoot, carefully, then the hind, stepped down into the pit of the empty flowerpot." And the "plot" — a cat finding its way — is an ordinary event seen every day. A good strategy in examining a poem is always to see why the poet wrote out its sentences in the way he or she did. Williams divided his sentence into four stanzas, each of three lines. How did he decide where to break his sentence, and why did he group the twelve pieces three-by-three? If we reread the poem asking the questions that the pause after each line encourages us to ask, we can see the meaning of Williams's line-breaks:

As the cat	*did what?*
climbed over	*over what?*
the top of	*of what?*
the jamcloset	*how?*
first the right	*paw? rear leg?*
forefoot	*then? (a mistaken question; it turns*
	out Williams wanted me to ask "how?")
carefully	*then what?*
then the hind	*did what?*
stepped down	*where?*
into the pit of	*oops! of what?*
the empty	*what has a "pit" anyhow?*
flowerpot	*not what you expected, kittycat!*

Well, this more or less shows me why Williams put his unsteady little pauses where he did. But why did he group his lines three by three? This action inserts three "major pauses" at certain points to punctuate the "minor pauses" at the end of each line. The first major pause comes when the cat stops before the descent into unknown regions (which it cannot see) from the top of the jamcloset. The second comes after the right forefoot has found (hurrah!) a place to poise. The third comes after the hind leg successfully (whee!) moves to follow the forefoot. Then comes the farcical end, when the poor cat finds itself trapped inside a deep flowerpot instead of safe on a flat surface.

Williams's lines consist, sometimes, of only a single word — "forefoot," "carefully," "flowerpot." Each line represents a cat-step, so these are particularly fraught steps. Some lines have two words — these are steps of medium difficulty. We end up feeling that the lines of *three* or even *four* words — "As the cat," "the top of," "first the right," "into the pit of," are almost carefree, almost lilting.

As for Williams's stanzas, they are all adverbial, ornaments attached to the central main verb, "stepped." There is the "as" stanza, the "first" stanza, the "then" stanza, and the "into" stanza. They are all equal in length, as though the cat had made four neat forays into what it hoped would be stability, but what it found was captivity. Clearly the initial confident tentativeness and the ultimate bewildering failure of the cat delighted Williams as a little emblem of human venturing. Whenever a poet calls a poem "Poem" it means that the story told in the poem resembles the making of poetry itself. Like the cat, the poet ventures out into the hazards of thin air, places a "foot" (a metrical foot, no doubt) on a possible landing, tries another foot after it, and may find farce instead of success.

It would be of no use to go to this poem looking for harmonious melody, or philosophical assertion, or nature description, or rhyme, or song-rhythm, or historical insight, or Freudian dreamwork, or gender problems. Each poem leads you to the questions it makes sense to ask it. It makes sense to ask this poem about its twelve lines and its four stanzas and its three white spaces and its line-breaks; it makes sense to ask what the cat expected and what the cat found; it makes sense to ask why the poet gave this humble anecdote the honorific name "Poem." It makes sense, too, to ask what the poet who writes such a poem understands poetry to be — to which we might answer that it is the imaginative perception of the ordinary; and the comic perception of hazards-and-landings; and the emblematic perception of how an animal's small ventures might be like ours.

Let us look for a moment at a very different sort of poem altogether, "We Real Cool," by Gwendolyn Brooks:

GWENDOLYN BROOKS
We Real Cool

> *The Pool Players.*
> *Seven at the Golden Shovel.*

We real cool. We
Left school. We

Lurk late. We
Strike straight. We

Sing sin. We
Thin gin. We

Jazz June. We
Die soon.

The first thing that strikes anyone reading this poem is that its sentences are arranged "wrong." It "should" read,

> We real cool.
> We left school.
>
> We lurk late.
> We strike straight.

And so on. The second thing that strikes the ear is that most of the poem is spoken in the present tense, but two things break that pattern — the past tense in "We *left* school" and the implied future tense — or is it? — in the "We die soon" that ends the poem.

The subtitle of the poem tells us who is speaking — seven pool players at the Golden Shovel pool room. The diction of the poem — "We real cool" instead of "We're real cool" — tells us the pool players are black, as they omit the verb "to be." Why are the poem's rhymes displaced to the "wrong" place in the lines, and why do its tenses change? How do these practices of the poet enact something about the seven pool players? And how, we might add, are we to explain that all their sentences consist of three words? And why do their sentences have so many internal binding sounds — "lurk late," "strike straight," "sing sin," "thin gin," "jazz June"? All the answers to such questions must be conjectural, but the analyst's aim is to make the conjectural answers as plausible as possible, so that they "account for" those patterns in which the composing poet, and the responsive reader, take pleasure.

In answering the questions that the poem makes us ask, we notice that instead of a "rhyme" at the end of each line, the insistent "We" appears down the right margin. "We" is the real word binding these seven adolescents together — they are a group giving each other solidarity. We get so used to seeing "We" at the end of every line — one, two, three, four, five, six, seven — that when we "miss" it at the end of line 8 we know that its absence is a sign of the imminent death of the group. The poverty-stricken sentences — after all, the first complete sentences made by babies consist of two or three words, "Me want that," "I go bed" — are a sign that indeed these young men have "left school" and its more complex possibilities of language. Nonetheless, their syntactically simple sentences are full of a feel for language — if they had stayed in school, they might have produced, among them, a poet or two. They like groups of words that sound "jazzy," and they like singing and playing games — all, inclinations characteristic of poets. The trouble is the gin and the sin and the gambling and the school leaving and the lurking into late hours.

It makes sense to ask this poem questions about its rhymes, its syntax, its tenses, its word placement, in order to know who these "cool" adolescents are, how the poet enacts their solidarity, their gifts, their appetites, and their mistakes. It makes sense, once one knows that this is a poem about young black dropouts, to ask what the poet's feelings about them are — "young, talented with words, doomed." It makes sense to ask this poem about its wit (these young men make their every word count — their three-word sentences have three full beats). It makes sense, too, to ask it about racial questions (the white world is entirely absent — why?). It makes sense to put the poem in a genre — the genre of elegy, especially the subgroup of elegies that mourn people who died much too young. This is an elegy with no visible offer of consolation — there is no better purpose served by the deaths of the young men, no envisaged heaven for them to go to after their death, no legacy they leave behind them of children begotten or accomplishments completed. It makes sense, as well, to ask to whom the young men are speaking. To us? To themselves? Highly literate readers may recall a "we" elegy spoken by the small band of Spartan soldiers who died in 480 B.C., at Thermopylae, an elegy that is perhaps the classical ancestor of this poem:

> Go tell the Spartans, thou who passest by,
> That here, obedient to their laws, we lie.

We can then see the poem not simply as an elegy by Gwendolyn Brooks for these young men, but as their self-epitaph, which could be inscribed on their grave: "We / Die soon." The apparent future tense of the last line then becomes a generalized present tense about the fate of all such adolescents: "We — people like us — always die soon."

The important thing is to be accustomed to looking, in any poem, at several levels — the sound, the rhythms and rhymes, the grammar, the images, the sentences, the plot, the assertions, the allusions, the self-contradictions. Somewhere the energy of the poem awaits you. The moment you see the main and subordinate patterns, you smile, and it "all makes sense."

Images

Though people sometimes refer to "images" in poems, a word is not the same thing as a picture. Words refer; images represent. When poets use nouns or phrases referring to something that an artist could represent by graphic means (a painting or sketch), they use them either for descriptive purposes or as illustrative examples. The images can be either literally pictorial ("This is the forest primeval") or figurative, as when Wordsworth says of a rural woman that she is "A violet by a mossy stone, / Half hidden from the eye." Shakespeare's three images in Sonnet 60 for time's action (ocean waves; a sun that rises and is eclipsed; a repeated destructive attack by a spear, a spade, a maw, a scythe) give three illustrative ways of thinking about life: life is a steady state in which each moment, wavelike, resembles the next; or, life is a glowing rise followed by a catastrophic blackout; or, life is experienced as a continuous and premature and universal execution. These are not compatible images, and the poem makes us see each later image obliterating the former model(s).

Images, in fact, serve in poems as a shorthand for argument. It is quicker to show than to tell. It is a rule of thumb in poems that when a second, different, image follows a first, the second one is somehow importantly supplementing, or indeed correcting or supplanting, the first, because of some perceived inadequacy in the first image (otherwise, the poem would not have needed the second). So, when William Blake wanders through London despairing at the evils of modern life, he first mentions, as a major evil that comes to mind, "the mind-forg'd manacles" of false beliefs. But he does not stop there. He replaces the manacles with the institution that imposes them, and which permits the exploitation of the poor and the powerless — the Church. Yet the Church is not the worst evil: after all, to lose one's life is worse than to be manacled in mind or to be poor, and so Blake goes on to indict the monarchy, which sends its sons off to be killed. Yet even that image of evil does not suffice. He must supplement Church and Palace with one more, the worst — the corruption of the sexual life which, by prostitution and syphilis, blinds the newborn infant in the cradle. Blake's images rise, supplementing and even replacing one another, to the fatal last word in the last line:

WILLIAM BLAKE
London

I wander thro' each charter'd street,
Near where the charter'd Thames does flow,
And mark in every face I meet
Marks of weakness, marks of woe.

In every cry of every man,
In every Infant's cry of fear,
In every voice, in every ban,
The mind-forg'd manacles I hear.

How the Chimney-sweeper's cry
Every blackning Church appalls;
And the hapless Soldier's sigh
Runs in blood down Palace walls.

But most thro' midnight streets I hear
How the youthful Harlot's curse
Blasts the new-born Infant's tear,
And blights with plagues the Marriage hearse.

It is necessary to see the climactic order of Blake's images ("But *most* I hear") in order to set them in relation to each other. Every image needs to be related to others in the same poem, but in an imaginative, not a mechanical, way. You need to enter the mind of the speaker, make yourself into the speaker, and ask yourself how you are connecting things in your ongoing expression.

Argument

A poem often looks as though it is making an argument. But "real" arguments are made in prose (theological tracts argue about God, philosophical books argue ethics or metaphysics, political papers argue politics). Arguments in poems are miniature imitations of "real" arguments, and are often designed to show the moves in the argumentative game rather than to make a full argument in order to persuade a "real-life" person. The debates in poems are often sophisticated games, as when a "shepherd" (really a courtier in pastoral disguise) tries to persuade a "nymph" (an aristocratic young woman playing at being a rustic shepherdess) to love him. She counters with a mini-sermon on the transience of all earthly love, relenting at the end to wish things were otherwise:

CHISTOPHER MARLOWE
The Passionate Shepherd to His Love

Come live with me and be my love,
And we will all the pleasures prove°   *experience*
That valleys, groves, hills, and fields,
Woods, or steepy mountain yields.

And we will sit upon the rocks,
Seeing the shepherds feed their flocks,
By shallow rivers to whose falls
Melodious birds sing madrigals.

And I will make thee beds of roses
And a thousand fragrant posies,
A cap of flowers, and a kirtle
Embroidered all with leaves of myrtle;

A gown made of the finest wool
Which from our pretty lambs we pull;
Fair lined slippers for the cold,
With buckles of the purest gold;

A belt of straw and ivy buds,
With coral clasps and amber studs:
And if these pleasures may thee move,
Come live with me, and be my love.

The shepherds' swains shall dance and sing
For thy delight each May morning:
If these delights thy mind may move,
Then live with me and be my love.

SIR WALTER RALEGH
The Nymph's Reply to the Shepherd

If all the world and love were young,
And truth in every shepherd's tongue,
These pretty pleasures might me move
To live with thee and be thy love.

Time drives the flocks from field to fold
When rivers rage and rocks grow cold,
And Philomel° becometh dumb;   *the nightingale*
The rest complains of cares to come.

The flowers do fade, and wanton fields
To wayward winter reckoning yields;
A honey tongue, a heart of gall,
Is fancy's spring, but sorrow's fall.

Thy gowns, thy shoes, thy beds of roses,
Thy cap, thy kirtle, and thy posies
Soon break, soon wither, soon forgotten —
In folly ripe, in reason rotten.

Thy belt of straw and ivy buds,
Thy coral clasps and amber studs,
All these in me no means can move
To come to thee and be thy love.

But could youth last and love still breed,
Had joys no date° nor age no need,   *end*
Then these delights my mind might move
To live with thee and be thy love.

There exist within poetic tradition debates between body and soul, between gardeners and mowers, between God and man, between the owl and the nightingale, between the flower and the leaf, between a philosopher and a poet. Such debates usually raise perennial questions — hedonism versus asceticism, night versus day, the mirthful man versus the pensive man, the active life versus the contemplative life, and so on. Partly *because* such questions cannot be settled, the pleasure in a poem of argument lies in seeing what strategic moves, and what new speakers, can be invented for such perennial arguments.

Poignancy

We often say a poem is "moving." What makes a poem moving? Normally, it is the relation between the situation implied in the poem (say, a lover at a girl's window) and the utterance of the poem (plaintive, or witty, or ecstatic).

Often, the situation in a poem changes as the poem develops, and the utterance changes along with the new event or the new perception. We never expect, for instance, that anyone we love will be taken from us, however logically we may "know" that death comes to everyone. Somehow we "repress" (as we now say) our knowledge that those we love most are themselves mortal. Wordsworth's speaker in a famous poem says that his mind (he calls it his "spirit") "slumbered" when it exempted his beloved from the threat of mortality. In the first stanza of the poem, the insidious word "seemed" holds the forthcoming catastrophe:

WILLIAM WORDSWORTH
A slumber did my spirit seal

A slumber did my spirit seal;
    I had no human fears:
She seemed a thing that could not feel
    The touch of earthly years.

A white space intervenes between stanza 1 and stanza 2. When we begin stanza 2, we see that the girl has died between the two stanzas — that the white space represents her death. The first stanza was delusion; the second is reality:

> No motion has she now, no force;
> > She neither hears nor sees;
> Rolled round in earth's diurnal course,
> > With rocks, and stones, and trees.

What is poignant here is, first of all, the speaker's total suppression of the narrative of her death. He does not say, "But then she sickened and she died" — it is too painful for him to say that bald sentence. He makes her still the subject of his second sentence, as she was the subject of the last part of his first sentence: "She seemed . . . She has now . . . ; She neither hears nor sees." But the sentence of stanza 2 is all negation in its predicates: Motion? No. Force? No. Hears? No. Sees? No. We then realize, looking back, that there was a comparable negation in stanza 1: Can feel earthly years? No. But that was preceded by the verb "seemed." Now, it proves untrue. She *can* feel the touch of earthly years, so much so that the word the speaker lightly used of her in stanza 1 — "thing" — turns out to be the accurate word. She is now a thing, as rocks and stones and trees are things, and she is as inertly rolled round, day and night, by the planet's motion as they are.

If the poignancy is partly in the speaker's mistake, and partly in his unwitting use of the word "thing," it lies also, in stanza 2, in his stern truthfulness. He speaks in strictly inorganic physical terms: motion, force, diurnal course, rocks, stones. He has mentioned hearing and seeing, organic functions, only to deny them. Nonetheless, he ultimately relents: in placing his beloved not only with rocks and stones and planetary motion, but also — and lastly — with organic and living trees, he gives her a posthumous association with life. The poem would be very different — and almost inhuman — if the last line read, "With granite, stones, and rocks." The poignancy of any poem comes with the struggle between uttering truth and honoring the undertow of strong feeling.

Wisdom

Poems descend in part from wisdom literature — prayers, spells, riddles, epigrams, proverbs, aphorisms. "What oft was thought but ne'er so well expressed" (Alexander Pope) is one description of poetry, and we respond (especially when we are young) to what poetry can tell us about human experience. Countless adolescents have memorized lines such as "How do I love thee? Let me count the ways" (Elizabeth Barrett Browning). Poetry is the most concise form of literature, and it has perfected techniques for rapid and deft exposition (partly by the short-hand arguments of imagery). Many people read poetry chiefly for the wisdom they find there, scarcely knowing that the wisdom seems wiser for having been expressed so memorably. There is a psychological wisdom in lyric: one of its functions is to give us a believable representation of what Matthew Arnold called "the dialogue of the mind with itself." When we see a credible representation of grief, or rebellion, or delusion, we feel the assuaging assent that comes from a ratification of something we have felt but have not previously seen represented. "Strength came where weakness was not known to be," as Wordsworth says of a similar experience. It is important to everyone to find his or her own experience mirrored back; some find this mirroring chiefly in novels, others in poetry, depending on personal taste. The dazzling variety of voices in lyric, each available to any reader as a vicarious voice in which to speak, lets us move through many experiences comparable to our own. Often we find (as we are being John Donne — "Sweetest love, I do not go / For weariness of thee" — or Elizabeth Bishop — "I caught a tremendous fish" —) that the exhilaration of having a new voice and new insight reverberates back into our "real" experiences of a comparable sort.

A New Language

Each major artist creates in a distinctive way. Though early Beethoven can sound like Mozart, or early Mozart like Haydn, in their maturity they end up sounding different from the predecessors whom they imitated in youth. We can walk into a museum and say, "That's a Van Gogh," or "That's a Picasso," because each major painter has a distinctive way of representing and coloring the world. Poets are the same: we can tell (after a while) Tennyson from William Butler Yeats, and Milton from Edmund Spenser, and Adrienne Rich from Anne Sexton, even though in many cases there are resemblances in subject matter. It is not subject matter that distinguishes artists, it is treatment. There are hundreds of portraits of distinguished-looking men, but anyone who has spent some time in museums can tell a Velásquez from a Hals, and either from a Cézanne.

A distinctive style is created in part by the artist and in part by the epoch in which the artist works. One can tell a Renaissance painting from a nineteenth-century painting, a piece of anonymous fifteenth-century music from a piece of anonymous seventeenth-century music. (I will say more about this in the chapter "History and Regionality.") Within what any given epoch permits, many styles are possible (as one can tell from looking at twentieth-century American painting or poetry). Wordsworth said that the poet must create the taste by which he is enjoyed; that is, the poet trains the audience to like a new sort of art. The training takes time, and each new poet you read is training you to like a new personal shorthand of images and a systematically original language. If a poet does not appeal to you now, look again at the work in ten years, and you may like it then. Acculturation is fast in some cases, slow in others. But if many people have found a poet's language memorable, you may some day find it memorable, too. Each person's taste hovers at a different evolutionary moment. A person brought up on Christian prayer comes to Christian religious poetry with great ease; someone who has never heard a Christian prayer or hymn may take a long time to get used to George Herbert or Christina Rossetti. An ecologist may not be put off by the scientific vocabulary in the poems of A. R. Ammons or Amy Clampitt; someone who has never heard of the Cambrian shield or pheromones may be more apprehensive. The rule of thumb is to let the poem work on you over time.

Finding Yourself

The strangest experience in reading poetry, as in writing it, is to find yourself in it, to be yourself in it. We sometimes speak of this as finding a "favorite poet." This is a poet whose writing is so close to your own way of seeing and thinking that there seems no barrier at all between you and the poet. Such a poet is a powerful reflecting mirror of your own sensibility and creativity. In that poet's work, you find yourself "more truly and more strange" (as Wallace Stevens put it in "Tea at the Palaz of Hoon"). Sometimes poets are mirrors for a whole generation, and become bestsellers on that account — as T. S. Eliot and Robert Frost and Adrienne Rich and Allen Ginsberg have been in the United States in the twentieth century. Other American poets, just as good, remain known to relatively few readers (who nonetheless claim them as intensely as the country at large claims the bestsellers). Samuel Johnson said (in his "Preface to Shakespeare") that it was only after a century had passed, and the topical interest of a piece of literature had died down, that one could tell whether it would last. Luckily, you do not have to worry about the potential durability of works in which you find a voice and a reflecting mirror; that question will take care of itself. The important thing is to feel companioned, as you go through life, by a host of poems which speak to your experience. And, in the long run, the poems you first read because you wanted to find out about love or death you will read again because of the living quality of the voice that speaks in them, that quality we call "style."

In Brief: Poems as Pleasure

No single poem offers all the pleasures of poetry. As you read, you will sometimes be caught up in the lilt of a rhythm, sometimes intrigued by plot; at other times you may be struck by an insight, moved by the poignancy of tone, or puzzled and pleased by a subversive and unexpected move by the text. The important thing is to be ready for whatever the poem offers, and to take it on its own terms, not requiring philosophical discourse from a song, or simplicity from a knotted problem-poem. The single best way to gain pleasure from a poem is to read it aloud; if you let the poem take you on its journey, you will know intuitively where it has led you. The next pleasure is to find words for what you felt and thought on that journey; and the next is to find what aspects of the poem — structure, images, argument — generated those feelings and those thoughts. Chapter 4 will suggest some ways by which you can describe the various aspects of poems from which these pleasures arise.

Reading Other Poems

All the following poems combine representation and strong patterning. Both Theodore Roethke and William Carlos Williams declare by their titles that they will employ strong rhythmic patterning. Can you graph the rhythms their lines enact?

Some poets can create strong patterns in very brief poems. William Blake's "The Sick Rose" consists (if one were to consider it clinically) of six lines of diagnosis followed by two of prognosis (or forecast of the course of the rose's disease). Do the rhymes in any way suggest the plot? Gerard Manley Hopkins's "sonnet" of reduced proportions — a six-line "octave" followed by a four-and-a-half-line "sestet" — is divided into two ways of talking about "dappled" beauty — beauty that is spotted, variegated, multiple. What is the pattern of discussion in the first part of the poem, offered in words like "skies," "trout," "trades"? And in the second, offered in words like "all things," "whatever is fickle," and so on?

Rhythms can differ greatly, from the lilt of "My Papa's Waltz" to the slow dark movement of D. H. Lawrence's "Bavarian Gentians" to the long-breathed lines of Derek Walcott's "The Season of Phantasmal Peace." Read each of these aloud to hear the difference in yourself as you become the person speaking the poem. How much can you say about the tones of voice of the speaker as they issue from you?

Sometimes a structural pattern can be borrowed, as we saw in this chapter with the passionate shepherd's invitation and the nymph's reply (in which she borrows the shepherd's stanza-form and vocabulary). The anterior structure generating a poem is sometimes well known in the poet's culture; sonneteers, for instance, were accustomed to praise their lady's beauties one by one. To understand Shakespeare's mocking reply to such a practice, you need to imagine that he has just read a poem beginning "My mistress' eyes shine brightly like the sun; / Coral is not more red than her lips' red, / She walks on air, she does not tread the ground," and so on. "I don't know about *your* mistress," says Shakespeare, "but *mine* has no such powers. *My* mistress' eyes are nothing *like* the sun." How precisely can you deduce from Shakespeare's reply the anterior claims of praise that he is mocking?

Description in lyric often proceeds by successive images, piled up in a montage of evidence. What is the picture you get of the speaker of "Domestic Mysticism" from her successive self-descriptions? Are these descriptions arranged in any rough order from beginning to end?

Look at the rhymes of William Wordsworth's eight-line stanza in "The Solitary Reaper." How is the first half of the stanza different from the second half? Does the poet make any use of the difference?

Both Robert Herrick's "To the Virgins, to Make Much of Time" and Thomas Hardy's "The Darkling Thrush" are poems giving moral advice, in the form of argument against an implied other moral position. Should virgins hasten to marry or not? At the end of the old century, should one despair or not? What means of persuasion does each author find to make the message seem not only wise but also moving? Rephrase the advice in a prose proposition. Does it lose its poignancy?

If you were asked by a friend to describe Blake's style in "The Sick Rose," or Lucie Brock-Broido's style in "Domestic Mysticism," can you think of three or four adjectives you might use for an answer?

Finally, can you see the patterning-by-pronouns ("I" versus "he") in Elizabeth Alexander's poem about a summer love affair? How does it change from stanza to stanza?

WILLIAM SHAKESPEARE
Sonnet 130

My mistress' eyes are nothing like the sun;
Coral is far more red than her lips' red;
If snow be white, why then her breasts are dun;
If hairs be wires, black wires grow on her head.
I have seen roses damasked,° red and white,   *variegated*
But no such roses see I in her cheeks;
And in some perfumes is there more delight
Than in the breath that from my mistress reeks.
I love to hear her speak, yet well I know
That music hath a far more pleasing sound;
I grant I never saw a goddess go;°   *walk*
My mistress, when she walks, treads on the ground.
And yet, by heaven, I think my love as rare
As any she belied with false compare.

ROBERT HERRICK
To the Virgins, to Make Much of Time

Gather ye rosebuds while ye may,
  Old time is still a-flying;
And this same flower that smiles today
  Tomorrow will be dying.

The glorious lamp of heaven, the sun,
  The higher he's a-getting,
The sooner will his race be run,
  And nearer he's to setting.

That age is best which is the first,
  When youth and blood are warmer;
But being spent, the worse, and worst
  Times still succeed the former.

Then be not coy, but use your time,
  And, while ye may, go marry;
For, having lost but once your prime,
  You may forever tarry.

WILLIAM BLAKE
The Sick Rose

O Rose, thou art sick!
The invisible worm
That flies in the night,
In the howling storm,

Has found out thy bed
Of crimson joy:
And his dark secret love
Does thy life destroy.

WILLIAM WORDSWORTH
The Solitary Reaper

Behold her, single in the field,
Yon solitary Highland Lass!
Reaping and singing by herself;
Stop here, or gently pass!
Alone she cuts and binds the grain,
And sings a melancholy strain;
O listen! for the Vale profound
Is overflowing with the sound.

No Nightingale did ever chaunt
More welcome notes to weary bands
Of travelers in some shady haunt,
Among Arabian sands;
A voice so thrilling ne'er was heard
In springtime from the Cuckoo bird,
Breaking the silence of the seas
Among the farthest Hebrides.

Will no one tell me what she sings? —
Perhaps the plaintive numbers flow
For old, unhappy, far-off things,
And battles long ago;
Or is it some more humble lay,
Familiar matter of today?
Some natural sorrow, loss, or pain,
That has been, and may be again?

Whate'er the theme, the Maiden sang
As if her song could have no ending;
I saw her singing at her work,
And o'er the sickle bending —
I listened, motionless and still;
And, as I mounted up the hill,
The music in my heart I bore,
Long after it was heard no more.

GERARD MANLEY HOPKINS
Pied Beauty

Glory be to God for dappled things —
    For skies of couple-colour as a brinded cow;
        For rose-moles all in stipple upon trout that swim;
Fresh-firecoal chestnut-falls; finches' wings;
    Landscape plotted and pieced — fold, fallow, and plough;
        And áll trádes, their gear and tackle and trim.
All things counter, original, spare, strange;
    Whatever is fickle, freckled (who knows how?)
        With swift, slow; sweet, sour; adazzle, dim;
He fathers-forth whose beauty is past change:
                Praise him.

THOMAS HARDY
The Darkling Thrush

I leant upon a coppice gate
    When Frost was spectre-gray,
And Winter's dregs made desolate
    The weakening eye of day.
The tangled bine-stems scored the sky
    Like strings of broken lyres,
And all mankind that haunted nigh
    Had sought their household fires.

The land's sharp features seemed to be
    The Century's corpse outleant,
His crypt the cloudy canopy,
    The wind his death-lament.
The ancient pulse of germ and birth
    Was shrunken hard and dry,

And every spirit upon earth
  Seemed fervourless as I.

At once a voice arose among
  The bleak twigs overhead
In a full-hearted evensong
  Of joy illimited;
An aged thrush, frail, gaunt, and small,
  In blast-beruffled plume,
Had chosen thus to fling his soul
  Upon the growing gloom.

So little cause for carolings
  Of such ecstatic sound
Was written on terrestrial things
  Afar or nigh around,
That I could think there trembled through
  His happy good-night air
Some blessed Hope, whereof he knew
  And I was unaware.

D. H. LAWRENCE
Bavarian Gentians

Not every man has gentians in his house
in soft September, at slow, sad Michaelmas.

Bavarian gentians, big and dark, only dark
darkening the daytime, torch-like with the smoking blueness of
    Pluto's gloom,
ribbed and torch-like, with their blaze of darkness spread blue
down flattening into points, flattened under the sweep of white
    day
torch-flower of the blue-smoking darkness, Pluto's dark-blue daze,
black lamps from the halls of Dis,[1] burning dark blue,
giving off darkness, blue darkness, as Demeter's pale lamps give off
    light,
lead me then, lead the way.

---

[1] Dis is a Roman name for Pluto, the ruler of the underworld. Dis abducted
Persephone (Roman Proserpine), the daughter of Demeter (Roman Ceres). Each year,
Persephone lived with him for six months and then spent six months with her mother.

Reach me a gentian, give me a torch!

let me guide myself with the blue, forked torch of this flower

down the darker and darker stairs, where blue is darkened on
 blueness

even where Persephone goes, just now, from the frosted Septem-
 ber

to the sightless realm where darkness is awake upon the dark

and Persephone herself is but a voice

or a darkness invisible enfolded in the deeper dark

of the arms Plutonic, and pierced with the passion of dense gloom,

among the splendor of torches of darkness, shedding darkness on
 the lost bride and her groom.

THEODORE ROETHKE
My Papa's Waltz

The whiskey on your breath
Could make a small boy dizzy;
But I hung on like death:
Such waltzing was not easy.

We romped until the pans
Slid from the kitchen shelf;
My mother's countenance
Could not unfrown itself.

The hand that held my wrist
Was battered on one knuckle;
At every step you missed
My right ear scraped a buckle.

You beat time on my head
With a palm caked hard by dirt,
Then waltzed me off to bed
Still clinging to your shirt.

WILLIAM CARLOS WILLIAMS
The Dance

In Breughel's[1] great picture, The Kermess,
the dancers go round, they go round and

---

[1] Pieter Bruegel (also spelled Breughel) the Elder (1521?–1569) was a Flemish painter famed for his pictures of peasant life, such as that of an open-air festival, or "Kermess."

around, the squeal and the blare and the
tweedle of bagpipes, a bugle and fiddles
tipping their bellies (round as the thick-
sided glasses whose wash they impound)
their hips and their bellies off balance
to turn them. Kicking and rolling about
the Fair Grounds, swinging their butts, those
shanks must be sound to bear up under such
rollicking measures, prance as they dance
in Breughel's great picture, The Kermess.

DEREK WALCOTT
The Season of Phantasmal° Peace   *imaginary*

Then all the nations of birds lifted together
the huge net of the shadows of this earth
in multitudinous dialects, twittering tongues,
stitching and crossing it. They lifted up
the shadows of long pines down trackless slopes,
the shadows of glass-faced towers down evening streets,
the shadow of a frail plant on a city sill —
the net rising soundless as night, the birds' cries soundless, until
there was no longer dusk, or season, decline, or weather,
only this passage of phantasmal light
that not the narrowest shadow dared to sever.

And men could not see, looking up, what the wild geese drew,
what the ospreys trailed behind them in silvery ropes
that flashed in the icy sunlight; they could not hear
battalions of starlings waging peaceful cries,
bearing the net higher, covering this world
like the vines of an orchard, or a mother drawing
the trembling gauze over the trembling eyes
of a child fluttering to sleep;
                              it was the light
that you will see at evening on the side of a hill
in yellow October, and no one hearing knew
what change had brought into the raven's cawing,
the killdeer's screech, the ember-circling chough
such an immense, soundless, and high concern
for the fields and cities where the birds belong,
except it was their seasonal passing, Love,

made seasonless, or, from the privilege of their birth,
something brighter than pity for the wingless ones
below them who shared dark holes in windows and in houses,
and higher they lifted the net with soundless voices
above all change, betrayals of falling suns,
and this season lasted one moment, like the pause
between dusk and darkness, between fury and peace,
but, for such as our earth is now, it lasted long.

LUCIE BROCK-BROIDO
Domestic Mysticism

In thrice 10,000 seasons, I will come back to this world
In a white cotton dress. Kingdom of After My Own Heart.
Kingdom of Fragile. Kingdom of Dwarves. When I come home,
Teacups will quiver in their Dresden saucers, pentatonic chimes
Will move in wind. A covey of alley cats will swarm on the side
Porch & perch there, portents with quickened heartbeats
You will feel against your ankles as you pass through.

After the first millennium, we were supposed to die out.
You had your face pressed up against the coarse dyed velvet
Of the curtain, always looking out for your own transmigration:
What colors you would wear, what cut of jewel,
What kind of pageantry, if your legs would be tied
Down, if there would be wandering tribes of minstrels
Following with woodwinds in your wake.

This work of mine, the kind of work which takes no arms to do,
Is least noble of all. It's peopled by Wizards, the Forlorn,
The Awkward, the Blinkers, the Spoon-Fingered, Agnostic Lispers,
Stutterers of Prayer, the Flatulent, the Closet Weepers,
The Charlatans. I am one of those. In January, the month the owls
Nest in, I am a witness & a small thing altogether. The Kingdom
Of Ingratitude. Kingdom of Lies. Kingdom of *How Dare I.*

I go on dropping words like little pink fish eggs, unawares, slightly
Illiterate, often on the mark. Waiting for the clear whoosh
Of fluid to descend & cover them. A train like a silver
Russian love pill for the sick at heart passes by
My bedroom window in the night at the speed of mirage.
In the next millennium, I will be middle aged. I do not do well
In the marrow of things. Kingdom of Trick. Kingdom of Drug.

In a lung-shaped suburb of Virginia, my sister will be childless
Inside the ice storm, forcing the narcissus. We will send
Each other valentines. The radio blowing out
Vaughan Williams on the highway's purple moor.
At nine o'clock, we will put away our sewing to speak
Of lofty things while, in the pantry, little plants will nudge
Their frail tips toward the light we made last century.

When I come home, the dwarves will be long
In their shadows & promiscuous. The alley cats will sneak
Inside, curl about the legs of furniture, close the skins
Inside their eyelids, sleep. Orchids will be intercrossed & sturdy.
The sun will go down as I sit, thin armed, small breasted
In my cotton dress, poked with eyelet stitches, a little lace,
In the queer light left when a room snuffs out.

I draw a bath, enter the water as a god enters water:
Fertile, knowing, kind, surrounded by glass objects
Which could break easily if mishandled or ill-touched.
Everyone knows an unworshipped woman will betray you.
There is always that promise, I like that. Kingdom of Kinesis.
Kingdom of Benevolent. I will betray as a god betrays,
With tenderheartedness. I've got this mystic streak in me.

ELIZABETH ALEXANDER
Nineteen

That summer in Culpepper, all there was to eat was white:
cauliflower, flounder, white sauce, white ice-cream.
I snuck around with an older man who didn't tell me
he was married. I was the baby, drinking rum and Coke
while the men smoked reefer they'd stolen from the campers.
I tiptoed with my lover to poison-ivied fields, camp vans.
I never slept. Each fortnight I returned to the city,
black and dusty, with a garbage bag of dirty clothes.

At nineteen it was my first summer away from home.
His beard smelled musty. His eyes were black. "The ladies love my
     hair,"
he'd say, and like a fool I'd smile. He knew everything
about marijuana, how dry it had to be to burn,
how to crush it, sniff it, how to pick the seeds out. He said
he learned it all in Vietnam. He brought his son to visit

after one of his days off. I never imagined a mother.
"Can I steal a kiss?" he said, the first thick night in the field.

I asked and asked about Vietnam, how each scar felt,
what combat was like, how the jungle smelled. He listened
to a lot of Marvin Gaye, was all he said, and grabbed
between my legs. I'd creep to my cot before morning.
I'd eat that white food. This was before I understood
that nothing could be ruined in one stroke. A sudden
storm came hard one night; he bolted up inside the van.
"The rain sounded just like that," he said, "on the roofs there."

4

Describing Poems

There are many ways of describing poems. As new sorts of poems are invented, as cross-fertilizing among cultures takes place, we need to come up with new descriptions. But it is useful to know some of the ways in which critics have described poems in the past, and to learn a handy set of methods for exploring a poem to find things worth describing in it. This chapter is a quick look at some techniques you can use to describe a poem you have read.

The large category "poetry" has often been divided into subcategories. We are concerned here not with the longer genres, epic poetry and dramatic poetry, but with the smaller kinds of relatively short poetry. Here are some of them. (A longer list can be found in the appendix "On Lyric Subgenres.")

Poetic Kinds

Narrative versus Lyric; Narrative in Lyric

We tend to distinguish *narrative* poems from *lyric* poems. A *narrative* poem (for instance, a ballad) tells a story — for example, about the murder of Lord Randall, or (as in the case of "Frankie and Johnny") about the revenge a woman took on her unfaithful lover. A *lyric*, on the other hand, may contain the germ of a story — say, a man's regret that a love affair is ending — but the poem dwells less on the plot than on the man's feelings (despair, grief, resentment, and so on). Wordsworth put the two kinds together and called some of his short poems "lyrical ballads" — meaning poems that, although they imply or even tell a story, make the characters' feelings more important than the plot. Narrative and lyric sometimes overlap, because most narrative poems include feeling and reflection as well as plot, and most lyric poems have an implied plot of sorts.

Lyric poems in which there is a distinct narrative interest often show changes in tense: "Once I *did* this but now I *can* no longer *do* it, and in the future I *will* never *do* it again." (Poems that are primarily lyric meditations on a single subject are often phrased in the present tense alone: "The expense of spirit in a waste of shame / Is lust in action"). To see the way verb tenses organize the narrative plot of a poem, let's look at a poem by Adrienne Rich, spoken by a woman who has emerged from the exhaustions of motherhood and is thinking that she will at last have a private life again. She retraces her own birth and ambitious adolescence, then shows her inner deprivation as her life (once she became a mother) was handed over to others in what sometimes seemed to her a form of slavery; she concludes with her present anticipation of a new — but aging — self. I have put the main verbs in uppercase so as to emphasize the tense changes; the present participles (which help make presentness) in italic; and the past participles (which help make pastness) in boldface:

ADRIENNE RICH
Necessities of Life

Piece by piece I SEEM	*present*
to re-enter the world: I first BEGAN	*past*
a small, **fixed** dot, still SEE	*present*
that old myself, a dark-blue thumbtack	
pushed into the scene,	
a hard little head *protruding*	
from the pointillist's buzz and bloom,	
After a time the dot	
BEGINS to ooze. Certain heats	*present*
MELT it. Now I WAS hurriedly	*present/past*
BLURRING into ranges	
of **burnt** red, *burning* green,	

whole biographies SWAM up and SWALLOWED me like Jonah.	*past*
Jonah! I WAS Wittgenstein, Mary Wollstonecraft, the soul	*past*
of Louis Jouvet, **dead** in a **blown-up** photograph.	
Till, **wolfed** almost to shreds, I LEARNED to make myself	*past*
unappetizing. Scaly as a dry bulb **thrown** into a cellar	
I USED myself, LET nothing use me. Like *being* on a private dole,	*past*
sometimes more like *kneading* bricks in Egypt. What life WAS then, WAS mine,	*past*
now and again TO LAY one hand on a warm brick	*infinitive*
and TOUCH the sun's ghost with economical joy,	*infinitive*
now and again TO NAME over the bare necessities.	*infinitive*
So much for those days. Soon practice MAY MAKE me middling-perfect, I'LL	*modal future*
DARE inhabit the world trenchant in motion as an eel, solid	*future*
as a cabbage-head. I HAVE invitations: a curl of mist STEAMS upward	*present* *present*
from a field, visible as my breath, houses along a road STAND waiting	*present*
like old women *knitting*, breathless TO TELL their tales.	*infinitive*

One can see the *narrative* here unfolding in the verbals (tensed verbs, infinitives, present and past participles), and can watch the past becoming momentarily present in memory (in present participles like "protruding" and "kneading"). The future becomes tenseless, and thereby infinitely extendable, by means of an infinitive ("breathless / to tell their tales"). It is always useful to look for the narrative in all poems, and to decide how much of the poem is narrative versus how much "stays the same" as it meditates for a while without changing its stance.

Some poems are almost purely *meditative*. Here is the contemporary poet Philip Larkin on estrangement between two people who have been lovers for a long time. You will notice that "nothing happens," that the speaker is still in the same predicament at the end as at the beginning. The whole poem, except for the general statement of the first line, takes place in the present tense, as many meditations do:

PHILIP LARKIN
Talking in Bed

Talking in bed ought to be easiest,
Lying together there goes back so far,
An emblem of two people being honest.

Yet more and more time passes silently.
Outside, the wind's incomplete unrest
Builds and disperses clouds about the sky,

And dark towns heap up on the horizon.
None of this cares for us. Nothing shows why
At this unique distance from isolation

It becomes still more difficult to find
Words at once true and kind,
Or not untrue and not unkind.

The *narrative* here — concerning the way talk becomes harder and harder as lovers gradually grow apart — is less important than the *meditation* on this problem conducted by the poet, as he says many things about it: that intimate talk should be easy, that he and his companion have a common past, that bed used to be the place where honesty had a chance, that the outside restless and menacing world is no help, and that there is no explanation for the increasing difficulty summed up in the last two lines. Here, the successive items reflected on in the meditation are the principle of interest, converging on the final redefinition of the problem in the last two lines. A meditative poem asks you to notice all its successive "takes" on the subject being considered.

In short, look for the *plot* in narrative lyrics where the tenses change, and look for *successive "takes"* on a subject in meditative lyrics.

Classifying Lyric Poems

Lyric poems themselves are generally classified in three ways: by *content*, by *speech act*, and by *outer form*.

> *Content:* We could classify the poems by Rich and Larkin according to their *content*, calling Rich's an *autobiography* and Larkin's a *love-poem*.
>
> *Speech act:* Or we could classify the two poems according to their *speech acts*, calling Rich's a *confessional narration* and Larkin's a *meditation* on estrangement.
>
> *Outer form:* Or we could classify the poems according to their *outer form*, describing Rich's as a *poem in unrhymed couplets* and Larkin's as a *poem in unrhymed tercets*.

Each of these classifications requires that we investigate the poem for something different — for what its content is, what sort of speech acts it is engaging in, and what outer form it displays.

CONTENT GENRES: Here are some of the most frequent kinds (or *genres*, the French word for "kinds") of lyric poems identified by *content:*

The love poem

The dawn poem (in which one of the lovers, usually, is waked by the sun and speaks)

The nocturne (a night scene)

The pastoral (a poem spoken by a shepherd; loosely, a poem in the countryside)

The elegy (a poem mourning a death)

The epithalamion (a poem celebrating a wedding)

The prayer

The autobiography

The flower poem

The sea poem

The travel poem

The birthday poem

There are enough poems of all the above sorts so that any poet writing a travel poem is bound to remember other travel poems, and so on. The poet expects the reader, often, to know how such poems usually go (a travel poem, for instance, normally reaches a destination).

The poet then often "changes the rules," and violates the very expectations that the poem has set up. The seventeenth-century poet George Herbert, for instance, in a poem called "Pilgrimage," leads us by his title to expect that he will find a destination, but all he finds is "a lake of brackish waters" instead of a place of spiritual healing. Flower poems, to give another example, usually praise the flower, but William Blake writes of a "sunflower, weary of time" and makes us wonder about the weariness of the flower. The dawn poem is usually spoken by one lover to the other, as in *Romeo and Juliet*; John Donne makes his dawn poem unusual by addressing the sun: "Busy old fool, unruly sun!" In every case, a poet writing with a known content will want to do something new and interesting with that content. The more poems you have read, the more pleasure you will get from reading a new poem, since you will be alert to the new thing the poet is doing. It is the "new twist," as well as the old thing done very well in a new way, that gives the pleasure.

The first poet to invent a kind sets a problem: What do lovers say when the sun comes up and interrupts their lovemaking? Every subsequent poet finds a new solution to the problem. No one solution is better, in theory, than any other; and a rich poetic problem is one that keeps on generating new solutions.

Emily Dickinson, for instance, wrote a prayer-poem describing a heart praying to an invisible power. The success of the poem depends on our having a sense that the usual prayer is addressed to God, has a reverential tone, and asks for some hoped-for good: only if we know these normal conditions will we see Dickinson's blasphemy. Dickinson tells us in the first stanza that *someone* is being addressed by the Heart, but it is not until the second stanza that that person addressed is described as an "inquisitor," a torturer. And the hoped-for good asked for by the Heart changes as the poem goes on, giving the poem its dynamic shape or inner form, as the praying Heart changes from someone demanding pleasure to an abject prisoner craving from God "the privilege to die":

EMILY DICKINSON
The Heart asks Pleasure — first —

The Heart asks Pleasure — first —	
And then — Excuse from Pain —	
And then — those little Anodynes°	*painkillers*
That deaden suffering —	

And then — to go to sleep —
And then — if it should be
The will of its Inquisitor
The privilege to die —

This two-stanza description of a prayer is organized as a list of goods
asked for. Its dynamic shape can be indicated as a long chain of petitions,
all of them the direct objects of the verb "asks":

The Heart asks:	Pleasure (first)
& then	Excuse from Pain
& then	Anodynes
& then	to go to sleep
& then	
(if it should be the will of its Inquisitor)	the privilege to die

Why does Dickinson divide this single list into two stanzas? What makes
stanza 2 worth separating from stanza 1? As soon as we ask this question
we realize that we don't know, in stanza 1, whom the Heart is addressing
with its prayer. If we translate Dickinson's narrative into the Heart's
direct pleas, the young Heart says: "I want Pleasure." Pleasure never
comes; that prayer goes unanswered. "Well, then, I want to have no
more Pain," says the Heart, still believing that its unknown Addressee in
heaven would prefer to bestow pleasure or at least painlessness on the
petitioner. But the pain goes on, unabated. "Well, then, please give me
some drugs to lessen the suffering," asks the Heart. Through the first
stanza the Heart still wants to maintain consciousness, even if it should
be consciousness dulled by a sedative. Through the first stanza the Heart
still believes in the potential benevolence of the Person listening to these
demands.

But no anodynes are forthcoming, and the Heart foresees that its
life will be one of unrelieved suffering. "At least let me sleep," prays
the Heart, now willing to forgo consciousness. But that prayer goes
unanswered, too; nights of insomniac suffering succeed days full of
undeadened pain. It is at this point that the Heart redefines the person
addressed. This person on high is clearly totally nonbenevolent, having
denied the Heart any morsel of pleasure, having even denied a letup
in pain, refusing to give painkilling medicines, withholding even the
relief from pain given by sleep. What can we call such a torturer?
Dickinson reaches to the Renaissance image of a church-licensed
torturer, an Inquisitor. The Inquisitor has total power; the tortured

Heart, none. Once you recognize that the person in charge of your destiny is a torturer and that you are totally in his power, nothing is left for you but to be abject, to cringe, to say, "Oh Inquisitor, if it be thy will, grant me the privilege of dying." It is to this suicidal point that the Heart comes at the end of her prayer, when she is willing (as she was not in the first stanza) to forgo consciousness entirely. She now clearly perceives (as she did not in the first stanza) that she is in the hands not of a benevolent God but of a relentlessly cruel one. At last we see why Dickinson divided her list of petitions in two.

The petitionary form described in this poem is that of a Christian prayer. A poem describing a "standard" Christian prayer might say:

> The soul asks peace of mind,
> And then for virtue's power,
> And then for hope and charity
> In every evil hour;
>
> And then for faith in grief,
> And then — if it should be
> The will of its Creator-God —
> His face at death to see.

A "conventional" prayer-poem of this sort is the "ghost-model" behind Dickinson's blasphemous rewriting of the genre. Dickinson expects her reader to react strongly to her departure from the conventional ways of talking to God. All poets expect readers to know (from ordinary social behavior) what sort of content would normally appear in the usual prayer, or the usual wedding song, or the conventional funeral speech, and to measure the poem's departures in content from the norm.

SPEECH ACTS: When we classify poems by their speech acts, we draw attention to their *manner* of expression more than to their content. I can apologize for any number of things — my tardiness, or my mistakes, or my clothing — but in each of these cases my speech act (whatever its content) is an *apology*. Similarly, I can protest about time, or death, or love — but in every case, my speech act is a *protest*. Since the language of most poems can be thought of as a series of utterances by a speaker, the poet expects you to track the person's successive speech acts, just as you might do in life when you might say, "First, she *criticized* me, then she *apologized,* then she *explained* why she was upset, and finally she *asked* if we could still be friends." A poem's speech acts need to be followed and identified in just this way: "The speaker *declares* his love, and then *vows* that he will always be faithful, while *protesting* the indifference of his beloved and *reproaching* her for it." Here are a few speech acts that often organize poems (a longer list is provided in the appendix "On Speech Acts"):

Apology

Apostrophe (a direct second-person address to another, usually of higher rank)

Declaration

Boast

Command

Interrogation

Exclamation

Description

Hypothesis

Rebuttal

Narration

Prayer

Debate or dialogue

Reproach

We have seen a *narration* of autobiography in Rich's poem "Necessities of Life," a *narration* of prayer in Dickinson's "The Heart asks Pleasure — first — ." A poem whose *speech act* was prayer would be, unlike the Dickinson poem, addressed directly to God, like George Herbert's "Discipline," which begins,

> Throw away thy rod,
> Throw away thy wrath,
>   O my God,
> Take the gentle path.

Or the speech act of a poem can be a *command*. Commands are normally given by people; one way of being original in a command-poem would be to have the commands given by something that normally doesn't talk. This is what Carl Sandburg does in his poem "Grass," where the grass speaks. This poem surveys the sites of famous battles during the Napoleonic Wars, the Civil War, and the First World War:

CARL SANDBURG
Grass

Pile the bodies high at Austerlitz and Waterloo.
Shovel them under and let me work —
    I am the grass; I cover all.

And pile them high at Gettysburg
And pile them high at Ypres and Verdun.
Shovel them under and let me work.
Two years, ten years, and passengers ask the conductor:

    What place is this?
    Where are we now?

    I am the grass.
    Let me work.

This poem contains other speech acts besides its repeated *commands* ("pile," "shovel under," "let me work"). It also contains a repeated *self-definition* ("I am the grass") and a piece of *narration* "Two years . . . and passengers ask . . . what place is this?" If we were mapping this poem by the grass's speech acts, numbering the commands in sequence (1, 2, and so on), it would read:

Command 1a ("pile")
Commands 2a and 3a ("shovel under," "let me work")
   Self-definition 1a ("I am the grass")

Command 1b ("and pile")
Command 1c ("and pile")
Commands 2b and 3b ("shovel under" and "let me work")
Narration ("passengers ask")

    (Inserted *question* by passengers: "What . . . ?")
    (Inserted *question* by passengers: "Where . . . ?")

   Self-definition 1b ("I am the grass")
   Command 3c ("let me work")

When we "map" a poem by its speech acts, we are often enabled to see its skeletal structure and to describe it precisely, saying, "This is a poem of repeated *commands* by the grass. The grass *defines itself* by its work of covering-over the dead of all battles, important in their day but soon forgotten, as the *questions* asked by later passers-by, *narrated* by the grass, reveal." This is a far more exact way of describing a poem than to mention only its theme, saying, "This poem is about the way in which past battles are soon forgotten." In noting the way the poet has made this thematic cliché memorable — by having the grass be the speaker, and by giving it relatively few and repeated speech acts to use — one sees the poem not merely as a statement about war but as a constructed piece of art. Since the language of most poems can be thought of as a series of utterances by a speaker, the poet expects the reader to track and identify the speech acts, just as we do in life. Here, the repetitiveness of form is used to emphasize the sameness of all wars, as burial follows burial repeatedly.

OUTER FORM: A poem can also be classified according to various aspects of its *outer form,* having to do with meter, rhyme, and stanza-form. (The appendix "On Prosody" describes these aspects more fully.) With respect to prosody, here are a few examples of kinds of naming.

Line-Width. Some form-names have to do with the *width* of the poetic *line.* A pentameter poem is a poem in lines *five* beats *wide:*

> When I / see BIRCH / es BEND / to LEFT / and RIGHT . . .
> I   LIKE / to   THINK / some   BOY'S / been   SWING / ing
>   THEM.

A trimeter poem is a poem in lines *three* beats *wide:*

> It is TIME / that I MADE / my WILL;
> I CHOOSE / upSTAND / ing MEN.

The single most important thing to remember in deciding how many beats a line has is that you cannot ascertain this in isolation. You need to look at the lines surrounding it, and, if it occurs in a poem with stanzas, at matching lines in other stanzas. The reason you need surrounding or matching lines is that many lines, taken by themselves, could be read in different ways. Take the line from Hamlet's famous soliloquy "To be or not to be: that is the question." You could read this line, taken by itself, in two different ways:

> To BE or NOT to be: THAT is the QUESTion.   (*4 beats*)
> To BE or NOT to BE: THAT is the QUESTion.   (*5 beats*)

We decide that the line is meant to have five beats because the lines surrounding it in Hamlet's speech mostly seem to fall into place if we read them with five beats:

> To DIE, to SLEEP; to SLEEP, perCHANCE to DREAM,   *(5)*
> And IN that SLEEP of DEATH what DREAMS may
>   COME   *(5)*
> When WE have SHUFFled OFF this MORtal COIL   *(5)*
> Must GIVE us PAUSE.

This gives us the evidence we need to decide that we should read our dubious line as "To BE or NOT to BE; THAT is the QUESTion," with five beats.

Similarly, the line with which William Butler Yeats begins his poem "Easter 1916" is "I have met them at close of day." Taken by itself, we could read this line perfectly reasonably as having four beats ("I HAVE met THEM at CLOSE of DAY") if it were followed by another four-beat line, as in this piece of doggerel:

> I have met them at close of day,   *(4)*
> But they have never greeted me,   *(4)*
> And though I now am old and gray,   *(4)*
> I think that we cannot agree.   *(4)*

In point of fact, though, Yeats's line is followed by a long series of lines that all have three beats each, which makes us read it, too, with a three-beat rhythm — "I have MET them at CLOSE of DAY":

> I have MET them at CLOSE of DAY   *(3)*
> COMing with VIVid FAces,   *(3)*
> From COUNTer or DESK among GREY   *(3)*
> EIGHTeenth-CENtury HOUSes.   *(3)*

The rule of thumb, then, is always to look at lines *in groups* when you are deciding how many beats they have. Find another stanza in the poem matching the one you are dubious about, and see if its pattern is clearer. (All similar stanzas in a poem have the same arrangement of beats.) The best way to "hear" the beats of a poem is to read it aloud, and to notice the natural stresses of the sentences as you read, deciding, in dubious cases, how to read the line by comparing it with others.

Rhythm. Some form-names have to do with the *rhythm* of the line. Rhythms are either *rising* (one-TWO, one-TWO would be an example) or *falling* (ONE-two-three, ONE-two-three would be an example). Shakespeare's blank verse has a two-syllable rising rhythmic unit represented as one-TWO, ˘ ´. Five of these building units make up the Shakespearean line — *five* beats *wide,* in a *rising* rhythm: ˘ ´ ˘ ´ ˘ ´ ˘ ´ ˘ ´; "To DIE, to SLEEP, to SLEEP, perCHANCE to DREAM." *Falling* rhythm is much heavier than rising rhythm, and is often used to imitate marching, hoofbeats, or some form of raw power, as in Blake's poem on the TYger that goes ONE-two, ONE-two: "TYger, TYger, BURNing BRIGHT / IN the FORests OF the NIGHT."

Poem-Length. Some form-names have to do with the *length* of the *whole poem*: Wallace Stevens's "Sunday Morning" is a poem in eight *cantos,* in which each *canto* (a single long stanza) has fifteen lines. The name *sonnet* normally means that the poem in question has fourteen lines.

Combinatorial Form-Names. Some form-names have to do with the width *and* rhythm *and* length *and* rhymes of the *whole poem*: a "Shakespearean sonnet" is a poem with lines *five* beats *wide* in a two-syllable *rising* rhythm; it is *fourteen* lines long, and the lines rhyme *abab cdcd efef gg* (making three quatrains in alternate rhyme and a rhyming couplet).

These qualities of form are explained systematically in the appendix "On Prosody." They need to be observed routinely, in the case of every poem you read. Once you have described its *content* (a spring poem, an elegy) and its successive *speech acts* (a narration, a plea), look at the *outer form.* How many lines does the whole poem have? How many stanzas? Are they all the same shape? How wide is the line? Where do the rhymes come? What is the overall rhythm? It helps to jot down what you observe in the margin next to the poem on the page ("Elegy; lament, protest, consolation; fifteen alternately rhymed pentameter quatrains in rising rhythm"). That way you have a handle on the poem the next time you look at it.

INNER STRUCTURAL FORM: Besides its *outer form* ("This is a poem in quatrains in falling rhythm rhyming *aabb*" — a description of Blake's "Tyger"), every poem has *internal structural form.* This is its dynamic shape, which derives from the curve traced by the emotions of the poem as they change over its duration. That emotional curve is plotted by connecting two, three, or more points of the poem, a rise from depression to hope to joy, for instance — or a decline from triumph through doubt to despair. Very few poems represent an unchanging steady state of the same emotion all through.

Some poems are two-part (*binary*) poems, like William Wordsworth's "A slumber did my spirit seal" (which we saw changing from illusion to stern knowledge), or like Dickinson's "The Heart asks Pleasure — first — " (which we saw changing its conception of God from benevolence to cruelty). Another fundamentally binary form is the debate poem, where A speaks, then B challenges A, then A replies to B, back and forth.

There are also many three-part (*ternary*) poems, which often take on the internal structure of beginning, modulation, end (a song-form preserved in lyric). We have seen an example of three-part form in Edmund Waller's "On the Last Poem in the Book."

Internal forms are infinitely variable, since they represent emotional response, always volatile. One well-known internal structure is that of the "surprise" ending, where the last few lines reverse everything that has gone before. George Herbert's poem "The Collar" is full of rebellion against God, until the very end:

> But as I raved, and grew more fierce and wilde
>   At every word,
> Methought I heard one calling, *Child!*
>   And I replied, *My Lord.*

In investigating the internal structure of a poem, one should try to divide it into parts along its "fault lines." Where does the logic of the argument seem to break? Where does the poem change from first person to second person? Where does the major change in tense or speech act take place? Here are some of the ingredients of internal structural form that will help you to explore a poem.

Sentences. Poems are, on the whole, made of sentences, and sentences are an important internal structuring principle of poems. For instance, there will often be a procession of short sentences, and then one very long sentence, or vice versa. The poet means us to notice how many sentences there are in a poem, and how they relate to one another. There may be a generalizing sentence ("How do I love thee? Let me count the ways") followed by many particulars; or many small instances leading up to more important ones, as in Robert Herrick's summary of his poetic subjects, ending at the hope of salvation:

Robert Herrick
The Argument of His Book

I sing of brooks, of blossoms, birds, and bowers,
Of April, May, of June, and July flowers.
I sing of Maypoles, hock carts, wassails, wakes,
Of bridegrooms, brides, and of their bridal cakes.
I write of youth, of love, and have access
By these to sing of cleanly wantonness.

I sing of dews, of rains, and, piece by piece,
Of balm, of oil, of spice, and ambergris.
I sing of times trans-shifting, and I write
How roses first came red and lilies white.
I write of groves, of twilights, and I sing
The court of Mab° and of the fairy king.   *queen of the fairies*
I write of hell; I sing (and ever shall)
Of heaven, and hope to have it after all.

You can often discover a lot about a poem by copying out its successive sentences in prose, putting each one under its predecessor. You can then ask yourself how they resemble one another, and how they differ, and why.

Person. Sentences are written either in the first person (*I/me* in the singular, *we/us* in the plural); the second person (*you* — archaic forms are *thou* in the nominative singular, *thee* in the objective singular, and *ye* in the plural); or the third person (*he/him, she/her,* and *it* in the singular; *they/them* in the plural). A *change of person* as a poem goes along is a significant structuring device. A change to the second person, addressing a person ("you") in the poem who hasn't appeared before, usually raises the temperature of a poem, as when Wordsworth, after a long monologue in "Tintern Abbey," turns to his sister, saying, "For thou art with me here upon the banks / Of this fair river," and we learn for the first time that he is not alone. An elegy often begins by trying to keep the dead person "alive" by directly addressing him or her, and may then subside into the third person, speaking no longer of "you" but of "the body," as Robert Lowell does in his elegy for his mother, "Sailing Home for Rapallo." He is bringing his mother's body from Italy (where she had died) home to New England, and we gradually see Charlotte Lowell turn from being a "you" to being "the corpse":

> **Your** nurse could only speak Italian,
> but after twenty minutes I could imagine **your** final week,
> and tears ran down my cheeks. . . .
>
> When I embarked from Italy with **my mother's body,**
> the whole shoreline of the *Golfo di Genova*°   *Gulf of Genoa*
> was breaking into fiery flower.
>
> .   .   .   .   .
>
> **Mother** travelled first-class in the hold.
>
> .   .   .   .   .
>
> In the grandiloquent lettering on **Mother's** coffin,

Lowell had been misspelled LOVEL.
The corpse
was wrapped like *panettone* in Italian tinfoil.

Person reveals the poet's relation to the world. Is the poet in the world of "you" or "we" — other persons — or in a solitary world inhabited only by the "I" of the poem? Or a world with no addressees, full of "its" and "thems"?

   Agency. Every sentence has a subject; the subject is the agent of the verb. Many poems have one subject ("I") for every sentence: in them, agency never changes. Others have a single *change in agency:* see, for instance, Randall Jarrell's "The Death of the Ball Turret Gunner," in which the subject of all the main verbs is "I" until the last line, when, because the ball turret gunner has been killed, the "I" vanishes and "they" take over. The "I" who acted becomes the "me" who is acted on. Here is the complete poem:

RANDALL JARRELL
The Death of the Ball Turret Gunner

From my mother's sleep I fell into the State,
And I hunched in its belly till my wet fur froze.
Six miles from earth, loosed from its dream of life,
I woke to black flak and the nightmare fighters.
When I died *they* washed *me* out of the turret with a hose.

   Some poems have a different subject for every sentence — these make the reader take on several different perspectives at once. See, for instance, Lowell's "Skunk Hour," where in the first stanza alone there are four different subjects which govern verbs:

Nautilus Island's hermit
heiress still lives through winter in her Spartan cottage;
her *sheep* still graze above the sea.
Her *son*'s a bishop. Her *farmer*
is first selectman in our village;
she's in her dotage.

Heiress, sheep, son, farmer: all govern verbs ("lives," "graze," "is," "is"). These agents are all linked in an elaborate system of center and satellites. The *hermit heiress* has *her* cottage, *her* sheep, *her* son, and *her* farmer (unfortunately, there is also *her* dotage, which she is in). The heiress still in some sense owns her sheep, her son, and her farmer (they are all *hers*); but because they are all given independent existence as agents in the poem, we know they are no longer hers, really. They are separate from her, separate subjects; and the only things that are really hers now are her cottage and her dotage; only these two rhyming nouns, among "her" possessions, are not independent agents governing a verb. *By tracing agency through a poem we can tell who is ruling it as it goes along.* In "Skunk Hour," the various inhabitants of the seaside town at first "own" the poem; then the disturbed speaker "owns" the poem while he carries out his voyeuristic acts; but finally it is the mother skunk with her column of kittens who "owns" the poem and the town, as in the last stanza the troubled speaker yields agency to the skunk:

> I **stand** on top
> of our back steps and **breathe** the rich air —
> *a mother skunk* with her column of kittens *swills* the garbage pail.
> *She jabs* her wedge-head in a cup
> of sour cream, *drops* her ostrich tail,
> and *will not scare.*

It is important to know who "owns," by agency, each part of every poem.

Tenses. Sentences are written in tenses, and tenses are also an important internal structuring aspect of the poem, making it move in time (as we saw in Adrienne Rich's "Necessities of Life") from past to present to future. *Tense-changes* ask to be noticed. Sometimes, even often, they are the main point of the poem. As we saw earlier, in Wordsworth's "A slumber did my spirit seal," the first stanza is in the past tense, the second in the present tense. The first stanza stands for delusion ("seemed"); the second stanza for reality; and the white gap between the two tenses represents the death of the beloved. Here are the tensed verbs:

WILLIAM WORDSWORTH
A slumber did my spirit seal

A slumber *did* my spirit *seal;*
    I *had* no human fears;
She *seemed* a thing that *could not feel*
    The touch of earthly years.

No motion *has* she now, no force;
    She neither *hears* nor *sees;*
Rolled round in earth's diurnal course,
    With rocks, and stones, and trees.

The main structuring agent of the poem is the *tense-change,* bracketing the invisible (infinite, untensed) white-space moment of the girl's death.

    Images, or Sensual Words. "We thought in images," said Robert Lowell in a poem to his friend and fellow poet John Berryman. Though words in poetry can only refer and not really picture, a linkage of references in the same category of sense-perceivable words — say, many words about the moon, such as "bright," "beams," "round," "white," and so on — tend to create the impression of the object to which they all refer. Linked words (referring especially to the senses of sight and hearing) help to structure many poems. These words can be all of one sort (a collection of names of different flowers, for instance, in Milton's "Lycidas") or they can be of different sorts: that is, a series of specific nouns like "flood," "earthquake," "fire," and "shipwreck" can all help to construct the single abstract category "catastrophe." There are systematic ways in which the concrete words that some refer to as "images" may be assembled, too: they may be arranged in *parallel,* or in *contrast,* or in a ranked *hierarchy.* When Edwin Arlington Robinson wrote a sonnet called "New England," he sketched the region by images:

EDWIN ARLINGTON ROBINSON
New England

Here where the wind is always north-north-east
And children learn to walk on frozen toes,
Wonder begets an envy of all those
Who boil elsewhere with such a lyric yeast
Of love that you will hear them at a feast
Where demons would appeal for some repose,
Still clamoring where the chalice overflows
And crying wildest who have drunk the least.

Passion is here a soilure of the wits,
We're told, and Love a cross for them to bear;
Joy shivers in the corner where she knits
And Conscience always has the rocking-chair,
Cheerful as when she tortured into fits
The first cat that was ever killed by Care.

We usually call the first sort of images (wind, children) "realistic" images, and the second kind (in which an abstract quality like Joy or Conscience is turned into a person who can sit in a rocking-chair) "personification." But of course in a definition-poem like this one the "realistic" chastising wind and freezing children are as symbolic of New England as Conscience in her rocking-chair. All concrete words in poems, even "realistic" ones like "wind" or "corner," work together to suggest something more than themselves alone. One could say that each of these word-images has a part-to-whole relation to the theme of the whole poem. In Robinson's poem, each is a mini-sketch of the meteorological and moral awfulness (to this New England poet) of New England. It is often useful to write out the series of concrete sense-words in a poem and see what meaningful emotional curve links them together, or see when the categories of words change sharply (as they do here from the concrete to the abstract), giving a dynamic shape to the whole list.

Exploring a Poem

What follows is a series of things to note when you run through a poem to see what its parts are and how they fit together. Let us use this list on a sonnet by John Keats, called "On First Looking into Chapman's Homer." The anthology will tell us, in footnotes, a few things we have to know to understand the references in the poem: Keats did not know Greek, and so he first read Homer's *Odyssey* in the Renaissance translation by George Chapman; Apollo is the Greek god of poetry; Keats believed (mistakenly) that it was the Spanish conquistador Cortez who, in exploring Panama ("Darien"), discovered the Pacific Ocean (in reality it was Balboa, but the historical error doesn't matter for the imaginative purposes of the poem). Keats tells us what it is like, even for a reader as experienced in poetry as he, to come across Homer's Odyssean epic (from which he draws his opening travel imagery) for the first time:

JOHN KEATS
On First Looking into Chapman's Homer

Much have I travell'd in the realms of gold,
    And many goodly states and kingdoms seen;
    Round many western islands have I been
Which bards in fealty° to Apollo hold.   *allegiance*
Oft of one wide expanse had I been told
    That deep-brow'd Homer ruled as his demesne°;   *domain*
    Yet did I never breathe its pure serene°   *atmosphere*

Till I heard Chapman speak out loud and bold:
Then felt I like some watcher of the skies
    When a new planet swims into his ken°;   *view*
Or like stout Cortez when with eagle eyes
    He star'd at the Pacific — and all his men
Look'd at each other with a wild surmise —
    Silent, upon a peak in Darien.

How do we go about exploring such a poem? Let us try a series of steps.

1. Meaning

This is the usual sort of information-retrieval reading that we do with any passage of prose or verse. We come up with a summary of greater or lesser length giving the import of the passage as we make sense of it. Here, we might arrive at something like "The speaker says that he had traveled through a lot of golden terrain — had read a lot of poems — and people had told him about the Homeric domain, but he had never breathed its air till he heard Chapman speak out. Then he felt like an astronomer discovering a new planet; or like the explorer who discovered the Pacific, whose men, astonished by his gaze, guessed at his discovery." This sort of meaning-paraphrase is necessary, but less useful in poetry than in prose. In many poems there is rather little in the way of plot or character or message or "information" in the ordinary sense, and that little can be quickly sketched (perhaps initially, especially in the case of a complex poem, by the teacher to the class). Hoping to learn things about the poem that are more interesting than simply "what it says" in prose, we try to construct its

2. Antecedent Scenario

What has been happening *before* the poem starts? What has disturbed the status quo and set the poem in motion? Here, we know what has happened: the speaker has picked up Homer (in Chapman's translation) for the first time, and has had a revelatory experience. But the antecedent scenario is not always given to us so clearly. If it is not evident right away, one moves on hopefully to

3. A Division into Structural Parts

Because small units are more easily handled than big ones, and because the process of a poem, even one as short as a sonnet, can't be addressed all at once with a single global question like "What's going on here?" we divide the poem into pieces. One way of dividing this poem up is to notice that it falls, by its rhymes, into two large parts: "I never knew Homer till I read Chapman" (*abbaabba*) and "Then I felt like this" (*cdcdcd*). The first part takes up the first eight lines, connected by the two rhyme-sounds represented by *-old* (rhyme *a*) and *-een* (rhyme *b*); and the second part takes up the last six lines, connected by a new set of rhyme-sounds, represented by *-ies* (rhyme *c*) and *-en* (rhyme *d*). There are other ways, besides this 8:6 division, to divide this poem into parts, as we shall see, but let us work first within this 8:6 division-by-rhyme. In order to suggest a meaningful relation of the parts, it is useful to look at

4. The Climax

In Keats's sonnet, the climax seems to come when Cortez stares at the Pacific — the high point of the poem. What is special about this experience? Why does it replace the image of the astronomer discovering a new planet? In lyric poems, the various parts tend to cluster around a moment of special significance — which its attendant parts lead up to, lead away from, help to clarify, and so on. The climax usually manifests itself by such things as greater intensity of tone, an especially significant metaphor, a change in rhythm, or a change in person. Having located the climax, one can now move back to

5. The Other Parts

About each part, it is useful to ask how it *differs* from the other parts. What is distinctive in it by contrast to the other members of the poem? Does something shift gears? Does the tense change? Does the predominant grammatical form change? (For example, does the poem stop emphasizing nouns and start emphasizing participles?) Is a new person addressed? Have we left a general overlook for certain particulars? Here, we notice that the first four lines talk in *general* about states, kingdoms, and islands. The next four lines talk about *one* special "wide expanse," the one ruled by Homer. The next part says, "I felt like an astronomer discovering a new planet." And the last part produces a new comparison: "I felt like an explorer discovering a new ocean, accompanied by his companions." Some questions immediately arise: Why doesn't the poem end after the poet says, "I felt as though I had discovered a new planet"? Why does he feel he needs a *second* comparison? And why, in the second comparison, does he need not only a single discoverer comparable to the astronomer, but a discoverer *accompanied by a group of companions* ("all his men")? Once these four parts (general realms; Homer's expanse; solo astronomer / planet; Cortez and men / Pacific Ocean) have been isolated, one can move on to the game called

6.   Find the Skeleton

What is the dynamic curve of emotion on which the whole poem is arranged? "I am much travelled, and have visited [presumably by ship] many islands; however, I had never visited the Homer-expanse till I heard Chapman; then I breathed the air of the Homer-expanse, and it was like finding" — like finding what? The first stab at comparison ("like finding a new planet") isn't quite right — you can't walk on a planet and explore it and get to know it the way you get to know islands and states. Well, what would be a better comparison? And the speaker realizes that whereas other poets seem feudal lords of a given piece of earth — a state, a kingdom, an island — Homer is different *not just in degree but in kind*. He is, all by himself, an *ocean*. A new ocean, unlike a planet, is something on one's own plane that one can actually explore; yet it is something so big that it must contain many new islands and realms within it. When we understand this, we can identify the curve of astonishment in the poem when the Homer-*expanse* (a carefully chosen word that doesn't give away too much) turns out to be not just another piece of land, and not some faraway uninhabitable body in the sky, but a whole unexplorable ocean, hitherto unguessed at. The tone has changed from one of ripe experience ("Much have I travelled") to one of ignorance (the speaker has never breathed the air of the vast Homeric expanse, though others had, and had told him about it), to the revelation of the "wild surmise" — we have found not just another bounded terrain, but an unsuspected ocean! This curve of emotion, rising from an almost complacent sense of experience to an astonished recognition, is the emotional skeleton of the poem. We can then ask about

7.   Games the Poet Plays with the Skeleton

If "On First Looking into Chapman's Homer," by its content, is a then/now poem ("I used not to know Homer / Now I do"), what is the event bridging the then and the now? It is reading Homer in Chapman's translation. "Reading" is not an "event" in the usual sense: most then/now poems (like "A slumber did my spirit seal") are about some more tangible event (a death, an absence, a catastrophe). Keats plays a game, then, with the then/now poem in making its fulcrum an experience of reading. By saying that reading, too, is an Event, Keats makes the then/now poem new.

If this is a riddle-poem (and it is: "What is Homer-land like?"), how is the riddle prepared? It is prepared by a series of alternatives: "I have seen realms, states, kingdoms, islands." Some "expanse" is ruled by Homer, but I have not seen it yet. Will it be a realm? a state? a kingdom?

another island? The first "answer" to the riddle is, "None of the above; Homer-land is a *new planet*!" But that is the wrong answer (one can't travel to and explore a new planet, and the speaker *is* exploring Homer), so the poem tries again to answer the riddle, and this time does it correctly: "None of the above; Homer-expanse is a *new ocean*!" The poet has played a game with our sense of the poem as a riddle by answering not in the category we anticipated from his former travels (a piece of land) but in an unexpected one (ocean), thus making the riddle-poem new.

Keats plays another game with the ignorance/discovery skeleton by making his poem a hero-poem. He makes the reward at the end of the emotional curve — the discovery of the new ocean — not a solitary experience (like that of the "watcher of the skies" seeing the planet), but a communal one. We normally think of reading as an uneventful private act. Why did Keats make it heroic? Furthermore, why did he show the heroic discovery being made not by a single explorer but by a company of explorers? Cortez is not alone on the isthmus of Panama, but is accompanied by "all his men / Look[ing] at each other with a wild surmise." When one discovers the Homeric "expanse" one reads alone, but one becomes thereby a member of a company of people who have discovered Homer — those people who had "oft . . . told" the speaker about Homer. A feat like Homer's writing the *Odyssey* is as heroic as the exploits of Achilles: mastery of such an intellectual discovery is itself a form of heroic exploration. Such a cultural discovery, Keats implies by the presence of Cortez's men, is collective, not private. Keats thought of himself as a poet among poets; a reader of Homer among readers of Homer; an explorer among explorers. And in this way he made the hero-poem both newly intellectual and newly communal and democratic.

Having seen the genre games that the poet plays with his skeleton — as a then/now poem, a riddle-poem, a hero-poem — one can go on to ask about

8. *Language*

Of course, we have been looking at language all along, but now we can do it more consciously. How many *sentences* does the poem have? (Two.) Where does the break between sentences come? (After line 4.) This gives us, as I promised earlier, a new division into parts: not the 8:6 of the then/now structure, but the 4:10 of the knowledge/discovery structure, which locates for us the moment in which traveled complacency turns to longing for Homeric acquaintance. *Poems often have several overlapping internal structures.* It is one of the signs of a complex poem that its rhymes may be dividing the poem one way, its theme another way, its action from inception through climax another way, its grammar another way, its sentences yet another way. Each of these divisions has something to tell us about the emotional dynamic of the poem.

What *parts of speech* predominate in the poem? (For a further explanation of these, see the appendix "On Grammar.") In Keats's sonnet, the chain of *nouns* of space — "realms," "states," "kingdoms," "islands," "expanse," "demesne," "planet," "Pacific" — stands out as one unifying link.

What other *words,* regardless of whether they are different parts of speech, make a *chain of significant relation?* You might notice how words of seeing and watching — "seen," "watcher," "ken," "eagle eyes," "stared," "looked at" — connect the parts of the poem as do the nouns of space.

What *contexts* are expressed in the diction? (We notice traveling, sailing, exploring, astronomical observation, feudal loyalty, and so on.)

Is the *diction* modern or ancient? (Keats uses archaic words like "realms of gold," "goodly," "bards," "fealty," "demesne," "pure serene," and "ken," which help us sense how long Homer has been alive in our culture.) A close look at language always leads to

9.   Tone

The calm beginning, in the voice of ripe experience ("Much have I travelled") mounts to the excitement of the "wild surmise," which then suddenly is confirmed by the breathless "silent" of the last line, and by the image of the "peak," corresponding to this heightened moment. Reading a poem aloud as if it were your own utterance makes you able to distinguish the various *tones of voice* it exhibits, and to name them. At this point, we can turn to

10.   Agency and Speech Acts

Who has agency in this poem? We notice that the main verbs are all governed by the "I" who speaks the poem: "I have travelled . . . and seen . . . [and] have been . . . [and] had been told . . . yet [never] did I breathe . . . I heard . . . Then felt I." But we notice that in the subordinate clauses a great many other subagencies are present. Bards hold islands, Homer rules an expanse, Chapman speaks out, the new planet swims into ken, Cortez stares at the Pacific, and his men look with wild surmise at each other. It is by the interpenetration of the rather colorless main verbs denoting the sedentary activity of reading, and the other more public or active actions of the other agents, that Keats draws his new acquaintance with the *Odyssey* into large realms of cultural activity. The speech act of this poem is a single long *narration* of the speaker's more remote and recent pasts. The unusual thing about the speech act (narration) and agency (a single main agent) is that they stop so soon: the last narrative verb by the agent is "Then felt I" in line 9. After that, the attention of the poem never comes back to the speaker, but instead expands out to the most exalting sorts of cultural discovery — that of an astronomer, that of explorers.

11. Roads Not Taken

What are the *roads not taken* in the poem? The sonnet might have ended with the comparison of the self to an astronomer. Would this have been as satisfactory? Or the expanse ruled over by Homer might have been shown as a new continent rather than as a new ocean. Would this have been equally revealing? Or the poem might have been written in the third person instead of the first person:

> Many have travelled in the realms of gold,
>> And they have goodly states and kingdoms seen;
>> Round many western islands have they been
> Which bards in fealty to Apollo hold.

Is this as dramatic as the first person? Or the poem might have *begun* with the reading of Chapman's Homer, instead of leading up to it:

> I once heard Chapman speak out loud and bold;
>> He told me of a wide expanse unseen,
> (Better than other states and realms of gold)
>> That deep-brow'd Homer ruled as his demesne.
> Then felt I like stout Cortez on his peak,
>> When with his eagle eyes he saw the sea. . . .

We can see how presenting the climax in line 5, as in this rewriting, creates a very different structural shape from the 4:10 knowledge/discovery structure building up to the Pacific. It is useful to think of plausible *roads not taken* by a poem, because they help to identify the roads that *were* taken. With a clear idea of the function of each piece of the poem within the whole, and of the dynamic curve of emotion governing the order in which the pieces appear, we can then pass on to

12. Genre, Form, and Rhythm

What is the *content* genre of the poem? A dramatic change between then and now; a poem about reading; a poem about a hero; a poem about collective experience. (It can be compared to other poems about newness, about reading, about heroes, about collectivity.)

What is the *speech act* genre of the poem? A *narration in the first person* of a significant event marking one life-period off from another; and an *asking-a-riddle*: "What is reading Homer like?" (It can be compared to other first-person narrations and to other riddle-poems.)

What is the *formal* genre of the poem? A sonnet (using the usual five-beat rising-rhythm line found in sonnets) rhyming *abbaabba cdcdcd*. (It can be compared to other sonnets rhyming the same way.) About form, we always need to ask how it has been made vivid; see below for remarks on Keats's rhythm. We can then move on to the last issue, which is always

13. The Imagination

What has the poet's *imagination invented* that is striking, or memorable, or beautiful? We can tell, from the metaphors of sailing, that before writing his poem Keats had been reading Homer's *Odyssey,* and had been thinking about what Odysseus had discovered as he sailed from realm to realm, from island to island. Wanting to describe his own first reading of Homer, Keats imaginatively borrows from the very book he has been reading, using the image of travel, saying that reading poetry in general is like voyaging from Shakespeare-land to Milton-kingdom to Spenser-state, but that reading Homer is not like finding just another piece of land to visit: it is like finding a new planet, or, even better, a whole unexpected new ocean to sail in. Keats *imagined* these large analogies — sailing, astronomical observation, discovering an ocean — for the act of reading in general, and for reading Homer in particular; they enliven the sonnet. What makes the poem touching is the imagined change from the complacency of the well-traveled speaker to the astonishment of the discoverer of Homer, and the poet's realization that in reading Homer he has joined a company of others who have also discovered the Homeric ocean, sharing his "wild surmise." It is characteristic of Keats to see poetry as a collective act: he said in a letter, "I think I shall be among the English poets after my death," not "I think I shall be famous after my death."

But the imagination is not invested in themes and images alone. The imagination of a poet has to extend to the rhythm of the poem as well. What the imagination has invented here that is *rhythmically* memorable is the change from the stately first ten lines — because even the astronomer doesn't have to do anything but look through his telescope — to the strenuous broken rhythms of the heroic last four lines, with their four sharply differentiated parts:

1. Or like stout Cortez when with eagle eyes he stared at the Pacific —
2. And all his men look'd at each other with a wild surmise —
3. Silent,
4. Upon a peak in Darien.

The intent, piercing stare of "stout Cortez"; the amazed mutual conjecture of his men; the sudden, short, transfixed silence of the whole group; the summit of foreign experience on which the action takes place — each of these four facts is given its own rhythmically irregular phrase, so different from the undisturbed and measured pentameter narration in "Then felt I like some watcher of the skies / When a new planet swims into his ken." A poem needs *imaginative rhythms* as well as *imaginative transformation* of content.

You will, of course, read most poems without investigating them in this detailed way for their inner processes. But as soon as you want to know *how a poem works,* as well as what it says, and *why it is poignant or compelling,* you will find yourself beginning to study it, using methods like the ones sketched here. Soon, it becomes almost second nature for you to notice sentences, tense-changes, speech acts, tonal variants, changes of agency, rhythms, rhymes, and other ingredients of internal and outer structure. Just as an archaeologist studies ruins, while the rest of us simply walk through Pompeii not understanding much of what we see, a student of poetry becomes more than simply a reader. You become more like a conductor who studies the musical score before conducting the piece in performance.

You can experience a poem with great pleasure as a general reader; or you can also learn how to explore it, to gain the more experienced pleasure that a student of architecture feels inside a Renaissance palace, or that an engineer feels looking at the San Francisco Bay Bridge. In every case, study adds to what you are able to perceive. Poems — because they are short and written in your own mother tongue — are very rewarding things to study as well as to read, to learn by heart as well as to study. They keep you company in life.

Exploring a poem under the broad headings given above will almost always lead you to a deeper understanding of the poem as a work of art, constructed in a dense and satisfying and surprising way. Though we almost always respond first to the quickly sensed "message" of a poem, the *reason* for our response (even if we do not at first know this) is the *arrangement* of the message (on many intersecting planes) into a striking and moving form. To give a poem its due as a work of art, we need to be able to see it as an *arranged* message. Looking through the poem thoroughly helps us realize the kind of work the poet puts into constructing this urgent expression of life as it is seen, sensed, and reflected on. Even the simplest of short poems will show imagination and architectural construction.

In Brief: Describing Poems

When you are looking for useful ways to describe a poem, this checklist of questions can guide your exploration:

1. *Meaning*: Can you paraphrase in prose the general outline of the poem?
2. *Antecedent scenario*: What has been happening before the poem begins? What has provoked the speaker into utterance? How has a previous equilibrium been unsettled? What is the speaker upset about?
3. *Division into parts*: How many? Where do the breaks come?
4. *The climax*: How do the other parts fall into place around it?
5. *The other parts*: What makes you divide the poem into these parts? Are there changes in person? In agency? In tense? In parts of speech?
6. *Find the skeleton*: What is the emotional curve on which the whole poem is strung? (It even helps to draw a shape — a crescendo, perhaps, or an hourglass-shape, or a sharp ascent followed by a steep decline — so you'll know how the poem looks to you as a whole.)
7. *Games with the skeleton*: How is this emotional curve made new?
8. *Language*: What are the contexts of diction; chains of significant relation; parts of speech emphasized; tenses; and so on?
9. *Tone*: Can you name the pieces of the emotional curve — the changes in tone you can hear in the speaker's voice as the poem goes along?
10. *Agency and its speech acts*: Who is the main agent in the poem, and does the main agent change as the poem progresses? See what the main speech act of the agent is, and whether that changes. Notice oddities about agency and speech acts.
11. *Roads not taken*: Can you imagine the poem written in a different person, or a different tense, or with the parts rearranged, or with an additional stanza, or with one stanza left out, conjecturing by such means why the poet might have wanted *these* pieces in *this* order?

12. *Genres*: What are they by content, by speech act, by outer form?

13. *The imagination*: What has it invented that is new, striking, memorable — in content, in genre, in analogies, in rhythm, in a speaker?

Reading Other Poems

If you were to give a genre-name by content to each of the poems below, you could begin, "Herbert: prayer-poem; Shakespeare: lust-poem; Marvell: poem of retreat," and go on through the list down to "Alexie: decline-poem." If you were to give a genre-name by form to each one, you could begin, "Herbert: shaped poem; Shakespeare: sonnet; Marvell: poem in eight-line, four-couplet stanzas," down to "Alexie: poem in tercets," and so on. If you were to group them according to what person they were spoken in, you could say, "Herbert: third person and first person; Shakespeare: third person; Marvell: first and third person," and so forth. If you were to name them by speech act, you could say, "Herbert: apostrophe; Shakespeare: definition; Marvell: mixed expostulation, narrative, question, commendation." Try making such a list, and see how each question — content? form? person? speech act? — gives you a different purchase on the poem. You can expand that purchase by expanding the number of questions you put to the poem. For instance, where is the climax? Does the poem have a happy ending? From what position — participant, observer, judge — does the speaker operate? The following are merely some sample questions.

What is the emotional curve traced by Shakespeare in his speaker's feelings about lust? By Ezra Pound in the young wife's feelings? Can you see how the tones of voice change with the feelings? How many different emotional responses to the fact of his blindness does Milton express?

How has the poet's imagination worked on the material? As Jorie Graham sees Piero della Francesca's painting of the young but majestic standing Virgin, pregnant and unbuttoning her dress before she goes into labor, how does the poet's imagination respond to the painting? As Mark Strand imagines courtship, how does he make it comic? As Heaney imagines that the anxiety of writing is like confronting police at a border checkpoint, how does he make that confrontation vivid? As Sherman Alexie imagines the decline of life on an Indian reservation, through what example does he convey it?

In longer poems like "Ode to a Nightingale," "Dover Beach," and "Mending Wall," the more scannings you make the more you see. You can begin anywhere that interests you. Anything you notice helps to build up your picture of the poem's world. In "Dover Beach" you might notice how one setting — on the English coast — leads to another — the Aegean Sea, and how one topic — love — leads to another — the ebbing of religious faith. These large structural blocks make you perceive how the poem is composed, and enable you to look at the micro-structures within each part. You can even begin your scanning at the end of the poem: when you look at the close of "Ode to a Nightingale" and see that it ends with two unresolved questions, you are more prepared for its inner vexations. Be patient with your scannings: each new run-through reveals more of the strategy of the poem, and enables you to describe the energies of the poem better.

GEORGE HERBERT

Easter Wings

Lord, who createdst man in wealth and store,
Though foolishly he lost the same,
Decaying more and more
Till he became
Most poor:
With thee
O let me rise
As larks, harmoniously,
And sing this day thy victories:
Then shall the fall further the flight in me.

My tender age in sorrow did begin;
And still with sicknesses and shame
Thou didst so punish sin,
That I became
Most thin.
With thee
Let me combine,
And feel this day thy victory;
For, if I imp[1] my wing on thine,
Affliction shall advance the flight in me.

---

[1] To graft feathers on a damaged wing so as to improve powers of flight. (A term from falconry.)

WILLIAM SHAKESPEARE
Sonnet 129

Th' expense of spirit in a waste of shame
Is lust in action; and till action, lust
Is perjured, murderous, bloody, full of blame,
Savage, extreme, rude, cruel, not to trust;
Enjoyed no sooner but despisèd straight:
Past reason hunted; and no sooner had,
Past reason hated, as a swallowèd bait,
On purpose laid to make the taker mad:
Mad in pursuit, and in possession so;
Had, having, and in quest to have, extreme;
A bliss in proof,° and proved, a very woe;   *in the experience*
Before, a joy proposed; behind, a dream.
All this the world well knows; yet none knows well
To shun the heaven that leads men to this hell.

ANDREW MARVELL
The Garden

  How vainly men themselves amaze
To win the palm, the oak, or bays,[1]
And their incessant labors see
Crowned from some single herb, or tree,
Whose short and narrow-vergèd shade
Does prudently their toils upbraid;
While all flowers and all trees do close
To weave the garlands of repose!

  Fair Quiet, have I found thee here,
And Innocence, thy sister dear?
Mistaken long, I sought you then
In busy companies of men.
Your sacred plants, if here below,
Only among the plants will grow;
Society is all but rude
To this delicious solitude.

[1] Awards for military, civic, or poetic achievement.

No white nor red was ever seen
So amorous as this lovely green.
Fond lovers, cruel as their flame,
Cut in these trees their mistress' name:
Little, alas, they know or heed
How far these beauties hers exceed!
Fair trees, wheresoe'er your barks I wound,
No name shall but your own be found.

When we have run our passion's heat,
Love hither makes his best retreat.
The gods, that mortal beauty chase,
Still in a tree did end their race:
Apollo hunted Daphne so,
Only that she might laurel grow;
And Pan did after Syrinx speed,
Not as a nymph, but for a reed.[2]

What wondrous life is this I lead!
Ripe apples drop about my head;
The luscious clusters of the vine
Upon my mouth do crush their wine;
The nectarine and curious peach
Into my hands themselves do reach;
Stumbling on melons, as I pass,
Insnared with flowers, I fall on grass.

Meanwhile the mind, from pleasure less,°   *from less pleasure*
Withdraws into its happiness;
The mind, that ocean where each kind
Does straight its own resemblance find;[3]
Yet it creates, transcending these,
Far other worlds and other seas,
Annihilating all that's made
To a green thought in a green shade.

Here at the fountain's sliding foot,
Or at some fruit tree's mossy root,
Casting the body's vest aside,

---

[2] Daphne, to escape Apollo, turned into a laurel tree. Syrinx, to escape Pan, turned into a reed. Marvell implies that Apollo and Pan desired these transformations.

[3] Alluding to the popular notion that the flora and fauna of the land have their parallels in the sea.

My soul into the boughs does glide:
There, like a bird, it sits and sings,
Then whets and combs its silver wings,
And, till prepared for longer flight,
Waves in its plumes the various light.

    Such was that happy garden-state,
While man there walked without a mate:
After a place so pure and sweet,
What other help could yet be meet!
But 'twas beyond a mortal's share
To wander solitary there:
Two paradises 'twere in one
To live in paradise alone.

    How well the skillful gardener drew
Of flowers and herbs this dial new,
Where, from above, the milder sun
Does through a fragrant zodiac run;
And as it works, th' industrious bee
Computes its time as well as we!
How could such sweet and wholesome hours
Be reckoned but with herbs and flowers?

JOHN MILTON
When I Consider How My Light Is Spent

When I consider how my light is spent
    Ere half my days in this dark world and wide,
    And that one talent which is death to hide
    Lodged with me useless, though my soul more bent
To serve therewith my Maker, and present
    My true account, lest he returning chide;
    "Doth God exact day-labor, light denied?"
    I fondly ask; but Patience to prevent
That murmur, soon replies, "God doth not need
    Either man's work or his own gifts; who best
    Bear his mild yoke, they serve him best. His state
Is kingly. Thousands at his bidding speed
    And post o'er land and ocean without rest:
    They also serve who only stand and wait."

JOHN KEATS
Ode to a Nightingale

1

My heart aches, and a drowsy numbness pains
 My sense, as though of hemlock[1] I had drunk,
Or emptied some dull opiate to the drains
 One minute past, and Lethe-wards[2] had sunk:
'Tis not through envy of thy happy lot,
 But being too happy in thine happiness —
  That thou, light-wingèd Dryad of the trees,
   In some melodious plot
 Of beechen green, and shadows numberless,
  Singest of summer in full-throated ease.

2

O, for a draught of vintage! that hath been
 Cooled a long age in the deep-delvèd earth,
Tasting of Flora° and the country green,   *goddess of flowers*
 Dance, and Provençal song,[3] and sunburnt mirth!
O for a beaker full of the warm South,
 Full of the true, the blushful Hippocrene,[4]
  With beaded bubbles winking at the brim,
   And purple-stainèd mouth;
 That I might drink, and leave the world unseen,
  And with thee fade away into the forest dim:

3

Fade far away, dissolve, and quite forget
 What thou among the leaves hast never known,
The weariness, the fever, and the fret
 Here, where men sit and hear each other groan;
Where palsy shakes a few, sad, last gray hairs,
 Where youth grows pale, and specter-thin, and dies,
  Where but to think is to be full of sorrow
   And leaden-eyed despairs,

---

[1] A plant which produces a powerful sedative, and from which it is also possible to produce a poison.

[2] Souls waiting in Hades to be reborn drink the waters of Lethe in order to forget their past existence.

[3] Provence was the home of the medieval troubadors.

[4] A fountain near Mount Helicon in Greece; its water induced poetic inspiration.

Where Beauty cannot keep her lustrous eyes,
    Or new Love pine at them beyond tomorrow.

4

Away! away! for I will fly to thee,
    Not charioted by Bacchus and his pards,[5]
But on the viewless° wings of Poesy,   *invisible*
    Though the dull brain perplexes and retards:
Already with thee! tender is the night,
    And haply the Queen-Moon is on her throne,
        Clustered around by all her starry Fays;°   *fairies*
           But here there is no light,
    Save what from heaven is with the breezes blown
        Through verdurous glooms and winding mossy ways.

5

I cannot see what flowers are at my feet,
    Nor what soft incense hangs upon the boughs,
But, in embalmèd° darkness, guess each sweet   *perfumed*
    Wherewith the seasonable month endows
The grass, the thicket, and the fruit tree wild;
    White hawthorn, and the pastoral eglantine;
        Fast fading violets covered up in leaves;
           And mid-May's eldest child,
    The coming musk-rose, full of dewy wine,
        The murmurous haunt of flies on summer eves.

6

Darkling° I listen; and for many a time   *in darkness*
    I have been half in love with easeful Death,
Called him soft names in many a musèd rhyme,
    To take into the air my quiet breath;
Now more than ever seems it rich to die,
    To cease upon the midnight with no pain,
        While thou art pouring forth thy soul abroad
           In such an ecstasy!
    Still wouldst thou sing, and I have ears in vain —
        To thy high requiem become a sod.

---

[5] Bacchus is the Greek god of wine, often represented in a chariot drawn by leopards ("pards").

7

Thou wast not born for death, immortal Bird!
    No hungry generations tread thee down;
The voice I hear this passing night was heard
    In ancient days by emperor and clown:
Perhaps the selfsame song that found a path
    Through the sad heart of Ruth,[6] when, sick for home,
        She stood in tears amid the alien corn;
            The same that ofttimes hath
    Charmed magic casements, opening on the foam
        Of perilous seas, in faery lands forlorn.

8

Forlorn! the very word is like a bell
    To toll me back from thee to my sole self!
Adieu! the fancy cannot cheat so well
    As she is famed to do, deceiving elf.
Adieu! adieu! thy plaintive anthem fades
    Past the near meadows, over the still stream,
        Up the hill side; and now 'tis buried deep
            In the next valley-glades:
    Was it a vision, or a waking dream?
        Fled is that music: — Do I wake or sleep?

MATTHEW ARNOLD

Dover Beach

The sea is calm tonight.
The tide is full, the moon lies fair
Upon the straits; on the French coast the light
Gleams and is gone; the cliffs of England stand,
Glimmering and vast, out in the tranquil bay.
Come to the window, sweet is the night-air!
Only, from the long line of spray
Where the sea meets the moon-blanched land,
Listen! you hear the grating roar
Of pebbles which the waves draw back, and fling,
At their return, up the high strand,

---

[6] In the Old Testament, Ruth was a faithful widow who followed her mother-in-law to a foreign land.

Begin, and cease, and then again begin,
With tremulous cadence slow, and bring
The eternal note of sadness in.

Sophocles long ago
Heard it on the Aegean, and it brought
Into his mind the turbid ebb and flow
Of human misery; we
Find also in the sound a thought,
Hearing it by this distant northern sea.

The Sea of Faith
Was once, too, at the full, and round earth's shore
Lay like the folds of a bright girdle furled.
But now I only hear
Its melancholy, long, withdrawing roar,
Retreating, to the breath
Of the night-wind, down the vast edges drear
And naked shingles of the world.

Ah, love, let us be true
To one another! for the world, which seems
To lie before us like a land of dreams,
So various, so beautiful, so new,
Hath really neither joy, nor love, nor light,
Nor certitude, nor peace, nor help for pain;
And we are here as on a darkling plain
Swept with confused alarms of struggle and flight,
Where ignorant armies clash by night.

ROBERT FROST
Mending Wall

Something there is that doesn't love a wall,
That sends the frozen-ground-swell under it,
And spills the upper boulders in the sun;
And makes gaps even two can pass abreast.
The work of hunters is another thing:
I have come after them and made repair
Where they have left not one stone on a stone,
But they would have the rabbit out of hiding,
To please the yelping dogs. The gaps I mean,
No one has seen them made or heard them made,

But at spring mending-time we find them there.
I let my neighbor know beyond the hill;
And on a day we meet to walk the line
And set the wall between us once again.
We keep the wall between us as we go.
To each the boulders that have fallen to each.
And some are loaves and some so nearly balls
We have to use a spell to make them balance:
"Stay where you are until our backs are turned!"
We wear our fingers rough with handling them.
Oh, just another kind of outdoor game,
One on a side. It comes to little more:
There where it is we do not need the wall:
He is all pine and I am apple orchard.
My apple trees will never get across
And eat the cones under his pines, I tell him.
He only says, "Good fences make good neighbors."
Spring is the mischief in me, and I wonder
If I could put a notion in his head:
"*Why* do they make good neighbors? Isn't it
Where there are cows? But here there are no cows.
Before I built a wall I'd ask to know
What I was walling in or walling out,
And to whom I was like to give offense.
Something there is that doesn't love a wall,
That wants it down." I could say "Elves" to him,
But it's not elves exactly, and I'd rather
He said it for himself. I see him there
Bringing a stone grasped firmly by the top
In each hand, like an old-stone savage armed.
He moves in darkness as it seems to me,
Not of woods only and the shade of trees.
He will not go behind his father's saying,
And he likes having thought of it so well
He says again, "Good fences make good neighbors."

EZRA POUND

The River-Merchant's Wife: a Letter[1]

While my hair was still cut straight across my forehead
I played about the front gate, pulling flowers.
You came by on bamboo stilts, playing horse,
You walked about my seat, playing with blue plums.
And we went on living in the village of Chokan:
Two small people, without dislike or suspicion.

At fourteen I married My Lord you.
I never laughed, being bashful.
Lowering my head, I looked at the wall.
Called to, a thousand times, I never looked back.

At fifteen I stopped scowling,
I desired my dust to be mingled with yours
Forever and forever and forever.
Why should I climb the look out?

At sixteen you departed,
You went into far Ku-to-yen, by the river of swirling eddies,
And you have been gone five months.
The monkeys make sorrowful noise overhead.

You dragged your feet when you went out.
By the gate now, the moss is grown, the different mosses,
Too deep to clear them away!
The leaves fall early this autumn, in wind.
The paired butterflies are already yellow with August
Over the grass in the West garden;
They hurt me. I grow older.
If you are coming down through the narrows of the river Kiang,
Please let me know beforehand,
And I will come out to meet you
      As far as Cho-fu-Sa.

---

[1] Adapted from the Chinese of Li Po (700?–762). Ernest Fenellosa (1853–1908), an American orientalist and collector, made the translation from which Pound worked.

MARK STRAND
Courtship

There is a girl you like so you tell her
your penis is big, but that you cannot get yourself
to use it. Its demands are ridiculous, you say,
even self-defeating, but to be honored somehow,
briefly, inconspicuously in the dark.

When she closes her eyes in horror,
you take it all back. You tell her you're almost
a girl yourself and can understand why she is shocked.
When she is about to walk away, you tell her
you have no penis, that you don't

know what got into you. You get on your knees.
She suddenly bends down to kiss your shoulder and you know
you're on the right track. You tell her you want
to bear children and that is why you seem confused.
You wrinkle your brow and curse the day you were born.

She tries to calm you, but you lose control.
You reach for her panties and beg forgiveness as you do.
She squirms and you howl like a wolf. Your craving
seems monumental. You know you will have her.
Taken by storm, she is the girl you will marry.

SEAMUS HEANEY
From the Frontier of Writing

The tightness and the nilness round that space
when the car stops in the road, the troops inspect
its make and number and, as one bends his face

towards your window, you catch sight of more
on a hill beyond, eyeing with intent
down cradled guns that hold you under cover

and everything is pure interrogation
until a rifle motions and you move
with guarded unconcerned acceleration —

a little emptier, a little spent
as always by that quiver in the self,
subjugated, yes, and obedient.

So you drive on to the frontier of writing
where it happens again. The guns on tripods;
the sergeant with his on-off mike repeating

data about you, waiting for the squawk
of clearance: the marksman training down
out of the sun upon you like a hawk.

And suddenly you're through, arraigned yet freed,
as if you'd passed from behind a waterfall
on the black current of a tarmac road

past armour-plated vehicles, out between
the posted soldiers flowing and receding
like tree shadows into the polished windscreen.

JORIE GRAHAM
San Sepolcro[1]

In this blue light
    I can take you there,
snow having made me
    a world of bone
seen through to. This
    is my house,

my section of Etruscan
    wall, my neighbor's
lemontrees, and, just below
    the lower church,
the airplane factory.
    A rooster

crows all day from mist
    outside the walls.
There's milk on the air,
    ice on the oily
lemonskins. How clean
    the mind is,

holy grave. It is this girl
    by Piero

---

[1] A town in Italy whose name translates to "holy grave."

della Francesca[1], unbuttoning
    her blue dress,
her mantle of weather,
    to go into

labor. Come, we can go in.
    It is before
the birth of god. No-one
    has risen yet
to the museums, to the assembly
    line — bodies

and wings — to the open air
    market. This is
what the living do: go in.
    It's a long way.
And the dress keeps opening
    from eternity

to privacy, quickening.
    Inside, at the heart,
is tragedy, the present moment
    forever stillborn,
but going in, each breath
    is a button

coming undone, something terribly
    nimble-fingered
finding all of the stops.

SHERMAN ALEXIE
Evolution

Buffalo Bill opens a pawn shop on the reservation
right across the border from the liquor store
and he stays open 24 hours a day, 7 days a week

and the Indians come running in with jewelry
television sets, a VCR, a full-length beaded buckskin outfit
it took Inez Muse 12 years to finish. Buffalo Bill

takes everything the Indians have to offer, keeps it

---

[1] Piero della Francesca (1420?–1492), Italian painter.

all catalogued and filed in a storage room. The Indians
pawn their hands, saving the thumbs for last, they pawn

their skeletons, falling endlessly from the skin
and when the last Indian has pawned everything
but his heart, Buffalo Bill takes that for twenty bucks

closes up the pawn shop, paints a new sign over the old
calls his venture THE MUSEUM OF NATIVE AMERICAN
        CULTURES
charges the Indians five bucks a head to enter.

5

The Play of Language

Language is the principal raw material out of which poets construct their experiments (rhythmic patterns are the other chief raw materials). By the single word "language" we mean many things:

Sound Units

The sound units of a poem are its syllables. The word "enemy" has three successive sounds, *en-eh-mee.* Readers are conscious of a sound effect when they hear two end-words rhyme; but poets are conscious of *all* the sounds in their lines, just as they are of the rhythms of a line. Poets "bind" words together in a line by having them share sounds, whether consonants (*alliteration*, as in "*br*oken *br*ead") or vowels (*assonance*, as in "wh*e*n . . . s*e*ssions"). This makes the words sound as if they "belong" together by natural affinity. Note how Shakespeare uses the vowel sounds *eh* and *uh* and the consonant sounds *n*, *t*, *th*, *s*, and *w* in this line from Sonnet 20: "When to the sessions of sweet silent thought . . ." Good poets tend to bind together words that have an important meaning-connection, as Robert Frost does in this line from "Birches": "When I see *b*irches *b*end to left and right . . ." and as Sylvia Plath does in these lines from "Ariel":

> *Stasis* in *dark*ness.
> Then the *sub*stance*less bl*ue
> *P*our of tor and *distances* . . .

Word Roots

These are the pieces of words that come from words in earlier languages, often Greek, Latin, or Anglo-Saxon. Poets usually are aware of the roots of the words they use. Many of these roots are preceded by prefixes, which also retain their original meanings, such as:

re- ("again"): return, revolve, repair, represent, etc.

ex- ("out of "): explain, expire, exhale, etc.

pre- ("in front of "): precede, prefer, preclude, etc.

com- (*cum*, "with"): compare, commemorate, commend, etc.

de- ("away from"): delete, defer, delay, defend, etc.

We have two main streams of language in English: our basic short words generally come from Anglo-Saxon, and our more complicated words from Latin (often through French). In the past, English was closer to Latin and French than it is today (during the Renaissance, for example, educated people usually knew several languages), and poets drew on that closeness. In Sonnet 15, Shakespeare wrote:

> When I *consider* everything that grows
> Holds in perfection but a little moment,
> That this huge stage presenteth naught but shows
> Whereon the *stars* in secret influence comment;
> When I *perceive* that men as plants increase,
> Cheerèd and checked even by the selfsame sky,
>
> .   .   .   .   .
>
> Then the *conceit* of this inconstant stay
> Sets *you* most rich in *you*th before my sight . . .

Here, he expected his readers to know that "consider" comes from a root (which we also find, for instance, in the word "sidereal") meaning "stars" — a word that appears in line 4. He also expected them to notice that the word "consider" is composed of two parts, *con-* and *-sider*, and that the next "I"-verb ("perceive") is followed by a noun ("conceit") which combines the *con-* of "consider" with the *-ceive* of "perceive." Perhaps he also expected at least some of his readers to see how the *con-* of "consider" and "conceit" is repeated in "in*con*stant" (and that the word "you" is contained in "youth").

We now live in an age when most readers are not schooled in Latin and therefore are less likely to recognize the Latin implications in English words. Still, we can easily find this information, especially for a word that seems unusually important in a poem, by consulting a dictionary.

Words

The meaning of a word in a poem is determined less by its dictionary definition (a single word like "stage" or "store" can have many definitions in a comprehensive dictionary) than by the words around it. Every word in a poem enters into relation with the other words in that poem. These relations can be of several kinds:

1. *thematic* (or meaning) relation — as we would connect "stars" and "sky" in the quotation above;
2. *phonemic* relation — as we would connect "stage," "stars," "secret," "selfsame," "sky," and "stay" in the quotation above by their initial *s*'s and *st*'s;
3. *grammatical* relation — as "cheerèd" and "checked" (already linked *phonemically* by their sounds, and *thematically* by their being antonyms of each other) are both verbal adjectives modifying "men";
4. *syntactic* relation — as "When I consider" and "When I perceive" introduce dependent clauses in "I," both modifying the main clause "Then the conceit . . . sets you."

Each word, then, exists in several "constellations" of relation, all of which the reader needs to notice in order to see the overlapping structures of language in the poem.

Sentences

When we think about a poem, it's useful to write out its sentences in ordinary prose order, and then see what has been done to them in verse. For each sentence, it's indispensable to identify the grammatical *subject* — the person, place, or thing in charge of the verb, so to speak — and the *predicate* — the verb telling what the grammatical subject is or does (present tense), was or did (past tense), or will be or will do (future tense). In the course of a poem, *subjects* can change (the poet can say, "*I* love you" and then say "*You* love me"), *predicates* can change (the poet can say, "I *love* you" and then, "I *hate* you"), and *tenses* can change (the poet can say, "I *love* you now," and later say, "But I *will* not *love* you tomorrow"). By tracking these changes of subject, predicate, and tense you can see the dynamic of the poem: where and with whom it began, what's happening to it, where it's going, and where it ends up.

The more complex the poem, the more necessary this tracking is, if you're to get a firm sense of who is doing (or saying) what when, in each part. But even a "simple" poem repays attention of this sort. In Robert Frost's "Stopping by Woods on a Snowy Evening," the grammatical *subject* alone changes from "I" to "house" to "he" (the owner) to "horse" to "he" (the horse) to "sound" to "woods" to "I".

ROBERT FROST
Stopping by Woods on a Snowy Evening

Whose woods these are *I* think *I* know.
His *house* is in the village though;
He will not see me stopping here
To watch his woods fill up with snow.

My little *horse* must think it queer
To stop without a farmhouse near
Between the woods and frozen lake
The darkest evening of the year.

He gives his harness bells a shake
To ask if there is some mistake.
The only other *sound*'s the sweep
Of easy wind and downy flake.

The *woods* are lovely, dark and deep
But *I* have promises to keep,
And miles to go before *I* sleep,
And miles to go before *I* sleep.

One can imagine a version of this poem (I apologize for its crudeness) in which the subject never changes, and is "I" throughout:

I know these woods, their owner too,
I feel in watching them some fear,
I sense my little horse's rue,
Pausing without a farmhouse near.

I hear his harness bells now shake
In wonder at my strange mistake.
I hear the sound of falling snow,
All easy wind and downy flake.

I love the woods so dark and deep,
But I have promises to keep,
And miles to go before I sleep,
And miles to go before I sleep.

Why does Frost, do you think, give a *subject*-position not only to himself but also to the owner of the woods and to his horse? And why does he also give it to inanimate things (the woods that fill up with snow, the sound of the wind)? The short answer is that everything in a poem that has subject-position is "alive" and can "do things": the owner of the woods is alive enough to see (but won't) the trespasser; the little horse is alive enough to query his master's odd behavior; the woods are alive enough to be "lovely, dark and deep"; and the silence in the snowy woods is deep enough to make the sound "of easy wind and downy flake" come alive, too. The whole world of the poem, in short, is animate and animated. This is far more interesting, at least in Frost's view of nature, than to have the speaker the only live person in the scene.

Sentences are, grammatically speaking, made up of words which function in different ways. Some words can function in several different ways: for instance, the word "stage" can be either a *noun* ("Have you built the *stage* yet?") or a *verb* ("Will they *stage* a Shakespeare play this season?"). The poet intends you to notice how each word *functions*, as well as what it *means*.

There are conventional names in grammar for words in their functions. You probably remember the basic names of most of the "parts of speech" (as they are called); if not, you might want to turn to the appendix "On Grammar" to refresh your memory.

In clarifying the *function* of each word in a poem, you can see the parade of main statements (nouns plus verbs) making up the logical skeleton of the poem, and you can distinguish these main clauses from the poet's ornamental or explanatory additions. Ask yourself, about each *main* piece of the skeleton, "What would be lost if I deleted this statement?" (What would be lost if we left out the little horse's query in "Stopping by Woods," for instance?) Then ask yourself what purpose is served by the pieces *outside* the noun-verb skeleton — explanations, additions, and ornaments. Sometimes, as in Dickinson's "The Heart asks," the "add-ons" to the main skeleton are of crucial importance. Here is the poem with its add-ons printed in italics:

EMILY DICKINSON
The Heart asks Pleasure — first —

The Heart asks Pleasure — *first* —
And *then* — Excuse *from Pain* —
And *then* — *those little* Anodynes
That deaden suffering —

And *then* — to go to sleep —
And *then* — *if it should be*
The will of its Inquisitor
The privilege to die.

Think what the bare skeleton would be: "The heart asks pleasure and excuse and anodynes and to go to sleep and the privilege to die." It is the adjectives and adverbs that punctuate the poem into its successive phases of torture.

Implication

Because poems are short, they depend more on implication than longer works, such as novels, do. A novel has time and leisure to spell things out; a poem compresses the maximum into each word. Because a poem can only suggest, not expatiate, it requires *you* to supply the concrete instances for each of its suggestions. At the end of his late poem "The Tower," William Butler Yeats draws an escalating list of the ills of old age, gradually arriving at the worst of all. He fears, he says,

> . . . the wreck of body,
> Slow decay of blood,
> Testy delirium
> Or dull decrepitude,
> Or what worse evil come —
> The death of friends, or death
> Of every brilliant eye
> That made a catch in the breath.

A lyric poet like Yeats expects *you to think concretely* as he speaks abstractly, since his words are to be yours. What do you mean when you tell me that you fear in yourself "the wreck of body"? Perhaps paralysis, perhaps a wasting disease — it doesn't matter, but you *must* (in reading the line to yourself or speaking it aloud) have *something* actively in mind that corresponds in *your* mind to Yeats's words. "Slow decay of blood":

perhaps, remembering Yeats's use of "blood" elsewhere, you will connect this phrase with the cooling of the hot blood of passion. "Testy delirium": you may think of brain damage from strokes, or incoherence from fever. "Dull decrepitude": you may think of senility. For "the death of friends," you might think of the friend you would miss the most. Then you arrive at the strange periphrasis (indirect way of speaking) marking the climax: What, Yeats makes us ask, is worse than bodily aging, worse than mental decay, worse than the death of friends? What is this "death / Of every brilliant eye / That made a catch in the breath"? The "death / Of every brilliant eye" is an indirect way of speaking of the death of a beautiful and beloved face — the worst event of all, the disappearance of the one face in the world that was everything to you. Perhaps, Yeats implies with "every," there were several such faces in his long life.

This process of paying attention to words, their functions, their logical arrangements in sentences, and their implications is what we really mean by "close" reading. It means spelling out, in your *own* mind — since the words of a poem are given to you to say *as if they were your own* — what the generalizing phrases of the poem mean *in your own case* as you extend their implications to yourself. Only then can you speak the words of the poem with conviction.

Lyric always generalizes. It is a blueprint of life, not a detailed transcription of it (as a novel can seem to be). Lyric, as Elizabeth Bishop said, is a map, not a photograph. Lyric is an algebraic equation, giving you x and y (decay, decrepitude, delirium) and asking you to fill in the poet's equation with your own "real numbers." A lyric asks you to be its co-creator, as you supply your own inner particulars for its generalizations.

Implication can be present in rhythm as well as in words. In Chapter 4, for instance, we saw the excited broken rhythms succeeding, in the close, the stately opening rhythms in Keats's "On First Looking into Chapman's Homer." In every case, you can discover implication by asking "Why?" Why is Yeats's list given in this order? Why do Keats's rhythms change at the end? Why isn't Keats's first metaphor (an astronomer discovering a new planet) good enough, so that he has to progress to a better metaphor (the discovery of the Pacific Ocean by an explorer and his men)? As Samuel Taylor Coleridge said, "Poetry is the best words in the best order." Your task, as a student of poetry, is to form hypotheses about why the poet arranged *these* words in *this* order till the poem seemed a satisfying whole. Your reflections on these matters will bring you into the heart of the poem, will give you increasing pleasure, and will make the poem an increasingly satisfying whole to you.

The Ordering of Language

Because poetry is a temporal art, it has to unfold sequentially, one piece after another. First I say *x*, then *y*, then *z*. But the *logical* relations among *x*, *y*, and *z* may not be additive or sequential ones. *X, y,* and *z* may instead be radii of the same circle, as in George Herbert's sonnet, "Prayer" where the successive definitions all relate radially to the one subject:

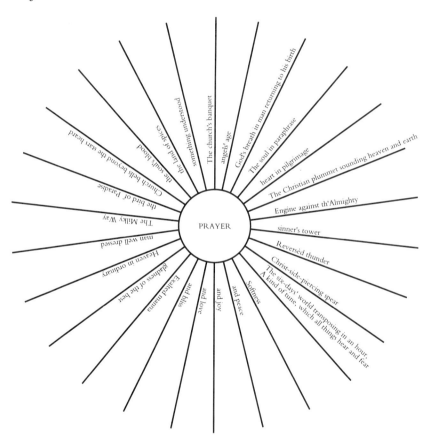

GEORGE HERBERT
Prayer (I)

Prayer, the church's banquet, angels' age,
    God's breath in man returning to his birth,
    The soul in paraphrase, heart in pilgrimage,
The Christian plummet sounding heaven and earth;

Engine against th'Almighty, sinner's tower,
    Reversèd thunder, Christ-side-piercing spear,

> The six-days' world transposing in an hour,
> A kind of tune, which all things hear and fear:
>
> Softness, and peace, and joy, and love, and bliss,
>   Exalted manna, gladness of the best,
>   Heaven in ordinary, man well dressed,
> The Milky Way, the bird of Paradise,
>   Church bells beyond the stars heard, the soul's blood,
>   The land of spices; something understood.

This list of all the things that prayer is might best be represented as radii of a circle: Herbert's order is one of radial amplification of one concept, prayer. But does the poem, in addition to its *radial* order, have a *temporal* order? That is, does something "happen" to the concept of prayer as the poem progresses? Most readers will be aware that thinking of prayer as "reversèd thunder" is not the same in feeling-tone as thinking of it as "softness, and peace, and joy, and love, and bliss." You may want to track the changes in mind of the speaker as the poem progresses, as the speaker exchanges one metaphor for another — only to give up entirely on metaphor at the end. In short, a poem can have more than one "shape" — here, it has both a static radial shape and a dynamic temporal unfolding.

Frequently the ordering of a poem's language offers a gradual clarification of meaning. At first, in Sonnet 66, Shakespeare's speaker sees only a procession of terrible miscarriages of justice in the world:

WILLIAM SHAKESPEARE
Sonnet 66

> Tired with all these, for restful death I cry:
> As to behold desert a beggar born,
> And needy nothing trimmed in jollity,
> And purest faith unhappily forsworn,
> And gilded honour shamefully misplaced,
> And maiden virtue rudely strumpeted,
> And right perfection wrongfully disgraced, . . .

At this point, most readers (especially those who have been imaginatively "filling in" the implications of Shakespeare's categories with their own current examples of the same vices) will begin to see that these actions have no agents. Who reduced the deserving ("desert") to beggary? Who misplaced honor, bestowing it on the unworthy instead of the worthy? Who has seduced the maiden? As the procession of wrongs continues in the poem, the speaker's vision becomes clarified: he can see now not only the victims but their victimizers accompanying them:

> And strength *by limping sway* disablèd,
> And art made tongue-tied *by authority*,
> And *folly, doctor-like*, controlling skill, . . .

The procession is now advancing two-by-two, instead of one-by-one; for instance, "strength" is hampered by "limping sway" (incompetent authority). Then, the two-by-two procession is interrupted by an anomalous solo figure:

> And simple truth miscalled simplicity,

Who can this be but the poem itself (in the person of its author)? Its "simple truth" is called, wrongly, "simplicity" ("political naïveté," in modern terms) by its detractors. Finally, we come, at the end, to the chief authority figure, who in a liturgical or court procession would be the Bishop or King. Here we see the chief agent of all the miscarriages of justice, leading his ultimate allegorical victim:

> And captive good attending captain ill.

Captain Ill is a secularized form of Satan, "the prince of this world." Just as the speaker of Shakespeare's sonnet sees more clearly as the procession winds on, so do we, until the author of all evil is revealed. This leaves the speaker with no hope of amelioration. Because Ill is Captain, and Good is always Captive in his power, there is no visible justice in this world. And so the speaker, though he is still longing for death, decides against it, not out of hope but out of protectiveness for his beloved:

> Tired with all these, from these would I be gone,
> Save that to die, I leave my love alone.

"Alone" is a terrible word in the evil world of this sonnet. In danger of being alone, strumpeted, tongue-tied, disgraced, disabled — who, in these circumstances, could abandon his beloved?

We can see the "shape" of this poem in several ways:

1. As a long procession bracketed by the speaker's two declarations of exhaustion;

2. More precisely, we can see the procession itself subdivided into three main parts: one-by-one, two-by-two, and a final archetype (generalizing personification) of Good in captivity to Ill;

3. Or we can see a single shape (disillusion and exhaustion) for the

first thirteen lines, "redeemed" by line 14, which reveals that the speaker has one value, love, as yet uncorrupted by the world.

The more ways we see the governing linguistic order of the poem, the more human complexity we can perceive within it.

The ordering of experience in shapes of radial or logical clarification — clarification by hierarchy, clarification by a comparison of then to now, clarification by here versus there, or clarification by rise-and-decline (to name only four common "shapes") — is what gives poetry its aura of mastery. Even when its "content" is tragic — as in Dickinson's list of the heart's requests, or Shakespeare's procession of injustice — the fact that the list has been ordered into an understood set or a hierarchy reassures us that the mind can understand what the heart cannot endure, and that the imagination can find a linguistic shape for the structures of reality, even for those that are most tragic.

There is no linguistic ingredient too small to attract the poet's interest. Wallace Stevens makes poems that turn on the difference between the definite and indefinite article ("the" versus "a"); Yeats constructs a poem ("In Memory of Eva Gore-Booth and Con Markiewicz") that turns on a movement from "I" to "you" to "we" as a sign of reconciliation of enemies. Shakespeare can build a whole sonnet ("Th'expense of spirit in a waste of shame," Sonnet 129) on a contrast between nouns and adjectives (nouns give essence, we are reminded; adjectives give qualities). The play of language is the chief cause for the aesthetic success of any poem. Without play at many levels of language, from phonemes to logical structures, a poem is merely prose with line-breaks added.

Let's look at a sample poem, Michael Drayton's "Since there's no help," to try to bring to bear on it what this chapter has said about examining the language of a poem very closely at several levels — its sound-units, its etymological roots, its sentences with their words functioning as parts of speech, its subjects and predicates, tenses and moods, its imaginative play of language, and its processes of implication. The poem is spoken by a young man whose beloved, we infer, has just declared that their love affair is over:

Michael Drayton
Since there's no help

Since there's no help, come let us kiss and part;
Nay, I have done, you get no more of me,
And I am glad, yea glad with all my heart
That thus so cleanly I myself can free;

> Shake hands forever, cancel all our vows,
> And when we meet at any time again,
> Be it not seen in either of our brows
> That we one jot of former love retain.
> Now at the last gasp of love's latest breath,
> When, his pulse failing, passion speechless lies,
> When faith is kneeling by his bed of death,
> And innocence is closing up his eyes;
> Now if thou wouldst, when all have given him over,
> From death to life thou mightst him yet recover.

Here are the main independent clauses of the first sentence of the poem, which occupies the octave, or first eight lines, of the sonnet. The clauses are here written out as statements, with the **subjects** in boldface and the *predicates* italicized:

> Come *let* **us** *kiss* and *part*
> **I** *have done*
> **You** *get* no more of me
> **I** *am* glad
> [*let* **us**] *shake* hands
> [*let* **us**] *cancel* vows
> *be* **it** not *seen*

The first sentence, then, moves through several verbs in the hortatory mood — "let us kiss and part," "let us shake hands," "let us cancel all our vows," "[let] it not be seen" — interspersed with verbs in the indicative mood, one in the past tense ("I have done") and two in the future tense ("you [will] get no more of me" and "when we [shall] meet at any [future] time"). The subjects change from **us** to **I** to **you** to **I** to **us** to **it**. All of these changes are indexes of the speaker's troubled state, as he darts from mood to mood, from tense to tense, and from subject position to object position. Although many of the dependent clauses add information ("Since there's no help," "that thus so cleanly I myself can free," "that we one jot of former love retain"), yet the skeleton above of the main clauses makes the import of the sentence clear.

The case is very different when we come to the second sentence, which takes up the last six lines (the sestet) of the sonnet. It has only one main clause: "**Thou** *mightst* him *recover*." All the other clauses are strung from this one. "Thou mightst him recover" — when?

> Now at the last gasp of love's latest breath
> [Now] when passion speechless lies

[Now] when faith is kneeling by his bed
[Now] when innocence is closing up his eyes
Now when all have given him over

All of these adverbial clauses "lead up" like the steps of a staircase to the main clause, giving the sestet its long suspense. In this way the relatively straightforward march of main clauses in the octave changes dramatically once we meet the long delay of the main clause in the sestet.

When we look at the kind of words these two sentences are composed of, we notice that with a few exceptions like "cancel" and "retain," most of the words of the octave are those short brisk words we tend to associate with our Anglo-Saxon linguistic heritage — "help," "come," "kiss," "get," "glad," "heart," "clean," and so on. When we come to the sestet, the number of Latin- or Romance-derived words rises — "pulse," "fail," "passion," "faith," "innocence," "close," "recover." Even if readers do not recognize the roots of all these words, they will sense how the more ceremonious sestet departs from the brisk colloquial nature of the words in the octave, not only because of the rise of Latin-derived words but also because of the suspended syntax.

It is clear that the speaker speaks about himself *in the first person* ("I") in the octave: "Nay, I have done, you get no more of me." But in the sestet, we see a change in language: instead of speaking directly about himself, the speaker speaks in the *third person* of someone called "Passion" who is lying on his "bed of death," whose "pulse [is] failing," who is emitting the last gasp of love's breath. This dying person is attended by two mourners: Faith is kneeling by his deathbed, and Innocence is closing the eyes of the dying man. This little third-person tableau is a way of avoiding first-person speech (otherwise, by the principle of inertia, the speaker would have continued as he began). The change to the third person makes us ask, "What would this closing tableau have been like if it, like the octave, had been put in the first person?"

Now, at the last gasp of my loving breath,
My passion has no words to say to thee,
I seem to lose the faith I had, and death
Of love is death of innocence in me.
Now if thou wouldst, when I have given love over,
From death to life thou mightst me yet recover.

We can see that it's more dignified to ask the woman to rescue "Passion" than to say, "Please, even at this last gasp of passion, rescue *me*."

Because the octave has been phrased in the *hortatory* ("let us") and *indicative* ("I am glad") moods, we especially notice, when we come to the sestet, that it turns for its main clause to the *conditional* mood: "Now *if* thou *wouldst* . . . / thou *mightst* him recover." This holds out a grain of hope — if she *would* do this, she *might* bring him back to life. This is "politer" than saying, in the imperative, "Do this, and he will be cured." It is a plea, not a command.

After the relatively plain octave, in which the words are linked by the concept of saying farewell and canceling vows, we come to two conspicuous sets of linked words in the sestet. One is a set of abstract nouns — Love, Passion, Faith, and Innocence. They are the actors in the little tableau. The other set of words is medical and funereal — "gasp," "breath," "pulse failing," "speechless," "bed of death," "closing . . . eyes," "life," "recover." Normally, we find human beings in the situation where here we find Passion — dying among mourners. Drayton brings together in the sestet two incompatible sets of linked words — one abstract, one medically concrete — and constructs his surprising little third-person tableau with them to show us how the lover feels: he is not *really* dying physically, but emotionally "a deathbed scene" is the best description for what is happening to his passion — and he hopes that externalizing his inward feelings in this theatrical tableau may persuade his beloved to have pity on him.

We see from the closing tableau, and the plea with which it ends, that the speaker put on his original bluster ("Nay, I have done, you get no more of me; / And I am glad, yea glad") to hide the real dismay and despair that his closing tableau reveals.

These are only some of the moves we could make in beginning to study the language of this poem, and to ask the questions it provokes: "Why the change in person between octave and sestet?" "Why the introduction of the little tableau?" "Why is the sestet so ceremoniously written after the colloquial language of the octave?" "Why is the main clause of the sestet in the conditional mood?" "Why is the main clause of the sestet so long suspended adverbially before we get to it?"

Of course, we eventually have to move on from the use of language to the wider purposes of the poem — Drayton's conception of passion, and its relation to love, faith, and innocence, and his apt psychological observation of the defenses put up by the jilted lover, before the lover breaks down into his final abject plea. But that is material for a longer study, in which we might compare this poem to others written by Drayton, and get a better idea of his general poetic procedures. In each case, though, the first place to begin is with the play of language. In it, we find the imagination at work.

In Brief: The Play of Language

Since the language of lyric is condensed, every word carries weight, and all aspects of grammar and syntax (parts of speech, speech acts, even word roots) are full of significance. Poets are people steeped in language: "For many years," said Emily Dickinson, "my lexicon was my only companion." It is helpful to look at each sentence by itself, and at its chief agent, and at what the agent does. What are the interesting or unusual words in the sentence? What speech acts are taking place? What is implied in the "white space" between sentences or stanzas? Is the organization linear (start-to-finish), radial (a cluster of phrases around a center), or recursive (doubling back on itself)? Does the language change from concrete to abstract, or vice versa? Language gives you the *manner* of the poem, as well as its matter.

Reading Other Poems

There is no poem that does not play with language. As the following poems demonstrate, some are more overt about it, some less so. Language is both spoken and written, and the poet thinks about both aspects: how the poem sounds, how it looks on the page. Not everything written can be spoken: see E. E. Cummings's poem on the way the grasshopper rearranges his limbs while leaping. If you trace the stages of the grasshopper's motions, how does Cummings mimic them?

Track the gestures implicit in the language of the Duke as he talks to the envoy arranging the new marriage. See how inconspicuously Robert Browning uses rhyme, and how the Duke's syntax shapes his powerful ongoing sentences. In the case of George Herbert's sonnet, you might ask how the language of the speaker reflects his initial mistake; in the case of Wallace Stevens's two-room poem, ask what you see in the first room, the kitchen, versus what you see in the second room, the bedroom, and how language is invented to match the reality in each room.

Sometimes a poet makes up a new personal language, as John Berryman often did in his *Dream Songs*. His protagonist, Henry, talks one way when he is drinking in a bar, angry with his wife; another way when he has a vision from an airplane; a third way when he's sick in the hospital, fearing death. Can you find adjectives to describe each phase of his language?

Repetition of language is one of the weapons in the armory of poetry, and certain verse-forms entail the "foregrounding" of one or two lines by repetition. What are the repeated lines in Elizabeth Bishop's villanelle "One Art"? Can you describe the effect on the reader of having them recur so often? To how many things are these lines applied?

The play of language is deeply felt when a poem has to convey changes over time. Can you see the time specified in each of Keats's stanzas in his autumn ode? What sort of language predominates in each stanza (for example, the infinitives in stanza 1)? What sort of noises end the poem? Can you compare the language used to guide the reader through the time sequence in Keats to the language that guides mentions of time in Yeats's poem about the swans? What sort of language does Yeats use about himself, by contrast to the language he uses about the swans?

Both John Donne's "Batter my heart" and H.D.'s "Oread" are poems structured by commands. Who is being commanded? Can they be commanded? What kind of language appears in the commands? Can the commands be obeyed? Do some commands differ from others? Imagine each poem rewritten as narrative rather than command: Can you then see the poet's attraction to this syntactic form?

Henry Reed's poem "The Naming of Parts" is structured by repetition and by puns: What are their expressive functions?

Sometimes the play of language is structured on the relation of one dialect to another (as Berryman uses slang and invented words along with standard English), sometimes on the relation of one language to another (as Lorna Dee Cervantes asserts the perpetual presence, in her mind, of both Spanish and English). What is your reaction to this mixed diction? (There is an old tradition of mixed diction in English poetry, beginning with poems written partly in English and partly in Latin.)

JOHN DONNE
Holy Sonnet 14

Batter my heart, three-personed God; for You
As yet but knock, breathe, shine, and seek to mend;
That I may rise and stand, o'erthrow me, and bend
Your force to break, blow, burn, and make me new.
I, like an usurped town, to another due,
Labor to admit You, but O, to no end;
Reason, Your viceroy in me, me should defend,
But is captívèd, and proves weak or untrue.
Yet dearly I love You, and would be lovèd fain,
But am betrothed unto Your enemy.

Divorce me, untie or break that knot again;
Take me to You, imprison me, for I,
Except You enthrall me, never shall be free,
Nor ever chaste, except You ravish me.

GEORGE HERBERT

Redemption

Having been tenant long to a rich lord,
    Not thriving, I resolvèd to be bold,
    And make a suit unto him, to afford°   *grant*
A new small-rented lease, and cancel the old.

In heaven at his manor I him sought;
    They told me there that he was lately gone
    About some land, which he had dearly bought
Long since on earth, to take possessïon.

I straight returned, and knowing his great birth,
    Sought him accordingly in great resorts;
    In cities, theaters, gardens, parks, and courts;
At length I heard a ragged noise and mirth

    Of thieves and murderers; there I him espied,
    Who straight, *Your suit is granted,* said, and died.

JOHN KEATS

To Autumn

1

Season of mists and mellow fruitfulness,
    Close bosom-friend of the maturing sun;
Conspiring with him how to load and bless
    With fruit the vines that round the thatch-eaves run;
To bend with apples the mossed cottage-trees,
    And fill all fruit with ripeness to the core;
        To swell the gourd, and plump the hazel shells
    With a sweet kernel; to set budding more,
And still more, later flowers for the bees,
Until they think warm days will never cease,
        For Summer has o'er-brimmed their clammy cells.

2

Who hath not seen thee oft amid thy store?
　　Sometimes whoever seeks abroad may find
Thee sitting careless on a granary floor,
　　Thy hair soft-lifted by the winnowing wind;
Or on a half-reaped furrow sound asleep,
　　Drowsed with the fume of poppies, while thy hook
　　　　Spares the next swath and all its twinèd flowers:
And sometimes like a gleaner thou dost keep
　　Steady thy laden head across a brook;
　　Or by a cider-press, with patient look,
　　　　Thou watchest the last oozings hours by hours.

3

Where are the songs of Spring? Aye, where are they?
　　Think not of them, thou hast thy music too —
While barrèd clouds bloom the soft-dying day,
　　And touch the stubble-plains with rosy hue;
Then in a wailful choir the small gnats mourn
　　Among the river sallows,° borne aloft　　　*low-growing willows*
　　　　Or sinking as the light wind lives or dies;
And full-grown lambs loud bleat from hilly bourn;
　　Hedge crickets sing; and now with treble soft
　　The redbreast whistles from a garden-croft;[1]
　　　　And gathering swallows twitter in the skies.

ROBERT BROWNING
My Last Duchess

Ferrara

That's my last duchess painted on the wall,
Looking as if she were alive. I call
That piece a wonder, now: Frà Pandolf's hands
Worked busily a day, and there she stands.
Will't please you sit and look at her? I said
"Frà Pandolf" by design, for never read
Strangers like you that pictured countenance,
The depth and passion of its earnest glance,

---

[1] Small field at the edge of a property, often leased to another proprietor.

But to myself they turned (since none puts by
The curtain I have drawn for you, but I)
And seemed as they would ask me, if they durst,
How such a glance came there; so, not the first
Are you to turn and ask thus. Sir, 'twas not
Her husband's presence only, called that spot
Of joy into the Duchess' cheek: perhaps
Frà Pandolf chanced to say "Her mantle laps
Over my lady's wrist too much," or "Paint
Must never hope to reproduce the faint
Half-flush that dies along her throat": such stuff
Was courtesy, she thought, and cause enough
For calling up that spot of joy. She had
A heart — how shall I say? — too soon made glad,
Too easily impressed; she liked whate'er
She looked on, and her looks went everywhere.
Sir, 'twas all one! My favor at her breast,
The dropping of the daylight in the West,
The bough of cherries some officious fool
Broke in the orchard for her, the white mule
She rode with round the terrace — all and each
Would draw from her alike the approving speech,
Or blush, at least. She thanked men — good! but thanked
Somehow — I know not how — as if she ranked
My gift of a nine-hundred-years-old name
With anybody's gift. Who'd stoop to blame
This sort of trifling? Even had you skill
In speech — which I have not — to make your will
Quite clear to such an one, and say, "Just this
Or that in you disgusts me; here you miss,
Or there exceed the mark" — and if she let
Herself be lessoned so, nor plainly set
Her wits to yours, forsooth, and made excuse,
— E'en then would be some stooping; and I choose
Never to stoop. Oh sir, she smiled, no doubt,
Whene'er I passed her; but who passed without
Much the same smile? This grew; I gave commands;
Then all smiles stopped together. There she stands
As if alive. Will't please you rise? We'll meet
The company below, then. I repeat,
The Count your master's known munificence
Is ample warrant that no just pretense

Of mine for dowry will be disallowed;
Though his fair daughter's self, as I avowed
At starting, is my object. Nay, we'll go
Together down, sir. Notice Neptune, though,
Taming a sea-horse, thought a rarity,
Which Claus of Innsbruck cast in bronze for me!

HENRY REED
Naming of Parts

Today we have naming of parts. Yesterday,
We had daily cleaning. And tomorrow morning,
We shall have what to do after firing. But today,
Today we have naming of parts. Japonica
Glistens like coral in all of the neighboring gardens,
    And today we have naming of parts.

This is the lower sling swivel. And this
Is the upper sling swivel, whose use you will see,
When you are given your slings. And this is the piling swivel,
Which in your case you have not got. The branches
Hold in the gardens their silent, eloquent gestures,
    Which in our case we have not got.

This is the safety-catch, which is always released
With an easy flick of the thumb. And please do not let me
See anyone using his finger. You can do it quite easy
If you have any strength in your thumb. The blossoms
Are fragile and motionless, never letting anyone see
    Any of them using their finger.

And this you can see is the bolt. The purpose of this
Is to open the breech, as you see. We can slide it
Rapidly backwards and forwards: we call this
Easing the spring. And rapidly backwards and forwards
The early bees are assaulting and fumbling the flowers:
    They call it easing the Spring.

They call it easing the Spring: it is perfectly easy
If you have any strength in your thumb: like the bolt,
And the breech, and the cocking-piece, and the point of balance,
Which in our case we have not got; and the almond-blossom
Silent in all of the gardens and the bees going backwards and
    forwards,
    For today we have naming of parts.

WILLIAM BUTLER YEATS
The Wild Swans at Coole

The trees are in their autumn beauty,
The woodland paths are dry,
Under the October twilight the water
Mirrors a still sky;
Upon the brimming water among the stones
Are nine-and-fifty swans.

The nineteenth autumn has come upon me
Since I first made my count;
I saw, before I had well finished,
All suddenly mount
And scatter wheeling in great broken rings
Upon their clamorous wings.

I have looked upon those brilliant creatures,
And now my heart is sore.
All's changed since I, hearing at twilight,
The first time on this shore,
The bell-beat of their wings above my head,
Trod with a lighter tread.

Unwearied still, lover by lover,
They paddle in the cold
Companionable streams or climb the air;
Their hearts have not grown old;
Passion or conquest, wander where they will,
Attend upon them still.

But now they drift on the still water,
Mysterious, beautiful;
Among what rushes will they build,
By what lake's edge or pool
Delight men's eyes when I awake some day
To find they have flown away?

WALLACE STEVENS
The Emperor of Ice-Cream

Call the roller of big cigars,
The muscular one, and bid him whip
In kitchen cups concupiscent curds.
Let the wenches dawdle in such dress

As they are used to wear, and let the boys
Bring flowers in last month's newspapers.
Let be be finale of seem.
The only emperor is the emperor of ice-cream.

Take from the dresser of deal,
Lacking the three glass knobs, that sheet
On which she embroidered fantails once
And spread it so as to cover her face.
If her horny feet protrude, they come
To show how cold she is, and dumb.
Let the lamp affix its beam.
The only emperor is the emperor of ice-cream.

H.D.
Oread[1]

Whirl up, sea —
whirl your pointed pines,
splash your great pines
on our rocks,
hurl your green over us,
cover us with your pools of fir.

E. E. CUMMINGS
r-p-o-p-h-e-s-s-a-g-r

                                 r-p-o-p-h-e-s-s-a-g-r
                 who
a)s w(e loo)k
upnowgath
        PPEGORHRASS
                     eringint (o-
aTHE) :l
      eA
         !p:
S   a
            (r
rIvInG   .gRrEaPsPhOs)
                        to
rea (be) rran (com) gi (e) ngly
,grasshopper;

---

[1] A nymph of the mountains and hills.

ELIZABETH BISHOP
One Art

The art of losing isn't hard to master;
so many things seem filled with the intent
to be lost that their loss is no disaster.

Lose something every day. Accept the fluster
of lost door keys, the hour badly spent.
The art of losing isn't hard to master.

Then practice losing farther, losing faster:
places, and names, and where it was you meant
to travel. None of these will bring disaster.

I lost my mother's watch. And look! my last, or
next-to-last, of three loved houses went.
The art of losing isn't hard to master.

I lost two cities, lovely ones. And, vaster,
some realms I owned, two rivers, a continent.
I miss them, but it wasn't a disaster.

— Even losing you (the joking voice, a gesture
I love) I shan't have lied. It's evident
the art of losing's not too hard to master
though it may look like (*Write it!*) like disaster.

JOHN BERRYMAN
Henry sats in de bar & was odd

Henry sats in de bar & was odd,
off in the glass from the glass,
at odds wif de world & its god,
his wife is a complete nothing,
St Stephen
getting even.

Henry sats in de plane & was gay.
Careful Henry nothing said aloud
but where a Virgin out of cloud
to her Mountain dropt in light,
his thought made pockets & the plane buckt.
'Parm, me, lady.' 'Orright.'

Henry lay in de netting, wild,
while the brainfever bird did scales;

Mr. Heartbreak, the New Man,
come to farm a crazy land;
an image of the dead on the fingernail
of a newborn child.

LORNA DEE CERVANTES
Poema para los Californios Muertos[1]

> *Once a refuge for Mexican Californios . . .*
> — PLAQUE OUTSIDE A RESTAURANT
> IN LOS ALTOS, CALIFORNIA, 1974

These older towns die
into stretches of freeway.
The high scaffolding cuts a clean cesarean[2]
across belly valleys and fertile dust.
What a bastard child, this city
lost in the soft
llorando de las madres.[3]
Californios moan like husbands of the raped,
husbands de la tierra,
tierra la madre.[4]

I run my fingers
across this brass plaque.
Its cold stirs in me a memory
of silver buckles and spent bullets,
of embroidered shawls and dark rebozos.[5]
Yo recuerdo los antepasados muertos.
Los recuerdo en la sangre,
la sangre fértil.[6]

What refuge did you find here,
ancient Californios?
Now at this restaurant nothing remains

---

[1] Poem for the dead Californios. (*Californios* — original inhabitants when California was still Mexico.)

[2] A caesarean is a surgical incision of the walls of the abdomen and uterus for delivery of offspring.

[3] Crying of the mothers.

[4] Of the land, the mother earth.

[5] A rebozo is a long shawl worn by Mexican women.

[6] I remember the dead ancestors. I remember them in my blood, my fertile blood.

but this old oak and an ill-placed plaque.
Is it true that you still live here
in the shadows of these white, high-class houses?
Soy la hija pobrecita
pero puedo maldecir estas fantasmas blancas.
Las fantasmas tuyas deben aquí quedarse,
solas las tuyas.[7]

In this place I see nothing but strangers.
On the shelves there are bitter antiques,
yanqui remnants
y estos no de los Californios.[8]
A blue jay shrieks
above the pungent odor of crushed
eucalyptus and the pure scent
of rage.

---

[7] I am only your poor daughter, but I can curse these white ghosts. Only your ghosts should remain here, only yours.

[8] And these not of the Californios.

6

Constructing a Self

If you are a poet wanting to create, on paper, a self into whose shoes a reader will be willing to step, a self whose voice a reader will willingly take on, you have probably only a short space (maybe 150 words) in which to give your lyric speaker credibility. You must create a personality provoked into speech; tones of voice tracking both provocation and response; and enough variability of expression to make for fictive robustness. How to do it?

Multiple Aspects

The single most successful way is to give your speaker not only a present but a past, and often not just a yesterday, but the day before that, and the year before that, and five years before that. (See Wordsworth's "Lines Composed a Few Miles above Tintern Abbey" for a stunning lengthy version of this process.) You invite your reader to "turn into" the speaker, uttering the sentences of the poem; you construct a whole temporal self available to be inhabited, a believable "thickly described" life to be entered. Here is Shakespeare's Sonnet 30, "When to the sessions of sweet silent thought," in which a speaker with a multiphased past comes alive:

William Shakespeare
Sonnet 30

When to the sessions of sweet silent thought
I summon up remembrance of things past,
I sigh the lack of many a thing I sought,
And with old woes new wail my dear time's waste:
Then can I drown an eye, unused to flow,
For precious friends hid in death's dateless night,
And weep afresh love's long since canceled woe,
And moan the expense of many a vanished sight:
Then can I grieve at grievances foregone,
And heavily from woe to woe tell o'er
The sad account of fore-bemoanèd moan,
Which I new pay as if not paid before.
But if the while I think on thee, dear friend,
All losses are restored and sorrows end.

The speaker (whose initial "when" means "whenever") is referring to a series of habitual actions. This in itself gives the speaker a continuous life stretching from the past to the present; he often has sessions of silent thought when he voluntarily summons past things to mind. In fact, when he does this, he finds himself in tears — an unusual event for him: "Then can I drown an eye, *unused to flow.*"

We're now in a better position to reconstruct the speaker's multiphased life. Let's call the time when he as yet did not have a friend T_1, the next phase T_2, and so on:

T_1: He doesn't yet have friends A, B, C.

T_2: He makes friends with A, B, C.

T_3: He enjoys the friendship over time.

T_4: Friends A, B, C die.

T_5: He weeps at the moment of their death.

T_6: Grief turns to stoicism; his tears stop.

T_7: He spends a long time without weeping; his tears are "unused to flow."

T_8: He often summons up, voluntarily, the old grief so that he can "drown" again in tears for his dead friends.

This pattern recurs throughout the poem, as, for instance: he "weep[s] *afresh* love's *long since canceled* woe." He was without love; then had it; then lost it, and wept in woe; that woe was (apparently) canceled, and he was dry-eyed for a long time; now he can weep afresh for that woe.

In fact, this process, many times safely and even luxuriously repeated, now suddenly awakens such grief in the speaker that he pays his debt of grief anew: "I new pay," he says, "*as if not paid before.*" This is a frightening experience. He thought he could summon up at will old griefs, and almost enjoy renewing them in "sessions of *sweet* silent thought." Yet suddenly the session is no longer sweet but painfully acute — grief recurs as if for the first time. It is this acute grief which pitches the speaker into looking for consolation in his present state; at least he has a friend now, friend Z:

> But if the while I think on thee, dear friend,
> All losses are restored and sorrows end.

This discovery of present joy stabilizes the character of the speaker at one point in his multiphased life. But the overall effect of the sonnet is to make us know the speaker as someone who has undergone many psychological phases — joy, grief, stoicism, loss, renewed grief — over time, and this confers on him a "reality" of prolonged existence which we take on as we speak his words.

Change of Discourse

Another way, if you are a poet, to give your speaker credibility is to let her change discourses in midstream. In "Diving into the Wreck," Adrienne Rich lets her practical, well-equipped speaker drift into hypnotic reverie once she's under water:

> I put on
> the body-armor of black rubber
> the absurd flippers
> the grave and awkward mask. . . .
>
> I go down.
> My flippers cripple me,
> I crawl like an insect down the ladder. . . .
>
> This is the place.
> And I am here, the mermaid whose dark hair
> streams black, the merman in his armored body.
> We circle silently
> about the wreck
> we dive into the hold.
> I am she: I am he
>
> whose drowned face sleeps with open eyes
> whose breasts still bear the stress. . . .

By the end, after this entrance to incantatory and androgynous language, the personality of the speaker seems to have more than one facet. The more facets — practical, mystical, baffled, exalted — the "thicker" the description.

Space and Time

Yet another way of giving historical believability to your speaker is, in the course of your poem, to relocate him or her in space and time. In "Mid-Term Break," the Irish poet Seamus Heaney (pronounced "Shāmus Hēney") writes about his return home from boarding school for the funeral of his four-year-old brother, killed by a car. ("College" in the first line refers to a boarding school.)

SEAMUS HEANEY
Mid-Term Break

I sat all morning in the college sick bay
Counting bells knelling classes to a close.
At two o'clock our neighbors drove me home.

In the porch I met my father crying —
He had always taken funerals in his stride —
And Big Jim Evans saying it was a hard blow.

The baby cooed and laughed and rocked the pram
When I came in, and I was embarrassed
By old men standing up to shake my hand

And tell me they were "sorry for my trouble."
Whispers informed strangers I was the eldest,
Away at school, as my mother held my hand

In hers and coughed out angry tearless sighs.
At ten o'clock the ambulance arrived
With the corpse, stanched and bandaged by the nurses.

Next morning I went up into the room. Snowdrops
And candles soothed the bedside; I saw him
For the first time in six weeks. Paler now,

Wearing a poppy bruise on his left temple,
He lay in the four foot box as in his cot.
No gaudy scars, the bumper knocked him clear.

A four foot box, a foot for every year.

We first see the speaker in the morning at his boarding school, after he has been notified of his brother's death; next we see him being driven home; next he is on the porch at home; next inside the house; next, present at evening when the body is brought from the hospital by an ambulance; next, the following morning, upstairs seeing the body of his brother laid out on the bed; next, seeing his brother in the coffin before the funeral. The living presence of the speaker over two days, in several places, makes him seem a "real person," into whose believable narrative we can enter. We track the changes in space and time by a series of markers in the poem:

Space	*Time*
in the college sick bay	all morning
home	two o'clock
in the porch	
I came in	
	whispers . . . as my mother held my hand
the ambulance arrived	at ten o'clock
up into the room . . . bedside	next morning
the four foot box	

Poets expect you to "track," even if unconsciously, such relocations of the speaker in space and time, as you "become" the person who goes from school to the porch, from the porch to the room inside, from the downstairs to the upstairs, and who, in the end, however reluctantly, takes up a mourner's position next to the coffin.

Testimony

Speakers also can be made credible by their intimate knowledge of a given historical time and place and its inhabitants. We feel this in E. E. Cummings's speaker who satirizes "the Cambridge ladies who live in furnished souls" and mocks their taste for Henry Wadsworth Longfellow; we feel it equally in the speaker of Andrew Marvell's "Horatian Ode" who seems to have observed the execution of Charles I, to know the details of Cromwell's campaign in Ireland, and to be aware of British parliamentary instability. Walt Whitman speaks as a witness to the events recounted in "Song of Myself": "I am the man; I suffered; I was there," and his Civil War poems offer vivid, almost cinematically detailed accounts of real events in "A March in the Night Hard Press'd" or "Cavalry Crossing a Ford." Even in a poem of symbolic experience, like Samuel Taylor

Coleridge's "Rime of the Ancient Mariner," the mariner tells so many particular details of his supernatural experiences, along with many natural ones, that we are drawn to find both halves of his tale reliable.

Motivations

How does the poet lead us to understand the selves that are so sketchily created on the page, in whose voices we find ourselves speaking? We tend, as the poem goes on, to fill in its gaps, and to think that Shakespeare's speaker weeping afresh has a whole "real life" in between his reported bouts of grief, stoicism, and renewed weeping. We assume that Coleridge's Ancient Mariner is being truthful about how he passes, like night, from land to land retelling his tale, and that he had a life before he shot the albatross. We also invent plausible reasons for the fact that a speaker who has formerly spoken of his estrangement from his beloved ("Since there's no help, come let us kiss and part") can say, only thirteen lines later, that his beloved could resuscitate love "from death to life." By postulating reasonable motivations, justifications, and conclusions in the gaps between words or lines, we ascribe to the speaker a "realness" that literature is designed to offer in order to persuade us of its insights about experience.

Typicality

Yet another aspect of credibility in a lyric speaker comes from typicality, a powerful resource of lyric. Anyone can put himself or herself into the unstipulated place and indefinite time of Shakespeare's speaker summoning up remembrance of things past. Even when the place and subject are specific (as they are in "the Cambridge ladies"), anyone, male or female, who lived in Cambridge might be the speaker of the poem. Even when the event is wholly personal, as in "Mid-Term Break," the emotions of the stunned adolescent recalled by the speaker are those that any adolescent in such a situation would probably experience. To create such a representative set of reactions, Heaney, like many lyric poets, deletes many particular autobiographical details (the presence of his siblings, the specific religious ceremonies surrounding a home wake in Ireland such as the recitation of the rosary) in order to make the experience related in the poem typical, rather than narrowly personal.

A lyric, then, wants us to be its speaker. We are not to *listen to* the speaker, but to *make ourselves into* the speaker. We speak the words of the poem as though we were their first utterers. The speaker's past is our past; his motivations are ours, his emotions ours, his excuses ours, his predictions ours. A poem is a set of instructions for voicing; listened to carefully, it tells us how to say its sentences — regretfully, apprehensively, bitterly, elatedly. We call these ways of voicing the *tones* of the poem. They are sufficiently typical that any reader can utter them.

Tone as Marker of Selfhood

Though poetry has become a written art, it has never lost its roots in speech. And since the first thing a poem asks of you is to read it aloud as though you were saying *it as your own words,* you must sound angry if "you" are angry, sad if "you" are sad. The poem itself tells you how to sound. Every lyric is uttered in response to a situation that has disturbed some former equilibrium: "you" have been told someone no longer loves you ("Since there's no help"), or that your brother has been killed in an accident ("Mid-Term Break"), or that "We don't like modern poetry" (the "Cambridge ladies," says Cummings, "believe in Christ and Longfellow, both dead"). Robert Frost went so far as to say, "Everything written is as good as it is dramatic. . . . [A poem is] heard as sung or spoken by a person in a scene — in character, in a setting." Because you cannot know the whole situation of the speaker till you have read the whole poem, you often are not sure what set of intonations to give the poem as you *first* read it aloud. But as you get to know it better, it begins to speak itself believably in your mind, and its speaker's character and emotions, mediated through the tones of utterance, become yours.

Take, for example, the first stanza of Emily Dickinson's poem, spoken above the many graves of her Dickinson ancestors in the cemetery of Amherst, Massachusetts:

> Safe in their Alabaster Chambers —
> Untouched by Morning
> And untouched by Noon —
> Sleep the meek members of the Resurrection —
> Rafter of satin
> And Roof of stone.

Is it good or bad for the dead to be "safe" in their mausoleums or graves? Is it good or bad to be "untouched" by morning and noon? Is it desirable to be ensconced under satin rafters and a roof of stone? In what tone are you to say these lines?

As you get to know the poem, you may decide that Dickinson thought it was certainly a deprivation to exist insensible to both morning and noon; that she is judging the dead as timid ("meek") people who always wanted to be "safe": now, indeed, and ironically, they are. When you learn that Dickinson rewrote the poem to remove the implication of resurrection — substituting "lie" for "sleep" in line 4 — you may decide that she thought her dead ancestors had been cheated by their credulous beliefs in an afterlife to which they would awaken. And however fine it may be to have satin rafters in your coffin, those rafters exist, after all, under that claustrophobic mausoleum-roof "of stone." Your tone might well then become ironic as you read the words "safe" and "untouched," seeing those words as the poet's gibe at the conventional timidity of her ancestors' lives.

In telling someone else how you see this poem, you probably would have to say, "I hear Dickinson being critical of the dead, with a dismissive and almost contemptuous tone in her description of them as 'safe' and 'untouched.'" And in speaking the poem aloud, you, as the speaker of these sentiments, would make your own voice take on that dismissive tone. In this way, every poem suggests to its readers the tones with which they might give voice to it; and conversely, the tones you feel to be present, as you get to know the poem well, give you clues to the perceptions and emotions of the self, constructed in the poem, that generates those tones.

Here, for instance, is a short poem in which an adult, who knows suffering well, comes upon a young girl who is crying because the leaves are falling from the trees in the wood called "Goldengrove." The adult thinks her grief trivial and childish, and rebukes her for wasting her tears on trees, prophesying that life soon enough will give her more serious things to cry about. But she continues nevertheless to cry, asking *why* the leaves have to fall. The poem turns on the adult's response to the child's "*Why?*" I've marked, next to the lines, the tones of voice they suggest. (In the third line from the end, "ghost guessed" means, approximately, "your spirit intuited.")

GERARD MANLEY HOPKINS
Spring and Fall

To a Young Child

Márgarét, áre you gríeving	*bantering disbelief*
Over Goldengrove unleaving?	
Leáves, líke the things of mán, you	*patronizing reproach*
With your fresh thoughts care for, can you?	

Áh, ás the héart grows ólder	*chilly prophecy of rational future*
It will come to ʂuch sights colder	
By and by, nor spare a sigh	
Though worlds of wanwood leafmeal lie;	*regret*
And yet you *will* weep and know why.	*impatience*
Now no matter, child, the name:	*insight, surprised*
Sórrow's spríngs áre the sáme.	*recognition and admission*
Nor mouth had, no, nor mind expressed	
What héart héard of, ghóst guéssed;	*self-reproach*
It ís the blíght mán was bórn for,	*universal despair*
It is Margaret you mourn for.	*grief*

By the end, the speaker is ashamed at rebuking Margaret's tears, and sees that adult grief and child grief are one; both lament the consequences of the fall of man — the temporality and mortality of all things. In "tracking the tones" of such a poem, readers can differ over the exact name of each tone, but every reader will hear changes of tone over the length of the poem. Uttering this poem, you must at first be the superior and patronizing adult; then, as you come to acknowledge your own shortsightedness, you feel the heavy weight of human destiny — that we are all born for blight, and that our tears, even when they seem to be shed for falling leaves, are in reality shed for our implicit recognition of our own fate. As you perceive the tones and say the words of this adult speaker, his selfhood — in his original pride of superior knowledge and his subsequent willingness to be ashamed of himself — becomes potentially credible.

The speaker's change in view has to be persuasively "put over" by your own voice as you speak (even if only mentally) the words, or the poem will lack its striking effect of self-rebuke and final shared grief. However, lyric poems are usually *inner meditations,* not dramatic or declaimed speeches; one can't be an orator or an actor in speaking a lyric aloud. One has to be a self, musing aloud over inner responses, not someone addressing an audience, or even someone speaking aloud in solitude like an actor delivering a soliloquy. Even when there is an auditor (here, Margaret), the lyric represents the *inner* speech or meditation of its utterer, and must sound inward and reflective rather than outer-directed and rhetorical. As William Butler Yeats said, "Out of the quarrel with others, we make rhetoric; out of the quarrel with ourselves, poetry." All the tones of a poem are the tones of an inward, not an outward, quarrel; the credible self in the lyric is the private divided self of the inner life. Even in a dramatic monologue (which is publicly addressed to another person, as Robert Browning's Duke addresses the ambassador), it is important to perceive the revelation of the inner life of the speaker by the poem. The Duke reveals himself to be jealous and homicidal, even though he may not be aware how much of himself is visible in his outwardly smooth and aristocratic speech. To see a dramatic monologue as simultaneously a self-protective public speech and an unconsciously self-revealing document is to read it as dramatic lyric demands, doubly.

Imagination

The selves constructed in poems needn't have original ideas (in fact, few of them do), but they must have imagination — and the imagination of the reader of the poem must somehow (by art) be drawn into the imagination of the speaker. The word "imagination" covers almost anything unusual and nonfactual in the way the self conveys thought. Often something said "imaginatively" is logically absurd, as in this couplet from William Blake's "Auguries of Innocence":

> If the Sun and Moon should doubt,
> They'd immediately go out.

This is an imaginative way of saying that life lives on faith, and that skepticism is corrosive to radiant living. Here is another example, this time from W. H. Auden's ballad "As I Walked Out One Evening":

> The glacier knocks in the cupboard,
> The desert sighs in the bed,
> And the crack in the teacup opens
> A lane to the land of the dead.

Such imaginativeness in the poetic self asks you to free-associate: even in the cupboard of the food supply, a coming Ice Age is making itself heard; even in the midst of lovemaking, aridity appears; a small flaw in a cup suggests the great Flaw in life, that we are not immortal.

Why — as the question is often put — do the poets (or their constructed poetic selves) say what they mean in "other" words? No poet would agree with putting the question this way. Poets tell us that in poems they say *exactly* what they mean in words chosen precisely to mean what they (the words) say. "Bed-desert-sigh" is an *exact* transcription, in Auden's speaker's mind, of what he felt in bed; "crack-lane-death," he thinks when he takes that teacup out of the cupboard; and even though he may close the door of the cupboard, a freezing-hidden-thing, the rigor mortis of the human relations in the house, makes its knocking heard behind the silent wood.

John Ashbery, in "Self-Portrait in a Convex Mirror," calls the surface of a poem its "visible core." The emotional core of Auden's poem, which we infer from the appearance on its surface of the glacier and the desert, is the inner feeling of dread that Auden's speaker feels even in the midst of the "safest" surroundings — his kitchen, his bed. And the dread seems to be lodged not in him but in his very cups and cupboards; *they* seem uneasy, disturbed, flawed. Psychologists call this reaction "projection" — when we "project" our inner emotion upon the world so that outside things seem uncanny or threatening. It would *not* be accurate, in this case, for the poet to say, "I feel dread and aridity" — that would be a generalizing summary, not a transcription of how concretely he feels a threat in every object at home. And poets wish to give accurate transcripts of feeling, as well as accurate transcripts of the structures of reality.

"How would I be feeling if I said *exactly this?*" is the question readers must ask as they read the words about the doubting sun uttered by the self that Blake constructs. And the answer is something like, "I'd be feeling that if the sun suddenly went out, it would be like my starting to doubt my belief in God — everything would go black." The animism by which the sun and moon become doubters like us, or by which a desert can sigh in a bed, is part of imagination's capacity to make the whole world alive. A credible self in poetry is one who can make us feel as he or she does. The poet shows; the poet does not simply tell. The poet transmits things "on the pulses," as Keats said; the senses are reproduced in words.

Words like "dread," "suspicion," "skepticism," and "faith" are words from the discourses of psychology and theology, rather than words from the senses or feelings. The senses and the feelings are poetry's stock in trade; words like "cup" and "desert," "sun" and "moon," never age in the way intellectual discourse does.

It is easy to describe, when reading striking excerpts like the ones from Blake and Auden, how the poet is using language "imaginatively" and creating a "flesh-and-blood self." But what about poems that seem factually written, without the odd personal deflections of language that characterize an idiosyncratic self? Here is a passage from Tennyson's "Mariana" which may seem largely like straightforward natural description, a passage transcribed by a camera rather than uttered by a defined self:

About a stone-cast from the wall
   A sluice with blacken'd waters slept,

And o'er it many, round and small,
    The cluster'd marish-mosses crept.
Hard by a poplar shook alway,
    All silver-green with gnarlèd bark:
    For leagues no other tree did mark
The level waste, the rounding gray.

There are in the stanza two relatively inconspicuous metaphors: the sluice *sleeps*, the mosses *creep*. Sleeping waters and creeping vegetation are not in themselves notably imaginative. Everything else — the wall, the sluice-channel, the round small marsh-grasses, the single shaking silver-green poplar with its gnarled bark, the level waste of land meeting the rounding gray of the horizon — seems factual, transcribed, uninflected by imagination. Of course the passage is highly decorative in terms of sound, but where is the imagination, or the imagining self?

It is only when we see the whole of "Mariana" — which contains seven of these stanzas — that we realize what the imagination is contributing to the poem. Tennyson is representing in "Mariana" the stream of consciousness of a girl waiting, with increasing hopelessness, for her lover to come. Because she has nothing else to occupy her mind, she notes, minutely and exhaustedly, every item in her surroundings, every small change of atmosphere during the long hours as they pass. It is in the accumulation of seven stanzas' worth of mounting ennui, apprehension, and loathing that we see Tennyson's imagination at work creating the imagination of Mariana. He gives each stanza its own peculiar atmosphere. We have already seen the unpromising "blacken'd waters" and "level waste" outside; here is a stanza in which Mariana perceives the inside atmosphere, as the day wears on without the arrival of her lover:

All day within the dreary house
    The doors upon their hinges creak'd;
The blue fly sung in the pane; the mouse
    Behind the moldering wainscot shriek'd.

The buzz of the fly, the shriek of the mouse, the creak of the hinges — by these details we understand the hope within hopelessness with which Mariana listens for the slightest sound of an arrival, and is rewarded only by these tiny interruptions of the deathly silence.

Where a poem offers such "facts" as the blackened waters or the creaking hinges, they are always facts seen through the lens of a particular feeling, which has been imagined by the poet, and ascribed to the imagination of the speaker. It is the *successive* feelings enacted by the poem which will lead you to see how the imagination is at work, even in the most "factual" lines. There is not a very great distance between Tennyson's "factual" mouse squeaking behind the wainscot and Auden's glacier knocking in the cupboard. Both of them serve chiefly as transcripts of the believable feelings of the constructed self rather than as a record of actual things.

Another way poets often show imagination operating in their fictive selves is to take a conventional timeline — birth, youth, maturity, old age, death (for example), or spring, summer, autumn, winter — and place the poem in a spot on the timeline that no one else has used. Dickinson (remembering Tennyson's "Mariana" where "the blue fly sung in the pane") inserts her (posthumous) speaker, who is recalling her own death, into the timeline of life at its very last gasp, the moment when she actually died. It is imaginative to employ a speaker speaking posthumously, but that had been done before — for instance, by George Herbert in "Love (III)." Dickinson's speaker takes the old tradition of "holy dying" and revises it blasphemously:

EMILY DICKINSON
I heard a Fly buzz — when I died —

I heard a Fly buzz — when I died —
The Stillness in the Room
Was like the Stillness in the Air —
Between the Heaves of Storm —

The Eyes around — had wrung them dry —
And Breaths were gathering firm
For that last Onset — when the King
Be witnessed — in the Room —

I willed my Keepsakes — Signed away
What portion of me be
Assignable — and then it was
There interposed a Fly —

With Blue — uncertain stumbling Buzz —
Between the light and me —
And then the Windows failed — and then
I could not see to see —

Dickinson is perfectly aware that the death of a Christian ought to take place when God, the "King," comes to take the soul to heaven, and she shows the mourners waiting precisely for "that last Onset." But instead of Christ's "This day thou shalt be with me in Paradise," the speaker reports a "Blue — uncertain stumbling Buzz," and dies. In inventing this sacrilegious rendering of the conventional "happy death" of the Christian believer, Dickinson has found a way for imagination to re-represent death, this time in wholly bodily and nihilistic form. Dickinson in this instance has inserted her fictive (and credibly blasphemous) self into the human timeline at the very last second.

Other poets, using the seasonal timeline, will also make their fictive selves speak out somewhere new. Wallace Stevens does not say, "At the beginning of spring" (a cliché), but rather, "At the earliest ending of winter" ("Not Ideas About the Thing But the Thing Itself"); he does not say, "The leaves have all fallen" (a cliché for autumn), but rather, "The last leaf that was going to fall had fallen" ("An Ordinary Evening in New Haven"). The poet can likewise choose an unusual moment in a timeline by referring to the hours of the day: "There's a certain slant of light," says Dickinson — the first time in literature that a writer has alluded to the light on late winter afternoons. These imaginative perceptions make a poetic self arresting, as well as believable.

Another strategy of the poetic imagination is to insert into a genre — say, the sonnet — where the reader might expect a conventional topic (love or death), a new topic, such as prayer (Herbert) or the massacre of "heretics" (Milton) or a car junkyard (Dave Smith). This "turn" of the speaker surprises the reader and refreshes the genre; the expectations of the sonnet form become roomier, deeper, riskier. Or the imagination can borrow a form from another literature and write a poem in that form in English, as Edward FitzGerald borrowed the Persian Rubáiyát and Allen Ginsberg borrowed the sutra (a Buddhist form) in his "Sunflower Sutra." Or a poet's imagination can flout the moral expectations of society: Thomas Hardy's "ruined maid" is quite happy in her new circumstances — " 'One's pretty lively when ruined,' said she."

An imaginative self can range freely through space and time, and can ask startling questions like, "What if this present were the world's last night?" (Donne). It can draw unusual comparisons, as when the birches bent by the weight of vanished snow seem to Frost "like girls on hands and knees that throw their hair / Before them over their heads to dry in the sun." It matters less *how* the imaginative self renews feeling — through a surreal phrase like Auden's "glacier . . . in the cupboard," through an old image like Pan revived as Cummings's balloonMan, through a genre-violation like Milton's sonnet of "slaughtered saints," or through blasphemy, as when Dickinson substitutes a fly for Christ in the deathroom — than *that* it renews feeling through a reconceiving of familiar circumstance.

The real appeal of the imagination, when it appears in a poetic speaker, is that one never knows what it will do next. Tonight the Last Judgment? Doubt eclipsing the sun and the moon? A speaker addressing us from beyond the grave? For every self you meet speaking in poetry, the first question — and the last question — to ask is: "Where in these words do I see the imagination at work?" Without imagination, the noblest idea is empty of *poetic* interest, and the most heartfelt confession merely a twice-told tale. With imagination, the world is made new, and seen sharply, clearly, at an angle. We go to poetry, as to fiction, for the shock of the newly seen. "Things seen," says Stevens, "are things as seen." It is in the "as" of a credible speaker that the imagination lives.

Persona

There are many ways to refer to the self who speaks a poem. Sometimes, in obviously autobiographical lyrics, we simply use the name of the author: "Keats writes about reading Homer for the first time." In this sort of shorthand, we mean, by the word "Keats," "the author as he lets us see himself in the speaker of this poem, in his fictive poetic self." The author's fictive self overlaps with, but is not identical to, his "real" self, because a poem obeys many laws (of form, of structure, of language) which may deflect it from factual accuracy.

Robert Lowell begins his poem "Bright Day in Boston" with the phrase, "Joy of standing up my dentist." In fact (as he later said) he *had* kept his dentist appointment, and only after it was over had he taken the walk recorded in the poem. But — as he also said — the felt impulse to skip the dentist, which in life he had *not* obeyed, made a "truer" emotional beginning to the poem. We can say, then, that "Lowell" stood up his dentist, while Lowell did not. It is often easiest, once one has made clear that one means the author rather than the person, to say "Keats" or "Lowell" in referring to the speaker of a poem.

But there are poems where the speaker is clearly not the author: Yeats, for instance, writes several poems in the voice of an old woman whom he calls "Crazy Jane." It is customary, in such cases, to refer to the speaker of the poem as a "persona" adopted by Yeats. The word "persona" comes from the Latin verb *personare* — "to *speak through* a mask." Only when the speaker is wearing a mask — that is, cannot possibly be seen as the actual author because of a difference of age, or sex, or national origin — does it make sense to speak of a "persona." Otherwise it is preferable to refer simply to "the speaker."

Why would a poet adopt a persona? Why does an educated, prosperous poet want to take on the voice of a poor old woman of the roads? What is there that the poet wants to express that he can utter only in Crazy Jane's voice? These are the questions that anyone writing on Yeats's late poetry must ask. Here is the most famous of Crazy Jane's poems. In it, Jane encounters the Bishop, who once (as we know from another poem in the sequence) was a priest in the parish where Jane and her lover, Jack, lived; he banned Jack from the parish, supposedly for religious reasons. Now, in old age, Crazy Jane and the Bishop once again exchange words:

WILLIAM BUTLER YEATS
Crazy Jane Talks with the Bishop

I met the Bishop on the road
And much said he and I.
"Those breasts are flat and fallen now,
Those veins must soon be dry;
Live in a heavenly mansion,
Not in some foul sty."

"Fair and foul are near of kin,
And fair needs foul," I cried.
"My friends are gone, but that's a truth
Nor grave nor bed denied,
Learned in bodily lowliness
And in the heart's pride.

"A woman can be proud and stiff
When on love intent;
But Love has pitched his mansion in
The place of excrement;
For nothing can be sole or whole
That has not been rent."

We can deduce, from the Bishop's opening remarks about the state of Crazy Jane's breasts — that they are "flat and fallen now" — that he had improperly noticed their unflat and unfallen shape in the past, and that when he banished Jack it was because of jealousy rather than piety. After the first stanza, the rest of the poem is Jane's. We notice that she can say things that a philosophical poet like Yeats might feel called upon, if he spoke in his own voice, to qualify further ("fair needs foul," for instance); but as the voice of peasant wisdom (speaking, we should notice, in an adaptation of an old folk ballad), Crazy Jane does not need to be philosophically subtle. And although her final assertion — that "Love has pitched his mansion in / The place of excrement" — is based on a dry proverbial remark ("We are born between urine and feces"), she can phrase that observation more passionately because it is her own female body that is in question; to the Bishop's stable "heavenly mansion" she opposes the nomadic "mansion" of Love, a tent pitched in "the place of excrement."

Crazy Jane says things, in short, that Yeats as a philosophically educated person, and as a man, could not say in his own person. That is the usefulness of adopting a persona. Well brought-up girls, in Dickinson's day, were not allowed to roam the fields barefoot; and so, when Dickinson wants to show the terror of encountering a snake underfoot, she has a boy speak her poem. When you see an obvious persona speaking a poem (as in so many of Browning's "dramatic monologues"), ask yourself what the persona is being used to express that the poet could not believably convey in a contemporary "real-life" voice. Poets often take on the voice of someone long dead: black poets like Robert Hayden and Rita Dove have written in the voice of slaves, to give vicarious utterance to those who were historically denied literacy and consequently expression in writing. William Blake did the same, when he spoke in the persona of a "little black boy," showing the boy already corrupted by Christian teaching:

> My mother bore me in the southern wild,
> And I am black, but O! my soul is white;
> White as an angel is the English child:
> But I am black as if bereav'd of light.

The assumption of the persona of a black child by a white poet, or of a female persona by a male poet, has been criticized by those who believe that only a black can speak of the black experience, only a woman of a woman's experience. Many have retorted that the very function of the imagination is to enable us to imagine the Other, and that only by such leaps of the imagination across the gaps of gender, race, and age can poetry induce its readers to practice that enabling fellow-feeling. Readers who might not have reflected on class issues, or issues of religious tyranny, or issues of the place of the sexual in the spiritual, can be brought, by Crazy Jane's encounter with the Bishop, to think of these issues afresh. It does not matter who wrote the lyric, if the self presented in the lyric is a credible one invested with imaginative power. Because every speaker of a lyric is a constructed speaker, made "alive" by the imagination, and delineated in the play of language, a poem asks that as you step into the shoes of the speaker, you notice how language has been arranged to make that act possible.

In Brief: Constructing a Self

As you read a poem, ask yourself questions about the speaker constructed within the poem. Where is he or she in time and space? Over how long a period? With what motivations? How typical? Speaking in what tones of voice? Imagining life how? Resembling the author or different from the author? The more you can deduce about the speaker, the better you understand the poem. If you think about what has been happening to the speaker *before* the poem begins (if that is implied by the poem), you will understand the speaker better.

Reading Other Poems

The constituents of selfhood that are being emphasized in any one poem can be seen from both content and form. What kind of a self do you feel you have if you find a tree to be a close relative, as Walt Whitman's speaker does? What kind of a self do you feel you have if you speak meditatively and slowly, as Whitman's fictive self does?

You can ask these questions of each of the poems that follow. What kind of a self do you feel you have if you call yourself "nobody," as Emily Dickinson's speaker does? You might expect that Thomas Hardy's "ruined maid" would feel herself to be a nobody (and so she might, in another poet's hands). But she feels herself quite a somebody. Why? Does the rhythm of Hardy's poem reinforce or contradict the attitude taken by the fictive speaker toward the prostitute?

What kind of a self usually utters a "love song"? Do you find that kind of a self in T. S. Eliot's poem? How does Prufrock's prophecy of his self in old age ("Do I dare to eat a peach? / I shall wear white flannel trousers, and walk upon the beach") help to construct your idea of his present self? The free-verse rhythms in which Prufrock speaks betray his personality, too. How? Eliot gradually assembles traits of Prufrock (beginning with his name) so that we understand him better and better as the poem proceeds. Can you characterize these traits?

A poem need not always say "I" for us to understand what the speaker is like, and what he or she values or regrets. A self can be constructed by analogy with another self, a persona (whether historical or imagined). A persona, by definition, differs markedly (by sex, by age, by country of origin, and so on) from the author. How much of Elizabeth Bishop's own self can you deduce from the things she makes her alter ego (fictive other self) Robinson Crusoe say? What does Crusoe regret? What does he value?

The self of the speaker can sometimes only be deduced from what he or she says observing another. As you address (speaking Marianne Moore's poem aloud) a person so overbearing as to be like a steamroller, what can you deduce (by contrast) about what Moore's speaker would prefer as social behavior? John Dryden's little song "Sylvia the Fair" enables you to deduce the speaker's attitude toward sexuality. How would you characterize it?

When we come to more explicitly social identities (often imposed by others rather than self-chosen), we arrive at speakers who must construct an identity in part from pregiven materials (as Countee Cullen and Carl Phillips do). How does Cullen's speaker confront this problem in "Heritage"? How are the contrasting positions imagined in this "dialogue of the mind with itself"? Can you speculate why Cullen gave his speaker the strong rhythmic form seen here (technically known as trochaic tetrameter rhyming couplets), rather than constructing the self of his speaker in, say, meditative blank verse, often used for such poems of internal debate (as, say, in Shakespeare's soliloquies)? How do Cullen's methods of defining himself vis-à-vis Africa compare with those of Phillips? To what extent is the speaker of each poet a type rather than a unique individual?

Because a self is often constructed, whether in a novel or a poem, around a decisive moment of crisis or choice, we can find the selfhood crystallizing around a single episode. William Butler Yeats's airman is an Irishman in the British army, defending England though he has never lived there, participating in a war in which his own country (Ireland) was neutral. Alone in his airplane, he sees his life clearly, and a young indeterminate self suddenly crystallizes. In what rhythms does he speak? Are they uncertain and wavering, or strong and emphatic? How, both negatively and positively, does he delineate his newly discovered self?

On the other hand, sometimes a self is constructed as much by social conditions as by a moment of decision. How did Elsie (in real life, William Carlos Williams's household help) end up the way she did? Williams imagines a group of social causes that cooperate to keep many Elsies from having a rewarding and independent life: each of them has contributed to the kind of self Elsie now is. Can you connect these causes to her self as it is described? And can you construct a plausible picture of the speaker's self from his personal and social feelings about Elsie?

In contrast to the self chosen in a moment, there is the self assumed to be stable: Anne Sexton's speaker assumes she belongs to a typical category of persons ("Her Kind"), and Charles Wright, though he writes many self-portraits, confers a temporary stability on the speaker of each one. How do Sexton and Wright assemble a stable speaking self through images?

JOHN DRYDEN
Sylvia the Fair

1

SYLVIA, the fair, in the bloom of fifteen,
Felt an innocent warmth as she lay on the green;
She had heard of a pleasure, and something she guess'd
By the towzing, and tumbling, and touching her breast.
She saw the men eager, but was at a loss,
What they meant by their sighing, and kissing so close;
      By their praying and whining,
      And clasping and twining,
      And panting and wishing,
      And sighing and kissing,
    And sighing and kissing so close.

2

"Ah!" she cried, "ah! for a languishing maid,
In a country of Christians, to die without aid!
Not a Whig, or a Tory, or Trimmer[1] at least,
Or a Protestant parson, or Catholic priest,
To instruct a young virgin, that is at a loss,
What they meant by their sighing, and kissing so close!
      By their praying and whining,
      And clasping and twining,
      And panting and wishing,
      And sighing and kissing,
    And sighing and kissing so close."

---

[1] A trimmer is one who inclines to either of two opposing political parties, as interest dictates.

3

Cupid, in shape of a swain, did appear,
He saw the sad wound, and in pity drew near;
Then show'd her his arrow, and bid her not fear,
For the pain was no more than a maiden may bear.
When the balm was infus'd, she was not at a loss,
What they meant by their sighing and kissing so close;
　　　By their praying and whining,
　　　And clasping and twining,
　　　And panting and wishing,
　　　And sighing and kissing,
　And sighing and kissing so close.

WALT WHITMAN

I Saw in Louisiana a Live-Oak Growing

I saw in Louisiana a live-oak growing,
All alone stood it and the moss hung down from the branches,
Without any companion it grew there uttering joyous leaves of
　　dark green,
And its look, rude, unbending, lusty, made me think of myself,
But I wonder'd how it could utter joyous leaves standing alone
　　there without its friend near, for I knew I could not,
And I broke off a twig with a certain number of leaves upon it, and
　　twined around it a little moss,
And brought it away, and have placed it in sight in my room,
It is not needed to remind me as of my own dear friends,
(For I believe lately I think of little else than of them,)
Yet it remains to me a curious token, it makes me think of manly
　　love;
For all that, and though the live-oak glistens there in Louisiana
　　solitary in a wide flat space,
Uttering joyous leaves all its life without a friend a lover near,
I know very well I could not.

EMILY DICKINSON

I'm Nobody! Who are you?

I'm Nobody! Who are you?
Are you — Nobody — Too?
Then there's a pair of us!
Don't tell! they'd advertise — you know!

How dreary — to be — Somebody!
How public — like a Frog —
To tell one's name — the livelong June —
To an admiring Bog!

WILLIAM BUTLER YEATS
An Irish Airman Foresees His Death

I know that I shall meet my fate
Somewhere among the clouds above;
Those that I fight I do not hate,
Those that I guard I do not love;
My country is Kiltartan Cross,
My countrymen Kiltartan's poor,
No likely end could bring them loss
Or leave them happier than before.
Nor law, nor duty bade me fight,
Nor public men, nor cheering crowds,
A lonely impulse of delight
Drove to this tumult in the clouds;
I balanced all, brought all to mind,
The years to come seemed waste of breath,
A waste of breath the years behind
In balance with this life, this death.

THOMAS HARDY
The Ruined Maid

"O'Melia, my dear, this does everything crown!
Who could have supposed I should meet you in Town?
And whence such fair garments, such prosperi-ty?"
"O didn't you know I'd been ruined?" said she.

"You left us in tatters, without shoes or socks,
Tired of digging potatoes, and spudding up docks;
And now you've gay bracelets and bright feathers three!"
"Yes: that's how we dress when we're ruined," said she.

"At home in the barton° you said 'thee' and 'thou,'   *farm*
And 'thik oon,' and 'theäs oon,' and 't'other'; but now
Your talking quite fits 'ee for high compa-ny!"
"Some polish is gained with one's ruin," said she.

"Your hands were like paws then, your face blue and bleak
But now I'm bewitched by your delicate cheek,
And your little gloves fit as on any la-dy!"
"We never do work when we're ruined," said she.

"You used to call home-life a hag-ridden dream,
And you'd sigh, and you'd sock; but at present you seem
To know not of megrims° or melancho-ly!"   low spirits
"True. One's pretty lively when ruined," said she.

"I wish I had feathers, a fine sweeping gown,
And a delicate face, and could strut about Town!"
"My dear — a raw country girl, such as you be,
Cannot quite expect that. You ain't ruined," said she.

T. S. ELIOT
The Love Song of J. Alfred Prufrock

> S'io credesse che mia risposta fosse
> A persona che mai tornasse al mondo,
> Questa fiamma staria senza più scosse.
> Ma perciocche giammai di questo fondo
> Non tornò vivo alcun, s'i'odo il vero,
> Senza tema d'infamia ti rispondo.[1]

Let us go then, you and I,
When the evening is spread out against the sky
Like a patient etherized upon a table;
Let us go, through certain half-deserted streets,
The muttering retreats
Of restless nights in one-night cheap hotels
And sawdust restaurants with oyster-shells:
Streets that follow like a tedious argument
Of insidious intent
To lead you to an overwhelming question . . .
Oh, do not ask, "What is it?"
Let us go and make our visit.

In the room the women come and go
Talking of Michelangelo.

---

[1] From Dante's *Inferno,* Canto 27, lines 61–66. Guido da Montefeltro speaks, after Dante questions him: "If I thought that my reply were to be to someone who would ever return to the world, this flame would be still, without further motion. But since no one has ever returned alive from this depth, if what I hear is true, I answer you without fear of shame."

The yellow fog that rubs its back upon the window-panes,
The yellow smoke that rubs its muzzle on the window-panes
Licked its tongue into the corners of the evening,
Lingered upon the pools that stand in drains,
Let fall upon its back the soot that falls from chimneys,
Slipped by the terrace, made a sudden leap,
And seeing that it was a soft October night,
Curled once about the house, and fell asleep.

And indeed there will be time
For the yellow smoke that slides along the street,
Rubbing its back upon the window-panes;
There will be time, there will be time
To prepare a face to meet the faces that you meet;
There will be time to murder and create,
And time for all the works and days² of hands
That lift and drop a question on your plate;
Time for you and time for me,
And time yet for a hundred indecisions,
And for a hundred visions and revisions,
Before the taking of a toast and tea.

In the room the women come and go
Talking of Michelangelo.

And indeed there will be time
To wonder, "Do I dare?" and, "Do I dare?"
Time to turn back and descend the stair,
With a bald spot in the middle of my hair —
[They will say: "How his hair is growing thin!"]
My morning coat, my collar mounting firmly to the chin,
My necktie rich and modest, but asserted by a simple pin —
[They will say: "But how his arms and legs are thin!"]
Do I dare
Disturb the universe?
In a minute there is time
For decisions and revisions which a minute will reverse.

For I have known them all already, known them all:
Have known the evenings, mornings, afternoons,
I have measured out my life with coffee spoons;

---

² The Greek poet Hesiod (eighth century B.C.) wrote *Works and Days,* a poem about country life.

I know the voices dying with a dying fall
Beneath the music from a farther room.
    So how should I presume?

    And I have known the eyes already, known them all —
The eyes that fix you in a formulated phrase,
And when I am formulated, sprawling on a pin,
When I am pinned and wriggling on the wall,
Then how should I begin
To spit out all the butt-ends of my days and ways?
    And how should I presume?

    And I have known the arms already, known them all —
Arms that are braceleted and white and bare
[But in the lamplight, downed with light brown hair!]
Is it perfume from a dress
That makes me so digress?
Arms that lie along a table, or wrap about a shawl.
    And should I then presume?
    And how should I begin?

    . . . . .

Shall I say, I have gone at dusk through narrow streets
And watched the smoke that rises from the pipes
Of lonely men in shirt-sleeves, leaning out of windows? . . .

    I should have been a pair of ragged claws
Scuttling across the floors of silent seas.

    . . . . .

And the afternoon, the evening, sleeps so peacefully!
Smoothed by long fingers,
Asleep . . . tired . . . or it malingers,
Stretched on the floor, here beside you and me.
Should I, after tea and cakes and ices,
Have the strength to force the moment to its crisis?
But though I have wept and fasted, wept and prayed,
Though I have seen my head [grown slightly bald] brought in
        upon a platter,[3]
I am no prophet — and here's no great matter;
I have seen the moment of my greatness flicker,

---

[3] The head of John the Baptist was delivered on a platter to Salome (Matthew 14: 1–11).

And I have seen the eternal Footman hold my coat, and snicker,
And in short, I was afraid.

    And would it have been worth it, after all,
After the cups, the marmalade, the tea,
Among the porcelain, among some talk of you and me,
Would it have been worth while,
To have bitten off the matter with a smile,
To have squeezed the universe into a ball
To roll it toward some overwhelming question,
To say: "I am Lazarus,[4] come from the dead,
Come back to tell you all, I shall tell you all" —
If one, settling a pillow by her head,
      Should say: "That is not what I meant at all.
      That is not it, at all."

    And would it have been worth it, after all,
Would it have been worth while,
After the sunsets and the dooryards and the sprinkled streets,
After the novels, after the teacups, after the skirts that trail along the
        floor —
And this, and so much more? —
It is impossible to say just what I mean!
But as if a magic lantern threw the nerves in patterns on a screen:
Would it have been worth while
If one, settling a pillow or throwing off a shawl,
And turning toward the window, should say:
      "That is not it at all,
      That is not what I meant, at all."

        · · · · ·

No! I am not Prince Hamlet, nor was meant to be;
Am an attendant lord, one that will do
To swell a progress,° start a scene or two,   *royal procession*
Advise the prince; no doubt, an easy tool,
Deferential, glad to be of use,
Politic, cautious, and meticulous;
Full of high sentence,° but a bit obtuse;   *sententiousness*
At times, indeed, almost ridiculous —
Almost, at times, the Fool.

---

[4] Lazarus was raised from the dead by Jesus (John 11: 1–44).

I grow old . . . I grow old . . .
I shall wear the bottoms of my trousers rolled.

Shall I part my hair behind? Do I dare to eat a peach?
I shall wear white flannel trousers, and walk upon the beach.
I have heard the mermaids singing, each to each.

I do not think that they will sing to me.

I have seen them riding seaward on the waves
Combing the white hair of the waves blown back
When the wind blows the water white and black.

We have lingered in the chambers of the sea
By sea-girls wreathed with seaweed red and brown
Till human voices wake us, and we drown.

WILLIAM CARLOS WILLIAMS
To Elsie

The pure products of America
go crazy —
mountain folk from Kentucky

or the ribbed north end of
Jersey
with its isolate lakes and

valleys, its deaf-mutes, thieves
old names
and promiscuity between

devil-may-care men who have taken
to railroading
out of sheer lust of adventure —

and young slatterns, bathed
in filth
from Monday to Saturday

to be tricked out that night
with gauds°   *jewelry*
from imaginations which have no

peasant traditions to give them
character
but flutter and flaunt

sheer rags — succumbing without
emotion
save numbed terror

under some hedge of choke-cherry
or viburnum —
which they cannot express —

Unless it be that marriage
perhaps
with a dash of Indian blood

will throw up a girl so desolate
so hemmed round
with disease or murder

that she'll be rescued by an
agent —
reared by the state and

sent out at fifteen to work in
some hard-pressed
house in the suburbs —

some doctor's family, some Elsie —
voluptuous water
expressing with broken

brain the truth about us —
her great
ungainly hips and flopping breasts

addressed to cheap
jewelry
and rich young men with fine eyes

as if the earth under our feet
were
an excrement of some sky

and we degraded prisoners
destined
to hunger until we eat filth

while the imagination strains
after deer
going by fields of goldenrod in

the stifling heat of September
Somehow
it seems to destroy us

It is only in isolate flecks that
something
is given off

No one
to witness
and adjust, no one to drive the car

COUNTEE CULLEN

Heritage

For Harold Jackman

What is Africa to me:
Copper sun or scarlet sea,
Jungle star or jungle track,
Strong bronzed men, or regal black
Women from whose loins I sprang
When the birds of Eden sang?
One three centuries removed
From the scenes his fathers loved,
Spicy grove, cinnamon tree,
What is Africa to me?

So I lie, who all day long
Want no sound except the song
Sung by wild barbaric birds
Goading massive jungle herds,
Juggernauts of flesh that pass
Trampling tall defiant grass
Where young forest lovers lie,
Plighting troth beneath the sky.
So I lie, who always hear,
Though I cram against my ear
Both my thumbs, and keep them there,
Great drums throbbing through the air.
So I lie, whose fount of pride,
Dear distress, and joy allied,
Is my somber flesh and skin,
With the dark blood dammed within
Like great pulsing tides of wine
That, I fear, must burst the fine
Channels of the chafing net
Where they surge and foam and fret.

Africa? A book one thumbs
Listlessly, till slumber comes.
Unremembered are her bats
Circling through the night, her cats
Crouching in the river reeds,
Stalking gentle flesh that feeds
By the river brink; no more
Does the bugle-throated roar
Cry that monarch claws have leapt
From the scabbards where they slept.
Silver snakes that once a year
Doff the lovely coats you wear,
Seek no covert in your fear
Lest a mortal eye should see;
What's your nakedness to me?
Here no leprous flowers rear
Fierce corollas in the air;
Here no bodies sleek and wet,
Dripping mingled rain and sweat,
Tread the savage measures of
Jungle boys and girls in love.
What is last year's snow to me,
Last year's anything? The tree
Budding yearly must forget
How its past arose or set —
Bough and blossom, flower, fruit,
Even what shy bird with mute
Wonder at her travail there,
Meekly labored in its hair.
One three centuries removed
From the scenes his fathers loved,
Spicy grove, cinnamon tree,
What is Africa to me?

So I lie, who find no peace
Night or day, no slight release
From the unremittent beat
Made by cruel padded feet
Walking through my body's street.
Up and down they go, and back,
Treading out a jungle track.
So I lie, who never quite

Safely sleep from rain at night —
I can never rest at all
When the rain begins to fall;
Like a soul gone mad with pain
I must match its weird refrain;
Ever must I twist and squirm,
Writhing like a baited worm,
While its primal measures drip
Through my body, crying, "Strip!
Doff this new exuberance.
Come and dance the Lover's Dance!"
In an old remembered way
Rain works on me night and day.

Quaint, outlandish heathen gods
Black men fashion out of rods,
Clay, and brittle bits of stone,
In a likeness like their own,
My conversion came high-priced;
I belong to Jesus Christ,
Preacher of Humility;
Heathen gods are naught to me.

Father, Son, and Holy Ghost,
So I make an idle boast;
Jesus of the twice-turned cheek,
Lamb of God, although I speak
With my mouth thus, in my heart
Do I play a double part.
Ever at Thy glowing altar
Must my heart grow sick and falter,
Wishing He I served were black,
Thinking then it would not lack
Precedent of pain to guide it,
Let who would or might deride it;
Surely then this flesh would know
Yours had borne a kindred woe.
Lord, I fashion dark gods, too,
Daring even to give You
Dark despairing features where,
Crowned with dark rebellious hair,
Patience wavers just so much as
Mortal grief compels, while touches

Quick and hot, of anger, rise
To smitten cheek and weary eyes.
Lord, forgive me if my need
Sometimes shapes a human creed.
All day long and all night through,
One thing only must I do:
Quench my pride and cool my blood,
Lest I perish in the flood,
Lest a hidden ember set
Timber that I thought was wet
Burning like the dryest flax,
Melting like the merest wax,
Lest the grave restore its dead.
Not yet has my heart or head
In the least way realized
They and I are civilized.

MARIANNE MOORE
To a Steam Roller

The illustration
is nothing to you without the application.
        You lack half wit. You crush all the particles down
                into close conformity, and then walk back and forth on
                        them.

Sparkling chips of rock
are crushed down to the level of the parent block.
        Were not "impersonal judgment in aesthetic
                matters, a metaphysical impossibility," you

might fairly achieve
it. As for butterflies, I can hardly conceive
        of one's attending upon you, but to question
                the congruence of the complement is vain, if it exists.

ELIZABETH BISHOP
Crusoe in England

A new volcano has erupted,
the papers say, and last week I was reading
where some ship saw an island being born:

at first a breath of steam, ten miles away;
and then a black fleck — basalt, probably —
rose in the mate's binoculars
and caught on the horizon like a fly.
They named it. But my poor old island's still
un-rediscovered, un-renamable.
None of the books has ever got it right.

Well, I had fifty-two
miserable, small volcanoes I could climb
with a few slithery strides —
volcanoes dead as ash heaps.
I used to sit on the edge of the highest one
and count the others standing up,
naked and leaden, with their heads blown off.
I'd think that if they were the size
I thought volcanoes should be, then I had
become a giant;
and if I had become a giant,
I couldn't bear to think what size
the goats and turtles were,
or the gulls, or the over-lapping rollers
— a glittering hexagon of rollers
closing and closing in, but never quite,
glittering and glittering, though the sky
was mostly overcast.

My island seemed to be
a sort of cloud-dump. All the hemisphere's
left-over clouds arrived and hung
above the craters — their parched throats
were hot to touch.
Was that why it rained so much?
And why sometimes the whole place hissed?
The turtles lumbered by, high-domed,
hissing like teakettles.
(And I'd have given years, or taken a few,
for any sort of kettle, of course.)
The folds of lava, running out to sea,
would hiss. I'd turn. And then they'd prove
to be more turtles.
The beaches were all lava, variegated,
black, red, and white, and gray;

the marbled colors made a fine display.
And I had waterspouts. Oh,
half a dozen at a time, far out,
they'd come and go, advancing and retreating,
their heads in cloud, their feet in moving patches
of scuffed-up white.
Glass chimneys, flexible, attenuated,
sacerdotal beings of glass . . . I watched
the water spiral up in them like smoke.
Beautiful, yes, but not much company.

I often gave way to self-pity.
"Do I deserve this? I suppose I must.
I wouldn't be here otherwise. Was there
a moment when I actually chose this?
I don't remember, but there could have been."
What's wrong about self-pity, anyway?
With my legs dangling down familiarly
over a crater's edge, I told myself
"Pity should begin at home." So the more
pity I felt, the more I felt at home.

The sun set in the sea; the same odd sun
rose from the sea,
and there was one of it and one of me.
The island had one kind of everything:
one tree snail, a bright violet-blue
with a thin shell, crept over everything,
over the one variety of tree,
a sooty, scrub affair.
Snail shells lay under these in drifts
and, at a distance,
you'd swear that they were beds of irises.
There was one kind of berry, a dark red.
I tried it, one by one, and hours apart.
Sub-acid, and not bad, no ill effects;
and so I made home-brew. I'd drink
the awful, fizzy, stinging stuff
that went straight to my head
and play my home-made flute
(I think it had the weirdest scale on earth)
and, dizzy, whoop and dance among the goats.
Home-made, home-made! But aren't we all?

I felt a deep affection for
the smallest of my island industries.
No, not exactly, since the smallest was
a miserable philosophy.

Because I didn't know enough.
Why didn't I know enough of something?
Greek drama or astronomy? The books
I'd read were full of blanks;
the poems — well, I tried
reciting to my iris-beds,
"They flash upon that inward eye,
which is the bliss . . ." The bliss of what?
One of the first things that I did
when I got back was look it up.

The island smelled of goat and guano.
The goats were white, so were the gulls,
and both too tame, or else they thought
I was a goat, too, or a gull.
Baa, baa, baa and *shriek, shriek, shriek,*
baa . . . shriek . . . baa . . . I still can't shake
them from my ears; they're hurting now.
The questioning shrieks, the equivocal replies
over a ground of hissing rain
and hissing, ambulating turtles
got on my nerves.

When all the gulls flew up at once, they sounded
like a big tree in a strong wind, its leaves.
I'd shut my eyes and think about a tree,
an oak, say, with real shade, somewhere.
I'd heard of cattle getting island-sick.
I thought the goats were.
One billy-goat would stand on the volcano
I'd christened *Mont d'Espoir* or *Mount Despair*
(I'd time enough to play with names),
and bleat and bleat, and sniff the air.
I'd grab his beard and look at him.
His pupils, horizontal, narrowed up
and expressed nothing, or a little malice.
I got so tired of the very colors!
One day I dyed a baby goat bright red
with my red berries, just to see

something a little different.
And then his mother wouldn't recognize him.

Dreams were the worst. Of course I dreamed of food
and love, but they were pleasant rather
than otherwise. But then I'd dream of things
like slitting a baby's throat, mistaking it
for a baby goat. I'd have
nightmares of other islands
stretching away from mine, infinities
of islands, islands spawning islands,
like frogs' eggs turning into polliwogs
of islands, knowing that I had to live
on each and every one, eventually,
for ages, registering their flora,
their fauna, their geography.

Just when I thought I couldn't stand it
another minute longer, Friday came.
(Accounts of that have everything all wrong.)
Friday was nice.
Friday was nice, and we were friends.
If only he had been a woman!
I wanted to propagate my kind,
and so did he, I think, poor boy.
He'd pet the baby goats sometimes,
and race with them, or carry one around.
— Pretty to watch; he had a pretty body.

And then one day they came and took us off.

Now I live here, another island,
that doesn't seem like one, but who decides?
My blood was full of them; my brain
bred islands. But that archipelago
has petered out. I'm old.
I'm bored, too, drinking my real tea,
surrounded by uninteresting lumber.
The knife there on the shelf —
it reeked of meaning, like a crucifix.
It lived. How many years did I
beg it, implore it, not to break?
I knew each nick and scratch by heart,
the bluish blade, the broken tip,

the lines of wood-grain on the handle . . .
Now it won't look at me at all.
The living soul has dribbled away.
My eyes rest on it and pass on.

The local museum's asked me to
leave everything to them:
the flute, the knife, the shrivelled shoes,
my shedding goatskin trousers
(moths have got in the fur),
the parasol that took me such a time
remembering the way the ribs should go.
It still will work but, folded up,
looks like a plucked and skinny fowl.
How can anyone want such things?
— And Friday, my dear Friday, died of measles
seventeen years ago come March.

ANNE SEXTON
Her Kind

I have gone out, a possessed witch,
haunting the black air, braver at night;
dreaming evil, I have done my hitch
over the plain houses, light by light:
lonely thing, twelve-fingered,[1] out of mind.
A woman like that is not a woman, quite.
I have been her kind.

I have found the warm caves in the woods,
filled them with skillets, carvings, shelves,
closets, silks, innumerable goods;
fixed the suppers for the worms and the elves:
whining, rearranging the disaligned.
A woman like that is misunderstood.
I have been her kind.

I have ridden in your cart, driver,
waved my nude arms at villages going by,
learning the last bright routes, survivor
where your flames still bite my thigh

---

[1] Witches were thought to have six fingers on each hand.

and my ribs crack where your wheels wind.[2]
A woman like that is not ashamed to die.
I have been her kind.

CHARLES WRIGHT
Self-Portrait

Someday they'll find me out, and my lavish hands,
Full moon at my back, fog groping the gone horizon, the edge
Of the continent scored in yellow, expectant lights,
White shoulders of surf, a wolf-colored sand,
The ashes and bits of char that will clear my name.

Till then, I'll hum to myself and settle the whereabouts.
Jade plants and oleander float in a shine.
The leaves of the pepper tree turn green.
My features are sketched with black ink in a slow drag through the
    sky,
Waiting to be filled in.

Hand that lifted me once, lift me again,
Sort me and flesh me out, fix my eyes.
From the mulch and the undergrowth, protect me and pass me on.
From my own words and my certainties,
From the rose and the easy cheek, deliver me, pass me on.

CARL PHILLIPS
Africa Says

Before you arrive, forget
the landscape the novels are filled with,
the dull retro-colonial glamour
of the British Sudan, Tunis's babble,
the Fat Man, Fez, the avenue that is Khartoum.
Forget the three words you know of
this continent: *baraka, baksheesh,*
assassin, words like chipped knives thrust
into an isolation of sand and night.
These will get you only so far.

---

[2] In the seventeenth century, women thought to be witches were often tortured
on the wheel (which stretched the victim's body till the bones broke), then burned at
the stake.

In the dreams of the first night,
Africa may seem just another body to
sleep with, a place where you can lay
your own broken equipment to rest.
You have leisure to wonder at her being
a woman, at your being disappointed
with this. You come around to asking
what became of her other four fingers,
how she operates on six alone.
You wipe the sweat from
your chest with her withered hand, raised
and two-fingered; observe, as she sleeps,
how that hand casts the perfect
jackal on a wall whose color
is the same as that of the country

itself, a dark, unpalatable thing who
uses a bulbed twig to paint her lids
in three parallel zones that meet and
kiss one another. She smells of henna or
attar, or rises steeped in musk that in other
women does not stray from between the legs.
She says she has no desire to return
with you. Don't be surprised if
she takes nothing you offer, and moves
on bare feet away from you, or if
you wake feeling close to something,
the gauze damp and loose at your face.

And should you choose to leave, know better
than to give the city a farewell sweep of
the eye. To the pith-helmeted mosques, the slim
and purposeless boulevardiers, the running
sores at the breasts of the women who beg
beside stalled trains, you were never here.
For this reason, you may decide to stay put,
thinking you have left nothing finished.
You may have an urge
to make each move count.
You may have learned nothing at all.

7

Poetry and Social Identity

The identity of the lyric speaker (by contrast to the speaker of satire or of dramatic monologue, for instance), has historically been "open-ended," meaning that the words of the speaker could be spoken by any reader within the culture. In the past, in literate cultures, both Western and Eastern, education was preliminary to the (male) professions; and writers, who usually came from the group of those so educated, directed their writings to people who belonged to the same group and possessed the same culture. As we look at the lyrics being produced today, especially in the United States, we can see a marked change in the conception of the lyric speaker. The speaker often is not "neutral," but is given a defined nationality, race, class, sex, or sexual preference, so that we may say, "This is a poem spoken by an African American," or "The speaker is a mother who addresses her sister," or "This is a gay love poem spoken by one man to another," or "This is a poem spoken in Hispanic dialect."

The choice of identity in a poem is up to the writer, for whom identity is never simple. All writers know that besides the forms of identity listed above (which can be combined into such a mixture as "African American middle-class gay male") there are other important identity components such as religion, generation (elder or younger), family roles, social roles, and so on. There is a riddle-game called "Who are you?" to test how people primarily identify themselves: answers by the same person could vary from "I'm a Marine" to "I'm Eric's father" to "I'm a Catholic" to "I'm a Chicano" to "I'm Joan's husband" to

"I'm the suspect" — all sayable by the very same person, depending on the situation and the context. When you read a poem with a clearly identified speaker, you need to ask yourself which *one or more* of his or her inevitably many identities the writer is invoking.

The poet Adrienne Rich, for instance, has poems entitled "A Marriage in the 'Sixties," "Sisters," "At the Jewish New Year," "Twenty-One Love Poems," "Mother-in-Law," "Heroines," and "Grandmothers," in which she presents herself, successively, as a wife, a sister, a perplexed Jew, a woman writing love poems to a woman, a lesbian daughter-in-law, an investigator of class privilege, and a grand-daughter. These are identities belonging to Rich insofar as she is an individual; in other poems Rich adopts a collective identity ("we" or "you") which makes the speaker representative of a class, such as "women" or "poets." Here are two of Rich's identity-poems. Can we say why the identities the poet chooses are relevant to the poems? The first poem is a dialogue between the mother-in-law (who speaks aloud, in italics) and the daughter-in-law (who silently replies when her mother-in-law says, "Tell me something"):

ADRIENNE RICH
Mother-in-Law

Tell me something

        you say
        Not: What are you working on now, is there anyone special,
        how is the job
        do you mind coming back to an empty house
        what do you do on Sundays
Tell me something . . .

        Some secret
        we both know and have never spoken?
        Some sentence that could flood with light
        your life, mine?
Tell me what daughters tell their mothers
everywhere in the world, and I and only I
even have to ask. . . .
Tell me something.

        Lately, I hear it: Tell me something true,
        daughter-in-law, before we part,
        tell me something true before I die

        And time was when I tried.
You married my son, and so
strange as you are, you're my daughter

Tell me. . . .
>   I've been trying to tell you, mother-in-law
>   that I think I'm breaking in two
>   and half of me doesn't even want to love
>   I can polish this table to satin because I don't care
>   I am trying to tell you, I envy
>   the people in mental hospitals their freedom
>   and I can't live on placebos
>   or Valium, like you

A cut lemon scours the smell of fish away
You'll feel better when the children are in school
>   I would try to tell you, mother-in-law
>   but my anger takes fire from yours and in the oven
>   the meal bursts into flames
Daughter-in-law, before we part
tell me something true
>   I polished the table, mother-in-law
>   and scrubbed the knives with half a lemon
>   the way you showed me to do
>   I wish I could tell you —
>   *Tell me!*
They think I'm weak and hold
things back from me. I agreed to this years ago.
Daughter-in-law, strange as you are,
tell me something true

tell me something
>   Your son is dead
>   ten years, I am a lesbian,
>   my children are themselves.
>   Mother-in-law, before we part
>   shall we try again? Strange as I am,
>   strange as you are? What do mothers
>   ask their own daughters, everywhere in the world?
>   Is there a question?
>   Ask me something.

If we sort out the speaker's multiple identities as she reveals them to us here, we find out that she is a daughter-in-law, a member of a younger generation addressing a member of the older generation, a person with a job, a person living alone, a mother, a widow, and a lesbian. We also are given a glimpse into her past, when she was the mother of young children not yet in school, a young woman taking lessons from her mother-in-law on how to polish a table and how to remove a fish smell from knives by rubbing them with a lemon, a young woman with a dangerously submerged anger. This double exposure — older identity superimposed on younger identity — is a familiar technique in lyric poetry, serving as it does to point up changes in identity over time. But the constant in the poem is the mother-in-law, saying now as she said then, "*Tell me something*," while the daughter-in-law answers now, as she did not then, "Ask me something." In her youth, the daughter-in-law was afraid to tell the truth because what she would have said ("I think I'm breaking in two") was too frightening to articulate even to herself. Now she is prepared to try to create a bridge of honest speaking between herself and her mother-in-law: "Your son is dead / ten years, I am a lesbian." But it is not enough to speak the truth; she wants an answering gesture from her mother-in-law, wants her to show some interest in her daughter-in-law's life — "What are you working on now?" "Is there anyone special?" "How is the job?" — almost anything. You will notice that in this poem Rich is *not* mobilizing identities ("I am a poet"; "I am half-Jewish") that she will use for other poems. Why not? In what way is each of the identities she *does* bring out here useful to the poem? A good rule of thumb is that in a poem where you see multiple identities, past as well as present, each of them is in some way necessary to make the poem work.

The relation between son and father (from the point of view of the son) has been frequently explored in literature. Rich broadens the topic of relation between the generations into daughter-in-law and mother-in-law — a relation not often explored, if ever, in lyric. And though the relation to one's mother-in-law has been made the subject of frequent jokes, Rich shows it as one which entails well-meaning gestures on both sides (the mother-in-law giving household advice, the daughter-in-law cooking a meal for the mother-in-law) but in which no truth-telling is possible, until, late in the day, the speaker senses that a desire for truth hovers in the mother-in-law's question, so that it becomes "Tell me something true before we part." The brutal answer — "Your son is dead / ten years, I am a lesbian, / my children are themselves" — surprises us. It is of course a clearing of the ground, as though the speaker demands that these facts be accepted before any further truths are possible. The tenuous relational links between the two women — "You married my son; we are both women; your children are my grandchildren" — are all true, but they are not the whole truth. "Your son is dead; I am a lesbian and you are not; the children are no longer children or grandchildren but adults" — these are the facts that must be accepted, says the daughter-in-law, before any further intimacy is possible. The hopeful end of the poem — "Ask me something" — is a request for that further intimacy, on a new basis, in the few years left.

The junctures at which mother-in-law and daughter-in-law meet are of course the son/husband, grandchildren, common-sex junctures. Being a daughter-in-law is an identity negotiated around these junctures. What happens when the people enabling the junctures disappear? With the son dead, and the children grown, does the daughter-in-law identity have any reality left? Is only an estranged generational relation present — older heterosexual woman, younger lesbian woman? Or can a new identity bond — a mother-daughter one — be formed? "What do mothers / ask their own daughters everywhere in the world? / Is there a question? // Ask me something."

By investigating a particular facet of identity — here, the unexplored one (in literature) of daughter-in-law-hood — the poet renews and deepens identity itself. At the same time, no poem was ever made viable by its topic alone. What does Rich do to stylize the identity juncture she wants to explore? And what do her chosen stylizations tell us about experience?

First of all, as I have said, Rich creates a double exposure of her young self and her older self; this tells us that although there is a separation between Rich as angry young mother and Rich as older lesbian living alone, the later self has not forgotten or obliterated her younger self — there is a continuity of the ego over time. Another principal tactic is Rich's use of a repeated refrain of double address ("Mother-in-law," "Daughter-in-law" — names people don't usually use in address); she borrows this repeated double address from a famous ballad, "Edward, Edward":

> "Why does your brand° so drop with blood,   *sword*
>   Edward, Edward?
> Why does your brand so drop with blood,
>   And why so sad gang ye,° O?"   *go you*
> "O, I have killed my hawk so good,
>   Mother, mother:
> O, I have killed my hawk so good,
>   And I had no more but he, O."

Yet another stylization is the repetition of request ("Tell me something," "Ask me something"). Fourteen times "tell" recurs, three times "ask." If we graphed the poem, it would be a series of spirals coming back, again and again, to those two points — "Tell me," "Ask me." This stylized recurrence represents the wish of the two women to stay in touch in spite of the disappearance of the former links between them. The poem is written in good faith, hoping that one will ask so that the other can tell.

It is not enough, therefore, to point out in what identity or identities a poem is written. We need to see how that identity, conferred by biology or by society, may be subjected to critique by the imagination (as it is here), and how it is stylized into poetry.

Here, by contrast, is one of Rich's poems in which the identity of the speaker is *not* very strongly particularized. The speaker, however, offers a new collective identity to a group of people addressed as "Prospective Immigrants." Presumably the speaker is someone who immigrated some time ago, and who speaks from the other side of the door that the new group may or may not choose to pass through:

ADRIENNE RICH
Prospective Immigrants Please Note

Either you will
go through this door
or you will not go through.

If you go through
there is always the risk
of remembering your name.

Things look at you doubly
and you must look back
and let them happen.

If you do not go through
it is possible
to live worthily

to maintain your attitudes
to hold your position
to die bravely

but much will blind you,
much will evade you,
at what cost who knows?

The door itself
makes no promises.
It is only a door.

To go through the door is to join a group of which the speaker is presumably one member. In this poem, Rich does not speak as a mother, a wife, a widow, a daughter-in-law, a Jew, a poet, a lesbian, or even as a woman. Her identity is "Immigrant," "One Who Has Gone through the Door." This is a slightly more particularized identity than "person" or "self" or "soul" (our names for the speaker of the normative generalized lyric of the past), but it is not very much more specific.

What can we deduce from the poem about the collective identity of those who immigrate to this new land? That it is painful to remember your old name here; that there is a double consciousness here, and an acquiescence in event; that you will see more clearly; that you will confront much. What can we deduce about those who choose not to go through the door? That they can retain their old names; that it is not ignoble to choose to stay where they are (they can live worthily, maintain their attitudes, hold on to their position, even die bravely). But they will be to some degree blind, to some degree unconscious, to some degree penalized.

This poem clearly draws on actual experiences of immigrants to the United States, who often lost their own names at Ellis Island when the Inspectors of Immigration affixed new ones to them. Immigrants to America found strange new things to look at and strange new events to undergo; they learned to live with the double consciousness of the hyphenated American. And the poem draws on the experience of those who stayed home in Europe and chose not to emigrate — who held to what they knew, and paid the price of never finding a New World.

Yet we feel that this is a poem not about physical immigration but about spiritual immigration. The "prospective immigrants" do not have to cross oceans or wait at Ellis Island or undergo quarantine; they have only to open a nameless door. Once through the door, they cannot go back. Clearly, however, the speaker is glad of his/her own past decision to join the immigrant group; the poem is, after all, an invitation to new vision and an abjuring of blindness. This poem is an example of an ancient literary genre: the immemorial promise of a better spiritual life.

How does Rich stylize her warning to prospective immigrants about joining the immigrant community? She does it by making her poem fork into the two possible decisions — to go through the door, or not:

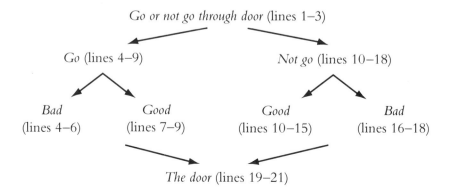

Go or not go through door (lines 1–3)

Go (lines 4–9)   *Not go* (lines 10–18)

Bad   *Good*   *Good*   *Bad*
(lines 4–6)   (lines 7–9)   (lines 10–15) (lines 16–18)

The door (lines 19–21)

At the end, Rich brings us back to the very door where we began, waiting for us to make our choice. Because entry to a more complex level of inner life is a choice open to all, Rich's speaker is neither gendered nor identified in any other way — nor are her co-immigrants or the prospective immigrants. In writing about an author who has, over the course of a career, spoken in many different identities, you will want to decide which identity is (or which identities are) operative in any given poem, and why.

An author who encounters an identity already preconstructed for him or her by society ("You are a woman"; "You are Boston Irish"; "You are a black male") is inevitably made conscious of identity questions by encountering the stereotypes attached by society to certain identities. Langston Hughes, writing not only about himself but about the wider Harlem community, shows particular awareness not only of race identity in itself, as society constructs it, but of alternative identities within the same group, constructed by the group about itself. Sometimes, as in the poem "Dream Variations," he writes about himself as black:

> Rest at pale evening . . .
> A tall, slim tree . . .
> Night coming tenderly
>   Black like me.

But sometimes, as in "Cross," he is a speaker of mixed race:

> My old man died in a fine big house.
> My ma died in a shack.
> I wonder where I'm gonna die,
> Being neither white nor black?

Sometimes, as in "I, Too," he is declaredly American as well as black:

> I, too, sing America.
>
> I am the darker brother.

Sometimes, as in "Afro-American Fragment," he is African American:

> Subdued and time-lost
> Are the drums — and yet
> Through some vast mist of race
> There comes this song
> I do not understand,

This song of atavistic land,
Of bitter yearnings lost
Without a place —
So long,
So far away
Is Africa's
Dark face.

And sometimes he is identified not by color, but only by his exceptional intelligence — which perhaps in childhood isolated him, even more than his color, as a social "monster." The North, as Hughes points out in other poems, does not lynch blacks as the South did — but the North finds victims it wants to kill spiritually, among them children distinguished by exceptional talent or intelligence:

LANGSTON HUGHES
Genius Child

This is a song for the genius child.
Sing it softly, for the song is wild.
Sing it softly as ever you can —
Lest the song get out of hand.

Nobody loves a genius child.

Can you love an eagle,
Tame or wild?

Wild or tame,
Can you love a monster
Of frightening name?

Nobody loves a genius child.
Kill him — and let his soul run wild!

How does Hughes bring imagination to the theme of the marginalized "genius child"? And how does he stylize his poem? He suggests that even to mention the genius child is dangerous — any song about him is "wild" and likely to "get out of hand." The tribe will recognize the song as something outside their culture, and will persecute the song and the singer as well as the genius child. But then the imagination of the poet does a 180-degree turn. He understands the feelings of the tribe. Could any of us love another species, a monster? And that is how the genius child appears to people. The refrain is absolute: nobody, absolutely nobody loves the child — and we are to believe that "nobody" includes the genius child's parents, his siblings, his teachers, his peers. The surprising and horrifying solution — a "lynching" to set the pariah free — is the most unsparing in all of Hughes's work. Culture no longer has any room for a wild soul; it is a kindness to put it to death.

Hughes was himself a genius at the assuming of different identities within the black community, male and female, upright and delinquent, upper-class and lower-class, educated and uneducated. Here he is in one of the poems written in "black English":

LANGSTON HUGHES
Me and the Mule

My old mule,
He's got a grin on his face.
He's been a mule so long
He's forgot about his race.

I'm that old mule —
Black — and don't give a damn!
You got to take me
Like I am.

A poem like this makes us think about the mule's "race" — half horse, half donkey. The gradual consolidation of the mule's "identity" consoles his owner, who makes the half-humorous, half-serious analogy with himself: live long enough and you become just yourself, not someone's notion of you. "You" says the black speaker to his white audience, "got to take me / Like I am." "You got to" — the whites have no choice, because this black knows himself so well he yields none of his individual autonomy to white society. Hughes stylizes his poem by giving us the mule's "success" first to "guarantee" his speaker's eventual triumph. By the end, the speaker's grin matches the one he imagines on the mule.

Our identities are constructed, according to the modern paradox, by others. We are taught to see ourselves first as our parents see us ("Sally's the one who's good at sports"), next as our peers see us ("You're black!" "You're just a girl!"), next as society as a whole sees us ("Statistics show that a high percentage of scientists are males"), and even as literature conceives us ("What are little girls made of? Sugar and spice and everything nice"). It is against these disabling conceptions from outside that inner authenticity makes its struggle. And the disabling conceptions — say, of race — do not have to come from "outside" the group itself. One of Hughes's most stinging poems embodies the mortified hatred of "upper-class" blacks for "lower-class" ones:

LANGSTON HUGHES
High to Low

God knows
We have our troubles, too —
One trouble is you:
you talk too loud,
cuss too loud,
look too black,
don't get anywhere,
and sometimes it seems
you don't even care.
The way you send your kids to school
stockings down,
(not Ethical Culture)
the way you shout out loud in church,
(not St. Phillips)
and the way you lounge on doorsteps
just as if you were down South,
(not at 409)
the way you clown —
the way, in other words,
you let me down —
me, trying to uphold the race
and you —
well, you can see,
we have our problems,
too, with you.

The blacks who are looked down on by the Ethical Culture / St. Phillips set (the names are those of a fashionable school and church) are already having pejorative identities ("loud," "too black," "don't care") constructed for them by their very own fellow blacks. Add these to the identities constructed for them by the surrounding whites, and the construction of an authentic self has two strikes against it before it can begin. Even the notion of what an "authentic self" might be is modeled by cultural expectations into which we are born.

Poetry is one of the great means in which one identity reaches out to another, tries to explain itself to another, brings up images to clarify itself (Rich's meal bursting into flames in the oven, Hughes's grinning and ornery mule), finds a diction that speaks its mind, and finds a stylized form to enact its appeal. There is a danger that a reader will take the identity in a lyric as more simple than it is, and will mentally invoke a stereotype of the female speaker or the black speaker or the gay speaker or the Catholic speaker. But good poems are thoroughly considered constructions; and in order for the poem to be interesting, the author must critique or reinvent the social stereotype. A lyric to keep in mind when reading identity-poems is Seamus Heaney's "Terminus," a poem announcing that a poet's identity is always at least a double one, because any poet worthy of the name has "second thoughts." Heaney, a Northern Irish poet, grew up on a farm but within sight of industry, in a rural place where people still used horses to draw wagons but took the train to go to the city. One "terminus" or border of the farm was the "march drain" — the creek marking the line ("march") between two parishes. Heaney, as a child, lived also along divides in the world of words — on the borderline between his parents' secular proverbs and their Biblical stories — both equally stimulating to the nascent poet's mind. And he lived between the present (Northern Ireland governed by England) and the better past (before the Irish earls, defeated by the British, fled to France in 1798, ending Irish independence). "Is it any wonder," the poet asks, given all these influences on my identity, that "when I thought / I would have second thoughts?" Any reflective poet has "second thoughts" about both inherited and acquired "identities," and it is those "second thoughts," and their origins, that Heaney so well identifies:

SEAMUS HEANEY
Terminus

I

When I hoked° there, I would find   *fished*
An acorn and a rusted bolt.

If I lifted my eyes, a factory chimney
And a dormant mountain.

If I listened, an engine shunting
And a trotting horse.

Is it any wonder when I thought
I would have second thoughts?

II

When they spoke of the prudent squirrel's hoard
It shone like gifts at a nativity.

When they spoke of the mammon of iniquity
The coins in my pockets reddened like stove-lids.

I was the march drain and the march drain's banks
Suffering the limit of each claim.

III

Two buckets were easier carried than one.
I grew up in between.

My left hand placed the standard iron weight.
My right tilted a last grain on the balance.

Baronies, parishes met where I was born.
When I stood on the central stepping stone

I was the last earl on horseback in midstream
Still parleying, in earshot of his peers.

Though a poem like Heaney's particularizes much about his identity (Irish, rural, Catholic, modern), it still does not specify idiosyncrasies that would point him out as a single individual. Even Rich's self-identification as lesbian widow, mother of children, daughter-in-law, could fit many people.

The most extreme reach of the "identity poem" is a poem that specifies its speaker so completely that he or she becomes entirely unique. No one but Frank O'Hara could speak the poem entitled "The Day Lady Died," a poem showing O'Hara's humdrum day suddenly brought to a stunned halt as he sees a newspaper headline announcing the death of the famous jazz singer Billie Holiday. The poem goes, in part:

It is 12:20 in New York a Friday
three days after Bastille day, yes
it is 1959 and I go get a shoeshine
because I will get off the 4:19 in Easthampton
at 7:15 and then go straight to dinner . . .
and in the GOLDEN GRIFFIN I get a little Verlaine
for Patsy with drawings by Bonnard . . .

and for Mike I just stroll into the PARK LANE
Liquor Store and ask for a bottle of Strega and
then I go back where I came from to 6th Avenue

and the tobacconist in the Ziegfeld Theatre and
casually ask for a carton of Gauloises and a carton
of Picayunes, and a NEW YORK POST with her face on it.

Nobody but Frank O'Hara is doing just these things in this order on this specified date, buying presents for specified friends named Patsy and Mike. In such a poem, not only are time and space fully specified, but personal identity is unmistakably that of only one person. The construction of a speaker in such a poem is as far as possible from the normative lyric construction of a "universal" or "representative" speaker, like the one in an anonymous English love song who says (as almost anyone in the world might say), "Love me little, love me long, / Is the burden of my song":

Constant love is moderate ever,
And it will through life persevere;
Give me that, with true endeavor
    I will it restore.

Why would the lyric poet sometimes want to construct a specified speaker instead of a universal one? Perhaps as modern life has grown more heterogeneous, it seems harder to some poets to speak for everyone. In England, before the turn of the century, there was a relatively small educated class confined to one island nation possessing only two universities. In such a country, with such an audience, the lyric poet could address his cultivated audience as though his speech and theirs were one. The poet in contemporary America, with its diversity of types and interests, may feel it only reasonable to speak more narrowly — not always, but sometimes. The uniqueness of each person is one modern article of faith — and by making himself unique, O'Hara suggests that each person lives a common shared event differently. Many people, on that day in New York, saw the headline about Billie Holiday's death: but, says the poet, your moment and mine were different. Let me tell you how it was for me; that will make you think how it was for you. The appeal to representativeness is still present, but it is an appeal to sameness-in-difference. Every lyric, no matter how socially specified, assumes that it speaks a language its readers can understand — even if in their own different terms.

In Brief: Poetry and Social Identity

Remembering Rich, remembering Hughes, remembering Heaney, remembering O'Hara, ask yourself, with respect to any identity-poem, "Between what borders, left and right, does this poem flow? What does it see when it looks up? or down? or around? Which words shine with morality? Which redden with shame? How does it see the past? the present? In what communities does it station itself? Against what others does it contend? To what degree does it specify its own uniqueness?" The rich contribution of identity formation to poetry, especially in the twentieth century, both criticizes and renews our inherited sense of the lyric speaker, reminding us that if we stand in the shoes of the poem, we do so not only in general ways but also in our own individualized way.

Reading Other Poems

Besides an idiosyncratic and unique personal identity, all of us have social identity, arising from groups to which we belong or are consigned. As you read the following poems, consider what portion of social identity each speaker claims as his or her own, or ascribes to his characters. Robert Southwell's speaker, for instance, has a vision identifying him as a Christian believer; Thomas Nashe's speaker is a victim of the plague for whom the whole world has narrowed into one great mortuary; John Milton's speaker shows himself solely as a supporter of a collective cause — he never says "I," only "we." In short, we may know only one identifying trait of the speaker from the *thematic* content of the poem. (We may know other traits from the speaker's tone, the images used, and so on.)

By contrast, how many personal identifying traits can you find in Anne Bradstreet's poem? What difference does it make in the effect of a poem to have the self of its speaker so narrowly specified? Would you rather read a poem that you can speak without feeling that a particular person uttered it — a poem that can be uttered by almost anyone, because its feelings are so general, and its speaker so apparently universal? Or would you rather feel that the poem is introducing you to the life and speech of a unique individual? (Neither one of these is better than the other; but we all have varying aesthetic responses, and you may prefer one to the other; reflect on why you do.)

If you are not a Christian, how are you able to read Southwell's poem with imaginative sympathy? If you deplore Cromwell's actions, how can you read Milton's poem and be convinced by it? Explore your own answers to these questions, which are profound ones and affect all art. Can a non-Christian respond to a painting of the nativity of Jesus, or a pacifist to a poem, like Milton's, about a military general? Can a white person respond to Rita Dove's portrait of her widowed grandmother's first participation in an "integrated" social occasion?

Is the drama of a poem spoken by a socially specified individual (Edward Lear describing himself as others might see him, Gerard Manley Hopkins speaking as a Catholic priest) different from that of a poem spoken by an abstract speaker? William Blake's persona, the little black boy, is a type rather than a person; but though we imagine ourselves in his shoes, speaking his words so full of pathos, are we not also objective observers, realizing the extent to which he is parroting what he has been taught (souls are white, angels are white, and so on)?

Sylvia Plath's "applicant" gets her identity from her envisaged social role. What is that role? Does it allow for any personal individuality? Can you compare Plath's view of the individuality allowed within marriage to Anne Bradstreet's view? (You do not have to choose: the very purpose of reading poetry is to let you see the world through many different lenses.)

What does it do to your perception of the identity of the speaker of the poem when he has the same name as the writer of the poem, as in Garrett Hongo's poem, "The Hongo Store?" Does this poem allow you to conflate author and speaker? If not, why not? What is the use, to Blake, of the persona of the little black boy, when the poet could equally well have written a poem protesting slavery in his own adult voice? And why do you think he had the little black boy speak in "heroic quatrains" — broad pentameter alternately rhyming quatrains, usually used for a philosophic or noble subject?

Poems exploring social identity must often face the fact that not all members of the social group share the same attitudes. In David Mura's poem about the internment of Japanese Americans during World War II, what are the attitudes dramatized? In what does the conflict consist?

ROBERT SOUTHWELL
The Burning Babe

As I in hoary winter's night stood shivering in the snow,
Surprised I was with sudden heat which made my heart to glow;
And lifting up a fearful eye to view what fire was near,
A pretty babe all burning bright did in the air appear;
Who, scorchèd with excessive heat, such floods of tears did shed

As though his floods should quench his flames which with his tears
    were fed.
"Alas," quoth he, "but newly born in fiery heats I fry,
Yet none approach to warm their hearts or feel my fire but I!
My faultless breast the furnace is, the fuel wounding thorns,
Love is the fire, and sighs the smoke, the ashes shame and scorns;
The fuel justice layeth on, and mercy blows the coals,
The metal in this furnace wrought are men's defilèd souls,
For which, as now on fire I am to work them to their good,
So will I melt into a bath to wash them in my blood."
With this he vanished out of sight and swiftly shrunk away,
And straight I callèd unto mind that it was Christmas day.

THOMAS NASHE
A Litany in Time of Plague

Adieu, farewell, earth's bliss;
This world uncertain is;
Fond are life's lustful joys;
Death proves them all but toys;
None from his darts can fly;
I am sick, I must die.
      Lord, have mercy on us!

Rich men, trust not in wealth,
Gold cannot buy you health;
Physic himself must fade.
All things to end are made,
The plague full swift goes by;
I am sick, I must die.
      Lord, have mercy on us!

Beauty is but a flower
Which wrinkles will devour;
Brightness falls from the air;
Queens have died young and fair;
Dust hath closed Helen's eye.
I am sick, I must die.
      Lord, have mercy on us!

Strength stoops unto the grave,
Worms feed on Hector brave;
Swords may not fight with fate,

Earth still holds ope her gate.
"Come, come!" the bells do cry.
I am sick, I must die.
    Lord, have mercy on us.

Wit with his wantonness
Tasteth death's bitterness;
Hell's executioner
Hath no ears for to hear
What vain art can reply.
I am sick, I must die.
    Lord, have mercy on us.

Haste, therefore, each degree,
To welcome destiny;
Heaven is our heritage,
Earth but a player's stage;
Mount we unto the sky.
I am sick, I must die.
    Lord, have mercy on us.

JOHN MILTON

To the Lord General Cromwell

Cromwell, our chief of men, who through a cloud,
    Not of war only, but detractions rude,
    Guided by faith and matchless fortitude,
    To peace and truth thy glorious way hast ploughed,
And on the neck of crownèd Fortune proud
    Hast reared God's trophies, and His work pursued,
    While Darwen stream,[1] with blood of Scots imbrued,
    And Dunbar field, resounds thy praises loud,
And Worcester's laureate wreath: yet much remains
    To conquer still; peace hath her victories
    No less renowned than war: new foes arise,
Threatening to bind our souls with secular chains.
    Help us to save free conscience from the paw
    Of hireling wolves, whose gospel is their maw.

---

[1] A river near Preston, where Cromwell won a victory in 1648. Dunbar and Worcester were also the sites of victories.

ANNE BRADSTREET

A Letter to Her Husband, Absent upon Public Employment

My head, my heart, mine eyes, my life, nay, more,
My joy, my magazine° of earthly store,   *storehouse*
If two be one, as surely thou and I,
How stayest thou there, whilst I at Ipswich lie?
So many steps, head from the heart to sever,
If but a neck, soon should we be together.
I, like the Earth this season, mourn in black,
My Sun is gone so far in's zodiac,
Whom whilst I joyed, nor storms, nor frost I felt,
His warmth such frigid colds did cause to melt.
My chillèd limbs now numbèd lie forlorn;
Return; return, sweet Sol, from Capricorn;
In this dead time, alas, what can I more
Than view those fruits which through thy heat I bore?
Which sweet contentment yield me for a space,
True living pictures of their father's face.
O strange effect! now thou art southward gone,
I weary grow the tedious day so long;
But when thou northward to me shalt return,
I wish my Sun may never set, but burn
Within the Cancer of my glowing breast,
The welcome house of him my dearest guest.
Where ever, ever stay, and go not thence,
Till nature's sad decree shall call thee hence;
Flesh of thy flesh, bone of thy bone,
I here, thou there, yet both but one.

WILLIAM BLAKE

The Little Black Boy

My mother bore me in the southern wild,
And I am black, but O! my soul is white;
White as an angel is the English child:
But I am black as if bereav'd of light.

My mother taught me underneath a tree,
And sitting down before the heat of day,
She took me on her lap and kissèd me,
And pointing to the east, began to say:

"Look on the rising sun: there God does live,
And gives his light, and gives his heat away;
And flowers and trees and beasts and men receive
Comfort in morning, joy in the noon day.

"And we are put on earth a little space,
That we may learn to bear the beams of love,
And these black bodies and this sun-burnt face
Is but a cloud, and like a shady grove.

"For when our souls have learn'd the heat to bear,
The cloud will vanish; we shall hear his voice,
Saying: 'Come out from the grove, my love & care,
And round my golden tent like lambs rejoice.' "

Thus did my mother say, and kissèd me;
And thus I say to little English boy:
When I from black and he from white cloud free,
And round the tent of God like lambs we joy,

I'll shade him from the heat till he can bear
To lean in joy upon our father's knee;
And then I'll stand and stroke his silver hair,
And be like him, and he will then love me.

EDWARD LEAR
How Pleasant to Know Mr. Lear

How pleasant to know Mr. Lear!
        Who has written such volumes of stuff!
Some think him ill-tempered and queer,
        But a few think him pleasant enough.

His mind is concrete and fastidious,
        His nose is remarkably big;
His visage is more or less hideous,
        His beard it resembles a wig.

He has ears, and two eyes, and ten fingers,
        Leastways if you reckon two thumbs;
Long ago he was one of the singers,
        But now he is one of the dumbs.

He sits in a beautiful parlor,
        With hundreds of books on the wall;

He drinks a great deal of Marsala,
    But never gets tipsy at all.

He has many friends, laymen and clerical;
    Old Foss is the name of his cat;
His body is perfectly spherical,
    He weareth a runcible hat.

When he walks in a waterproof white,
    The children run after him so!
Calling out, "He's come out in his night-
    Gown, that crazy old Englishman, oh!"

He weeps by the side of the ocean,
    He weeps on the top of the hill;
He purchases pancakes and lotion,
    And chocolate shrimps from the mill.

He reads but he cannot speak Spanish,
    He cannot abide ginger-beer:
Ere the days of his pilgrimage vanish,
    How pleasant to know Mr. Lear!

GERARD MANLEY HOPKINS
Felix Randal

Felix Randal the farrier,° O is he dead then?   *blacksmith*
    my duty all ended,
Who have watched his mould of man, big-boned and
    hardy-handsome
Pining, pining, till time when reason rambled in it and some
Fatal four disorders, fleshed there, all contended?

Sickness broke him. Impatient, he cursed at first, but mended
Being anointed and all; though a heavenlier heart began some
Months earlier, since I had our sweet reprieve and ransom
Tendered to him. Ah well, God rest him all road ever he offended!

This seeing the sick endears them to us, us too it endears.
My tongue had taught thee comfort, touch had quenched
    thy tears,
Thy tears that touched my heart, child, Felix, poor Felix Randal;

How far from then forethought of, all thy more boisterous years,
When thou at the random° grim forge, powerful   *ramshackle*
    amidst peers,

Didst fettle° for the great grey drayhorse his bright   *shape*
    and battering sandal!

SYLVIA PLATH
The Applicant

First, are you our sort of a person?
Do you wear
A glass eye, false teeth or a crutch,
A brace or a hook,
Rubber breasts or a rubber crotch,

Stitches to show something's missing? No, no? Then
How can we give you a thing?
Stop crying.
Open your hand.
Empty? Empty. Here is a hand

To fill it and willing
To bring teacups and roll away headaches
And do whatever you tell it.
Will you marry it?
It is guaranteed

To thumb shut your eyes at the end
And dissolve of sorrow.
We make new stock from the salt.
I notice you are stark naked.
How about this suit —

Black and stiff, but not a bad fit.
Will you marry it?
It is waterproof, shatterproof, proof
Against fire and bombs through the roof.
Believe me, they'll bury you in it.

Now your head, excuse me, is empty.
I have the ticket for that.
Come here, sweetie, out of the closet.
Well, what do you think of *that?*
Naked as paper to start

But in twenty-five years she'll be silver,
In fifty, gold.
A living doll, everywhere you look.
It can sew, it can cook,
It can talk, talk, talk.

It works, there is nothing wrong with it.
You have a hole, it's a poultice.
You have an eye, it's an image.
My boy, it's your last resort.
Will you marry it, marry it, marry it.

GARRETT HONGO

The Hongo Store
29 Miles Volcano
Hilo, Hawaii

From a Photograph

My parents felt those rumblings
Coming deep from the earth's belly,
Thudding like the bell of the Buddhist Church.
Tremors in the ground swayed the bathinette
Where I lay squalling in soapy water.

My mother carried me around the house,
Back through the orchids, ferns, and plumeria
Of that greenhouse world behind the store,
And jumped between gas pumps into the car.

My father gave it the gun
And said, "Be quiet," as he searched
The frequencies, flipping for the right station
(The radio squealing more loudly than I could cry).

And then even the echoes stopped —
The only sound the Edsel's grinding
And the bark and crackle of radio news
Saying stay home or go to church.

"Dees time she no blow!"
My father said, driving back
Over the red ash covering the road.
"I worried she went go for broke already!"

So in this print the size of a matchbook,
The dark skinny man, shirtless and grinning,
A toothpick in the corner of his smile,
Lifts a naked baby above his head —
Behind him the plate glass of the store only cracked.

DAVID MURA
An Argument: On 1942

For My Mother

Near Rose's Chop Suey and Jinosuke's grocery,
the temple where incense hovered and inspired
dense evening chants (prayers for Buddha's mercy,
colorless and deep), that day he was fired . . .

—No, no, no, she tells me. Why bring it back?
The camps are over. (Also overly dramatic.)
Forget *shoyu*°-stained *furoshiki*,°   soy sauce / scarf
    mochi° on a stick: rice cakes
You're like a terrier, David, gnawing a bone, an old, old trick . . .

Mostly we were bored. Women cooked and sewed,
men played blackjack, dug gardens, a *benjo*.°   toilet
Who noticed barbed wire, guards in the towers?
We were children, hunting stones, birds, wild flowers.

Yes, Mother hid tins of *utskemono* and eel
beneath the bed. And when the last was peeled,
clamped tight her lips, growing thinner and thinner.
But cancer not the camps made her throat blacker

. . . And she didn't die then . . . after the war, in St. Paul,
you weren't even born. Oh I know, I know, it's all
part of your job, your way, but why can't you glean
how far we've come, how much I can't recall —

David, it was so long ago — how useless it seems . . .

RITA DOVE
Wingfoot Lake

(Independence Day, 1964)

On her 36th birthday, Thomas had shown her
her first swimming pool. It had been
his favorite color, exactly — just
so much of it, the swimmers' white arms jutting
into the chevrons of high society.
She had rolled up her window
and told him to drive on, fast.

Now this *act of mercy:* four daughters
dragging her to their husbands' company picnic,
white families on one side and them
on the other, unpacking the same
squeeze bottles of Heinz, the same
waxy beef patties and Salem potato chip bags.
So he was dead for the first time
on Fourth of July — ten years ago

had been harder, waiting for something to happen,
and ten years before that, the girls
like young horses eyeing the track.
Last August she stood alone for hours
in front of the T.V. set
as a crow's wing moved slowly through
the white streets of government.
That brave swimming

scared her, like Joanna saying
Mother, we're Afro-Americans now!
What did she know about Africa?
Were there lakes like this one
with a rowboat pushed under the pier?
Or Thomas' Great Mississippi
with its sullen silks? (There was
the Nile but the Nile belonged

to God.) Where she came from
was the past, 12 miles into town
where nobody had locked their back door,
and Goodyear hadn't begun to dream of a park
under the company symbol, a white foot
sprouting two small wings.

8

History and Regionality

Poetry is always interested in time and space. Sometimes these can be very generally expressed, as we saw in "A slumber did my spirit seal." Time in this poem means simply past versus present; space encloses first two individuals, then the whole planet:

WILLIAM WORDSWORTH
A slumber did my spirit seal

A slumber did my spirit seal;
    I had no human fears:
She seemed a thing that could not feel
    The touch of earthly years.

No motion has she now, no force;
    She neither hears nor sees;
Rolled round in earth's diurnal course,
    With rocks, and stones, and trees.

But poetry is not only interested in such large general uses of space and time. It is also interested in time specified — in history. Especially for nations emerging from colonial status — America after the Revolution, Ireland after 1916 — history needs to be made freshly significant, newly sacred. Important dates need to be memorialized (as "The Star-Spangled Banner" commemorates the battle of Fort McHenry; as

William Butler Yeats's "Easter 1916" meditates on Ireland's Easter Rising). Important heroes and heroines need to be immortalized (as John Greenleaf Whittier's "Barbara Frietchie" salutes a semilegendary heroine of the Revolution; as Yeats's "A Rose Tree" salutes Padraic Pearse, executed for his part in the Easter Rising). And poetry about history is not only celebratory. Problematic aspects of history have to be investigated (as Herman Melville queries war enthusiasm in "The March into Virginia" during the Civil War; as Adrienne Rich decries the 1953 execution of Ethel Rosenberg in "For Ethel Rosenberg"; as Seamus Heaney scrutinizes the violent conflicts in Northern Ireland in "North").

History

Immediate challenges arise for a lyric poet who is writing a poem about (or within or against) history. In the first place, written history is a narrative genre, and the history of a complex event (the American Revolution, the Civil War in England leading to the execution of Charles I, the Easter Rising) is not only narratively complicated, but always politically disputed. The English narrate the American Revolution from a point of view (that of the losing side) very different from the celebratory view taken in American history books. Propaganda always exists on both sides of any historical question, as on both sides of any disputed ethical question. It is up to the poet to see beyond the simplifications of propaganda (always unfair to the intricacy of any disputed event) and to present the crises of history in a way that does not diminish their ambiguity and their painfulness.

How does the poet incorporate history within the miniature dimensions of the lyric? There are several central techniques:

1. Focusing on a problem rather than on incidents;
2. Finding an emblematic scene or scenes;
3. Finding a symbolic or mythological equivalent for a historical episode;
4. Seeing the human inside of the event as corresponding to the historical outside;
5. Finding an epigrammatic summation;
6. Adopting a prophetic or philosophic view larger than that of a mere eyewitness.

Let us see how these techniques come into play in Melville's Civil War poem written in fear and dismay after the Union forces were twice routed by the Confederate army in the first and second battles of Manassas (sometimes called the first and second battles of Bull Run). The Union army — composed of young, patriotic, impulsive, untried recruits — marched gaily into battle, only to suffer carnage. The few who survived had to march into battle once again, knowing, this time, the horrors ahead. Was their original innocence of any value? Can naive ignorance be of ultimate political use? Melville begins his consideration by reflecting on this problem: he admits how little we would undertake if we knew beforehand the "lets and bars" — obstacles and hindrances — that we would encounter:

HERMAN MELVILLE
The March into Virginia

Ending in the First Manassas (July 1861)

Did all the lets and bars appear
    To every just or larger end,
Whence should come the trust and cheer?
    Youth must its ignorant impulse lend —
Age finds place in the rear.
    All wars are boyish, and are fought by boys,
The champions and enthusiasts of the state:
    Turbid ardours and vain joys
        Not barrenly abate —
Stimulants to the power mature,
    Preparatives of fate.

Having stated the paradox that enthusiasm for war is both ignorant ("All wars are boyish, and are fought by boys") and useful (the boys' "vain joys" and patriotic ardor bring forth the fruit of mature power, through which one can hope for the reinstatement of the Union), Melville can go on to set the scene of the boys' heedless march into Virginia:

Who here forecasteth the event?
What heart but spurns at precedent
And warnings of the wise,
Contemned foreclosures of surprise?
The banners play, the bugles call,
The air is blue and prodigal.
    No berrying party, pleasure-wooed,
No picnic party in the May,
Ever went less loth than they
    Into that leafy neighbourhood.

After this naturalistic scene painting, Melville breaks into a foreboding symbolic discourse of myth. The intoxicated glee of the boys, comparable to that of the devotees of the wine god Bacchus, will lead them into being sacrificed. They resemble, in fact, the Hebrew children sacrificed to the idol Moloch:

> In Bacchic glee they file toward Fate,
> Moloch's uninitiate;
> Expectancy, and glad surmise
> Of battle's unknown mysteries.

From his prophetic and mythological distance, Melville then returns, in close focus, to a last snapshot of the emotional state of the naive boys as they "file toward Fate":

> All they feel is this: 'tis glory,
> A rapture sharp, though transitory,
> Yet lasting in belaureled story.
> So they gaily go to fight,
> Chatting left and laughing right.

At this point, the speaker of the poem, who had begun philosophically and had continued scenically, becomes once again a prophet, foreseeing the end of these boys, some dead, some surviving the shame of defeat to fight, a year later, the battle of second Manassas:

> But some who this blithe mood present,
> > As on in lightsome files they fare,
> Shall die experienced ere three days are spent —
> > Perish, enlightened by the volleyed glare;
> Or shame survive, and, like to adamant,
> > The throe of Second Manassas share.

We can now see that Melville epitomizes the war for us by showing us three stages in an emblematic young soldier's experience: his initial gaiety and desire for fame and glory, his "enlightenment" in the volleyed glare as he learns, perishing, what war is; or, for one who survives the shame of defeat, a third stage, beyond mere "enlightenment," in which the soldier becomes "like to adamant" in his stony and steeled knowledge of degradation, violence, and death. By his philosophic problematizing of ignorance and courage, by his visual scenes of carefree young soldiers, by his penetration of their emotional attitudes, by his shorthand references to the mythic Bacchus and Moloch to represent poles of blithe ignorance and pitiless extinction, by his schematizing the experience of war in three stages, and by his final prophecy — that the boys "shall die experienced" or shall share "the throe of Second Manassas" — Melville puts a year of the Civil War, and the problems it raised for him, into the short confines of lyric.

Not all of these techniques appear in every historical poem, but the poet always needs some of these strategies to make history pliable to lyric. Though Melville intermittently takes a philosophic position above the scene of battle, it is clear from his inner snapshots of the recruits' feelings that he sympathizes with the Union side, hoping that the youthful Union forces' "turbid ardours" will be useful to the country in stimulating its ultimate Fate.

In some history poems, the poet is immediately engaged, writing from within a particular moment, representing himself or herself as a historically specified person, of specified political or historical allegiance, and (as we will see) of specified geographic origin. This tradition in American verse begins with *Leaves of Grass,* in which the author named himself and his home: "Walt Whitman, a kosmos, of Manhattan the son," and specified even his age, "I, now thirty-seven years old in perfect health begin." However, we notice that even this socially specified self also identifies himself as "a kosmos," that is, a representative universe. The lyric poet, even when engaged in social self-specification, intends representativeness as well. This is the case in Robert Lowell's unrhymed sonnet about the March on the Pentagon in 1967 protesting the Vietnam War. Lowell took part in the March (vividly described later by Norman Mailer in *The Armies of the Night*), as the protesters went, several abreast, toward the Pentagon — only to be routed by the Army:

ROBERT LOWELL
The March 1

For Dwight Macdonald
Under the too white marmoreal Lincoln Memorial,
the too tall marmoreal Washington Obelisk,
gazing into the too long reflecting pool,
the reddish trees, the withering autumn sky,
the remorseless, amplified harangues for peace —
lovely to lock arms, to march absurdly locked
(unlocking to keep my wet glasses from slipping)
to see the cigarette match quaking in my fingers,

then to step off like green Union Army recruits
for the first Bull Run, sped by photographers,
the notables, the girls . . . fear, glory, chaos, rout . . .
our green army staggered out on the miles-long green fields,
met by the other army, the Martian, the ape, the hero,
his new-fangled rifle, his green new steel helmet.

It is clear that Lowell is remembering Melville's poem about the "green Union Army recruits / for the first Bull Run" as he writes of his own first foray into battle. But he is a middle-aged man, feeling absurd in the fraternal political gesture of locked arms, hating (as only a poet could) the awful propaganda slogans of the March being relentlessly boomed out over his head by the marchers' public address system. Nor does the poet feel akin to the ideology affirmed by the state architecture of Washington: its marble monuments inspired by Rome ("marmoreal") and Egypt ("obelisk"), its supersized conception of itself (which he sees as too white, too tall, too long). He is no hero — his glasses keep slipping, his hands quake with fear. The poem is scenic with a vengeance for its first eight lines, but the scenes are always infused with the poet's attitude toward what they show. Just when we wonder whether anything philosophic, epigrammatic, prophetic, or emblematic might come along to sum up and give point to Lowell's procession of scenes, we meet just what we have been expecting — first the allusion to Melville as an epigrammatic summing up of ignorance about to be turned into experience, then an emblematic series of nouns ("fear, glory, chaos, rout") summing up the stages of both political protest and armed war. The poem returns, at the end, to a scenic mode, this time a scene not of a march but of a confrontation, as the "green army" of the protesters is met by the real Army in tactical gear. We see three "green's" in succession: the green (inexperienced) protesters, the "miles-long" ideologically too-big green (grass) fields of the Washington Mall, and the literal green metal of the Army soldier's helmet. This "irrational" repetition of "green" in several different contexts makes the closing scene feel epigrammatic, "tied together," "final."

And the closing scene, unlike the literal scenes preceding it, has elements of the surreal. What does it seem like when you find yourself, as an American protester, being confronted inimically by your own American Army, composed of green recruits like yourself? And how do you feel about the Army now? You have a confused set of impressions as you see your first soldier in riot gear: "He looks like a Martian, something out of science fiction; no, with his hulking posture he looks more like an ape; but wait, this is *our* Army, he's a hero; odd, he seems to have a new-fangled kind of rifle, not the kind I remember from newsreels; he's the archetypal warrior, archaic, helmeted, like the warriors of Troy, only his helmet is new, and it is made of steel, not bronze." Some such latent content is contained within the last two lines, a content more "intellectual" than the scenes with which the poem opened, and therefore able to satisfy our desire that the poet "make something" — if only by revealing how confusing it is to be opposing your own American Army — of his experience. Though Lowell's poem is about a specific historical event, and represents the poet himself not only in his physical being (his fear, his glasses) but also in his political taking of sides, it is a representative poem, too, about the confused emotions Lowell feels in protesting the actions of his own government — a set of emotions anyone might feel.

A simpler "propaganda" poem written by a participant in the March would probably not have shown a sweating and awkward protagonist with his glasses slipping down his nose; it would certainly not have called the peace messages "the *remorseless*, amplified *harangues* for peace"; and it would not have seen the Army soldier as *both* ape and hero. It is Lowell's accuracy, both to his own motives for marching (the critique of America's imperial ambitions) and to his own sense of absurdity (including his mixed reactions to the Army soldier) that makes the poem humanly believable.

Even the simplest "history" poem usually has scene, epigram, feeling, and "philosophic" comment. Here is Langston Hughes's little song-and-echo poem, "World War II":

LANGSTON HUGHES
World War II

What a grand time was the war!
   Oh, my, my!
What a grand time was the war!
   My, my, my!
In wartime we had fun,
Sorry that old war is done!
What a grand time was the war,
   My, my!

Echo:
   Did
   Somebody
   Die?

Here, Hughes is not writing as a socially specified singular self — as a black poet or as "Langston Hughes," a man of a certain age living in a certain city; rather, he writes a public chorus for the late 1940s, and counterpoints the chorus with a single satiric and epigrammatic echo. Hughes can sympathize with the chorus of voices praising wartime: following the catastrophe of the 1929 Depression and its long dreary aftermath of stinted lives, the plentiful jobs (in defense, in war work, in communications and services) brought about by the war effort rejuvenated many a poor family. The chorus has not a single dissenting voice, as all join in for the refrain, "Oh, my, my." Who utters the haunting echo? Is it the philosophic poet? Is it a forgotten Gold Star mother? Is it the voice of history? Whoever it is, each of its words is significant. The chorus' words all run together horizontally — "In wartime we had fun." But the Echo's voice runs vertically:

> *Did*
> *Somebody*
> *Die?*

This is the way oracles speak: every word with a line to itself, every word capitalized, every word in italics. These are sacred words, whereas the words of the chorus are profane words. By such simple means Hughes shows us two comments on history, both "correct," but irreconcilable.

One of the problems in reading history poems is that one has to know something about history, and about the import of historical events within a given culture. Someone who knew nothing about the Civil War, or the March on Washington, or about the economic boom brought by World War II, would have difficulty taking in the attitudes and implications of these poems by Melville, Lowell, and Hughes. To this extent, lyric poets writing history poems have to depend on the shared knowledge of a common culture — and American readers wishing to understand an English poem about, say, the English Civil War have to learn, perhaps, many things that an English reader would have learned in school and that the poet took for granted in composing the poem. It is up to the poet to give the reader as much information as possible in the poem, but there is a limit to what can be conveyed in a short space. The generalized lyric usually has a longer shelf-life than the historically specified lyric because it does not make such particular demands on the reader. Yet nothing matches the vivid scenic, topical, and philosophic intensity of the best history poems, especially as they are first encountered by the audience to whom their topic is an urgent and contemporary one.

"Revisionary" history poems aim to turn the received view of a given historical circumstance upside down. War was treated heroically by classical literature, and the quotation from the Roman poet Horace, "Dulce et decorum est pro patria mori" ("It is sweet and fitting to die for one's country"), had been taken as the epitome of the proper attitude for young men going off to war. The introduction of such inhuman fighting methods as poison gas in World War I made a revisionary view of war almost inevitable, and the most famous poem of that war, dismantling armed struggle as a noble act, was composed by the English poet Wilfred Owen, who died in the war in 1918. You will see that in spite of the revisionary aims of the poem, it uses the familiar strategies of scenic presentation, crucial event, emotional insight, a mythic interlude (here, a recurrent dream), and epigrammatic summation (via Horace). It is spoken not by someone removed at a philosophic distance, but by one of the soldiers undergoing a gas attack:

WILFRED OWEN
Dulce Et Decorum Est

Bent double, like old beggars under sacks,
Knock-kneed, coughing like hags, we cursed through sludge,
Till on the haunting flares we turned our backs
And towards our distant rest began to trudge.
Men marched asleep. Many had lost their boots
But limped on, blood-shod. All went lame; all blind;
Drunk with fatigue; deaf even to the hoots
Of tired, outstripped Five-Nines° that dropped behind. *gas shells*

Gas! GAS! Quick, boys! — An ecstasy of fumbling,
Fitting the clumsy helmets just in time;
But someone still was yelling out and stumbling
And flound'ring like a man in fire or lime . . .
Dim, through the misty panes and thick green light,
As under a green sea, I saw him drowning.

In all my dreams, before my helpless sight,
He plunges at me, guttering, choking, drowning.

If in some smothering dreams you too could pace
Behind the wagon that we flung him in,
And watch the white eyes writhing in his face,
His hanging face, like a devil's sick of sin;
If you could hear, at every jolt, the blood

Come gargling from the froth-corrupted lungs,
Obscene as cancer, bitter as the cud
Of vile, incurable sores on innocent tongues, —
My friend, you would not tell with such high zest
To children ardent for some desperate glory,
The old Lie: Dulce et decorum est
Pro patria mori.

Owen chooses as a form for his poem the alternately rhyming iambic pentameter four-line stanza known as the "heroic quatrain" because it was used for noble narratives. The irony of attaching its heroic lineage to the squalor and tragedy of gas warfare must have appealed to the revisionary poet. "Dulce Et Decorum Est" reads at first like a realistic, unshaped report. Owen jams his quatrains together to obscure the regularity of his form (one can read the poem without realizing, at first, that it is written in rhyming quatrains). However, his report is "broken" by the shortest passage — the two-line recurrent dream of the dying gassed man — which is marked off from the rest of the poem not only by its brevity and its dream-based present tense, but also by its repetition of an identical rhyme-word: "drowning" rhymes with "drowning."

Regionality

When the generalized space of lyric — the vague spatial context, say, of "A slumber did my spirit seal" — gives way to a particular climate, geography, and scenery, we say that we have a regional poem. Wordsworth's poetry has made the Lake District of northern England a place of tourism and literary pilgrimage; Hopkins made the scenery of North Wales enter English poetry; Longfellow, Whittier, Frost, and Lowell became famous for their poems of New England; Robinson Jeffers immortalized Big Sur on the California coast; and Elizabeth Bishop, though American by birth, wrote many memorable poems about the landscapes of Brazil. These are only a few relatively recent examples. In older countries, descriptive poems (and landscape paintings) blanket the whole landscape: there is scarcely a town in Italy that has not been represented by a painter or a poet of classical or modern times.

The power of imagination to clothe a landscape in powerful allusive images is nowhere better seen than in Robert Lowell's "The Quaker Graveyard in Nantucket." This is a powerful, violent, and tumultuous poem, boiling up from the page as it follows the poet's meditations as he looks at the graveyard in Nantucket where the Quaker whalers buried their dead. Yet when one goes and looks at that very graveyard, it is simply a placid green slope, for the most part unmarked by headstones. It is Lowell's poem that has transformed that placid and uninformative space into a powerful container of ocean combers, whaling ships, wounded whales, harpoons, dead bodies, and fearful prayers. To visit the graveyard before, and then after, reading Lowell's poem is to see how regional poetry clothes the land in reminiscence, intimations of history, and imaginative power. The same is true of Longfellow's poem "The Jewish Cemetery in Newport." One might easily pass by an old cemetery with graves inscribed in Hebrew letters; but after reading Longfellow's meditation on the early Jewish settlers, now vanished into "the long, mysterious Exodus of death," one sees the cemetery with different eyes.

Though European colonizers thought the New World bare of culture, Native Americans had already consecrated certain lands and mountains as sacred, and had composed poetry about them. This first acculturation of space in the United States has been in great part lost, with many of the Indian languages and their oral literatures fallen into extinction. But an imaginative claim to American territory is now being repeated by Native American poets like Sherman Alexie, who recalls, in his poem "On the Amtrak from Boston to New York City," a well-meaning woman whose ideas of American history, American landscape, and American literature start with the Revolutionary period and end with Thoreau:

SHERMAN ALEXIE

On the Amtrak from Boston to New York City

The white woman across the aisle from me says, "Look,
look at all the history, that house
on the hill there is over two hundred years old,"
as she points out the window past me

into what she has been taught. I have learned
little more about American history during my few days
back East than what I expected and far less
of what we should all know of the tribal stories

whose architecture is 15,000 years older
than the corners of the house that sits
museumed on the hill. "Walden Pond,"
the woman on the train asks, "Did you see Walden Pond?"

and I don't have a cruel enough heart to break
her own by telling her there are five Walden Ponds
on my little reservation out West
and at least a hundred more surrounding Spokane,

the city I pretend to call my home. "Listen,"
I could have told her. "I don't give a shit
about Walden. I know the Indians were living stories
around that pond before Walden's grandparents were born

and before his grandparents' grandparents were born.
I'm tired of hearing about Don-fucking-Henley[1] saving it, too,
because that's redundant. If Don Henley's brothers and sisters
and mothers and fathers hadn't come here in the first place

then nothing would need to be saved."
But I didn't say a word to the woman about Walden
Pond because she smiled so much and seemed delighted
that I thought to bring her an orange juice

back from the food car. I respect elders
of every color. All I really did was eat
my tasteless sandwich, drink my Diet Pepsi
and nod my head whenever the woman pointed out

another little piece of her country's history
while I, as all Indians have done
since this war began, made plans
for what I would do and say the next time

somebody from the enemy thought I was one of their own.

The first English colonists, as Robert Frost says in "The Gift Outright," felt estranged in America because their own culture was English. They lived on land they had conquered, but they were still "unpossessed" by it. It was not until they (we) broke the tie to England, Frost argues, that we could give ourselves to the land "vaguely realizing westward, / But still unstoried, artless, unenhanced." It was the hope of writers to give that land stories, art, enhancement. By writing narrative poems like "The Wreck of the Hesperus" (about a wreck off the New England shore), "Evangeline" (about the exile of the Acadians), and Hiawatha (about Indians of New England), Longfellow hoped to give to

---

[1] Don Henley: A popular musician who organized benefit concerts to save Walden Pond from real estate developers.

the unstoried land the aura of legend. But Longfellow also wrote New England regional lyrics without narrative aim, like his famous poem about the coastal waters, "The Tide Rises, the Tide Falls":

> The tide rises, the tide falls,
> The twilight darkens, the curlew calls;
> Along the sea-sands damp and brown
> The traveller hastens toward the town,
>   And the tide rises, the tide falls.

Is this a poem that a poet who had grown up in Tulsa would write? Probably not; and in sensing that a child of the desert or the prairie would find rhythms not in the tides but perhaps in the winds, would write not about the wreck of the Hesperus but about the devastation caused by a tornado, we begin to see how the poetry of a large country like the United States (or Russia, or China) necessarily begins to have a large component of regional difference.

But the "regional" poet can also be one whose sense of a place is sharpened by coming to that landscape late in life. Elizabeth Bishop's poems of Brazil, such as "Questions of Travel," convey the mixed sense of estrangement combined with wonder and amazement that is felt by one to whom the tropics were a late revelation:

> There are too many waterfalls here; the crowded streams
> hurry too rapidly down to the sea,
> and the pressure of so many clouds on the mountaintops
> makes them spill over the sides in soft slow-motion,
> turning to waterfalls under our very eyes. . . .
>
> Should we have stayed at home and thought of here? . . .
>
> But surely it would have been a pity
> not to have seen the trees along this road,
> really exaggerated in their beauty,
> not to have seen them gesturing
> like noble pantomimists, robed in pink. . . .

The poet never describes landscape without entering it kinesthetically, feeling the motion of the crowded streams, humanizing the trees into noble pantomimists. Landscape in poetry is always *projected outward from the writing self*, which has, before the composition of the poem, absorbed it and colored it with the personality of the writer. It is not "London" that we see in William Blake's "London," which begins, "I wander through each charter'd street," but rather London-as-interpreted-by-Blake. Similarly, it is not "London" that we see in Wordsworth's "Composed upon Westminster Bridge," but rather "London-as-interpreted-by-Wordsworth" or "Wordsworth-turned-into-London." Because Wordsworth loved tranquil and sublime scenery, the bustle of daytime London repelled him; yet he found a way to discover "his" London, a London that could resemble him and his way of being. It was the London of dawn, when the air was free of smoke and the Thames was free of barges and the streets free of noise, when the architectural features of the city seemed almost like items in a natural landscape:

WILLIAM WORDSWORTH
Composed upon Westminster Bridge, September 3, 1802

Earth hath not anything to show more fair:
Dull would he be of soul who could pass by
A sight so touching in its majesty:
This City now doth, like a garment, wear
The beauty of the morning; silent, bare,
Ships, towers, domes, theatres, and temples lie
Open unto the fields, and to the sky;
All bright and glittering in the smokeless air.
Never did sun more beautifully steep
In his first splendour, valley, rock, or hill;
Ne'er saw I, never felt, a calm so deep!
The river glideth at his own sweet will:
Dear God! the very houses seem asleep;
And all that mighty heart is lying still!

Just as the "history poem" must have a problem, and scenes to illustrate it, and a point of view from which to consider it, and a summing-up of insight somewhere in its close, so the "geography poem" must have a problem — and scenes, and a point of view, and a "solution," if only temporary, to the problem. That is, description is never "merely description." Wordsworth's powerful visual sense, repelled by daytime London, is nonetheless forced to concede aesthetic beauty to dawn London — is forced even to concede that the sight of man's most ambitious creative product — a city — is more impressive than the sight of nature: "Never did sun more beautifully steep . . . valley, rock, or hill." As the list "valley, rock, or hill" is compared to the list "Ships, towers, domes, theatres, and temples," it is clear that the City wins.

Nature has "majesty," of course, but its majesty is not "touching" as the majesty of the human city, a human product, is. Yet the beauty of the morning is only a temporary "garment" that the City briefly wears; and the tension between the satisfying, because unchanging, beauty of the valley or hill and the temporary, but touching, majesty of the City gives the poem its oscillations of feeling as the poet wrestles with his own taste, and concedes to the fallen majesty of the human over the serene majesty of his beloved nature.

In Brief: History and Regionality

In thinking about history poems, the main thing to remember is that there is always a tension between the copiousness of history and the brevity of lyric. To see how a structure as brief as lyric can present, speculate on, and judge history is to see a form straining against its own limits. When it succeeds, it strikes us as a triumph of style over difficulty. It is also useful to remember that the history poem has been a genre chiefly undertaken, until recently, by men, since they were the group admitted to warfare, political rights, and historical decision making. As women increasingly take on political responsibility, history will be "owned" by women as much as by men, and "poems on affairs of state" will be written by men and women alike. The notable public poems written in the last several years by such poets as Adrienne Rich, Amy Clampitt, and Jorie Graham (on such topics as the atomic bomb, the Vietnam War Memorial, and the B-52 bombers on perpetual alert) show the increasing intervention of women's poetry in political life.

When you encounter a poem of geography or regionality, ask yourself how it embodies a problem and how landscape has been "lyricized" — that is, made a bearer of human feeling. Usually there will be at least two points of view in the poem (as in Bishop's mixed feelings about Brazil, and Wordsworth's mixed feelings about London). These points of view represent an emotional, and even a moral, quarrel within the poet. As Marianne Moore says in "The Steeple-Jack," speaking of a New England town in a storm, "It is a privilege to see so / much confusion." And that is indubitably true. At the same time, her protagonist "sees boats // at sea progress white and rigid as if in / a groove" and likes that "elegance of which / the source is not bravado." Should the modern American poem throw itself open to the privilege of confusion, or should it have a formal elegance not defensive but self-generated? Moore wants — and attains — both; she is famous for her profusion of detail and her unobtrusive elegance of formulation. Her New England town is herself, and she becomes its displays, whether dynamic or rigid. It is always the author that the landscape reveals to us; and the landscape of lyric is always revelatory because the author is within it, projecting it from its preliminary reconstitution in the imagination.

Reading Other Poems

Ask yourself what the time-axis and the space-axis is for each of the poems that follow. Does the poem take place over time, and if so, how many episodes does it show? (You can trace, through "Tintern Abbey," Wordsworth's entire development to adulthood, from his "glad animal movements" as a child to his political disillusion to his present restoration.) Does the poem bring in several different spaces? (Look at "Tintern Abbey" and see whether it all takes place outdoors.) Some poems, like W. S. Merwin's "The Asians Dying" (about the Vietnam War) treat only one episode of time. How is that episode made significant? Does the poem refer as Robert Hayden's does to a time in the historical past? If so, what does that epoch mean to the speaker? Why would a nineteenth-century man such as Keats write a poem about ancient Greece, or a twentieth-century woman such as Bishop write a poem about sixteenth-century Brazil? If the poem treats a contemporary episode (as Whitman treats Lincoln's death, as Yeats treats the 1916 Irish insurrection), how is the chaos of history ordered into the brief space of a lyric?

Does the poem move from space to space as it goes along, or does it remain in one place? How big is the space delineated in the poem? (That is, would Stevens's "Anecdote" be a different poem if it lacked the words "wilderness" or "Tennessee"?) If the poem treats imagined spaces (as Coleridge does in the fantastic visions of "Kubla Khan"), how are those spaces laid out and demarcated? Derek Walcott writes the relatively new genre, the airplane poem: he takes off from Love Field, Dallas, and contemplates the state of the nation from an enormous height (a height no one could see from prior to the twentieth century). What advantages (and disadvantages) come from writing at such a spatial distance? Does his adaptation of Dante's *terza rima* suggest a (perhaps hellish) expanse to be gazed at?

Jorie Graham contemplates a barbed-wire-enclosed field full of B-52 bombers on perpetual alert, kept running always in case they must respond instantly to an enemy threat. Her field of vision then takes in two more episodes — one of a marriage, one of the murder of the first poet, Orpheus. Can you link these three episodes, one in public space, one in private space, one in mythological space? Lowell's "For the Union Dead," too, takes place in several spaces, and also over several times, stretching from the Revolutionary War to the poet's current America of forced school integration and New England decline (symbolized by the destruction of the Boston Common to make an underground garage for the cars that have invaded the city). Can you track Lowell's spaces and times, and suggest some reasons why the poem does not proceed chronologically in time or in some ordered spatial way? Simon Ortiz's poem, too, is ordered by both space and time, as are many quest-poems. What are its temporal and spatial coordinates? What is the object of its quest? Robert Hayden's poem enacts itself in a time and place tersely announced by its title. What do the two parts of the poem tell us about "night" and "Mississippi"?

SAMUEL TAYLOR COLERIDGE
Kubla Khan[1]

Or a Vision in a Dream. A Fragment
In Xanadu did Kubla Khan
A stately pleasure dome decree:
Where Alph, the sacred river, ran
Through caverns measureless to man
   Down to a sunless sea.
So twice five miles of fertile ground
With walls and towers were girdled round:
And there were gardens bright with sinuous rills,
Where blossomed many an incense-bearing tree;
And here were forests ancient as the hills,
Enfolding sunny spots of greenery.

But oh! that deep romantic chasm which slanted
Down the green hill athwart a cedarn cover!
A savage place! as holy and enchanted
As e'er beneath a waning moon was haunted
By woman wailing for her demon lover!
And from this chasm, with ceaseless turmoil seething,

---

[1] Ruler of the Mongol dynasty in thirteenth-century China. Coleridge has invented the topography and place names in the poem.

As if this earth in fast thick pants were breathing,
A mighty fountain momently was forced:
Amid whose swift half-intermitted burst
Huge fragments vaulted like rebounding hail,
Or chaffy grain beneath the thresher's flail:
And 'mid these dancing rocks at once and ever
It flung up momently the sacred river.
Five miles meandering with a mazy motion
Through wood and dale the sacred river ran,
Then reached the caverns measureless to man,
And sank in tumult to a lifeless ocean:
And 'mid this tumult Kubla heard from far
Ancestral voices prophesying war!

    The shadow of the dome of pleasure
    Floated midway on the waves;
    Where was heard the mingled measure
    From the fountain and the caves.
It was a miracle of rare device,
A sunny pleasure dome with caves of ice!

    A damsel with a dulcimer
    In a vision once I saw:
    It was an Abyssinian maid,
    And on her dulcimer she played,
    Singing of Mount Abora.
    Could I revive within me
    Her symphony and song,
    To such a deep delight 'twould win me,
That with music loud and long,
I would build that dome in air,
That sunny dome! those caves of ice!
And all who heard should see them there,
And all should cry, Beware! Beware!
His flashing eyes, his floating hair!
Weave a circle round him thrice,
And close your eyes with holy dread,
For he on honey-dew hath fed,
And drunk the milk of Paradise.

WILLIAM WORDSWORTH

Lines Composed a Few Miles above Tintern Abbey on Revisiting the Banks of the Wye During a Tour

July 13, 1798

      Five years have passed; five summers, with the length
Of five long winters! and again I hear
These waters, rolling from their mountain-springs
With a soft inland murmur. Once again
Do I behold these steep and lofty cliffs,
That on a wild secluded scene impress
Thoughts of more deep seclusion; and connect
The landscape with the quiet of the sky.
The day is come when I again repose
Here, under this dark sycamore, and view
These plots of cottage ground, these orchard tufts,
Which at this season, with their unripe fruits,
Are clad in one green hue, and lose themselves
'Mid groves and copses. Once again I see
These hedgerows, hardly hedgerows, little lines
Of sportive wood run wild; these pastoral farms,
Green to the very door; and wreaths of smoke
Sent up, in silence, from among the trees!
With some uncertain notice, as might seem
Of vagrant dwellers in the houseless woods,
Or of some Hermit's cave, where by his fire
The Hermit sits alone.
                   These beauteous forms,
Through a long absence, have not been to me
As is a landscape to a blind man's eye;
But oft, in lonely rooms, and 'mid the din
Of towns and cities, I have owed to them,
In hours of weariness, sensations sweet,
Felt in the blood, and felt along the heart;
And passing even into my purer mind,
With tranquil restoration — feelings too
Of unremembered pleasure; such, perhaps,
As have no slight or trivial influence
On that best portion of a good man's life,
His little, nameless, unremembered, acts
Of kindness and of love. Nor less, I trust,
To them I may have owed another gift,

Of aspect more sublime; that blessed mood,
In which the burthen of the mystery,
In which the heavy and the weary weight
Of all this unintelligible world,
Is lightened — that serene and blessed mood,
In which the affections gently lead us on —
Until, the breath of this corporeal frame
And even the motion of our human blood
Almost suspended, we are laid asleep
In body, and become a living soul;
While with an eye made quiet by the power
Of harmony, and the deep power of joy,
We see into the life of things.

                    If this
Be but a vain belief, yet, oh! how oft —
In darkness and amid the many shapes
Of joyless daylight; when the fretful stir
Unprofitable, and the fever of the world,
Have hung upon the beatings of my heart —
How oft, in spirit, have I turned to thee,
O sylvan Wye! thou wanderer through the woods,
How often has my spirit turned to thee!

        And now, with gleams of half-extinguished thought,
With many recognitions dim and faint,
And somewhat of a sad perplexity,
The picture of the mind revives again;
While here I stand, not only with the sense
Of present pleasure, but with pleasing thoughts
That in this moment there is life and food
For future years. And so I dare to hope,
Though changed, no doubt, from what I was when first
I came among these hills; when like a roe
I bounded o'er the mountains, by the sides
Of the deep rivers, and the lonely streams,
Wherever nature led — more like a man
Flying from something that he dreads than one
Who sought the thing he loved. For nature then
(The coarser pleasures of my boyish days,
And their glad animal movements all gone by)
To me was all in all. — I cannot paint
What then I was. The sounding cataract
Haunted me like a passion; the tall rock,

The mountain, and the deep and gloomy wood,
Their colors and their forms, were then to me
An appetite; a feeling and a love,
That had no need of a remoter charm,
By thought supplied, nor any interest
Unborrowed from the eye. — That time is past,
And all its aching joys are now no more,
And all its dizzy raptures. Not for this
Faint I, nor mourn nor murmur; other gifts
Have followed; for such loss, I would believe,
Abundant recompense. For I have learned
To look on nature, not as in the hour
Of thoughtless youth; but hearing oftentimes
The still, sad music of humanity,
Nor harsh nor grating, though of ample power
To chasten and subdue. And I have felt
A presence that disturbs me with the joy
Of elevated thoughts; a sense sublime
Of something far more deeply interfused,
Whose dwelling is the light of setting suns,
And the round ocean and the living air,
And the blue sky, and in the mind of man:
A motion and a spirit, that impels
All thinking things, all objects of all thought,
And rolls through all things. Therefore am I still
A lover of the meadows and the woods,
And mountains; and of all that we behold
From this green earth; of all the mighty world
Of eye, and ear — both what they half create,
And what perceive; well pleased to recognize
In nature and the language of the sense
The anchor of my purest thoughts, the nurse,
The guide, the guardian of my heart, and soul
Of all my moral being.

                   Nor perchance,
If I were not thus taught, should I the more
Suffer my genial spirits to decay:
For thou art with me here upon the banks
Of this fair river; thou my dearest Friend,[1]

---

[1] He is referring to his sister, Dorothy Wordsworth (1771–1855), writer and diarist.

My dear, dear Friend; and in thy voice I catch
The language of my former heart, and read
My former pleasures in the shooting lights
Of thy wild eyes. Oh! yet a little while
May I behold in thee what I was once,
My dear, dear Sister! and this prayer I make,
Knowing that Nature never did betray
The heart that loved her; 'tis her privilege,
Through all the years of this our life, to lead
From joy to joy: for she can so inform
The mind that is within us, so impress
With quietness and beauty, and so feed
With lofty thoughts, that neither evil tongues,
Rash judgments, nor the sneers of selfish men,
Nor greetings where no kindness is, nor all
The dreary intercourse of daily life,
Shall e'er prevail against us, or disturb
Our cheerful faith, that all which we behold
Is full of blessings. Therefore let the moon
Shine on thee in thy solitary walk;
And let the misty mountain winds be free
To blow against thee: and, in after years,
When these wild ecstasies shall be matured
Into a sober pleasure; when thy mind
Shall be a mansion for all lovely forms,
Thy memory be as a dwelling place
For all sweet sounds and harmonies; oh! then,
If solitude, or fear, or pain, or grief
Should be thy portion, with what healing thoughts
Of tender joy wilt thou remember me,
And these my exhortations! Nor, perchance —
If I should be where I no more can hear
Thy voice, nor catch from thy wild eyes these gleams
Of past existence — wilt thou then forget
That on the banks of this delightful stream
We stood together; and that I, so long
A worshipper of Nature, hither came
Unwearied in that service; rather say
With warmer love — oh! with far deeper zeal
Of holier love. Nor wilt thou then forget,
That after many wanderings, many years

Of absence, these steep woods and lofty cliffs,
And this green pastoral landscape, were to me
More dear, both for themselves and for thy sake!

JOHN KEATS
Ode on a Grecian Urn

1

Thou still unravished bride of quietness,
　　Thou foster child of silence and slow time,
Sylvan historian, who canst thus express
　　A flowery tale more sweetly than our rhyme:
What leaf-fringed legend haunts about thy shape
　　Of deities or mortals, or of both,
　　　　In Tempe or the dales of Arcady?[1]
　　What men or gods are these? What maidens loath?
What mad pursuit? What struggle to escape?
　　　　What pipes and timbrels? What wild ecstasy?

2

Heard melodies are sweet, but those unheard
　　Are sweeter; therefore, ye soft pipes, play on;
Not to the sensual ear, but, more endeared,
　　Pipe to the spirit ditties of no tone:
Fair youth, beneath the trees, thou canst not leave
　　Thy song, nor ever can those trees be bare;
　　　　Bold Lover, never, never canst thou kiss,
Though winning near the goal — yet, do not grieve;
　　　　She cannot fade, though thou hast not thy bliss,
　　Forever wilt thou love, and she be fair!

3

Ah, happy, happy boughs! that cannot shed
　　Your leaves, nor ever bid the Spring adieu;
And, happy melodist, unwearièd,
　　Forever piping songs forever new;
More happy love! more happy, happy love!
　　Forever warm and still to be enjoyed,

---

[1] Traditional pastoral landscapes.

Forever panting, and forever young;
All breathing human passion far above,
      That leaves a heart high-sorrowful and cloyed,
            A burning forehead, and a parching tongue.

4

Who are these coming to the sacrifice?
      To what green altar, O mysterious priest,
Lead'st thou that heifer lowing at the skies,
      And all her silken flanks with garlands dressed?
What little town by river or sea shore,
      Or mountain-built with peaceful citadel,
            Is emptied of this folk, this pious morn?
And, little town, thy streets forevermore
      Will silent be; and not a soul to tell
            Why thou art desolate, can e'er return.

5

O Attic shape! Fair attitude! with brede°   *embroidery*
      Of marble men and maidens overwrought,
With forest branches and the trodden weed;
      Thou, silent form, dost tease us out of thought
As doth eternity: Cold Pastoral!
      When old age shall this generation waste,
            Thou shalt remain, in midst of other woe
Than ours, a friend to man, to whom thou say'st,
"Beauty is truth, truth beauty, — that is all
            Ye know on earth, and all ye need to know."

WALT WHITMAN
When Lilacs Last in the Dooryard Bloom'd

1

When lilacs last in the dooryard bloom'd,
And the great star early droop'd in the western sky in the night,
I mourn'd, and yet shall mourn with ever-returning spring.
Ever-returning spring, trinity sure to me you bring,
Lilac blooming perennial and drooping star in the west,
And thought of him I love.

2

O powerful western fallen star!
O shades of night — O moody, tearful night!
O great star disappear'd — O the black murk that hides the star!
O cruel hands that hold me powerless — O helpless soul of me!
O harsh surrounding cloud that will not free my soul.

3

In the dooryard fronting an old farm-house near the white-wash'd
    palings,
Stands the lilac-bush tall-growing with heart-shaped leaves of rich
    green,
With many a pointed blossom rising delicate, with the perfume
    strong I love,
With every leaf a miracle — and from this bush in the dooryard,
With delicate-color'd blossoms and heart-shaped leaves of rich
    green,
A sprig with its flower I break.

4

In the swamp in secluded recesses,
A shy and hidden bird is warbling a song.

Solitary the thrush,
The hermit withdrawn to himself, avoiding the settlements,
Sings by himself a song.

Song of the bleeding throat,
Death's outlet song of life, (for well dear brother I know,
If thou wast not granted to sing thou would'st surely die.)

5

Over the breast of the spring, the land, amid cities,
Amid lanes and through old woods, where lately the violets peep'd
    from the ground, spotting the gray debris,
Amid the grass in the fields each side of the lanes, passing the
    endless grass,
Passing the yellow-spear'd wheat, every grain from its shroud in
    the dark-brown fields uprisen,
Passing the apple-tree blows of white and pink in the orchards,
Carrying a corpse to where it shall rest in the grave,
Night and day journeys a coffin.

6

Coffin that passes through lanes and streets,[1]
Through day and night with the great cloud darkening the land,
With the pomp of the inloop'd flags with the cities draped in black,
With the show of the States themselves as of crape-veil'd women
    standing,
With processions long and winding and the flambeaus of the night,
With the countless torches lit, with the silent sea of faces and the
    unbared heads,
With the waiting depot, the arriving coffin, and the sombre faces,
With dirges through the night, with the thousand voices rising
    strong and solemn,
With all the mournful voices of the dirges pour'd around the
    coffin,
The dim-lit churches and the shuddering organs — where amid
    these you journey,
With the tolling tolling bells' perpetual clang,
Here, coffin that slowly passes,
I give you my sprig of lilac.

7

(Nor for you, for one alone,
Blossoms and branches green to coffins all I bring,
For fresh as the morning, thus would I chant a song for you O sane
    and sacred death.

All over bouquets of roses,
O death, I cover you over with roses and early lilies,
But mostly and now the lilac that blooms the first,
Copious I break, I break the sprigs from the bushes,
With loaded arms I come, pouring for you,
For you and the coffins all of you O death.)

8

O western orb sailing the heaven,
Now I know what you must have meant as a month since I walk'd,
As I walk'd in silence the transparent shadowy night,
As I saw you had something to tell as you bent to me night after
    night,

---

[1] Lincoln's funeral procession traveled from Washington, D.C., to Springfield, Illinois, stopping along the way so that people could honor the slain president.

As you droop'd from the sky low down as if to my side, (while the
    other stars all look'd on,)
As we wander'd together the solemn night, (for something I know
    not what kept me from sleep,)
As the night advanced, and I saw on the rim of the west how full
    you were of woe,
As I stood on the rising ground in the breeze in the cool trans-
    parent night,
As I watch'd where you pass'd and was lost in the netherward black
    of the night,
As my soul in its trouble dissatisfied sank, as where you sad orb,
Concluded, dropt in the night, and was gone.

9

Sing on there in the swamp,
O singer bashful and tender, I hear your notes, I hear your call,
I hear, I come presently, I understand you,
But a moment I linger, for the lustrous star has detain'd me,
The star my departing comrade holds and detains me.

10

O how shall I warble myself for the dead one there I loved?
And how shall I deck my song for the large sweet soul that has
    gone?
And what shall my perfume be for the grave of him I love?

Sea-winds blown from east and west,
Blown from the Eastern sea and blown from the Western sea, till
    there on the prairies meeting,
These and with these and the breath of my chant,
I'll perfume the grave of him I love.

11

O what shall I hang on the chamber walls?
And what shall the pictures be that I hang on the walls,
To adorn the burial-house of him I love?

Pictures of growing spring and farms and homes,
With the Fourth-month eve at sundown, and the gray smoke lucid
    and bright,
With floods of the yellow gold of the gorgeous, indolent, sinking
    sun, burning, expanding the air,
With the fresh sweet herbage under foot, and the pale green leaves
    of the trees prolific,

In the distance the flowing glaze, the breast of the river, with a
    wind-dapple here and there,
With ranging hills on the banks, with many a line against the sky,
    and shadows,
And the city at hand with dwellings so dense, and stacks of chim-
    neys,
And all the scenes of life and the workshops, and the workmen
    homeward returning.

12

Lo, body and soul — this land,
My own Manhattan with spires, and the sparkling and hurrying
    tides, and the ships,
The varied and ample land, the South and the North in the light,
    Ohio's shores and flashing Missouri,
And ever the far-spreading prairies cover'd with grass and corn.

Lo, the most excellent sun so calm and haughty,
The violet and purple morn with just-felt breezes,
The gentle soft-born measureless light,
The miracle spreading bathing all, the fulfill'd noon,
The coming eve delicious, the welcome night and the stars,
Over my cities shining all, enveloping man and land.

13

Sing on, sing on you gray-brown bird,
Sing from the swamps, the recesses, pour your chant from the
    bushes,
Limitless out of the dusk, out of the cedars and pines.

Sing on dearest brother, warble your reedy song,
Loud human song, with voice of uttermost woe.

O liquid and free and tender!
O wild and loose to my soul — O wondrous singer!
You only I hear — yet the star holds me, (but will soon depart,)
Yet the lilac with mastering odor holds me.

14

Now while I sat in the day and look'd forth,
In the close of the day with its light and the fields of spring, and the
    farmers preparing their crops,
In the large unconscious scenery of my land with its lakes and
    forests,

In the heavenly aerial beauty, (after the perturb'd winds and the
    storms,)
Under the arching heavens of the afternoon swift passing, and the
    voices of children and women,
The many-moving sea-tides, and I saw the ships how they sail'd,
And the summer approaching with richness, and the fields all busy
    with labor,
And the infinite separate houses, how they all went on, each with
    its meals and minutia of daily usages,
And the streets how their throbbings throbb'd, and the cities
    pent — lo, then and there,
Falling upon them all and among them all, enveloping me with the
    rest,
Appear'd the cloud, appear'd the long black trail,
And I knew death, its thought, and the sacred knowledge of death.

Then with the knowledge of death as walking one side of me,
And the thought of death close-walking the other side of me,
And I in the middle as with companions, and as holding the hands
    of companions,
I fled forth to the hiding receiving night that talks not,
Down to the shores of the water, the path by the swamp in the
    dimness,
To the solemn shadowy cedars and ghostly pines so still.

And the singer so shy to the rest receiv'd me,
The gray-brown bird I know receiv'd us comrades three,
And he sang the carol of death, and a verse for him I love.

From deep secluded recesses,
From the fragrant cedars and the ghostly pines so still,
Came the carol of the bird.

And the charm of the carol rapt me,
As I held as if by their hands my comrades in the night,
And the voice of my spirit tallied the song of the bird.

Come lovely and soothing death,
Undulate round the world, serenely arriving, arriving,
In the day, in the night, to all, to each,
Sooner or later delicate death.

Prais'd be the fathomless universe,
For life and joy, and for objects and knowledge curious,

And for love, sweet love — but praise! praise! praise!
For the sure-enwinding arms of cool-enfolding death.

Dark mother always gliding near with soft feet,
Have none chanted for thee a chant of fullest welcome?
Then I chant it for thee, I glorify thee above all,
I bring thee a song that when thou must indeed come, come unfalteringly.

Approach strong deliveress,
When it is so, when thou hast taken them I joyously sing the dead,
Lost in the loving floating ocean of thee,
Laved in the flood of thy bliss O death.

From me to thee glad serenades,
Dances for thee I propose saluting thee, adornments and feastings for thee,
And the sights of the open landscape and the high-spread sky are fitting,
And life and the fields, and the huge and thoughtful night.

The night in silence under many a star,
The ocean shore and the husky whispering wave whose voice I know,
And the soul turning to thee O vast and well-veil'd death,
And the body gratefully nestling close to thee.

Over the tree-tops I float thee a song,
Over the rising and sinking waves, over the myriad fields and the prairies
*   wide,*
Over the dense-pack'd cities all and the teeming wharves and ways,
I float this carol with joy, with joy to thee O death.

15

To the tally of my soul,
Loud and strong kept up the gray-brown bird,
With pure deliberate notes spreading filling the night.

Loud in the pines and cedars dim,
Clear in the freshness moist and the swamp-perfume,
And I with my comrades there in the night.

While my sight that was bound in my eyes unclosed,
As to long panoramas of visions.

And I saw askant the armies,
I saw as in noiseless dreams hundreds of battle-flags,
Borne through the smoke of the battles and pierc'd with missiles I
    saw them,
And carried hither and yon through the smoke, and torn and
    bloody,

And at last but a few shreds left on the staffs, (and all in silence,)
And the staffs all splinter'd and broken.

I saw battle-corpses, myriads of them,
And the white skeletons of young men, I saw them,
I saw the debris and debris of all the slain soldiers of the war,
But I saw they were not as was thought,
They themselves were fully at rest, they suffer'd not,
The living remain'd and suffer'd, the mother suffer'd,
And the wife and the child and the musing comrade suffer'd,
And the armies that remain'd suffer'd.

16

Passing the visions, passing the night,
Passing, unloosing the hold of my comrades' hands,
Passing the song of the hermit bird and the tallying song of my
    soul,
Victorious song, death's outlet song, yet varying ever-altering song,
As low and wailing, yet clear the notes, rising and falling, flooding
    the night,
Sadly sinking and fainting, as warning and warning, and yet again
    bursting with joy,
Covering the earth and filling the spread of the heaven,
As that powerful psalm in the night I heard from recesses,
Passing, I leave thee lilac with heart-shaped leaves,
I leave thee there in the door-yard, blooming, returning with
    spring.

I cease from my song for thee,
From my gaze on thee in the west, fronting the west, communing
    with thee,
O comrade lustrous with silver face in the night.

Yet each to keep and all, retrievements out of the night,
The song, the wondrous chant of the gray-brown bird,
And the tallying chant, the echo arous'd in my soul,
With the lustrous and drooping star with the countenance full of
    woe,
With the holders holding my hand nearing the call of the bird,
Comrades mine and I in the midst, and their memory ever to keep,
    for the dead I loved so well,
For the sweetest, wisest soul of all my days and lands — and this for
    his dear sake,
Lilac and star and bird twined with the chant of my soul,
There in the fragrant pines and the cedars dusk and dim.

William Butler Yeats
Easter 1916[1]

I have met them at close of day
Coming with vivid faces
From counter or desk among grey
Eighteenth-century houses.
I have passed with a nod of the head
Or polite meaningless words,
Or have lingered awhile and said
Polite meaningless words,
And thought before I had done
Of a mocking tale or a gibe
To please a companion
Around the fire at the club,
Being certain that they and I
But lived where motley is worn:
All changed, changed utterly:
A terrible beauty is born.

That woman's days were spent
In ignorant good-will,
Her nights in argument
Until her voice grew shrill.
What voice more sweet than hers
When, young and beautiful,
She rode to harriers?[2]
This man had kept a school
And rode our wingèd horse;[3]
This other his helper and friend[4]
Was coming into his force;
He might have won fame in the end,
So sensitive his nature seemed,
So daring and sweet his thought.
This other man I had dreamed

---

[1] The title refers to the Easter Rebellion on April 24, 1916. Republicans seized buildings and a park in the center of Dublin. They were killed or captured by April 29 and the leaders were executed in May.

[2] Yeats's friend, Countess Markiewicz, née Constance Gore-Booth (1868–1927), was involved in the rebellion.

[3] Patrick Pearse (1879–1916), the founder of St. Enda's School for Boys at Rathfarnham near Dublin, was one of the leaders of the rebellion. He was also a poet. (The winged horse is Pegasus, a symbol of poetic inspiration.)

[4] Thomas MacDonagh (1878–1916), poet and dramatist.

A drunken, vainglorious lout.[5]
He had done most bitter wrong
To some who are near my heart,
Yet I number him in the song;
He, too, has resigned his part
In the casual comedy;
He, too, has been changed in his turn,
Transformed utterly:
A terrible beauty is born.

Hearts with one purpose alone
Through summer and winter seem
Enchanted to a stone
To trouble the living stream.
The horse that comes from the road,
The rider, the birds that range
From cloud to tumbling cloud,
Minute by minute they change;
A shadow of cloud on the stream
Changes minute by minute;
A horse-hoof slides on the brim,
And a horse plashes within it;
The long-legged moor-hens dive,
And hens to moor-cocks call;
Minute by minute they live:
The stone's in the midst of all.

Too long a sacrifice
Can make a stone of the heart.
O when may it suffice?
That is Heaven's part, our part
To murmur name upon name,
As a mother names her child
When sleep at last has come
On limbs that had run wild.
What is it but nightfall?
No, no, not night but death;
Was it needless death after all?
For England may keep faith
For all that is done and said.[6]

---

[5] Major Thomas MacBride was married to Maud Gonne, whom Yeats loved.
[6] England had promised Home Rule for Ireland.

We know their dream; enough
To know they dreamed and are dead;
And what if excess of love
Bewildered them till they died?
I write it out in a verse —
MacDonagh and MacBride
And Connolly and Pearse
Now and in time to be,
Wherever green is worn,
Are changed, changed utterly:
A terrible beauty is born.

WALLACE STEVENS
Anecdote of the Jar

I placed a jar in Tennessee,
And round it was, upon a hill.
It made the slovenly wilderness
Surround that hill.

The wilderness rose up to it,
And sprawled around, no longer wild.
The jar was round upon the ground
And tall and of a port in air.

It took dominion everywhere.
The jar was gray and bare.
It did not give of bird or bush,
Like nothing else in Tennessee.

ROBERT LOWELL
For the Union Dead[1]

"Relinquunt Omnia Servare Rem Publicam."[2]

The old South Boston Aquarium stands
in a Sahara of snow now. Its broken windows are boarded.

---

[1] Soldiers who died fighting for the North in the Civil War. The poem is written about a bronze bas-relief opposite the Massachusetts State House on Beacon Street, in Boston; the monument, by Augustus St. Gaudens (1848–1897), commemorates Colonel Robert Gould Shaw (1837–1897), who commanded the first all-Negro regiment in the North, and who was killed while leading an attack on Fort Wagner in South Carolina. The monument represents Shaw on horseback flanked by Negro foot soldiers.

[2] Lowell has changed the inscription on the monument from the singular to the plural, so that it reads: "They leave everything behind to serve the Republic."

The bronze weathervane cod[3] has lost half its scales.
The airy tanks are dry.

Once my nose crawled like a snail on the glass;
my hand tingled
to burst the bubbles
drifting from the noses of the cowed, compliant fish.

My hand draws back. I often sigh still
for the dark downward and vegetating kingdom
of the fish and reptile. One morning last March,
I pressed against the new barbed and galvanized

fence on the Boston Common.[4] Behind their cage,
yellow dinosaur steamshovels were grunting
as they cropped up tons of mush and grass
to gouge their underworld garage.[5]

Parking spaces luxuriate like civic
sandpiles in the heart of Boston.
A girdle of orange, Puritan-pumpkin colored girders
braces the tingling Statehouse,

shaking over the excavations, as it faces Colonel Shaw
and his bell-cheeked Negro infantry
on St. Gaudens' shaking Civil War relief,
propped by a plank splint against the garage's earthquake.

Two months after marching through Boston,
half the regiment was dead;
at the dedication,
William James[6] could almost hear the bronze Negroes breathe.

Their monument sticks like a fishbone
in the city's throat.
Its Colonel is as lean
as a compass-needle.

He has an angry wrenlike vigilance,
a greyhound's gentle tautness;

---

[3] Codfish, the symbol of Boston.

[4] Park facing the State House.

[5] The construction of the garage beneath the Common was attended by graft and corruption.

[6] Philosopher and psychologist (1842–1910).

he seems to wince at pleasure,
and suffocate for privacy.

He is out of bounds now. He rejoices in man's lovely,
peculiar power to choose life and die —
when he leads his black soldiers to death,
he cannot bend his back.

On a thousand small town New England greens,
the old white churches hold their air
of sparse, sincere rebellion; frayed flags
quilt the graveyards of the Grand Army of the Republic.

The stone statues of the abstract Union Soldier
grow slimmer and younger each year —
wasp-waisted, they doze over muskets
and muse through their sideburns . . .

Shaw's father wanted no monument
except the ditch,
where his son's body was thrown
and lost with his "niggers."[7]

The ditch is nearer.
There are no statues for the last war here;
on Boylston Street, a commercial photograph
shows Hiroshima boiling

over a Mosler Safe, the "Rock of Ages"
that survived the blast. Space is nearer.
When I crouch to my television set,
the drained faces of Negro school-children[8] rise like balloons.

Colonel Shaw
is riding on his bubble,
he waits
for the blessèd break.

The Aquarium is gone. Everywhere,
giant finned cars nose forward like fish;
a savage servility
slides by on grease.

---

[7] Shaw's father could have had his son's body brought home (officers had that privilege, while infantry were buried where they fell), but he refused, knowing his son's affection for his men.

[8] Schools in the South were being forcibly desegregated in 1960.

ELIZABETH BISHOP
Brazil, January 1, 1502

> *. . . embroidered nature . . . tapestried landscape.*
> — *LANDSCAPE INTO ART,*
> SIR KENNETH CLARK

Januaries, Nature greets our eyes
exactly as she must have greeted theirs:
every square inch filling in with foliage —
big leaves, little leaves, and giant leaves,
blue, blue-green, and olive,
with occasional lighter veins and edges,
or a satin underleaf turned over;
monster ferns
in silver-gray relief,
and flowers, too, like giant water lilies
up in the air — up, rather, in the leaves —
purple, yellow, two yellows, pink,
rust red and greenish white;
solid but airy; fresh as if just finished
and taken off the frame.

A blue-white sky, a simple web,
backing for feathery detail:
brief arcs, a pale-green broken wheel,
a few palms, swarthy, squat, but delicate;
and perching there in profile, beaks agape,
the big symbolic birds keep quiet,
each showing only half his puffed and padded,
pure-colored or spotted breast.
Still in the foreground there is Sin:
five sooty dragons near some massy rocks.
The rocks are worked with lichens, gray moonbursts
splattered and overlapping,
threatened from underneath by moss
in lovely hell-green flames,
attacked above
by scaling-ladder vines, oblique and neat,
"one leaf yes and one leaf no" (in Portuguese).
The lizards scarcely breathe; all eyes
are on the smaller, female one, back-to,
her wicked tail straight up and over,
red as a red-hot wire.

Just so the Christians, hard as nails,
tiny as nails, and glinting,
in creaking armor, came and found it all,
not unfamiliar:
no lovers' walks, no bowers,
no cherries to be picked, no lute music,
but corresponding, nevertheless,
to an old dream of wealth and luxury
already out of style when they left home —
wealth, plus a brand-new pleasure.
Directly after Mass, humming perhaps
L'Homme armé or some such tune,
they ripped away into the hanging fabric,
each out to catch an Indian for himself —
those maddening little women who kept calling,
calling to each other (or had the birds waked up?)
and retreating, always retreating, behind it.

ROBERT HAYDEN
Night, Death, Mississippi

I

A quavering cry. Screech-owl?
Or one of them?
The old man in his reek
and gauntness laughs —

One of them, I bet —
and turns out the kitchen lamp,
limping to the porch to listen
in the windowless night.

Be there with Boy and the rest
if I was well again.
Time was. Time was.
White robes like moonlight

In the sweetgum dark.
Unbucked that one then
and him squealing bloody Jesus
as we cut it off.

Time was. A cry?
A cry all right.

He hawks and spits,
fevered as by groinfire.

Have us a bottle,
Boy and me —
he's earned him a bottle —
when he gets home.

                    II

Then we beat them, he said,
beat them till our arms was tired
and the big old chains
messy and red.

O Jesus burning on the lily cross

Christ, it was better
than hunting bear
which don't know why
you want him dead.

O night, rawhead and bloodybones night

You kids fetch Paw
some water now so's he
can wash that blood
off him, she said.

O night betrayed by darkness not its own

W. S. MERWIN
The Asians Dying

When the forests have been destroyed their darkness remains
The ash the great walker follows the possessors
Forever
Nothing they will come to is real
Nor for long
Over the watercourses
Like ducks in the time of the ducks
The ghosts of the villages trail in the sky
Making a new twilight

Rain falls into the open eyes of the dead
Again again with its pointless sound
When the moon finds them they are the color of everything

The nights disappear like bruises but nothing is healed
The dead go away like bruises
The blood vanishes into the poisoned farmlands

Pain the horizon
Remains
Overhead the seasons rock
They are paper bells
Calling to nothing living

The possessors move everywhere under Death their star
Like columns of smoke they advance into the shadows
Like thin flames with no light
They with no past
And fire their only future

DEREK WALCOTT
The Gulf

For Jack and Barbara Harrison

I

The airport coffee tastes less of America.
Sour, unshaven, dreading the exertion
of tightening, racked nerves fuelled with liquor,

some smoky, resinous bourbon,
the body, buckling at its casket hole,
a roar like last night's blast racing its engines,

watches the fumes of the exhausted soul
as the trans-Texas jet, screeching, begins
its flight and friends diminish. So, to be aware

of the divine union the soul detaches
itself from created things. "We're in the air,"
the Texan near me grins. All things: these matches

from LBJ's[1] campaign hotel, this rose
given me at dawn in Austin by a child,
this book of fables by Borges,[2] its prose

---

[1] Lyndon Baines Johnson (1908–1975), thirty-sixth president of the United States.
[2] Jorge Luis Borges (1899–1986), Argentine writer.

a stalking, moonlit tiger. What was willed
on innocent, sun-streaked Dallas, the beast's claw
curled round that hairspring rifle[3] is revealed

on every page as lunacy or feral law;
circling that wound we leave Love Field.
Fondled, these objects conjure hotels,

quarrels, new friendships, brown limbs
nakedly moulded as these autumn hills
memory penetrates as the jet climbs

the new clouds over Texas; their home means
an island suburb, forest, mountain water;
they are the simple properties for scenes

whose joy exhausts like grief, scenes where we learn,
exchanging the least gifts, this rose, this napkin,
that those we love are objects we return,

that this lens on the desert's wrinkled skin
has priced our flesh, all that we love in pawn
to that brass ball, that the gifts, multiplying,

clutter and choke the heart, and that I shall
watch love reclaim its things as I lie dying.
My very flesh and blood! Each seems a petal

shrivelling from its core. I watch them burn,
by the nerves' flare I catch their skeletal
candour! Best never to be born,

the great dead cry. Their works shine on our shelves,
by twilight tour their gilded gravestone spines,
and read until the lamplit page revolves

to a white stasis whose detachment shines
like a propeller's rainbowed radiance.
Circling like us; no comfort for their loves!

II

The cold glass darkens. Elizabeth wrote once
that we make glass the image of our pain;
I watch clouds boil past the cold, sweating pane

---

[3] Reference to the assassination of President John F. Kennedy in Dallas on November 22, 1963.

above the Gulf. All styles yearn to be plain
as life. The face of the loved object under glass
is plainer still. Yet, somehow, at this height,

above this cauldron boiling with its wars,
our old earth, breaking to familiar light,
that cloud-bound mummy with self-healing scars

peeled of her cerements again looks new;
some cratered valley heals itself with sage,
through that grey, fading massacre a blue

lighthearted creek flutes of some siege
to the amnesia of drumming water.
Their cause is crystalline: the divine union

of these detached, divided states, whose slaughter
darkens each summer now, as one by one,
the smoke of bursting ghettos clouds the glass

down every coast where filling station signs
proclaim the Gulf, an air, heavy with gas,
sickens the state, from Newark to New Orleans.

III

Yet the South felt like home. Wrought balconies,
the sluggish river with its tidal drawl,
the tropic air charged with the extremities

of patience, a heat heavy with oil,
canebrakes, that legendary jazz. But fear
thickened my voice, that strange, familiar soil

prickled and barbed the texture of my hair,
my status as a secondary soul.
The Gulf, your gulf, is daily widening,

each blood-red rose warns of that coming night
when there's no rock cleft to go hidin' in
and all the rocks catch fire, when that black might,

their stalking, moonless panthers turn from Him
whose voice they can no more believe, when the black X's
mark their passover with slain seraphim.

IV

The Gulf shines, dull as lead. The coast of Texas
glints like a metal rim. I have no home
as long as summer bubbling to its head

boils for that day when in the Lord God's name
the coals of fire are heaped upon the head
of all whose gospel is the whip and flame,

age after age, the uninstructing dead.

SIMON J. ORTIZ
Bend in the River

Flicker flies by.
His ochre wing
is tied to prayer sticks.
Pray for mountains,
the cold strong shelter.

Sun helps me to see
where Arkansas River
ripples over pebbles.
Glacial stone moves slowly;
it will take a while.

A sandbank cuts sharply
down to a poplar log
buried in damp sand.
Shadow lengths tell me
it is afternoon.

There are tracks
at river's edge, raccoon,
coyote, deer, crow,
and now my own.

My sight follows
the river upstream
until it bends.
Beyond the bend
is more river
and, soon, the mountains.
We shall arrive,
to see, soon.

Jorie Graham
What the End Is For

Grand Forks, North Dakota

A boy just like you took me out to see them,
    the five hundred B-52's on alert on the runway,
fully loaded fully manned pointed in all the directions,
    running every minute
of every day.
    They sound like a sickness of the inner ear,

where the heard foams up into the noise of listening,
    where the listening arrives without being extinguished.
The huge hum soaks up into the dusk.
    The minutes spring open. Six is too many.
From where we watch,
    from where even watching is an anachronism,

from the 23rd of March from an open meadow,
    the concertina wire in its double helix
designed to tighten round a body if it turns
    is the last path the sun can find to take out,
each barb flaring gold like a braille being read,
    then off with its knowledge and the sun
is gone. . . .

That's when the lights on all the extremities, like an outline like a
        dress,
    become loud in the story,
and a dark I have not seen before
    sinks in to hold them one
by one.
    Strange plot made to hold so many inexhaustible
screams.
    Have you ever heard in a crowd mutterings of
blame

that will not modulate that will not rise?
    He tells me, your stand-in, they *stair-step* up.
He touches me to have me look more deeply
    in
to where for just a moment longer
    color still lives:
the belly white so that it looks like sky, the top
    some kind of brown, some soil — How does it look

from up there now
    this meadow we lie on our bellies in, this field Iconography
tells me stands for sadness
    because the wind can move through it uninterrupted?
What is it the wind
    would have wanted to find and didn't

leafing down through this endless admiration unbroken
    because we're too low for it
to find us?
    Are you still there for me now in that dark
we stood in for hours
    letting it sweep as far as it could down over us
unwilling to move, irreconcilable? What *he*
    wants to tell me,

his whisper more like a scream
    over this eternity of engines never not running,
is everything: how the crews assigned to each plane
    for a week at a time, the seven boys, must live
inseparable,
    how they stay together for life,
how the wings are given a life of
    seven feet of play,

how they drop practice bombs called *shapes* over Nevada,
    how the measures for counterattack in air
have changed and we
    now forego firepower for jamming, for the throwing
of false signals. The meadow, the meadow hums, love, with the
        planes,
    as if every last blade of grass were wholly possessed

by this practice, wholly prepared. The last time I saw you,
    we stood facing each other as dusk came on.
I leaned against the refrigerator, you leaned against the door.
    The picture window behind you was slowly extinguished,
the tree went out, the two birdfeeders, the metal braces on them.
    The light itself took a long time,

bits in puddles stuck like the useless
    splinters of memory, the chips
of history, hopes, laws handed down. *Here, hold these* he says, these
    grasses these
torn pods, he says, smiling over the noise another noise, *take these*
    he says, my hands wrong for

the purpose, here,
    not-visible-from-the-sky, prepare yourself with these, boy
        and
bouquet of
    thistleweed and wort and william and
timothy. We stood there. Your face went out a long time
    before the rest of it. Can't see you anymore I said. *Nor I,*
you, whatever you still were
    replied.
When I asked you to hold me you refused.
    When I asked you to cross the six feet of room to hold me

you refused. Until I
    couldn't rise out of the patience either any longer
to make us
    take possession.
Until we were what we must have wanted to be:
    shapes the shapelessness was taking back.
Why should I lean out?
    Why should I move?
When the Maenads tear Orpheus limb from limb,
    they throw his head

out into the river.[1]
    Unbodied it sings
all the way downstream, all the way to the single ocean,
    head floating in current downriver singing,
until the sound of the cataracts grows,
    until the sound of the open ocean grows and the voice.

---

[1] Orpheus was torn to pieces by Maenads, savage female followers of Dionysus, god of drunkenness and revelry. Orpheus's severed head, floating down the Thracian river, Hebrus, reached the island of Lesbos, the home of lyric poetry, where it was buried.

9

Attitudes, Values, Judgments

You're under no obligation to like all the remarks or attitudes you come across in art. Past artists reflect the prejudices and beliefs of their time, just as our twentieth-century writers will reveal, to later readers, the (frequently unconscious) presumptions and beliefs of our era. It is notoriously hard to believe that morally we are much superior to our ancestors. Social attitudes may progress in one or another area (we in America no longer recommend public hangings or beheadings), but we are sure to seem as backward and ignorant to our descendants as even our recent ancestors seem to us.

Nor are artists necessarily morally better than others in their private or public actions. Genius does not guarantee moral probity in the ordinary activities of life. What, then, are the moral obligations of artists insofar as they are artists? (As people, they exist under the same moral imperatives as anyone else, and are conditioned by their cultures in their interpretation of those imperatives.) How — to put our question another way — can artists betray their artistic principles?

They can betray themselves as artists, and their art itself, by saying what society wants to hear, rather than what seems true; by papering over the actual with the agreeable or the socially enjoined; by falling into the comfortable habits of the past instead of reinventing their medium. If, however, the artist has the talent to work the medium accurately — to reveal in stylized language the structure of reality as it is delivered by perception, emotion, and thought — without being cowed by convention or audience response, there is a chance that the artwork will succeed.

This does not mean that a work has to be composed entirely freely, with no external conditions laid upon it. On the contrary. Many commissioned artworks have been spectacularly successful — Michelangelo's paintings in the Sistine Chapel, Bach's cantatas for Sunday services, Milton's "Lycidas," written for an anthology of verse compiled in honor of a schoolfellow who was drowned. In fact, nothing is more stimulating to some artists than a patron's saying, "I'd like you to make a painting in a semicircular shape to fit that space over the door; and I'd like it to represent Apollo; and you may have exactly four ounces of gold leaf to decorate it with." Poetry is less often commissioned than music, sculpture, or painting, yet William Blake represents his *Songs of Innocence* as "commissioned" by a child-Muse:

> Piping down the valleys wild
> Piping songs of pleasant glee
> On a cloud I saw a child,
> And he laughing said to me,
>
> "Pipe a song about a Lamb";
> So I piped with merry cheer.
> "Piper, pipe that song again" —
> So I piped, he wept to hear.

And Shakespeare's sonnets seem to have begun as a commissioned sequence urging an aristocratic young man to marry and beget an heir.

A poem sometimes seeks out its own commissions, so to speak, by casting itself as a letter replying to a request or a question. Gerard Manley Hopkins's friend and fellow poet Robert Bridges asks Hopkins, in a letter, why he has sent him no poems lately. In response, Hopkins sends a verse-letter in the form of a sonnet ("To R.B.") explaining that inspiration has forsaken him:

> Sweet fire, the sire of muse, my soul needs this;
> I want the one rapture of an inspiration.
> Oh then if in my lagging lines you miss
> The roll, the rise, the carol, the creation,
> My winter world, that scarcely breathes that bliss,
> Now yields you, with some sighs, our explanation.

We may suppose that this poem might never have been written without the pressure of Bridges's "commissioning" question. It is always useful, in considering the attitudes of a poem, to ask what has occasioned it. Has an anterior question, reproach, or command brought it into being? If we do not ask this question, we are likely to mistake the poem's attitudes, values, and tone.

Let me give an example. Shakespeare's Sonnet 76 has usually been read as a self-interrogation in which Shakespeare laments the barrenness and sameness of his poems. Improbably enough, according to this reading, Shakespeare thought ill of his own work, accusing himself of a boring similarity in all his poems:

WILLIAM SHAKESPEARE
Sonnet 76

Why is my verse so barren of new pride?
So far from variation or quick change?
Why with the time do I not glance aside
To new-found methods and to compounds strange?
Why write I still all one, ever the same,
And keep invention in a noted weed,°   *well-known garment*
That every word doth almost tell my name,
Showing their birth and where they did proceed?

If this were all we had of the poem, we might indeed think Shakespeare is reproaching himself. But the next part of the sonnet shows that this is an "answer-poem," replying to an implied question previously asked by Shakespeare's young patron: "Why do you bring me nothing but sonnets, old-fashioned poems?" Shakespeare replies, "O know, sweet love, I always write of you":

And you and love are still my argument;
So all my best is dressing old words new,
Spending again what is already spent:
    For as the sun is daily new and old,
    So is my love still telling what is told.

Armed with this knowledge of implied question and answer, we can now better imagine the "antecedent scenario" of the poem. The fashionable young man, who has by now received many sonnets from Shakespeare, is surprised that his poet keeps writing in this old-fashioned form, already in existence for over two hundred years. Other poets have gone on to new things. Why can't his poet write a satire, or a picturesque mini-narrative, or a debate-poem? "Why," says the up-to-date young man to the poet, "are you always writing the same old sonnets, all the same sort, so that everyone who sees them says, 'Oh, of course, another piece by Shakespeare'? " And he continues, "How about doing something new next time?" Shakespeare, only too conscious of the young man's ignorant and trendy dismissal of his incomparable poems, gives the soft answer that turns away wrath, repeating and quoting the young man's reproach, but finding nonetheless a way to defend himself. We can now reconstruct the poem as it should be read: not as Shakespeare's reproach to himself but as his reproof of the young man:

> *Why* [you ask] is my verse so barren of "new pride"?
> So far from "variation" or "quick change"?
> *Why* with the time do I not glance aside
> To "new-found methods" and to "compounds" strange?
> *Why* write I still "all one," "ever the same,"
> And keep invention in a "noted weed,"
> That every word doth almost "tell my name,"
> Showing their birth and where they did proceed?
> O know, sweet love, I always write of you,
> And you and love are still my argument;
> So all my best is dressing old words new,
> Spending again what is already spent:
> > For as the sun is daily new and old,
> > So is my love still telling what is told.

This deft but gentle rebuke reminds the young man, at the close, that nobody looks up at the sky at dawn and says, "The sun again! How boring and repetitive!" There are things so precious — the sun and love being among them — that we never have enough of them. And poetry, after all, never has new *words* — all the words are already present in the language. The only thing *any* poet can do is "dress [that is, arrange] old words new," re-spending the words that poetic predecessors have already spent.

Our view of the attitudes expressed by the speaker in this sonnet depends very much on whether we see it as *self-reproach* or as a *rebuke to the young man*. This reminds us that before we can evaluate the attitudes and values expressed in a poem we must try to be as accurate as possible in describing them. These are delicate questions; and the sophistication of poems (and of the people who write them) warns us against too hasty a judgment. One has to understand a poem well before judging it. (And really understanding the implications of a poem usually depends on having read many other poems by that poet.)

Evaluation depends on where you stand with respect to the things described in a poem. Until fairly recently, the poems that Langston Hughes wrote about Harlem — representing such realities as sexual intercourse before marriage, marital infidelity, children born out of wedlock, prostitution and pimping, and the strife between Jewish landlords and black tenants — were simply not represented in general anthologies of American poetry or anthologies of poetry by blacks. Much of Hughes's subject matter seemed indecent to whites and blacks alike; and black anthologists wanted to print poems that were "a credit to the race." Hughes's veracity — his refusal to betray the structure of reality as he saw it for something more acceptable — is today much admired, but was in his lifetime often criticized. Judges were judging not his art — represented in his striking sequences on Harlem and his adaptation of jazz rhythms — but what they saw as his failure to condemn immorality, on the one hand, and his washing dirty social linen in public, on the other.

It is not desirable to let a difference in values blind us to the imaginative mastery of language and form in such poets as the atheist Robinson Jeffers (whose nihilism was much criticized) or the social realists Langston Hughes and Allen Ginsberg. The nineteenth-century anthologists who censored Charles Baudelaire's depiction of lesbianism are replaced in our day by those who censor Ginsberg's depiction of homosexuality. The accurate representation of reality is, for the artist, the highest morality. It is immoral to conceal the way human beings live, or what human beings think. The tension between allowing an artist free expression and, for instance, shielding the sensibilities of the young is a real one; and most societies have worked out a gradual scale according to which the young can be exposed to art of increasing moral complexity.

However, in countries with active political or religious censorship, where free expression is not permitted at all, artists perform marvelous end-runs around forbidden topics. During the Cold War years, ingenious Eastern European poets in Russia, Poland, Hungary, and other Iron Curtain countries constructed allegorical poems which were seemingly "harmless" but which everyone could read as a coded critique of the regime. Even under censorship, art will find a way to be free — though sometimes the artist may suffer imprisonment and death.

It is impossible not to notice the attitudes and values expressed in a poem. In fact, they are often the first thing we do notice. Yet a criticism of attitudes and values alone does not come to grips with what a poet really has to offer, which is a personal sense of the world, an idiosyncratic temperament, a unique imagination, and a new linguistic lens through which readers may see the world afresh.

How, then, are we to evaluate the success of a poem if we cannot base our judgment on its attitudes and values? Robert Lowell, in the poem "Epilogue," printed last in his final book, *Day by Day,* suggests one way. Despairing of his unrhymed modern "snapshots" of reality, he asks why he can't make something as beautiful as the radiant interiors painted by the seventeenth-century Dutch artist Jan Vermeer. He is thinking particularly of one painting, which shows a girl reading a letter; Lowell imagines her "yearning" for its absent writer. She stands by a casement window from which light steals across the wall behind her, illuminating the map on the wall (which is, in Vermeer and elsewhere, a figure for the abstraction of art). Here is the poem:

ROBERT LOWELL
Epilogue

Those blessèd structures, plot and rhyme —
why are they no use to me now
I want to make
something imagined, not recalled?
I hear the noise of my own voice:
The painter's vision is not a lens,
it trembles to caress the light.
But sometimes everything I write
with the threadbare art of my eye
seems a snapshot
lurid, rapid, garish, grouped,
heightened from life,
yet paralyzed by fact.
All's misalliance.
Yet why not say what happened?
Pray for the grace of accuracy
Vermeer gave to the sun's illumination
stealing like the tide across a map
to his girl solid with yearning.
We are poor passing facts,
warned by that to give
each figure in the photograph
his living name.

At its middle, the poem collapses in despair: "All's misalliance." But then the poet gets a second wind: What is wrong with describing his life truthfully as he sees it? "Yet why not say what happened?" He resolves his poem by realizing that though his "snapshots" may not look superficially like Vermeer's paintings, he and Vermeer have in common the artist's truest motive — accuracy of representation. The artist can vow accuracy, but he or she must pray for the other ingredient in successful art — grace. "Pray for *the grace of accuracy,*" the poet tells himself. One part of his function as a poet is a duty to set down contemporary facts of life before they disappear; but he can only hope and pray that by the grace of aesthetic power he can give to the people of his century (who will otherwise be anonymous numbers in a census, "poor passing facts") their "living name." That living name is conferred only by the *grace* of art — its aesthetic power that often seems bestowed from the outside, like religious "grace." By the end of the poem, the poet can stop referring to his work by the ugly and clipped word "snapshot," and can speak of it as "writing with light" — a "photo-graph." He, like Vermeer, will also become a writer with light if he can attain "the grace of accuracy."

This poem suggests that we must judge any poem we read as a representation of its author's perception of reality; but we must also judge it as an experiment in its medium, according to its portion of "grace" — what Hopkins called "the roll, the rise, the carol, the creation."

If, in one direction, we judge poetry, it is also true that in another direction the poem judges us. It looks at us with a steady gaze and dares us to judge ourselves by its revelations. "The poet judges, not as the judge judges but as the sun falling around a helpless thing," said Walt Whitman. To observe and convey reality is itself a judgment on reality, even if the poem makes no explicit judgment on the reality conveyed.

Rita Dove, a contemporary African American poet, writes about the "poetic justice" of art in a poem about a painting she saw in Germany by a modern painter, Christian Schad. He had painted, in the twenties, in Berlin, a portrait of two circus "freaks": one of them was a man with a bone disease that caused his shoulder bones to protrude like wings. He was billed as "Agosta the Winged Man." The other "freak" was a perfectly normal black woman who, billed as "Rasha, the Black Dove," was displayed as an exotic jungle creature, dancing entwined with a boa constrictor. The black Rita Dove, seeing "the Black Dove" — who, but for an accident of time, could have been herself — depicts Schad, the painter, planning the double portrait he is about to begin, attempting to decide where its power will lie. Is it in the mercilessness of his unsparing view of his subjects? No,

                    The canvas,
        not his eye, was merciless. . . .

        Schad would place him°   *Agosta*
        on a throne, a white sheet tucked
        over his loins, the black suit jacket
        thrown off like a cloak.
        Agosta had told him
                    of the medical students
        at the Charité,°   *a hospital*
        that chill arena

                    where he perched on
        a cot, his torso
        exposed, its crests and fins
        a colony of birds, trying
        to get out . . .
                    and the students,
        lumps caught
        in their throats, taking notes.

        Ah, Rasha's
                    foot on the stair.
        She moved slowly, as if she carried
        the snake around her body
        always. . . .

                    Agosta in
        classical drapery, then,
        and Rasha at his feet.
        Without passion. Not
        the canvas
                    but their gaze,
                    so calm,
        was merciless.

Is it the painter's eye, seeing the social marginalization of his subjects (one black, one deformed) that is merciless in its accuracy? Or is it the canvas, demanding how paint shall be used, and how the picture will be composed, that is merciless? Schad decides that neither of these is true. It is neither his eye nor the canvas that is merciless, but the gaze of his two subjects, saying, "Here we are. This is how we were seen, in Berlin, in 1929." The gaze is merciless because it is, like the portrait which depicts it, "without passion." The painting is not propaganda; it is not "social protest art"; it is simply an accurate transcription (with the "grace" of its compositional arrangements with which Schad has taken such care) of "Reality, Berlin, 1929." Nothing more than this is necessary; but how hard it is to ensure that the eye and the canvas and the gaze maintain this accuracy of perception — without exaggeration, without deletion.

There have been other suggestions by poets on how to make and judge art, each understandable within its culture and its century. The religious poet George Herbert thought that if one wrote for God alone, one would write well: "If I please him, I write fine and wittie." Similarly, Milton said, in "Lycidas," that the poet should look for true fame only from the "pure eyes / And perfect witness of all-judging Jove." These reflections suggest that the poets did not find the immediate judgment of contemporaries a reliable measure for any poet.

We, too, can be warned by such remarks that poems that last for a long time tend to satisfy many criteria of success, and to interest many generations of future writers. It is, in the last analysis, chiefly by the admiration of other writers that writers become "canonized." In one strand of the canonical male line (male because until recently only males were educated in complex uses of language) Spenser admires Chaucer, John Milton admires Spenser, Wordsworth admires Milton, Keats admires Wordsworth, Tennyson admires Keats, Eliot admires Tennyson, Auden admires Eliot, Merrill admires Auden, and so it has gone. It is no accident that almost every contemporary woman poet in America, from Adrienne Rich through Jorie Graham to Lucie Brock-Broido, has written a poem to or about Emily Dickinson, or that Dickinson herself wrote a poem about her favorite woman poet, Elizabeth Barrett Browning, or that Elizabeth Bishop wrote a poem to Marianne Moore, creating a comparable ongoing line of female "canonization." It is also true that canonization crosses gender lines: T. S. Eliot and Wallace Stevens and William Carlos Williams and A. R. Ammons admired the poetry of Marianne Moore; Hopkins admired Christina Rossetti; Dickinson admired Emerson; and Moore admired La Fontaine. It is the admiration of poets for each other's accomplishments in the medium of language that keeps poetry alive; and poets keep poetry honest in their fine-tuned admiration of any writing that is not only "accurate with respect to the structures of reality" but also full of "the grace of accuracy," giving the "poor passing facts" of every era their "living name."

In Brief: Attitudes, Values, Judgments

If we keep the honorific name "poetry" to mean "verse that suceeds in achieving lasting interest over time," we are still uncertain of the amount of "poetry" being produced by our own century. There is a great deal of verse being written, all of it, of course, of documentary interest to sociologists or anthropologists or cultural critics. For such scholars, the overt message, or representation of life in a poem, means more than the skill with which that message or representation has been arranged. We all read for message and picture, but readers with a strong commitment to poetry as an art require in it those new symbolic structures, invented by talented artists of every age, that both affront and refresh. An experienced reader of poetry is soon bored by the already known and the clichéd; but the previously unheard, the previously unknown, arranged in a form true to a temperament, and transmitting a shock of pleasure — this makes for the renewal of both life and art. It is this capacity of poetry to rewrite the old that we value in it, that we search out in it, and that we judge it by.

Reading Other Poems

Each of the following poems expresses a strong moral attitude: that is, at least two sets of opposing values are presented, and the poet (through a sympathetic or unsympathetic speaker) comes out in favor of one set. This entails describing, or at least implying, the contrasting set of values that the poet repudiates. In each poem, trace the way the repudiated value is presented — whether in John Milton's corrupt bishops, or Rita Dove's dictator, or Walt Whitman's astronomer, or William Butler Yeats's imperial rulers, or Robinson Jeffers's decayed democracy, or Louise Glück's speaker's sexual partner. Does the poet imply that the reader already agrees with his or her preferred value?

Sometimes the poet's preference may be surprising (see Jonson, Lovelace, Whitman, and Glück). The pacifist poet has to set himself against the public values of his society (see Jeffers). The woman poet has to examine the clichés of women's advancement. In these cases, when the poet cannot count on the agreement of the reader, what sort of persuasive means does he or she employ?

Sometimes a poem which seems to express values admired by the poet's contemporaries can later be subject to question. Robert Frost was invited to read his sonnet "The Gift Outright" at the inauguration of President John F. Kennedy. What are the patriotic values expressed in the sonnet? How might they be viewed now by a Native American reader? How do you respond when you read both "with the grain" of the poem and also "against the grain"?

It is a useful exercise to read strongly moral poems from the poet's view and also from a different viewpoint. What might Lucasta have said back to the man going off to war; or Ben Jonson's addressee back to the poet; or an astronomer back to Whitman? Or how might the recipient of Elizabeth Barrett Browning's love-sonnet have felt? (Would you want to be loved "with the passion put to use" of abandoned religious belief?) What would a believer in original sin make of Ginsberg's "Sunflower Sutra," with its belief in original innocence?

Dove, though she opposes the slave-holding and slave-murdering Dominican dictator Rafael Trujillo, lets him speak and articulate his motives in order that her reader may get inside his mind. Though finally, in reading these poems, you may come to sympathize with the poet's view, it is useful to position yourself, at least temporarily, on both sides of the question being debated. That way you sharpen your sense of the attitudes being expressed, the values being contested, and the judgments being made. In Michael Weaver's "Picnic," the only mention of the oppositions aroused by the Civil Rights movement of the 1960s comes at the end, in the phrase "reluctant laws and bloodied heads." Can you expand this phrase to show the reasons for the joy of the picnickers?

John Milton
Lycidas

In this monody[1] the author bewails a learned friend, unfortunately drowned in his passage from Chester on the Irish seas, 1637. And by occasion foretells the ruin of our corrupted clergy, then in their height.

> Yet once more, O ye laurels, and once more
> Ye myrtles brown, with ivy never sere,
> I come to pluck your berries harsh and crude,
> And with forced fingers rude,
> Shatter your leaves before the mellowing year.
> Bitter constraint, and sad occasion dear,
> Compels me to disturb your season due;
> For Lycidas is dead, dead ere his prime,
> Young Lycidas, and hath not left his peer.

---

[1] A dirge sung by a single voice.

Who would not sing for Lycidas? He knew
Himself to sing, and build the lofty rhyme.
He must not float upon his watery bier
Unwept, and welter to the parching wind,
Without the meed of some melodious tear.
 Begin then, sisters of the sacred well°   *muses*
That from beneath the seat of Jove doth spring,
Begin, and somewhat loudly sweep the string.
Hence with denial vain, and coy excuse;
So may some gentle Muse°   *poet*
With lucky words favor my destined urn,
And as he passes turn,
And bid fair peace be to my sable shroud.
For we were nursed upon the selfsame hill,
Fed the same flock, by fountain, shade, and rill.
 Together both, ere the high lawns appeared
Under the opening eyelids of the morn,
We drove afield, and both together heard
What time the grayfly winds her sultry horn,
Battening our flocks with the fresh dews of night,
Oft till the star that rose at evening bright
Toward Heaven's descent had sloped his westering wheel.
Meanwhile the rural ditties were not mute,
Tempered to th' oaten flute,
Rough satyrs danced, and fauns with cloven heel
From the glad sound would not be absent long,
And old Damoetas² loved to hear our song.
 But O the heavy change, now thou art gone,
Now thou art gone, and never must return!
Thee, shepherd, thee the woods and desert caves,
With wild thyme and the gadding vine o'ergrown,
And all their echoes mourn.
The willows and the hazel copses green
Shall now no more be seen,
Fanning their joyous leaves to thy soft lays.
As killing as the canker° to the rose,   *cankerworm*
Or taint-worm to the weanling herds that graze,
Or frost to flowers that their gay wardrobe wear,

---

² A conventional name from pastoral poetry, possibly referring to a Cambridge tutor.

When first the white thorn blows;°   *blossoms*
Such, Lycidas, thy loss to shepherd's ear.
    Where were ye, nymphs, when the remorseless deep
Closed o'er the head of your loved Lycidas?
For neither were ye playing on the steep,
Where your old Bards, the famous Druids lie,
Nor on the shaggy top of Mona high,
Nor yet where Deva spreads her wizard stream:[3]
Ay me! I fondly dream —
Had ye been there — for what could that have done?
What could the Muse[4] herself that Orpheus bore,
The Muse herself, for her inchanting son
Whom universal Nature did lament,
When by the rout that made the hideous roar,
His gory visage down the stream was sent,
Down the swift Hebrus to the Lesbian shore?
    Alas! What boots° it with uncessant care   *profits*
To tend the homely slighted shepherd's trade,
And strictly meditate the thankless Muse?
Were it not better done as others use,
To sport with Amaryllis in the shade,
Or with the tangles of Neaera's hair?[5]
Fame is the spur that the clear spirit doth raise
(That last infirmity of noble mind)
To scorn delights, and live laborious days;
But the fair guerdon° when we hope to find,   *reward*
And think to burst out into sudden blaze,
Comes the blind Fury[6] with th' abhorrèd shears,
And slits the thin spun life. "But not the praise,"
Phoebus° replied, and touched my trembling   *Apollo, god of*
    ears;   *poetic inspiration*
"Fame is no plant that grows on mortal soil,
Nor in the glistering foil
Set off to th' world, nor in broad rumor lies,

---

[3] Mona is the Roman name for the Isle of Anglesey, off the Welsh coast. Deva is the river Dee, which flows into the Irish Sea. Its changes were said to foretell good or ill for England and Wales.

[4] Calliope, the muse of epic poetry. Her son, Orpheus, was slain by Thracian women, and his head cast into the river Hebrus.

[5] Amaryllis and Neaera: conventional names for shepherdesses.

[6] Atropos, not one of the Furies, but the Fate who cuts the thread of life.

But lives and spreads aloft by those pure eyes,
And perfect witness of all-judging Jove;
As he pronounces lastly on each deed,
Of so much fame in Heaven expect thy meed."
    O fountain Arethuse,[7] and thou honored flood,
Smooth-sliding Mincius crowned with vocal reeds,
That strain I heard was of a higher mood.
But now my oat° proceeds,   *oaten-pipe song*
And listens to the herald of the sea°   *Triton*
That came in Neptune's plea.
He asked the waves, and asked the felon winds,
"What hard mishap hath doomed this gentle swain?"
And questioned every gust of rugged wings
That blows from off each beakèd promontory;
They knew not of his story,
And sage Hippotades° their answer brings,   *god of winds*
That not a blast was from his dungeon strayed,
The air was calm, and on the level brine,
Sleek Panope° with all her sisters played.   *sea nymph*
It was that fatal and perfidious bark
Built in th' eclipse, and rigged with curses dark,
That sunk so low that sacred head of thine.
    Next Camus,[8] reverend sire, went footing slow,
His mantle hairy, and his bonnet sedge,
Inwrought with figures dim, and on the edge
Like to that sanguine flower inscribed with woe.[9]
"Ah! who hath reft," quoth he, "my dearest pledge?"
Last came and last did go
The pilot of the Galilean lake,°   *Saint Peter*
Two massy keys he bore of metals twain
(The golden opes, the iron shuts amain).
He shook his mitered locks, and stern bespake:
"How well could I have spared for thee, young swain,
Enow of such as for their bellies' sake,
Creep and intrude, and climb into the fold!
Of other care they little reckoning make,
Than how to scramble at the shearers' feast,

---

[7] Arethusa was a nymph pursued by Alpheus. She fled under the sea to Sicily, where she came up as a fountain.

[8] God of the river Cam, representing Cambridge University.

[9] The hyacinth, supposedly marked with the Greek cry of lamentation, "aiai."

And shove away the worthy bidden guest.
Blind mouths! That scarce themselves know how to hold
A sheep-hook, or have learned aught else the least
That to the faithful herdsman's art belongs!
What recks it them? What need they? They are sped;
And when they list, their lean and flashy songs
Grate on their scrannel° pipes of wretched straw.   *meager*
The hungry sheep look up, and are not fed,
But swoln with wind, and the rank mist they draw,
Rot inwardly, and foul contagion spread,
Besides what the grim wolf with privy paw°   *Roman Catholic agents*
Daily devours apace, and nothing said.
But that two-handed engine at the door
Stands ready to smite once, and smite no more."[10]
    Return, Alpheus,° the dread voice is past,   *(see note 6)*
That shrunk thy streams; return, Sicilian muse,
And call the vales, and bid them hither cast
Their bells and flowerets of a thousand hues.
Ye valleys low where the mild whispers use,
Of shades and wanton winds, and gushing brooks,
On whose fresh lap the swart star[11] sparely looks,
Throw hither all your quaint enameled eyes,
That on the green turf suck the honeyed showers,
And purple all the ground with vernal flowers.
Bring the rathe° primrose that forsaken dies,   *early*
The tufted crow-toe, and pale jessamine,
The white pink, and the pansy freaked° with jet,   *dappled*
The glowing violet,
The musk-rose, and the well attired woodbine.
With cowslips wan that hang the pensive head,
And every flower that sad embroidery wears:
Bid amaranthus all his beauty shed,
And daffadillies fill their cups with tears,
To strew the laureate hearse where Lycid lies.
For so to interpose a little ease,
Let our frail thoughts dally with false surmise.
Ay me! Whilst thee the shores and sounding seas
Wash far away, where'er thy bones are hurled,

---

[10] Milton has in mind some instrument of retribution which will punish the corrupt clergy.

[11] Sirius, the Dog Star, associated with the hot days of late summer.

Whether beyond the stormy Hebrides,
Where thou perhaps under the whelming tide
Visit'st the bottom of the monstrous world;
Or whether thou, to our moist vows denied,
Sleep'st by the fable of Bellerus old,
Where the great vision of the guarded mount
Looks toward Namancos and Bayona's hold;[12]
Look homeward angel now, and melt with ruth:
And, O ye dolphins, waft the hapless youth.
    Weep no more, woeful shepherds, weep no more,
For Lycidas your sorrow is not dead,
Sunk though he be beneath the watery floor,
So sinks the day-star° in the ocean bed,   *sun*
And yet anon repairs his drooping head,
And tricks° his beams, and with new-spangled ore,   *dresses*
Flames in the forehead of the morning sky:
So Lycidas sunk low, but mounted high,
Through the dear might of him that walked the waves,
Where other groves, and other streams along,
With nectar pure his oozy locks he laves,
And hears the unexpressive° nuptial song,   *inexpressible*
In the blest kingdoms meek of joy and love.
There entertain him all the saints above,
In solemn troops and sweet societies
That sing, and singing in their glory move,
And wipe the tears forever from his eyes.
Now, Lycidas, the shepherds weep no more;
Henceforth thou art the genius° of the shore,   *protective deity*
In thy large recompense, and shalt be good
To all that wander in that perilous flood.
    Thus sang the uncouth swain to th' oaks and rills,
While the still morn went out with sandals gray;
He touched the tender stops of various quills,
With eager thought warbling his Doric° lay: *rustic*
And now the sun had stretched out all the hills,
And now was dropped into the western bay;
At last he rose, and twitched his mantle blue:
Tomorrow to fresh woods, and pastures new.

---

[12] Bellerus is a giant said to be buried at Land's End in Cornwall. St. Michael's Mount is also in Cornwall. The angel looks toward Namancos and Bayona on the Spanish coast.

BEN JONSON
Still to Be Neat

Still to be neat, still to be dressed,
As you were going to a feast;
Still to be powdered, still perfumed;
Lady, it is to be presumed,
Though art's hid causes are not found,
All is not sweet, all is not sound.

Give me a look, give me a face
That makes simplicity a grace;
Robes loosely flowing, hair as free;
Such sweet neglect more taketh me
Then all th' adulteries of art.
They strike mine eyes, but not my heart.

RICHARD LOVELACE
To Lucasta, Going to the Wars

Tell me not, sweet, I am unkind
That from the nunnery
Of thy chaste breast and quiet mind,
To war and arms I fly.

True, a new mistress now I chase,
The first foe in the field;
And with a stronger faith embrace
A sword, a horse, a shield.

Yet this inconstancy is such
As you too shall adore;
I could not love thee, dear, so much,
Loved I not honor more.

ELIZABETH BARRETT BROWNING
How Do I Love Thee?

How do I love thee? Let me count the ways.
I love thee to the depth and breadth and height
My soul can reach, when feeling out of sight
For the ends of Being and ideal Grace.
I love thee to the level of everyday's
Most quiet need, by sun and candle-light.

I love thee freely, as men strive for Right;
I love thee purely, as they turn from Praise.
I love thee with the passion put to use
In my old griefs, and with my childhood's faith.
I love thee with a love I seemed to lose
With my lost saints — I love thee with the breath,
Smiles, tears, of all my life! — and, if God choose,
I shall but love thee better after death.

WALT WHITMAN
When I Heard the Learn'd Astronomer

When I heard the learn'd astronomer,
When the proofs, the figures, were ranged in columns before me,
When I was shown the charts and diagrams, to add, divide, and
      measure them,
When I sitting heard the astronomer where he lectured with much
      applause in the lecture-room,
How soon unaccountable I became tired and sick,
Till rising and gliding out I wander'd off by myself,
In the mystical moist night-air, and from time to time,
Look'd up in perfect silence at the stars.

WILLIAM BUTLER YEATS
Meru[1]

Civilisation is hooped together, brought
Under a rule, under the semblance of peace
By manifold illusion; but man's life is thought,
And he, despite his terror, cannot cease
Ravening through century after century,
Ravening, raging, and uprooting that he may come
Into the desolation of reality:
Egypt and Greece, good-bye, and good-bye, Rome!
Hermits upon Mount Meru or Everest,
Caverned in night under the drifted snow,
Or where that snow and winter's dreadful blast

---

[1] In Hindu mythology, Meru is a sacred mountain at the center of the world. It
is the home of Vishnu, the god who preserves humanity.

Beat down upon their naked bodies, know
That day brings round the night, that before dawn
His glory and his monuments are gone.

ROBINSON JEFFERS
Shine, Perishing Republic

While this America settles in the mould of its vulgarity, heavily
    thickening to empire,
And protest, only a bubble in the molten mass, pops and sighs out,
    and the mass hardens,

I sadly smiling remember that the flower fades to make fruit, the
    fruit rots to make earth.
Out of the mother; and through the spring exultances, ripeness and
    decadence; and home to the mother.

You making haste haste on decay: not blameworthy; life is good,
    be it stubbornly long or suddenly
A mortal splendor: meteors are not needed less than mountains:
    shine, perishing republic.

But for my children, I would have them keep their distance from
    the thickening center; corruption
Never has been compulsory, when the cities lie at the monster's
    feet there are left the mountains.

And boys, be in nothing so moderate as in love of man, a clever
    servant, insufferable master.
There is the trap that catches noblest spirits, that caught — they
    say — God, when he walked on earth.

ROBERT FROST
The Gift Outright

The land was ours before we were the land's.
She was our land more than a hundred years
Before we were her people. She was ours
In Massachusetts, in Virginia,
But we were England's, still colonials,
Possessing what we still were unpossessed by,
Possessed by what we now no more possessed.
Something we were withholding made us weak

Until we found it was ourselves
We were withholding from our land of living,
And forthwith found salvation in surrender.
Such as we were we gave ourselves outright
(The deed of gift was many deeds of war)
To the land vaguely realizing westward,
But still unstoried, artless, unenhanced,
Such as she was, such as she would become.

ALLEN GINSBERG
Sunflower Sutra[1]

I walked on the banks of the tincan banana dock and sat down
under the huge shade of a Southern Pacific locomotive to
look at the sunset over the box house hills and cry.
Jack Kerouac[2] sat beside me on a busted rusty iron pole, compan-
ion, we thought the same thoughts of the soul, bleak and blue
and sad-eyed, surrounded by the gnarled steel roots of trees of
machinery.
The oily water on the river mirrored the red sky, sun sank on top
of final Frisco peaks, no fish in that stream, no hermit in those
mounts, just ourselves rheumy-eyed and hungover like old
bums on the riverbank, tired and wily.
Look at the Sunflower, he said, there was a dead gray shadow
against the sky, big as a man, sitting dry on top of a pile of
ancient sawdust —
— I rushed up enchanted — it was my first sunflower, memories
of Blake[3] — my visions — Harlem
and Hells of the Eastern rivers, bridges, clanking Joes Greasy Sand-
wiches, dead baby carriages, black treadless tires forgotten
and unretreaded, the poem of the riverbank, condoms &
pots, steel knives, nothing stainless, only the dank muck and
the razor sharp artifacts passing into the past —
and the gray Sunflower poised against the sunset, crackly bleak and
dusty with the smut and smog and smoke of olden locomo-
tives in its eye —

---

[1] Buddhist religious text.
[2] Jack Kerouac (1922–1969), friend of Ginsberg's and author of *On the Road* and other autobiographical novels.
[3] William Blake (1757–1827), English poet and author of "Ah! Sun-flower." Ginsberg in 1948 had had a vision in which he heard Blake's voice reciting his poems.

corolla of bleary spikes pushed down and broken like a battered
  crown, seeds fallen out of its face, soon-to-be-toothless
  mouth of sunny air, sunrays obliterated on its hairy head like
  a dried wire spiderweb,

leaves stuck out like arms out of the stem, gestures from the saw-
  dust root, broke pieces of plaster fallen out of the black twigs,
  a dead fly in its ear,

Unholy battered old thing you were, my sunflower O my soul, I
  loved you then!

The grime was no man's grime but death and human locomotives,

all that dress of dust, that veil of darkened railroad skin, that smog
  of cheek, that eyelid of black mis'ry, that sooty hand or
  phallus or protuberance of artificial worse-than-dirt —
  industrial — modern — all that civilization spotting your
  crazy golden crown —

and those blear thoughts of death and dusty loveless eyes and ends
  and withered roots below, in the home-pile of sand and
  sawdust, rubber dollar bills, skin of machinery, the guts and
  innards of the weeping coughing car, the empty lonely tin-
  cans with their rusty tongues alack, what more could I name,
  the smoked ashes of some cock cigar, the cunts of wheelbar-
  rows and the milky breasts of cars, wornout asses out of chairs
  & sphincters of dynamos — all these

entangled in your mummied roots — and you there standing be-
  fore me in the sunset, all your glory in your form!

A perfect beauty of a sunflower! a perfect excellent lovely sun-
  flower existence! a sweet natural eye to the new hip moon,
  woke up alive and excited grasping in the sunset shadow
  sunrise golden monthly breeze!

How many flies buzzed round you innocent of your grime, while
  you cursed the heavens of the railroad and your flower soul?

Poor dead flower? when did you forget you were a flower? when
  did you look at your skin and decide you were an impotent
  dirty old locomotive? the ghost of a locomotive? the specter
  and shade of a once powerful mad American locomotive?

You were never no locomotive, Sunflower, you were a sunflower!

And you Locomotive, you are a locomotive, forget me not!

So I grabbed up the skeleton thick sunflower and stuck it at my
  side like a scepter,

and deliver my sermon to my soul, and Jack's soul too, and anyone
  who'll listen,

— We're not our skin of grime, we're not our dread bleak dusty imageless locomotive, we're all beautiful golden sunflowers inside, we're blessed by our own seed & golden hairy naked accomplishment-bodies growing into mad black formal sunflowers in the sunset, spied on by our eyes under the shadow of the mad locomotive riverbank sunset Frisco hilly tincan evening sitdown vision.

LOUISE GLÜCK
Mock Orange

It is not the moon, I tell you.
It is these flowers
lighting the yard.

I hate them.
I hate them as I hate sex,
the man's mouth
sealing my mouth, the man's
paralyzing body —

and the cry that always escapes,
the low, humiliating
premise of union —

In my mind tonight
I hear the question and pursuing answer
fused in one sound
that mounts and mounts and then
is split into the old selves,
the tired antagonisms. Do you see?
We were made fools of.
And the scent of mock orange
drifts through the window.

How can I rest?
How can I be content
when there is still
that odor in the world?

RITA DOVE
Parsley[1]

1.   The Cane Fields

There is a parrot imitating spring
in the palace, its feathers parsley green.
Out of the swamp the cane appears

to haunt us, and we cut it down. El General
searches for a word; he is all the world
there is. Like a parrot imitating spring,

we lie down screaming as rain punches through
and we come up green. We cannot speak an R —
out of the swamp, the cane appears

and then the mountain we call in whispers *Katalina.*[2]
The children gnaw their teeth to arrowheads.
There is a parrot imitating spring.

El General has found his word: *perejil.*
Who says it, lives. He laughs, teeth shining
out of the swamp. The cane appears

in our dreams, lashed by wind and streaming.
And we lie down. For every drop of blood
there is a parrot imitating spring.
Out of the swamp the cane appears.

2.   The Palace

The word the general's chosen is parsley.
It is fall, when thoughts turn
to love and death; the general thinks
of his mother, how she died in the fall
and he planted her walking cane at the grave
and it flowered, each spring stolidly forming
four-star blossoms. The general

pulls on his boots, he stomps to
her room in the palace, the one without
curtains, the one with a parrot

---

[1] Dove's note: "*Parsley:* On October 2, 1937, Rafael Trujillo (1891–1961), dictator of the Dominican Republic, ordered 20,000 blacks killed because they could not roll the letter *r* in *perejil,* the Spanish word for parsley."

[2] Properly "Katarina."

in a brass ring. As he paces he wonders
Who can I kill today. And for a moment
the little knot of screams
is still. The parrot, who has traveled

all the way from Australia in an ivory
cage, is, coy as a widow, practising
spring. Ever since the morning
his mother collapsed in the kitchen
while baking skull-shaped candies
for the Day of the Dead,[3] the general
has hated sweets. He orders pastries
brought up for the bird; they arrive

dusted with sugar on a bed of lace.
The knot in his throat starts to twitch;
he sees his boots the first day in battle
splashed with mud and urine
as a soldier falls at his feet amazed —
how stupid he looked! — at the sound
of artillery. *I never thought it would sing*
the soldier said, and died. Now

the general sees the fields of sugar
cane, lashed by rain and streaming.
He sees his mother's smile, the teeth
gnawed to arrowheads. He hears
the Haitians sing without R's
as they swing the great machetes:
Katalina, they sing, *Katalina,*

mi madle, mi amol en muelte.[4] God knows
his mother was no stupid woman; she
could roll an R like a queen. Even
a parrot can roll an R! In the bare room
the bright feathers arch in a parody
of greenery, as the last pale crumbs
disappear under the blackened tongue. Someone

---

[3] November 1, the Feast of All Souls.

[4] "My mother, my love in death." In the Spanish, the *r*'s have been changed to *l*'s to simulate the Haitians' inability to roll their *r*'s.

calls out his name in a voice
so like his mother's, a startled tear
splashes the tip of his right boot.
My mother, my love in death.
The general remembers the tiny green sprigs
men of his village wore in their capes
to honor the birth of a son. He will
order many, this time, to be killed

for a single, beautiful word.

MICHAEL S. WEAVER
The Picnic, an Homage to Civil Rights

We spread torn quilts and blankets,
mashing the grass under us until it was hard,
piled the baskets of steamed crabs
by the trees in columns that hid the trunk,
put our water coolers of soda pop
on the edges to mark the encampment,
like gypsies settling in for revelry
in a forest in Rumania or pioneers
blazing through the land of the Sioux,
the Apache, and the Arapaho, looking guardedly
over our perimeters for poachers
or the curious noses of fat women
ambling past on the backs of their shoes.
The sun crashed through the trees,
tumbling down and splattering in shadows
on the baseball diamond like mashed bananas.
We hunted for wild animals in the clumps
of forests, fried hot dogs until the odor
turned solid in our nostrils like wood.
We were in the park.

One uncle talked incessantly, because he knew
the universe; another was the griot[1]
who stomped his foot in syncopation
to call the details from the base of his mind;

---

[1] African tribal storyteller.

another was a cynic who doubted everything,
toasting everyone around with gin.
The patriarchal council mumbled on,
while the women took the evening to tune
their hearts to the slow air and buzzing flies,
to hold their hands out so angels could stand
in their palms and give dispensation,
as we played a rough game of softball
in the diamond with borrowed gloves,
singing Chuck Berry and Chubby Checker,
diving in long lines into the public pool,
throwing empty peanut shells to the lion,
buying cotton candy in the aviary
of the old mansion, laughing at monkeys,
running open-mouthed and full in the heat
until our smell was pungent and natural,
while the sun made our fathers and uncles
fall down in naps on their wives' laps, and
we frolicked like wealthy children on an English estate,
as reluctant laws and bloodied heads
tacked God's theses on wooden doors,[2]
guaranteed the canopy of the firmament above us.

---

[2] tacked . . . theses: As did Martin Luther, beginning the Protestant Reformation.

II

ANTHOLOGY

ELIZABETH ALEXANDER

Ode

The sky was a street map with stars for
house parties, where blue-lit basements
were fever-dreams of the closest a boy
could get to home after yucca fritters,
rice, pigeon peas, and infinite chicken
made by anyone's mother before the night's
charioteer arrived in his beat-up boat
to spirit the three, or the four, or the five, or
as many would fit in the car to the party.
Pennies and pennies bought one red bottle
of Mad Dog Double-Twenty or Boone's Farm.
"Que pasa, y'all, que pasa," Mister James
Brown sweated, and the Chi-Lites whispered pink.
White Catholic school girls never would dance
or grind or neck or lift their skirts to these
black boys with mothers who spoke little
English and guarded their young with candles
for *los santos,* housework, triple-locked
doors, jars of tinted water, fierce arm-pinches.
Love is a platter of *plátanos.*°   *plantains*
"Did you hear? Did you hear?" — the young men whisper,
but church calls its altar boys Sunday noon —
"They danced Latin at the Mocambo Room!"
The tale has been told again and again
of boys growing old, going bad, making good,
leaving home while the neighborhood rises
or falls, and this story ends the same.
Now dreadlocked vendors sell mechanized monkeys
programmed to beat *guaguanco.*°   *Latin-American music*

SHERMAN ALEXIE

Reservation Love Song

I can meet you
in Springdale buy you beer
& take you home
in my one-eyed Ford

I can pay your rent
on HUD house get you free
food from the BIA
get your teeth fixed at IHS

I can buy you alcohol
& not drink it all
while you're away I won't fuck
any of your cousins

if I don't get too drunk
I can bring old blankets
to sleep with in winter
they smell like grandmother

hands digging up roots
they have powerful magic
we can sleep good
we can sleep warm

PAULA GUNN ALLEN
Zen Americana

Un is okay.
Un pretentious. Un decided. Un known.
Un ego is where I want to be. How do you open
the door to Un? What does the un place look like,
look alikes?

Un beginning; can I un wake myself, un sleep
motionless in a bright green chair?
Maybe un lamps light the room (the un place).
When I get there, maybe it will be dark, un lit
where it has no occasion to be any way.

(Un celebrated.)
(Un repentant.)
(Un regenerate.)
(Un believed.)

A. R. AMMONS
The City Limits

When you consider the radiance, that it does not withhold
itself but pours its abundance without selection into every
nook and cranny not overhung or hidden; when you consider

that birds' bones make no awful noise against the light but
lie low in the light as in a high testimony; when you consider
the radiance, that it will look into the guiltiest

swervings of the weaving heart and bear itself upon them,
not flinching into disguise or darkening; when you consider
the abundance of such resource as illuminates the glow-blue

bodies and gold-skeined wings of flies swarming the dumped
guts of a natural slaughter or the coil of shit and in no
way winces from its storms of generosity; when you consider

that air or vacuum, snow or shale, squid or wolf, rose or lichen,
each is accepted into as much light as it will take, then
the heart moves roomier, the man stands and looks about, the

leaf does not increase itself above the grass, and the dark
work of the deepest cells is of a tune with May bushes
and fear lit by the breadth of such calmly turns to praise.

Easter Morning

I have a life that did not become,
that turned aside and stopped,
astonished:
I hold it in me like a pregnancy or
as on my lap a child
not to grow or grow old but dwell on

it is to his grave I most
frequently return and return
to ask what is wrong, what was
wrong, to see it all by
the light of a different necessity
but the grave will not heal
and the child,
stirring, must share my grave
with me, an old man having
gotten by on what was left

when I go back to my home country in these
fresh far-away days, it's convenient to visit
everybody, aunts and uncles, those who used to say,
look how he's shooting up, and the
trinket aunts who always had a little
something in their pocketbooks, cinnamon bark
or a penny or nickel, and uncles who
were the rumored fathers of cousins
who whispered of them as of great, if
troubled, presences, and school
teachers, just about everybody older
(and some younger) collected in one place
waiting, particularly, but not for
me, mother and father there, too, and others
close, close as burrowing
under skin, all in the graveyard
assembled, done for, the world they
used to wield, have trouble and joy
in, gone

the child in me that could not become
was not ready for others to go,
to go on into change, blessings and
horrors, but stands there by the road
where the mishap occurred, crying out for
help, come and fix this or we
can't get by, but the great ones who
were to return, they could not or did
not hear and went on in a flurry and
now, I say in the graveyard, here
lies the flurry, now it can't come
back with help or helpful asides, now
we all buy the bitter
incompletions, pick up the knots of
horror, silently raving, and go on
crashing into empty ends not
completions, not rondures the fullness
has come into and spent itself from
I stand on the stump
of a child, whether myself
or my little brother who died, and
yell as far as I can, I cannot leave this place, for
for me it is the dearest and the worst,

it is life nearest to life which is
life lost: it is my place where
I must stand and fail,
calling attention with tears
to the branches not lofting
boughs into space, to the barren
air that holds the world that was my world

though the incompletions
(& completions) burn out
standing in the flash high-burn
momentary structure of ash, still it
is a picture-book, letter-perfect
Easter morning: I have been for a
walk: the wind is tranquil: the brook
works without flashing in an abundant
tranquility: the birds are lively with
voice: I saw something I had
never seen before: two great birds,
maybe eagles, blackwinged, whitenecked
and -headed, came from the south oaring
the great wings steadily; they went
directly over me, high up, and kept on
due north: but then one bird,
the one behind, veered a little to the
left and the other bird kept on seeming
not to notice for a minute: the first
began to circle as if looking for
something, coasting, resting its wings
on the down side of some of the circles:
the other bird came back and they both
circled, looking perhaps for a draft;
they turned a few more times, possibly
rising — at least, clearly resting —
then flew on falling into distance till
they broke across the local bush and
trees: it was a sight of bountiful
majesty and integrity: the having
patterns and routes, breaking
from them to explore other patterns or
better ways to routes, and then the
return: a dance sacred as the sap in
the trees, permanent in its descriptions

as the ripples round the brook's
ripplestone: fresh as this particular
flood of burn breaking across us now
from the sun.

ANONYMOUS
Sir Patrick Spens

1

The king sits in Dumferling town,
    Drinking the blude-reid° wine: *blood-red*
"O whar will I get guid sailor,
    To sail this ship of mine?"

2

Up and spak an eldern knicht,
    Sat at the king's richt knee:
"Sir Patrick Spens is the best sailor
    That sails upon the sea."

3

The king has written a braid° letter   *broad*
    And signed it wi' his hand,
And sent it to Sir Patrick Spens,
    Was walking on the sand.

4

The first line that Sir Patrick read,
    A loud lauch° lauchèd he;   *laugh*
The next line that Sir Patrick read,
    The tear blinded his ee.°   *eye*

5

"O wha is this has done this deed,
    This ill deed done to me,
To send me out this time o' the year,
    To sail upon the sea?

6

"Mak haste, mak haste, my mirry men all,
    Our guid ship sails the morn."
"O say na sae,° my master dear,   *so*
    For I fear a deadly storm.

7

"Late, late yestre'en I saw the new moon
    Wi' the auld moon in hir arm,
And I fear, I fear, my dear master,
    That we will come to harm."

8

O our Scots nobles were richt laith°   *loath*
    To weet° their cork-heeled shoon,°   *wet / shoes*
But lang or° a' the play were played   *before*
    Their hats they swam aboon.°   *above*

9

O lang, lang may their ladies sit,
    Wi' their fans into their hand,
Or ere they see Sir Patrick Spens
    Come sailing to the land.

10

O lang, lang may the ladies stand
    Wi' their gold kems° in their hair,   *combs*
Waiting for their ain dear lords,
    For they'll see them na mair.

11

Half o'er, half o'er to Aberdour
    It's fifty fadom deep,
And there lies guid Sir Patrick Spens
    Wi' the Scots lords at his feet.

ANONYMOUS
Western Wind

Western wind, when will thou blow,
    The small rain down can rain?
Christ, if my love were in my arms
    And I in my bed again!

MATTHEW ARNOLD
Shakespeare

Others abide our question. Thou art free.
We ask and ask — thou smilest and art still,

Out-topping knowledge. For the loftiest hill,
Who to the stars uncrowns his majesty,

Planting his stedfast footsteps in the sea,
Making the heaven of heavens his dwelling-place,
Spares but the cloudy border of his base
To the foiled searching of mortality;

And thou, who didst the stars and sunbeams know,
Self-schooled, self-scanned, self-honored, self-secure,
Didst tread on earth unguessed at — better so!

All pains the immortal spirit must endure,
All weakness which impairs, all griefs which bow,
Find their sole speech in that victorious brow.

To Marguerite

Yes! in the sea of life enisled,
With echoing straits between us thrown,
Dotting the shoreless watery wild,
We mortal millions live *alone*.
The islands feel the enclasping flow,
And then their endless bounds they know.

But when the moon their hollows lights,
And they are swept by balms of spring,
And in their glens, on starry nights,
The nightingales divinely sing;
And lovely notes, from shore to shore,
Across the sounds and channels pour —

Oh! then a longing like despair
Is to their farthest caverns sent;
For surely once, they feel, we were
Parts of a single continent!
Now round us spreads the watery plain —
Oh might our marges meet again!

Who ordered, that their longing's fire
Should be, as soon as kindled, cooled?
Who renders vain their deep desire? —
A God, a God their severance ruled!
And bade betwixt their shores to be
The unplumbed, salt, estranging sea.

JOHN ASHBERY
The Painter

Sitting between the sea and the buildings
He enjoyed painting the sea's portrait.
But just as children imagine a prayer
Is merely silence, he expected his subject
To rush up the sand, and, seizing a brush,
Plaster its own portrait on the canvas.

So there was never any paint on his canvas
Until the people who lived in the buildings
Put him to work: "Try using the brush
As a means to an end. Select, for a portrait,
Something less angry and large, and more subject
To a painter's moods, or, perhaps, to a prayer."

How could he explain to them his prayer
That nature, not art, might usurp the canvas?
He chose his wife for a new subject,
Making her vast, like ruined buildings,
As if, forgetting itself, the portrait
Had expressed itself without a brush.

Slightly encouraged, he dipped his brush
In the sea, murmuring a heartfelt prayer:
"My soul, when I paint this next portrait
Let it be you who wrecks the canvas."
The news spread like wildfire through the buildings:
He had gone back to the sea for his subject.

Imagine a painter crucified by his subject!
Too exhausted even to lift his brush,
He provoked some artists leaning from the buildings
To malicious mirth: "We haven't a prayer
Now, of putting ourselves on canvas,
Or getting the sea to sit for a portrait!"

Others declared it a self-portrait.
Finally all indications of a subject
Began to fade, leaving the canvas
Perfectly white. He put down the brush.
At once a howl, that was also a prayer,
Arose from the overcrowded buildings.

They tossed him, the portrait, from the tallest of the buildings;
And the sea devoured the canvas and the brush
As though his subject had decided to remain a prayer.

Paradoxes and Oxymorons

This poem is concerned with language on a very plain level.
Look at it talking to you. You look out a window
Or pretend to fidget. You have it but you don't have it.
You miss it, it misses you. You miss each other.

The poem is sad because it wants to be yours, and cannot.
What's a plain level? It is that and other things,
Bringing a system of them into play. Play?
Well, actually, yes, but I consider play to be

A deeper outside thing, a dreamed role-pattern,
As in the division of grace these long August days
Without proof. Open-ended. And before you know
It gets lost in the steam and chatter of typewriters.

It has been played once more. I think you exist only
To tease me into doing it, on your level, and then you aren't there
Or have adopted a different attitude. And the poem
Has set me softly down beside you. The poem is you.

Street Musicians

One died, and the soul was wrenched out
Of the other in life, who, walking the streets
Wrapped in an identity like a coat, sees on and on
The same corners, volumetrics, shadows
Under trees. Farther than anyone was ever
Called, through increasingly suburban airs
And ways, with autumn falling over everything:
The plush leaves the chattels in barrels
Of an obscure family being evicted
Into the way it was, and is. The other beached
Glimpses of what the other was up to:
Revelations at last. So they grew to hate and forget each other.

So I cradle this average violin that knows
Only forgotten showtunes, but argues
The possibility of free declamation anchored
To a dull refrain, the year turning over on itself

In November, with the spaces among the days
More literal, the meat more visible on the bone.
Our question of a place of origin hangs
Like smoke: how we picnicked in pine forests,
In coves with the water always seeping up, and left
Our trash, sperm and excrement everywhere, smeared
On the landscape, to make of us what we could.

W. H. AUDEN

As I Walked Out One Evening

As I walked out one evening,
    Walking down Bristol Street,
The crowds upon the pavement
    Were fields of harvest wheat.

And down by the brimming river
    I heard a lover sing
Under an arch of the railway:
    "Love has no ending.

"I'll love you, dear, I'll love you
    Till China and Africa meet,
And the river jumps over the mountain
    And the salmon sing in the street,

"I'll love you till the ocean
    Is folded and hung up to dry
And the seven stars go squawking
    Like geese about the sky.

"The years shall run like rabbits,
    For in my arms I hold
The Flower of the Ages,
    And the first love of the world."

But all the clocks in the city
    Began to whirr and chime:
"O let not Time deceive you,
    You cannot conquer Time.

"In the burrows of the Nightmare
    Where Justice naked is,
Time watches from the shadow
    And coughs when you would kiss.

"In headaches and in worry
    Vaguely life leaks away,
And Time will have his fancy
    Tomorrow or today.

"Into many a green valley
    Drifts the appalling snow;
Time breaks the threaded dances
    And the diver's brilliant bow.

"O plunge your hands in water,
    Plunge them in up to the wrist;
Stare, stare in the basin
    And wonder what you've missed.

"The glacier knocks in the cupboard,
    The desert sighs in the bed,
And the crack in the teacup opens
    A lane to the land of the dead.

"Where the beggars raffle the banknotes
    And the Giant is enchanting to Jack,
And the Lily-white Boy is a Roarer,
    And Jill goes down on her back.

"O look, look in the mirror,
    O look in your distress;
Life remains a blessing
    Although you cannot bless.

"O stand, stand at the window
    As the tears scald and start;
You shall love your crooked neighbor
    With your crooked heart."

It was late, late in the evening,
    The lovers they were gone;
The clocks had ceased their chiming,
    And the deep river ran on.

Musée des Beaux Arts[1]

About suffering they were never wrong,
The Old Masters: how well they understood

---

[1] French for "Museum of Fine Arts."

Its human position; how it takes place
While someone else is eating or opening a window or just walking
  dully along;
How, when the aged are reverently, passionately waiting
For the miraculous birth, there always must be
Children who did not specially want it to happen, skating
On a pond at the edge of the wood:
They never forgot
That even the dreadful martyrdom must run its course
Anyhow in a corner, some untidy spot
Where the dogs go on with their doggy life and the torturer's horse
Scratches its innocent behind on a tree.

In Brueghel's *Icarus,* for instance: how everything turns away
Quite leisurely from the disaster; the ploughman may
Have heard the splash, the forsaken cry,
But for him it was not an important failure; the sun shone
As it had to on the white legs disappearing into the green
Water; and the expensive delicate ship that must have seen
Something amazing, a boy falling out of the sky,
Had somewhere to get to and sailed calmly on.

JOHN BERRYMAN
Dream Song 4

Filling her compact & delicious body
with chicken páprika, she glanced at me
twice.
Fainting with interest, I hungered back
and only the fact of her husband & four other people
kept me from springing on her

or falling at her little feet and crying
"You are the hottest one for years of night
Henry's dazed eyes
have enjoyed, Brilliance." I advanced upon
(despairing) my spumoni. — Sir Bones: is stuffed,
de world, wif feeding girls.

— Black hair, complexion Latin, jeweled eyes
downcast . . . The slob beside her feasts . . . What wonders is
she sitting on, over there?
The restaurant buzzes. She might as well be on Mars.

Where did it all go wrong? There ought to be a law against Henry.
— Mr. Bones: there is.

Dream Song 45

He stared at ruin. Ruin stared straight back.
He thought they was old friends. He felt on the stair
where her papa found them bare
they became familiar. When the papers were lost
rich with pals' secrets, he thought he had the knack
of ruin. Their paths crossed

and once they crossed in jail; they crossed in bed;
and over an unsigned letter their eyes met,
and in an Asian city
directionless & lurchy at two & three,
or trembling to a telephone's fresh threat,
and when some wired his head

to reach a wrong opinion, 'Epileptic'.
But he noted now that: they were not old friends.
He did not know this one.   ·
This one was a stranger, come to make amends
for all the imposters, and to make it stick.
Henry nodded, un-.

Dream Song 384

The marker slants, flowerless, day's almost done,
I stand above my father's grave with rage,
often, often before
I've made this awful pilgrimage to one
who cannot visit me, who tore his page
out: I come back for more,

I spit upon this dreadful banker's grave
who shot his heart out in a Florida dawn
O ho alas alas
When will indifference come, I moan & rave
I'd like to scrabble till I got right down
away down under the grass

and ax the casket open ha to see
just how he's taking it, which he sought so hard
we'll tear apart

the mouldering grave clothes ha & then Henry
will heft the ax once more, his final card,
and fell it on the start.

FRANK BIDART
Ellen West

I love sweets, —
                    heaven
would be dying on a bed of vanilla ice cream . . .

But my true self
is thin, all profile

and effortless gestures, the sort of blond
elegant girl whose
                    body is the image of her soul.

— My doctors tell me I must give up
this ideal;
            but I
WILL NOT . . . cannot.

Only to my husband I'm not simply a "case."

But he is a fool. He married
meat, and thought it was a wife.

                •   •   •

Why am I a girl?

I ask my doctors, and they tell me they
don't know, that it is just "given."

But it has such
implications — ;
                    and sometimes,
I even feel like a girl.

                •   •   •

Now, at the beginning of Ellen's thirty-second year, her physical
condition has deteriorated still further. Her use of laxatives in-
creases beyond measure. Every evening she takes sixty to seventy
tablets of a laxative, with the result that she suffers tortured vom-
iting at night and violent diarrhea by day, often accompanied by a

weakness of the heart. She has thinned down to a skeleton, and
weighs only 92 pounds.

•   •   •

About five years ago, I was in a restaurant,
eating alone
        with a book. I was
not married, and often did that . . .

— I'd turn down
dinner invitations, so I could eat alone;

I'd allow myself two pieces of bread, with
butter, at the beginning, and three scoops of
vanilla ice cream, at the end, —

                sitting there alone
with a book, both in the book
and out of it, waited on, idly
watching people, —

        when an attractive young man
and woman, both elegantly dressed,
sat next to me.
        She was beautiful — ;

with sharp, clear features, a good
bone structure — ;
        if she took her make-up off
in front of you, rubbing cold cream
again and again across her skin, she still would be
beautiful —
      more beautiful.

And he, —
        I couldn't remember when I had seen a man
so attractive. I didn't know why. He was almost

a male version
        of her, —

I had the sudden, mad notion that I
wanted to be his lover . . .

— Were they married?
            were *they* lovers?

They didn't wear wedding rings.

Their behavior was circumspect. They discussed
politics. They didn't touch . . .

— How could I discover?

                    Then, when the first course
arrived, I noticed the way

each held his fork out for the other

to taste what he had ordered . . .

                        They did this
again and again, with pleased looks, indulgent
smiles, for each course,

                more than once for *each* dish — ;
much too much for just friends . . .

— Their behavior somehow sickened me;

the way each *gladly*
put the *food* the other had offered *into his mouth* — ;

I knew what they were. I knew they slept together.

An immense depression came over me . . .

— I knew I could never
with such ease allow another to put food into my mouth:

happily *myself* put food into another's mouth — ;

I knew that to become a wife I would have to give up my ideal.

              •   •   •

Even as a child,
I saw that the "natural" process of aging

is for one's middle to thicken —
one's skin to blotch;

as happened to my mother.
And her mother.
                I loathed "Nature."

At twelve, pancakes
became the most terrible thought there is . . .

I shall *defeat* "Nature."

In the hospital, when they
weigh me, I wear weights secretly sewn into my belt.

•   •   •

January 16. The patient is allowed to eat in her room, but comes readily with her husband to afternoon coffee. Previously she had stoutly resisted this on the ground that she did not really eat but devoured like a wild animal. This she demonstrated with utmost realism. . . . Her physical examination showed nothing striking. Salivary glands are markedly enlarged on both sides.

January 21. Has been reading *Faust*[1] again. In her diary, writes that art is the "mutual permeation" of the "world of the body" and the "world of the spirit." Says that her own poems are "hospital poems . . . weak — without skill or perseverance; only managing to beat their wings softly."

February 8. Agitation, quickly subsided again. Has attached herself to an elegant, very thin female patient. Homo-erotic component strikingly evident.

February 15. Vexation, and torment. Says that her mind forces her always to think of eating. Feels herself degraded by this. Has entirely, for the first time in years, stopped writing poetry.

•   •   •

Callas[2] is my favorite singer, but I've only
seen her once — ;

I've never forgotten that night . . .

— It was in *Tosca*,[3] she had long before
lost weight, her voice
had been, for years,

                    deteriorating, half itself . . .

When her career began, of course, she was fat,

enormous — ; in the early photographs,
sometimes I almost don't recognize her . . .

The voice too then was enormous —

healthy; robust; subtle; but capable of
crude effects, even vulgar,

                    almost out of
high spirits, too much health . . .

---

[1] Work by Johann Wolfgang von Goethe (1749–1842) about the magician of German legend who enters into a compact with the devil.

[2] Maria Callas (1923–1977), Greek-American soprano.

[3] An opera by Giacomo Puccini (1858–1924).

But soon she felt that she must lose weight, —
that all she was trying to express

was obliterated by her body,
buried in flesh — ;
                  abruptly, within
four months, she lost at least sixty pounds . . .

— The gossip in Milan was that Callas
had swallowed a tapeworm.

But of course she hadn't.

                  The *tapeworm*
was her *soul* . . .

— How her soul, uncompromising,
insatiable,
              must have loved eating the flesh from her bones,

revealing this extraordinarily
mercurial; fragile; masterly creature . . .

— But irresistibly, nothing
stopped there; the huge voice

also began to change: at first, it simply diminished
in volume, in size,
                then the top notes became
shrill, unreliable — at last,
usually not there at all . . .

— No one knows *why*. Perhaps her mind,
ravenous, still insatiable, sensed

that to struggle with the *shreds* of a voice

must make her artistry subtler, more refined,
more capable of expressing humiliation,
rage, betrayal . . .

— Perhaps the opposite. Perhaps her spirit
loathed the unending struggle

to *embody* itself, to *manifest* itself, on a stage whose

mechanics, and suffocating customs,
seemed expressly designed to annihilate spirit . . .

— I know that in *Tosca*, in the second act,
when, humiliated, hounded by Scarpia,

she sang *Vissi d'arte*

        — "I lived for art" —

and in torment, bewilderment, at the end she asks,
with a voice reaching

        harrowingly for the notes,

"Art has *repaid* me LIKE THIS?"

        I felt I was watching

autobiography —

        an art; skill;

virtuosity

miles distant from the usual soprano's
athleticism, —

        the usual musician's dream
of virtuosity *without* content . . .

— I wonder what she feels, now,
listening to her recordings.

For they have already, within a few years,
begun to date . . .

Whatever they express
they express through the style of a decade
and a half — ;

        a style *she* helped create . . .

— She must know that now
she probably would *not* do a trill in
exactly that way, —

        that the whole sound, atmosphere,
dramaturgy of her recordings

have just slightly become those of the past . . .

— Is it bitter? Does her soul
tell her

that she was an *idiot* ever to think
anything

        material wholly could satisfy? . . .

— Perhaps it says: *The only way*
to escape
the History of Styles

is not to have a body.

●   ●   ●

When I open my eyes in the morning, my great
mystery
        stands before me . . .

— I *know* that I am intelligent; therefore

the inability not to fear food
day-and-night; this unending hunger
ten minutes after I have eaten . . .
                      a childish
dread of eating; hunger which can have no cause, —

half my mind says that all this
is *demeaning* . . .

         Bread
for days on end
drives all real thought from my brain . . .

— Then I think, No. The ideal of being thin

conceals the ideal
not to have a body — ;
             which is NOT trivial . . .

This wish seems now as much a "given" of my existence

as the intolerable
fact that I am dark-complexioned; big-boned;
and once weighed
one hundred and sixty-five pounds . . .

— But then I think, *No.* That's too simple, —

without a body, who can
know himself at all?
            Only by
acting; choosing; rejecting; have I
made myself —
           discovered who and what *Ellen* can be . . .

— But then again I think, *NO.* This *I* is anterior

to name; gender; action;
fashion;
      MATTER ITSELF, —

. . . trying to stop my hunger with FOOD

is like trying to appease thirst

          with ink.

         •   •   •

March 30. Result of the consultation: Both gentlemen agree completely with my prognosis and doubt any therapeutic usefulness of commitment even more emphatically than I. All three of us are agreed that it is not a case of obsessional neurosis and not one of manic-depressive psychosis, and that no definitely reliable therapy is possible. We therefore resolved to give in to the patient's demand for discharge.

         •   •   •

The train-ride yesterday
was far *worse* than I expected . . .

                In our compartment
were ordinary people: a student;
a woman; her child; —

they had ordinary bodies, pleasant faces;

              but I thought
I was surrounded by creatures

with the pathetic, desperate
desire to be *not* what they were: —

the student was short,
and carried his body as if forcing
it to be taller — ;

the woman showed her gums when she smiled,
and often held her
hand up to hide them — ;

the child
seemed to cry simply because it was
small; a dwarf, and helpless . . .

— I was hungry. I had insisted that my husband
not bring food . . .

After about thirty minutes, the woman
peeled an orange

to quiet the child. She put a section
into its mouth — ;

         immediately it spit it out.

The piece fell to the floor.

— She pushed it with her foot through the dirt
toward me
several inches.

My husband saw me staring
down at the piece . . .

— I didn't move; how I wanted
to reach out,
                    and as if invisible

shove it in my mouth — ;

my body
became rigid. As I stared at him,
I could see him staring

at me, —
                    then he looked at the student — ; at the woman — ; then
back to me . . .

I didn't move.

— At last, he bent down, and
casually
            threw it out the window.

He looked away.

— I got up to leave the compartment, then
saw his face, —

his eyes
were red;
                    and I saw

— *I'm sure I saw* —

disappointment.

>   •   •   •

On the third day of being home she is as if transformed. At break-
fast she eats butter and sugar, at noon she eats so much that — for
the first time in thirteen years! — she is satisfied by her food and
gets really full. At afternoon coffee she eats chocolate creams and
Easter eggs. She takes a walk with her husband, reads poems, listens
to recordings, is in a positively festive mood, and all heaviness
seems to have fallen away from her. She writes letters, the last one

a letter to the fellow patient here to whom she had become so attached. In the evening she takes a lethal dose of poison, and on the following morning she is dead. "She looked as she had never looked in life — calm and happy and peaceful."

• • •

Dearest. — I remember how
at eighteen,
            on hikes with friends, when
they rested, sitting down to joke or talk,

I circled
around them, afraid to hike ahead alone,

yet afraid to rest
when I was not yet truly thin.

You and, yes, my husband, —
you and he

have by degrees drawn me within the circle;
forced me to sit down at last on the ground.

I am grateful.

But something in me *refuses* it.

— How eager I have been
to compromise, to kill this *refuser*, —

but each compromise, each attempt
to poison an ideal
which often seemed to *me* sterile and unreal,

heightens my hunger.

I am crippled. I disappoint you.

Will you greet with anger, or
happiness,

the news which might well reach you
before this letter?

Your *Ellen.*

To My Father

I walked into the room.
There were objects in the room. I thought I needed nothing

from them. They began to speak,
but the words were unintelligible, a painful cacophony . . .
Then I realized they were saying
                                        the name
of the man who had chosen them, owned them,
ordered, arranged them, their deceased cause,
the secret pattern that made these things order.
I strained to hear: but
the sound remained unintelligible . . .
senselessly getting louder, urgent, deafening.

Hands over my ears, at last I knew
                                        they would remain
inarticulate; your name was not in my language.

ELIZABETH BISHOP
At the Fishhouses

Although it is a cold evening,
down by one of the fishhouses
an old man sits netting,
his net, in the gloaming almost invisible,
a dark purple-brown,
and his shuttle worn and polished.
The air smells so strong of codfish
it makes one's nose run and one's eyes water.
The five fishhouses have steeply peaked roofs
and narrow, cleated gangplanks slant up
to storerooms in the gables
for the wheelbarrows to be pushed up and down on.
All is silver: the heavy surface of the sea,
swelling slowly as if considering spilling over,
is opaque, but the silver of the benches,
the lobster pots, and masts, scattered
among the wild jagged rocks,
is of an apparent translucence
like the small old buildings with an emerald moss
growing on their shoreward walls.
The big fish tubs are completely lined
with layers of beautiful herring scales
and the wheelbarrows are similarly plastered
with creamy iridescent coats of mail,

with small iridescent flies crawling on them.
Up on the little slope behind the houses,
set in the sparse bright sprinkle of grass,
is an ancient wooden capstan,[1]
cracked, with two long bleached handles
and some melancholy stains, like dried blood,
where the ironwork has rusted.
The old man accepts a Lucky Strike.
He was a friend of my grandfather.
We talk of the decline in the population
and of codfish and herring
while he waits for a herring boat to come in.
There are sequins on his vest and on his thumb.
He has scraped the scales, the principal beauty,
from unnumbered fish with that black old knife,
the blade of which is almost worn away.

Down at the water's edge, at the place
where they haul up the boats, up the long ramp
descending into the water, thin silver
tree trunks are laid horizontally
across the gray stones, down and down
at intervals of four or five feet.

Cold dark deep and absolutely clear,
element bearable to no mortal,
to fish and to seals . . . One seal particularly
I have seen here evening after evening.
He was curious about me. He was interested in music;
like me a believer in total immersion,[2]
so I used to sing him Baptist hymns.
I also sang "A Mighty Fortress Is Our God."[3]
He stood up in the water and regarded me
steadily, moving his head a little.
Then he would disappear, then suddenly emerge
almost in the same spot, with a sort of shrug
as if it were against his better judgment.
Cold dark deep and absolutely clear,

---

[1] Machine for raising weights by winding cable around a vertical rotating drum.

[2] Form of baptism practiced by some Christian sects.

[3] Hymn of which the original German version was written by Martin Luther (1483–1546).

the clear gray icy water . . . Back, behind us,
the dignified tall firs begin.
Bluish, associating with their shadows,
a million Christmas trees stand
waiting for Christmas. The water seems suspended
above the rounded gray and blue-gray stones.
I have seen it over and over, the same sea, the same,
slightly, indifferently swinging above the stones,
icily free above the stones,
above the stones and then the world.
If you should dip your hand in,
your wrist would ache immediately,
your bones would begin to ache and your hand would burn
as if the water were a transmutation of fire
that feeds on stones and burns with a dark gray flame.
If you tasted it, it would first taste bitter,
then briny, then surely burn your tongue.
It is like what we imagine knowledge to be:
dark, salt, clear, moving, utterly free,
drawn from the cold hard mouth
of the world, derived from the rocky breasts
forever, flowing and drawn, and since
our knowledge is historical, flowing, and flown.

The Fish

I caught a tremendous fish
and held him beside the boat
half out of water, with my hook
fast in a corner of his mouth.
He didn't fight.
He hadn't fought at all.
He hung a grunting weight,
battered and venerable
and homely. Here and there
his brown skin hung in strips
like ancient wall-paper,
and its pattern of darker brown
was like wall-paper:
shapes like full-blown roses
stained and lost through age.
He was speckled with barnacles,

fine rosettes of lime,
and infested
with tiny white sea-lice,
and underneath two or three
rags of green weed hung down.
While his gills were breathing in
the terrible oxygen
— the frightening gills,
fresh and crisp with blood,
that can cut so badly —
I thought of the coarse white flesh
packed in like feathers,
the big bones and the little bones,
the dramatic reds and blacks
in his shiny entrails,
and the pink swim-bladder
like a big peony.
I looked into his eyes
which were far larger than mine
but shallower, and yellowed,
the irises backed and packed
with tarnished tinfoil
seen through the lenses
of old scratched isinglass.
They shifted a little, but not
to return my stare.
— It was more like the tipping
of an object toward the light.
I admired his sullen face,
the mechanism of his jaw,
and then I saw
that from his lower lip
— if you could call it a lip —
grim, wet, and weapon-like,
hung five old pieces of fish-line,
or four and a wire leader
with the swivel still attached,
with all their five big hooks
grown firmly in his mouth.
A green line, frayed at the end
where he broke it, two heavier lines,
and a fine black thread

still crimped from the strain and snap
when it broke and he got away.
Like medals with their ribbons
frayed and wavering,
a five-haired beard of wisdom
trailing from his aching jaw.
I stared and stared
and victory filled up
the little rented boat,
from the pool of bilge
where oil had spread a rainbow
around the rusted engine
to the bailer rusted orange,
the sun-cracked thwarts,
the oarlocks on their strings,
the gunnels — until everything
was rainbow, rainbow, rainbow!
And I let the fish go.

Poem

About the size of an old-style dollar bill,
American or Canadian,
mostly the same whites, gray greens, and steel grays
— this little painting (a sketch for a larger one?)
has never earned any money in its life.
Useless and free, it has spent seventy years
as a minor family relic
handed along collaterally to owners
who looked at it sometimes, or didn't bother to.

It must be Nova Scotia; only there
does one see gabled wooden houses
painted that awful shade of brown.
The other houses, the bits that show, are white.
Elm trees, low hills, a thin church steeple
— that gray-blue wisp — or is it? In the foreground
a water meadow with some tiny cows,
two brushstrokes each, but confidently cows;
two minuscule white geese in the blue water,
back-to-back, feeding, and a slanting stick.
Up closer, a wild iris, white and yellow,
fresh-squiggled from the tube.

The air is fresh and cold; cold early spring
clear as gray glass; a half inch of blue sky
below the steel-gray storm clouds.
(They were the artist's specialty.)
A specklike bird is flying to the left.
Or is it a flyspeck looking like a bird?

Heavens, I recognize the place, I know it!
It's behind — I can almost remember the farmer's name.
His barn backed on that meadow. There it is,
titanium white, one dab. The hint of steeple,
filaments of brush-hairs, barely there,
must be the Presbyterian church.
Would that be Miss Gillespie's house?
Those particular geese and cows
are naturally before my time.

A sketch done in an hour, "in one breath,"
once taken from a trunk and handed over.
Would you like this? I'll probably never
have room to hang these things again.
Your Uncle George, no, mine, my Uncle George,
he'd be your great-uncle, left them all with Mother
when he went back to England.
You know, he was quite famous, an R.A. . . .

I never knew him. We both knew this place,
apparently, this literal small backwater,
looked at it long enough to memorize it,
our years apart. How strange. And it's still loved,
or its memory is (it must have changed a lot).
Our visions coincided — "visions" is
too serious a word — our looks, two looks:
art "copying from life" and life itself,
life and the memory of it so compressed
they've turned into each other. Which is which?
Life and the memory of it cramped,
dim, on a piece of Bristol board,
dim, but how live, how touching in detail
— the little that we get for free,
the little of our earthly trust. Not much.
About the size of our abidance
along with theirs: the munching cows,
the iris, crisp and shivering, the water

still standing from spring freshets,
the yet-to-be-dismantled elms, the geese.

Sestina

September rain falls on the house.
In the failing light, the old grandmother
sits in the kitchen with the child
beside the Little Marvel Stove,
reading the jokes from the almanac,
laughing and talking to hide her tears.

She thinks that her equinoctial tears
and the rain that beats on the roof of the house
were both foretold by the almanac,
but only known to a grandmother.
The iron kettle sings on the stove.
She cuts some bread and says to the child,

It's time for tea now; but the child
is watching the teakettle's small hard tears
dance like mad on the hot black stove,
the way the rain must dance on the house.
Tidying up, the old grandmother
hangs up the clever almanac

on its string. Birdlike, the almanac
hovers half open above the child,
hovers above the old grandmother
and her teacup full of dark brown tears.
She shivers and says she thinks the house
feels chilly, and puts more wood in the stove.

It was to be, says the Marvel Stove.
I know what I know, says the almanac.
With crayons the child draws a rigid house
and a winding pathway. Then the child
puts in a man with buttons like tears
and shows it proudly to the grandmother.

But secretly, while the grandmother
busies herself about the stove,
the little moons fall down like tears
from between the pages of the almanac

into the flower bed the child
has carefully placed in the front of the house.

Time to plant tears, says the almanac.
The grandmother sings to the marvelous stove
and the child draws another inscrutable house.

Ah Sun-flower

Ah Sun-flower, weary of time,
Who countest the steps of the Sun,
Seeking after that sweet golden clime
Where the traveller's journey is done:

Where the Youth pined away with desire,
And the pale Virgin shrouded in snow
Arise from their graves and aspire
Where my Sun-flower wishes to go.

The Garden of Love

I went to the Garden of Love,
And saw what I never had seen:
A Chapel was built in the midst,
Where I used to play on the green.

And the gates of this Chapel were shut,
And "Thou shalt not" writ over the door;
So I turn'd to the Garden of Love,
That so many sweet flowers bore,

And I saw it was filled with graves,
And tomb-stones where flowers should be:
And Priests in black gowns were walking their rounds,
And binding with briars my joys & desires.

The Lamb

    Little Lamb, who made thee?
    Dost thou know who made thee?
Gave thee life & bid thee feed,
By the stream & o'er the mead;
Gave thee clothing of delight,
Softest clothing, wooly, bright;

Gave thee such a tender voice,
Making all the vales rejoice?
    Little Lamb, who made thee?
    Dost thou know who made thee?

    Little Lamb, I'll tell thee,
    Little Lamb, I'll tell thee:
He is callèd by thy name,
For he calls himself a Lamb.
He is meek & he is mild,
He became a little child.
I a child, & thou a lamb,
We are callèd by his name.
    Little Lamb, God bless thee.
    Little Lamb, God bless thee.

The Tyger

Tyger! Tyger! burning bright
In the forests of the night,
What immortal hand or eye
Could frame thy fearful symmetry?

In what distant deeps or skies
Burnt the fire of thine eyes?
On what wings dare he aspire?
What the hand, dare seize the fire?

And what shoulder, & what art,
Could twist the sinews of thy heart?
And when thy heart began to beat,
What dread hand? & what dread feet?

What the hammer? what the chain?
In what furnace was thy brain?
What the anvil? what dread grasp
Dare its deadly terrors clasp?

When the stars threw down their spears,
And water'd heaven with their tears,
Did he smile his work to see?
Did he who made the Lamb make thee?

Tyger! Tyger! burning bright
In the forests of the night,
What immortal hand or eye
Dare frame thy fearful symmetry?

MICHAEL BLUMENTHAL

A Marriage

For Margie Smigel and Jon Dopkeen

You are holding up a ceiling
with both arms. It is very heavy,
but you must hold it up, or else
it will fall down on you. Your arms
are tired, terribly tired,
and, as the day goes on, it feels
as if either your arms or the ceiling
will soon collapse.

But then,
unexpectedly,
something wonderful happens:
Someone,
a man or a woman,
walks into the room
and holds their arms up
to the ceiling beside you.

So you finally get
to take down your arms.
You feel the relief of respite,
the blood flowing back
to your fingers and arms.
And when your partner's arms tire,
you hold up your own
to relieve him again.

And it can go on like this
for many years
without the house falling.

Wishful Thinking

I like to think that ours will be more than just another story
of failed love and the penumbras of desire. I like to think
that the moon that day was in whatever house the astrologists
would have it in for a kind of quiet, a trellis lust could climb
easily and then subside, resting against the sills and ledges,
giving way like shore to an occasional tenderness, coddling
the cold idiosyncrasies of impulse and weather that pound it

as it holds to its shape against the winds and duststorms of
temptation and longing. I like to think that some small canister
of hope and tranquility washed ashore that day and we, in
the right place, found it. These are the things I imagine
all lovers wish for amid the hot commencements of love
and promises, their histories and failures washing ashore
like flotsam, their innards girthed against those architects
of misery, desire and restlessness, their hope rising
against the air as it fondles the waves and frolics them skywards.
I like to think that, if the heart pauses awhile in a single place,
it finds a home somewhere, like a vagabond lured by fatigue
to an unlikely town and, with a sudden peacefulness, deciding
to stay there. I like to think these things because, whether
or not they reach fruition, they provide the heart with a kind
of solace, the way poetry does, or all forms of tenderness
that issue out amid the deserts of failed love and petulant desire.
I like to think them because, meditated on amid this pattern
of off-white and darkness, they lend themselves to a kind of
music, not unlike the music a dove makes as it circles the trees,
not unlike the sun and the earth and their orbital brothers,
the planets, as they chant to the heavens their longing for hope
and repetition amid orderly movement, not unlike the music
these humble wishes make with their cantata of willfulness
and good intentions, looking for some pleasant abstractions
amid our concretized lives, something tender and lovely to
defy the times with, quiet and palpable amid the flickers of flux
and the flames of longing: a bird rising over the ashes, a dream.

LUCIE BROCK-BROIDO
Carrowmore

All about Carrowmore[1] the lambs
Were blotched blue, belonging.

They were waiting for carnage or
Snuff. This is why they are born

To begin with, to end.
Ruminants do not frighten

---

[1] A location in County Sligo, Ireland, where there is a large prehistoric megalithic
cemetery.

At anything — gorge in the soil, butcher
Noise, the mere graze of predators.

All about Carrowmore
The rain quells for three days.

I remember how cold I was, the botched
Job of travelling. And just so.

Wherever I went I came with me.
She buried her bone barrette

In the ground's woolly shaft.
A tear of her hair, an old gift

To the burnt other who went
First. My thick braid, my ornament —

My belonging I
Remember how cold I will be.

EMILY BRONTË
No Coward Soul Is Mine

No coward soul is mine,
No trembler in the world's storm-troubled sphere!
I see Heaven's glories shine,
And Faith shines equal, arming me from Fear.

O God within my breast,
Almighty ever-present Deity!
Life, that in me hast rest
As I, undying Life, have power in thee!

Vain are the thousand creeds
That move men's hearts, unutterably vain;
Worthless as withered weeds,
Or idlest froth, amid the boundless main

To waken doubt in one
Holding so fast by thy infinity,
So surely anchored on
The steadfast rock of Immortality.

With wide-embracing love
Thy spirit animates eternal years,
Pervades and broods above,
Changes, sustains, dissolves, creates and rears.

Though earth and moon were gone,
And suns and universes ceased to be,
And thou were left alone,
Every Existence would exist in thee.

There is not room for Death,
Nor atom that his might could render void
Since thou art Being and Breath,
And what thou art may never be destroyed.

Remembrance

Cold in the earth — and the deep snow piled above thee,
Far, far removed, cold in the dreary grave!
Have I forgot, my only Love, to love thee,
Severed at last by Time's all-severing wave?

Now, when alone, do my thoughts no longer hover
Over the mountains, on that northern shore,
Resting their wings where heath and fern leaves cover
Thy noble heart forever, ever more?

Cold in the earth — and fifteen wild Decembers,
From those brown hills, have melted into spring;
Faithful, indeed, is the spirit that remembers
After such years of change and suffering!

Sweet Love of youth, forgive, if I forget thee,
While the world's tide is bearing me along;
Other desires and other hopes beset me,
Hopes which obscure, but cannot do thee wrong!

No later light has lightened up my heaven,
No second morn has ever shone for me;
All my life's bliss from thy dear life was given,
All my life's bliss is in the grave with thee.

But, when the days of golden dreams had perished,
And even Despair was powerless to destroy,
Then did I learn how existence could be cherished,
Strengthened, and fed without the aid of joy.

Then did I check the tears of useless passion —
Weaned my young soul from yearning after thine;
Sternly denied its burning wish to hasten
Down to that tomb already more than mine.

And, even yet, I dare not let it languish,
Dare not indulge in memory's rapturous pain;
Once drinking deep of that divinest anguish,
How could I seek the empty world again?

GWENDOLYN BROOKS
The Bean Eaters

They eat beans mostly, this old yellow pair.
Dinner is a casual affair.
Plain chipware on a plain and creaking wood,
Tin flatware.

Two who are Mostly Good.
Two who have lived their day,
But keep on putting on their clothes
And putting things away.

And remembering . . .
Remembering, with twinklings and twinges,
As they lean over the beans in their rented back room that is full
     of beads and receipts and dolls and clothes, tobacco crumbs,
     vases and fringes.

Kitchenette Building

We are things of dry hours and the involuntary plan,
Grayed in, and gray. "Dream" makes a giddy sound, not strong
Like "rent," "feeding a wife," "satisfying a man."

But could a dream send up through onion fumes
Its white and violet, fight with fried potatoes
And yesterday's garbage ripening in the hall,
Flutter, or sing an aria down these rooms

Even if we were willing to let it in,
Had time to warm it, keep it very clean,
Anticipate a message, let it begin?

We wonder. But not well! not for a minute!
Since Number Five is out of the bathroom now,
We think of lukewarm water, hope to get in it.

The Mother

Abortions will not let you forget.
You remember the children you got that you did not get,
The damp small pulps with a little or with no hair,
The singers and workers that never handled the air.
You will never neglect or beat
Them, or silence or buy with a sweet.
You will never wind up the sucking-thumb
Or scuttle off ghosts that come.
You will never leave them, controlling your luscious sigh,
Return for a snack of them, with gobbling mother-eye.

I have heard in the voices of the wind the voices of my dim killed
      children.
I have contracted. I have eased
My dim dears at the breasts they could never suck.
I have said, Sweets, if I sinned, if I seized
Your luck
And your lives from your unfinished reach,
If I stole your births and your names,
Your straight baby tears and your games,
Your stilted or lovely loves, your tumults, your marriages, aches,
      and your deaths,
If I poisoned the beginnings of your breaths,
Believe that even in my deliberateness I was not deliberate.
Though why should I whine,
Whine that the crime was other than mine? —
Since anyhow you are dead.
Or rather, or instead,
You were never made.
But that too, I am afraid,
Is faulty: oh, what shall I say, how is the truth to be said?
You were born, you had body, you died.
It is just that you never giggled or planned or cried.
Believe me, I loved you all.
Believe me, I knew you, though faintly, and I loved, I loved you
All.

ELIZABETH BARRETT BROWNING

From *Sonnets from the Portuguese*

1

I thought once how Theocritus[1] had sung
    Of the sweet years, the dear and wished-for years,
    Who each one in a gracious hand appears
To bear a gift for mortals, old or young:
And, as I mused it in his antique tongue,
    I saw, in gradual vision through my tears,
    The sweet, sad years, the melancholy years,
Those of my own life, who by turns had flung
A shadow across me. Straightway I was 'ware,
    So weeping, how a mystic Shape did move
Behind me, and drew me backward by the hair;
    And a voice said in mastery, while I strove, —
"Guess now who holds thee?" — "Death," I said. But, there,
    The silver answer rang, — "Not Death, but Love."

A Musical Instrument

What was he doing, the great god Pan,
    Down in the reeds by the river?
Spreading ruin and scattering ban,°   *baleful influence*
Splashing and paddling with hoofs of a goat,
And breaking the golden lilies afloat
    With the dragonfly on the river.

He tore out a reed, the great god Pan,
    From the deep cool bed of the river;
The limpid water turbidly ran,
And the broken lilies a-dying lay,
And the dragonfly had fled away,
    Ere he brought it out of the river.

High on the shore sat the great god Pan
    While turbidly flowed the river;
And hacked and hewed as a great god can,
With his hard bleak steel at the patient reed,
Till there was not a sign of the leaf indeed
    To prove it fresh from the river.

---

[1] Greek pastoral poet of the third century B.C.

He cut it short, did the great god Pan
    (How tall it stood in the river!),
Then drew the pith, like the heart of a man,
Steadily from the outside ring,
And notched the poor dry empty thing
    In holes, as he sat by the river.

"This is the way," laughed the great god Pan
    (Laughed while he sat by the river),
"The only way, since gods began
To make sweet music, they could succeed."
Then, dropping his mouth to a hole in the reed,
    He blew in power by the river.

Sweet, sweet, sweet, O Pan!
    Piercing sweet by the river!
Blinding sweet, O great god Pan!
The sun on the hill forgot to die,
And the lilies revived, and the dragonfly
    Came back to dream on the river.

Yet half a beast is the great god Pan,
    To laugh as he sits by the river,
Making a poet out of a man;
The true gods sigh for the cost and pain —
For the reed which grows nevermore again
    As a reed with the reeds in the river.

ROBERT BROWNING
"Childe Roland to the Dark Tower Came"[1]

(*See Edgar's Song in* Lear)

1

My first thought was, he lied in every word,
    That hoary cripple, with malicious eye
    Askance to watch the working of his lie
On mine, and mouth scarce able to afford
Suppression of the glee, that pursed and scored
    Its edge, at one more victim gained thereby.

---

[1] The title is taken from Shakespeare's *King Lear* (III. iv. 173). A "childe" is a medieval term for a youth awaiting knighthood.

2

What else should he be set for, with his staff?
    What, save to waylay with his lies, ensnare
    All travelers who might find him posted there,
And ask the road? I guessed what skull-like laugh
Would break, what crutch 'gin° write my epitaph   *begin to*
    For pastime in the dusty thoroughfare,

3

If at his counsel I should turn aside
    Into that ominous tract which, all agree,
    Hides the Dark Tower. Yet acquiescingly
I did turn as he pointed: neither pride
Nor hope rekindling at the end descried,
    So much as gladness that some end might be.

4

For, what with my whole world-wide wandering,
    What with my search drawn out through years, my hope
    Dwindled into a ghost not fit to cope
With that obstreperous joy success would bring, —
I hardly tried now to rebuke the spring
    My heart made, finding failure in its scope.

5

As when a sick man very near to death
    Seems dead indeed, and feels begin and end
    The tears, and takes the farewell of each friend,
And hears one bid the other go, draw breath
Freelier outside, ("since all is o'er," he saith,
    "And the blow fallen no grieving can amend;")

6

While some discuss if near the other graves
    Be room enough for this, and when a day
    Suits best for carrying the corpse away,
With care about the banners, scarves and staves:
And still the man hears all, and only craves
    He may not shame such tender love and stay.

7

Thus, I had so long suffered in this quest,
    Heard failure prophesied so oft, been writ
    So many times among "The Band" — to wit,

The knights who to the Dark Tower's search addressed
Their steps — that just to fail as they, seemed best,
    And all the doubt was now — should I be fit?

8

So, quiet as despair, I turned from him,
    That hateful cripple, out of his highway
    Into the path he pointed. All the day
Had been a dreary one at best, and dim
Was settling to its close, yet shot one grim
    Red leer to see the plain catch its estray.[2]   ¹

9

For mark! no sooner was I fairly found
    Pledged to the plain, after a pace or two,
    Than, pausing to throw backward a last view
O'er the safe road, 'twas gone; gray plain all round:
Nothing but plain to the horizon's bound.
    I might go on; naught else remained to do.

10

So, on I went. I think I never saw
    Such starved ignoble nature; nothing throve:
    For flowers — as well expect a cedar grove!
But cockle, spurge, according to their law
Might propagate their kind, with none to awe,
    You'd think: a burr had been a treasure trove.

11

No! penury, inertness and grimace,
    In some strange sort, were the land's portion. "See
    Or shut your eyes," said Nature peevishly,
"It nothing skills: I cannot help my case:
'Tis the Last Judgment's fire must cure this place,
    Calcine° its clods and set my prisoners free."   *reduce to ash*

12

If there pushed any ragged thistle-stalk
    Above its mates, the head was chopped;
        the bents°   *coarse grasses*
    Were jealous else. What made those holes and rents

---

[2] Potential victim who has strayed.

In the dock's harsh swarth leaves, bruised as to balk
All hope of greenness? 'tis a brute must walk
    Pashing° their life out, with a brute's intents.   *crushing*

13

As for the grass, it grew as scant as hair
    In leprosy; thin dry blades pricked the mud
    Which underneath looked kneaded up with blood.
One stiff blind horse, his every bone a-stare,
Stood stupefied, however he came there:
    Thrust out past service from the devil's stud!

14

Alive? he might be dead for aught I know,
    With that red gaunt colloped° neck a-strain,   *ridged*
    And shut eyes underneath the rusty mane;
Seldom went such grotesqueness with such woe;
I never saw a brute I hated so;
    He must be wicked to deserve such pain.

15

I shut my eyes and turned them on my heart.
    As a man calls for wine before he fights,
    I asked one draught of earlier, happier sights,
Ere fitly I could hope to play my part.
Think first, fight afterwards — the soldier's art:
    One taste of the old time sets all to rights.

16

Not it! I fancied Cuthbert's reddening face
    Beneath its garniture of curly gold,
    Dear fellow, till I almost felt him fold
An arm in mine to fix me to the place,
That way he used. Alas, one night's disgrace!
    Out went my heart's new fire and left it cold.

17

Giles then, the soul of honor — there he stands
    Frank as ten years ago when knighted first.
    What honest man should dare (he said) he durst.
Good — but the scene shifts — faugh! what hangman hands
Pin to his breast a parchment? His own bands
    Read it. Poor traitor, spit upon and curst!

18

Better this present than a past like that;
    Back therefore to my darkening path again!
    No sound, no sight as far as eye could strain.
Will the night send a howlet° or a bat?   *owl*
I asked: when something on the dismal flat
    Came to arrest my thoughts and change their train.

19

A sudden little river crossed my path
    As unexpected as a serpent comes.
    No sluggish tide congenial to the glooms;
This, as it frothed by, might have been a bath
For the fiend's glowing hoof — to see the wrath
    Of its black eddy bespate° with flakes   *bespattered*
        and spumes.

20

So petty yet so spiteful! All along,
    Low scrubby alders kneeled down over it;
    Drenched willows flung them headlong in a fit
Of mute despair, a suicidal throng:
The river which had done them all the wrong,
    Whate'er that was, rolled by, deterred no whit.

21

Which, while I forded, — good saints, how I feared
    To set my foot upon a dead man's cheek,
    Each step, or feel the spear I thrust to seek
For hollows, tangled in his hair or beard!
— It may have been a water-rat I speared,
    But, ugh! it sounded like a baby's shriek.

22

Glad was I when I reached the other bank.
    Now for a better country. Vain presage!
    Who were the strugglers, what war did they wage,
Whose savage trample thus could pad the dank
Soil to a plash? Toads in a poisoned tank,
    Or wild cats in a red-hot iron cage —

23

The fight must so have seemed in that fell cirque.
    What penned them there, with all the plain to choose?
    No footprint leading to that horrid mews,

None out of it. Mad brewage set to work
Their brains, no doubt, like galley-slaves the Turk
    Pits for his pastime, Christians against Jews.

24

And more than that — a furlong on — why, there!
    What bad use was that engine for, that wheel,
    Or brake, not wheel — that harrow fit to reel
Men's bodies out like silk? with all the air
Of Tophet's° tool, on earth left unaware,   *Hell's*
    Or brought to sharpen its rusty teeth of steel.

25

Then came a bit of stubbed ground, once a wood,
    Next a marsh, it would seem, and now mere earth
    Desperate and done with; (so a fool finds mirth,
Makes a thing and then mars it, till his mood
Changes and off he goes!) within a rood° —   *quarter-acre*
    Bog, clay and rubble, sand and stark black dearth.

26

Now blotches rankling, colored gay and grim,
    Now patches where some leanness of the soil's
    Broke into moss or substances like boils;
Then came some palsied oak, a cleft in him
Like a distorted mouth that splits its rim
    Gaping at death, and dies while it recoils.

27

And just as far as ever from the end!
    Nought in the distance but the evening, nought
    To point my footstep further! At the thought,
A great black bird, Apollyon's[3] bosom-friend,
Sailed past, nor beat his wide wing
        dragon-penned°   *dragon-feathered*
    That brushed my cap — perchance the guide I sought.

28

For, looking up, aware I somehow grew,
    'Spite of the dusk, the plain had given place
    All round to mountains — with such name to grace

---

[3] In Revelation 9:11, an angel of the bottomless pit.

Mere ugly heights and heaps now stolen in view.
How thus they had surprised me, — solve it, you!
    How to get from them was no clearer case.

29

Yet half I seemed to recognize some trick
    Of mischief happened to me, God knows when —
    In a bad dream perhaps. Here ended, then,
Progress this way. When, in the very nick
Of giving up, one time more, came a click
    As when a trap shuts — you're inside the den!

30

Burningly it came on me all at once,
    This was the place! those two hills on the right,
    Crouched like two bulls locked horn in horn in fight;
While to the left, a tall scalped mountain . . . Dunce,
Dotard, a-dozing at the very nonce,
    After a life spent training for the sight!

31

What in the midst lay but the Tower itself?
    The round squat turret, blind as the fool's heart,
    Built of brown stone, without a counterpart
In the whole world. The tempest's mocking elf
Points to the shipman thus the unseen shelf
    He strikes on, only when the timbers start.

32

Not see? because of night perhaps? — why, day
    Came back again for that! before it left,
    The dying sunset kindled through a cleft:
The hills, like giants at a hunting, lay,
Chin upon hand, to see the game at bay, —
    "Now stab and end the creature — to the heft!"

33

Not hear? when noise was everywhere! it tolled
    Increasing like a bell. Names in my ears
    Of all the lost adventurers my peers, —
How such a one was strong, and such was bold,
And such was fortunate, yet each of old
    Lost, lost! one moment knelled the woe of years.

34

There they stood, ranged along the hillsides, met
    To view the last of me, a living frame
    For one more picture! in a sheet of flame
I saw them and I knew them all. And yet
Dauntless the slug-horn[4] to my lips I set,
    And blew. *"Childe Roland to the Dark Tower came."*

Memorabilia

1

Ah, did you once see Shelley plain,
    And did he stop and speak to you
And did you speak to him again?
    How strange it seems and new!

2

But you were living before that,
    And also you are living after;
And the memory I started at —
    My starting moves your laughter.

3

I crossed a moor, with a name of its own
    And a certain use in the world no doubt,
Yet a hand's-breadth of it shines alone
    'Mid the blank miles round about:

4

For there I picked up on the heather
    And there I put inside my breast
A moulted feather, an eagle-feather!
    Well, I forget the rest.

ROBERT BURNS

O, Wert Thou in the Cauld Blast

O, wert thou in the cauld blast
    On yonder lea, on yonder lea,
My plaidie to the angry airt,°   *quarter (of the wind)*
    I'd shelter thee, I'd shelter thee.

---

[4] A rough trumpet made from the horn of an ox or cow.

Or did misfortune's bitter storms
    Around thee blaw, around thee blaw,
Thy bield° should be my bosom,   *shelter*
    To share it a', to share it a'.

Or were I in the wildest waste,
    Sae black and bare, sae black and bare,
The desert were a paradise,
    If thou wert there, if thou wert there.
Or were I monarch o' the globe,
    Wi' thee to reign, wi' thee to reign,
The brightest jewel in my crown
    Wad be my queen, wad be my queen.

A Red, Red Rose

O my luve's like a red, red rose,
    That's newly sprung in June;
O my luve's like the melodie
    That's sweetly played in tune.

As fair art thou, my bonnie lass,
    So deep in luve am I;
And I will luve thee still, my dear,
    Till a' the seas gang dry.

Till a' the seas gang dry, my dear,
    And the rocks melt wi' the sun:
O I will luve thee still, my dear,
    While the sands o' life shall run.

And fare thee weel, my only luve,
    And fare thee weel awhile!
And I will come again, my luve,
    Though it were ten thousand mile.

GEORGE GORDON, LORD BYRON
She Walks in Beauty

1

She walks in beauty, like the night
    Of cloudless climes and starry skies;
And all that's best of dark and bright
    Meet in her aspect and her eyes:

Thus mellowed to that tender light
 Which heaven to gaudy day denies.

2

One shade the more, one ray the less,
 Had half impaired the nameless grace
Which waves in every raven tress,
 Or softly lightens o'er her face;
Where thoughts serenely sweet express
 How pure, how dear their dwelling place.

3

And on that cheek, and o'er that brow,
 So soft, so calm, yet eloquent,
The smiles that win, the tints that glow,
 But tell of days in goodness spent,
A mind at peace with all below,
 A heart whose love is innocent!

When We Two Parted

When we two parted
 In silence and tears,
Half broken-hearted
 To sever for years,
Pale grew thy cheek and cold,
 Colder thy kiss;
Truly that hour foretold
 Sorrow to this.

The dew of the morning
 Sunk chill on my brow —
It felt like the warning
 Of what I feel now.
Thy vows are all broken,
 And light is thy fame;
I hear thy name spoken,
 And share in its shame.

They name thee before me,
 A knell to mine ear;
A shudder comes o'er me —
 Why wert thou so dear?
They know not I knew thee,
 Who knew thee too well —

Long, long shall I rue thee,
    Too deeply to tell.

In secret we met —
    In silence I grieve,
That thy heart could forget,
    Thy spirit deceive.
If I should meet thee
    After long years,
How should I greet thee? —
    With silence and tears.

LORNA DEE CERVANTES

Poem for the Young White Man Who Asked Me How I, An Intelligent, Well-Read Person Could Believe in the War Between Races

In my land there are no distinctions.
The barbed wire politics of oppression
have been torn down long ago. The only reminder
of past battles, lost or won, is a slight
rutting in the fertile fields.

In my land
people write poems about love,
full of nothing but contented childlike syllables.
Everyone reads Russian short stories and weeps.
There are no boundaries.
There is no hunger, no
complicated famine or greed.

I am not a revolutionary.
I don't even like political poems.
Do you think I can believe in a war between races?
I can deny it. I can forget about it
when I'm safe,
living on my own continent of harmony
and home, but I am not
there.

I believe in revolution
because everywhere the crosses are burning,

sharp-shooting goose-steppers round every corner,
there are snipers in the schools . . .
(I know you don't believe this.
You think this is nothing
but faddish exaggeration. But they
are not shooting at you.)

I'm marked by the color of my skin.
The bullets are discrete and designed to kill slowly.
They are aiming at my children.
These are facts.
Let me show you my wounds: my stumbling mind, my
"excuse me" tongue, and this
nagging preoccupation
with the feeling of not being good enough.

These bullets bury deeper than logic.
Racism is not intellectual.
I can not reason these scars away.

Outside my door
there is a real enemy
who hates me.

I am a poet
who yearns to dance on rooftops,
to whisper delicate lines about joy
and the blessings of human understanding.
I try. I go to my land, my tower of words and
bolt the door, but the typewriter doesn't fade out
the sounds of blasting and muffled outrage.
My own days bring me slaps on the face.
Every day I am deluged with reminders
that this is not
my land

and this is my land.

I do not believe in the war between races
but in this country
there is war.

Refugee Ship

Like wet cornstarch, I slide
past my grandmother's eyes. Bible

at her side, she removes her glasses.
The pudding thickens.

Mama raised me without language.
I'm orphaned from my Spanish name.
The words are foreign, stumbling
on my tongue. I see in the mirror
my reflection: bronzed skin, black hair.

I feel I am a captive
aboard the refugee ship.
The ship that will never dock.
El barco que nunca atraca.

MARILYN CHIN
Altar

I tell her she has outlived her usefulness.
I point to the corner where dust gathers,
where light has never touched. But there she sits,
a thousand years, hands folded, in a tattered armchair,
with yesterday's news, "the Golden Mountain Edition."
The morning sun slants down the broken eaves,
shading half of her sallow face.

On the upper northwest corner (I'd consulted a geomancer),
a deathtrap shines on the dying bougainvillea.
The carcass of a goatmoth hangs upsidedown,
hollowed out. The only evidence
of her seasonal life is a dash
of shimmery powder, a last cry.

She, who was attracted to that bare bulb,
who danced around that immigrant dream,
will find her end here, this corner,
this solemn altar.

Autumn Leaves

My dead piled up, thick, fragrant, on the fire escape.
My mother ordered me again, and again, to sweep it clean.
All that blooms must fall. I learned this not from the Tao,
    but from high school biology.

Oh, the contradictions of having a broom and not a dustpan!
I swept the leaves down, down through the iron grille
and let the dead rain over the Wong family's patio.

And it was Achilles Wong who completed the task.
    We called her:
The-one-who-cleared-away-another-family's-autumn.
She blossomed, tall, benevolent, notwithstanding.

AMY CLAMPITT
A Procession at Candlemas[1]

1

Moving on or going back to where you came from,
bad news is what you mainly travel with:
a breakup or a breakdown, someone running off

or walking out, called up or called home:
death in the family. Nudged from their stanchions
outside the terminal, anonymous of purpose

as a flock of birds, the bison of the highway
funnel westward onto Route 80, mirroring
an entity that cannot look into itself and know

what makes it what it is. Sooner or later
every trek becomes a funeral procession.
The mother curtained in Intensive Care —

a scene the mind leaves blank, fleeing instead
toward scenes of transhumance,° the belled sheep   *transport of*
moving up the Pyrenees, red-tassled pack llamas   *flocks*

footing velvet-green precipices, the Kurdish
women, jingling with bangles, gorgeous
on their rug-piled mounts — already lying dead,

bereavement altering the moving lights
to a processional, a feast of Candlemas.
Change as child-bearing, birth as a kind

---

[1] February 2. Observed as a church festival in commemoration of the presentation of Christ in the temple and the purification of the Virgin Mary after childbirth.

of shucking off: out of what began
as a Mosaic[2] insult — such a loathing
of the common origin, even a virgin,

having given birth, needs purifying —
to carry fire as though it were a flower,
the terror and the loveliness entrusted

into naked hands, supposing God might have,
might actually need a mother: people have
at times found this a way of being happy.

A Candlemas of moving lights along Route 80;
lighted candles in a corridor from Arlington[3]
over the Potomac, for every carried flame

the name of a dead soldier: an element
fragile as ego, frightening as parturition,°   *giving birth*
necessary and intractable as dreaming.

The lapped, wheelborne integument, layer
within layer, at the core a dream of
something precious, ripped: Where are we?

The sleepers groan, stir, rewrap themselves
about the self's imponderable substance,
or clamber down, numb-footed, half in a drowse

of freezing dark, through a Stonehenge
of fuel pumps, the bison hulks slantwise
beside them, drinking. What is real except

what's fabricated? The jellies glitter
cream-capped in the cafeteria showcase;
gumball globes, Life Savers cinctured

in parcel gilt, plop from their housings
perfect, like miracles. Comb, nail clipper,
lip rouge, mirrors and emollients embody,

niched into the washroom wall case,
the pristine seductiveness of money.
Absently, without inhabitants, this

---

[2] Of or related to Moses or the institutions or writings attributed to him; here, the
Mosaic law that forty days after childbirth a woman must present herself at the temple
for ritual purification.

[3] Arlington National Cemetery.

nowhere oasis wears the place name
of Indian Meadows. The westward-trekking
transhumance, once only, of a people who,

in losing everything they had, lost even
the names they went by, stumbling past
like caribou, perhaps camped here. Who

can assign a trade-in value to that sorrow?
The monk in sheepskin over tucked-up saffron
intoning to a drum becomes the metronome

of one more straggle up Pennsylvania Avenue
in falling snow, a whirl of tenderly
remorseless corpuscles, street gangs

amok among magnolias' pregnant wands,
a stillness at the heart of so much whirling:
beyond the torn integument of childbirth,

sometimes, wrapped like a papoose into a grief
not merely of the ego, you rediscover almost
the rest-in-peace of the placental coracle.

2

Of what the dead were, living, one knows
so little as barely to recognize
the fabric of the backward-ramifying

antecedents, half-noted presences
in darkened rooms: the old, the feared,
the hallowed. Never the same river

drowns the unalterable doorsill. An effigy
in olive wood or pear wood, dank
with the sweat of age, walled in the dark

at Brauron, Argos, Samos:[4] even the unwed
Athene,[5] who had no mother, born — it's declared —
of some man's brain like every other pure idea,

had her own wizened cult object, kept
out of sight like the incontinent whimperer
in the backstairs bedroom, where no child

---

[4] Brauron was a site known from ancient times for the worship of Artemis. Hera
was worshiped at Argos. Samos is an island in the Aegean Sea.

[5] Athena emerged, fully armed, from the head of her father, Zeus.

ever goes — to whom, year after year,
the fair linen of the sacred peplos[6]
was brought in ceremonial procession —

flutes and stringed instruments, wildflower-
hung cattle, nubile Athenian girls, young men
praised for the beauty of their bodies. Who

can unpeel the layers of that seasonal
returning to the dark where memory fails,
as birds re-enter the ancestral flyway?

Daylight, snow falling, knotting of gears:
Chicago. Soot, the rotting backsides
of tenements, grimed trollshapes of ice

underneath the bridges, the tunnel heaving
like a birth canal. Disgorged, the infant
howling in the restroom; steam-table cereal,

pale coffee; wall-eyed TV receivers, armchairs
of molded plastic: the squalor of the day
resumed, the orphaned litter taken up again

unloved, the spawn of botched intentions,
grief a mere hardening of the gut,
a set piece of what can't be avoided:

parents by the tens of thousands living
unthanked, unpaid but in the sour coin
of resentment. Midmorning gray as zinc

along Route 80, corn-stubble quilting
the underside of snowdrifts, the cadaverous
belvedere of windmills, the sullen stare

of feedlot cattle; black creeks puncturing
white terrain, the frozen bottomland
a mush of willow tops; dragnetted in ice,

the Mississippi. Westward toward the dark,
the undertow of scenes come back to, fright
riddling the structures of interior history:

Where is it? Where, in the shucked-off
bundle, the hampered obscurity that has been
for centuries the mumbling lot of women,

---

[6] A linen shawl, cult symbol of Athena; object of the Panathenaic procession in ancient Athens, represented on the Parthenon.

did the thread of fire, too frail
ever to discover what it meant, to risk
even the taking of a shape, relinquish

the seed of possibility, unguessed-at
as a dream of something precious? Memory,
that exquisite blunderer, stumbling

like a migrant bird that finds the flyway
it hardly knew it knew except by instinct,
down the long-unentered nave of childhood,

late on a midwinter afternoon, alone
among the snow-hung hollows of the windbreak
on the far side of the orchard, encounters

sheltering among the evergreens, a small
stilled bird, its cap of clear yellow
slit by a thread of scarlet — the untouched

nucleus of fire, the lost connection
hallowing the wizened effigy, the mother
curtained in Intensive Care: a Candlemas

of moving lights along Route 80, at nightfall,
in falling snow, the stillness and the sorrow
of things moving back to where they came from.

JOHN CLARE
Badger

When midnight comes a host of dogs and men
Go out and track the badger to his den,
And put a sack within the hole, and lie
Till the old grunting badger passes by.
He comes and hears — they let the strongest loose.
The old fox hears the noise and drops the goose.
The poacher shoots and hurries from the cry,
And the old hare half wounded buzzes by.
They get a forkèd stick to bear him down
And clap the dogs and take him to the town,
And bait him all the day with many dogs,
And laugh and shout and fright the scampering hogs.
He runs along and bites at all he meets:
They shout and hollo down the noisy streets.

He turns about to face the loud uproar
And drives the rebels to their very door.
The frequent stone is hurled where'er they go;
When badgers fight, then everyone's a foe.
The dogs are clapped and urged to join the fray;
The badger turns and drives them all away.
Though scarcely half as big, demure and small,
He fights with dogs for hours and beats them all.
The heavy mastiff, savage in the fray,
Lies down and licks his feet and turns away.
The bulldog knows his match and waxes cold,
The badger grins and never leaves his hold.
He drives the crowd and follows at their heels
And bites them through — the drunkard swears and reels.

The frighted women take the boys away,
The blackguard laughs and hurries on the fray.
He tries to reach the woods, an awkward race,
But sticks and cudgels quickly stop the chase.
He turns again and drives the noisy crowd
And beats the many dogs in noises loud.
He drives away and beats them every one,
And then they loose them all and set them on.
He falls as dead and kicked by boys and men,
Then starts and grins and drives the crowd again;
Till kicked and torn and beaten out he lies
And leaves his hold and crackles, groans, and dies.

First Love

I ne'er was struck before that hour
    With love so sudden and so sweet,
Her face it bloomed like a sweet flower
    And stole my heart away complete.
My face turned pale as deadly pale.
    My legs refused to walk away,
And when she looked, what could I ail?
    My life and all seemed turned to clay.

And then my blood rushed to my face
    And took my eyesight quite away,
The trees and bushes round the place
    Seemed midnight at noonday.

I could not see a single thing,
    Words from my eyes did start —
They spoke as chords do from the string,
    And blood burnt round my heart.

Are flowers the winter's choice?
    Is love's bed always snow?
She seemed to hear my silent voice,
    Not love's appeals to know.
I never saw so sweet a face
    As that I stood before.
My heart has left its dwelling-place
    And can return no more.

I Am

I am: yet what I am none cares or knows
    My friends forsake me like a memory lost,
I am the self-consumer of my woes —
    They rise and vanish in oblivious host,
Like shadows in love's frenzied, stifled throes —
And yet I am, and live — like vapors tossed

Into the nothingness of scorn and noise,
    Into the living sea of waking dreams,
Where there is neither sense of life or joys,
    But the vast shipwreck of my life's esteems;
Even the dearest, that I love the best,
Are strange — nay, rather stranger than the rest.

I long for scenes, where man hath never trod,
    A place where woman never smiled or wept —
There to abide with my Creator, God,
    And sleep as I in childhood sweetly slept,
Untroubling, and untroubled where I lie,
The grass below — above the vaulted sky.

Henri Cole
40 Days and 40 Nights

Opening a vein he called my radial,
the phlebotomist introduced himself as Angel.
Since the counseling it had been ten days
of deep inversion — self-recrimination weighed

against regret, those useless emotions.
Now there would be thirty more enduring the notion
of some self-made doom foretold in the palm.

Waiting for blood work with aristocratic calm,
big expectant mothers from Spanish Harlem
appeared cut-out, as if Matisse had conceived them.
Their bright smocks ruffling like plumage before the fan,
they might themselves have been angels, come by land.

Consent and disclosure signed away, liquid gold
of urine glimmering in a plastic cup, threshold
of last doubt crossed, the red fluid was drawn
in a steady hematic ooze from my arm.
"Now, darling, the body doesn't lie," Angel said.
DNA and enzymes and antigens in his head
true as lines in the face in the mirror
on his desk.

      I smiled, pretending to be cheered.
In the way that some become aware of God
when they cease becoming overawed
with themselves, no less than the artist concealed
behind the surface of whatever object or felt
words he builds, so I in my first week
of waiting let the self be displaced by each
day's simplest events, letting them speak
with emblematic voices that might teach me.
They did . . . until I happened on the card
from the clinic, black-framed as a graveyard.
Could the code 12 22 90 have represented
some near time, December 22, 1990, for repentance?
The second week I believed it. The fourth I
rejected it and much else loved, until the eyes
teared those last days and the lab phoned.

Back at the clinic — someone's cheap cologne,
Sunday lamb yet on the tongue, the mind cool as a pitcher
of milk, a woman's knitting needles aflutter,
Angel's hand in mind — I watched the verdict-lips move,
rubbed my arm, which, once pricked, had tingled then bruised.

SAMUEL TAYLOR COLERIDGE

Dejection: An Ode

Late, late yestreen I saw the new Moon,
With the old Moon in her arms;
And I fear, I fear, my master dear!
We shall have a deadly storm.
        — BALLAD OF SIR PATRICK SPENCE

1

Well! If the Bard was weather-wise, who made
        The grand old ballad of Sir Patrick Spence,
        This night, so tranquil now, will not go hence
Unroused by winds, that ply a busier trade
Than those which mold yon cloud in lazy flakes,
Or the dull sobbing draft, that moans and rakes
Upon the strings of this Aeolian lute,[1]
        Which better far were mute.
    For lo! the New-moon winter-bright!
    And overspread with phantom light,
    (With swimming phantom light o'erspread
    But rimmed and circled by a silver thread)
I see the old Moon in her lap, foretelling
        The coming-on of rain and squally blast.
And oh! that even now the gust were swelling,
        And the slant night shower driving loud and fast!
Those sounds which oft have raised me, whilst they awed,
        And sent my soul abroad,
Might now perhaps their wonted impulse give,
Might startle this dull pain, and make it move and live!

2

A grief without a pang, void, dark, and drear,
        A stifled, drowsy, unimpassioned grief,
        Which finds no natural outlet, no relief,
            In word, or sigh, or tear —
O Lady! in this wan and heartless mood,
To other thoughts by yonder throstle wooed,
        All this long eve, so balmy and serene,
Have I been gazing on the western sky,
        And its peculiar tint of yellow green:

---

[1] An Aeolian lute or harp is a stringed instrument that produces musical sounds when touched by a current of air.

And still I gaze — and with how blank an eye!
And those thin clouds above, in flakes and bars,
That give away their motion to the stars;
Those stars, that glide behind them or between,
Now sparkling, now bedimmed, but always seen:
Yon crescent Moon, as fixed as if it grew
In its own cloudless, starless lake of blue;
I see them all so excellently fair,
I see, not feel, how beautiful they are!

3

My genial spirits fail;
And what can these avail
To lift the smothering weight from off my breast?
It were a vain endeavor,
Though I should gaze forever
On that green light that lingers in the west:
I may not hope from outward forms to win
The passion and the life, whose fountains are within.

4

O Lady! we receive but what we give,
And in our life alone does Nature live:
Ours is her wedding garment, ours her shroud!
And would we aught behold, of higher worth,
Than that inanimate cold world allowed
To the poor loveless ever-anxious crowd,
Ah! from the soul itself must issue forth
A light, a glory, a fair luminous cloud
Enveloping the Earth —
And from the soul itself must there be sent
A sweet and potent voice, of its own birth,
Of all sweet sounds the life and element!

5

O pure of heart! thou need'st not ask of me
What this strong music in the soul may be!
What, and wherein it doth exist,
This light, this glory, this fair luminous mist,
This beautiful and beauty-making power.
Joy, virtuous Lady! Joy that ne'er was given,
Save to the pure, and in their purest hour,
Life, and Life's effluence, cloud at once and shower,
Joy, Lady! is the spirit and the power,

Which wedding Nature to us gives in dower
    A new Earth and new Heaven,
Undreamt of by the sensual and the proud —
Joy is the sweet voice, Joy the luminous cloud —
        We in ourselves rejoice!
And thence flows all that charms or ear or sight,
    All melodies the echoes of that voice,
All colors a suffusion from that light.

6

There was a time when, though my path was rough,
    This joy within me dallied with distress,
And all misfortunes were but as the stuff
    Whence Fancy made me dreams of happiness:
For hope grew round me, like the twining vine,
And fruits, and foliage, not my own, seemed mine.
But now afflictions bow me down to earth:
Nor care I that they rob me of my mirth;
        But oh! each visitation
Suspends what nature gave me at my birth,
    My shaping spirit of Imagination.

For not to think of what I needs must feel,
    But to be still and patient, all I can;
And haply by abstruse research to steal
    From my own nature all the natural man —
This was my sole resource, my only plan:
Till that which suits a part infects the whole,
And now is almost grown the habit of my soul.

7

Hence, viper thoughts, that coil around my mind,
    Reality's dark dream!
I turn from you, and listen to the wind,
    Which long has raved unnoticed. What a scream
Of agony by torture lengthened out
That lute sent forth! Thou Wind, that rav'st without,
    Bare crag, or mountain tairn,° or blasted tree,   *pool*
Or pine grove whither woodman never clomb,
Or lonely house, long held the witches' home,
    Methinks were fitter instruments for thee,
Mad Lutanist! who in this month of showers,
Of dark-brown gardens, and of peeping flowers,
Mak'st Devils' yule, with worse than wintry song,

The blossoms, buds, and timorous leaves among.
     Thou Actor, perfect in all tragic sounds!
Thou mighty Poet, e'en to frenzy bold!
        What tell'st thou now about?
        'Tis of the rushing of an host in rout,
    With groans, of trampled men, with smarting wounds —
At once they groan with pain, and shudder with the cold!
But hush! there is a pause of deepest silence!
     And all that noise, as of a rushing crowd,
With groans, and tremulous shudderings — all is over —
    It tells another tale, with sounds less deep and loud!
       A tale of less affright,
       And tempered with delight,
As Otway's[2] self had framed the tender lay —
      'Tis of a little child
      Upon a lonesome wild,
Not far from home, but she hath lost her way:
And now moans low in bitter grief and fear,
And now screams loud, and hopes to make her mother hear.

8

'Tis midnight, but small thoughts have I of sleep:
Full seldom may my friend such vigils keep!
Visit her, gentle Sleep! with wings of healing,
    And may this storm be but a mountain birth,
May all the stars hang bright above her dwelling,
    Silent as though they watched the sleeping Earth!
       With light heart may she rise,
       Gay fancy, cheerful eyes,
    Joy lift her spirit, joy attune her voice;
To her may all things live, from pole to pole,
Their life the eddying of her living soul!
    O simple spirit, guided from above,
Dear Lady! friend devoutest of my choice,
Thus mayest thou ever, evermore rejoice.

---

[2] Thomas Otway (1652–1685), a dramatist whose plays emphasize pathos and sentiment.

The Rime of the Ancient Mariner

In Seven Parts

> *Facile credo, plures esse Naturas invisibiles quam visi-*
> *biles in rerum universitate. Sed horum* [sic] *omnium*
> *familiam quis nobis enarrabit? et gradus et cognationes*
> *et discrimina et singulorum munera? Quid agunt? quae*
> *loca habitant? Harum rerum notitiam semper ambivit*
> *ingenium humanum, nunquam attigit. Juvat, interea,*
> *non diffiteor, quandoque in animo, tanquam in tabulà,*
> *majoris et melioris mundi imaginem contemplari: ne*
> *mens assuefacta hodiernae vitae minutiis se contrahat*
> *nimis, et tota subsidat in pusillas cogitationes. Sed*
> *veritati interea invigilandum est, modusque servandus,*
> *ut certa ab incertis, diem a nocte, distinguamus.*[1]

— T. BURNET

Part I

An ancient Mariner meeteth three Gallants bidden to a wedding feast, and detaineth one.

It is an ancient Mariner
And he stoppeth one of three.
— "By thy long gray beard and glittering eye,
Now wherefore stopp'st thou me?

The Bridegroom's doors are opened wide,
And I am next of kin;
The guests are met, the feast is set:
May'st hear the merry din."

He holds him with his skinny hand,
"There was a ship," quoth he.
"Hold off! unhand me, graybeard loon!"
Eftsoons° his hand dropped he.   *immediately*

---

[1] From Burnet's *Archaeologiae Philosophiae:* "I can easily believe that there are more invisible than visible beings in the universe. But of their families, degrees, connections, distinctions, and functions, who shall tell us? How do they act? Where are they found? About such matters the human mind has always circled without attaining knowledge. Yet I do not doubt that sometimes it is well for the soul to contemplate as in a picture the image of a larger and better world, lest the mind, habituated to the small concerns of daily life, limit itself too much and sink entirely into trivial thinking. But meanwhile we must be on watch for the truth, avoiding extremes, so that we may distinguish certain from uncertain, day from night." Burnet was a seventeenth-century English theologian.

The Wedding Guest is spellbound by the eye of the old seafaring man, and constrained to hear his tale.

He holds him with his glittering eye —
The Wedding Guest stood still,
And listens like a three years' child:
The Mariner hath his will.

The Wedding Guest sat on a stone:
He cannot choose but hear;
And thus spake on that ancient man,
The bright-eyed Mariner.

"The ship was cheered, the harbor cleared,
Merrily did we drop
Below the kirk,° below the hill,   *church*
Below the lighthouse top.

The Mariner tells how the ship sailed southward with a good wind and fair weather, till it reached the line.

The Sun came up upon the left,
Out of the sea came he!
And he shone bright, and on the right
Went down into the sea.

Higher and higher every day,
Till over the mast at noon — "
The Wedding Guest here beat his breast,
For he heard the loud bassoon.

The Wedding Guest heareth the bridal music; but the Mariner continueth his tale.

The bride hath paced into the hall,
Red as a rose is she;
Nodding their heads before her goes
The merry minstrelsy.

The Wedding Guest he beat his breast,
Yet he cannot choose but hear;
And thus spake on that ancient man,
The bright-eyed Mariner.

The ship driven by a storm toward the South Pole.

"And now the STORM-BLAST came, and he
Was tyrannous and strong;
He struck with his o'ertaking wings,
And chased us south along.

With sloping masts and dipping prow,
As who pursued with yell and blow
Still treads the shadow of his foe,
And forward bends his head,
The ship drove fast, loud roared the blast,
And southward aye we fled.

And now there came both mist and snow,
And it grew wondrous cold:
And ice, mast-high, came floating by,
As green as emerald.

The land of ice, and of fearful sounds where no living thing was to be seen. And through the drifts the snowy clifts°   *cliffs*
Did send a dismal sheen:
Nor shapes of men nor beasts we ken —
The ice was all between.

The ice was here, the ice was there,
The ice was all around:
It cracked and growled, and roared and howled,
Like noises in a swound!°   *swoon*

Till a great sea bird, called the Albatross, came through the snow-fog and was received with great joy and hospitality. At length did cross an Albatross,
Thorough the fog it came;
As if it had been a Christian soul,
We hailed it in God's name.

It ate the food it ne'er had eat,
And round and round it flew.
The ice did split with a thunder-fit;
The helmsman steered us through!

And lo! the Albatross proveth a bird of good omen, and followeth the ship as it returned northward through fog and floating ice. And a good south wind sprung up behind;
The Albatross did follow,
And every day, for food or play,
Came to the mariners' hollo!

In mist or cloud, on mast or shroud,
It perched for vespers nine;
Whiles all the night, through fog-smoke white,
Glimmered the white Moon-shine."

The ancient Mariner inhospitably killeth the pious bird of good omen. "God save thee, ancient Mariner!
From the fiends, that plague thee thus! —
Why look'st thou so?" — With my crossbow
I shot the ALBATROSS.

Part II

The Sun now rose upon the right:
Out of the sea came he,
Still hid in mist, and on the left
Went down into the sea.

And the good south wind still blew behind,
But no sweet bird did follow,
Nor any day for food or play
Came to the mariners' hollo!

His shipmates cry out against the ancient Mariner, for killing the bird of good luck.

And I had done a hellish thing,
And it would work 'em woe:
For all averred, I had killed the bird
That made the breeze to blow.
Ah wretch! said they, the bird to slay,
That made the breeze to blow!

But when the fog cleared off, they justify the same, and thus make themselves accomplices in the crime.

Nor dim nor red, like God's own head,
The glorious Sun uprist:
Then all averred, I had killed the bird
That brought the fog and mist.
'Twas right, said they, such birds to slay,
That bring the fog and mist.

The fair breeze continues; the ship enters the Pacific Ocean, and sails northward, even till it reaches the Line.

The fair breeze blew, the white foam flew,
The furrow followed free;
We were the first that ever burst
Into that silent sea.

The ship hath been suddenly becalmed.

Down dropped the breeze, the sails dropped down,
'Twas sad as sad could be;
And we did speak only to break
The silence of the sea!

All in a hot and copper sky,
The bloody Sun, at noon,
Right up above the mast did stand,
No bigger than the Moon.

Day after day, day after day,
We stuck, nor breath nor motion;
As idle as a painted ship
Upon a painted ocean.

And the Albatross begins to be avenged.

Water, water, everywhere,
And all the boards did shrink;
Water, water, everywhere,
Nor any drop to drink.

The very deep did rot: O Christ!
That ever this should be!

Yea, slimy things did crawl with legs
Upon the slimy sea.

About, about, in reel and rout
The death-fires danced at night;
The water, like a witch's oils,
Burnt green, and blue and white.

And some in dreams assurèd were
A Spirit had fol-   Of the Spirit that plagued us so;
lowed them; one of   Nine fathom deep he had followed us
the invisible inhab-   From the land of mist and snow.
itants of this
planet, neither departed souls nor angels; concerning whom the learned Jew, Josephus, and
the Platonic and Constantinopolitan, Michael Psellus, may be consulted. They are very
numerous, there is no climate or element without one or more.

And every tongue, through utter drought,
Was withered at the root;
We could not speak, no more than if
We had been choked with soot.

The shipmates, in   Ah! well-a-day! what evil looks
their sore distress,   Had I from old and young!
would fain throw   Instead of the cross, the Albatross
the whole guilt on   About my neck was hung.
the ancient Mari-
ner: in sign whereof they hang the dead sea bird round his neck.

Part III

There passed a weary time. Each throat
Was parched, and glazed each eye.
A weary time! a weary time!
How glazed each weary eye,
The ancient Mar-   When looking westward, I beheld
iner beholdeth a   A something in the sky.
sign in the ele-
ment afar off.

At first it seemed a little speck,
And then it seemed a mist;
It moved and moved, and took at last
A certain shape, I wist.°   *knew*

A speck, a mist, a shape, I wist!
And still it neared and neared:
As if it dodged a water sprite,
It plunged and tacked and veered.

At its nearer approach, it seemeth him to be a ship; and at a dear ransom he freeth his speech from the bonds of thirst.

With throats unslaked, with black lips baked,
We could nor laugh nor wail;
Through utter drought all dumb we stood!
I bit my arm, I sucked the blood,
And cried, A sail! a sail!

A flash of joy;

With throats unslaked, with black lips baked,
Agape they heard me call:
Gramercy! they for joy did grin,
And all at once their breath drew in,
As they were drinking all.

And horror follows. For can it be a ship that comes onward without wind or tide?

See! see! (I cried) she tacks no more!
Hither to work us weal;
Without a breeze, without a tide,
She steadies with upright keel!

The western wave was all aflame.
The day was well nigh done!
Almost upon the western wave
Rested the broad bright Sun;
When that strange shape drove suddenly
Betwixt us and the Sun.

It seemeth him but the skeleton of a ship.

And straight the Sun was flecked with bars,
(Heaven's Mother send us grace!)
As if through a dungeon grate he peered
With broad and burning face.

Alas! (thought I, and my heart beat loud)
How fast she nears and nears!
Are those *her* sails that glance in the Sun,
Like restless gossameres?

And its ribs are seen as bars on the face of the setting Sun.

The Specter-Woman and her Deathmate, and no other on board the skeleton ship.

Are those *her* ribs through which the Sun
Did peer, as through a grate?
And is that Woman all her crew?
Is that a DEATH? and are there two?
Is DEATH that woman's mate?

Like vessel, like crew!

Her lips were red, *her* looks were free,
Her locks were yellow as gold:
Her skin was as white as leprosy,
The Nightmare LIFE-IN-DEATH was she,
Who thicks man's blood with cold.

*Death and Life-
in-Death have
diced for the ship's
crew, and she (the
latter) winneth the
ancient Mariner.*

The naked hulk alongside came,
And the twain were casting dice;
"The game is done! I've won! I've won!"
Quoth she, and whistles thrice.

*No twilight within
the courts of the
Sun.*

The Sun's rim dips; the stars rush out:
At one stride comes the dark;
With far-heard whisper, o'er the sea,
Off shot the specter-bark.

*At the rising of the
Moon,*

We listened and looked sideways up!
Fear at my heart, as at a cup,
My lifeblood seemed to sip!
The stars were dim, and thick the night,
The steersman's face by his lamp gleamed white;
From the sails the dew did drip —
Till clomb above the eastern bar
The hornèd Moon, with one bright star
Within the nether tip.

One after another,

One after one, by the star-dogged Moon,
Too quick for groan or sigh,
Each turned his face with ghastly pang,
And cursed me with his eye.

*His shipmates drop
down dead.*

Four times fifty living men,
(And I heard nor sigh nor groan)
With heavy thump, a lifeless lump,
They dropped down one by one.

*But Life-in-Death
begins her work on
the ancient Mari-
ner.*

The souls did from their bodies fly —
They fled to bliss or woe!
And every soul, it passed me by,
Like the whizz of my cross-bow!

Part IV

*The Wedding
Guest feareth that
a Spirit is talking
to him;*

"I fear thee, ancient Mariner!
I fear thy skinny hand!
And thou art long, and lank, and brown,
As is the ribbed sea-sand.

I fear thee and thy glittering eye,
And thy skinny hand, so brown." —

But the ancient Mariner assureth him of his bodily life, and pro- ceedeth to relate his horrible pen- ance.

Fear not, fear not, thou Wedding Guest!
This body dropped not down.

Alone, alone, all, all alone,
Alone on a wide wide sea!
And never a saint took pity on
My soul in agony.

He despiseth the creatures of the calm,

The many men, so beautiful!
And they all dead did lie:
And a thousand thousand slimy things
Lived on; and so did I.

And envieth that they should live, and so many lie dead.

I looked upon the rotting sea,
And drew my eyes away;
I looked upon the rotting deck,
And there the dead men lay.

I looked to heaven, and tried to pray;
But or ever a prayer had gushed,
A wicked whisper came, and made
My heart as dry as dust.

I closed my lids, and kept them close,
And the balls like pulses beat,
For the sky and the sea, and the sea and the sky
Lay like a load on my weary eye,
And the dead were at my feet.

But the curse liveth for him in the eye of the dead men.

The cold sweat melted from their limbs,
Nor rot nor reek did they:
The look with which they looked on me
Had never passed away.

An orphan's curse would drag to hell
A spirit from on high;
But oh! more horrible than that
Is the curse in a dead man's eye!
Seven days, seven nights, I saw that curse,
And yet I could not die.

In his loneliness and fixedness he yearneth towards the journeying Moon, and the stars that still sojourn, yet still

The moving Moon went up the sky,
And nowhere did abide:
Softly she was going up,
And a star or two beside —

Her beams bemocked the sultry main,
Like April hoar-frost spread;

move onward; and But where the ship's huge shadow lay,
everywhere the blue The charméd water burnt alway
sky belongs to A still and awful red.
them, and is their
appointed rest, and their native country and their own natural homes, which they enter
unannounced, as lords that are certainly expected and yet there is a silent joy at their arrival.

By the light of the Beyond the shadow of the ship,
Moon he beholdeth I watched the water snakes:
God's creatures of They moved in tracks of shining white,
the great calm. And when they reared, the elfish light
Fell off in hoary flakes.

Within the shadow of the ship
I watched their rich attire:
Blue, glossy green, and velvet black,
They coiled and swam; and every track
Was a flash of golden fire.

Their beauty and O happy living things! no tongue
their happiness. Their beauty might declare:
A spring of love gushed from my heart,
He blesseth them And I blessed them unaware:
in his heart. Sure my kind saint took pity on me,
And I blessed them unaware.

The spell begins to The self-same moment I could pray;
break. And from my neck so free
The Albatross fell off, and sank
Like lead into the sea.

Part V

Oh sleep! it is a gentle thing,
Beloved from pole to pole!
To Mary Queen the praise be given!
She sent the gentle sleep from Heaven,
That slid into my soul.

By grace of the The silly° buckets on the deck,   *lowly*
holy Mother, the That had so long remained,
ancient Mariner is I dreamt that they were filled with dew;
refreshed with rain. And when I awoke, it rained.

My lips were wet, my throat was cold,
My garments all were dank;
Sure I had drunken in my dreams,
And still my body drank.

I moved, and could not feel my limbs:
I was so light — almost
I thought that I had died in sleep,
And was a blessèd ghost.

He heareth sounds
and seeth strange
sights and commo-
tions in the sky
and the element.

And soon I heard a roaring wind:
It did not come anear;
But with its sound it shook the sails,
That were so thin and sere.

The upper air burst into life!
And a hundred fire-flags sheen,
To and fro they were hurried about!
And to and fro, and in and out,
The wan stars danced between.

And the coming wind did roar more loud,
And the sails did sigh like sedge;
And the rain poured down from one black cloud;
The Moon was at its edge.

The thick black cloud was cleft, and still
The Moon was at its side:
Like waters shot from some high crag,
The lightning fell with never a jag,
A river steep and wide.

The bodies of the
ship's crew are in-
spirited, and the
ship moves on;

The loud wind never reached the ship,
Yet now the ship moved on!
Beneath the lightning and the Moon
The dead men gave a groan.

They groaned, they stirred, they all uprose,
Nor spake, nor moved their eyes;
It had been strange, even in a dream,
To have seen those dead men rise.

The helmsman steered, the ship moved on;
Yet never a breeze up-blew;
The mariners all 'gan work the ropes,
Where they were wont to do;
They raised their limbs like lifeless tools —
We were a ghastly crew.

The body of my brother's son
Stood by me, knee to knee:
The body and I pulled at one rope,
But he said nought to me.

"I fear thee, ancient Mariner!"
Be calm, thou Wedding Guest!
'Twas not those souls that fled in pain,
Which to their corses came again,
But a troop of spirits blest:

*But not by the
souls of the men,
nor by demons of
earth or middle air,
but by a blèssed
troop of angelic
spirits, sent down
by the invocation of
the guardian saint.*

For when it dawned — they dropped their arms,
And clustered round the mast;
Sweet sounds rose slowly through their mouths,
And from their bodies passed.

Around, around, flew each sweet sound,
Then darted to the Sun;
Slowly the sounds came back again,
Now mixed, now one by one.

Sometimes a-dropping from the sky
I heard the sky-lark sing;
Sometimes all little birds that are,
How they seemed to fill the sea and air
With their sweet jargoning!°   *warbling*

And now 'twas like all instruments,
Now like a lonely flute;
And now it is an angel's song,
That makes the heavens be mute.

It ceased; yet still the sails made on
A pleasant noise till noon,
A noise like of a hidden brook
In the leafy month of June,
That to the sleeping woods all night
Singeth a quiet tune.

Till noon we quietly sailed on,
Yet never a breeze did breathe:
Slowly and smoothly went the ship,
Moved onward from beneath.

*The lonesome
Spirit from the
South Pole carries
on the ship as far
as the Line, in
obedience to the
angelic troop, but
still requireth vengeance.*

Under the keel nine fathom deep,
From the land of mist and snow,
The spirit slid: and it was he
That made the ship to go.
The sails at noon left off their tune,
And the ship stood still also.

The Sun, right up above the mast,
Had fixed her to the ocean:
But in a minute she 'gan stir,
With a short uneasy motion —
Backwards and forwards half her length
With a short uneasy motion.

Then like a pawing horse let go,
She made a sudden bound:
It flung the blood into my head,
And I fell down in a swound.

The Polar Spirit's fellow demons, the invisible inhabitants of the element, take part in his wrong; and two of them relate, one to the other, that penance long and heavy for the ancient Mariner hath been accorded to the Polar Spirit, who returneth southward.

How long in that same fit I lay,
I have not° to declare;   *cannot*
But ere my living life returned,
I heard and in my soul discerned
Two voices in the air.

"Is it he?" quoth one, "Is this the man?
By him who died on cross,
With his cruel bow he laid full low
The harmless Albatross.

The spirit who bideth by himself
In the land of mist and snow,
He loved the bird that loved the man
Who shot him with his bow."

The other was a softer voice,
As soft as honey-dew:
Quoth he, "The man hath penance done,
And penance more will do."

Part VI

FIRST VOICE
"But tell me, tell me! speak again,
Thy soft response renewing —
What makes that ship drive on so fast?
What is the ocean doing?"

SECOND VOICE
"Still as a slave before his lord,
The ocean hath no blast;
His great bright eye most silently
Up to the Moon is cast —

If he may know which way to go;
For she guides him smooth or grim.
See, brother, see! how graciously
She looketh down on him."

FIRST VOICE

The Mariner hath
been cast into a
trance; for the an-
gelic power causeth
the vessel to drive
northward faster
than human life
could endure.

"But why drives on that ship so fast,
Without or wave or wind?"

SECOND VOICE

"The air is cut away before,
And closes from behind.

Fly, brother, fly! more high, more high!
Or we shall be belated:
For slow and slow that ship will go,
When the Mariner's trance is abated."

The supernatural
motion is retarded;
the Mariner
awakes, and his
penance begins
anew.

I woke, and we were sailing on
As in a gentle weather:
'Twas night, calm night, the moon was high;
The dead men stood together.

All stood together on the deck,
For a charnel-dungeon fitter:
All fixed on me their stony eyes,
That in the Moon did glitter.

The pang, the curse, with which they died,
Had never passed away:
I could not draw my eyes from theirs,
Nor turn them up to pray.

The curse is finally
expiated.

And now this spell was snapped: once more
I viewed the ocean green,
And looked far forth, yet little saw
Of what had else been seen —

Like one, that on a lonesome road
Doth walk in fear and dread,
And having once turned round walks on,
And turns no more his head;
Because he knows, a frightful fiend
Doth close behind him tread.

But soon there breathed a wind on me,
Nor sound nor motion made:

Its path was not upon the sea,
In ripple or in shade.

It raised my hair, it fanned my cheek
Like a meadow-gale of spring —
It mingled strangely with my fears,
Yet it felt like a welcoming.

Swiftly, swiftly flew the ship,
Yet she sailed softly too:
Sweetly, sweetly blew the breeze —
On me alone it blew.

And the ancient   Oh! dream of joy! is this indeed
Mariner beholdeth   The lighthouse top I see?
his native country.   Is this the hill? is this the kirk?
Is this mine own countree?

We drifted o'er the harbor-bar,
And I with sobs did pray —
O let me be awake, my God!
Or let me sleep alway.

The harbor bay was clear as glass,
So smoothly it was strewn!
And on the bay the moonlight lay,
And the shadow of the Moon.

The rock shone bright, the kirk no less,
That stands above the rock:
The moonlight steeped in silentness
The steady weathercock.

And the bay was white with silent light,
The angelic spirits   Till rising from the same,
leave the dead bod-   Full many shapes, that shadows were,
ies,   In crimson colors came.

A little distance from the prow
And appear in their   Those crimson shadows were:
own forms of light.   I turned my eyes upon the deck —
Oh, Christ! what saw I there!

Each corse lay flat, lifeless and flat,
And, by the holy rood!°   *cross of Christ*
A man all light, a seraph°-man,   *angel-like*
On every corse there stood.

This seraph-band, each waved his hand:
It was a heavenly sight!
They stood as signals to the land,
Each one a lovely light;

This seraph-band, each waved his hand,
No voice did they impart —
No voice; but oh! the silence sank
Like music on my heart.

But soon I heard the dash of oars,
I heard the Pilot's cheer;
My head was turned perforce away
And I saw a boat appear.

The Pilot and the Pilot's boy,
I heard them coming fast:
Dear Lord in Heaven! it was a joy
The dead men could not blast.

I saw a third — I heard his voice:
It is the Hermit good!
He singeth loud his godly hymns
That he makes in the wood.
He'll shrieve my soul, he'll wash away
The Albatross's blood.

Part VII

The Hermit of the Wood

This Hermit good lives in that wood
Which slopes down to the sea.
How loudly his sweet voice he rears!
He loves to talk with marineres
That come from a far countree.

He kneels at morn, and noon, and eve —
He hath a cushion plump:
It is the moss that wholly hides
The rotted old oak stump.

The skiff-boat neared: I heard them talk,
"Why, this is strange, I trow!
Where are those lights so many and fair,
That signal made but now?"

Approacheth the ship with wonder.

"Strange, by my faith!" the Hermit said —
"And they answered not our cheer!
The planks looked warped! and see those sails,

How thin they are and sere!
I never saw aught like to them,
Unless perchance it were

Brown skeletons of leaves that lag
My forest-brook along;
When the ivy tod° is heavy with snow,   *bushy clump*
And the owlet whoops to the wolf below,
That eats the she-wolf's young."

"Dear Lord! it hath a fiendish look,"
The Pilot made reply,
"I am a-feared" — "Push on, push on!"
Said the Hermit cheerily.

The boat came closer to the ship,
But I nor spake nor stirred;
The boat came close beneath the ship,
And straight a sound was heard.

The ship suddenly
sinketh.

Under the water it rumbled on,
Still louder and more dread:
It reached the ship, it split the bay;
The ship went down like lead.

The ancient Mari-
ner is saved in the
Pilot's boat.

Stunned by that loud and dreadful sound,
Which sky and ocean smote,
Like one that hath been seven days drowned
My body lay afloat;
But swift as dreams, myself I found
Within the Pilot's boat.

Upon the whirl, where sank the ship,
The boat spun round and round;
And all was still, save that the hill
Was telling of the sound.

I moved my lips — the Pilot shrieked
And fell down in a fit;
The holy Hermit raised his eyes,
And prayed where he did sit.

I took the oars: the Pilot's boy,
Who now doth crazy go,
Laughed loud and long, and all the while
His eyes went to and fro.
"Ha! ha!" quoth he, "full plain I see,
The Devil knows how to row."

And now, all in my own countree,
I stood on the firm land!
The Hermit stepped forth from the boat,
And scarcely he could stand.

The ancient Mari-
ner earnestly en-
treateth the Hermit
to shrieve him; and
the penance of life
falls on him.

"O shrieve me, shrieve me, holy man!"
The Hermit crossed his brow.
"Say quick," quoth he, "I bid thee say —
What manner of man art thou?"

Forthwith this frame of mine was wrenched
With a woeful agony,
Which forced me to begin my tale;
And then it left me free.

And ever and anon
throughout his
future life an agony
constraineth him to
travel from land to
land;

Since then, at an uncertain hour,
That agony returns:
And till my ghastly tale is told,
This heart within me burns.

I pass, like night, from land to land;
I have strange power of speech;
That moment that his face I see,
I know the man that must hear me:
To him my tale I teach.

What loud uproar bursts from that door!
The wedding guests are there:
But in the garden-bower the bride
And bridemaids singing are:
And hark the little vesper bell,
Which biddeth me to prayer!

O Wedding Guest! this soul hath been
Alone on a wide wide sea:
So lonely 'twas, that God himself
Scarce seemèd there to be.

O sweeter than the marriage feast,
'Tis sweeter far to me,
To walk together to the kirk
With a goodly company!

To walk together to the kirk,
And all together pray,
While each to his great Father bends,
Old men, and babes, and loving friends
And youths and maidens gay!

And to teach, by
his own example,
love and reverence
to all things that
God made and
loveth.

Farewell, farewell! but this I tell
To thee, thou Wedding Guest!
He prayeth well, who loveth well
Both man and bird and beast.

He prayeth best, who loveth best
All things both great and small;
For the dear God who loveth us,
He made and loveth all.

The Mariner, whose eye is bright,
Whose beard with age is hoar,
Is gone: and now the Wedding Guest
Turned from the bridegroom's door.

He went like one that hath been stunned,
And is of sense forlorn:
A sadder and a wiser man,
He rose the morrow morn.

WILLIAM COWPER

The Castaway

Obscurest night involved the sky,
    The Atlantic billows roared,
When such a destined wretch as I,
    Washed headlong from on board,
Of friends, of hope, of all bereft,
His floating home forever left.

No braver chief could Albion boast
    Than he with whom he went,[1]
Nor ever ship left Albion's coast,
    With warmer wishes sent.
He loved them both, but both in vain,
Nor him beheld, nor her again.

Not long beneath the whelming brine,
    Expert to swim, he lay;
Nor soon he felt his strength decline,
    Or courage die away;
But waged with death a lasting strife,
Supported by despair of life.

---

[1] Cowper's poem is based on an incident in Richard Walter's *A Voyage Round the World by . . . George Anson* (1748).

He shouted; nor his friends had failed
    To check the vessel's course,
But so the furious blast prevailed,
    That, pitiless perforce,
They left their outcast mate behind,
And scudded still before the wind.

Some succor yet they could afford;
    And, such as storms allow,
The cask, the coop, the floated cord,
    Delayed not to bestow.
But he (they knew) nor ship, nor shore,
Whate'er they gave, should visit more.

Nor, cruel as it seemed, could he
    Their haste himself condemn,
Aware that flight, in such a sea,
    Alone could rescue them;
Yet bitter felt it still to die
Deserted, and his friends so nigh.

He long survives, who lives an hour
    In ocean, self-upheld;
And so long he, with unspent power,
    His destiny repelled;
And ever, as the minutes flew,
Entreated help, or cried, "Adieu!"

At length, his transient respite past,
    His comrades, who before
Had heard his voice in every blast,
    Could catch the sound no more.
For then, by toil subdued, he drank
The stifling wave, and then he sank.

No poet wept him; but the page
    Of narrative sincere,
That tells his name, his worth, his age,
    Is wet with Anson's tear.
And tears by bards or heroes shed
Alike immortalize the dead.

I therefore purpose not, or dream,
    Descanting on his fate,
To give the melancholy theme
    A more enduring date:

But misery still delights to trace
Its semblance in another's case.

No voice divine the storm allayed,
    No light propitious shone,
When, snatched from all effectual aid,
    We perished, each alone;
But I beneath a rougher sea,
And whelmed in deeper gulfs than he.

Epitaph on a Hare

Here lies, whom hound did ne'er pursue,
    Nor swifter greyhound follow,
Whose foot ne'er tainted morning dew,
    Nor ear heard huntsman's hallo',

Old Tiney, surliest of his kind,
    Who, nursed with tender care,
And to domestic bounds confined,
    Was still a wild jack-hare.

Though duly from my hand he took
    His pittance every night,
He did it with a jealous look,
    And, when he could, would bite.

His diet was of wheaten bread,
    And milk, and oats, and straw,
Thistles, or lettuces instead,
    With sand to scour his maw.

On twigs of hawthorn he regaled,
    On pippins' russet peel;
And, when his juicy salads failed,
    Sliced carrot pleased him well.

A Turkey carpet was his lawn,
    Whereon he loved to bound,
To skip and gambol like a fawn,
    And swing his rump around.

His frisking was at evening hours,
    For then he lost his fear;
But most before approaching showers,
    Or when a storm drew near.

Eight years and five round-rolling moons
    He thus saw steal away,
Dozing out all his idle noons,
    And every night at play.

I kept him for his humor's sake,
    For he would oft beguile
My heart of thoughts that made it ache,
    And force me to a smile.

But now, beneath this walnut-shade
    He finds his long, last home,
And waits in snug concealment laid,
    Till gentler Puss shall come.

He, still more agèd, feels the shocks
    From which no care can save,
And, partner once of Tiney's box,
    Must soon partake his grave.

HART CRANE
The Broken Tower

The bell-rope that gathers God at dawn
Dispatches me as though I dropped down the knell
Of a spent day — to wander the cathedral lawn
From pit to crucifix, feet chill on steps from hell.

Have you not heard, have you not seen that corps
Of shadows in the tower, whose shoulders sway
Antiphonal carillons launched before
The stars are caught and hived in the sun's ray?

The bells, I say, the bells break down their tower;
And swing I know not where. Their tongues engrave
Membrane through marrow, my long-scattered score
Of broken intervals . . . And I, their sexton slave!

Oval encyclicals in canyons heaping
The impasse high with choir. Banked voices slain!
Pagodas, campaniles° with reveilles outleaping —   *bell towers*
O terraced echoes prostrate on the plain! . . .

And so it was I entered the broken world
To trace the visionary company of love, its voice

An instant in the wind (I know not whither hurled)
But not for long to hold each desperate choice.

My word I poured. But was it cognate, scored
Of that tribunal monarch of the air
Whose thigh embronzes earth, strikes crystal Word
In wounds pledged once to hope — cleft to despair?

The steep encroachments of my blood left me
No answer (could blood hold such a lofty tower
As flings the question true?) — or is it she
Whose sweet mortality stirs latent power?

And through whose pulse I hear, counting the strokes
My veins recall and add, revived and sure
The angelus of wars my chest evokes:
What I hold healed, original now, and pure . . .

And builds, within, a tower that is not stone
(Not stone can jacket heaven) — but slip
Of pebbles — visible wings of silence sown
In azure circles, widening as they dip

The matrix of the heart, lift down the eye
That shrines the quiet lake and swells a tower . . .
The commodious, tall decorum of that sky
Unseals her earth, and lifts love in its shower.

To Brooklyn Bridge

How many dawns, chill from his rippling rest
The seagull's wings shall dip and pivot him,
Shedding white rings of tumult, building high
Over the chained bay waters Liberty —

Then, with inviolate curve, forsake our eyes
As apparitional as sails that cross
Some page of figures to be filed away;
— Till elevators drop us from our day . . .

I think of cinemas, panoramic sleights
With multitudes bent toward some flashing scene
Never disclosed, but hastened to again,
Foretold to other eyes on the same screen;

And Thee, across the harbor, silver-paced
As though the sun took step of thee, yet left

Some motion ever unspent in thy stride, —
Implicitly thy freedom staying thee!

Out of some subway scuttle, cell or loft
A bedlamite° speeds to thy parapets,   *madman*
Tilting there momently, shrill shirt ballooning,
A jest falls from the speechless caravan.

Down Wall,° from girder into street noon leaks,   *Wall Street*
A rip-tooth of the sky's acetylene;
All afternoon the cloud-flown derricks turn . . .
Thy cables breathe the North Atlantic still.

And obscure as that heaven of the Jews,
Thy guerdon° . . . Accolade thou dost bestow   *reward*
Of anonymity time cannot raise:
Vibrant reprieve and pardon thou dost show.

O harp and altar, of the fury fused,
(How could mere toil align thy choiring strings!)
Terrific threshold of the prophet's pledge,
Prayer of pariah and the lover's cry, —

Again the traffic lights that skim thy swift
Unfractioned idiom, immaculate sigh of stars,
Beading thy path — condense eternity:
And we have seen night lifted in thine arms.

Under thy shadow by the piers I waited;
Only in darkness is thy shadow clear.
The City's fiery parcels all undone,
Already snow submerges an iron year . . .

O Sleepless as the river under thee,
Vaulting the sea, the prairies' dreaming sod,
Unto us lowliest sometime sweep, descend
And of the curveship lend a myth to God.

ROBERT CREELEY
A Marriage

The first retainer
he gave to her
was a golden
wedding ring.

The second — late at night
he woke up,
leaned over on an elbow,
and kissed her.

The third and the last —
he died with
and gave up loving
and lived with her.

COUNTEE CULLEN
Incident

For Eric Walrond

Once riding in old Baltimore,
      Heart-filled, head-filled with glee,
I saw a Baltimorean
      Keep looking straight at me.

Now I was eight and very small,
      And he was no whit bigger,
And so I smiled, but he poked out
      His tongue, and called me, "Nigger."

I saw the whole of Baltimore
      From May until December;
Of all the things that happened there
      That's all that I remember.

E. E. CUMMINGS
anyone lived in a pretty how town

anyone lived in a pretty how town
(with up so floating many bells down)
spring summer autumn winter
he sang his didn't he danced his did.

Women and men (both little and small)
cared for anyone not at all
they sowed their isn't they reaped their same
sun moon stars rain

children guessed (but only a few
and down they forgot as up they grew
autumn winter spring summer)
that noone loved him more by more

when by now and tree by leaf
she laughed his joy she cried his grief
bird by snow and stir by still
anyone's any was all to her

someones married their everyones
laughed their cryings and did their dance
(sleep wake hope and then) they
said their nevers they slept their dream

stars rain sun moon
(and only the snow can begin to explain
how children are apt to forget to remember
with up so floating many bells down)

one day anyone died i guess
(and noone stooped to kiss his face)
busy folk buried them side by side
little by little and was by was

all by all and deep by deep
and more by more they dream their sleep
noone and anyone earth by april
wish by spirit and if by yes.

Women and men (both dong and ding)
summer autumn winter spring
reaped their sowing and went their came
sun moon stars rain

may i feel said he

may i feel said he
(i'll squeal said she
just once said he)
it's fun said she

(may i touch said he
how much said she
a lot said he)
why not said she

(let's go said he
not too far said she
what's too far said he
where you are said she)

may i stay said he
(which way said she
like this said he
if you kiss said she

may i move said he
is it love said she)
if you're willing said he
(but you're killing said she

but it's life said he
but your wife said she
now said he)
ow said she

(tiptop said he
don't stop said she
oh no said he)
go slow said she

(cccome? said he
ummm said she)
you're divine! said he
(you are Mine said she)

EMILY DICKINSON
After great pain, a formal feeling comes —

After great pain, a formal feeling comes —
The Nerves sit ceremonious, like Tombs —
The stiff Heart questions was it He, that bore,
And Yesterday, or Centuries before?

The Feet, mechanical, go round —
Of Ground, or Air, or Ought° —   *nothing, void*
A Wooden way
Regardless grown,
A Quartz contentment, like a stone —

This is the Hour of Lead —
Remembered, if outlived,
As Freezing persons, recollect the Snow —
First — Chill — then Stupor — then the letting go —

The Brain — is wider than the Sky —

The Brain — is wider than the Sky —
For — put them side by side —
The one the other will contain
With ease — and You — beside —

The Brain is deeper than the sea —
For — hold them — Blue to Blue —
The one the other will absorb —
As Sponges — Buckets — do —

The Brain is just the weight of God —
For — Heft them — Pound for Pound —
And they will differ — if they do —
As Syllable from Sound —

I like a look of Agony

I like a look of Agony,
Because I know it's true —
Men do not sham Convulsion,
Nor simulate, a Throe —

The Eyes glaze once — and that is Death —
Impossible to feign
The Beads upon the Forehead
By homely Anguish strung.

Much Madness is divinest Sense —

Much Madness is divinest Sense —
To a discerning Eye —
Much Sense — the starkest Madness —
'Tis the Majority
In this, as All, prevail —
Assent — and you are sane —
Demur — you're straightway dangerous —
And handled with a Chain —

My Life had stood — a Loaded Gun —

My Life had stood — a Loaded Gun —
In Corners — till a Day
The Owner passed — identified —
And carried Me away —

And now We roam in Sovereign Woods —
And now We hunt the Doe —
And every time I speak for Him —
The Mountains straight reply —

And do I smile, such cordial light
Upon the Valley glow —
It is as a Vesuvian face
Had let its pleasure through —

And when at Night — Our good Day done —
I guard My Master's Head —
'Tis better than the Eider-Duck's
Deep Pillow — to have shared —

To foe of His — I'm deadly foe —
None stir the second time —
On whom I lay a Yellow Eye —
Or an emphatic Thumb —

Though I than He — may longer live
He longer must — than I —
For I have· but the power to kill,
Without — the power to die —

Safe in their Alabaster Chambers —

(Version of 1859)

Safe in their Alabaster Chambers —
Untouched by Morning
And untouched by Noon —
Sleep the meek members of the Resurrection —
Rafter of satin,
And Roof of stone.

Light laughs the breeze
In her Castle above them —
Babbles the Bee in a stolid Ear,
Pipe the Sweet Birds in ignorant cadence —
Ah, what sagacity perished here!

Safe in their Alabaster Chambers —

(Version of 1861)

Safe in their Alabaster Chambers —
Untouched by Morning —
And untouched by Noon —
Lie the meek members of the Resurrection —
Rafter of Satin — and Roof of Stone!

Grand go the Years — in the Crescent — above them —
Worlds scoop their Arcs —
And Firmaments — row —
Diadems — drop — and Doges[1] — surrender —
Soundless as dots — on a Disc of Snow —

The Soul selects her own Society —

The Soul selects her own Society —
Then — shuts the Door —
To her divine Majority —
Present no more —

Unmoved — she notes the Chariots — pausing —
At her low Gate —
Unmoved — an Emperor be kneeling
Upon her Mat —

I've known her — from an ample nation —
Choose One —
Then — close the Valves of her attention —
Like Stone —

Success is counted sweetest

Success is counted sweetest
By those who ne'er succeed.
To comprehend a nectar
Requires sorest need.

Not one of all the purple Host
Who took the Flag today
Can tell the definition
So clear of Victory

---

[1] Chief magistrates in Venice from the eleventh through the sixteenth centuries.

As he defeated — dying —
On whose forbidden ear
The distant strains of triumph
Burst agonized and clear!

There's a certain Slant of light

There's a certain Slant of light,
Winter Afternoons —
That oppresses, like the Heft
Of Cathedral Tunes —

Heavenly Hurt, it gives us —
We can find no scar,
But internal difference,
Where the Meanings, are —

None may teach it — Any —
'Tis the Seal Despair —
An imperial affliction
Sent us of the Air —

When it comes, the Landscape listens —
Shadows — hold their breath —
When it goes, 'tis like the Distance
On the look of Death —

Wild Nights — Wild Nights!

Wild Nights — Wild Nights!
Were I with thee
Wild Nights should be
Our luxury!

Futile — the Winds —
To a Heart in port —
Done with the Compass —
Done with the Chart!

Rowing in Eden —
Ah, the Sea!
Might I but moor — Tonight —
In Thee!

J O H N D O N N E
The Canonization

For God's sake hold your tongue, and let me love,
    Or chide my palsy, or my gout,
My five gray hairs, or ruined fortune, flout,
      With wealth your state, your mind with arts improve,
         Take you a course, get you a place,
         Observe His Honor, or His Grace,
Or the King's real, or his stampèd face
      Contémplate; what you will, approve,°   *experience*
    So you will let me love.

Alas, alas, who's injured by my love?
    What merchant's ships have my sighs drowned?
Who says my tears have overflowed his ground?
      When did my colds a forward spring remove?
         When did the heats which my veins fill
         Add one more to the plaguy bill?[1]
Soldiers find wars, and lawyers find out still
      Litigious men, which quarrels move,
    Though she and I do love.

Call us what you will, we're made such by love;
    Call her one, me another fly,
We're tapers too, and at our own cost die,[2]
      And we in us find th' eagle and the dove.
         The phoenix[3] riddle hath more wit°   *meaning*
         By us: we two being one, are it.
So, to one neutral thing both sexes fit.
      We die and rise the same, and prove
    Mysterious by this love.

We can die by it, if not live by love,
    And if unfit for tombs and hearse
Our legend be, it will be fit for verse;
      And if no piece of chronicle we prove,
         We'll build in sonnets pretty rooms;
         As well a well-wrought urn becomes

---

[1] Weekly list of people who died of the plague.

[2] "Die" was slang for consummating the sexual act. It was believed that this act reduced one's life span.

[3] Mythical unique bird, periodically regenerated from its own ashes.

The greatest ashes, as half-acre tombs;
    And by these hymns, all shall approve
    Us canonized for love:

And thus invoke us: You whom reverend love
    Made one another's hermitage;
You, to whom love was peace, that now is rage;
    Who did the whole world's soul contract, and drove
        Into the glasses of your eyes
        (So made such mirrors, and such spies,
That they did all to you epitomize)
    Countries, towns, courts: Beg from above
    A pattern of your love!

Death, be not proud

Death, be not proud, though some have callèd thee
Mighty and dreadful, for thou art not so;
For those whom thou think'st thou dost overthrow
Die not, poor Death, nor yet canst thou kill me.
From rest and sleep, which but thy pictures be,
Much pleasure; then from thee much more must flow,
And soonest our best men with thee do go,
Rest of their bones, and soul's delivery.
Thou art slave to fate, chance, kings, and desperate men,
And dost with poison, war, and sickness dwell,
And poppy or charms can make us sleep as well
And better than thy stroke; why swell'st thou then?
One short sleep past, we wake eternally,
And death shall be no more; Death, thou shalt die.

The Sun Rising

    Busy old fool, unruly sun,
    Why dost thou thus,
Through windows and through curtains call on us?
Must to thy motions lovers' seasons run?
    Saucy pedantic wretch, go chide
    Late school boys and sour prentices,
    Go tell court huntsmen that the king will ride,
    Call country ants to harvest offices;
Love, all alike, no season knows nor clime,
Nor hours, days, months, which are the rags of time.

Thy beams, so reverend and strong
Why shouldst thou think?
I could eclipse and cloud them with a wink,
But that I would not lose her sight so long;
If her eyes have not blinded thine,
Look, and tomorrow late tell me,
Whether both th' Indias of spice and mine
Be where thou leftst them, or lie here with me.
Ask for those kings whom thou saw'st yesterday,
And thou shalt hear, All here in one bed lay.

She's all states, and all princes, I,
Nothing else is.
Princes do but play us; compared to this,
All honor's mimic, all wealth alchemy.
Thou, sun, art half as happy as we,
In that the world's contracted thus;
Thine age asks ease, and since thy duties be
To warm the world, that's done in warming us.
Shine here to us, and thou art everywhere;
This bed thy center is, these walls, thy sphere.

RITA DOVE
Adolescence — II

Although it is night, I sit in the bathroom, waiting.
Sweat prickles behind my knees, the baby-breasts are alert.
Venetian blinds slice up the moon; the tiles quiver in pale strips.

Then they come, the three seal men with eyes as round
As dinner plates and eyelashes like sharpened tines.
They bring the scent of licorice. One sits in the washbowl,

One on the bathtub edge; one leans against the door.
"Can you feel it yet?" they whisper.
I don't know what to say, again. They chuckle,

Patting their sleek bodies with their hands.
"Well, maybe next time." And they rise,
Glittering like pools of ink under moonlight,

And vanish. I clutch at the ragged holes
They leave behind, here at the edge of darkness.
Night rests like a ball of fur on my tongue.

Dusting

Every day a wilderness — no
shade in sight. Beulah
patient among knicknacks,
the solarium a rage
of light, a grainstorm
as her gray cloth brings
dark wood to life.

Under her hand scrolls
and crests gleam
darker still. What
was his name, that
silly boy at the fair with
the rifle booth? And his kiss and
the clear bowl with one bright
fish, rippling
wound!

Not Michael —
something finer. Each dust
stroke a deep breath and
the canary in bloom.
Wavery memory: home
from a dance, the front door
blown open and the parlor
in snow, she rushed
the bowl to the stove, watched
as the locket of ice
dissolved and he
swam free.

That was years before
Father gave her up
with her name, years before
her name grew to mean
Promise, then
Desert-in-Peace.
Long before the shadow and
sun's accomplice, the tree.

Maurice.

JOHN DRYDEN
To the Memory of Mr. Oldham

Farewell, too little, and too lately known,
Whom I began to think and call my own: .
For sure our souls were near allied, and thine
Cast in the same poetic mold with mine.
One common note on either lyre did strike,
And knaves and fools we both abhorred alike.
To the same goal did both our studies drive;
The last set out the soonest did arrive.
Thus Nisus[1] fell upon the slippery place,
While his young friend performed and won the race.
O early ripe! to thy abundant store
What could advancing age have added more?
It might (what nature never gives the young)
Have taught the numbers of thy native tongue.
But satire needs not those, and wit will shine
Through the harsh cadence of a rugged line:
A noble error, and but seldom made,
When poets are by too much force betrayed.
Thy generous fruits, though gathered ere their prime,
Still showed a quickness, and maturing time
But mellows what we write to the dull sweets of rhyme.
Once more, hail and farewell; farewell, thou young,
But ah too short, Marcellus[2] of our tongue;
Thy brows with ivy, and with laurels bound;
But fate and gloomy night encompass thee around.

PAUL LAURENCE DUNBAR
Harriet Beecher Stowe[1]

She told the story, and the whole world wept
 At wrongs and cruelties it had not known

---

[1] In Book V of Virgil's *Aeneid,* two friends, Nisus and Euryalus, run together in a foot race. Nisus, the older man, is on the point of winning the race when he slips and falls. He trips the next runner, thereby enabling his friend Euryalus to win.

[2] The nephew and adopted son of Augustus, who was expected to succeed him as emperor, but who died in 23 B.C.

[1] Harriet Beecher Stowe (1811–1896) wrote *Uncle Tom's Cabin* (1852), an antislavery novel that had an enormous impact on American attitudes toward slavery.

But for this fearless woman's voice alone.
She spoke to consciences that long had slept:
Her message, Freedom's clear reveille, swept
From heedless hovel to complacent throne.
Command and prophecy were in the tone
And from its sheath the sword of justice leapt.
Around two peoples swelled a fiery wave,
But both came forth transfigured from the flame.
Blest be the hand that dared be strong to save,
And blest be she who in our weakness came —
Prophet and priestess! At one stroke she gave
A race to freedom and herself to fame.

Robert Gould Shaw[1]

Why was it that the thunder voice of Fate
Should call thee, studious, from the classic groves,
Where calm-eyed Pallas[2] with still footstep roves,
And charge thee seek the turmoil of the state?
What bade thee hear the voice and rise elate,
Leave home and kindred and thy spicy loaves,
To lead th' unlettered and despisèd droves
To manhood's home and thunder at the gate?

Far better the slow blaze of Learning's light,
The cool and quiet of her dearer fane,
Than this hot terror of a hopeless fight,
This cold endurance of the final pain, —
Since thou and those who with thee died for right
Have died, the Present teaches, but in vain!

We Wear the Mask

We wear the mask that grins and lies,
It hides our cheeks and shades our eyes —
This debt we pay to human guile;
With torn and bleeding hearts we smile,
And mouth with myriad subtleties.

---

[1] Robert Gould Shaw (1837–1863) commanded the first all-Negro regiment in the North. He was killed while leading an attack on Fort Wagner in South Carolina.

[2] Pallas Athena, Greek goddess of wisdom.

Why should the world be over-wise,
In counting all our tears and sighs?
Nay, let them only see us, while
      We wear the mask.

We smile, but, O great Christ, our cries
To thee from tortured souls arise.
We sing, but oh the clay is vile
Beneath our feet, and long the mile;
But let the world dream otherwise,
      We wear the mask!

T. S. ELIOT
Marina [1]

Quis hic locus, quae regio, quae mundi plaga? [2]

What seas what shores what grey rocks and what islands
What water lapping the bow
And scent of pine and the woodthrush singing through the fog
What images return
O my daughter.

    Those who sharpen the tooth of the dog, meaning
Death
Those who glitter with the glory of the humming-bird, meaning
Death
Those who sit in the stye of contentment, meaning
Death
Those who suffer the ecstasy of the animals, meaning
Death

    Are become unsubstantial, reduced by a wind,
A breath of pine, and the woodsong fog
By this grace dissolved in place

    What is this face, less clear and clearer
The pulse in the arm, less strong and stronger —
Given or lent? more distant than stars and nearer than the eye

---

[1] In Shakespeare's *Pericles,* the name of the miraculously regained daughter.

[2] This epigraph comes from the play *Hercules Furens (The Madness of Hercules)* by the Roman writer Seneca (4? B.C.–A.D. 65). Hercules, upon discovering that in his madness he has killed his wife and children, says: "What place is this, what region, what quarter of the world?"

Whispers and small laughter between leaves and hurrying feet
Under sleep, where all the waters meet.

Bowsprit cracked with ice and paint cracked with heat.
I made this, I have forgotten
And remember.
The rigging weak and the canvas rotten
Between one June and another September.
Made this unknowing, half conscious, unknown, my own.
The garboard strake leaks, the seams need caulking.

This form, this face, this life
Living to live in a world of time beyond me; let me
Resign my life for this life, my speech for that unspoken,
The awakened, lips parted, the hope, the new ships.

What seas what shores what granite islands towards my
            timbers
And woodthrush calling through the fog
My daughter.

Preludes

I

The winter evening settles down
With smell of steaks in passageways.
Six o'clock.
The burnt-out ends of smoky days.
And now a gusty shower wraps
The grimy scraps
Of withered leaves about your feet
And newspapers from vacant lots;
The showers beat
On broken blinds and chimney-pots,
And at the corner of the street
A lonely cab-horse steams and stamps.
And then the lighting of the lamps.

II

The morning comes to consciousness
Of faint stale smells of beer
From the sawdust-trampled street
With all its muddy feet that press
To early coffee-stands.

With the other masquerades
That time resumes,
One thinks of all the hands
That are raising dingy shades
In a thousand furnished rooms.

III

You tossed a blanket from the bed,
You lay upon your back, and waited;
You dozed, and watched the night revealing
The thousand sordid images
Of which your soul was constituted;
They flickered against the ceiling.
And when all the world came back
And the light crept up between the shutters
And you heard the sparrows in the gutters,
You had such a vision of the street
As the street hardly understands;
Sitting along the bed's edge, where
You curled the papers from your hair,
Or clasped the yellow soles of feet
In the palms of both soiled hands.

IV

His soul stretched tight across the skies
That fade behind a city block,
Or trampled by insistent feet
At four and five and six o'clock;
And short square fingers stuffing pipes,
And evening newspapers, and eyes
Assured of certain certainties,
The conscience of a blackened street
Impatient to assume the world.

   I am moved by fancies that are curled
Around these images, and cling:
The notion of some infinitely gentle
Infinitely suffering thing.

   Wipe your hand across your mouth, and laugh;
The worlds revolve like ancient women
Gathering fuel in vacant lots.

Sweeney among the Nightingales

ὦμοι, πέπληγμαι καιρίαν πληγὴν εσω[1]

Apeneck Sweeney spreads his knees
Letting his arms hang down to laugh,
The zebra stripes along his jaw
Swelling to maculate° giraffe.   *spotted*

    The circles of the stormy moon
Slide westward toward the River Plate,[2]
Death and the Raven drift above
And Sweeney guards the hornèd gate.[3]

    Gloomy Orion[4] and the Dog
Are veiled; and hushed the shrunken seas;
The person in the Spanish cape
Tries to sit on Sweeney's knees

    Slips and pulls the table cloth
Overturns a coffee-cup,
Reorganized upon the floor
She yawns and draws a stocking up;

    The silent man in mocha brown
Sprawls at the window-sill and gapes;
The waiter brings in oranges
Bananas figs and hothouse grapes;

    The silent vertebrate in brown
Contracts and concentrates, withdraws;
Rachel *née* Rabinovitch
Tears at the grapes with murderous paws;

    She and the lady in the cape
Are suspect, thought to be in league;
Therefore the man with heavy eyes
Declines the gambit, shows fatigue,

    Leaves the room and reappears
Outside the window, leaning in,
Branches of wistaria
Circumscribe a golden grin;

[1] "Alas I am struck a mortal blow within": Agamemnon's cry as he is murdered by his wife and her lover (Aeschylus, *Agamemnon*, I. 1343).

[2] A river in Argentina.

[3] In Hades, the gate through which true dreams pass.

[4] The constellation Orion and the Dog Star, Sirius.

The host with someone indistinct
Converses at the door apart,
The nightingales are singing near
The Convent of the Sacred Heart,

And sang within the bloody wood
When Agamemnon cried aloud,
And let their liquid siftings fall
To stain the stiff dishonoured shroud.

RALPH WALDO EMERSON
Concord Hymn

Sung at the Completion of the Battle Monument,[1] *July 4, 1837*

By the rude bridge that arched the flood,
    Their flag to April's breeze unfurled,
Here once the embattled farmers stood
    And fired the shot heard round the world.

The foe long since in silence slept;
    Alike the conqueror silent sleeps;
And Time the ruined bridge has swept
    Down the dark stream which seaward creeps.

On this green bank, by this soft stream,
    We set to-day a votive stone;
That memory may their deed redeem,
    When, like our sires, our sons are gone.

Spirit, that made those heroes dare
    To die, and leave their children free,
Bid Time and Nature gently spare
    The shaft we raise to them and thee.

The Snowstorm

Announced by all the trumpets of the sky,
Arrives the snow, and, driving o'er the fields,
Seems nowhere to alight: the whited air
Hides hills and woods, the river, and the heaven,
And veils the farmhouse at the garden's end.

---

[1] Commemorating the battles of Lexington and Concord, April 19, 1775.

The sled and traveler stopped, the courier's feet
Delayed, all friends shut out, the housemates sit
Around the radiant fireplace, enclosed
In a tumultuous privacy of storm.

     Come see the north wind's masonry.
Out of an unseen quarry evermore
Furnished with tile, the fierce artificer
Curves his white bastions with projected roof
Round every windward stake, or tree, or door.
Speeding, the myriad-handed, his wild work
So fanciful, so savage, nought cares he
For number or proportion. Mockingly,
On coop or kennel he hangs Parian[1] wreaths;
A swan-like form invests the hidden thorn;
Fills up the farmer's lane from wall to wall,
Maugre° the farmer's sighs; and, at the gate,   *in spite of*
A tapering turret overtops the work.
And when his hours are numbered, and the world
Is all his own, retiring, as he were not,
Leaves, when the sun appears, astonished Art
To mimic in slow structures, stone by stone,
Built in an age, the mad wind's night-work,
The frolic architecture of the snow.

LOUISE ERDRICH
I Was Sleeping Where the Black Oaks Move

We watched from the house
as the river grew, helpless
and terrible in its unfamiliar body.
Wrestling everything into it,
the water wrapped around trees
until their life-hold was broken.
They went down, one by one,
and the river dragged off their covering.

Nests of the herons, roots washed to bones,
snags of soaked bark on the shoreline:
a whole forest pulled through the teeth

---

[1] Resembling the fine white marble from the Greek island of Paros.

of the spillway. Trees surfacing
singly, where the river poured off
into arteries for fields below the reservation.

When at last it was over, the long removal,
they had all become the same dry wood.
We walked among them, the branches
whitening in the raw sun.
Above us drifted herons,
alone, hoarse-voiced, broken,
settling their beaks among the hollows.

Grandpa said, *These are the ghosts of the tree people,*
moving above us, unable to take their rest.

Sometimes now, we dream our way back to the heron dance.
Their long wings are bending the air
into circles through which they fall.
They rise again in shifting wheels.
How long must we live in the broken figures
their necks make, narrowing the sky.

The Strange People

> The antelope are strange people . . . they are beautiful to look at, and yet they
> are tricky. We do not trust them. They appear and disappear; they are like
> shadows on the plains. Because of their great beauty, young men sometimes
> follow the antelope and are lost forever. Even if those foolish ones find them-
> selves and return, they are never again right in their heads.
>
> — PRETTY SHIELD, MEDICINE WOMAN OF THE CROWS,
> TRANSCRIBED AND EDITED BY FRANK LINDERMAN (1932)

All night I am the doe, breathing
his name in a frozen field,
the small mist of the word
drifting always before me.

And again he has heard it
and I have gone burning
to meet him, the jacklight
fills my eyes with blue fire;
the heart in my chest
explodes like a hot stone.

Then slung like a sack
in the back of his pickup,
I wipe the death scum

from my mouth, sit up laughing,
and shriek in my speeding grave.

Safely shut in the garage,
when he sharpens his knife
and thinks to have me, like that,
I come toward him,
a lean gray witch,
through the bullets that enter and dissolve.

I sit in his house
drinking coffee till dawn,
and leave as frost reddens on hubcaps,
crawling back into my shadowy body.
All day, asleep in clean grasses,
I dream of the one who could really wound me.

ROBERT FROST
Birches

When I see birches bend to left and right
Across the lines of straighter darker trees,
I like to think some boy's been swinging them.
But swinging doesn't bend them down to stay
As ice-storms do. Often you must have seen them
Loaded with ice a sunny winter morning
After a rain. They click upon themselves
As the breeze rises, and turn many-colored
As the stir cracks and crazes their enamel.
Soon the sun's warmth makes them shed crystal shells
Shattering and avalanching on the snow-crust —
Such heaps of broken glass to sweep away
You'd think the inner dome of heaven had fallen.
They are dragged to the withered bracken by the load,
And they seem not to break; though once they are bowed
So low for long, they never right themselves:
You may see their trunks arching in the woods
Years afterwards, trailing their leaves on the ground
Like girls on hands and knees that throw their hair
Before them over their heads to dry in the sun.
But I was going to say when Truth broke in
With all her matter-of-fact about the ice-storm
I should prefer to have some boy bend them

As he went out and in to fetch the cows —
Some boy too far from town to learn baseball,
Whose only play was what he found himself,
Summer or winter, and could play alone.
One by one he subdued his father's trees
By riding them down over and over again
Until he took the stiffness out of them,
And not one but hung limp, not one was left
For him to conquer. He learned all there was
To learn about not launching out too soon
And so not carrying the tree away
Clear to the ground. He always kept his poise
To the top branches, climbing carefully
With the same pains you use to fill a cup
Up to the brim, and even above the brim.
Then he flung outward, feet first, with a swish,
Kicking his way down through the air to the ground.
So was I once myself a swinger of birches.
And so I dream of going back to be.
It's when I'm weary of considerations,
And life is too much like a pathless wood
Where your face burns and tickles with the cobwebs
Broken across it, and one eye is weeping
From a twig's having lashed across it open.
I'd like to get away from earth awhile
And then come back to it and begin over.
May no fate willfully misunderstand me
And half grant what I wish and snatch me away
Not to return. Earth's the right place for love:
I don't know where it's likely to go better.
I'd like to go by climbing a birch tree,
And climb black branches up a snow-white trunk
Toward heaven, till the tree could bear no more,
But dipped its top and set me down again.
That would be good both going and coming back.
One could do worse than be a swinger of birches.

Design[1]

I found a dimpled spider, fat and white,
On a white heal-all, holding up a moth
Like a white piece of rigid satin cloth —
Assorted characters of death and blight
Mixed ready to begin the morning right,
Like the ingredients of a witches' broth —
A snow-drop spider, a flower like froth,
And dead wings carried like a paper kite.

What had that flower to do with being white,
The wayside blue and innocent heal-all?
What brought the kindred spider to that height,
Then steered the white moth thither in the night?
What but design of darkness to appall? —
If design govern in a thing so small.

JAMES GALVIN
Independence Day, 1956: A Fairy Tale

I think this house's mouth is full of dirt.

                        Smoke is nothing up its sleeve.
I think it could explode.

                    Where I am, in the dirt under the floor, I hear
them.

    They don't know.

                        My mother leaves each room my father enters.

                                                            Now
she is cleaning things that are already clean.

                            My father is in the living
room.

        He's pouring.

                Rum into a glass, gas into a lamp, kerosene into a can.

He pours capped fuses, matches, dynamite sticks into his pockets.

                                                        He pours
rounds into the .45 which he will point skyward and hold next to
        his ear

---

[1] The argument from design (order in nature) was often used as a proof for the existence of God.

as if it were telling him things.
                              Where I am, the spider spins.
                                                  The broken
mouse drags a trap through lunar talc of dust.
                                        Where the bitch whelps is
where I wriggle on my belly, cowardly, ashamed, to escape the
        Fourth of July.
I think the house is very ready.
                              It seems to hover like an "exploded
view" in a repair manual.
                        Parts suspended in disbelief.
                                            Nails pulled back,
aimed.
        My father goes out.
                        My mother whimpers.
                                        There'll be no supper.
She opens the firebox and stuffs it full of forks.

ALLEN GINSBERG
America

America I've given you all and now I'm nothing.
America two dollars and twentyseven cents January 17, 1956.
I can't stand my own mind.
America when will we end the human war?
Go fuck yourself with your atom bomb.
I don't feel good don't bother me.
I won't write my poem till I'm in my right mind.
America when will you be angelic?
When will you take off your clothes?
When will you look at yourself through the grave?
When will you be worthy of your million Trotskyites?[1]
America why are your libraries full of tears?
America when will you send your eggs to India?[2]
I'm sick of your insane demands.
When can I go into the supermarket and buy what I need with my
        good looks?

---

[1] Communist idealists, followers of Leon Trotsky (1879–1940), the opponent of Stalin.

[2] India was suffering a famine, while America had an agricultural surplus.

America after all it is you and I who are perfect not the next world.
Your machinery is too much for me.
You made me want to be a saint.
There must be some other way to settle this argument.
Burroughs is in Tangiers[3] I don't think he'll come back it's sinister.
Are you being sinister or is this some form of practical joke?
I'm trying to come to the point.
I refuse to give up my obsession.
America stop pushing I know what I'm doing.
America the plum blossoms are falling.
I haven't read the newspapers for months, everyday somebody
    goes on trial for murder.
America I feel sentimental about the Wobblies.[4]
America I used to be a communist when I was a kid I'm not sorry.
I smoke marijuana every chance I get.
I sit in my house for days on end and stare at the roses in the closet.
When I go to Chinatown I get drunk and never get laid.
My mind is made up there's going to be trouble.
You should have seen me reading Marx.[5]
My psychoanalyst thinks I'm perfectly right.
I won't say the Lord's Prayer.
I have mystical visions and cosmic vibrations.
America I still haven't told you what you did to Uncle Max after
    he came over from Russia.

I'm addressing you.
Are you going to let your emotional life be run by Time Magazine?
I'm obsessed by Time Magazine.
I read it every week.
Its cover stares at me every time I slink past the corner candystore.
I read it in the basement of the Berkeley Public Library.
It's always telling me about responsibility. Businessmen are serious.
    Movie producers are serious. Everybody's serious but me.
It occurs to me that I am America.
I am talking to myself again.

---

[3] William Burroughs (b. 1914), a friend of Ginsberg's and author of the novel
Naked Lunch (1959), was living in Morocco.

[4] Nickname for members of the Industrial Workers of the World, a union founded
in 1905.

[5] Karl Marx (1818–1883), German political theorist and coauthor, with Friedrich
Engels, of *The Communist Manifesto* (1848).

Asia is rising against me.

I haven't got a chinaman's chance.

I'd better consider my national resources.

My national resources consist of two joints of marijuana millions of
    genitals an unpublishable private literature that goes 1400
    miles an hour and twentyfive-thousand mental institutions.

I say nothing about my prisons nor the millions of underprivileged
    who live in my flowerpots under the light of five hundred
    suns.

I have abolished the whorehouses of France, Tangiers is the next
    to go.

My ambition is to be President despite the fact that I'm a Catholic.

America how can I write a holy litany in your silly mood?

I will continue like Henry Ford my strophes are as individual as his
    automobiles more so they're all different sexes.

America I will sell you strophes $2500 apiece $500 down on your
    old strophe

America free Tom Mooney[6]

America save the Spanish Loyalists[7]

America Sacco & Vanzetti[8] must not die

America I am the Scottsboro boys.[9]

America when I was seven momma took me to Communist Cell
    meetings they sold us garbanzos[10] a handful per ticket a ticket
    costs a nickel and the speeches were free everybody was
    angelic and sentimental about the workers it was all so sincere
    you have no idea what a good thing the party was in 1935
    Scott Nearing was a grand old man a real mensch Mother
    Bloor made me cry I once saw Israel Amter[11] plain. Every-
    body must have been a spy.

---

[6] American labor agitator in California, accused of bomb killings and sentenced to
death in 1916 but pardoned in 1939.

[7] Those fighting against Franco in the Spanish Civil War.

[8] Nicola Sacco and Bartolomeo Vanzetti were executed in Massachusetts in 1927
for a murder connected with a robbery. Sentiment ran high against them because of their
radical beliefs.

[9] The "Scottsboro boys" were nine blacks who were convicted in Alabama of the
rape of two white women in 1931. Liberals and radicals believed the conviction to be
unproved. Four years later the sentences were reduced in four cases and the charges
dropped in five.

[10] Chickpeas.

[11] Scott Nearing (1883–1983), Ella ("Mother") Bloor (1862–1951), and Israel
Amter (1881–1954): well-known American Socialists and Communists.

America you don't really want to go to war.

America it's them bad Russians.

Them Russians them Russians and them Chinamen. And them
  Russians.

The Russia wants to eat us alive. The Russia's power mad. She
  wants to take our cars from out our garages.

Her wants to grab Chicago. Her needs a Red Readers' Digest. Her
  wants our auto plants in Siberia. Him big bureaucracy run-
  ning our fillingstations.

That no good. Ugh. Him make Indians learn read. Him need big
  black niggers. Hah. Her make us all work sixteen hours a day.
  Help.

America this is quite serious.

America this is the impression I get from looking in the television
  set.

America is this correct?

I'd better get right down to the job.

It's true I don't want to join the Army or turn lathes in precision
  parts factories, I'm nearsighted and psychopathic anyway.

America I'm putting my queer shoulder to the wheel.

LOUISE GLÜCK
All Hallows[1]

Even now this landscape is assembling.
The hills darken. The oxen
sleep in their blue yoke,
the fields having been
picked clean, the sheaves
bound evenly and piled at the roadside
among cinquefoil,[2] as the toothed moon rises:

This is the barrenness
of harvest or pestilence.
And the wife leaning out the window
with her hand extended, as in payment,
and the seeds
distinct, gold, calling

---

[1] Halloween (short for "All Hallows Even"), October 31, the evening before All
Saints' Day.

[2] Plant with five-lobed leaves.

Come here
Come here, little one

And the soul creeps out of the tree.

The White Lilies

As a man and woman make
a garden between them like
a bed of stars, here
they linger in the summer evening
and the evening turns
cold with their terror: it
could all end, it is capable
of devastation. All, all
can be lost, through scented air
the narrow columns
uselessly rising, and beyond,
a churning sea of poppies —

Hush, beloved. It doesn't matter to me
how many summers I live to return:
this one summer we have entered eternity.
I felt your two hands
bury me to release its splendor.

JORIE GRAHAM

Of Forced Sightes and Trusty Ferefulness

Stopless wind, here are the columbine seeds I have
collected. What we would do with them is
different. Though both your trick and mine flower blue
and white

with four stem tails and yellow underpetals. Stopless
and unessential, half-hiss, half-
lullaby, if I fell in among your laws,
if I fell down into your mind your snow, into the miles

of spirit-drafts you drive, frenetic multitudes,
out from timber to the open ground and back to no
avail, if I fell down, warmblooded, ill, into your endless
evenness,

into this race you start them on and will not let them win . . . ?
If I fell in?

What is your law to my law, unhurried hurrying?
At my remove from you, today, in your supremest

calculation, re-
adjustment, are these three birds scratching for dead
bark beetles, frozen seeds, too late for being here yet only
     here,
in the stenchfree

cold. This is another current, river of rivers, this thrilling
third-act love. Who wouldn't want to stay
behind? They pack the rinds away, the blazing applecores,
the frantic shadow-wings scribbling the fenceposts, window-

panes. Meanwhile you turn, white jury, draft, away,
deep justice done.
I don't presume to cross the distances, the clarity,
but what grows in your only open hands? Or is

digressive love,
row after perfect greenhouse row,
the garden you're out of for good, wind of the theorems,
of proof, square root of light,

chaos of truth,
blinder than the mice that wait you out
     in any crack?
This is the best I can do now for prayer — to you,
for you — these scraps I throw

my lonely acrobats
that fall
of your accord
right to my windowsill: they pack it away, the grains, the

accidents, they pack it deep into the rent
heart of the blue
spruce, skins in with spiky needles. . . . Oh
     hollow
charged with forgetfulness,

through wind, through winter nights, we'll pass,
steering with crumbs, with words,
making of every hour
a thought, remembering

by pain and rhyme and arabesques of foraging
the formula for theft
under your sky that keeps
sliding away

married to hurry
and grim song.

Soul Says

(Afterword)

To be so held by brittleness, shapeliness.
By meaning. As where I *have to go where you go,*
I *have to touch what you must touch,*
in hunger, in boredom, the spindrift, the ticket . . .
Distilled in you (can you hear me)
the idiom in you, the why —

The flash *of a voice.* The river *glints.*
The mother *opens the tablecloth up into the wind.*
There as the fabric descends — the alphabet of ripenesses,
what is, what could have been.
The bread on the tablecloth. Crickets shrill in the grass.

O pluck my magic garment from me. So.

[lays down his robe]

Lie there, my art —

(This is a form of matter of matter she sang)

(Where the hurry is stopped) (and held) (but not extinguished)
    (no)

(So listen, listen, this will soothe you) (if that is what you want)

Now then, I said, I go to meet that which I liken to
(even though the wave break and drown me in laughter)
the wave breaking, the wave drowning me in laughter —

THOMAS GRAY

Elegy Written in a Country Churchyard

The curfew tolls the knell of parting day,
    The lowing herd wind slowly o'er the lea,
The plowman homeward plods his weary way,
    And leaves the world to darkness and to me.

Now fades the glimmering landscape on the sight,
    And all the air a solemn stillness holds,
Save where the beetle wheels his droning flight,
    And drowsy tinklings lull the distant folds;

Save that from yonder ivy-mantled tower
    The moping owl does to the moon complain
Of such, as wandering near her secret bower,
    Molest her ancient solitary reign.

Beneath those rugged elms, that yew tree's shade,
    Where heaves the turf in many a moldering heap,
Each in his narrow cell forever laid,
    The rude° forefathers of the hamlet sleep.   *rustic*

The breezy call of incense-breathing morn,
    The swallow twittering from the straw-built shed,
The cock's shrill clarion, or the echoing horn,
    No more shall rouse them from their lowly bed.

For them no more the blazing hearth shall burn,
    Or busy housewife ply her evening care;
No children run to lisp their sire's return,
    Or climb his knees the envied kiss to share.

Oft did the harvest to their sickle yield,
    Their furrow oft the stubborn glebe° has broke;   *clot of soil*
How jocund did they drive their team afield!
    How bowed the woods beneath their sturdy stroke!

Let not Ambition mock their useful toil,
    Their homely joys, and destiny obscure;
Nor Grandeur hear with a disdainful smile
    The short and simple annals of the poor.

The boast of heraldry, the pomp of power,
    And all that beauty, all that wealth e'er gave,
Awaits alike the inevitable hour.
    The paths of glory lead but to the grave.

Nor you, ye proud, impute to these the fault,
    If Memory o'er their tomb no trophies raise,
Where through the long-drawn aisle and fretted vault
    The pealing anthem swells the note of praise.

Can storied urn or animated bust
    Back to its mansion call the fleeting breath?

Can Honor's voice provoke the silent dust,
    Or Flattery soothe the dull cold ear of Death?

Perhaps in this neglected spot is laid
    Some heart once pregnant with celestial fire;
Hands that the rod of empire might have swayed,
    Or waked to ecstasy the living lyre.

But Knowledge to their eyes her ample page
    Rich with the spoils of time did ne'er unroll;
Chill Penury repressed their noble rage,
    And froze the genial current of the soul.

Full many a gem of purest ray serene,
    The dark unfathomed caves of ocean bear:
Full many a flower is born to blush unseen,
    And waste its sweetness on the desert air.

Some village Hampden,[1] that with dauntless breast
    The little tyrant of his fields withstood;
Some mute inglorious Milton here may rest,
    Some Cromwell guiltless of his country's blood.

The applause of listening senates to command,
    The threats of pain and ruin to despise,
To scatter plenty o'er a smiling land,
    And read their history in a nation's eyes,

Their lot forbade: nor circumscribed alone
    Their growing virtues, but their crimes confined;
Forbade to wade through slaughter to a throne,
    And shut the gates of mercy on mankind,

The struggling pangs of conscious truth to hide,
    To quench the blushes of ingenuous shame,
Or heap the shrine of Luxury and Pride
    With incense kindled at the Muse's flame.

Far from the madding crowd's ignoble strife,
    Their sober wishes never learned to stray;
Along the cool sequestered vale of life
    They kept the noiseless tenor of their way.

---

[1] One of the leaders of the opposition to Charles I. He was killed in battle in the English Civil War.

Yet even these bones from insult to protect
    Some frail memorial still erected nigh,
With uncouth rhymes and shapeless sculpture decked,
    Implores the passing tribute of a sigh.

Their name, their years, spelt by the unlettered Muse,
    The place of fame and elegy supply:
And many a holy text around she strews,
    That teach the rustic moralist to die.

For who to dumb Forgetfulness a prey,
    This pleasing anxious being e'er resigned,
Left the warm precincts of the cheerful day,
    Nor cast one longing lingering look behind?

On some fond breast the parting soul relies,
    Some pious drops the closing eye requires;
Even from the tomb the voice of Nature cries,
    Even in our ashes live their wonted fires.

For thee, who mindful of the unhonored dead
    Dost in these lines their artless tale relate;
If chance, by lonely contemplation led,
    Some kindred spirit shall inquire thy fate,

Haply some hoary-headed swain may say,
    "Oft have we seen him at the peep of dawn
Brushing with hasty steps the dews away
    To meet the sun upon the upland lawn.

"There at the foot of yonder nodding beech
    That wreathes its old fantastic roots so high,
His listless length at noontide would he stretch,
    And pore upon the brook that babbles by.

"Hard by yon wood, now smiling as in scorn,
    Muttering his wayward fancies he would rove,
Now drooping, woeful wan, like one forlorn,
    Or crazed with care, or crossed in hopeless love.

"One morn I missed him on the customed hill,
    Along the heath and near his favorite tree;
Another came; nor yet beside the rill,
    Nor up the lawn, nor at the wood was he;

"The next with dirges due in sad array
    Slow through the churchway path we saw him borne.

Approach and read (for thou canst read) the lay,
    Graved on the stone beneath yon aged thorn.''

The Epitaph

Here rests his head upon the lap of Earth
    A youth to Fortune and to Fame unknown.
Fair Science° frowned not on his humble birth,   *general knowledge*
    And Melancholy marked him for her own.

Large was his bounty, and his soul sincere,
    Heaven did a recompense as largely send:
He gave to Misery all he had, a tear,
    He gained from Heaven ('twas all he wished) a friend.

No farther seek his merits to disclose,
    Or draw his frailties from their dread abode
(There they alike in trembling hope repose),
    The bosom of his Father and his God.

THOM GUNN
The Man with Night Sweats

I wake up cold, I who
Prospered through dreams of heat
Wake to their residue,
Sweat, and a clinging sheet.

My flesh was its own shield:
Where it was gashed, it healed.

I grew as I explored
The body I could trust
Even while I adored
The risk that made robust,

A world of wonders in
Each challenge to the skin.

I cannot but be sorry
The given shield was cracked,
My mind reduced to hurry,
My flesh reduced and wrecked.

I have to change the bed,
But catch myself instead

Stopped upright where I am
Hugging my body to me
As if to shield it from
The pains that will go through me,

As if hands were enough
To hold an avalanche off.

My Sad Captains

One by one they appear in
the darkness: a few friends, and
a few with historical
names. How late they start to shine!
but before they fade they stand
perfectly embodied, all

the past lapping them like a
cloak of chaos. They were men
who, I thought, lived only to
renew the wasteful force they
spent with each hot convulsion.
They remind me, distant now.

True, they are not at rest yet,
but now that they are indeed
apart, winnowed from failures,
they withdraw to an orbit
and turn with disinterested
hard energy, like the stars.

H. D.
Helen[1]

All Greece hates
the still eyes in the white face,
the lustre as of olives
where she stands,
and the white hands.

---

[1] The beautiful wife of Menelaus. Her abduction by Paris was the cause of the
Trojan War.

All Greece reviles
the wan face when she smiles,
hating it deeper still
when it grows wan and white,
remembering past enchantments
and past ills.

Greece sees unmoved,
God's daughter, born of love,
the beauty of cool feet
and slenderest knees,
could love indeed the maid,
only if she were laid,
white ash amid funereal cypresses.

THOMAS HARDY
Afterwards

When the Present has latched its postern behind my tremulous
      stay,
    And the May month flaps its glad green leaves like wings,
Delicate-filmed as new-spun silk, will the neighbors say,
    "He was a man who used to notice such things"?

If it be in the dusk when, like an eyelid's soundless blink,
    The dewfall-hawk comes crossing the shades to alight
Upon the wind-warped upland thorn, a gazer may think,
    "To him this must have been a familiar sight."

If I pass during some nocturnal blackness, mothy and warm,
    When the hedgehog travels furtively over the lawn,
One may say, "He strove that such innocent creatures should
      come to no harm,
    But he could do little for them; and now he is gone."

If, when hearing that I have been stilled at last, they stand at the
      door,
    Watching the full-starred heavens that winter sees,
Will this thought rise on those who will meet my face no more,
    "He was one who had an eye for such mysteries"?

And will any say when my bell of quittance is heard in the gloom,
    And a crossing breeze cuts a pause in its outrollings,
Till they rise again, as they were a new bell's boom,
    "He hears it not now, but used to notice such things"?

Channel Firing

That night your great guns, unawares,
Shook all our coffins as we lay,
And broke the chancel window-squares,
We thought it was the Judgment-day

And sat upright. While drearisome
Arose the howl of wakened hounds:
The mouse let fall the altar-crumb,
The worms drew back into the mounds,

The glebe° cow drooled. Till God called, "No;   *plot of land*
It's gunnery practice out at sea
Just as before you went below;
The world is as it used to be:

"All nations striving strong to make
Red war yet redder. Mad as hatters
They do no more for Christés sake
Than you who are helpless in such matters.

"That this is not the judgment-hour
For some of them's a blessed thing,
For if it were they'd have to scour
Hell's floor for so much threatening. . . .

"Ha, ha. It will be warmer when
I blow the trumpet (if indeed
I ever do; for you are men,
And rest eternal sorely need)."

So down we lay again. "I wonder,
Will the world ever saner be,"
Said one, "than when He sent us under
In our indifferent century!"

And many a skeleton shook his head.
"Instead of preaching forty year,"
My neighbour Parson Thirdly said,
"I wish I had stuck to pipes and beer."

Again the guns disturbed the hour,
Roaring their readiness to avenge,
As far inland as Stourton Tower,
And Camelot, and starlit Stonehenge.

JOY HARJO
Santa Fe

The wind blows lilacs out of the east. And it isn't lilac season. And
I am walking the street in front of St. Francis Cathedral in Santa Fe.
Oh, and it's a few years earlier and more. That's how you tell real
time. It is here, it is there. The lilacs have taken over everything:
the sky, the narrow streets, my shoulders, my lips. I talk lilac. And
there is nothing else until a woman the size of a fox breaks through
the bushes, breaks the purple web. She is tall and black and gor-
geous. She is the size of a fox on the arm of a white man who looks
and tastes like cocaine. She lies for cocaine, dangles on the arm of
cocaine. And lies to me now from a room in the DeVargas Hotel,
where she has eaten her lover, white powder on her lips. That is
true now; it is not true anymore. Eventually space curves, walks
over and taps me on the shoulder. On the sidewalk I stand near St.
Francis; he has been bronzed, a perpetual tan, with birds on his
hand, his shoulder, deer at his feet. I am Indian and in this town I
will never be a saint. I am seventeen and shy and wild. I have been
up until three at a party, but there is no woman in the DeVargas
Hotel for that story hasn't yet been invented. A man whose face I
will never remember, and never did, drives up on a Harley Dav-
idson. There are lilacs on his arm, they spill out from the spokes of
his wheels. He wants me on his arm, on the back of his lilac bike
touring the flower kingdom of San Francisco. And for a piece of
time the size of a nickel, I think, maybe. But maybe is vapor, has
no anchor here in the sun beneath St. Francis Cathedral. And space
is as solid as the bronze statue of St. Francis, the fox breaking
through the lilacs, my invention of this story, the wind blowing.

MICHAEL HARPER
Nightmare Begins Responsibility[1]

I place these numbed wrists to the pane
watching white uniforms whisk over
him in the tube-kept
prison

---

[1] A play on William Butler Yeats's epigraph to his volume *Responsibilities* (1913):
"In dreams begin responsibilities." This poem is an elegy for Harper's son, who died one
day after birth. Another son had also died shortly after birth.

fear what they will do in experiment
watch my gloved stickshifting gasolined hands
breathe *boxcar-information-please* infirmary tubes
distrusting white-pink mending paperthin
silkened end hairs, distrusting tubes
shrunk in his *trunk-skincapped*
shaven head, in thighs
distrusting-white-hands-picking-baboon-light
on this son who will not make his second night
of this wardstrewn intensive airpocket
where his father's asthmatic
hymns of *night-train,* train done gone
his mother can only know that he has flown
up into essential calm unseen corridor
going boxscarred home, *mamaborn, sweetsonchild*
gonedowntown into *researchtestingwarehousebatteryacid*
mama-son-done-gone / me telling her 'nother
train tonight, no music, no breathstroked
heartbeat in my infinite distrust of them:

and of my distrusting self
white-doctor-who-breathed-for-him-all-night
say it for two sons gone,
say nightmare, say it loud
panebreaking heartmadness:
nightmare begins responsibility.

ROBERT HAYDEN
Frederick Douglass[1]

When it is finally ours, this freedom, this liberty, this beautiful
and terrible thing, needful to man as air,
usable as earth; when it belongs at last to all,
when it is truly instinct, brain matter, diastole, systole,
reflex action; when it is finally won; when it is more
than the gaudy mumbo jumbo of politicians:
this man, this Douglass, this former slave, this Negro
beaten to his knees, exiled, visioning a world
where none is lonely, none hunted, alien,

---

[1] Frederick Douglass (ca. 1817–1895), who escaped from slavery in 1838, became an abolitionist, writer, and statesman.

this man, superb in love and logic, this man
shall be remembered. Oh, not with statues' rhetoric,
not with legends and poems and wreaths of bronze alone,
but with the lives grown out of his life, the lives
fleshing his dream of the beautiful, needful thing.

Mourning Poem for the Queen of Sunday

> Lord's lost Him His mockingbird,
> His fancy warbler;
> Satan sweet-talked her,
> four bullets hushed her.
> Who would have thought
> she'd end that way?

Four bullets hushed her. And the world a-clang with evil.
Who's going to make old hardened sinner men tremble now
and the righteous rock?
Oh who and oh who will sing Jesus down
to help with struggling and doing without and being colored
all through blue Monday?
Till way next Sunday?

> All those angels
> in their cretonne clouds and finery
> the true believer saw
> when she rared back her head and sang,
> all those angels are surely weeping.
> Who would have thought
> she'd end that way?

Four holes in her heart. The gold works wrecked.
But she looks so natural in her big bronze coffin
among the Broken Hearts and Gates-Ajar,
it's as if any moment she'd lift her head
from its pillow of chill gardenias
and turn this quiet into shouting Sunday
and make folks forget what she did on Monday.

> Oh, Satan sweet-talked her,
> and four bullets hushed her.
> Lord's lost Him His diva,
> His fancy warbler's gone.
> Who would have thought,
> who would have thought she'd end that way?

SEAMUS HEANEY
Bogland

For T. P. Flanagan

We have no prairies
To slice a big sun at evening —
Everywhere the eye concedes to
Encroaching horizon,

Is wooed into the cyclops' eye
Of a tarn. Our unfenced country
Is bog that keeps crusting
Between the sights of the sun.

They've taken the skeleton
Of the Great Irish Elk
Out of the peat, set it up,
An astounding crate full of air.

Butter sunk under
More than a hundred years
Was recovered salty and white.
The ground itself is kind, black butter

Melting and opening underfoot,
Missing its last definition
By millions of years.
They'll never dig coal here,

Only the waterlogged trunks
Of great firs, soft as pulp.
Our pioneers keep striking
Inwards and downwards,

Every layer they strip
Seems camped on before.
The bogholes might be Atlantic seepage.
The wet centre is bottomless.

Punishment

I can feel the tug
of the halter at the nape
of her neck, the wind
on her naked front.

It blows her nipples
to amber beads,
it shakes the frail rigging
of her ribs.

I can see her drowned
body in the bog,
the weighing stone,
the floating rods and boughs.

Under which at first
she was a barked sapling
that is dug up
oak-bone, brain-firkin:°   *container*

her shaved head
like a stubble of black corn,
her blindfold a soiled bandage,
her noose a ring

to store
the memories of love.
Little adulteress,
before they punished you

you were flaxen-haired,
undernourished, and your
tar-black face was beautiful.
My poor scapegoat,

I almost love you
but would have cast, I know,
the stones of silence.
I am the artful voyeur

of your brain's exposed
and darkened combs,
your muscles' webbing
and all your numbered bones:

I who have stood dumb
when your betraying sisters,
cauled in tar,
wept by the railings,

who would connive
in civilized outrage

yet understand the exact
and tribal, intimate revenge.

GEORGE HERBERT
The Collar

I struck the board° and cried, "No more;   *table*
    I will abroad!
What? shall I ever sigh and pine?
My lines and life are free, free as the road,
    Loose as the wind, as large as store.
        Shall I be still in suit?
    Have I no harvest but a thorn
    To let me blood, and not restore
What I have lost with cordial fruit?
        Sure there was wine
    Before my sighs did dry it; there was corn
        Before my tears did drown it.
    Is the year only lost to me?
        Have I no bays to crown it,
No flowers, no garlands gay? All blasted?
        All wasted?
    Not so, my heart; but there is fruit,
        And thou hast hands.
    Recover all thy sigh-blown age
On double pleasures: leave thy cold dispute
Of what is fit and not. Forsake thy cage,
        Thy rope of sands,
Which petty thoughts have made, and made to thee
    Good cable, to enforce and draw,
        And be thy law,
    While thou didst wink and wouldst not see.
        Away! take heed;
        I will abroad.
Call in thy death's-head there; tie up thy fears.
        He that forbears
    To suit and serve his need,
        Deserves his load."
But as I raved and grew more fierce and wild
        At every word,
Methought I heard one calling, *Child!*
        And I replied, *My Lord.*

Redemption

Having been tenant long to a rich lord,
    Not thriving, I resolvèd to be bold,
    And make a suit unto him, to afford°   *grant*
A new small-rented lease, and cancel the old.

In heaven at his manor I him sought;
    They told me there that he was lately gone
    About some land, which he had dearly bought
Long since on earth, to take possessiön.

I straight returned, and knowing his great birth,
    Sought him accordingly in great resorts;
    In cities, theaters, gardens, parks and courts;
At length I heard a ragged noise and mirth

    Of thieves and murderers; there I him espied,
    Who straight, *Your suit is granted,* said, and died.

ROBERT HERRICK
Corinna's Going A-Maying

Get up! get up for shame! the blooming morn
Upon her wings presents the god unshorn.° *Apollo, god of the sun*
    See how Aurora° throws her fair   *goddess of dawn*
    Fresh-quilted colors through the air:
    Get up, sweet slug-a-bed, and see
    The dew bespangling herb and tree.
Each flower has wept and bowèd toward the east
Above an hour since, yet you not dressed;
    Nay, not so much as out of bed?
    When all the birds have matins said,
    And sung their thankful hymns, 'tis sin,
    Nay, profanation to keep in,
Whenas a thousand virgins on this day
Spring, sooner than the lark, to fetch in May.

Rise, and put on your foliage, and be seen
To come forth, like the springtime, fresh and green,
    And sweet as Flora.° Take no care   *goddess of flowers*
    For jewels for your gown or hair;
    Fear not; the leaves will strew
    Gems in abundance upon you;

Besides, the childhood of the day has kept,
Against you come, some orient pearls unwept;
    Come and receive them while the light
    Hangs on the dew-locks of the night,
    And Titan° on the eastern hill   *the sun*
    Retires himself, or else stands still
Till you come forth. Wash, dress, be brief in praying:
Few beads° are best when once we go a-Maying.   *prayers*

Come, my Corinna, come; and, coming mark
How each field turns a street, each street a park
    Made green and trimmed with trees; see how
    Devotion gives each house a bough
    Or branch: each porch, each door ere this,
    An ark, a tabernacle is,
Made up of whitethorn neatly interwove,
As if here were those cooler shades of love.
    Can such delights be in the street
    And open fields, and we not see 't?
    Come, we'll abroad; and let's obey
    The proclamation made for May,
And sin no more, as we have done, by staying;
But, my Corinna, come, let's go a-Maying.

There's not a budding boy or girl this day
But is got up and gone to bring in May;
    A deal of youth, ere this, is come
    Back, and with whitethorn laden home.
    Some have dispatched their cakes and cream
    Before that we have left to dream;
And some have wept, and wooed, and plighted troth,
And chose their priest, ere we can cast off sloth.
    Many a green-gown has been given,
    Many a kiss, both odd and even,
    Many a glance, too, has been sent
    From out the eye, love's firmament;
Many a jest told of the keys betraying
This night, and locks picked; yet we're not a-Maying.

Come, let us go while we are in our prime,
And take the harmless folly of the time.
    We shall grow old apace, and die
    Before we know our liberty.

Our life is short, and our days run
As fast away as does the sun;
And, as a vapor or a drop of rain
Once lost, can ne'er be found again;
So when or you or I are made
A fable, song, or fleeting shade,
All love, all liking, all delight
Lies drowned with us in endless night.
Then while time serves, and we are but decaying,
Come, my Corinna, come, let's go a-Maying.

GERARD MANLEY HOPKINS
God's Grandeur

The world is charged with the grandeur of God.
It will flame out, like shining from shook foil;
It gathers to a greatness, like the ooze of oil
Crushed. Why do men then now not reck his rod?
Generations have trod, have trod, have trod;
And all is seared with trade; bleared, smeared with toil;
And wears man's smudge and shares man's smell: the soil
Is bare now, nor can foot feel, being shod.

And for all this, nature is never spent;
There lives the dearest freshness deep down things;
And though the last lights off the black West went
Oh, morning, at the brown brink eastward, springs —
Because the Holy Ghost over the bent
World broods with warm breast and with ah! bright wings.

No worst, there is none. Pitched past pitch of grief

No worst, there is none. Pitched past pitch of grief,
More pangs will, schooled at forepangs, wilder wring.
Comforter, where, where is your comforting?
Mary, mother of us, where is your relief?

My cries heave, herds-long; huddle in a main, a chief-
woe, world-sorrow; on an age-old anvil wince and sing —
Then lull, then leave off. Fury had shrieked "No ling-
ering! Let me be fell:° force° I must be brief."   *fierce / perforce*

O the mind, mind has mountains; cliffs of fall
Frightful, sheer, no-man-fathomed. Hold them cheap
May who ne'er hung there. Nor does long our small
Durance deal with that steep or deep. Here! creep,
Wretch, under a comfort serves in a whirlwind: all
Life death does end and each day dies with sleep.

The Windhover

To Christ Our Lord

I caught this morning morning's minion, king-
    dom of daylight's dauphin, dapple-dawn-drawn Falcon, in his
             riding
    Of the rolling level underneath him steady air, and striding
High there, how he rung upon the rein of a wimpling wing
In his ecstasy! then off, off forth on swing,
    As a skate's heel sweeps smooth on a bow-bend: the hurl and
        gliding
    Rebuffed the big wind. My heart in hiding
Stirred for a bird, — the achieve of, the mastery of the thing!

Brute beauty and valour and act, oh, air, pride, plume, here
    Buckle! AND the fire that breaks from thee then, a billion
Times told lovelier, more dangerous, O my chevalier!

    No wonder of it: shéer plód makes plough down sillion
Shine, and blue-bleak embers, ah my dear,
    Fall, gall themselves, and gash gold-vermilion.

A. E. HOUSMAN
Loveliest of Trees, the Cherry Now

Loveliest of trees, the cherry now
Is hung with bloom along the bough,
And stands about the woodland ride
Wearing white for Eastertide.

Now, of my threescore years and ten,
Twenty will not come again,
And take from seventy springs a score,
It only leaves me fifty more.

And since to look at things in bloom
Fifty springs are little room,
About the woodlands I will go
To see the cherry hung with snow.

With Rue My Heart Is Laden

With rue my heart is laden
  For golden friends I had,
For many a rose-lipt maiden
  And many a lightfoot lad.

By brooks too broad for leaping
  The lightfoot boys are laid;
The rose-lipt girls are sleeping
  In fields where roses fade.

Harlem

What happens to a dream deferred?

  Does it dry up
  like a raisin in the sun?
  Or fester like a sore —
  And then run?
  Does it stink like rotten meat?
  Or crust and sugar over —
  like a syrupy sweet?

  Maybe it just sags
  like a heavy load.

  Or does it explode?

LANGSTON HUGHES
I, Too

I, too, sing America.

I am the darker brother.
They send me to eat in the kitchen
When company comes,
But I laugh,
And eat well,
And grow strong.

Tomorrow,
I'll be at the table
When company comes.
Nobody'll dare
Say to me,

"Eat in the kitchen,"
Then.

Besides,
They'll see how beautiful I am
And be ashamed —

I, too, am America.

Suicide's Note

The calm,
Cool face of the river
Asked me for a kiss.

The Weary Blues

Droning a drowsy syncopated tune,
Rocking back and forth to a mellow croon,
    I heard a Negro play.
Down on Lenox Avenue the other night
By the pale dull pallor of an old gas light
       He did a lazy sway. . . .
       He did a lazy sway. . . .
To the tune o' those Weary Blues.
With his ebony hands on each ivory key
He made that poor piano moan with melody.
     O Blues!
Swaying to and fro on his rickety stool
He played that sad raggy tune like a musical fool.
     Sweet Blues!
Coming from a black man's soul.
     O Blues!
In a deep song voice with a melancholy tone
I heard that Negro sing, that old piano moan —
    "Ain't got nobody in all this world,
    Ain't got nobody but ma self.
    I's gwine to quit ma frownin'
    And put ma troubles on the shelf."
Thump, thump, thump, went his foot on the floor.
He played a few chords then he sang some more —
    "I got the Weary Blues
    And I can't be satisfied.
    Got the Weary Blues

> And can't be satisfied —
> I ain't happy no mo'
> And I wish that I had died."
And far into the night he crooned that tune.
The stars went out and so did the moon.
The singer stopped playing and went to bed
While the Weary Blues echoed through his head.
He slept like a rock or a man that's dead.

BEN JONSON
Come, My Celia[1]

Come, my Celia, let us prove,°   *experience*
While we can, the sports of love;
Time will not be ours forever;
He at length our good will sever.
Spend not then his gifts in vain.
Suns that set may rise again;
But if once we lose this light,
'Tis with us perpetual night.
Why should we defer our joys?
Fame and rumor are but toys.
Cannot we delude the eyes
Of a few poor household spies,
Or his easier ears beguile,
So removèd by our wile?
'Tis no sin love's fruit to steal;
But the sweet thefts to reveal,
To be taken, to be seen,
These have crimes accounted been.

To the Memory of My Beloved, the Author Mr. William Shakespeare

And What He Hath Left Us[1]

To draw no envy, Shakespeare, on thy name,
Am I thus ample to thy book and fame,
While I confess thy writings to be such

---

[1] From *Volpone*.
[1] Prefixed to the First Folio edition of Shakespeare's works (1623).

As neither man nor Muse can praise too much.
'Tis true, and all men's suffrage. But these ways
Were not the paths I meant unto thy praise:
For silliest ignorance on these may light,
Which, when it sounds at best, but echoes right;
Or blind affection, which doth ne'er advance
The truth, but gropes, and urgeth all by chance;
Or crafty malice might pretend this praise,
And think to ruin where it seemed to raise.
These are as some infamous bawd or whore
Should praise a matron. What could hurt her more?
But thou art proof against them, and, indeed,
Above th' ill fortune of them, or the need.
I therefore will begin. Soul of the age!
The applause! delight! the wonder of our stage!
My Shakespeare, rise; I will not lodge thee by
Chaucer or Spenser, or bid Beaumont lie
A little further to make thee a room:
Thou art a monument without a tomb,
And art alive still while thy book doth live,
And we have wits to read and praise to give.
That I not mix thee so, my brain excuses,
I mean with great, but disproportioned Muses;
For, if I thought my judgment were of years,
I should commit thee surely with thy peers,
And tell how far thou didst our Lyly outshine,
Or sporting Kyd, or Marlowe's mighty line.
And though thou hadst small Latin and less Greek,
From thence to honor thee I would not seek
For names, but call forth thund'ring Aeschylus,
Euripides, and Sophocles to us,
Pacuvius, Accius, him of Cordova dead,[2]
To life again, to hear thy buskin[3] tread
And shake a stage; or, when thy socks were on,
Leave thee alone for the comparison
Of all that insolent Greece or haughty Rome
Sent forth, or since did from their ashes come.
Triumph, my Britain; thou hast one to show

---

[2] Aeschylus, Sophocles, and Euripides, the three writers of Greek tragedy, are grouped with Pacuvius, Accius, and Seneca, three writers of Roman tragedy.

[3] The buskin was associated with Greek tragedy, the socks with comedy.

To whom all scenes° of Europe homage owe.   *stages*
He was not of an age, but for all time!
And all the Muses still were in their prime
When like Apollo he came forth to warm
Our ears, or like a Mercury to charm.
Nature herself was proud of his designs,
And joyed to wear the dressing of his lines,
Which were so richly spun, and woven so fit,
As, since, she will vouchsafe no other wit:
The merry Greek, tart Aristophanes,
Neat Terence, witty Plautus[4] now not please,
But antiquated and deserted lie,
As they were not of Nature's family.
Yet must I not give Nature all; thy Art,
My gentle Shakespeare, must enjoy a part.
For though the poet's matter Nature be,
His Art doth give the fashion; and that he
Who casts to write a living line must sweat
(Such as thine are) and strike the second heat
Upon the muses' anvil; turn the same,
And himself with it, that he thinks to frame,
Or for the laurel he may gain a scorn;
For a good poet's made as well as born.
And such wert thou! Look how the father's face
Lives in his issue, even so the race
Of Shakespeare's mind and manners brightly shines
In his well-turnèd and true-filèd lines,
In each of which he seems to shake a lance,
As brandished at the eyes of ignorance.
Sweet swan of Avon, what a sight it were
To see thee in our waters yet appear,
And make those flights upon the banks of Thames
That so did take Eliza and our James!
But stay; I see thee in the hemisphere
Advanced and made a constellation there!
Shine forth, thou star of poets, and with rage
Or influence chide or cheer the drooping stage,
Which, since thy flight from hence, hath mourned like night,
And despairs day, but for thy volume's light.

---

[4] Aristophanes, Terence, and Plautus were the most renowned comic writers of classical times.

JOHN KEATS
In drear nighted December

In drear nighted December,
    Too happy, happy tree,
Thy branches ne'er remember
    Their green felicity —
The north cannot undo them
With a sleety whistle through them,
Nor frozen thawings glue them
    From budding at the prime.

In drear nighted December,
    Too happy, happy brook,
Thy bubblings ne'er remember
    Apollo's summer look;
But with a sweet forgetting
They stay their crystal fretting,
Never, never petting
    About the frozen time.

Ah! would 'twere so with many
    A gentle girl and boy —
But were there ever any
    Writh'd not of passèd joy?
The feel of not to feel it,
When there is none to heal it,
Nor numbèd sense to steel it,
    Was never said in rhyme.

On Sitting Down to Read King Lear Once Again

O golden-tongued Romance with serene lute!
    Fair plumèd Siren!° Queen of far away!   *enchantress*
    Leave melodizing on this wintry day,
Shut up thine olden pages, and be mute:
Adieu! for once again the fierce dispute
    Betwixt damnation and impassioned clay
    Must I burn through; once more humbly assay
The bitter-sweet of this Shakespearean fruit.
Chief Poet! and ye clouds of Albion,°   *England*
    Begetters of our deep eternal theme,
When through the old oak forest I am gone,
    Let me not wander in a barren dream,

But when I am consumèd in the fire,
Give me new Phoenix[1] wings to fly at my desire.

This Living Hand[1]

This living hand, now warm and capable
Of earnest grasping, would, if it were cold
And in the icy silence of the tomb,
So haunt thy days and chill thy dreaming nights
That thou wouldst wish thine own heart dry of blood
So in my veins red life might stream again,
And thou be conscience-calmed — see here it is —
I hold it towards you.

ETHERIDGE KNIGHT

A Poem for Myself
(Or Blues for a Mississippi Black Boy)

I was born in Mississippi;
I walked barefooted thru the mud.
Born black in Mississippi,
Walked barefooted thru the mud.
But, when I reached the age of twelve
I left that place for good.
My daddy he chopped cotton
And he drank his liquor straight.
Said my daddy chopped cotton
And he drank his liquor straight.
When I left that Sunday morning
He was leaning on the barnyard gate.
I left my momma standing
With the sun shining in her eyes.
Left her standing in the yard
With the sun shining in her eyes.
And I headed North
As straight as the Wild Goose Flies,
I been to Detroit & Chicago —
Been to New York city too.
I been to Detroit and Chicago

---

[1] Legendary bird that lives for centuries, then consumes itself in fire and is reborn.
[1] Written on a manuscript page of Keats's unfinished poem, "The Cap and Bells."

Been to New York city too.
Said I done strolled all those funky avenues
I'm still the same old black boy with the same old blues.
Going back to Mississippi
This time to stay for good
Going back to Mississippi
This time to stay for good —
Gonna be free in Mississippi
Or dead in the Mississippi mud.

KENNETH KOCH

Variations on a Theme by William Carlos Williams

1

I chopped down the house that you had been saving to live in next
    summer.
I am sorry, but it was morning, and I had nothing to do
and its wooden beams were so inviting.

2

We laughed at the hollyhocks together
and then I sprayed them with lye.
Forgive me. I simply do not know what I am doing.

3

I gave away the money that you had been saving to live on for the
    next ten years.
The man who asked for it was shabby
and the firm March wind on the porch was so juicy and cold.

4

Last evening we went dancing and I broke your leg.
Forgive me. I was clumsy, and
I wanted you here in the wards, where I am the doctor!

YUSEF KOMUNYAKAA

Boat People

After midnight they load up.
A hundred shadows move about blindly.
Something close to sleep
hides low voices drifting
toward a red horizon. Tonight's

a black string, the moon's pull —
this boat's headed somewhere.
Lucky to have gotten past
searchlights low-crawling the sea,
like a woman shaking water
from her long dark hair.

Twelve times in three days
they've been lucky,
clinging to each other in gray mist.
Now Thai fishermen gaze out across
the sea as it changes color,
hands shading their eyes
the way sailors do,
minds on robbery & rape.
Sunlight burns blood-orange.

Storm warnings crackle on a radio.
The Thai fishermen turn away.
Not enough water for the trip.
The boat people cling to each other,
faces like yellow sea grapes,
wounded by doubt & salt.
Dusk hangs over the water.
Seasick, they daydream Jade Mountain
a whole world away, half-drunk
on what they hunger to become.

My Father's Loveletters

On Fridays he'd open a can of Jax,
Close his eyes, & ask me to write
The same letter to my mother
Who sent postcards of desert flowers
Taller than a man. He'd beg her
Return & promised to never
Beat her again. I was almost happy
She was gone, & sometimes wanted
To slip in something bad.
His carpenter's apron always bulged
With old nails, a claw hammer
Holstered in a loop at his side
& extension cords coiled around his feet.
Words rolled from under
The pressure of my ballpoint:

Love, Baby, Honey, Please.
We lingered in the quiet brutality
Of voltage meters & pipe threaders,
Lost between sentences . . . the heartless
Gleam of a two-pound wedge
On the concrete floor,
A sunset in the doorway
Of the tool shed.
I wondered if she'd laugh
As she held them over a flame.
My father could only sign
His name, but he'd look at blueprints
& tell you how many bricks
Formed each wall. This man
Who stole roses & hyacinth
For his yard, stood there
With eyes closed & fists balled,
Laboring over a simple word,
Opened like a fresh wound, almost
Redeemed by what he tried to say.

PHILIP LARKIN
High Windows

When I see a couple of kids
And guess he's fucking her and she's
Taking pills or wearing a diaphragm,
I know this is paradise

Everyone old has dreamed of all their lives —
Bonds and gestures pushed to one side
Like an outdated combine harvester,
And everyone young going down the long slide

To happiness, endlessly. I wonder if
Anyone looked at me, forty years back,
And thought, *That'll be the life;*
No God any more, or sweating in the dark

About hell and that, or having to hide
What you think of the priest. He
And his lot will all go down the long slide
Like free bloody birds. And immediately

Rather than words comes the thought of high windows:
The sun-comprehending glass,
And beyond it, the deep blue air, that shows
Nothing, and is nowhere, and is endless.

Mr Bleaney

"This was Mr Bleaney's room. He stayed
The whole time he was at the Bodies, till
They moved him." Flowered curtains, thin and frayed,
Fall to within five inches of the sill,

Whose window shows a strip of building land,
Tussocky, littered. "Mr Bleaney took
My bit of garden properly in hand."
Bed, upright chair, sixty-watt bulb, no hook

Behind the door, no room for books or bags —
"I'll take it." So it happens that I lie
Where Mr Bleaney lay, and stub my fags
On the same saucer-souvenir, and try

Stuffing my ears with cotton-wool, to drown
The jabbering set he egged her on to buy.
I know his habits — what time he came down,
His preference for sauce to gravy, why

He kept on plugging at the four aways —
Likewise their yearly frame: the Frinton folk
Who put him up for summer holidays,
And Christmas at his sister's house in Stoke.

But if he stood and watched the frigid wind
Tousling the clouds, lay on the fusty bed
Telling himself that this was home, and grinned,
And shivered, without shaking off the dread

That how we live measures our own nature,
And at his age having no more to show
Than one hired box should make him pretty sure
He warranted no better, I don't know.

Reasons for Attendance

The trumpet's voice, loud and authoritative,
Draws me a moment to the lighted glass

To watch the dancers — all under twenty-five —
Shifting intently, face to flushed face,
Solemnly on the beat of happiness.

— Or so I fancy, sensing the smoke and sweat,
The wonderful feel of girls. Why be out here?
But then, why be in there? Sex, yes, but what
Is sex? Surely, to think the lion's share
Of happiness is found by couples — sheer

Inaccuracy, as far as I'm concerned.
What calls me is that lifted, rough-tongued bell
(Art, if you like) whose individual sound
Insists I too am individual.
It speaks; I hear; others may hear as well,

But not for me, nor I for them; and so
With happiness. Therefore I stay outside,
Believing this; and they maul to and fro,
Believing that; and both are satisfied,
If no one has misjudged himself. Or lied.

This Be The Verse

They fuck you up, your mum and dad.
    They may not mean to, but they do.
They fill you with the faults they had
    And add some extras, just for you.

But they were fucked up in their turn
    By fools in old-style hats and coats,
Who half the time were soppy-stern
    And half at one another's throats.

Man hands on misery to man.
    It deepens like a coastal shelf.
Get out as early as you can,
    And don't have any kids yourself.

D. H. LAWRENCE
The English Are So Nice!

The English are so nice
So awfully nice
They are the nicest people in the world.

And what's more, they're very nice about being nice
About your being nice as well!
If you're not nice they soon make you feel it.

Americans and French and Germans and so on
They're all very well
But they're not *really* nice, you know.
They're not nice in *our* sense of the word, are they now?

That's why one doesn't have to take them seriously.
We must be nice to them, of course,
Of course, naturally.
But it doesn't really matter what you say to them,
They don't really understand
You can just say anything to them:
Be nice, you know, just nice
But you must never take them seriously, they wouldn't
    understand,
Just be nice, you know! oh, fairly nice,
Not too nice of course, they take advantage
But nice enough, just nice enough
To let them feel they're not quite as nice as they might be.

DENISE LEVERTOV
The Ache of Marriage

The ache of marriage:

thigh and tongue, beloved,
are heavy with it,
it throbs in the teeth

We look for communion
and are turned away, beloved,
each and each

It is leviathan and we
in its belly
looking for joy, some joy
not to be known outside it

two by two in the ark of
the ache of it.

O Taste and See

The world is
not with us enough.
O taste and see

the subway Bible poster said,
meaning The Lord, meaning
if anything all that lives
to the imagination's tongue,

grief, mercy, language,
tangerine, weather, to
breathe them, bite,
savor, chew, swallow, transform

into our flesh our
deaths, crossing the street, plum, quince,
living in the orchard and being

hungry, and plucking
the fruit.

LI-YOUNG LEE

The Interrogation

Two streams: one dry, one poured all night by our beds.

I'll wonder
about neither.

The dry one was clogged with bodies.

I'm through
with memory.

At which window of what house did light teach you tedium?
On which step of whose stairway did you learn indecision?

I'm through
sorting avenues and doors,
curating houses and deaths.

Which house did we flee by night? Which house did we flee by day?

Don't ask me.

We stood and watched one burn; from one we ran away.

I'm neatly folding
the nights and days, notes
to be forgotten.

We were diminished. We were not spared. There was no pity.
Neither was their sanctuary. Neither rest.
There were fires in the streets. We stood among men, at the level
of their hands, all those wrists, dead or soon to die.

No more
letting my survival
depend on memory.

There was the sea; its green volume brought despair.
There was waiting, there was leaving. There was
astonishment too. The astonishment of
"I thought you died!" "How did you get out?"
"And Little Fei Fei walked right by the guards!"

I grow
leaden with stories,
my son's eyelids
grow heavy.

Who rowed the boat when our father tired?

Don't ask me.

Who came along? Who got left behind?

Ask the sea.

Through it all there was no song, and weeping
came many years later.

I'm through
with memory.

Sometimes a song,
even when there was weeping.

I'm through with memory.

Can't you still smell the smoke on my body?

HENRY WADSWORTH LONGFELLOW
Aftermath

When the summer fields are mown,
When the birds are fledged and flown,
    And the dry leaves strew the path;
With the falling of the snow,
With the cawing of the crow,
Once again the fields we mow
    And gather in the aftermath.

Not the sweet, new grass with flowers
Is this harvesting of ours;
    Not the upland clover bloom;
But the rowen mixed with weeds,
Tangled tufts from marsh and meads,
Where the poppy drops its seeds
    In the silence and the gloom.

The Jewish Cemetery at Newport

How strange it seems! These Hebrews in their graves,
    Close by the street of this fair seaport town,
Silent beside the never-silent waves,
    At rest in all this moving up and down!

The trees are white with dust, that o'er their sleep
    Wave their broad curtains in the southwind's breath,
While underneath these leafy tents they keep
    The long, mysterious Exodus of Death.

And these sepulchral stones, so old and brown,
    That pave with level flags their burial-place,
Seem like the tablets of the Law, thrown down
    And broken by Moses at the mountain's base.

The very names recorded here are strange,
    Of foreign accent, and of different climes;
Alvares and Rivera interchange
    With Abraham and Jacob of old times.

"Blessed be God! for he created Death!"
    The mourners said, "and Death is rest and peace;"
Then added, in the certainty of faith,
    "And giveth Life that nevermore shall cease."

Closed are the portals of their Synagogue,
　　No Psalms of David now the silence break,
No Rabbi reads the ancient Decalogue°　　　*Ten Commandments*
　　In the grand dialect the Prophets spake.

Gone are the living, but the dead remain,
　　And not neglected; for a hand unseen,
Scattering its bounty, like a summer rain,
　　Still keeps their graves and their remembrance green.

How came they here? What burst of Christian hate,
　　What persecution, merciless and blind,
Drove o'er the sea — that desert desolate —
　　These Ishmaels and Hagars of mankind?

They lived in narrow streets and lanes obscure,
　　Ghetto and Judenstrass,[1] in mirk and mire;
Taught in the school of patience to endure
　　The life of anguish and the death of fire.

All their lives long, with the unleavened bread
　　And bitter herbs of exile and its fears,
The wasting famine of the heart they fed,
　　And slaked its thirst with marah[2] of their tears.

Anathema maranatha![3] was the cry
　　That rang from town to town, from street to street;
At every gate the accursed Mordecai[4]
　　Was mocked and jeered, and spurned by Christian feet.

Pride and humiliation hand in hand
　　Walked with them through the world where'er they went;
Trampled and beaten were they as the sand,
　　And yet unshaken as the continent.

For in the background figures vague and vast
　　Of patriarchs and of prophets rose sublime,
And all the great traditions of the Past
　　They saw reflected in the coming time.

---

[1] German for "Street of Jews."

[2] The Hebrew word for bitterness.

[3] A curse; literally, "Let him be cursed, the Lord has come" (I Corinthians 16: 22).

[4] See the Book of Esther, in which Mordecai represents the Jew devoted to his people's welfare.

And thus forever with reverted look
    The mystic volume of the world they read,
Spelling it backward, like a Hebrew book,
    Till life became a Legend of the Dead.

But ah! what once has been shall be no more!
    The groaning earth in travail and in pain
Brings forth its races, but does not restore,
    And the dead nations never rise again.

The Tide Rises, the Tide Falls

The tide rises, the tide falls,
The twilight darkens, the curlew° calls;   *migratory bird*
Along the sea-sands damp and brown
The traveller hastens toward the town,
    And the tide rises, the tide falls.

Darkness settles on roofs and walls,
But the sea, the sea in the darkness calls;
The little waves, with their soft, white hands,
Efface the footprints in the sands,
    And the tide rises, the tide falls.

The morning breaks; the steeds in their stalls
Stamp and neigh, as the hostler calls;
The day returns, but nevermore
Returns the traveller to the shore,
    And the tide rises, the tide falls.

AUDRE LORDE
Hanging Fire

I am fourteen
and my skin has betrayed me
the boy I cannot live without
still sucks his thumb
in secret
how come my knees are
always so ashy
what if I die
before morning

and momma's in the bedroom
with the door closed.

I have to learn how to dance
in time for the next party
my room is too small for me
suppose I die before graduation
they will sing sad melodies
but finally
tell the truth about me
There is nothing I want to do
and too much
that has to be done
and momma's in the bedroom
with the door closed.

Nobody even stops to think
about my side of it
I should have been on Math Team
my marks were better than his
why do I have to be
the one
wearing braces
I have nothing to wear tomorrow
will I live long enough
to grow up
and momma's in the bedroom
with the door closed.

ROBERT LOWELL
Sailing Home from Rapallo[1]

[*February 1954*]

Your nurse could only speak Italian,
but after twenty minutes I could imagine your final week,
and tears ran down my cheeks. . . .

When I embarked from Italy with my Mother's body,
the whole shoreline of the *Golfo di Genova*[2]
was breaking into fiery flower.

---

[1] A city in northern Italy.
[2] Gulf of Genoa.

The crazy yellow and azure sea-sleds
blasting like jack-hammers across
the *spumante*[3]-bubbling wake of our liner,
recalled the clashing colors of my Ford.
Mother traveled first-class in the hold;
her *Risorgimento*[4] black and gold casket
was like Napoleon's at the *Invalides*.[5] . . .

While the passengers were tanning
on the Mediterranean in deck-chairs,
our family cemetery in Dunbarton[6]
lay under the White Mountains
in the sub-zero weather.
The graveyard's soil was changing to stone —
so many of its deaths had been midwinter.
Dour and dark against the blinding snowdrifts,
its black brook and fir trunks were as smooth as masts.
A fence of iron spear-hafts
black-bordered its mostly Colonial grave-slates.
The only "unhistoric" soul to come here
was Father, now buried beneath his recent
unweathered pink-veined slice of marble.
Even the Latin of his Lowell motto:
Occasionem cognosce,[7]
seemed too businesslike and pushing here,
where the burning cold illuminated
the hewn inscriptions of Mother's relatives:
twenty or thirty Winslows and Starks.
Frost had given their names a diamond edge. . . .

In the grandiloquent lettering on Mother's coffin,
Lowell had been misspelled LOVEL.
The corpse
was wrapped like *panettone*[8] in Italian tinfoil.

---

[3] Italian for "sparkling," as of wine.

[4] A reference to the period of Italy's national revival in the mid-nineteenth century.

[5] The building in Paris where Napoleon is buried.

[6] A town in New Hampshire near the Lowell's family home in Concord.

[7] Latin for "Recognize (your) opportunity."

[8] A Milanese sweet cake.

ARCHIBALD MacLEISH
Ars Poetica

A poem should be palpable and mute
As a globed fruit,

Dumb
As old medallions to the thumb,

Silent as the sleeve-worn stone
Of casement ledges where the moss has grown —

A poem should be wordless
As the flight of birds.

A poem should be motionless in time
As the moon climbs,

Leaving, as the moon releases
Twig by twig the night-entangled trees,

Leaving, as the moon behind the winter leaves,
Memory by memory the mind —

A poem should be motionless in time
As the moon climbs.

A poem should be equal to:
Not true.

For all the history of grief
An empty doorway and a maple leaf.

For love
The leaning grasses and two lights above the sea —

A poem should not mean
But be.

ANDREW MARVELL
An Horatian Ode

Upon Cromwell's Return from Ireland[1]

The forward youth that would appear
Must now forsake his Muses dear,

---

[1] Cromwell returned from conquering Ireland in May 1650, eighteen months after the execution of Charles I. In July he would invade Scotland.

Nor in the shadows sing
His numbers° languishing: *poems*

'Tis time to leave the books in dust,
And oil the unusèd armor's rust,
        Removing from the wall
        The corslet of the hall.

So restless Cromwell could not cease
In the inglorious arts of peace,
        But through adventurous war
        Urgèd his active star;

And like the three-forked lightning, first
Breaking the clouds where it was nursed,
        Did thorough his own side
        His fiery way divide.[2]

For 'tis all one to courage high,
The emulous or enemy;
        And with such to inclose
        Is more than to oppose.

Then burning through the air he went,
And palaces and temples rent;
        And Caesar's head at last
        Did through his laurels blast.

'Tis madness to resist or blame
The force of angry heaven's flame;
        And if we would speak true,
        Much to the man is due,

Who, from his private gardens, where
He lived reservèd and austere
        (As if his highest plot
        To plant the bergamot[3]),

Could by industrious valor climb
To ruin the great work of time,
        And cast the kingdom old
        Into another mold;

---

[2] Cromwell, after 1644, opened a way for himself among rival parliamentary leaders.

[3] A species of pear, also known as prince's pear or the pear of kings.

Though Justice against Fate complain,
And plead the ancient rights in vain;
    But those do hold or break,
    As men are strong or weak.

Nature, that hateth emptiness,
Allows of penetration less,[4]
    And therefore must make room
    Where greater spirits come.

What field of all the civil wars,
Where his were not the deepest scars?
    And Hampton shows what part
    He had of wiser art;[5]

Where, twining subtle fears with hope,
He wove a net of such a scope
    That Charles himself might chase
    To Carisbrooke's narrow case,

That thence the royal actor borne
The tragic scaffold might adorn;
    While round the armèd bands
    Did clap their bloody hands.

He nothing common did or mean
Upon that memorable scene,
    But with his keener eye
    The axe's edge did try;

Nor called the gods with vulgar spite
To vindicate his helpless right;
    But bowed his comely head
    Down, as upon a bed.

This was that memorable hour
Which first assured the forcèd power:
    So, when they did design
    The Capitol's first line,

---

[4] Although abhorring a vacuum, Nature is even more averse to the occupation of the same space by two bodies at the same time.

[5] Charles I fled to Carisbrooke Castle, which turned out to be a cage ("narrow case") for him. It was long believed that Cromwell connived at the flight of Charles from Hampton Court to Carisbrooke Castle in order to prod Parliament into executing him.

A bleeding head, where they begun,
Did fright the architects to run;
  And yet in that the state
  Foresaw its happy fate.[6]

And now the Irish are ashamed
To see themselves in one year tamed;
  So much one man can do
  That does both act and know.

They can affirm his praises best,
And have, though overcome, confessed
  How good he is, how just,
  And fit for highest trust.

Nor yet grown stiffer with command,
But still in the republic's hand —
  How fit he is to sway
  That can so well obey!

He to the Commons' feet presents
A kingdom for his first year's rents;
  And, what he may, forbears
  His fame to make it theirs;

And has his sword and spoils ungirt,
To lay them at the public's skirt:
  So when the falcon high
  Falls heavy from the sky,

She, having killed, no more does search
But on the next green bough to perch;
  Where, when he first does lure,
  The falconer has her sure.

What may not, then, our isle presume,
While victory his crest does plume?
  What may not others fear,
  If thus he crown each year?

A Caesar he, ere long, to Gaul
To Italy an Hannibal,

---

 [6] Pliny tells, in his *Natural History* (28:4), an anecdote about workmen who found a head while digging the foundation of a temple to Jupiter on the Tarpeian hill in Rome. The omen was interpreted as indicating a prosperous future for Rome.

And to all states not free
Shall climactèric be.

The Pict no shelter now shall find
Within his parti-colored mind,[7]
But from this valor sad
Shrink underneath the plaid;

Happy if in the tufted brake
The English hunter him mistake,
Nor lay his hounds in near
The Caledonian° deer.   *Scottish*

But thou, the war's and fortune's son,
March indefatigably on!
And for the last effect,
Still keep thy sword erect;

Besides the force it has to fright
The spirits of the shady night,
The same arts that did gain
A power must it maintain.

To His Coy Mistress

Had we but world enough, and time,
This coyness, lady, were no crime.
We would sit down, and think which way
To walk, and pass our long love's day.
Thou by the Indian Ganges' side
Shouldst rubies find; I by the tide
Of Humber[1] would complain. I would
Love you ten years before the flood,
And you should, if you please, refuse
Till the conversion of the Jews.[2]
My vegetable love should grow
Vaster than empires and more slow;
An hundred years should go to praise

---

[7] The early inhabitants of Scotland were called Picts because the warriors painted themselves with many colors for battle. (*Pictus* is Latin for "painted.") Marvell implies that the Scots are divided into many parties or factions.

[1] The Humber flows through Hull, Marvell's native town.

[2] Supposed to occur at the end of time.

Thine eyes, and on thy forehead gaze;
Two hundred to adore each breast,
But thirty thousand to the rest;
An age at least to every part,
And the last age should show your heart.
For, lady, you deserve this state,
Nor would I love at lower rate.
　　　But at my back I always hear
Time's wingèd chariot hurrying near;
And yonder all before us lie
Deserts of vast eternity.
Thy beauty shall no more be found;
Nor, in thy marble vault, shall sound
My echoing song; then worms shall try
That long-preserved virginity,
And your quaint honor turn to dust,
And into ashes all my lust:
The grave's a fine and private place,
But none, I think, do there embrace.
　　　Now therefore, while the youthful hue
Sits on thy skin like morning dew,
And while thy willing soul transpires
At every pore with instant fires,
Now let us sport us while we may,
And now, like amorous birds of prey,
Rather at once our time devour
Than languish in his slow-chapped power.
Let us roll all our strength and all
Our sweetness up into one ball,
And tear our pleasures with rough strife
Thorough the iron gates of life:
Thus, though we cannot make our sun
Stand still, yet we will make him run.

HERMAN MELVILLE
The Berg

A Dream

I saw a ship of martial build
(Her standards set, her brave apparel on)

Directed as by madness mere
Against a stolid iceberg steer,
Nor budge it, though the infatuate ship went down.
The impact made huge ice-cubes fall
Sullen, in tons that crashed the deck;
But that one avalanche was all —
No other movement save the foundering wreck.

Along the spurs of ridges pale,
Not any slenderest shaft and frail,
A prism over glass-green gorges lone,
Toppled; nor lace of traceries fine,
Nor pendent drops in grot or mine
Were jarred, when the stunned ship went down.

Nor sole the gulls in cloud that wheeled
Circling one snow-flanked peak afar,
But nearer fowl the floes that skimmed
And crystal beaches, felt no jar.
No thrill transmitted stirred the lock
Of jack-straw needle-ice at base;
Towers undermined by waves — the block
Atilt impending — kept their place.
Seals, dozing sleek on sliddery ledges
Slipt never, when by loftier edges
Through very inertia overthrown,
The impetuous ship in bafflement went down.

Hard Berg (methought), so cold, so vast,
With mortal damps self-overcast;
Exhaling still thy dankish breath —
Adrift dissolving, bound for death;
Though lumpish thou, a lumbering one —
A lumbering lubbard loitering slow,
Impingers rue thee and go down,
Sounding thy precipice below,
Nor stir the slimy slug that sprawls
Along thy dead indifference of walls.

Fragments of a Lost Gnostic[1] Poem of the Twelfth Century

. . . . .

Found a family, build a state,
The pledged event is still the same:
Matter in end will never abate
His ancient brutal claim.

. . . . .

Indolence is heaven's ally here,
And energy the child of hell:
The good man pouring from his pitcher clear
But brims the poisoned well.

Monody[1]

To have known him, to have loved him,
    After loneness long;
And then to be estranged in life,
    And neither in the wrong;
And now for death to set his seal —
    Ease me, a little ease, my song!

By wintry hills his hermit-mound
    The sheeted snow-drifts drape,
And houseless there the snow-bird flits
    Beneath the fir-tree's crape:
Glazed now with ice the cloistral vine
    That hid the shyest grape.

JAMES MERRILL
The Broken Home

Crossing the street,
I saw the parents and the child
At their window, gleaming like fruit
With evening's mild gold leaf.

---

[1] Gnosticism was a religious movement of late antiquity and the early Christian era.

[1] This poem is perhaps an elegy for Nathaniel Hawthorne, called "Vine" in Melville's long poem *Clarel.*

In a room on the floor below,
Sunless, cooler — a brimming
Saucer of wax, marbly and dim —
I have lit what's left of my life.

I have thrown out yesterday's milk
And opened a book of maxims.
The flame quickens. The word stirs.

Tell me, tongue of fire,
That you and I are as real
At least as the people upstairs.

My father,[1] who had flown in World War I,
Might have continued to invest his life
In cloud banks well above Wall Street and wife.
But the race was run below, and the point was to win.

Too late now, I make out in his blue gaze
(Through the smoked glass of being thirty-six)
The soul eclipsed by twin black pupils, sex
And business; time was money in those days.

Each thirteenth year he married. When he died
There were already several chilled wives
In sable orbit — rings, cars, permanent waves.
We'd felt him warming up for a green bride.

He could afford it. He was "in his prime"
At three score ten. But money was not time.

When my parents were younger this was a popular act:
A veiled woman would leap from an electric, wine-dark car
To the steps of no matter what — the Senate or the Ritz Bar —
And bodily, at newsreel speed, attack

No matter whom — Al Smith or José Maria Sert
Or Clemenceau[2] — veins standing out on her throat
As she yelled *War mongerer! Pig! Give us the vote!*,
And would have to be hauled away in her hobble skirt.

---

[1] Charles Merrill, who was a financier and founder of the brokerage firm Merrill, Lynch. He and Merrill's mother eventually divorced.

[2] Alfred E. Smith (1873–1944) and Georges Clemenceau (1841–1929) were politicians; José Maria Sert (1876–1945) was a painter.

What had the man done? Oh, made history.
Her business (he had implied) was giving birth,
Tending the house, mending the socks.

Always that same old story —
Father Time and Mother Earth,[3]
A marriage on the rocks.

One afternoon, red, satyr-thighed
Michael, the Irish setter, head
Passionately lowered, led
The child I was to a shut door. Inside,

Blinds beat sun from the bed.
The green-gold room throbbed like a bruise.
Under a sheet, clad in taboos
Lay whom we sought, her hair undone, outspread,

And of a blackness found, if ever now, in old
Engravings where the acid bit.
I must have needed to touch it
Or the whiteness — was she dead?
Her eyes flew open, startled strange and cold.
The dog slumped to the floor. She reached for me. I fled.

Tonight they have stepped out onto the gravel.
The party is over. It's the fall
Of 1931. They love each other still.

She: Charlie, I can't stand the pace.
He: Come on, honey — why, you'll bury us all!

A lead soldier guards my windowsill:
Khaki rifle, uniform, and face.
Something in me grows heavy, silvery, pliable.

How intensely people used to feel!
Like metal poured at the close of a proletarian novel,
Refined and glowing from the crucible,
I see those two hearts, I'm afraid,
Still. Cool here in the graveyard of good and evil,
They are even so to be honored and obeyed.

---

[3] In mythology, Cronus (Time) and Rhea (mother of the gods) were the parents
of Zeus, who dethroned his father.

. . . Obeyed, at least, inversely. Thus
I rarely buy a newspaper, or vote.
To do so, I have learned, is to invite
The tread of a stone guest[4] within my house.

Shooting this rusted bolt, though, against him,
I trust I am no less time's child than some
Who on the heath impersonate Poor Tom[5]
Or on the barricades risk life and limb.

Nor do I try to keep a garden, only
An avocado in a glass of water —
Roots pallid, gemmed with air. And later,

When the small gilt leaves have grown
Fleshy and green, I let them die, yes, yes,
And start another. I am earth's no less.

A child, a red dog roam the corridors,
Still, of the broken home. No sound. The brilliant
Rag runners halt before wide-open doors.
My old room! Its wallpaper — cream, medallioned
With pink and brown — brings back the first nightmares,
Long summer colds, and Emma, sepia-faced,
Perspiring over broth carried upstairs
Aswim with golden fats I could not taste.

The real house became a boarding-school.
Under the ballroom ceiling's allegory
Someone at last may actually be allowed
To learn something; or, from my window, cool
With the unstiflement of the entire story,
Watch a red setter[6] stretch and sink in cloud.

An Upward Look

O heart green acre   sown with salt
by the departing   occupier

lay down your gallant   spears of wheat
Salt of the earth   each stellar pinch

---

[4] In Mozart's opera *Don Giovanni,* the Commendatore's statue comes to life and enters the Don's house, seeking vengeance for his daughter's seduction.

[5] The name adopted, in Shakespeare's *King Lear,* by Edgar, disinherited by his father, Gloucester.

[6] This is a pun on "setter" — the dog and the setting sun.

flung in blind   defiance backwards
now takes its toll   Up from his quieted

quarry the lover   colder and wiser
hauling himself   finds the world turning

toys triumphs   toxins into
this vast facility   the living come
dearest to die in   How did it happen

In bright alternation   minutely mirrored
within the thinking   of each and every

mortal creature   halves of a clue
approach the earthlights   Morning star

evening star   salt of the sky
First the grave   dissolving into dawn

then the crucial   recrystallizing
from inmost depths   of clear dark blue

W. S. MERWIN
For a Coming Extinction

Gray whale
Now that we are sending you to The End
That great god
Tell him
That we who follow you invented forgiveness
And forgive nothing

I write as though you could understand
And I could say it
One must always pretend something
Among the dying
When you have left the seas nodding on their stalks
Empty of you
Tell him that we were made
On another day

The bewilderment will diminish like an echo
Winding along your inner mountains
Unheard by us
And find its way out
Leaving behind it the future

Dead
And ours

When you will not see again
The whale calves trying the light
Consider what you will find in the black garden
And its court
The sea cows the Great Auks the gorillas
The irreplaceable hosts ranged countless
And fore-ordaining as stars
Our sacrifices

Join your word to theirs
Tell him
That it is we who are important

For the Anniversary of My Death

Every year without knowing it I have passed the day
When the last fires will wave to me
And the silence will set out
Tireless traveller
Like the beam of a lightless star

Then I will no longer
Find myself in life as in a strange garment
Surprised at the earth
And the love of one woman
And the shamelessness of men
As today writing after three days of rain
Hearing the wren sing and the falling cease
And bowing not knowing to what

JOHN MILTON
L'Allegro[1]

Hence loathèd Melancholy
    Of Cerberus and blackest midnight born,
In Stygian cave forlorn
    'Mongst horrid shapes, and shrieks, and sights unholy,
Find out some uncouth cell,
    Where brooding Darkness spreads his jealous wings,

---

[1] The title is Italian for "The Cheerful Man."

And the night-raven sings;
    There under ebon shades, and low-browed rocks,
As ragged as thy locks,
    In dark Cimmerian[2] desert ever dwell.
But come thou goddess fair and free,
In Heaven yclept° Euphrosyne,[3]   *called*
And by men, heart-easing Mirth,
Whom lovely Venus at a birth
With two sister Graces more
To ivy-crownèd Bacchus bore;
Or whether (as some sager sing)[4]
The frolic wind that breathes the spring,
Zephyr with Aurora playing,
As he met her once a-Maying,
There on beds of violets blue,
And fresh-blown roses washed in dew,
Filled her with thee a daughter fair,
So buxom, blithe, and debonair.
Haste thee nymph, and bring with thee
Jest and youthful Jollity,
Quips and Cranks, and wanton Wiles,
Nods, and Becks, and wreathèd Smiles,
Such as hang on Hebe's° cheek,   *goddess of youth*
And love to live in dimple sleek;
Sport that wrinkled Care derides,
And Laughter holding both his sides.
Come, and trip it as ye go
On the light fantastic toe,
And in thy right hand lead with thee,
The mountain nymph, sweet Liberty;
And if I give thee honor due,
Mirth, admit me of thy crew
To live with her and live with thee,
In unreprovèd pleasures free;
To hear the lark begin his flight,
And, singing, startle the dull night,
From his watch-tower in the skies,
Till the dappled dawn doth rise;
Then to come in spite of sorrow,

---

[2] A land in which, according to Homer, the sun never shone.

[3] Mirth, one of the three Graces.

[4] This genealogy is invented by Milton.

And at my window bid good morrow,
Through the sweetbriar, or the vine,
Or the twisted eglantine.
While the cock with lively din,
Scatters the rear of darkness thin,
And to the stack, or the barn door,
Stoutly struts his dames before;
Oft listening how the hounds and horn
Cheerly rouse the slumbering morn,
From the side of some hoar hill,
Through the high wood echoing shrill.
Sometime walking not unseen
By hedgerow elms, on hillocks green,
Right against the eastern gate,
Where the great sun begins his state,
Robed in flames, and amber light,
The clouds in thousand liveries dight;°   *clad*
While the plowman near at hand,
Whistles o'er the furrowed land,
And the milkmaid singeth blithe,
And the mower whets his scythe,
And every shepherd tells his tale,
Under the hawthorn in the dale.
Straight mine eye hath caught new pleasures
Whilst the landscape round it measures,
Russet lawns and fallows gray,
Where the nibbling flocks do stray,
Mountains on whose barren breast
The laboring clouds do often rest;
Meadows trim with daisies pied,
Shallow brooks, and rivers wide.
Towers and battlements it sees
Bosomed high in tufted trees,
Where perhaps some beauty lies,
The cynosure of neighboring eyes.
Hard by, a cottage chimney smokes,
From betwixt two aged oaks,
Where Corydon and Thyris[5] met,
Are at their savory dinner set
Of herbs, and other country messes,

---

[5] Corydon, Thyrsis, Phyllis (line 86), and Thestylis (line 88) are conventional names from pastoral poetry.

Which the neat-handed Phyllis dresses;
And then in haste her bower she leaves,
With Thestylis to bind the sheaves;
Or if the earlier season lead
To the tanned haycock in the mead.
Sometimes with secure delight
The upland hamlets will invite,
When the merry bells ring round
And the jocund rebecks° sound   *fiddles*
To many a youth and many a maid,
Dancing in the checkered shade;
And young and old come forth to play
On a sunshine holiday,
Till the livelong daylight fail;
Then to the spicy nut-brown ale,
With stories told of many a feat,
How fairy Mab the junkets eat;
She was pinched and pulled, she said,
And he, by Friar's lantern° led,   *will-o'-the-wisp*
Tells how the drudging goblin sweat
To earn his cream-bowl, duly set,
When in one night, ere glimpse of morn,
His shadowy flail hath threshed the corn
That ten day-laborers could not end;
Then lies him down the lubber° fiend,   *drudging*
And, stretched out all the chimney's° length,   *fireplace's*
Basks at the fire his hairy strength;
And crop-full out of doors he flings
Ere the first cock his matin rings.
Thus done the tales, to bed they creep,
By whispering winds soon lulled asleep.
Towered cities please us then,
And the busy hum of men,
Where throngs of knights and barons bold,
In weeds of peace high triumphs hold,
With store of ladies, whose bright eyes
Rain influence, and judge the prize
Of wit, or arms, while both contend
To win her grace, whom all commend.
There let Hymen° oft appear   *god of marriage*
In saffron robe, with taper clear,
And pomp, and feast, and revelry,
With masque, and antique pageantry;

Such sights as youthful poets dream
On summer eves by haunted stream.
Then to the well-trod stage anon,
If Jonson's learnèd sock[6] be on,
Or sweetest Shakespeare, fancy's child,
Warble his native wood-notes wild.
And ever against eating cares
Lap me in soft Lydian airs
Married to immortal verse
Such as the meeting soul may pierce
In notes, with many a winding bout°   *turn*
Of linkèd sweetness long drawn out,
With wanton heed, and giddy cunning,
The melting voice through mazes running;
Untwisting all the chains that tie
The hidden soul of harmony;
That Orpheus' self[7] may heave his head
From golden slumber on a bed
Of heaped Elysian flowers, and hear
Such strains as would have won the ear
Of Pluto, to have quite set free
His half-regained Eurydice.
These delights if thou canst give,
Mirth, with thee I mean to live.

On Shakespeare

What needs my Shakespeare for his honored bones
The labor of an age in pilèd stones?
Or that his hallowed reliques should be hid
Under a star-ypointing pyramid?
Dear son of Memory, great heir of Fame,
What need'st thou such weak witness of thy name?
Thou in our wonder and astonishment
Hast built thyself a livelong monument.
For whilst, to th' shame of slow-endeavoring art,
Thy easy numbers flow, and that each heart
Hath from the leaves of thy unvalued° book   *invaluable*

---

[6] The light shoe of ancient comic actors, a symbol of comedy.

[7] Orpheus, the great musician of classical mythology, pleaded with Pluto, god of the underworld, to allow him to rescue his wife, Eurydice. Pluto consented to let Eurydice return; but Orpheus, by looking back to be sure she was following, broke the terms of his agreement with Pluto, and Eurydice remained in Hades.

Those Delphic lines with deep impression took,
Then thou, our fancy of itself bereaving,
Dost make us marble with too much conceiving,
And so sepúlchred in such pomp dost lie
That kings for such a tomb would wish to die.

MARIANNE MOORE
Poetry

I, too, dislike it: there are things that are important beyond all
this fiddle.
Reading it, however, with a perfect contempt for it, one
discovers in
it after all, a place for the genuine.
Hands that can grasp, eyes
that can dilate, hair that can rise
if it must, these things are important not because a
high-sounding interpretation can be put upon them but because
they are
useful. When they become so derivative as to become
unintelligible,
the same thing may be said for all of us, that we
do not admire what
we cannot understand: the bat
holding on upside down or in quest of something to
eat, elephants pushing, a wild horse taking a roll, a tireless wolf
under
a tree, the immovable critic twitching his skin like a horse
that feels a flea, the base-
ball fan, the statistician —
nor is it valid
to discriminate against "business documents and
school-books";[1] all these phenomena are important. One must
make a distinction
however: when dragged into prominence by half poets, the
result is not poetry,

---

[1] Moore's note: "*Diary of Tolstoy* (Dutton), p. 84. 'Where the boundary between prose and poetry lies, I shall never be able to understand. The question is raised in manuals of style, yet the answer to it lies beyond me. Poetry is verse; prose is not verse. Or else poetry is everything with the exception of business documents and school books.'"

nor till the poets among us can be
    "literalists of
    the imagination"[2] — above
        insolence and triviality and can present

for inspection, "imaginary gardens with real toads in them,"
                              shall we have
    it. In the meantime, if you demand on the one hand,
    the raw material of poetry in
        all its rawness and
        that which is on the other hand
            genuine, you are interested in poetry.

The Steeple-Jack

    Revised, 1961

Dürer would have seen a reason for living
    in a town like this, with eight stranded whales
to look at; with the sweet sea air coming into your house
on a fine day, from water etched
    with waves as formal as the scales
on a fish.

One by one in two's and three's, the seagulls keep
    flying back and forth over the town clock,
or sailing around the lighthouse without moving their wings —
rising steadily with a slight
    quiver of the body — or flock
mewing where

a sea the purple of the peacock's neck is
    paled to greenish azure as Dürer changed
the pine green of the Tyrol to peacock blue and guinea
gray. You can see a twenty-five-
    pound lobster; and fish nets arranged
to dry. The

whirlwind fife-and-drum of the storm bends the salt
    marsh grass, disturbs stars in the sky and the
star on the steeple; it is a privilege to see so

---

[2] Moore's note: "*Yeats: Ideas of Good and Evil* (A. H. Bullen, 1903), p. 182. 'The limitation of his view was from the very intensity of his vision; he was a too literal realist of imagination, as others are of nature; and because he believed that the figures seen by the mind's eye, when exalted by inspiration, were "eternal existences," symbols of divine essences, he hated every grace of style that might obscure their lineaments.' "

much confusion. Disguised by what
      might seem the opposite, the sea-
side flowers and

trees are favored by the fog so that you have
      the tropics at first hand: the trumpet vine,
foxglove, giant snapdragon, a salpiglossis that has
spots and stripes; morning-glories, gourds,
      or moon-vines trained on fishing twine
at the back door:

cattails, flags, blueberries and spiderwort,
      striped grass, lichens, sunflowers, asters, daisies —
yellow and crab-claw ragged sailors with green bracts — toad-
            plant,
petunias, ferns; pink lilies, blue
      ones, tigers; poppies; black sweet-peas.
The climate

is not right for the banyan, frangipani, or
      jack-fruit trees; or for exotic serpent
life. Ring lizard and snakeskin for the foot, if you see fit;
but here they've cats, not cobras, to
      keep down the rats. The diffident
little newt

with white pin-dots on black horizontal spaced-
      out bands lives here; yet there is nothing that
ambition can buy or take away. The college student
named Ambrose sits on the hillside
      with his not-native books and hat
and sees boats

at sea progress white and rigid as if in
      a groove. Liking an elegance of which
the source is not bravado, he knows by heart the antique
sugar-bowl shaped summerhouse of
      interlacing slats, and the pitch
of the church

spire, not true, from which a man in scarlet lets
      down a rope as a spider spins a thread;
he might be part of a novel, but on the sidewalk a
sign says C. J. Poole, Steeple Jack,
      in black and white; and one in red
and white says

Danger. The church portico has four fluted
      columns, each a single piece of stone, made
modester by whitewash. This would be a fit haven for
waifs, children, animals, prisoners,
      and presidents who have repaid
sin-driven

senators by not thinking about them. The
      place has a schoolhouse, a post-office in a
store, fish-houses, hen-houses, a three-masted
      schooner on
the stocks. The hero, the student,
      the steeple jack, each in his way,
is at home.

It could not be dangerous to be living
      in a town like this, of simple people,
who have a steeple-jack placing danger signs by the church
while he is gliding the solid-
      pointed star, which on a steeple
stands for hope.

To a Snail

If "compression is the first grace of style,"
you have it. Contractility is a virtue
as modesty is a virtue.
It is not the acquisition of any one thing
that is able to adorn,
or the incidental quality that occurs
as a concomitant of something well said,
that we value in style,
but the principle that is hid:
in the absence of feet, "a method of conclusions";
"a knowledge of principles,"
in the curious phenomenon of your occipital horn.

THYLIAS MOSS
Lunchcounter Freedom

I once wanted a white man's eyes upon
me, my beauty riveting him to my slum
color. Forgetting his hands are made for my

curves, he would raise them to shield his eyes
and they would fly to my breasts with gentleness
stolen from doves.

I've made up my mind not to order a sandwich on
light bread if the waitress approaches me
with a pencil. My hat is the one I wear
the Sundays my choir doesn't sing. A dark
bird on it darkly sways to the gospel music,
trying to pull nectar from a cloth flower.
Psalms are mice in my mind, nibbling,
gnawing, tearing up my thoughts.
White men are the walls. I can't tell anyone
how badly I want water. In the mirage that
follows, the doves unfold into hammers.
They still fly to my breasts.

Because I'm nonviolent I don't act or
react. When knocked from the stool
my body takes its shape from what
it falls into. The white man cradles
his tar baby. Each magus in turn.
He fathered it, it looks just like him,
the spitting image. He can't let go of
his future. The menu offers tuna fish,
grits, beef in a sauce like desire.
He is free to choose from available
choices. The asterisk marks the special.

FRANK O'HARA
Ave Maria[1]

Mothers of America
        let your kids go to the movies!
get them out of the house so they won't know what you're up to
it's true that fresh air is good for the body
        but what about the soul
that grows in darkness, embossed by silvery images
and when you grow old as grow old you must
        they won't hate you

---

[1] Latin: "Hail Mary," prayer to the Virgin Mary saluting her as the Mother of God.

they won't criticize you they won't know
　　　　　　　　　　　they'll be in some glamorous country
they first saw on a Saturday afternoon or playing hookey
they may even be grateful to you
　　　　　　　　　　　　　for their first sexual experience
which only cost you a quarter
　　　　　　　　　　　and didn't upset the peaceful home
they will know where candy bars come from
　　　　　　　　　　　　and gratuitous bags of popcorn
as gratuitous as leaving the movie before it's over
with a pleasant stranger whose apartment is in the Heaven on Earth
　　　Bldg
near the Williamsburg Bridge
　　　　　　　　　　oh mothers you will have made the little tykes
so happy because if nobody does pick them up in the movies
they won't know the difference
　　　　　　　　　　　and if somebody does it'll be sheer gravy
and they'll have been truly entertained either way
instead of hanging around the yard
　　　　　　　　　　　　or up in their room
　　　　　　　　　　　　　　　hating you
prematurely since you won't have done anything horribly mean
　　　yet
except keeping them from the darker joys
　　　　　　　　　　　　　it's unforgivable the latter
so don't blame me if you won't take this advice
　　　　　　　　　　　and the family breaks up
and your children grow old and blind in front of a TV set
　　　　　　　　　　　　　　　seeing
movies you wouldn't let them see when they were young

Why I Am Not a Painter

I am not a painter, I am a poet.
Why? I think I would rather be
a painter, but I am not. Well,

for instance, Mike Goldberg
is starting a painting. I drop in.
"Sit down and have a drink" he
says. I drink; we drink. I look
up. "You have SARDINES in it."
"Yes, it needed something there."
"Oh." I go and the days go by

and I drop in again. The painting
is going on, and I go, and the days
go by. I drop in. The painting is
finished. "Where's SARDINES?"
All that's left is just
letters, "It was too much," Mike says.

But me? One day I am thinking of
a color: orange. I write a line
about orange. Pretty soon it is a
whole page of words, not lines.
Then another page. There should be
so much more, not of orange, of
words, of how terrible orange is
and life. Days go by. It is even in
prose, I am a real poet. My poem
is finished and I haven't mentioned
orange yet. It's twelve poems, I call
it ORANGES. And one day in a gallery
I see Mike's painting, called SARDINES.

WILFRED OWEN
Anthem for Doomed Youth

What passing-bells for these who die as cattle?
    — Only the monstrous anger of the guns.
    Only the stuttering rifles' rapid rattle
Can patter out their hasty orisons.
No mockeries now for them; no prayers nor bells;
    Nor any voice of mourning save the choirs, —
The shrill, demented choirs of wailing shells;
    And bugles calling for them from sad shires.

What candles may be held to speed them all?
    Not in the hands of boys, but in their eyes
Shall shine the holy glimmers of goodbyes.
    The pallor of girls' brows shall be their pall;
Their flowers the tenderness of patient minds,
And each slow dusk a drawing-down of blinds.

Disabled

He sat in a wheeled chair, waiting for dark,
And shivered in his ghastly suit of grey,

Legless, sewn short at elbow. Through the park
Voices of boys rang saddening like a hymn,
Voices of play and pleasure after day,
Till gathering sleep had mothered them from him.

About this time Town used to swing so gay
When glow-lamps budded in the light blue trees,
And girls glanced lovelier as the air grew dim,
— In the old times, before he threw away his knees.
Now he will never feel again how slim
Girls' waists are, or how warm their subtle hands.
All of them touch him like some queer disease.

There was an artist silly for his face,
For it was younger than his youth, last year.
Now, he is old; his back will never brace;
He's lost his colour very far from here,
Poured it down shell-holes till the veins ran dry,
And half his lifetime lapsed in the hot race
And leap of purple spurted from his thigh.

One time he liked a bloodsmear down his leg,
After the matches, carried shoulder-high.
It was after football, when he'd drunk a peg,
He thought he'd better join. — He wonders why.
Someone had said he'd look a god in kilts,
That's why; and maybe, too, to please his Meg,
Aye, that was it, to please the giddy jilts
He asked to join. He didn't have to beg;
Smiling they wrote his lie: aged nineteen years.
Germans he scarcely thought of; all their guilt
And Austria's, did not move him. And no fears
Of Fear came yet. He thought of jewelled hilts
For daggers in plaid socks; of smart salutes;
And care of arms; and leave; and pay arrears;
Esprit de corps; and hints for young recruits.
And soon, he was drafted out with drums and cheers.

Some cheered him home, but not as crowds cheer Goal.
Only a solemn man who brought him fruits
Thanked him; and then inquired about his soul.

Now, he will spend a few sick years in institutes,
And do what things the rules consider wise,
And take whatever pity they may dole.

Tonight he noticed how the women's eyes
Passed from him to the strong men that were whole.
How cold and late it is! Why don't they come
And put him into bed? Why don't they come?

CARL PHILLIPS

Passing

When the Famous Black Poet speaks,
I understand

that his is the same unnervingly slow
rambling method of getting from A to B
that I hated in my father,
my father who always told me
don't shuffle.

The Famous Black Poet is
speaking of the dark river in the mind
that runs thick with the heroes of color,
Jackie R., Bessie, Billie, Mr. Paige, anyone
who knew how to sing or when to run.
I think of my grandmother, said
to have dropped dead from the evil eye,
of my lesbian aunt who saw cancer and
a generally difficult future headed her way
in the still water
of her brother's commode.
I think of voodoo in the bottoms of soup-cans,
and I want to tell the poet that the blues
is *not* my name, that Alabama
is something I cannot use
in my business.

He is so like my father,
I don't ask the Famous Black Poet,
afterwards,
to remove his shoes,
knowing the inexplicable black
and pink I will find there, a cut
gone wrong in five places.
I don't ask him to remove
his pants, since that too

is known, what has never known
a blade, all the spaces between,
where we differ . . .

I have spent years tugging
between my legs,
and proved nothing, really.
I wake to the sheets I kicked aside,
and examine where they've failed to mend
their own creases, resembling some silken
obstruction, something pulled
from my father's chest, a bad heart,
a lung,

the lung of the Famous Black Poet
saying nothing I want to understand.

SYLVIA PLATH

Blackberrying

Nobody in the lane, and nothing, nothing but blackberries,
Blackberries on either side, though on the right mainly,
A blackberry alley, going down in hooks, and a sea
Somewhere at the end of it, heaving. Blackberries
Big as the ball of my thumb, and dumb as eyes
Ebon in the hedges, fat
With blue-red juices. These they squander on my fingers.
I had not asked for such a blood sisterhood; they must love me.
They accommodate themselves to my milkbottle, flattening their
       sides.

Overhead go the choughs in black, cacophonous flocks —
Bits of burnt paper wheeling in a blown sky.
Theirs is the only voice, protesting, protesting.
I do not think the sea will appear at all.
The high, green meadows are glowing, as if lit from within.
I come to one bush of berries so ripe it is a bush of flies,
Hanging their bluegreen bellies and their wing panes in a Chinese
       screen.
The honey-feast of the berries has stunned them; they believe in
       heaven.
One more hook, and the berries and bushes end.

The only thing to come now is the sea.
From between two hills a sudden wind funnels at me,
Slapping its phantom laundry in my face.
These hills are too green and sweet to have tasted salt.
I follow the sheep path between them. A last hook brings me
To the hills' northern face, and the face is orange rock
That looks out on nothing, nothing but a great space
Of white and pewter lights, and a din like silversmiths
Beating and beating at an intractable metal.

Edge

The woman is perfected.
Her dead

Body wears the smile of accomplishment,
The illusion of a Greek necessity

Flows in the scrolls of her toga,
Her bare

Feet seem to be saying:
We have come so far, it is over.

Each dead child coiled, a white serpent,
One at each little

Pitcher of milk, now empty.
She has folded

Them back into her body as petals
Of a rose close when the garden

Stiffens and odors bleed
From the sweet, deep throats of the night flower.

The moon has nothing to be sad about,
Staring from her hood of bone.

She is used to this sort of thing.
Her blacks crackle and drag.

Lady Lazarus[1]

I have done it again.
One year in every ten
I manage it —

---

[1] Lazarus was raised from the dead by Jesus.

A sort of walking miracle, my skin
Bright as a Nazi lampshade,[2]
My right foot

A paperweight,
My face a featureless, fine
Jew linen.

Peel off the napkin[3]
O my enemy.
Do I terrify? —

The nose, the eye pits, the full set of teeth?
The sour breath
Will vanish in a day.

Soon, soon the flesh
The grave cave ate will be
At home on me

And I a smiling woman.
I am only thirty.
And like the cat I have nine times to die.

This is Number Three.
What a trash
To annihilate each decade.

What a million filaments.
The peanut-crunching crowd
Shoves in to see

Them unwrap me hand and foot —
The big strip tease.
Gentleman, ladies,

These are my hands,
My knees.
I may be skin and bone,

Nevertheless, I am the same, identical woman.
The first time it happened I was ten.
It was an accident.

---

[2] The Nazis, in concentration camps, made lampshades of human skin.
[3] According to legend, the veil or napkin with which Veronica wiped Jesus' face, as he bore the Cross, was then impressed with his features.

The second time I meant
To last it out and not come back at all.
I rocked shut

As a seashell.
They had to call and call
And pick the worms off me like sticky pearls.

Dying
Is an art, like everything else.
I do it exceptionally well.

I do it so it feels like hell.
I do it so it feels real.
I guess you could say I've a call.

It's easy enough to do it in a cell.
It's easy enough to do it and stay put.
It's the theatrical

Comeback in broad day
To the same place, the same face, the same brute
Amused shout:

"A miracle!"
That knocks me out.
There is a charge

For the eyeing of my scars, there is a charge
For the hearing of my heart —
It really goes.

And there is a charge, very large charge,
For a word or a touch
Or a bit of blood

Or a piece of my hair or my clothes.
So, so, Herr Doktor.
So, Herr Enemy.

I am your opus,
I am your valuable,
The pure gold baby

That melts to a shriek.
I turn and burn.
Do not think I underestimate your great concern.

Ash, ash —
You poke and stir.
Flesh, bone, there is nothing there —

A cake of soap,
A wedding ring,
A gold filling.[4]

Herr God, Herr Lucifer,
Beware
Beware.

Out of the ash
I rise with my red hair
And I eat men like air.

Morning Song

Love set you going like a fat gold watch.
The midwife slapped your footsoles, and your bald cry
Took its place among the elements.

Our voices echo, magnifying your arrival. New statue.
In a drafty museum, your nakedness
Shadows our safety. We stand round blankly as walls.

I'm no more your mother
Than the cloud that distills a mirror to reflect its own slow
Effacement at the wind's hand.

All night your moth-breath
Flickers among the flat pink roses. I wake to listen:
A far sea moves in my ear.

One cry, and I stumble from bed, cow-heavy and floral
In my Victorian nightgown.
Your mouth opens clean as a cat's. The window square

Whitens and swallows its dull stars. And now you try
Your handful of notes;
The clear vowels rise like balloons.

---

[4] Items left in the crematoria of the Nazi concentration camps after the bodies of
prisoners had been burned. (The rendered fat of the bodies was used to make soap.)

EDGAR ALLAN POE
Annabel Lee

It was many and many a year ago,
  In a kingdom by the sea,
That a maiden there lived whom you may know
  By the name of Annabel Lee;
And this maiden she lived with no other thought
  Than to love and be loved by me.

She was a child and *I* was a child,
  In this kingdom by the sea,
But we loved with a love that was more than love —
  I and my Annabel Lee —
With a love that the wingéd seraphs of Heaven
  Coveted her and me.

And this was the reason that, long ago,
  In this kingdom by the sea,
A wind blew out of a cloud by night
  Chilling my Annabel Lee;
So that her highborn kinsmen came
  And bore her away from me,
To shut her up in a sepulchre
  In this kingdom by the sea.

The angels, not half so happy in Heaven,
  Went envying her and me:
Yes! that was the reason (as all men know,
  In this kingdom by the sea)
That the wind came out of the cloud, chilling
  And killing my Annabel Lee.

But our love it was stronger by far than the love
  Of those who were older than we —
  Of many far wiser than we —
And neither the angels in Heaven above
  Nor the demons down under the sea,
Can ever dissever my soul from the soul
  Of the beautiful Annabel Lee:

For the moon never beams without bringing me dreams
  Of the beautiful Annabel Lee;
And the stars never rise but I see the bright eyes
  Of the beautiful Annabel Lee;

And so, all the night-tide, I lie down by the side
Of my darling, my darling, my life and my bride,
　　In her sepulchre there by the sea —
　　In her tomb by the side of the sea.

To Helen

Helen, thy beauty is to me
　　Like those Nicean barks of yore,
That gently, o'er a perfumed sea,
　　The weary, way-worn wanderer bore
　　To his own native shore.

On desperate seas long wont to roam,
　　Thy hyacinth hair, thy classic face,
Thy Naiad airs have brought me home
　　To the glory that was Greece
And the grandeur that was Rome.

Lo! in yon brilliant window-niche
　　How statue-like I see thee stand!
　　The agate lamp within thy hand,
Ah! Psyche,[1] from the regions which
　　Are Holy Land!

ALEXANDER POPE

From *An Essay on Man* (Epistle I)

　　Heav'n from all creatures hides the book of Fate,
All but the page prescrib'd, their present state:
From brutes what men, from men what spirits know:
Or who could suffer Being here below?
The lamb thy riot dooms to bleed to-day,
Had he thy Reason, would he skip and play?
Pleas'd to the last, he crops the flow'ry food,
And licks the hand just rais'd to shed his blood.
Oh blindness to the future! kindly giv'n,
That each may fill the circle mark'd by Heav'n;

---

[1] Psyche was married to Cupid, who came to her only at night; she was forbidden to look at him. When she stole a glimpse of him sleeping, he awoke and disappeared. She asked Venus to help her find him. Venus, required, among other things, that Psyche bring back, unopened, a box from the underworld.

Who sees with equal eye, as God of all,
A hero perish, or a sparrow fall,
Atoms or systems into ruin hurl'd,
And now a bubble burst, and now a world.

(lines 77–90)

What would this Man? Now upward will he soar,
And little less than Angel, would be more;
Now looking downwards, just as griev'd appears
To want the strength of bulls, the fur of bears.
Made for his use all creatures if he call,
Say what their use, had he the pow'rs of all?
Nature to these, without profusion, kind,
The proper organs, proper pow'rs assign'd;
Each seeming want compénsated of course,
Here with degrees of swiftness, there of force;
All in exact proportion to the state;
Nothing to add, and nothing to abate.
Each beast, each insect, happy in its own;
Is Heav'n unkind to Man, and Man alone?
Shall he alone, whom rational we call,
Be pleas'd with nothing, if not bless'd with all?
The bliss of Man (could Pride that blessing find)
Is not to think or act beyond mankind;
No pow'rs of body or of soul to share,
But what his nature and his state can bear.
Why has not Man a microscopic eye?
For this plain reason, Man is not a Fly.
Say what the use, were finer optics giv'n,
T' inspect a mite, not comprehend the heav'n?
Or touch, if tremblingly alive all o'er,
To smart and agonize at ev'ry pore?
Or quick effluvia darting thro' the brain,
Die of a rose in aromatic pain?

(lines 173–200)

Far as Creation's ample range extends,
The scale of sensual, mental pow'rs ascends:
Mark how it mounts, to Man's imperial race,
From the green myriads in the peopled grass:
What modes of sight betwixt each wide extreme,
The mole's dim curtain, and the lynx's beam:
Of smell, the headlong lioness between,

And hound sagacious on the tainted green:
Of hearing, from the life that fills the flood,
To that which warbles thro' the vernal wood:
The spider's touch, how exquisitely fine!
Feels at each thread, and lives along the line:
In the nice° bee, what sense so subtly true   *exact*
From pois'nous herbs extracts the healing dew:
How Instinct varies in the grov'ling swine,
Compar'd, half-reas'ning elephant, with thine:
'Twixt that, and Reason, what a nice barrier,
For ever sep'rate, yet for ever near!
Remembrance and Reflection how ally'd;
What thin partitions Sense from Thought divide:
And Middle natures, how they long to join,
Yet never pass th' insuperable line!
Without this just gradation, could they be
Subjected these to those, or all to thee?
The pow'rs of all subdu'd by thee alone,
Is not thy Reason all these pow'rs in one?

(lines 207–232)

EZRA POUND
The Garden

En robe de parade.[1]
— SAMAIN

Like a skein of loose silk blown against a wall
She walks by the railing of a path in Kensington Gardens,
And she is dying piecemeal
        of a sort of emotional anemia.

And round about there is a rabble
Of the filthy, sturdy, unkillable infants of the very poor.
They shall inherit the earth.

In her is the end of breeding.
Her boredom is exquisite and excessive.
She would like some one to speak to her,
And is almost afraid that I
        will commit that indiscretion.

---

[1] French: "dressed for going out."

In a Station of the Metro

The apparition of these faces in the crowd;
Petals on a wet, black bough.

SIR WALTER RALEGH
The Lie

Go, soul, the body's guest,
Upon a thankless errand;
Fear not to touch the best;
The truth shall be thy warrant.
Go, since I needs must die,
And give the world the lie.

Say to the court, it glows
And shines like rotten wood;
Say to the church, it shows
What's good, and doth no good.
If church and court reply,
Then give them both the lie.

Tell potentates, they live
Acting by others' action;
Not loved unless they give,
Not strong but by a faction.
If potentates reply,
Give potentates the lie.

Tell men of high condition,
That manage the estate,
Their purpose is ambition,
Their practice only hate.
And if they once reply,
Then give them all the lie.

Tell them that brave it most,
They beg for more by spending,
Who, in their greatest cost,
Seek nothing but commending.
And if they make reply,
Then give them all the lie.

Tell zeal it wants° devotion;   *lacks*
Tell love it is but lust;

Tell time it is but motion;
Tell flesh it is but dust.
And wish them not reply,
For thou must give the lie.

Tell age it daily wasteth;
Tell honor how it alters;
Tell beauty how she blasteth;
Tell favor how it falters.
And as they shall reply,
Give every one the lie.

Tell wit how much it wrangles
In tickle° points of niceness;   *fine*
Tell wisdom she entangles
Herself in overwiseness.
And when they do reply,
Straight give them both the lie.

Tell physic of her boldness;
Tell skill it is pretension;
Tell charity of coldness;
Tell law it is contention.
And as they do reply,
So give them still the lie.

Tell fortune of her blindness;
Tell nature of decay;
Tell friendship of unkindness;
Tell justice of delay.
And if they will reply,
Then give them all the lie.

Tell arts they have no soundness,
But vary by esteeming;
Tell schools they want profoundness,
And stand too much on seeming.
If arts and schools reply,
Give arts and schools the lie.

Tell faith it's fled the city;
Tell how the country erreth;
Tell manhood shakes off pity;
Tell virtue least preferreth.
And if they do reply,
Spare not to give the lie.

So when thou hast, as I
Commanded thee, done blabbing —
Although to give the lie
Deserves no less than stabbing —
Stab at thee he that will,
No stab the soul can kill.

ADRIENNE RICH
Diving into the Wreck

First having read the book of myths,
and loaded the camera,
and checked the edge of the knife-blade,
I put on
the body-armor of black rubber
the absurd flippers
the grave and awkward mask.
I am having to do this
not like Cousteau[1] with his
assiduous team
aboard the sun-flooded schooner
but here alone.

There is a ladder.
The ladder is always there
hanging innocently
close to the side of the schooner.
We know what it is for,
we who have used it.
Otherwise
it's a piece of maritime floss
some sundry equipment.

I go down.
Rung after rung and still
the oxygen immerses me
the blue light
the clear atoms
of our human air.
I go down.
My flippers cripple me,

---

[1]Jacques Cousteau (b. 1910), French underwater explorer, inventor of the aqualung, author, and filmmaker.

I crawl like an insect down the ladder
and there is no one
to tell me when the ocean
will begin.

First the air is blue and then
it is bluer and then green and then
black I am blacking out and yet
my mask is powerful
it pumps my blood with power
the sea is another story
the sea is not a question of power
I have to learn alone
to turn my body without force
in the deep element.

And now: it is easy to forget
what I came for
among so many who have always
lived here
swaying their crenellated fans
between the reefs
and besides
you breathe differently down here.

I came to explore the wreck.
The words are purposes.
The words are maps.
I came to see the damage that was done
and the treasures that prevail.
I stroke the beam of my lamp
slowly along the flank
of something more permanent
than fish or weed

the thing I came for:
the wreck and not the story of the wreck
the thing itself and not the myth
the drowned face always staring
toward the sun
the evidence of damage
worn by salt and sway into this threadbare beauty
the ribs of the disaster
curving their assertion
among the tentative haunters.

This is the place.
And I am here, the mermaid whose dark hair
streams black, the merman in his armored body
We circle silently
about the wreck
we dive into the hold.
I am she: I am he

whose drowned face sleeps with open eyes
whose breasts still bear the stress
whose silver, copper, vermeil cargo lies
obscurely inside barrels
half-wedged and left to rot
we are the half-destroyed instruments
that once held to a course
the water-eaten log
the fouled compass

We are, I am, you are
by cowardice or courage
the one who find our way
back to this scene
carrying a knife, a camera
a book of myths
in which
our names do not appear.

The Middle-Aged

Their faces, safe as an interior
Of Holland tiles and Oriental carpet,
Where the fruit-bowl, always filled, stood in a light
Of placid afternoon — their voices' measure,
Their figures moving in the Sunday garden
To lay the tea outdoors or trim the borders,
Afflicted, haunted us. For to be young
Was always to live in other peoples' houses
Whose peace, if we sought it, had been made by others,
Was ours at second-hand and not for long.
The custom of the house, not ours, the sun
Fading the silver-blue Fortuny[1] curtains,
The reminiscence of a Christmas party

---

[1] Manufacturers of expensive cloth.

Of fourteen years ago — all memory,
Signs of possession and of being possessed,
We tasted, tense with envy. They were so kind,
Would have given us anything; the bowl of fruit
Was filled for us, there was a room upstairs
We must call ours: but twenty years of living
They could not give. Nor did they ever speak
Of the coarse stain on that polished balustrade,
The crack in the study window, or the letters
Locked in a drawer and the key destroyed.
All to be understood by us, returning
Late, in our own time — how that peace was made,
Upon what terms, with how much left unsaid.

Snapshots of a Daughter-in-Law

1

You, once a belle in Shreveport,
with henna-colored hair, skin like a peachbud,
still have your dresses copied from that time,
and play a Chopin[1] prelude
called by Cortot[2]: *"Delicious recollections
float like perfume through the memory."*[3]

Your mind now, moldering like wedding-cake,
heavy with useless experience, rich
with suspicion, rumor, fantasy,
crumbling to pieces under the knife-edge
of mere fact. In the prime of your life.

Nervy, glowering, your daughter
wipes the teaspoons, grows another way.

2

Banging the coffee-pot into the sink
she hears the angels chiding, and looks out
past the raked gardens to the sloppy sky.
Only a week since They said: *Have no patience.*

---

[1]Frederick François Chopin (1810–1849), Polish composer and pianist who settled in Paris in 1831.

[2] Alfred Cortot (1877–1962), French pianist.

[3] Cortot's notation on one of Chopin's preludes.

The next time it was: *Be insatiable.*
Then: *Save yourself; others you cannot save.*
Sometimes she's let the tapstream scald her arm,
a match burn to her thumbnail,

or held her hand above the kettle's snout
right in the woolly steam. They are probably angels,
since nothing hurts her anymore, except
each morning's grit blowing into her eyes.

3

A thinking woman sleeps with monsters.
The beak that grips her, she becomes. And Nature,
that sprung-lidded, still commodious
steamer-trunk of *tempora* and *mores*[4]
gets stuffed with it all: the mildewed orange-flowers,
the female pills, the terrible breasts
of Boadicea[5] beneath flat foxes' heads and orchids.

Two handsome women, gripped in argument,
each proud, acute, subtle, I hear scream
across the cut glass and majolica
like Furies cornered from their prey:
The argument *ad feminam,* all the old knives
that have rusted in my back, I drive in yours,
ma semblable, ma soeur![6]

4

Knowing themselves too well in one another:
their gifts no pure fruition, but a thorn,
the prick filed sharp against a hint of scorn . . .
Reading while waiting
for the iron to heat,
writing, *My Life had stood — a Loaded Gun —*[7]
in that Amherst pantry while the jellies boil and scum,

---

[4] A reference to Cicero's phrase "O Tempora! O Mores!" ("Alas for the degeneracy of the times and the low standard of our morals!")

[5] British queen in the time of the Roman emperor Nero. She led an unsuccessful revolt against Roman rule.

[6] The last line of the poem "Au Lecteur" by Charles Baudelaire reads, "Hypocrite lecteur! — mon semblable, — mon frere!" ("Hypocrite reader, my double, my brother!") Rich alters the line to read, "my sister."

[7] A poem by Emily Dickinson, reproduced earlier in this anthology.

or, more often,
iron-eyed and beaked and purposed as a bird,
dusting everything on the whatnot every day of life.

5

Dulce ridens, dulce loquens,[8]
she shaves her legs until they gleam
like petrified mammoth-tusk.

6

When to her lute Corinna sings[9]
neither words nor music are her own;
only the long hair dipping
over her cheek, only the song
of silk against her knees
and these
adjusted in reflections of an eye.

Poised, trembling and unsatisfied, before
an unlocked door, that cage of cages,
tell us, you bird, you tragical machine —
is this *fertilisante douleur?*[10] Pinned down
by love, for you the only natural action,
are you edged more keen
to prise the secrets of the vault? has Nature shown
her household books to you, daughter-in-law,
that her sons never saw?

7

"To have in this uncertain world some stay
which cannot be undermined, is
of the utmost consequence."[11]
                    Thus wrote
a woman, partly brave and partly good,
who fought with what she partly understood.
Few men about her would or could do more,
hence she was labeled harpy, shrew and whore.

---

[8] Latin for "sweetly laughing, sweetly speaking." The line is adapted from Horace's Ode 22.

[9] First line of a poem by Thomas Campion (1567–1620).

[10] French for "fertilizing sorrow," "life-giving sorrow."

[11] From Mary Wollstonecraft, *Thoughts on the Education of Daughters* (1787).

8

"You all die at fifteen," said Diderot,[12]
and turn part legend, part convention.
Still, eyes inaccurately dream
behind closed windows blankening with steam.
Deliciously, all that we might have been,
all that we were — fire, tears,
wit, taste, martyred ambition —
stirs like the memory of refused adultery
the drained and flagging bosom of our middle years.

9

*Not that it is done well, but
that it is done at all?*[13] Yes, think
of the odds! or shrug them off forever.
This luxury of the precocious child,
Time's precious chronic invalid, —
would we, darlings, resign it if we could?
Our blight has been our sinecure:
mere talent was enough for us —
glitter in fragments and rough drafts.

Sigh no more, ladies.
                    Time is male
and in his cups drinks to the fair.
Bemused by gallantry, we hear
our mediocrities over-praised,
indolence read as abnegation,
slattern thought styled intuition,
every lapse forgiven, our crime
only to cast too bold a shadow
or smash the mold straight off.

For that, solitary confinement,
tear gas, attrition shelling.
Few applicants for that honor.

---

[12] Denis Diderot (1713–1784) was a French philosopher.

[13] An allusion to Samuel Johnson's remark to Boswell, "Sir, a woman's preaching is like a dog's walking on his hinder legs. It is not done well; but you are surprised to find it done at all."

10

Well,

she's long about her coming, who must be
more merciless to herself than history.
Her mind full to the wind, I see her plunge
breasted and glancing through the currents,
taking the light upon her
at least as beautiful as any boy
or helicopter,

poised, still coming,

her fine blades making the air wince

but her cargo
no promise then:
delivered
palpable
ours.

ALBERTO RÍOS
Mi Abuelo[1]

Where my grandfather is is in the ground
where you can hear the future
like an Indian with his ear at the tracks.
A pipe leads down to him so that sometimes
he whispers what will happen to a man
in town or how he will meet the best
dressed woman tomorrow and how the best
man at her wedding will chew the ground
next to her. Mi abuelo is the man
who speaks through all the mouths in my house.
An echo of me hitting the pipe sometimes
to stop him from saying *my hair is a*
sieve is the only other sound. It is a phrase
that among all others is the best,
he says, and *my hair is a sieve* is sometimes
repeated for hours out of the ground
when I let him, which is not often.
An abuelo should be much more than a man

---

[1] Spanish: "my grandfather."

like you! He stops then, and speaks: *I am a man*
who has served ants with the attitude
of a waiter, who has made each smile as only
an ant who is fat can, and they liked me best,
but there is nothing left. Yet I know he ground
green coffee beans as a child, and sometimes
he will talk about his wife, and sometimes
about when he was deaf and a man
cured him by mail and he heard groundhogs
talking, or about how he walked with a cane
he chewed on when he got hungry.
At best, mi abuelo is a liar.
I see an old picture of him at nani's with an
off-white yellow center mustache and sometimes
that's all I know for sure. He talks best
about these hills, *slowest waves,* and where this man
is going, and I'm convinced his hair is a sieve,
that his fever is cooled now underground.
Mi abuelo is an ordinary man.
I look down the pipe, sometimes, and see a
ripple-topped stream in its best suit, in the ground.

Teodoro Luna's Two Kisses

Mr. Teodoro Luna in his later years had taken to kissing
His wife
Not so much with his lips as with his brows.
This is not to say he put his forehead
Against her mouth —
Rather, he would lift his eyebrows, once, quickly:
Not so vigorously he might be confused with the villain
Famous in the theaters, but not so little as to be thought
A slight movement, one of accident. This way
He kissed her
Often and quietly, across tables and through doorways,
Sometimes in photographs, and so through the years themselves.
This was his passion, that only she might see. The chance
He might feel some movement on her lips
Toward laughter.

EDWIN ARLINGTON ROBINSON

Eros Turannos[1]

She fears him, and will always ask
    What fated her to choose him;
She meets in his engaging mask
    All reasons to refuse him;
But what she meets and what she fears
Are less than are the downward years,
Drawn slowly to the foamless weirs
    Of age, were she to lose him.

Between a blurred sagacity
    That once had power to sound him,
And Love, that will not let him be
    The Judas that she found him,
Her pride assuages her almost,
As if it were alone the cost.
He sees that he will not be lost,
    And waits and looks around him.

A sense of ocean and old trees
    Envelopes and allures him;
Tradition, touching all he sees,
    Beguiles and reassures him;
And all her doubts of what he says
Are dimmed with what she knows of days —
Till even prejudice delays
    And fades, and she secures him.

The falling leaf inaugurates
    The reign of her confusion;
The pounding wave reverberates
    The dirge of her illusion;
And home, where passion lived and died,
Becomes a place where she can hide,
While all the town and harbor side
    Vibrate with her seclusion.

We tell you, tapping on our brows,
    The story as it should be,

---

[1] "Eros Turannos" means "tyrannical love."

As if the story of a house
    Were told, or ever could be;
We'll have no kindly veil between
Her visions and those we have seen,
As if we guessed what hers have been,
    Or what they are or would be.

Meanwhile we do no harm; for they
    That with a god have striven,
Not hearing much of what we say,
    Take what the god has given;
Though like waves breaking it may be,
Or like a changed familiar tree,
Or like a stairway to the sea
    Where down the blind are driven.

Richard Cory

Whenever Richard Cory went down town,
We people on the pavement looked at him:
He was a gentleman from sole to crown,
Clean favored, and imperially slim.

And he was always quietly arrayed,
And he was always human when he talked;
But still he fluttered pulses when he said,
"Good-morning," and he glittered when he walked.

And he was rich — yes, richer than a king —
And admirably schooled in every grace:
In fine, we thought that he was everything
To make us wish that we were in his place.

So on we worked, and waited for the light,
And went without the meat, and cursed the bread;
And Richard Cory, one calm summer night,
Went home and put a bullet through his head.

THEODORE ROETHKE

Elegy for Jane

My Student, Thrown by a Horse

I remember the neckcurls, limp and damp as tendrils;
And her quick look, a sidelong pickerel smile;
And how, once startled into talk, the light syllables leaped for her,
And she balanced in the delight of her thought,
A wren, happy, tail into the wind,
Her song trembling the twigs and small branches.
The shade sang with her;
The leaves, their whispers turned to kissing;
And the mold sang in the bleached valleys under the rose.

Oh, when she was sad, she cast herself down into such a pure
    depth,
Even a father could not find her:
Scraping her cheek against straw;
Stirring the clearest water.

My sparrow, you are not here,
Waiting like a fern, making a spiny shadow.
The sides of wet stones cannot console me,
Nor the moss, wound with the last light.

If only I could nudge you from this sleep,
My maimed darling, my skittery pigeon.
Over this damp grave I speak the words of my love:
I, with no rights in this matter,
Neither father nor lover.

The Waking

I wake to sleep, and take my waking slow.
I feel my fate in what I cannot fear.
I learn by going where I have to go.

We think by feeling. What is there to know?
I hear my being dance from ear to ear.
I wake to sleep, and take my waking slow.

Of those so close beside me, which are you?
God bless the Ground! I shall walk softly there,
And learn by going where I have to go.

Light takes the Tree; but who can tell us how?
The lowly worm climbs up a winding stair;
I wake to sleep, and take my waking slow.

Great Nature has another thing to do
To you and me; so take the lively air,
And, lovely, learn by going where to go.

This shaking keeps me steady. I should know.
What falls away is always. And is near.
I wake to sleep, and take my waking slow.
I learn by going where I have to go.

CHRISTINA ROSSETTI
Up-Hill

Does the road wind up-hill all the way?
    Yes, to the very end.
Will the day's journey take the whole long day?
    From morn to night, my friend.

But is there for the night a resting-place?
    A roof for when the slow dark hours begin.
May not the darkness hide it from my face?
    You cannot miss that inn.

Shall I meet other wayfarers at night?
    Those who have gone before.
Then must I knock, or call when just in sight?
    They will not keep you standing at that door.

Shall I find comfort, travel-sore and weak?
    Of labor you shall find the sum.
Will there be beds for me and all who seek?
    Yea, beds for all who come.

ANNE SEXTON
Snow White and the Seven Dwarfs

No matter what life you lead
the virgin is a lovely number:
cheeks as fragile as cigarette paper,

arms and legs made of Limoges,[1]
lips like Vin Du Rhone,[2]
rolling her china-blue doll eyes
open and shut.
Open to say,
Good Day Mama,
and shut for the thrust
of the unicorn.
She is unsoiled.
She is as white as a bonefish.

Once there was a lovely virgin
called Snow White.
Say she was thirteen.
Her stepmother,
a beauty in her own right,
though eaten, of course, by age,
would hear of no beauty surpassing her own.
Beauty is a simple passion,
but, oh my friends, in the end
you will dance the fire dance in iron shoes.
The stepmother had a mirror to which she referred —
something like the weather forecast —
a mirror that proclaimed
the one beauty of the land.
She would ask,
Looking glass upon the wall,
who is fairest of us all?
And the mirror would reply,
You are fairest of us all.
Pride pumped in her like poison.

Suddenly one day the mirror replied,
Queen, you are full fair, 'tis true,
but Snow White is fairer than you.
Until that moment Snow White
had been no more important
than a dust mouse under the bed.
But now the queen saw brown spots on her hand
and four whiskers over her lip

---

[1] Fine porcelain made in Limoges, France.
[2] Rhone wine (French).

so she condemned Snow White
to be hacked to death.
Bring me her heart, she said to the hunter,
and I will salt it and eat it.
The hunter, however, let his prisoner go
and brought a boar's heart back to the castle.
The queen chewed it up like a cube steak.
Now I am fairest, she said,
lapping her slim white fingers.

Snow White walked in the wildwood
for weeks and weeks.
At each turn there were twenty doorways
and at each stood a hungry wolf,
his tongue lolling out like a worm.
The birds called out lewdly,
talking like pink parrots,
and the snakes hung down in loops,
each a noose for her sweet white neck.
On the seventh week
she came to the seventh mountain
and there she found the dwarf house.
It was as droll as a honeymoon cottage
and completely equipped with
seven beds, seven chairs, seven forks
and seven chamber pots.
Snow White ate seven chicken livers
and lay down, at last, to sleep.

The dwarfs, those little hot dogs,
walked three times around Snow White,
the sleeping virgin. They were wise
and wattled like small czars.
Yes. It's a good omen,
they said, and will bring us luck.
They stood on tiptoes to watch
Snow White wake up. She told them
about the mirror and the killer-queen
and they asked her to stay and keep house.
Beware of your stepmother,
they said.
Soon she will know you are here.
While we are away in the mines

during the day, you must not
open the door.

Looking glass upon the wall . . .
The mirror told
and so the queen dressed herself in rags
and went out like a peddler to trap Snow White.
She went across seven mountains.
She came to the dwarf house
and Snow White opened the door
and bought a bit of lacing.
The queen fastened it tightly
around her bodice,
as tight as an Ace bandage,
so tight that Snow White swooned.
She lay on the floor, a plucked daisy.
When the dwarfs came home they undid the lace
and she revived miraculously.
She was as full of life as soda pop.
Beware of your stepmother,
they said.
She will try once more.

Looking glass upon the wall . . .
Once more the mirror told
and once more the queen dressed in rags
and once more Snow White opened the door.
This time she bought a poison comb,
a curved eight-inch scorpion,
and put it in her hair and swooned again.
The dwarfs returned and took out the comb
and she revived miraculously.
She opened her eyes as wide as Orphan Annie.
Beware, beware, they said,
but the mirror told,
the queen came,
Snow White, the dumb bunny,
opened the door
and she bit into a poison apple
and fell down for the final time.
When the dwarfs returned
they undid her bodice,
they looked for a comb,

but it did no good.
Though they washed her with wine
and rubbed her with butter
it was to no avail.
She lay as still as a gold piece.

The seven dwarfs could not bring themselves
to bury her in the black ground
so they made a glass coffin
and set it upon the seventh mountain
so that all who passed by
could peek in upon her beauty.
A prince came one June day
and would not budge.
He stayed so long his hair turned green
and still he would not leave.
The dwarfs took pity upon him
and gave him the glass Snow White —
its doll's eyes shut forever —
to keep in his far-off castle.
As the prince's men carried the coffin
they stumbled and dropped it
and the chunk of apple flew out
of her throat and she woke up miraculously.

And thus Snow White became the prince's bride.
The wicked queen was invited to the wedding feast
and when she arrived there were
red-hot iron shoes,
in the manner of red-hot roller skates,
clamped upon her feet.
First your toes will smoke
and then your heels will turn black
and you will fry upward like a frog,
she was told.
And so she danced until she was dead,
a subterranean figure,
her tongue flicking in and out
like a gas jet.
Meanwhile Snow White held court,
rolling her china-blue doll eyes open and shut
and sometimes referring to her mirror
as women do.

WILLIAM SHAKESPEARE

Fear No More the Heat o' the Sun[1]

Fear no more the heat o' the sun,
    Nor the furious winter's rages;
Thou thy worldly task hast done,
    Home art gone, and ta'en thy wages:
Golden lads and girls all must,
As chimney-sweepers, come to dust.

Fear no more the frown o' the great;
    Thou art past the tyrant's stroke;
Care no more to clothe and eat;
    To thee the reed is as the oak:
The scepter, learning, physic, must
All follow this, and come to dust.

Fear no more the lightning flash,
    Nor the all-dreaded thunder stone;
Fear not slander, censure rash;
    Thou hast finished joy and moan:
All lovers young, all lovers must
Consign to thee, and come to dust.

No exorciser harm thee!
Nor no witchcraft charm thee!
Ghost unlaid forbear thee!
Nothing ill come near thee!
Quiet consummation have;
And renownèd be thy grave!

Full Fathom Five[1]

Full fathom five thy father lies;
    Of his bones are coral made;
Those are pearls that were his eyes:
    Nothing of him that doth fade,
But doth suffer a sea change
Into something rich and strange.

---

[1] From *Cymbeline.*
[1] From *The Tempest.*

Sea nymphs hourly ring his knell:
    Ding-dong.
Hark! now I hear them — Ding-dong, bell.

Sonnet 18

Shall I compare thee to a summer's day?
Thou art more lovely and more temperate:
Rough winds do shake the darling buds of May,
And summer's lease hath all too short a date:
Sometimes too hot the eye of heaven shines,
And often is his gold complexion dimmed;
And every fair from fair sometimes declines,
By chance or nature's changing course
    untrimmed;°   *divested of beauty*
But thy eternal summer shall not fade,
Nor lose possession of that fair thou ow'st;°   *ownest*
Nor shall death brag thou wander'st in his shade,
When in eternal lines to time thou grow'st:
So long as men can breathe, or eyes can see,
So long lives this, and this gives life to thee.

Sonnet 116

Let me not to the marriage of true minds
Admit impediments. Love is not love
Which alters when it alteration finds,
Or bends with the remover to remove:
Oh, no! it is an ever-fixèd mark,
That looks on tempests and is never shaken;
It is the star to every wandering bark,
Whose worth's unknown, although his height be taken.
Love's not Time's fool, though rosy lips and cheeks
Within his bending sickle's compass come;
Love alters not with his brief hours and weeks,
But bears it out even to the edge of doom.
If this be error and upon me proved,
I never writ, nor no man ever loved.

PERCY BYSSHE SHELLEY
England in 1819

An old, mad, blind, despised, and dying king[1] —
Princes, the dregs of their dull race, who flow
Through public scorn — mud from a muddy spring;
Rulers who neither see, nor feel, nor know,
But leechlike to their fainting country cling,
Till they drop, blind in blood, without a blow;
A people starved and stabbed in the untilled field —
An army, which liberticide and prey
Makes as a two-edged sword to all who wield;
Golden and sanguine laws which tempt and slay;
Religion Christless, Godless — a book sealed;
A Senate — Time's worst statute[2] unrepealed —
Are graves, from which a glorious Phantom[3] may
Burst, to illumine our tempestuous day.

Ode to the West Wind

1

O wild West Wind, thou breath of Autumn's being,
Thou, from whose unseen presence the leaves dead
Are driven, like ghosts from an enchanter fleeing,

Yellow, and black, and pale, and hectic red,
Pestilence-stricken multitudes: O thou,
Who chariotest to their dark wintry bed

The wingèd seeds, where they lie cold and low,
Each like a corpse within its grave, until
Thine azure sister of the Spring shall blow

Her clarion o'er the dreaming earth, and fill
(Driving sweet buds like flocks to feed in air)
With living hues and odors plain and hill:

Wild Spirit, which art moving everywhere;
Destroyer and preserver; hear, oh, hear!

---

[1] George III was eighty-one and hopelessly insane in 1819.
[2] The laws excluding Catholics from office.
[3] The spirit of political liberty.

2

Thou on whose stream, mid the steep sky's commotion,
Loose clouds like earth's decaying leaves are shed,
Shook from the tangled boughs of Heaven and Ocean,

Angels of rain and lightning: there are spread
On the blue surface of thine aëry surge,
Like the bright hair uplifted from the head

Of some fierce Maenad,[1] even from the dim verge
Of the horizon to the zenith's height,
The locks of the approaching storm. Thou dirge

Of the dying year, to which this closing night
Will be the dome of a vast sepulcher,
Vaulted with all thy congregated might

Of vapors, from whose solid atmosphere
Black rain, and fire, and hail will burst: oh, hear!

3

Thou who didst waken from his summer dreams
The blue Mediterranean, where he lay,
Lulled by the coil of his crystálline streams,

Beside a pumice isle in Baiae's bay,[2]
And saw in sleep old palaces and towers
Quivering within the wave's intenser day,

All overgrown with azure moss and flowers
So sweet, the sense faints picturing them! Thou
For whose path the Atlantic's level powers

Cleave themselves into chasms, while far below
The sea-blooms and the oozy woods which wear
The sapless foliage of the ocean, know

Thy voice, and suddenly grow gray with fear,
And tremble and despoil themselves: oh, hear!

4

If I were a dead leaf thou mightest bear;
If I were a swift cloud to fly with thee;
A wave to pant beneath thy power, and share

---

[1] Women inspired with ecstatic frenzy by the Greek god Dionysus.
[2] Near Naples, Italy.

The impulse of thy strength, only less free
Than thou, O uncontrollable! If even
I were as in my boyhood, and could be

The comrade of thy wanderings over Heaven,
As then, when to outstrip thy skyey speed
Scarce seemed a vision; I would ne'er have striven

As thus with thee in prayer in my sore need.
Oh, lift me as a wave, a leaf, a cloud!
I fall upon the thorns of life! I bleed!

A heavy weight of hours has chained and bowed
One too like thee: tameless, and swift, and proud.

5

Make me thy lyre, even as the forest is:
What if my leaves are falling like its own!
The tumult of thy mighty harmonies

Will take from both a deep, autumnal tone,
Sweet though in sadness. Be thou, Spirit fierce,
My spirit! Be thou me, impetuous one!

Drive my dead thoughts over the universe
Like withered leaves to quicken a new birth!
And, by the incantation of this verse,

Scatter, as from an unextinguished hearth
Ashes and sparks, my words among mankind!
Be through my lips to unawakened earth

The trumpet of a prophecy! O Wind,
If Winter comes, can Spring be far behind?

Ozymandias[1]

I met a traveler from an antique land
Who said: Two vast and trunkless legs of stone
Stand in the desert . . . Near them, on the sand,
Half sunk, a shattered visage lies, whose frown,
And wrinkled lip, and sneer of cold command,
Tell that its sculptor well those passions read
Which yet survive, stamped on these lifeless things,
The hand that mocked them, and the heart that fed:

---

[1] Greek name for the Egyptian monarch Ramses II (1304–1237 B.C.).

And on the pedestal these words appear:
"My name is Ozymandias, king of kings:
Look on my works, ye Mighty, and despair!"
Nothing beside remains. Round the decay
Of that colossal wreck, boundless and bare
The lone and level sands stretch far away.

SIR PHILIP SIDNEY
From *Astrophel and Stella*

1

Loving in truth, and fain in verse my love to show,
That she, dear she, might take some pleasure of my pain,
Pleasure might cause her read, reading might make her know,
Knowledge might pity win, and pity grace obtain,
I sought fit words to paint the blackest face of woe:
Studying inventions fine, her wits to entertain,
Oft turning others' leaves, to see if thence would flow
Some fresh and fruitful showers upon my sunburned brain.
But words came halting forth, wanting Invention's stay;
Invention, Nature's child, fled stepdame Study's blows;
And others' feet still seemed but strangers in my way.
Thus, great with child to speak, and helpless in my throes,
Biting my truant° pen, beating myself for spite: *idle*
"Fool," said my Muse to me, "look in thy heart, and write."

31

With how sad steps, Oh Moon, thou climb'st the skies,
How silently, and with how wan a face!
What, may it be that even in heav'nly place
That busy archer° his sharp arrows tries?   *Cupid*
Sure, if that long-with-love-acquainted eyes
Can judge of love, thou feel'st a lover's case;
I read it in thy looks: thy languished grace,
To me that feel the like, thy state descries.
Then even of fellowship, Oh Moon, tell me,
Is constant love deemed there but want of wit?
Are beauties there as proud as here they be?
Do they above love to be loved, and yet
Those lovers scorn whom that love doth possess?
Do they call virtue there ungratefulness?

LESLIE MARMON SILKO
Prayer to the Pacific

I traveled to the ocean
        distant
                from my southwest land of sandrock
                to the moving blue water
        Big as the myth of origin.

Pale
pale water in the yellow-white light of
           sun   floating west
                to China
          where ocean herself was born.
Clouds that blow across the sand are wet.

Squat in the wet sand and speak to the Ocean:
      I return to you   turquoise   the red coral you sent us,
                sister spirit of Earth.
Four round stones in my pocket   I carry back the ocean
               to suck and to taste.

Thirty thousand years ago
             Indians came riding across the ocean
             carried by giant sea turtles.
Waves were high that day
      great sea turtles waded   slowly out
              from the gray sundown sea.
Grandfather Turtle rolled in the sand   four times
          and disappeared
              swimming into the sun.

And so   from that time
        immemorial,
           as the old people say,
rain clouds drift from the west
         gift from the ocean.

Green leaves in the wind
Wet earth on my feet
       swallowing raindrops
         clear from China.

CHARLES SIMIC
Charon's° Cosmology   *ferryman of the dead*

With only his feeble lantern
To tell him where he is
And every time a mountain
Of fresh corpses to load up

Take them to the other side
Where there are plenty more
I'd say by now he must be confused
As to which side is which

I'd say it doesn't matter
No one complains he's got
Their pockets to go through
In one a crust of bread in another a sausage

Once in a long while a mirror
Or a book which he throws
Overboard into the dark river
Swift cold and deep

Fork

This strange thing must have crept
Right out of hell.
It resembles a bird's foot
Worn around the cannibal's neck.

As you hold it in your hand,
As you stab with it into a piece of meat,
It is possible to imagine the rest of the bird:
Its head which like your fist
Is large, bald, beakless and blind.

CHRISTOPHER SMART
From *Jubilate Agno*[1]

For I will consider my Cat Jeoffry.
For he is the servant of the Living God, duly and daily serving him.

---

[1] "Jubilate Agno" was written during Smart's incarceration in a private madhouse from 1758 to 1763. The manuscript remained unknown to the public until 1939.

For at the first glance of the glory of God in the East he worships
in his way.

For is this done by wreathing his body seven times round with
elegant quickness.

For then he leaps up to catch the musk, which is the blessing of
God upon his prayer.

For he rolls upon prank to work it in.

For having done duty and received blessing he begins to consider
himself.

For this he performs in ten degrees.

For first he looks upon his fore-paws to see if they are clean.

For secondly he kicks up behind to clear away there.

For thirdly he works it upon stretch with the fore paws extended.

For fourthly he sharpens his paws by wood.

For fifthly he washes himself.

For sixthly he rolls upon wash.

For Seventhly he fleas himself, that he may not be interrupted
upon the beat.

For Eighthly he rubs himself against a post.

For Ninthly he looks up for his instructions.

For Tenthly he goes in quest of food.

For having consider'd God and himself he will consider his neigh-
bour.

For if he meets another cat he will kiss her in kindness.

For when he takes his prey he plays with it to give it chance.

For one mouse in seven escapes by his dallying.

For when his day's work is done his business more properly begins.

For he keeps the Lord's watch in the night against the adversary.

For he counteracts the powers of darkness by his electrical skin &
glaring eyes.

For he counteracts the Devil, who is death, by brisking about the
life.

For in his morning orisons he loves the sun and the sun loves him.

For he is of the tribe of Tiger.

For the Cherub Cat is a term of the Angel Tiger.

For he has the subtlety and hissing of a serpent, which in goodness
he suppresses.

For he will not do destruction, if he is well-fed, neither will he spit
without provocation.

For he purrs in thankfulness, when God tells him he's a good Cat.

For he is an instrument for the children to learn benevolence upon.

For every house is incompleat without him & a blessing is lacking
in the spirit.

For the Lord commanded Moses concerning the cats at the de-
parture of the Children of Israel from Egypt.[2]

For every family had one cat at least in the bag.

For the English Cats are the best in Europe.

For he is the cleanest in the use of his fore-paws of any quadrupede.

For the dexterity of his defence is an instance of the love of God
to him exceedingly.

For he is the quickest to his mark of any creature.

For he is tenacious of his point.

For he is a mixture of gravity and waggery.

For he knows that God is his Saviour.

For there is nothing sweeter than his peace when at rest.

For there is nothing brisker than his life when in motion.

For he is of the Lord's poor and so indeed is he called by benev-
olence perpetually — Poor Jeoffry! poor Jeoffry! the rat has
bit thy throat.

For I bless the name of the Lord Jesus that Jeoffry is better.

For the divine spirit comes about his body to sustain it in compleat
cat.

For his tongue is exceeding pure so that it has in purity what it
wants in musick.

For he is docile and can learn certain things.

For he can set up with gravity which is patience upon approbation.

For he can fetch and carry, which is patience in employment.

For he can jump over a stick which is patience upon proof positive.

For he can spraggle upon waggle at the word of command.

For he can jump from an eminence into his master's bosom.

For he can catch the cork and toss it again.

For he is hated by the hypocrite and miser.

For the former is affraid of detection.

For the latter refuses the charge.

For he camels his back to bear the first notion of business.

For he is good to think on, if a man would express himself neatly.

For he made a great figure in Egypt for his signal services.

For he killed the Icneumon-rat[3] very pernicious by land.

---

[2] No cats are mentioned in the Bible.

[3] The Ichneumon, which resembles a weasel, was domesticated (and highly val-
ued) by the ancient Egyptians.

For his ears are so acute that they sting again.

For from this proceeds the passing quickness of his attention.

For by stroaking of him I have found out electricity.

For I perceived God's light about him both wax and fire.

For the Electrical fire is the spiritual substance, which God sends
    from heaven to sustain the bodies both of man and beast.

For God has blessed him in the variety of his movements.

For, tho he cannot fly, he is an excellent clamberer.

For his motions upon the face of the earth are more than any other
    quadrupede.

For he can tread to all the measures upon the musick.

For he can swim for life.

For he can creep.

On a Bed of Guernsey Lilies

Written in September 1763

Ye beauties! O how great the sum
    Of sweetness that ye bring;
On what a charity ye come
    To bless the latter spring!
How kind the visit that ye pay,
Like strangers on a rainy day,
    When heartiness despair'd of guests:
No neighbour's praise your pride alarms,
No rival flow'r surveys your charms,
    Or heightens, or contests!

Lo, thro' her works gay nature grieves
    How brief she is and frail,
As ever o'er the falling leaves
    Autumnal winds prevail.
Yet still the philosophic mind
Consolatory food can find,
    And hope her anchorage maintain:
We never are deserted quite;
'Tis by succession of delight
    That love supports his reign.

DAVE SMITH
On a Field Trip at Fredericksburg[1]

The big steel tourist shield says maybe
fifteen thousand got it here. No word
of either Whitman[2] or one uncle
I barely remember in the smoke
that filled his tiny mountain house.

If each finger were a thousand of them
I could clap my hands and be dead
up to my wrists. It was quick
though not so fast as we can do it
now, one bomb, atomic or worse,
one silly pod slung on wing-tip,
high up, an egg cradled
by some rapacious mockingbird.

Hiroshima[3] canned nine times their number
in a flash. Few had the time
to moan or feel the feeling
ooze back in the groin.

In a ditch I stand
above Marye's Heights, the book-
boned faces of Brady's[4] fifteen-year-old
drummers, before battle, rigid
as August's dandelions
all the way to the Potomac
rolling in my skull.

If Audubon[5] came here, the names
of birds would gush, the marvel
single feathers make
evoke a cloud, a nation,
a gray blur preserved
on a blue horizon, but

---

[1] Site in Virginia of a Civil War battle (December 13, 1862), a Union defeat.

[2] Although Walt Whitman (1819–1892) wrote about the Civil War, his poems do not mention the Battle of Fredericksburg.

[3] City in Japan where the first atomic bomb was dropped.

[4] Matthew Brady (ca. 1823–1896), Civil War photographer.

[5] John James Audubon (1785–1851), Haitian-born American ornithologist and painter of birds.

there is only a wandering child,
one dark stalk snapped off
in her hand, held out to me.
Taking it, I try to help her
hold its obscure syllables
one instant in her mouth,
like a drift of wind
at the forehead, the front door,
the black, numb fingernails.

STEVIE SMITH
Not Waving but Drowning

Nobody heard him, the dead man,
But still he lay moaning:
I was much further out than you thought
And not waving but drowning.

Poor chap, he always loved larking
And now he's dead
It must have been too cold for him his heart gave way,
They said.

Oh, no no no, it was too cold always
(Still the dead one lay moaning)
I was much too far out all my life
And not waving but drowning.

Pretty

Why is the word pretty so underrated?
In November the leaf is pretty when it falls
The stream grows deep in the woods after rain
And in the pretty pool the pike stalks

He stalks his prey, and this is pretty too,
The prey escapes with an underwater flash
But not for long, the great fish has him now
The pike is a fish who always has his prey

And this is pretty. The water rat is pretty
His paws are not webbed, he cannot shut his nostrils
As the otter can and the beaver, he is torn between
The land and water. Not "torn," he does not mind.

The owl hunts in the evening and it is pretty
The lake water below him rustles with ice
There is frost coming from the ground, in the air mist
All this is pretty, it could not be prettier.

GARY SNYDER
Axe Handles

One afternoon the last week in April
Showing Kai how to throw a hatchet
One-half turn and it sticks in a stump.
He recalls the hatchet-head
Without a handle, in the shop
And go gets it, and wants it for his own.
A broken-off axe handle behind the door
Is long enough for a hatchet,
We cut it to length and take it
With the hatchet head
And working hatchet, to the wood block.
There I begin to shape the old handle
With the hatchet, and the phrase
First learned from Ezra Pound
Rings in my ears!
"When making an axe handle
        the pattern is not far off."
And I say this to Kai
"Look: We'll shape the handle
By checking the handle
Of the axe we cut with — "
And he sees. And I hear it again:
It's in Lu Ji's *Wên Fu,* fourth century
A.D. "Essay on Literature" — in the
Preface: "In making the handle
Of an axe
By cutting wood with an axe
The model is indeed near at hand."
My teacher Shih-hsiang Chen
Translated that and taught it years ago
And I see: Pound was an axe,
Chen was an axe, I am an axe
And my son a handle, soon
To be shaping again, model

And tool, craft of culture,
How we go on.

How Poetry Comes to Me

It comes blundering over the
Boulders at night, it stays
Frightened outside the
Range of my campfire
I go to meet it at the
Edge of the light

Riprap[1]

Lay down these words
Before your mind like rocks.
        placed solid, by hands
In choice of place, set
Before the body of the mind
        in space and time:
Solidity of bark, leaf, or wall
        riprap of things:
Cobble of milky way,
        straying planets,
These poems, people,
        lost ponies with
Dragging saddles
        and rocky sure-foot trails.
The world's like an endless
        four-dimensional
Game of *Go*.
        ants and pebbles
In the thin loam, each rock a word
        a creek-washed stone
Granite: ingrained
        with torment of fire and weight
Crystal and sediment linked hot
        all change, in thoughts,
As well as things.

---

[1] Snyder's note: "Riprap: a cobble of stone laid on steep slick rock to make a trail for horses in the mountains."

EDMUND SPENSER

Epithalamion

Ye learned sisters° which have oftentimes   *the muses*
Beene to me ayding, others to adorne:
Whom ye thought worthy of your gracefull rymes,
That even the greatest did not greatly scorne
To heare theyr names sung in your simple layes,
But joyéd in theyr prayse.
And when ye list your owne mishaps to mourne,
Which death, or love, or fortunes wreck did rayse,
Your string could soone to sadder tenor turne,
And teach the woods and waters to lament
Your dolefull dreriment.
Now lay those sorrowfull complaints aside,
And having all your heads with girland crownd,
Helpe me mine owne loves prayses to resound,
Ne let the same of any be envíde:
So Orpheus did for his owne bride,
So I unto my selfe alone will sing,
The woods shall to me answer and my Eccho ring.

Early before the worlds light giving lampe,
His golden beame upon the hils doth spred,
Having disperst the nights unchearefull dampe,
Doe ye awake, and with fresh lustyhed
Go to the bowre of my belovèd love,
My truest turtle dove,
Bid her awake; for Hymen° is awake,   *god of marriage*
And long since ready forth his maske to move,
With his bright Tead° that flames with many a flake,   *torch*
And many a bachelor to waite on him,
In theyr fresh garments trim.
Bid her awake therefore and soone her dight,°   *dress*
For lo the wishèd day is come at last,
That shall for al the paynes and sorrowes past,
Pay to her usury of long delight:
And whylest she doth her dight,
Doe ye to her of joy and solace sing,
That all the woods may answer and your eccho ring.

Bring with you all the Nymphes that you
    can heare°   *that can hear you*
Both of the rivers and the forrests greene:

And of the sea that neighbours to her neare,
Al with gay girlands goodly wel beseene.
And let them also with them bring in hand,
Another gay girland
For my fayre love of lillyes and of roses,
Bound truelove wize with a blew silke riband.
And let them make great store of bridale poses,
And let them eeke° bring store of other flowers   *also*
To deck the bridale bowers.
And let the ground whereas her foot shall tread,
For feare the stones her tender foot should wrong
Be strewed with fragrant flowers all along,
And diapred lyke the
    discolored mead.°   *patterned like the multicolored meadow*
Which done, doe at her chamber dore awayt,
For she will waken strayt,
The whiles doe ye this song unto her sing,
The woods shall to you answer and your Eccho ring.

Ye Nymphes of Mulla[1] which with carefull heed,
The silver scaly trouts doe tend full well,
And greedy pikes which use therein to feed,
(Those trouts and pikes all others doo excell)
And ye likewise which keepe the rushy lake,
Where none doo fishes take,
Bynd up the locks the which hang scatterd light,
And in his waters which your mirror make,
Behold your faces as the christall bright,
That when you come whereas my love doth lie,
No blemish she may spie.
And eke ye lightfoot mayds which keepe the deere,
That on the hoary mountayne use to towre,[2]
And the wylde wolves which seeke them to devoure,
With your steele darts doo chace from comming neer
Be also present heere,
To helpe to decke her and to help to sing,
That all the woods may answer and your eccho ring.

Wake, now my love, awake; for it is time,
The Rosy Morne long since left Tithones bed,

---

[1] The vale of Mulla, near Spenser's home in Ireland.
[2] To climb high, a term from falconry.

All ready to her silver coche to clyme,
And Phoebus gins to shew his glorious hed.
Hark how the cheerefull birds do chaunt theyr laies
And carroll of loves praise.
The merry Larke hir mattins sings aloft.
The thrush replyes, the Mavis
  descant° playes,   *melodic counterpoint*
The Ouzell shrills, the Ruddock warbles soft,
So goodly all agree with sweet consent,
To this dayes merriment.
Ah my deere love why doe ye sleepe thus long,
When meeter° were that ye should now awake,   *fitter*
T' awayt the comming of your joyous make,°   *mate*
And hearken to the birds lovelearnèd song,
The deawy leaves among.
For they of joy and pleasance to you sing,
That all the woods them answer and theyr eccho ring.

My love is now awake out of her dreame,
And her fayre eyes like stars that dimmèd were
With darksome cloud, now shew theyr goodly beams
More bright then Hesperus° his head doth rere.   *evening star*
Come now ye damzels, daughters of delight,
Helpe quickly her to dight,°   *adorn*
But first come ye fayre houres which were begot
In Joves sweet paradice, of Day and Night,
Which doe the seasons of the yeare allot,
And al that ever in this world is fayre
Doe make and still repayre.
And ye three handmayds of the Cyprian Queene,°   *Venus*
The which doe still adorne her beauties pride,
Helpe to addorne my beautifullest bride:
And as ye her array, still throw betweene°   *now and then*
Some graces to be seene,
And as ye use to Venus, to her sing,
The whiles the woods shal answer and your eccho ring.

Now is my love all ready forth to come,
Let all the virgins therefore well awayt,
And ye fresh boyes that tend upon her groome
Prepare your selves; for he is comming strayt.
Set all your things in seemely good aray
Fit for so joyfull day,

The joyfulst day that ever sunne did see.
Faire Sun, shew forth thy favourable ray,
And let thy lifull heat not fervent be
For feare of burning her sunshyny face,
Her beauty to disgrace.
O fayrest Phoebus, father of the Muse,
If ever I did honour thee aright,
Or sing the thing, that mote thy mind delight,
Doe not thy servants simple boone° refuse,   *request*
But let this day let this one day be myne,
Let all the rest be thine.
Then I thy soverayne prayses loud wil sing,
That all the woods shal answer and theyr eccho ring.

Harke how the Minstrels gin to shrill aloud
Their merry Musick that resounds from far
The pipe, the tabor,° and the trembling Croud,°   *drum / viol*
That well agree withouten breach or jar
But most of all the Damzels doe delite,
When they their tymbrels° smyte,   *tambourines*
And thereunto doe daunce and carrol sweet,
That all the sences they doe ravish quite,
The whyles the boyes run up and downe the street,
Crying aloud with strong confusèd noyce,
As if it were one voyce.
Hymen iô Hymen, Hymen they do shout,
That even to the heavens theyr shouting shrill
Doth reach, and all the firmament doth fill,
To which the people standing all about,
As in approvance doe thereto applaud
And loud advaunce her laud,°   *praise*
And evermore they *Hymen Hymen* sing,
That al the woods them answer and theyr eccho ring.

Loe where she comes along with portly° pace   *majestic*
Lyke Phoebe° from her chamber of the East,   *moon goddess*
Arysing forth to run her mighty race,
Clad all in white, that seemes° a virgin best.   *suits*
So well it her beseemes that ye would weene
Some angell she had beene.
Her long loose yellow locks lyke golden wyre,
Sprinckled with perle, and perling flowres a tweene,
Doe lyke a golden mantle her attyre,

And being crownèd with a girland greene,
Seeme lyke some mayden Queene.
Her modest eyes abashèd to behold
So many gazers, as on her do stare,
Upon the lowly ground affixèd are.
Ne dare lift up her countenance too bold,
But blush to heare her prayses sung so loud,
So farre from being proud.
Nathlesse doe ye still loud her prayses sing.
That all the woods may answer and your eccho ring.

Tell me ye merchants daughters did ye see
So fayre a creature in your towne before,
So sweet, so lovely, and so mild as she,
Adornd with beautyes grace and vertues store,
Her goodly eyes lyke Saphyres shining bright,
Her forehead yvory white,
Her cheekes lyke apples which the sun hath rudded,
Her lips lyke cherryes charming men to byte,
Her brest like to a bowle of creame uncrudded,°   *uncurdled*
Her paps° lyke lyllies budded,   *breasts*
Her snowie necke lyke to a marble towre,
And all her body lyke a pallace fayre,
Ascending uppe with many a stately stayre,
To honors seat and chastities sweet bowre.
Why stand ye still ye virgins in amaze,
Upon her so to gaze,
Whiles ye forget your former lay to sing,
To which the woods did answer and your eccho ring.

But if ye saw that which no eyes can see,
The inward beauty of her lively spright,
Garnisht with heavenly guifts of high degree,
Much more then would ye wonder at that sight,
And stand astonisht lyke to those which red°   *saw*
Medusaes mazeful hed.
There dwels sweet love and constant chastity,
Unspotted fayth and comely womanhood,
Regard of honour and mild modesty,
There vertue raynes as Queene in royal throne,
And giveth lawes alone.
The which the base affections doe obay,
And yeeld theyr services unto her will,

Ne thought of thing uncomely ever may
Thereto approach to tempt her mind to ill.
Had ye once seene these her celestial threasures,
And unrevealèd pleasures,
Then would ye wonder and her prayses sing,
That al the woods should answer and your eccho ring.

Open the temple gates unto my love,
Open them wide that she may enter in,
And all the postes adorne as doth behove,°   *as is proper*
And all the pillours deck with girlands trim,
For to recyve this Saynt with honour dew,
That commeth in to you.
With trembling steps and humble reverence,
She commeth in, before th' almighties vew,
Of her ye virgins learne obedience,
When so ye come into those holy places,
To humble your proud faces:
Bring her up to th' high altar, that she may
The sacred ceremonies there partake,
The which do endlesse matrimony make,
And let the roring Organs loudly play
The praises of the Lord in lively notes,
The whiles with hollow throates
The Choristers the joyous Antheme sing,
That al the woods may answere and their eccho ring.

Behold whiles she before the altar stands
Hearing the holy priest that to her speakes
And blesseth her with his two happy hands,
How the red roses flush up in her cheekes,
And the pure snow with goodly vermill stayne,
Like crimsin dyde in grayne,°   *fast color*
That even th' Angels which continually,
About the sacred Altare doe remaine,
Forget their service and about her fly,
Ofte peeping in her face that seemes more fayre,
The more they on it stare.
But her sad° eyes still fastened on the ground,   *serious*
Are governèd with goodly modesty,
That suffers not one looke to glaunce awry,
Which may let in a little thought unsownd.

Why blush ye love to give to me your hand,
The pledge of all our band?°   *bond*
Sing ye sweet Angels, Alleluya sing,
That all the woods may answere and your eccho ring.

Now al is done; bring home the bride againe,
Bring home the triumph of our victory,
Bring home with you the glory
     of her gaine,°   *the glory of gaining her*
With joyance bring her and with jollity.
Never had man more joyfull day then this,
Whom heaven would heape with blis.
Make feast therefore now all this live long day,
This day for ever to me holy is,
Poure out the wine without restraint or stay,
Poure not by cups, but by the belly full,
Poure out to all that wull
And sprinkle all the postes and wals with wine,
That they may sweat, and drunken be withall.
Crowne ye God Bacchus with a coronall,
And Hymen also crowne with wreathes of vine,
And let the Graces daunce unto the rest;
For they can doo it best:
The whiles the maydens doe theyr carroll sing,
To which the woods shal answer and theyr eccho ring.

Ring ye the bels, ye yong men of the towne,
And leave your wonted labors for this day:
This day is holy; doe ye write it downe,
That ye for ever it remember may.
This day the sunne is in his chiefest hight,
With Barnaby the bright,[3]
From whence declining daily by degrees,
He somewhat loseth of his heat and light,
When once the Crab behind his back he sees.
But for this time it ill ordainèd was,
To chose the longest day in all the yeare,
And shortest night, when longest fitter weare:
Yet never day so long, but late° would passe.   *at last*

---

[3] Saint Barnabas's Day was the day of the summer solstice in Spenser's time.

Ring ye the bels, to make it weare away,
And bonefiers make all day,
And daunce about them, and about them sing:
That all the woods may answer, and your eccho ring.

Ah when will this long weary day have end,
And lende me leave to come unto my love?
How slowly do the houres theyr numbers spend?
How slowly does sad Time his feathers move?
Hast thee O fayrest Planet° to thy home   *the sun*
Within the Westerne fome:
Thy tyred steedes long since have need of rest.
Long though it be, at last I see it gloome,
And the bright evening star with golden creast
Appeare out of the East.
Fayre childe of beauty, glorious lampe of love
That all the host of heaven in rankes doost lead,
And guydest lovers through the nightès dread,
How chearefully thou lookest from above,
And seemst to laugh atweene thy twinkling light
As joying in the sight
Of these glad many which for joy doe sing,
That all the woods them answer and their eccho ring.

Now ceasse ye damsels your delights forepast;
Enough is it, that all the day was youres:
Now day is doen, and night is nighing fast:
Now bring the Bryde into the brydall boures.
Now night is come, now soone her disaray,
And in her bed her lay;
Lay her in lillies and in violets,
And silken courteins over her display,
And odourd sheetes, and Arras° coverlets.   *tapestry*
Behold how goodly my faire love does ly
In proud humility;
Like unto Maia,[4] when as Jove her tooke,
In Tempe, lying on the flowry gras,
Twixt sleepe and wake, after she weary was,
With bathing in the Acidalian brooke.
Now it is night, ye damsels may be gon,

---

[4] The eldest and most beautiful of the Pleiades.

And leave my love alone,
And leave likewise your former lay to sing:
The woods no more shal answere, nor your eccho ring.

Now welcome night, thou night so long expected,
That long daies labour doest at last defray,°   *pay*
And all my cares, which cruell love collected,
Hast sumd in one, and cancellèd for aye:
Spread thy broad wing over my love and me,
That no man may us see,
And in thy sable mantle us enwrap,
From feare of perrill and foule horror free.
Let no false treason seeke us to entrap,
Nor any dread disquiet once annoy
The safety of our joy:
But let the night be calme and quietsome,
Without tempestuous storms or sad afray:
Lyke as when Jove with fayre Alcmena° lay,   *mother of Hercules*
When he begot the great Tirynthian groome:
Or lyke as when he with thy selfe did lie,
And begot Majesty.
And let the mayds and yongmen cease to sing:
Ne let the woods them answer, nor theyr eccho ring.

Let no lamenting cryes, nor dolefull teares,
Be heard all night within nor yet without:
Ne let false whispers, breeding hidden feares,
Breake gentle sleepe with misconceivèd dout.
Let no deluding dreames, nor dreadful sights
Make sudden sad affrights;
Ne let housefyres, nor lightnings helpelesse harmes,
Ne let the Pouke,[5] nor other evill sprights,
Ne let mischívous witches with theyr charmes,
Ne let hob Goblins, names whose sence we see not,
Fray us with things that be not.
Let not the shriech Oule, nor the Storke be heard:
Nor the night Raven that still° deadly yels,   *continually*
Nor damnèd ghosts cald up with mighty spels,
Nor griesly vultures make us once affeard:

---

[5] The same Puck as in Shakespeare's *A Midsummer Night's Dream*. This Puck, however, is an "evil spright."

Ne let th' unpleasant Quyre of Frogs still croking
Make us to wish theyr choking.
Let none of these theyr drery accents sing;
Ne let the woods them answer, nor theyr eccho ring.

But let stil Silence trew night watches keepe,
That sacred peace may in assurance rayne,
And tymely sleep, when it is tyme to sleepe,
May poure his limbs forth on your pleasant playne,
The whiles an hundred little wingèd loves,
Like divers fethered doves,
Shall fly and flutter round about your bed,
And in the secret darke, that none reproves,
Their prety stealthes shal worke, and snares shal spread
To filch away sweet snatches of delight,
Conceald through covert night.
Ye sonnes of Venus, play your sports at will,
For greedy pleasure, carelesse of your toyes,°   *amorous dallying*
Thinks more upon her paradise of joyes,
Then what ye do, albe it good or ill.
All night therefore attend your merry play,
For it will soone be day:
Now none doth hinder you, that say or sing,
Ne will the woods now answer, nor your Eccho ring.

Who is the same, which at my window peepes?
Or whose is that faire face, that shines so bright,
Is it not Cinthia,° she that never sleepes,   *moon goddess*
But walkes about high heaven al the night?
O fayrest goddesse, do thou not envy
My love with me to spy:
For thou likewise didst love, though now
      unthought,°   *unsuspected*
And for a fleece of woll, which privily,
The Latmian shephard⁶ once unto thee brought,
His pleasures with thee wrought.
Therefore to us be favorable now;
And sith of wemens labours thou hast charge,
And generation goodly dost enlarge,
Encline thy will t' effect our wishfull vow,
And the chast wombe informe with timely seed,
That may our comfort breed:

---

⁶ Endymion, with whom Cynthia/Diana fell in love.

Till which we cease our hopefull hap to sing,
Ne let the woods us answere, nor our Eccho ring.

And thou great Juno, which with awful might
The lawes of wedlock still dost patronize,
And the religion° of the faith first plight   *sanctity*
With sacred rites hast taught to solemnize:
And eeke for comfort often callèd art
Of women in their smart,°   *labor*
Eternally bind thou this lovely band,
And all thy blessings unto us impart.
And thou glad Genius, in whose gentle hand,
The bridale bowre and geniall bed remaine,
Without blemish or staine,
And the sweet pleasures of theyr loves delight
With secret ayde doest succour and supply,
Till they bring forth the fruitfull progeny,
Send us the timely fruit of this same night.
And thou fayre Hebe,° and thou Hymen free,   *goddess of youth*
Grant that it may so be.
Til which we cease your further prayse to sing,
Ne any woods shal answer, nor your Eccho ring.

And ye high heavens, the temple of the gods,
In which a thousand torches flaming bright
Doe burne, that to us wretched earthly clods,
In dreadful darknesse lend desiréd light;
And all ye powers which in the same remayne,
More then we men can fayne,°   *imagine*
Poure out your blessing on us plentiously,
And happy influence upon us raine,
That we may raise a large posterity,
Which from the earth, which they may long possesse,
With lasting happinesse,
Up to your haughty pallaces may mount,
And for the guerdon° of theyr glorious merit   *reward*
May heavenly tabernacles there inherit,
Of blessed Saints for to increase the count.
So let us rest, sweet love, in hope of this,
And cease till then our tymely joyes to sing,
The woods no more us answer, nor our eccho ring.

Song made in lieu of many ornaments,
With which my love should duly have bene dect,
Which cutting off through hasty accidents,

Ye would not stay your dew time to expect,
But promist both to recompens,
Be unto her a goodly ornament,
And for short time an endlesse moniment.

Sonnet 75

From "Amoretti"

One day I wrote her name upon the strand,
But came the waves and washéd it away:
Agayne I wrote it with a second hand,
But came the tyde, and made my paynes his pray.
"Vayne man," sayd she, "that doest in vaine assay,
A mortall thing so to immortalize,
For I my selve shall lyke to this decay,
And eek° my name bee wypéd out lykewize."   *also*
"Not so," quod I, "let baser things devize°   *contrive*
To dy in dust, but you shall live by fame:
My verse your vertues rare shall eternize,
And in the hevens wryte your glorious name.
Where whenas death shall all the world subdew,
Our love shall live, and later life renew."

WALLACE STEVENS
The Idea of Order at Key West

She sang beyond the genius of the sea.
The water never formed to mind or voice,
Like a body wholly body, fluttering
Its empty sleeves; and yet its mimic motion
Made constant cry, caused constantly a cry,
That was not ours although we understood,
Inhuman, of the veritable ocean.

The sea was not a mask. No more was she.
The song and water were not medleyed sound
Even if what she sang was what she heard,
Since what she sang was uttered word by word.
It may be that in all her phrases stirred
The grinding water and the gasping wind;
But it was she and not the sea we heard.
For she was the maker of the song she sang.
The ever-hooded, tragic-gestured sea

Was merely a place by which she walked to sing.
Whose spirit is this? we said, because we knew
It was the spirit that we sought and knew
That we should ask this often as she sang.

If it was only the dark voice of the sea
That rose, or even colored by many waves;
If it was only the outer voice of sky
And cloud, of the sunken coral water-walled,
However clear, it would have been deep air,
The heaving speech of air, a summer sound
Repeated in a summer without end
And sound alone. But it was more than that,
More even than her voice, and ours, among
The meaningless plungings of water and the wind,
Theatrical distances, bronze shadows heaped
On high horizons, mountainous atmospheres
Of sky and sea.
                    It was her voice that made
The sky acutest at its vanishing.
She measured to the hour its solitude.
She was the single artificer of the world
In which she sang. And when she sang, the sea,
Whatever self it had, became the self
That was her song, for she was the maker. Then we,
As we beheld her striding there alone,
Knew that there never was a world for her
Except the one she sang and, singing, made.

Ramon Fernandez,[1] tell me, if you know,
Why, when the singing ended and we turned
Toward the town, tell why the glassy lights,
The lights in the fishing boats at anchor there,
As the night descended, tilting in the air,
Mastered the night and portioned out the sea,
Fixing emblazoned zones and fiery poles,
Arranging, deepening, enchanting night.

Oh! Blessed rage for order, pale Ramon,
The maker's rage to order words of the sea,
Words of the fragrant portals, dimly-starred,
And of ourselves and of our origins,
In ghostlier demarcations, keener sounds.

---

[1] No particular person is intended.

The Planet on the Table[1]

Ariel[2] was glad he had written his poems.
They were of a remembered time
Or of something seen that he liked.

Other makings of the sun
Were waste and welter
And the ripe shrub writhed.

His self and the sun were one
And his poems, although makings of his self,
Were no less makings of the sun.

It was not important that they survive.
What mattered was that they should bear
Some lineament or character,

Some affluence, if only half-perceived,
In the poverty of their words,
Of the planet of which they were part.

The Snow Man

One must have a mind of winter
To regard the frost and the boughs
Of the pine-trees crusted with snow;

And have been cold a long time
To behold the junipers shagged with ice,
The spruces rough in the distant glitter

Of the January sun; and not to think
Of any misery in the sound of the wind,
In the sound of a few leaves,

Which is the sound of the land
Full of the same wind
That is blowing in the same bare place

For the listener, who listens in the snow,
And, nothing himself, beholds
Nothing that is not there and the nothing that is.

---

[1] The "planet" is an image for Stevens's *Collected Poems* (1954).

[2] Ariel, the tree spirit in Shakespeare's play, *The Tempest,* here represents the poet.

Sunday Morning

1

Complacencies of the peignoir, and late
Coffee and oranges in a sunny chair,[1]
And the green freedom of a cockatoo
Upon a rug mingle to dissipate
The holy hush of ancient sacrifice.[2]
She dreams a little, and she feels the dark
Encroachment of that old catastrophe,
As a calm darkens among water-lights.
The pungent oranges and bright, green wings
Seem things in some procession of the dead,
Winding across wide water, without sound.
The day is like wide water, without sound,
Stilled for the passing of her dreaming feet
Over the seas, to silent Palestine,
Dominion of the blood and sepulchre.[3]

2

Why should she give her bounty to the dead?
What is divinity if it can come
Only in silent shadows and in dreams?
Shall she not find in comforts of the sun,
In pungent fruit and bright, green wings, or else
In any balm or beauty of the earth,
Things to be cherished like the thought of heaven?
Divinity must live within herself:
Passions of rain, or moods in falling snow;
Grievings in loneliness, or unsubdued
Elations when the forest blooms; gusty
Emotions on wet roads on autumn nights;
All pleasures and all pains, remembering
The bough of summer and the winter branch.
These are the measures destined for her soul.

3

Jove in the clouds had his inhuman birth.
No mother suckled him, no sweet land gave

---

[1] The woman in the poem does not attend a Sunday church service; instead, she remains in her peignoir and has breakfast.

[2] The death of Jesus.

[3] The passion and entombment of Jesus.

Large-mannered motions to his mythy mind.
He moved among us, as a muttering king,
Magnificent, would move among his hinds,°   *shepherds*
Until our blood, commingling, virginal,
With heaven, brought such requital to desire
The very hinds discerned it, in a star.
Shall our blood fail? Or shall it come to be
The blood of paradise? And shall the earth
Seem all of paradise that we shall know?
The sky will be much friendlier then than now,
A part of labor and a part of pain,
And next in glory to enduring love,
Not this dividing and indifferent blue.

4

She says, "I am content when wakened birds,
Before they fly, test the reality
Of misty fields, by their sweet questionings;
But when the birds are gone, and their warm fields
Return no more, where, then, is paradise?"
There is not any haunt of prophecy,
Nor any old chimera° of the grave,   *ghost*
Neither the golden underground,[4] nor isle
Melodious,[5] where spirits gat them home,
Nor visionary south, nor cloudy palm[6]
Remote on heaven's hill, that has endured
As April's green endures; or will endure
Like her remembrance of awakened birds,
Or her desire for June and evening, tipped
By the consummation of the swallow's wings.

5

She says, "But in contentment I still feel
The need of some imperishable bliss."
Death is the mother of beauty; hence from her,
Alone, shall come fulfilment to our dreams
And our desires. Although she strews the leaves
Of sure obliteration on our paths,

---

[4] The Elysian fields — in Greek mythology, the heaven of heroes.
[5] Avalon, where King Arthur was taken after his death.
[6] The palm was the reward given to Christian martyrs in heaven.

The path sick sorrow took, the many paths
Where triumph rang its brassy phrase, or love
Whispered a little out of tenderness,
She makes the willow shiver in the sun
For maidens who were wont to sit and gaze
Upon the grass, relinquished to their feet.
She causes boys to pile new plums and pears
On disregarded plate.° The maidens taste   *silver dishes*
And stray impassioned in the littering leaves.

6

Is there no change of death in paradise?
Does ripe fruit never fall? Or do the boughs
Hang always heavy in that perfect sky,
Unchanging, yet so like our perishing earth,
With rivers like our own that seek for seas
They never find, the same receding shores
That never touch with inarticulate pang?
Why set the pear upon those river-banks
Or spice the shores with odors of the plum?
Alas, that they should wear our colors there,
The silken weavings of our afternoons,
And pick the strings of our insipid lutes!
Death is the mother of beauty, mystical,
Within whose burning bosom we devise
Our earthly mothers waiting, sleeplessly.

7

Supple and turbulent, a ring of men
Shall chant in orgy on a summer morn
Their boisterous devotion to the sun,
Not as a god, but as a god might be,
Naked among them, like a savage source.
Their chant shall be a chant of paradise,
Out of their blood, returning to the sky;
And in their chant shall enter, voice by voice,
The windy lake wherein their lord delights,
The trees, like serafin,° and echoing hills,   *angels*
That choir among themselves long afterward.
They shall know well the heavenly fellowship
Of men that perish and of summer morn.
And whence they came and whither they shall go
The dew upon their feet shall manifest.

8

She hears, upon that water without sound,
A voice that cries, "The tomb in Palestine
Is not the porch of spirits lingering.
It is the grave of Jesus, where he lay."
We live in an old chaos of the sun,
Or old dependency of day and night,
Or island solitude, unsponsored, free,
Of that wide water, inescapable.
Deer walk upon our mountains, and the quail
Whistle about us their spontaneous cries;
Sweet berries ripen in the wilderness;
And, in the isolation of the sky,
At evening, casual flocks of pigeons make
Ambiguous undulations as they sink,
Downward to darkness, on extended wings.

Thirteen Ways of Looking at a Blackbird

1

Among twenty snowy mountains,
The only moving thing
Was the eye of the blackbird.

2

I was of three minds,
Like a tree
In which there are three blackbirds.

3

The blackbird whirled in the autumn winds.
It was a small part of the pantomime.

4

A man and a woman
Are one.
A man and a woman and a blackbird
Are one.

5

I do not know which to prefer,
The beauty of inflections
Or the beauty of innuendoes,

The blackbird whistling
Or just after.

6

Icicles filled the long window
With barbaric glass.
The shadow of the blackbird
Crossed it to and fro.
The mood
Traced in the shadow
An indecipherable cause.

7

O thin men of Haddam,[1]
Why do you imagine golden birds?
Do you not see how the blackbird
Walks around the feet
Of the women about you?

8

I know noble accents
And lucid, inescapable rhythms;
But I know, too,
That the blackbird is involved
In what I know.

9

When the blackbird flew out of sight,
It marked the edge
Of one of many circles.

10

At the sight of blackbirds
Flying in a green light,
Even the bawds of euphony
Would cry out sharply.

11

He rode over Connecticut
In a glass coach.
Once, a fear pierced him,

---

[1] Town in Connecticut.

In that he mistook
The shadow of his equipage
For blackbirds.

12

The river is moving.
The blackbird must be flying.

13

It was evening all afternoon.
It was snowing
And it was going to snow.
The blackbird sat
In the cedar-limbs.

MARK STRAND
Keeping Things Whole

In a field
I am the absence
of field.
This is
always the case.
Wherever I am
I am what is missing.

When I walk
I part the air
and always
the air moves in
to fill the spaces
where my body's been.

We all have reasons
for moving.
I move
to keep things whole.

JONATHAN SWIFT
A Description of the Morning

Now hardly here and there a hackney coach
Appearing, showed the ruddy morn's approach.
Now Betty from her master's bed has flown,
And softly stole to discompose her own.
The slipshod prentice from his master's door
Had pared the dirt, and sprinkled round the floor.
Now Moll had whirled her mop with dexterous airs,
Prepared to scrub the entry and the stairs.
The youth with broomy stumps began to trace
The kennel-edge,° where wheels had worn the place.   *gutter*
The smallcoal man was heard with cadence deep;[1]
Till drowned in shriller notes of chimney-sweep.
Duns[2] at his Lordship's gate began to meet;
And Brickdust[3] Moll had screamed through half a street.
The turnkey now his flock returning sees,
Duly let out a-nights to steal for fees.[4]
The watchful bailiffs take their silent stands;
And schoolboys lag with satchels in their hands.

ALFRED, LORD TENNYSON
From *In Memoriam A. H. H.*

7

Dark house, by which once more I stand
    Here in the long unlovely street,
    Doors, where my heart was used to beat
So quickly, waiting for a hand,

A hand that can be clasped no more —
    Behold me, for I cannot sleep,
    And like a guilty thing I creep
At earliest morning to the door.

---

[1] Coal was hawked in the street.
[2] Bailiffs acting as debt collectors.
[3] Tanned; a tanned complexion was a mark of the working classes.
[4] Prisoners were let out to get money to pay their jailers.

He[1] is not here; but far away
    The noise of life begins again,
    And ghastly through the drizzling rain
On the bald street breaks the blank day.

99

Risest thou thus, dim dawn, again,
    So loud with voices of the birds,
    So thick with lowings of the herds,
Day, when I lost the flower of men;

Who tremblest thro' thy darkling red
    On yon swollen brook that bubbles fast
    By meadows breathing of the past,
And woodlands holy to the dead;

Who murmurest in the foliage eaves
    A song that slights the coming care,
    And Autumn laying here and there
A fiery finger on the leaves;

Who wakenest with thy balmy breath
    To myriads on the genial earth,
    Memories of bridal, or of birth,
And unto myriads more, of death.

O, wheresoever those may be,
    Betwixt the slumber of the poles,
    To-day they count as kindred souls;
They know me not, but mourn with me.

106

Ring out, wild bells, to the wild sky,
    The flying cloud, the frosty light:
    The year is dying in the night;
Ring out, wild bells, and let him die.

Ring out the old, ring in the new,
    Ring, happy bells, across the snow:
    The year is going, let him go;
Ring out the false, ring in the true.

---

[1] Arthur Henry Hallam (1811–1833), Tennyson's brilliantly promising friend. He died suddenly in Vienna, while on a tour of the Continent with his father.

Ring out the grief that saps the mind,
    For those that here we see no more;
    Ring out the feud of rich and poor,
Ring in redress to all mankind.

Ring out a slowly dying cause
    And ancient forms of party strife;
    Ring in the nobler modes of life,
With sweeter manners, purer laws.

Ring out the want, the care, the sin,
    The faithless coldness of the times;
    Ring out, ring out my mournful rhymes,
But ring the fuller minstrel in.

Ring out false pride in place and blood,
    The civic slander and the spite;
    Ring in the love of truth and right,
Ring in the common love of good.

Ring out old shapes of foul disease;
    Ring out the narrowing lust of gold;
    Ring out the thousand wars of old,
Ring in the thousand years of peace.

Ring in the valiant man and free,
    The larger heart, the kindlier hand;
    Ring out the darkness of the land,
Ring in the Christ that is to be.

121

Sad Hesper° o'er the buried sun   *the evening star*
    And ready, thou, to die with him,
    Thou watchest all things ever dim
And dimmer, and a glory done.

The team is loosened from the wain,°   *wagon*
    The boat is drawn upon the shore;
    Thou listenest to the closing door,
And life is darkened in the brain.

Bright Phosphor,° fresher for the night,   *the morning star*
    By thee the world's great work is heard
    Beginning, and the wakeful bird;
Behind thee comes the greater light.

The market boat is on the stream,
    And voices hail it from the brink;
    Thou hear'st the village hammer clink,
And see'st the moving of the team.

Sweet Hesper-Phosphor, double name[2]
    For what is one, the first, the last,
    Thou, like my present and my past,
Thy place is changed; thou art the same.

Tears, Idle Tears

From "The Princess"

Tears, idle tears, I know not what they mean,
Tears from the depth of some divine despair
Rise in the heart, and gather to the eyes,
In looking on the happy autumn-fields,
And thinking of the days that are no more.

    Fresh as the first beam glittering on a sail,
That brings our friends up from the underworld,
Sad as the last which reddens over one
That sinks with all we love below the verge;
So sad, so fresh, the days that are no more.

    Ah, sad and strange as in dark summer dawns
The earliest pipe of half-awakened birds
To dying ears, when unto dying eyes
The casement slowly grows a glimmering square;
So sad, so strange, the days that are no more.

    Dear as remembered kisses after death,
And sweet as those by hopeless fancy feigned
On lips that are for others; deep as love,
Deep as first love, and wild with all regret;
O Death in Life, the days that are no more!

Ulysses[1]

It little profits that an idle king,
By this still hearth, among these barren crags,
Matched with an aged wife, I mete and dole

---

[2] The morning star and evening star are both the planet Venus.
[1] This poem derives from Ulysses' description of his last voyage in Dante's *Inferno* (Canto 26).

Unequal laws unto a savage race,
That hoard, and sleep, and feed, and know not me.
I cannot rest from travel; I will drink
Life to the lees. All times I have enjoyed
Greatly, have suffered greatly, both with those
That loved me, and alone; on shore, and when
Through scudding drifts the rainy Hyades[2]
Vext the dim sea. I am become a name;
For always roaming with a hungry heart
Much have I seen and known — cities of men
And manners, climates, councils, governments,
Myself not least, but honored of them all, —
And drunk delight of battle with my peers,
Far on the ringing plains of windy Troy.
I am a part of all that I have met;
Yet all experience is an arch wherethrough
Gleams that untraveled world whose margin fades
For ever and for ever when I move.
How dull it is to pause, to make an end,
To rust unburnished, not to shine in use!
As though to breathe were life! Life piled on life
Were all too little, and of one to me
Little remains; but every hour is saved
From that eternal silence, something more,
A bringer of new things; and vile it were
For some three suns to store and hoard myself,
And this gray spirit yearning in desire
To follow knowledge like a sinking star,
Beyond the utmost bound of human thought.
     This is my son, mine own Telemachus,
To whom I leave the scepter and the isle, —
Well-loved of me, discerning to fulfill
This labor, by slow prudence to make mild
A rugged people, and through soft degrees
Subdue them to the useful and the good.
Most blameless is he, centered in the sphere
Of common duties, decent not to fail
In offices of tenderness, and pay
Meet adoration to my household gods,
When I am gone. He works his work, I mine.

---

[2] A cluster of five stars in the constellation Taurus. They were supposed to foretell rain.

There lies the port; the vessel puffs her sail;
There gloom the dark, broad seas. My mariners,
Souls that have toiled, and wrought, and thought with me,
That ever with a frolic welcome took
The thunder and the sunshine, and opposed
Free hearts, free foreheads — you and I are old;
Old age hath yet his honor and his toil.
Death closes all; but something ere the end,
Some work of noble note, may yet be done,
Not unbecoming men that strove with gods.
The lights begin to twinkle from the rocks;
The long day wanes; the slow moon climbs; the deep
Moans round with many voices. Come, my friends,
'Tis not too late to seek a newer world.
Push off, and sitting well in order smite
The sounding furrows; for my purpose holds
To sail beyond the sunset, and the baths
Of all the western stars, until I die.
It may be that the gulfs will wash us down;
It may be we shall touch the Happy Isles,[3]
And see the great Achilles, whom we knew.
Though much is taken, much abides; and though
We are not now that strength which in old days
Moved earth and heaven, that which we are, we are,
One equal temper of heroic hearts,
Made weak by time and fate, but strong in will
To strive, to seek, to find, and not to yield.

DYLAN THOMAS
Fern Hill

Now as I was young and easy under the apple boughs
About the lilting house and happy as the grass was green,
    The night above the dingle starry,
        Time let me hail and climb
      Golden in the heydays of his eyes,
And honored among wagons I was prince of the apple towns
And once below a time I lordly had the trees and leaves
        Trail with daisies and barley
      Down the rivers of the windfall light.

---

[3] The abode after death of those favored by the gods.

And as I was green and carefree, famous among the barns
About the happy yard and singing as the farm was home,
    In the sun that is young once only,
        Time let me play and be
      Golden in the mercy of his means,
And green and golden I was huntsman and herdsman, the calves
Sang to my horn, the foxes on the hills barked clear and cold,
        And the sabbath rang slowly
      In the pebbles of the holy streams.

All the sun long it was running, it was lovely, the hay
Fields high as the house, the tunes from the chimneys, it was air
      And playing, lovely and watery
        And fire green as grass.
    And nightly under the simple stars
As I rode to sleep the owls were bearing the farm away,
All the moon long I heard, blessed among stables, the night-jars
      Flying with the ricks, and the horses
        Flashing into the dark.

And then to awake, and the farm, like a wanderer white
With the dew, come back, the cock on his shoulder: it was all
      Shining, it was Adam and maiden,
        The sky gathered again
    And the sun grew round that very day.
So it must have been after the birth of the simple light
In the first, spinning place, the spellbound horses walking warm
      Out of the whinnying green stable
        On to the fields of praise.

And honored among foxes and pheasants by the gay house
Under the new made clouds and happy as the heart was long,
      In the sun born over and over,
        I ran my heedless ways,
      My wishes raced through the house high hay
And nothing I cared, at my sky blue trades, that time allows
In all his tuneful turning so few and such morning songs
      Before the children green and golden
        Follow him out of grace,

Nothing I cared, in the lamb white days, that time would take me
Up to the swallow thronged loft by the shadow of my hand,
      In the moon that is always rising,
        Nor that riding to sleep
      I should hear him fly with the high fields

And wake to the farm forever fled from the childless land.
Oh as I was young and easy in the mercy of his means,
      Time held me green and dying
    Though I sang in my chains like the sea.

In My Craft or Sullen Art

In my craft or sullen art
Exercised in the still night
When only the moon rages
And the lovers lie abed
With all their griefs in their arms,
I labor by singing light
Not for ambition or bread
Or the strut and trade of charms
On the ivory stages
But for the common wages
Of their most secret heart.

Not for the proud man apart
From the raging moon I write
On these spindrift pages
Nor for the towering dead
With their nightingales and psalms
But for the lovers, their arms
Round the griefs of the ages,
Who pay no praise or wages
Nor heed my craft or art.

Henry Vaughan

They Are All Gone into the World of Light!

They are all gone into the world of light!
    And I alone sit lingering here;
Their very memory is fair and bright,
    And my sad thoughts doth clear.

It glows and glitters in my cloudy breast
    Like stars upon some gloomy grove,
Or those faint beams in which this hill is dressed
    After the sun's remove.

I see them walking in an air of glory,
 Whose light doth trample on my days;
My days, which are at best but dull and hoary,
 Mere glimmering and decays.

O holy hope, and high humility,
 High as the heavens above!
These are your walks, and you have showed them me
 To kindle my cold love.

Dear, beauteous death! the jewel of the just,
 Shining nowhere but in the dark;
What mysteries do lie beyond thy dust,
 Could man outlook that mark!

He that hath found some fledged bird's nest may know
 At first sight if the bird be flown;
But what fair well or grove he sings in now,
 That is to him unknown.

And yet, as angels in some brighter dreams
 Call to the soul when man doth sleep,
So some strange thoughts transcend our wonted themes,
 And into glory peep.

If a star were confined into a tomb,
 Her captive flames must needs burn there;
But when the hand that locked her up gives room,
 She'll shine through all the sphere.

O Father of eternal life, and all
 Created glories under Thee!
Resume° Thy spirit from this world of thrall   *take back*
 Into true liberty!

Either disperse these mists, which blot and fill
 My pérspective° still as they pass;   *telescope*
Or else remove me hence unto that hill
 Where I shall need no glass.

DEREK WALCOTT
Ruins of a Great House

> *Though our longest sun sets at right declensions and*
> *makes but winter arches, it cannot be long before we lie*
> *down in darkness, and have our light in ashes . . .*
>   — BROWNE, *URN BURIAL*[1]

Stones only, the disjecta membra° of this
    Great House,   *fragments*
Whose moth-like girls are mixed with candledust,
Remain to file the lizard's dragonish claws.
The mouths of those gate cherubs shriek with stain;
Axle and coach wheel silted under the muck
Of cattle droppings.
              Three crows flap for the trees
And settle, creaking the eucalyptus boughs.
A smell of dead limes quickens in the nose
The leprosy of empire.
          "Farewell, green fields,
          Farewell, ye happy groves!"°   *Satan in*
Marble like Greece, like Faulkner's[2] South in stone,   *Paradise*
Deciduous beauty prospered and is gone,   *Lost*
But where the lawn breaks in a rash of trees
A spade below dead leaves will ring the bone
Of some dead animal or human thing
Fallen from evil days, from evil times.

It seems that the original crops were limes
Grown in the silt that clogs the river's skirt;
The imperious rakes are gone, their bright girls gone,
The river flows, obliterating hurt.
I climbed a wall with the grille ironwork
Of exiled craftsmen protecting that great house
From guilt, perhaps, but not from the worm's rent
Nor from the padded cavalry of the mouse.
And when a wind shook in the limes I heard
What Kipling[3] heard, the death of a great empire, the abuse
Of ignorance by Bible and by sword.

---

[1] Sir Thomas Browne (1605–1682), author of the treatise *Hydriotaphia: Urn Burial.*
[2] William Faulkner (1897–1962), American novelist.
[3] Rudyard Kipling (1865–1936), English novelist and poet.

A green lawn, broken by low walls of stone,
Dipped to the rivulet, and pacing, I thought next
Of men like Hawkins, Walter Raleigh, Drake,[4]
Ancestral murderers and poets, more perplexed
In memory now by every ulcerous crime.
The world's green age then was a rotting lime
Whose stench became the charnel galleon's text.
The rot remains with us, the men are gone.
But, as dead ash is lifted in a wind
That fans the blackening ember of the mind,
My eyes burned from the ashen prose of Donne.[5]

Ablaze with rage I thought,
Some slave is rotting in this manorial lake,
But still the coal of my compassion fought
That Albion[6] too was once
A colony like ours, "part of the continent, piece of the main,"[7]
Nook-shotten, rook o'erblown, deranged
By foaming channels and the vain expense
Of bitter faction.

     All in compassion ends
So differently from what the heart arranged:
"as well as if a manor of thy friend's . . ."

EDMUND WALLER

Song

 Go, lovely rose!
Tell her that wastes her time and me
 That now she knows,
When I resemble° her to thee,   *compare*
How sweet and fair she seems to be.

---

 [4] Sir John Hawkins (1532–1595); Sir Walter Raleigh (1552?–1618); Sir Francis Drake (1540?–1596). Leading English explorers.

 [5] John Donne (1572–1631), English poet.

 [6] A poetic name for Great Britain.

 [7] John Donne, Meditation 17, from his "Devotions upon Emergent Occasions." "No man is an island entire of itself; every man is a piece of the continent, a part of the main; if a clod be washed away by the sea, Europe is the less, as well as if a promontory were, as well as if a manor of thy friend's or of thine own were." Walcott quotes the closing phrase of this quotation to close his poem.

   Tell her that's young,
And shuns to have her graces spied,
   That hadst thou sprung
In deserts, where no men abide,
Thou must have uncommended died.

   Small is the worth
Of beauty from the light retired;
   Bid her come forth,
Suffer herself to be desired,
And not blush so to be admired.

   Then die! that she
The common fate of all things rare
   May read in thee;
How small a part of time they share
That are so wondrous sweet and fair!

ROSANNA WARREN
In Creve Coeur, Missouri

(Pulitzer Prize for Photojournalism, 1989)

Only in Creve Coeur
would an amateur photographer
firebug snap a shot so
unconsolable: fireman bent low

over the rag of body held
like impossible laundry pulled
too soon from the line, too pale,
too sodden with smoke to flail

in his huge, dark, crumpled embrace.
He leans to the tiny face.
Her hair stands out like flame.
She is naked, she has no name.

No longer a baby, almost
a child, not yet a ghost,
she presses a doll-like fist
to his professional chest.

Her head falls back to his hand.
Tell us that she will stand

again, quarrel and misbehave.
He is trying to make her breathe.

Strong man, you know how it's done,
you've done it again and again
sucking the spirit back
to us from its lair of smoke.

We'll call it a fine surprise.
The snapshot won a prize
though it couldn't revive *her*
that night in Creve Coeur.

JAMES WELCH
Harlem, Montana: Just Off the Reservation

We need no runners here. Booze is law
and all the Indians drink in the best tavern.
Money is free if you're poor enough.
Disgusted, busted whites are running
for office in this town. The constable,
a local farmer, plants the jail with wild
raven-haired stiffs who beg just one more drink.
One drunk, a former Methodist, becomes a saint
in the Indian church, bugs the plaster man
on the cross with snakes. If his knuckles broke,
he'd see those women wail the graves goodbye.

Goodbye, goodbye, Harlem on the rocks,
so bigoted, you forget the latest joke,
so lonely, you'd welcome a battalion of Turks
to rule your women. What you don't know,
what you will never know or want to learn —
Turks aren't white. Turks are olive, unwelcome
alive in any town. Turks would use
your one dingy park to declare a need for loot.
Turks say bring it, step quickly, lay down and dead.

Here we are when men were nice. This photo, hung
in the New England Hotel lobby, shows them nicer
than pie, agreeable to the warring bands of redskins
who demanded protection money for the price of food.
Now, only Hutterites out north are nice. We hate

them. They are tough and their crops are always good.
We accuse them of idiocy and believe their belief all wrong.

Harlem, your hotel is overnamed, your children
are raggedy-assed but you go on, survive
the bad food from the two cafes and peddle
your hate for the wild who bring you money.
When you die, if you die, will you remember
the three young bucks who shot the grocery up,
locked themselves in and cried for days, we're rich,
help us, oh God, we're rich.

The Man from Washington

The end came easy for most of us.
Packed away in our crude beginnings
in some far corner of a flat world,
we didn't expect much more
than firewood and buffalo robes
to keep us warm. The man came down,
a slouching dwarf with rainwater eyes,
and spoke to us. He promised
that life would go on as usual,
that treaties would be signed, and everyone —
man, woman and child — would be inoculated
against a world in which we had no part,
a world of money, promise and disease.

WALT WHITMAN
A Hand-Mirror

Hold it up sternly — see this it sends back, (who is it? is it you?)
Outside fair costume, within ashes and filth,
No more a flashing eye, no more a sonorous voice or
    springy step,
Now some slave's eye, voice, hands, step,
A drunkard's breath, unwholesome eater's face, venerealee's[1]
    flesh,
Lungs rotting away piecemeal, stomach sour and cankerous,
Joints rheumatic, bowels clogged with abomination,

---

[1] Victim of venereal disease.

Blood circulating dark and poisonous streams,
Words babble, hearing and touch callous,
No brain, no heart left, no magnetism of sex;
Such from one look in this looking-glass ere you go hence,
Such a result so soon — and from such a beginning!

From *Song of Myself*

1

I celebrate myself, and sing myself,
And what I assume you shall assume,
For every atom belonging to me as good belongs to you.

I loaf and invite my soul,
I lean and loaf at my ease observing a spear of summer grass.

My tongue, every atom of my blood, formed from this soil, this air,
Born here of parents born here from parents the same, and their
      parents the same,
I, now thirty-seven years old in perfect health begin,
Hoping to cease not till death.

Creeds and schools in abeyance,
Retiring back a while sufficed at what they are, but never forgotten,
I harbor for good or bad, I permit to speak at every hazard,
Nature without check with original energy.

6

A child said *What is the grass?* fetching it to me with full hands;
How could I answer the child? I do not know what it is any more
      than he.

I guess it must be the flag of my disposition, out of hopeful green
      stuff woven.

Or I guess it is the handkerchief of the Lord,
A scented gift and remembrancer designedly dropped,
Bearing the owner's name someway in the corners, that we may
      see and remark, and say *Whose?*

Or I guess the grass is itself a child, the produced babe of the
      vegetation.

Or I guess it is a uniform hieroglyphic,
And it means, Sprouting alike in broad zones and narrow zones,
Growing among black folks as among white,

Kanuck, Tuckahoe, Congressman, Cuff,[1] I give them the same,
    I receive them the same.

And now it seems to me the beautiful uncut hair of graves.

Tenderly will I use you curling grass,
It may be you transpire from the breasts of young men,
It may be if I had known them I would have loved them,
It may be you are from old people, or from offspring taken soon
    out of their mothers' laps,
And here you are the mothers' laps.

This grass is very dark to be from the white heads of old mothers,
Darker than the colorless beards of old men,
Dark to come from under the faint red roofs of mouths.

O I perceive after all so many uttering tongues,
And I perceive they do not come from the roofs of mouths for
    nothing.

I wish I could translate the hints about the dead young men and
    women,
And the hints about old men and mothers, and the offspring taken
    soon out of their laps.

What do you think has become of the young and old men?
And what do you think has become of the women and children?

They are alive and well somewhere,
The smallest sprout shows there is really no death,
And if ever there was it led forward life, and does not wait at the
    end to arrest it,
And ceased the moment life appeared.

All goes onward and outward, nothing collapses,
And to die is different from what anyone supposed, and luckier.

52

The spotted hawk swoops by and accuses me, he complains of my
    gab and my loitering.

I too am not a bit tamed, I too am untranslatable,
I sound my barbaric yawp over the roofs of the world.

---

[1] A "Kanuck" refers to a French Canadian, a "Tuckahoe" refers to a native of
Tidewater, Virginia, and a "Cuff" refers to an African American.

The last scud of day holds back for me,
It flings my likeness after the rest and true as any on the shadowed
    wilds,
It coaxes me to the vapor and the dusk.

I depart as air, I shake my white locks at the runaway sun,
I effuse my flesh in eddies, and drift it in lacy jags.

I bequeath myself to the dirt to grow from the grass I love,
If you want me again look for me under your boot-soles.

You will hardly know who I am or what I mean,
But I shall be good health to you nevertheless,
And filter and fiber your blood.

Failing to fetch me at first keep encouraged,
Missing me one place search another,
I stop somewhere waiting for you.

Vigil Strange I Kept on the Field One Night

Vigil strange I kept on the field one night;
When you my son and my comrade dropt at my side that day,
One look I but gave which your dear eyes return'd with a look I
    shall never forget,
One touch of your hand to mine O boy, reach'd up as you lay on
    the ground,
Then onward I sped in the battle, the even-contested battle,
Till late in the night reliev'd to the place at last again I made my
    way,
Found you in death so cold dear comrade, found your body son of
    responding kisses, (never again on earth responding,)
Bared your face in the starlight, curious the scene, cool blew the
    moderate night-wind,
Long there and then in vigil I stood, dimly around me the battle-
    field spreading,
Vigil wondrous and vigil sweet there in the fragrant silent night,
But not a tear fell, not even a long-drawn sigh, long I gazed,
Then on the earth partially reclining sat by your side leaning my
    chin in my hands,
Passing sweet hours, immortal and mystic hours with you dearest
    comrade — not a tear, not a word,
Vigil of silence, love and death, vigil for you my son and my
    soldier,
As onward silently stars aloft, eastward new ones upward stole,

Vigil final for you brave boy, (I could not save you, swift was your
 death,
I faithfully loved you and cared for you living, I think we shall
 surely meet again,)
Till at latest lingering of the night, indeed just as the dawn appear'd,
My comrade I wrapt in his blanket, envelop'd well his form,
Folded the blanket well, tucking it carefully over head and care-
 fully under feet,
And there and then and bathed by the rising sun, my son in his
 grave, in his rude-dug grave I deposited,
Ending my vigil strange with that, vigil of night and battle-field dim,
Vigil for boy of responding kisses, (never again on earth respond-
 ing,)
Vigil for comrade swiftly slain, vigil I never forget, how as day
 brighten'd,
I rose from the chill ground and folded my soldier well in his
 blanket,
And buried him where he fell.

RICHARD WILBUR
Cottage Street, 1953

Framed in her phoenix fire-screen, Edna Ward
Bends to the tray of Canton,[1] pouring tea
For frightened Mrs. Plath; then, turning toward
The pale, slumped daughter, and my wife, and me,

Asks if we would prefer it weak or strong.
Will we have milk or lemon, she enquires?
The visit seems already strained and long.
Each in his turn, we tell her our desires.

It is my office to exemplify
The published poet in his happiness,
Thus cheering Sylvia, who has wished to die;[2]
But half-ashamed, and impotent to bless,

---

[1] Blue-and-white patterned Chinese-export porcelain ware; in this case, the tea
service.

[2] The poet Sylvia Plath (1932–1963) attempted suicide after her junior year at
Smith College. Later, she died by suicide, at thirty-one.

I am a stupid life-guard who has found,
Swept to his shallows by the tide, a girl
Who, far from shore, has been immensely drowned,
And stares through water now with eyes of pearl.

How large is her refusal; and how slight
The genteel chat whereby we recommend
Life, of a summer afternoon, despite
The brewing dusk which hints that it may end.

And Edna Ward shall die in fifteen years,
After her eight-and-eighty summers of
Such grace and courage as permit no tears,
The thin hand reaching out, the last word *love,*

Outliving Sylvia who, condemned to live,
Shall study for a decade, as she must,
To state at last her brilliant negative
In poems free and helpless and unjust.

The Writer

In her room at the prow of the house
Where light breaks, and the windows are tossed with linden,
My daughter is writing a story.

I pause in the stairwell, hearing
From her shut door a commotion of typewriter-keys
Like a chain hauled over a gunwale.

Young as she is, the stuff
Of her life is a great cargo, and some of it heavy:
I wish her a lucky passage.

But now it is she who pauses,
As if to reject my thought and its easy figure.
A stillness greatens, in which

The whole house seems to be thinking,
And then she is at it again with a bunched clamor
Of strokes, and again is silent.

I remember the dazed starling
Which was trapped in that very room, two years ago;
How we stole in, lifted a sash

And retreated, not to affright it;
And how for a helpless hour, through the crack of the door,
We watched the sleek, wild, dark

And iridescent creature
Batter against the brilliance, drop like a glove
To the hard floor, or the desk-top,

And wait then, humped and bloody,
For the wits to try it again; and how our spirits
Rose when, suddenly sure,

It lifted off from a chair-back,
Beating a smooth course for the right window
And clearing the sill of the world.

It is always a matter, my darling,
Of life or death, as I had forgotten. I wish
What I wished you before, but harder.

WILLIAM CARLOS WILLIAMS
Landscape with the Fall of Icarus

According to Breughel
when Icarus fell
it was spring

a farmer was ploughing
his field
the whole pageantry

of the year was
awake tingling
near

the edge of the sea
concerned
with itself

sweating in the sun
that melted
the wings' wax

unsignificantly
off the coast
there was

a splash quite unnoticed
this was
Icarus drowning

The Raper from Passenack

was very kind. When she regained
her wits, he said, It's all right, Kid,
I took care of you.

What a mess she was in. Then he added,
You'll never forget me now.
And drove her home.

Only a man who is sick, she said
would do a thing like that.
It must be so.

No one who is not diseased could be
so insanely cruel. He wants to give it
to someone else —

to justify himself. But if I get a
venereal infection out of this
I won't be treated.

I refuse. You'll find me dead in bed
first. Why not? That's
the way she spoke,

I wish I could shoot him. How would
you like to know a murderer?
I may do it.

I'll know by the end of this week.
I wouldn't scream. I bit him
several times

but he was too strong for me.
I can't yet understand it. I don't
faint so easily.

When I came to myself and realized
what had happened all I could do
was to curse

and call him every vile name I could
think of. I was so glad
to be taken home.

I suppose it's my mind — the fear of
infection. I'd rather a million times
have been got pregnant.

But it's the foulness of it can't
be cured. And hatred, hatred of all men
— and disgust.

Spring and All

By the road to the contagious hospital
under the surge of the blue
mottled clouds driven from the
northeast — a cold wind. Beyond, the
waste of broad, muddy fields
brown with dried weeds, standing and fallen

patches of standing water
the scattering of tall trees

All along the road the reddish
purplish, forked, upstanding, twiggy
stuff of bushes and small trees
with dead, brown leaves under them
leafless vines —

Lifeless in appearance, sluggish
dazed spring approaches —

They enter the new world naked,
cold, uncertain of all
save that they enter. All about them
the cold, familiar wind —

Now the grass, tomorrow
the stiff curl of wildcarrot leaf
One by one objects are defined —
It quickens: clarity, outline of leaf

But now the stark dignity of
entrance — Still, the profound change
has come upon them: rooted, they
grip down and begin to awaken

This Is Just to Say

I have eaten
the plums
that were in
the icebox

and which
you were probably
saving
for breakfast

Forgive me
they were delicious
so sweet
and so cold

WILLIAM WORDSWORTH
My Heart Leaps Up

My heart leaps up when I behold
    A rainbow in the sky:
So was it when my life began;
So is it now I am a man;
So be it when I shall grow old,
    Or let me die!
The Child is father of the Man;
And I could wish my days to be
Bound each to each by natural piety.

Ode

INTIMATIONS OF IMMORTALITY FROM RECOLLECTIONS
OF EARLY CHILDHOOD

> *The Child is father of the Man;*
> *And I could wish my days to be*
> *Bound each to each by natural piety.*

1

There was a time when meadow, grove, and stream,
The earth, and every common sight,
    To me did seem
   Appar6led in celestial light,
The glory and the freshness of a dream.
It is not now as it hath been of yore —
    Turn whereso'er I may,
     By night or day,
The things which I have seen I now can see no more.

2

The Rainbow comes and goes,
  And lovely is the Rose,
  The Moon doth with delight
Look round her when the heavens are bare,
    Waters on a starry night
    Are beautiful and fair;
The sunshine is a glorious birth;
But yet I know, where'er I go,
That there hath passed away a glory from the earth.

3

Now, while the birds thus sing a joyous song,
  And while the young lambs bound
    As to the tabor's° sound,   *small drum*
To me alone there came a thought of grief:
A timely utterance gave that thought relief,
    And I again am strong:
The cataracts blow their trumpets from the steep;
No more shall grief of mine the season wrong;
I hear the Echoes through the mountains throng,
The Winds come to me from the fields of sleep,
  And all the earth is gay;
    Land and sea
  Give themselves up to jollity,
    And with the heart of May
  Doth every Beast keep holiday —
    Thou Child of Joy,
Shout round me, let me hear thy shouts, thou happy Shepherd-
  boy!

4

Ye blessèd Creatures, I have heard the call
  Ye to each other make; I see
The heavens laugh with you in your jubilee;
  My heart is at your festival,
    My head hath its coronal,
The fullness of your bliss, I feel — I feel it all.
    — Oh, evil day! if I were sullen
    While Earth herself is adorning,
     This sweet May morning,

And the Children are culling
    On every side,
In a thousand valleys far and wide,
  Fresh flowers; while the sun shines warm,
And the Babe leaps up on his Mother's arm —
    I hear, I hear, with joy I hear!
    — But there's a Tree, of many, one,
A single Field which I have looked upon,
Both of them speak of something that is gone:
      The Pansy at my feet
      Doth the same tale repeat:
Whither is fled the visionary gleam?
Where is it now, the glory and the dream?

5

Our birth is but a sleep and a forgetting:
The Soul that rises with us, our life's Star,
    Hath had elsewhere its setting,
      And cometh from afar:
    Not in entire forgetfulness,
    And not in utter nakedness,
But trailing clouds of glory do we come
    From God, who is our home:
Heaven lies about us in our infancy!
Shades of the prison-house begin to close
    Upon the growing Boy
But he beholds the light, and whence it flows,
    He sees it in his joy;
The Youth, who daily farther from the east
    Must travel, still is Nature's Priest,
    And by the vision splendid
    Is on his way attended;
At length the Man perceives it die away,
And fade into the light of common day.

6

Earth fills her lap with pleasures of her own;
Yearnings she hath in her own natural kind,
And, even with something of a Mother's mind,
    And no unworthy aim,
    The homely Nurse doth all she can

To make her foster child, her Inmate Man,
    Forget the glories he hath known,
And that imperial palace whence he came.

7

Behold the Child among his newborn blisses,
A six-years' Darling of a pygmy size!
See, where 'mid work of his own hand he lies,
Fretted by sallies of his mother's kisses,
With light upon him from his father's eyes!
See, at his feet, some little plan or chart,
Some fragment from his dream of human life,
Shaped by himself with newly-learnèd art;
    A wedding or a festival,
    A mourning or a funeral;
        And this hath now his heart,
    And unto this he frames his song;
        Then will he fit his tongue
To dialogues of business, love, or strife;
    But it will not be long
    Ere this be thrown aside,
    And with new joy and pride
The little Actor cons another part;
Filling from time to time his "humorous stage"
With all the Persons, down to palsied Age,
That Life brings with her in her equipage;
    As if his whole vocation
    Were endless imitation.

8

Thou, whose exterior semblance doth belie
    Thy Soul's immensity;
Thou best Philosopher, who yet dost keep
Thy heritage, thou Eye among the blind,
That, deaf and silent, read'st the eternal deep,
Haunted forever by the eternal mind —
    Mighty Prophet! Seer blest!
    On whom those truths do rest,
Which we are toiling all our lives to find,
In darkness lost, the darkness of the grave;
Thou, over whom thy Immortality
Broods like the Day, a Master o'er a Slave,
A Presence which is not to be put by;

Thou little Child, yet glorious in the might
Of heaven-born freedom on thy being's height,
Why with such earnest pains dost thou provoke
The years to bring the inevitable yoke,
Thus blindly with thy blessedness at strife?
Full soon thy Soul shall have her earthly freight,
And custom lie upon thee with a weight,
Heavy as frost, and deep almost as life!

9

O joy! that in our embers
Is something that doth live,
That nature yet remembers
What was so fugitive!
The thought of our past years in me doth breed
Perpetual benediction: not indeed
For that which is most worthy to be blest;
Delight and liberty, the simple creed
Of Childhood, whether busy or at rest,
With new-fledged hope still fluttering in his breast —
Not for these I raise
The song of thanks and praise;
But for those obstinate questionings
Of sense and outward things,
Fallings from us, vanishings;
Blank misgivings of a Creature
Moving about in worlds not realized,
High instincts before which our mortal Nature
Did tremble like a guilty Thing surprised;
But for those first affections,
Those shadowy recollections,
Which, be they what they may,
Are yet the fountain-light of all our day,
Are yet a master-light of all our seeing;
Uphold us, cherish, and have power to make
Our noisy years seem moments in the being
Of the eternal Silence: truths that wake,
To perish never;
Which neither listlessness, nor mad endeavor,
Nor Man nor Boy,
Nor all that is at enmity with joy,
Can utterly abolish or destroy!

Hence in a season of calm weather
       Though inland far we be,
Our Souls have sight of that immortal sea
       Which brought us hither,
     Can in a moment travel thither,
And see the Children sport upon the shore,
And hear the mighty waters rolling evermore.

10

Then sing, ye Birds, sing, sing a joyous song!
        And let the young Lambs bound
        As to the tabor's sound!
We in thought will join your throng,
        Ye that pipe and ye that play,
        Ye that through your hearts today
        Feel the gladness of the May!
What though the radiance which was once so bright
Be now forever taken from my sight,
     Though nothing can bring back the hour
Of splendor in the grass, of glory in the flower;
        We will grieve not, rather find
        Strength in what remains behind;
        In the primal sympathy
        Which having been must ever be;
        In the soothing thoughts that spring
        Out of human suffering;
        In the faith that looks through death,
In years that bring the philosophic mind.

11

And O, ye Fountains, Meadows, Hills, and Groves,
Forebode not any severing of our loves!
Yet in my heart of hearts I feel your might;
I only have relinquished one delight
To live beneath your more habitual sway.
I love the Brooks which down their channels fret,
Even more than when I tripped lightly as they;
The innocent brightness of a newborn Day
        Is lovely yet;
The clouds that gather round the setting sun
Do take a sober coloring from an eye
That hath kept watch o'er man's mortality;

Another race hath been, and other palms°   *symbols of victory*
    are won.
Thanks to the human heart by which we live,
Thanks to its tenderness, its joys, and fears,
To me the meanest° flower that blows°   *most ordinary / blooms*
    can give
Thoughts that do often lie too deep for tears.

The World Is Too Much with Us

The world is too much with us; late and soon,
Getting and spending, we lay waste our powers;
Little we see in Nature that is ours;
We have given our hearts away, a sordid boon!°   *gift*
This Sea that bares her bosom to the moon,
The winds that will be howling at all hours,
And are up-gathered now like sleeping flowers,
For this, for everything, we are out of tune;
It moves us not. — Great God! I'd rather be
A Pagan suckled in a creed outworn;
So might I, standing on this pleasant lea,
Have glimpses that would make me less forlorn;
Have sight of Proteus rising from the sea;
Or hear old Triton blow his wreathèd horn.[1]

CHARLES WRIGHT
Laguna Blues

It's Saturday afternoon at the edge of the world.
White pages lift in the wind and fall.
Dust threads, cut loose from the heart, float up and fall.
Something's off-key in my mind.
Whatever it is, it bothers me all the time.

It's hot, and the wind blows on what I have had to say.
I'm dancing a little dance.
The crows pick up a thermal that angles away from the sea.

---

[1] In Greek mythology, Proteus is a lesser sea god, to whom Poseidon gave the ability to change his form. Triton, a merman, is usually represented as blowing on a shell or conch, calming the waves.

I'm singing a little song.
Whatever it is, it bothers me all the time.

It's Saturday afternoon and the crows glide down,
Black pages that lift and fall.
The castor beans and the pepper plant trundle their weary heads.
Something's off-key and unkind.
Whatever it is, it bothers me all the time.

JAMES WRIGHT
A Blessing

Just off the highway to Rochester, Minnesota,
Twilight bounds softly forth on the grass.
And the eyes of those two Indian ponies
Darken with kindness.
They have come gladly out of the willows
To welcome my friend and me.
We step over the barbed wire into the pasture
Where they have been grazing all day, alone.
They ripple tensely, they can hardly contain their happiness
That we have come.
They bow shyly as wet swans. They love each other.
There is no loneliness like theirs.
At home once more,
They begin munching the young tufts of spring in the darkness.
I would like to hold the slenderer one in my arms,
For she has walked over to me
And nuzzled my left hand.
She is black and white,
Her mane falls wild on her forehead,
And the light breeze moves me to caress her long ear
That is delicate as the skin over a girl's wrist.
Suddenly I realize
That if I stepped out of my body I would break
Into blossom.

Small Frogs Killed on the Highway

Still,
I would leap too
Into the light,

If I had the chance.
It is everything, the wet green stalk of the field
On the other side of the road.
They crouch there, too, faltering in terror
And take strange wing. Many
Of the dead never moved, but many
Of the dead are alive forever in the split second
Auto headlights more sudden
Than their drivers know.
The drivers burrow backward into dank pools
Where nothing begets
Nothing.

Across the road, tadpoles are dancing
On the quarter thumbnail
Of the moon. They can't see,
Not yet.

SIR THOMAS WYATT
Forget Not Yet

Forget not yet the tried intent
Of such a truth as I have meant;
My great travail so gladly spent
    Forget not yet.

Forget not yet when first began
The weary life ye know, since whan
The suit, the service none tell can;
    Forget not yet.

Forget not yet the great assays,°   *trials*
The cruel wrong, the scornful ways,
The painful patience in denays,°   *denials*
    Forget not yet.

Forget not yet, forget not this,
How long ago hath been and is
The mind that never meant amiss;
    Forget not yet.

Forget not then thine own approved,
The which so long hath thee so loved,
Whose steadfast faith yet never moved;
    Forget not this.

WILLIAM BUTLER YEATS
Among School Children

I

I walk through the long schoolroom questioning;
A kind old nun in a white hood replies;
The children learn to cipher and to sing,
To study reading-books and history,
To cut and sew, be neat in everything
In the best modern way — the children's eyes
In momentary wonder stare upon
A sixty-year-old smiling public man.

II

I dream of a Ledaean body,[1] bent
Above a sinking fire, a tale that she
Told of a harsh reproof, or trivial event
That changed some childish day to tragedy —
Told, and it seemed that our two natures blent
Into a sphere from youthful sympathy,
Or else, to alter Plato's parable,
Into the yolk and white of the one shell.[2]

III

And thinking of that fit of grief or rage
I look upon one child or t'other there
And wonder if she stood so at that age —
For even daughters of the swan can share
Something of every paddler's heritage —
And had that colour upon cheek or hair,
And thereupon my heart is driven wild:
She stands before me as a living child.

IV

Her present image floats into the mind —
Did Quattrocento[3] finger fashion it
Hollow of cheek as though it drank the wind

---

[1] A body like Leda's. Leda was, in Greek myth, a maiden ravished by Zeus, who took the form of a swan.

[2] Plato, in *The Symposium,* suggests that man was originally both male and female but fell into division. Each half now longs for the other half.

[3] Italian name for the fifteenth century.

And took a mess of shadows for its meat?
And I though never of Ledaean kind
Had pretty plumage once — enough of that,
Better to smile on all that smile, and show
There is a comfortable kind of old scarecrow.

V

What youthful mother, a shape upon her lap
Honey of generation had betrayed,
And that must sleep, shriek, struggle to escape
As recollection or the drug decide,
Would think her son, did she but see that shape
With sixty or more winters on its head,
A compensation for the pang of his birth,
Or the uncertainty of his setting forth?

VI

Plato thought nature but a spume that plays
Upon a ghostly paradigm of things;
Solider Aristotle played the taws
Upon the bottom of a king of kings;[4]
World-famous golden-thighed Pythagoras
Fingered upon a fiddle-stick or strings
What a star sang and careless Muses heard:[5]
Old clothes upon old sticks to scare a bird.

VII

Both nuns and mothers worship images,
But those the candles light are not as those
That animate a mother's reveries,
But keep a marble or a bronze repose.
And yet they too break hearts — O Presences
That passion, piety or affection knows,
And that all heavenly glory symbolise —
O self-born mockers of man's enterprise;

---

[4] Yeats wrote to a friend, "Here is a fragment of my last curse upon old age. It means that even the greatest men are owls, scarecrows, by the time their fame has come. Aristotle, remember, was Alexander [the Great's] tutor, hence the taws [form of birch]," i.e., Aristotle flogged his pupil into learning.

[5] Yeats is referring to the fact that Pythagoras measured the intervals between notes on a stretched string.

VIII

Labour is blossoming or dancing where
The body is not bruised to pleasure soul,
Nor beauty born out of its own despair,
Nor blear-eyed wisdom out of midnight oil.
O chestnut-tree, great-rooted blossomer,
Are you the leaf, the blossom or the bole?
O body swayed to music, O brightening glance,
How can we know the dancer from the dance?

Down by the Salley Gardens

Down by the salley gardens my love and I did meet;
She passed the salley gardens with little snow-white feet.
She bid me take love easy, as the leaves grow on the tree;
But I, being young and foolish, with her would not agree.
In a field by the river my love and I did stand,
And on my leaning shoulder she laid her snow-white hand.
She bid me take life easy, as the grass grows on the weirs;
But I was young and foolish, and now am full of tears.

The Lake Isle of Innisfree

I will arise and go now, and go to Innisfree,
And a small cabin build there, of clay and wattles made:
Nine bean-rows will I have there, a hive for the honeybee,
And live alone in the bee-loud glade.

And I shall have some peace there, for peace comes dropping slow,
Dropping from the veils of the morning to where the cricket sings;
There midnight's all a glimmer, and noon a purple glow,
And evening full of the linnet's wings.

I will arise and go now, for always night and day
I hear lake water lapping with low sounds by the shore;
While I stand on the roadway, or on the pavements grey,
I hear it in the deep heart's core.

Leda and the Swan[1]

A sudden blow: the great wings beating still
Above the staggering girl, her thighs caressed
By the dark webs, her nape caught in his bill,
He holds her helpless breast upon his breast.

How can those terrified vague fingers push
The feathered glory from her loosening thighs?
And how can body, laid in that white rush,
But feel the strange heart beating where it lies?

A shudder in the loins engenders there
The broken wall, the burning roof and tower
And Agamemnon dead.
                              Being so caught up,
So mastered by the brute blood of the air,
Did she put on his knowledge with his power
Before the indifferent beak could let her drop?

Sailing to Byzantium

I

That is no country for old men. The young
In one another's arms, birds in the trees
— Those dying generations — at their song,
The salmon-falls, the mackerel-crowded seas,
Fish, flesh, or fowl, commend all summer long
Whatever is begotten, born, and dies.
Caught in that sensual music all neglect
Monuments of unageing intellect.

II

An aged man is but a paltry thing,
A tattered coat upon a stick, unless
Soul clap its hands and sing, and louder sing
For every tatter in its mortal dress,
Nor is there singing school but studying[1]

---

[1] In Greek myth, Leda was ravished by Zeus, who took the form of a swan. She gave birth to Helen. Helen left her husband, Menelaus, to go with Paris to Troy, thus causing the Trojan War.

[1] That is, "Nor is there any way to learn to sing except by studying."

Monuments of its own magnificence;
And therefore I have sailed the seas and come
To the holy city of Byzantium.

III

O sages standing in God's holy fire
As in the gold mosaic of a wall,
Come from the holy fire, perne in a gyre,[2]
And be the singing-masters of my soul.
Consume my heart away; sick with desire
And fastened to a dying animal
It knows not what it is; and gather me
Into the artifice of eternity.

IV

Once out of nature I shall never take
My bodily form from any natural thing,
But such a form as Grecian goldsmiths make
Of hammered gold and gold enamelling
To keep a drowsy Emperor awake;[3]
Or set upon a golden bough to sing
To lords and ladies of Byzantium
Of what is past, or passing, or to come.

The Second Coming

Turning and turning in the widening gyre[1]
The falcon cannot hear the falconer;
Things fall apart; the centre cannot hold;
Mere anarchy is loosed upon the world,
The blood-dimmed tide is loosed, and everywhere
The ceremony of innocence is drowned,
The best lack all conviction, while the worst
Are full of passionate intensity.

---

[2] Swoop down in a whirling movement.
[3] Yeats's note: "I have read somewhere that in the Emperor's palace at Byzantium was a tree made of gold and silver, and artificial birds sang."
[1] Yeats used the image of two interlocking gyres or cones to symbolize the conflicting forces of life.

Surely some revelation is at hand;
Surely the Second Coming is at hand.
The Second Coming! Hardly are those words out
When a vast image out of *Spiritus Mundi*[2]
Troubles my sight: somewhere in sands of the desert
A shape with lion body and the head of a man
A gaze blank and pitiless as the sun,
Is moving its slow thighs, while all about it
Reel shadows of the indignant desert birds.
The darkness drops again; but now I know
That twenty centuries of stony sleep
Were vexed to nightmare by a rocking cradle,
And what rough beast, its hour come round at last,
Slouches towards Bethlehem to be born?

---

[2] Yeats's term for the collective human memory.

Appendices

Appendix 1. On Prosody

Prosody concerns the measure in which poems are written. There are three kinds of poems, prosodically speaking:

poems in counted lines (where lines have a regular number of beats);

poems in free verse (where lines have an irregular number of beats);

poems in prose (usually a short symbolic paragraph).

This appendix is concerned with poems in counted lines and poems in free verse. Since free verse is a relatively recent form (Walt Whitman is the earliest significant American poet of free verse), we will take up counted poetry first.

Poems in Counted Lines

Poems in counted lines are written in units we call feet. A foot consists of one stressed syllable (one "beat," to use the musical term), usually accompanied by one or two unstressed syllables. We represent a stressed syllable by an accent (´) and an unstressed syllable by a symbol called a breve (˘). Here is an example of a line with four feet:

Whose woóds / these áre / I thínk / I knów

The number of feet in a line gives the line its (Greek-derived) name, and tells you how *wide* the line is. Natural intonation makes you stress some words and leave others unstressed, helping you to see how many beats are in the line. We characterize a line by how many stresses (beats) exist in it: the word "meter" (meaning measure) is the general name for the length of a counted line:

> one beat per line = *monometer* (from Greek meaning "one," as in "monologue");
>
> two beats per line = *dimeter* (from Greek meaning "two," as in "dialogue");
>
> three beats per line = *trimeter* (from Greek meaning "three," as in "triangle");
>
> four beats per line = *tetrameter* (from Greek meaning "four," as in "tetrahedron");
>
> five beats per line = *pentameter* (from Greek meaning "five," as in "Pentagon");
>
> six beats per line = *hexameter* (from Greek meaning "six," as in "hexagram");
>
> seven beats per line = *heptameter* (from Greek meaning "seven," as in "heptathlon");
>
> eight beats per line = *octameter* (from Greek meaning "eight," as in "octopus").

Most poems written in English have lines four or five beats wide. Shakespeare wrote all of his plays in pentameter lines five beats wide (though he also inserted prose and short songs from time to time).

When you are looking to see how many beats are in a line, it helps sometimes to see how many syllables are in the line. Ten-syllable lines tend to have five beats each; eight-syllable lines tend to have four beats each. But it is still natural intonation that tells you where to put the stresses:

> When Í / see bír / ches bénd / to léft / and ríght [ten syllables, five beats]
>
> Gólden / láds and / gírls all / múst [eight syllables, four beats]

Here are samples of all the line-widths. It helps to read these aloud, so that you can hear the beats.

1. *Monometer* (one beat per line, a rare meter), as in the little poem called "Fleas":

Adam
Had 'em.

2. *Dimeter* (two beats), which is likewise rare:

> Take her up tenderly,
> Lift her with care,
> Fashioned so slenderly,
> Young and so fair.
> — THOMAS HOOD, "The Bridge of Sighs"

3. *Trimeter* (three beats):

> It is time that I wrote my will;
> I choose upstanding men
> That climb the streams until
> The fountain leap, and at dawn
> Drop their cast at the side
> Of dripping stone; I declare
> They shall inherit my pride.
> — W. B. YEATS, "The Tower"

4. *Tetrameter* (four beats):

> Whose woods these are I think I know
> His house is in the village though,
> He will not see me stopping here
> To watch his woods fill up with snow.
> — ROBERT FROST, "Stopping by Woods"

5. *Pentameter* (five beats)

> The woods decay, the woods decay and fall,
> The vapours weep their burthens to the ground,
> Man comes and tills the soil and lies beneath,
> And after many a summer dies the swan.
> — ALFRED, LORD TENNYSON, "Tithonus"

6. *Hexameter* (six beats), which is sometimes called an Alexandrine (from the French usage) and which is rare in English verse:

> I will arise and go now, and go to Innisfree,
> And a small cabin build there, of clay and wattles made.
> — W. B. YEATS, "The Lake Isle of Innisfree"

The common meters (line-lengths) have been trimeter, tetrameter, and pentameter, used singly or in combination.

RHYTHM

You have probably noticed that the lilts (swings) in each of the above examples of line-length differ. That is because the lines are written in different rhythms. Two dimeter poems can sound very different from each other because they are written in two different rhythms. You can see this by comparing Hood's "The Bridge of Sighs," given above as an example of dimeter, with Dorothy Parker's satirical poem on suicide, "Résumé," also in dimeter:

Táke her up / ténderly,   Rázors / páin you
Líft her with / cáre,   Rívers are / dámp;
Fáshioned so / slénderly,   Ácids / stáin you;
Yóung and so / fáir.   And drúgs cause / crámp.

To describe the versification of a poem, you have to say not only how wide its lines are, but also what rhythm they are written in. English rhythms are based on *stressed* and *unstressed* syllables. Each stressed syllable with its associated unstressed syllable(s) makes a single unit, which we call a foot.

There are two main kinds of rhythm in English: *rising* rhythms and *falling* rhythms. In a *rising* rhythm, a foot consists of one or more unstressed syllables leading up to a stressed syllable: ˘′ or ˘ ˘′.

Where the yóuth / pined awáy / with desíre
And the pále / virgin shroúd / ed in snów
Aríse / from their gráves / and aspíre
Where my sún / flower wísh / es to gó.
— WILLIAM BLAKE, "Ah Sun-flower"

In a *falling* rhythm, a foot begins with the stressed syllable, which is followed by one or more unstressed syllables: ′˘ or ′˘˘.

Týger, / týger, / búrning / bríght
Ín the / fórests / óf the / níght.
— WILLIAM BLAKE, "The Tyger"

Metrical feet are named according to where their stress appears and how many unstressed syllables they possess. Rising rhythms are either *iambic* (with two syllables, ˘′) or *anapestic* (with three syllables, ˘ ˘′). We speak of an *iamb* or an *iambic foot* when we mean ˘′; an *anapest* or an *anapestic foot* when we mean ˘ ˘′. Falling rhythms are either *trochaic* (with two syllables, ′˘) or *dactylic* (with three syllables, ′˘˘). The corresponding nouns are *trochee* and *dactyl*.

When you read a poem in counted lines, try to see whether the general movement is a rising one or a falling one. In the two examples from Blake given above, "Ah Sun-flower" is written in rising anapestic (three-syllable) feet, and "The Tyger" in falling trochaic (two-syllable) feet.

In each *line* of "Ah Sun-flower" there are three *feet* (because there are three stressed syllables):

Where the yoúth / pined awáy / with desíre

In each *line* of "The Tyger" there are four *feet* (because there are four stressed syllables):

Týger, / týger, / búrning / bríght

If you think of each *stressed* syllable as a musical beat, the lines of "Ah Sun-flower" have three beats each ("and a *one* and a *two* and a *three*"); the lines of "The Tyger" have four beats each (*"one* and *two* and *three* and *four"*).

Feet can shed one or more of their unstressed syllables. You can see that at the end of each line in "The Tyger," an unstressed syllable is "missing." And in "Ah Sun-flower," in the line "Aríse / from their gráves / and aspíre," an unstressed syllable is missing in the first foot, which has only two syllables, "Arise." These irregularities do not occur so often that they destroy the general impression of the metrical scheme underlying the poem.

If you hear these rhythms in your ear as you read, you will soon recognize them. Here are two more examples, to fill our scheme:

I found a dimpled spider, fat and white.
— ROBERT FROST, "Design"

Read aloud, this reveals itself to have five beats (five stressed syllables): "and *one* and *two* and *three* and *four* and *five*." Each of the five units consists of an unstressed syllable followed by a stressed syllable (iambic foot):

I foúnd / a dímp / led spí / der, fát / and whíte.

Listen to Longfellow's description of the original American forest:

This is the forest primeval, the murmuring pines and the hemlocks.
— HENRY WADSWORTH LONGFELLOW, "Evangeline"

Read aloud, this reveals itself to have six beats (six stressed syllables): "*one* and a *two* and a *three* and // a *four* and a *five* and a *six* and." Each foot (except the last, which has shed one unstressed syllable) consists of a stressed syllable followed by two unstressed syllables (dactylic foot):

This is the / fórest prim / éval // the / múrmuring / pínes and
the / hémlocks.

These rising and falling feet occur in lines of different widths.
We have seen, above, trimeter lines ("Ah Sun-flower") and tetrameter
lines ("The Tyger"). We have seen pentameter lines ("Design") and
hexameter lines ("Evangeline"). *A full description of a line describes its*
rhythm and then its width. "Ah Sun-flower" is written in anapestic tri-
meter. "The Tyger" is written in trochaic tetrameter. "Design" is
written in iambic pentameter. "Evangeline" is written in dactylic hex-
ameter.

It is less important that you know these names than that you
recognize a rhythm by ear. Practice tapping out the rhythms above until
they become familiar. Counting out the rhythm and length of a line is
called *scanning* it.

It is often difficult, even impossible, to scan a single line taken by
itself. One line can be scanned two or more ways, depending on the
intonation we give it. The rule of thumb is to look at the other lines
matching it. If they are all five-beat lines, then the dubious line is
probably a five-beat line, too. But do not allow the prevailing rhythm,
when you read a line aloud, to ride roughshod over the sense; the sense
will usually tell you what syllables ought to be stressed.

In all rhythms, some feet are irregular, so that the cadence does not
become intolerably inflexible. Feet of comparable length can freely sub-
stitute for each other. Shakespeare often begins one of his iambic (˘′)
lines with an initial trochaic foot (′˘) to give energy to the line:

Whý is / my verse / so bar / ren of / new pride?

Each of these metrical schemes is merely a grid underlying a line. The
line itself must, by its intonation pattern, indicate the grid (or you cannot
know what the basic rhythm is supposed to be), but it can depart from
the grid in various ways — by substituting a different foot, by having a
light foot called the *pyrrhic* (˘˘) for unimportant words, or a heavy foot
called the *spondee* (′′) for important words, and so on. What you are
asked to do in scanning the line is to see the underlying grid, first of all,
and then to note any departures from it. Poets enjoy varying their
rhythms to accord with dramatic emphasis, tone of voice, and so on.
They also enjoy breaking their lines with a pause in the middle, which
we call a *caesura* and represent with a double slash. An iambic pentameter
line can be broken one or more times:

I grant I never saw a goddess go;
My mistress, // when she walks, // treads on the ground.
And yet, // by heaven, // I think my love as rare
As any she belied with false compare.
— SHAKESPEARE, Sonnet 130

RHYMES AND STANZA-FORMS

Not all counted poetry is written in rhymes. But because lyric began as song (the name "lyric" comes from "lyre"), simple rhyming stanza-forms such as those found in the ballad or the hymn became important in the English tradition. Gradually, as oral poetry gave way to printed poetry (meant to be read rather than sung), stanza-forms of considerable complexity arose. Here are some of the most common rhyming forms in English. When rhyming units are separated by white space, they are called *stanzas*.

1. A pair of rhyming lines is called a *couplet*. Couplets are frequently run together, not separated as stanzas:

While the plowman near at hand,
Whistles o'er the furrowed land,
And the milkmaid singeth blithe,
And the mower whets his scythe,
And every shepherd tells his tale,
Under the hawthorn in the dale.
— JOHN MILTON, "L'Allegro"

These couplets are written in trochaic tetrameter. The rhyme scheme of these lines is indicated thus: *aabbcc.* That is, because the first two lines rhyme ("hand," "land"), they can be indicated by *aa,* and because the next two rhyme, they can be indicated by *bb.* We indicate the *rhyme scheme* by these abbreviated lowercase italicized letters.

The *heroic couplet* is an iambic pentameter couplet that is end-stopped (marked by a heavy pause after the second line of the couplet), and frequently pointed and witty. Alexander Pope and John Dryden used it with brio:

Meanwhile, declining from the noon of day,
The sun obliquely shoots his burning ray;
The hungry judges soon the sentence sign,
And wretches hang that jurymen may dine.
— ALEXANDER POPE, "The Rape of the Lock"

2.   A stanza of three lines is called a *tercet*:

Light the first light of evening, as in a room
In which we sit, and for small reason, think
The world imagined is the ultimate good.
— WALLACE STEVENS,
"Final Soliloquy of the Interior Paramour"

Terza rima is a form of pentameter tercet with interlinked rhymes (*aba bcb cdc* and so on) used by Dante in the *Divine Comedy*. It is difficult to carry off in English, though Shelley used it for his "Ode to the West Wind." Many poets intend an allusion to Dante when they use loosely rhymed pentameter tercets.

3.   A stanza of four lines is called a *quatrain*. The commonest quatrain is the *ballad stanza,* in which the first and third lines are un-rhymed and have four beats, while the second and fourth lines rhyme and have three beats:

It is an ancient Mariner,
And he stoppeth one of three.
"By thy long grey beard and glittering eye,
Now wherefore stopp'st thou me?"
— SAMUEL TAYLOR COLERIDGE,
"The Rime of the Ancient Mariner"

Some tetrameter quatrains are rhymed *abba,* like those in Shakespeare's "The Phoenix and the Turtle" and Tennyson's "In Memoriam." This stanza is generally referred to as the *"In Memoriam" stanza:*

Ring out, wild bells, to the wild sky,
      The flying cloud, the frosty light,
      The year is dying in the night;
Ring out, wild bells, and let him die.

The *heroic quatrain* is an iambic pentameter quatrain, rhyming *abab*:

I know my life's a pain and but a span;
I know my sense is mock'd with everything;
And, to conclude, I know myself a man,
Which is a proud and yet a wretched thing.
— SIR JOHN DAVIES, "Nosce Teipsum"

4.   A stanza of six lines is sometimes called a *sixain* (its French name) or a *sestet.* The commonest sixain rhyme-form is *ababcc.* A pen-

tameter quatrain rhyming this way is called the *"Venus and Adonis" stanza,* from the poem of that name by Shakespeare:

> Look how a bird lies tangled in a net,
> So fast'nd in her arms Adonis lies,
> Pure shame and awed resistance made him fret,
> Which bred more beauty in his angry eyes.
>> Rain added to a river that is rank
>> Perforce will force it overflow the bank.

5. The only common seven-line stanza is *rime royal* (so called because King James I used it) — iambic pentameter rhyming *ababbcc.* This is the meter of many long poems on high themes — Chaucer's *Troilus and Criseyde,* for instance. Spenser uses it for his "Four Hymns":

> For love is a celestial harmony
> Of likely hearts composed of stars' consent,
> Which join together in sweet sympathy,
> To work each other's joy and true content,
> Which they have harbored since their first descent
> Out of their heavenly bowers, where they did see
> And know each other here beloved to be.
>> — EDMUND SPENSER, "Hymn to Love"

6. The best-known eight-line form is *ottava rima* — iambic pentameter rhyming *abababcc.* The final couplet can give this stanza epigrammatic point, and Byron used it with notable wit in his long poem *Don Juan.* Its greatest modern practitioner has been W. B. Yeats:

> Labour is blossoming or dancing where
> The body is not bruised to pleasure soul,
> Nor beauty born out of its own despair,
> Nor blear-eyed wisdom out of midnight oil.
> O chestnut-tree, great-rooted blossomer,
> Are you the leaf, the blossom or the bole?
> O body swayed to music, O brightening glance,
> How can we know the dancer from the dance?
>> — W. B. YEATS, "Among School Children"

7. The best-known nine-line form is the *Spenserian stanza* (so called because Spenser used it in *The Faerie Queene*). Keats adopted it for "The Eve of St. Agnes." All its lines are pentameter, except the last, which is a hexameter. It rhymes in a closely linked way: *ababbcbcc.*

St. Agnes' Eve — Ah, bitter chill it was!
The owl, for all his feathers, was a-cold;
The hare limped trembling through the frozen grass,
And silent was the flock in woolly fold:
Numb were the Beadsman's fingers, while he told
His rosary, and while his frosted breath,
Like pious incense from a censer old,
Seemed taking flight for heaven, without a death,
Past the sweet Virgin's picture, while his prayer he saith.
— JOHN KEATS, "The Eve of St. Agnes"

There are many unnamed stanza-forms, some of them common ones. For instance, an extra line or two is often added to the ballad stanza, to make a five- or six-line stanza. Or a *refrain* (a line repeated after every stanza) can be added to lengthen the ballad quatrain.

TYPES OF RHYMING POEMS

1. The *sonnet* is a fourteen-line pentameter poem. There are two chief forms:

The *Italian (Petrarchan) sonnet* consists of an octave and a sestet. There are embraced rhymes in the octave (the first eight lines): *abbaabba*. The sestet of a Petrarchan sonnet can rhyme in several different ways, but the most common are *cdecde* and (as below) *cdcdee*:

Who will in fairest book of Nature know
    How Virtue may best lodged in beauty be,
    Let him but learn of *Love* to read in thee,
Stella, those fair lines which true goodness show.
There shall he find all vices' overthrow,
    Not by rude force, but sweetest sovereignty
    Of reason, from whose light those nightbirds fly,
That inward sun in thine eyes shineth so.
    And, not content to be Perfection's heir
Thyself, dost strive all minds that way to move,
Who mark in thee what is in thee most fair.
So while thy beauty draws the heart to love,
    As fast thy Virtue bends that love to good.
    "But ah," Desire still cries, "give me some food."
— SIR PHILIP SIDNEY, *Astrophel and Stella,* 71

The *English (Shakespearean) sonnet* consists of three four-line quatrains, alternately rhymed (*ababcdcdefef*), and a couplet, *gg*:

Let me not to the marriage of true minds
Admit impediments. Love is not love
Which alters when it alteration finds,
Or bends with the remover to remove.
O no, it is an ever fixèd mark
That looks on tempests and is never shaken;
It is the star to every wand'ring bark,
Whose worth's unknown, although his height be taken.
Love's not Time's fool, though rosy lips and cheeks
Within his bending sickle's compass come,
Love alters not with his brief hours and weeks,
But bears it out even to the edge of doom.
    If this be error and upon me proved,
    I never writ, nor no man ever loved.

There have been many variations on the two basic sonnet forms. Spenser wrote sonnets that were composed of linked rhymes: *abab bcbc cdcd ee*. Some poets (Herbert, Yeats) have made hybrid sonnets by attaching Petrarchan sestets to Shakespearean octaves, or vice versa. Others, like George Meredith and Stevens, have written sonnet-like poems with thirteen or fifteen lines. The odes of Keats basically form their stanzas by combining a Shakespearean quatrain with a Petrarchan sestet (they vary the length of line and sometimes double a rhyme, but it is clear that their elements come from the two sonnet traditions).

2.   The *sestina* is a pentameter poem consisting of six stanzas of six lines plus a three-line coda (known as the *envoy* or *envoi*). The sestina "rhymes" on six end-words, which must be repeated in each stanza in a controlled order, whereby the last end-word in each stanza becomes the first end-word of the next stanza: *abcdef, fabcde, efabcd, defabc, cdefab, bcdefa*. The envoi must employ two of the end-words in each of its three lines. A good sestina makes this difficult pattern seem natural. The sestina is easier seen than described. Here is one (called "Sestina") by Elizabeth Bishop. The six end-words are "house," "grandmother," "child," "stove," "almanac," and "tears." It may help to know that Bishop was raised by her grandmother, since her father was dead and her mother was confined to an insane asylum:

September rain falls on the house.
In the failing light, the old grandmother
sits in the kitchen with the child
beside the Little Marvel Stove,
reading the jokes from the almanac,
laughing and talking to hide her tears.

She thinks that her equinoctial tears
and the rain that beats on the roof of the house
were both foretold by the almanac,
but only known to a grandmother.
The iron kettle sings on the stove.
She cuts some bread and says to the child,

It's time for tea now; but the child
is watching the teakettle's small hard tears
dance like mad on the hot black stove,
the way the rain must dance on the house.
Tidying up, the old grandmother
hangs up the clever almanac

on its string. Birdlike, the almanac
hovers half open above the child,
hovers above the old grandmother
and her teacup full of dark brown tears.
She shivers and says she thinks the house
feels chilly, and puts more wood in the stove.

It was to be, says the Marvel Stove.
I know what I know, says the almanac.
With crayons the child draws a rigid house
and a winding pathway. Then the child
puts in a man with buttons like tears
and shows it proudly to the grandmother.

But secretly, while the grandmother
busies herself about the stove,
the little moons fall down like tears
from between the pages of the almanac
into the flower bed the child
has carefully placed in the front of the house.

Time to plant tears, says the almanac.
The grandmother sings to the marvelous stove
and the child draws another inscrutable house.

    3.   The *villanelle* is a French form that has been used with notable success by many modern poets, among them Theodore Roethke, William Empson, Dylan Thomas, and Bishop. A villanelle is a poem of five pentameter tercets rhyming *aba,* followed by a pentameter quatrain rhyming *abaa.* In a villanelle, lines 1 and 3 of the first tercet are repeated alternately at the end of each following tercet, and they close the final

quatrain. Again, this is easier seen than described, and in a good villanelle the repetitions are made to seem natural. Here is Dylan Thomas's villanelle "Do Not Go Gentle into That Good Night," a poem he wrote when his father was dying:

> Do not go gentle into that good night,
> Old age should burn and rave at close of day;
> Rage, rage against the dying of the light.
>
> Though wise men at their end know dark is right,
> Because their words had forked no lightning they
> Do not go gentle into that good night.
>
> Good men, the last wave by, crying how bright
> Their frail deeds might have danced in a green bay,
> Rage, rage against the dying of the light.
>
> Wild men who caught and sang the sun in flight,
> And learn, too late, they grieved it on its way,
> Do not go gentle into that good night.
>
> Grave men, near death, who see with blinding sight
> Blind eyes could blaze like meteors and be gay,
> Rage, rage against the dying of the light.
>
> And you, my father, there on the sad height,
> Curse, bless, me now with your fierce tears, I pray.
> Do not go gentle into that good night.
> Rage, rage against the dying of the light.

There are many other rhymed poem-forms, such as the *rondeau,* the *ballade,* the *pantoum.* A poet using one of the rhymed poem-forms expects the reader to recall the tradition of such forms.

4. The *ode* in English is usually a stanzaic poem, but it has no set form. An ode is defined by its content: it is a poem of a lofty or sublime sort, often using the figure of speech called *apostrophe,* which is an address to some divine or quasi-divine person or thing. "O wild West Wind," says Shelley; "Thou still unravished bride of quietness," says Keats addressing the Grecian urn.

COUNTED VERSE THAT DOES NOT RHYME

The most common form of counted unrhymed verse is *blank verse,* unrhymed iambic pentameter lines. This is the verse of Shakespeare's plays and of Milton's epic poem, *Paradise Lost:*

That space the evil one abstracted stood
From his own evil, and for the time remained
Stupidly good, of enmity disarmed,
Of guile, of hate, of envy, of revenge.

Blank verse can also be used in a lyric, as Coleridge uses it in his poem "Frost at Midnight":

Therefore all seasons shall be sweet to thee,
Whether the summer clothe the general earth
With greenness, or the redbreast sit and sing
Betwixt the tufts of snow on the bare branch.

Most of the unrhymed verse in English is blank verse, though poets have also written unrhymed four-beat poems that imitate Anglo-Saxon meter. Some poets have experimented with stanzas of unrhymed verse in imitation of Greek and Latin verse (which did not rhyme, but depended on a quantitative system contrasting long vowels with short vowels). Here are two stanzas of Thomas Campion's "Rose-Cheeked Laura," an imitation of the Greek meter called, after the poet Sappho, *sapphic*. The first three lines have four beats each, the fourth line two beats:

Róse-cheéked Laúra, cóme,
Síng thou smoóthly wíth thy beaúty's
Sílent músic, eíther óther
        Sweétly grácing.

Lovely forms do flow
From concent divinely framed;
Heav'n is music, and thy beauty's
        Birth is heavenly.

Every so often a new poet will once again imitate classical unrhymed forms.

Free Verse

Free verse — verse in which the lines are of different widths, and which does not rhyme in any regular way — was invented by poets who had been brought up on rhymed and counted verse. Poets like Whitman, Pound, Eliot, Stevens, Williams, Lowell, and Bishop all began by writing conventional verse. Whitman was drawn to free verse because he saw it as a primitive, "bardic" form. Eliot wrote it in imitation of the

French poet Jules Laforgue. Pound wrote it in an attempt to achieve poetic effects he thought inhered in the Chinese ideogram. Williams and Stevens adopted it as a way to free themselves from the hold of English poets such as Keats. But behind their free verse there lurked always the shadow of counted verse. Eliot's "The Love Song of J. Alfred Prufrock" keeps threatening to turn into regular pentameter. Pound's largely free-verse "Cantos" include counted and rhymed segments.

The history of free verse is not yet entirely understood. The United States was a more hospitable environment for it than England, and a nativist wish to throw off inherited English forms certainly motivated many American poets. The unit of free verse seems to be the breath: there is a breath limit to the long line of free verse (reached by Whitman and Ginsberg, to give two notable examples). The theoretical appeal of free verse is that it admits an element of chance; it offers a model not of a teleological or providential universe but of an *aleatory* one, where the casual, rather than the fated, holds sway.

Free verse must justify its reasons for breaking a line here rather than there. If we look at a small free-verse poem, William Carlos Williams's "The Red Wheelbarrow," we must ask why the lines break where they do:

So much depends
upon

a red wheel
barrow

glazed with rain
water

beside the white
chickens

We might notice that in each little "stanza" the second line has only two syllables. This gives symmetry to the poem. The word "upon" literally hangs off the word "depends," acting out the meaning of something which depends (Latin: *dependere*, "to hang from") on something else. The red "wheel" turns into a "wheelbarrow" as we turn the line. Rain turns into rainwater, in the same way. After the inorganic wheelbarrow and rainwater, we may expect an inorganic object to follow the word "white" — say "the white / fence." Instead, the scene comes alive with chickens.

This very mannered little poem says that if the eye didn't see something inviting in the landscape (the shiny glaze the rain has put on the redness of the wheelbarrow; the composition of the still wheelbarrow and the living chickens; the contrast of red and white), there would be nothing to write about. "So much depends" on there being something out there to gratify and focus the eye. When we understand the poem, we understand its line-breaks. A free-verse poem that doesn't justify its line-breaks hardly deserves the name "poem."

Summary

When you come across a new poem, look at the way it displays itself on the page. Is it a skinny poem or a wide poem? A short poem or a long one? Are all the lines the same length, or are some shorter than others? Does it rhyme? Does it have stanzas?

Think of the look of the poem as its body. Is it a symmetrical body or a ragged body? A solid-looking body or an emaciated one?

As you read it aloud and listen to its rhythms, feel what it is telling you. Is it serious or even ponderous? Or does it move with a lilt and a skip? Does it change its manner of walking, from indolent to hurried? Does it manifest leisure or anxiety in its rhythms?

These are questions to ask even before you begin to note a rhyme scheme or count how many beats there are in a line. After you have done the technical noticing and counting, ask yourself how these formal features match up with the sentiments and emotions that the poem is expressing. Do the formal features align with those sentiments, or do they contradict them? It is always worthwhile to pay attention to the technical work the poet has done on the external form of the poem; it is, after all, the body the poet has chosen to live in for a determined period.

For a more complete survey of metrical forms, see Paul Fussell, *Poetic Meter and Poetic Form* (New York: Random House, 1965; revised 1979); or John Hollander, *Rhyme's Reason* (New Haven, Conn., Yale University Press, 1981). For fuller definitions of terms used here, see the *Princeton Encyclopedia of Poetry and Poetics*, ed. Alex Preminger et al. (Princeton, N.J.: Princeton University Press, 1965; rpt. 1993).

Appendix 2. On Grammar

A familiarity with grammatical terms can help you to analyze and to describe poetry. This appendix provides a brief review of some of the most common and useful grammatical terms.

Noun

A word that names a person, place, thing, or idea. Examples: "Adam," "garden," "chair," "destiny." In short, a noun names an *essence*.

Adjective

A word that tells you something about that essence. An adjective modifies a noun by limiting or describing it. Examples: "the *early* bird," "a *false* alarm." An adjective expresses something present with or connected to a noun, but not essential: "a *red* wheelbarrow" (not all wheelbarrows are red). Adjectives are the chief resource of descriptive language, as when Shakespeare says (Sonnet 129) that lust is "perjur'd, murderous, bloody, full of blame, / Savage, extreme, rude, cruel, not to trust." The plainness of nouns is fleshed out by adjectives; and the complexity of life is such that poems need a wealth of adjectives to describe their essential nouns.

Pronoun

A word that stands in for a noun. Pronouns can be used as subjects (nominative case, as in "On a cloud *I* saw a child") or as objects (objective case, as in "And he laughing said to *me*"). In what follows I'll give the objective case in brackets after the nominative case.

The *first-person singular* is "I" [objective: "me"]; the *first-person plural* is "we" ["us"].

The modern *second-person pronoun* is "you" in both the singular and plural, nominative and objective, though in the past it was more complex. Then, the second-person singular was "thou" ["thee"], and the plural was "ye." "Thou" was used both in familiar address and in an exalted form of address to God or a monarch; over time, "you" took its place.

The *third-person singular* pronouns are "he" ["him"], "she" ["her"], and "it"; the plural is "they" ["them"].

A change in person ("I" to "you") or in number ("I" to "we") in a poem is always of profound significance, since, on the general principle of inertia, a speaker tends to continue in the same person rather than change, unless the change is somehow provoked. In the poem "In

Memory of Eva Gore-Booth and Con Markiewicz," Yeats himself changes significantly from "I" to "we," as he finally makes common cause with the sisters he had begun by opposing; and his reference to the sisters changes from "one or the other" (third-person, people other than the poet) to "you" (people he addresses) to "we" (part of a group which also contains the poet):

> Many a time *I* think to seek
> *One or the other* out. . . .

> Dear shadows, now *you* know it all. . . .

> *We* the great gazebo built. . . .

A reader who misses the changes in person and number here misses the essential drama of the poem, as the poet changes his mind about the sisters and his relation to them.

Verb

A word that usually conveys either action ("My mother *bore* me in the southern wild") or state ("And I *am* black"). Verbs may be

> *Linking* verbs, which join two things that are equivalent ("He *seems* tired"; "I *will become* a teacher"; "Mary *is* a doctor");
>
> *Transitive* verbs, which take objects both direct and indirect ("I *gave* him the book"); or
>
> *Intransitive* verbs, which do not take an object ("The building *fell* down").

Verbs can appear in two *voices:*

> *Active:* "I do this."
>
> *Passive:* "This is done to me."

They can take on different *tenses* (past, present, future, and so on):

> *Simple present:* "I *sing* of heaven."
>
> *Present of habitual action:* "Whenever it *rains,* I *take* my umbrella."
>
> *Present of perpetual truth:* "Water *boils* at 212°F."
>
> *Present of state:* "I *am* a lawyer."

Present progressive: "It *is raining.*"

Simple past: "I *knew* him, Horatio."

Compound past: "I *have known* him a long time."

Past progressive: "It *was snowing.*"

Pluperfect: "I *had known* him for several years before I met his wife."

Simple future: "I *will call* him tomorrow."

Future perfect: "I *will have called* him by Wednesday."

Future progressive: "I *will be telling* this with a sigh."

They can appear in different *moods* (statement, question, wish, and so on):

Indicative (states an assertion): "I *like* him."

Interrogative (asks a question): "*Do* you *like* him?"

Imperative (gives a command): "*Do* this."

Subjunctive (often contrary to fact or hypothetical): "If I *were to do* this, I would be prosecuted."

Optative (wish): "Oh, if I *could* only *do* [*have done*] this!"

Hortatory (enjoining something): "*Let us kiss* and part."

Conditional: "I *should like* to come if you *would let* me."

Poems can achieve multiple effects by changing tenses and moods as they go along.

Adverb

A word that characterizes (limits or describes) a verb, just as an adjective characterizes a noun. Adverbs answer the questions "Where?" "How?" "In what manner?" "When?" "Why?" and so on. Examples: "Till noon we *quietly* sailed on"; "my collar mounting *firmly* to my chin." Since verbs, like nouns, tend to be bare things, the poet uses adverbs to put a halo of circumstance around the verbs of the poem. Verbs are also amplified by adverbial phrases: "From you have I been absent *in the spring.*"

Appendix 3. On Speech Acts

There are numberless speech acts in which a lyric speaker may engage. The list that follows is merely a sampling of common ones in lyric. It is always a good idea to name the successive speech acts in a poem. Does it begin with an apology? Is that followed by a plea? Is that followed by a claim? Is that followed by a boast? This classifying helps you to track the emotions that structure a poem.

ACKNOWLEDGING	The darkness drops again, but now I know. . . .
ADDRESS	Old trooper, I see your child's red crayon pass.
ADMISSION	Alas, 'tis true, I have gone here and there, And made myself a motley to the view.
APOLOGY	Sweet Love of youth, forgive, if I forget thee.
APOSTROPHE	O wild West Wind!
BANISHING	Hence, loathèd Melancholy!
BOAST	Not marble, nor the gilded monuments Of princes, shall outlive this powerful rhyme.
CELEBRATION	I celebrate myself, and sing myself.
CLAIM	Mine — by the Right of the White Election!
COMMAND	Irish poets, learn your trade, Sing whatever is well made.
CONJECTURE	Thou mayst be false, and yet I know it not.
CONSOLATION	Fear no more the heat o' the sun.
DEFINITION	Remorse — is Memory — awake —
DESCRIPTION	No cloud, no relique of the sunken day Distinguishes the West.
DIALOGUE	Does the road wind uphill all the way? Yes, to the very end.
DREAMING	I dream of a Ledaean body, bent Above a sinking fire.
EXCLAMATION	What a piece of work is a man!

EXHORTATION	Be shellèd, eyes, with double dark And find the uncreated light.
EXPOSTULATION	Up, up, my friend, and quit your books!
GENERALIZATION	All this the world well knows, yet none knows well To shun the heaven that leads men to this hell.
IMPRECATION	For God's sake hold your tongue, and let me love.
INSTRUCTION	He who binds to himself a joy Does the wingèd life destroy.
INVITATION	Come live with me and be my love.
INVOCATION	But come, thou goddess fair and free.
LAMENT	Alas! I have nor hope nor health.
NARRATION	
PRESENT	It is an ancient Mariner And he stoppeth one of three.
PAST	I wandered lonely as a cloud.
HABITUAL	For oft, when on my couch I lie . . . They flash upon that inward eye.
HISTORICAL	Calvert and Wilson, Blake and Claude, Prepared a peace for the people of God.
OATH	I will not harm her, by all saints I swear.
PLEA	Say, may I be for aye thy vassal blest?
PRAYER	Mine, O thou Lord of life, send my roots rain.
PROPHECY	Therefore all seasons shall be sweet to thee.
QUESTION	Did he who made the Lamb make thee?
REBUTTAL	Love's not Time's fool.
REMINISCENCE	I was thy neighbor once, thou rugged Pile!
REQUEST	Permit me voyage, love, into your hands.
RESOLVE	Despair I will not.
RETRACTION	But I am by her death (which word wrongs her) . . .

RHETORICAL QUESTION	O chestnut-tree, great-rooted blossomer, Are you the leaf, the blossom, or the bole?
SCORNING	How vainly men themselves amaze To win the palm, the oak, the bays.

SELF-BLAME	I see
	The lost are like this, and their scourge to
	    be
	As I am mine, their sweating selves, but
	    worse.

SELF-CORRECTION	Alas, but Morrison fell young: He never fell, thou fall'st, my toungue. He stood, a soldier to the last right end.
SELF-PRESENTATION	I am the mower Damon.
SPELL	No exorciser harm thee! Nor no witchcraft charm thee!
SUPPOSITION	Had we but world enough, and time.

SURMISE	I cannot see what flowers are at my
	    feet . . .
	But, in embalmèd darkness, guess each
	    sweet.

VOW	Yes, I will be thy priest.

Appendix 4. On Rhetorical Devices

These devices, sometimes called "figures of speech," appear in all speech and writing (you can find them in advertising, political speeches, and newspapers, as well as in essays, letters, and poems). It helps, if you wish to give a brief description of what a writer is doing at a given moment, to know some of these shorthand terms for frequent practices.

ALTERNATIVE ORDERING	A man that looks on glass, On it may stay his eye, Or, if he pleaseth, through it pass, And then the heaven espy.
ANALOGY *(comparison of A and B)*	No more be grieved at that which thou hast done: Roses have thorns, and silver fountains mud.
ANAPHORA *(repetition of opening word)*	All shuffle there, all cough in ink, All wear the carpet with their shoes, All think what other people think; All know the man their neighbor knows.
ANTICLIMAX	In silk, in crepes, in Garters, and in rags.
ANTITHESIS *(opposition of A and B)*	For I have sworn thee fair, and thought thee bright, Who art as dark as hell, as black as night.
APPOSITION *(list of different formulations of the same thing)*	The Mind of Man, My haunt, and the main region of my song.
CATALOGUE	The leaden-eyed shark, the walrus, the turtle, the hairy sea-leopard.
CHIASMUS *(an X-like arrangement)*	By brooks too broad for leaping The lightfoot boys are laid; The rose-lipt girls are sleeping In fields where roses fade. [brooks : boys :: girls : fields]
HIERARCHICAL ORDERING	Such sweet neglect more taketh me Than all th' adulteries of art.
METAPHOR *(comparison without "like" or "as")*	Church bells beyond the stars heard, the soul's blood, The land of spices; something understood.

METONYMY
(assemblage by parts)

Four beating wings, two beaks, a swirling
    mass.

ONOMATOPOEIA
(imitative sound)

And murmuring of innumerable bees.

PARADOX
*(union of dissimilar
qualities)*

There is in God, some say,
A deep but dazzling darkness.

PARALLELISM

These are thy wonders, Lord of Power . . .
These are thy wonders, Lord of Love.

PERIPHRASIS
(circumlocution)

The Peer now spreads the glittering forfex
    wide
[= opens scissors]

PERSONIFICATION
*(an abstraction made
into a person)*

Love is swift of foot,
Love's a man of war.

PUN
*(a play on two
meanings of one
word)*

Therefore I lie with her, and she with me,
And in our faults by lies we flattered be.

QUOTATION

My flesh began unto my soul in pain,
"Sicknesses cleave my bones."

SIMILE
*(comparison with
"like" or "as")*

Like as the waves make toward the peb-
    bled shore,
So do our minutes hasten to their end.

SYNECDOCHE
*(use of the part for
the whole)*

Diadems — drop — and Doges — surren-
    der.

ZEUGMA
*(two dissimilar ob-
jects of same verb)*

Or stain her honor, or her new brocade.

Appendix 5. On Lyric Subgenres

This is a summary of the kinds of poems that lyric poets return to most frequently. It is convenient to be able to name a poem by its kind, because you can then compare it to others of the same kind.

ADDRESS TO THE READER	Pray thee, take care, that tak'st my book.
BALLAD	There lived a wife at Usher's well, / And a wealthy wife was she; / She had three stout and stalwart sons, / And sent them o'er the sea.
CHILD'S POEM	"The Little Black Boy" (Blake)
DAWN POEM *(aubade)*	Get up! get up for shame! the blooming morn / Upon her wings presents the god unshorn.
DEATHBED POEM	I heard a Fly buzz — when I died —
DEBATE-POEM	*Body* / O who shall me deliver whole / From bonds of this tyrannic soul? . . . / *Soul* / What magic could me thus confine / Within another's grief to pine?
ECHO-POEM	Then tell me, what is that supreme delight? Light. / Light to the mind, what shall the will enjoy? Joy.
EKPHRASIS *(poem on an art object)*	"Ode on a Grecian Urn" (Keats)
ELEGY	Felix Randal the farrier, O is he dead then, my duty all ended?
EMBLEM-POEM *(allegorical object)*	"The Sick Rose" (Blake)
EPIGRAM *(short, pointed poem)*	I am his Highness' dog at Kew: / And pray, good sir, whose dog are you?
EPITAPH	Underneath this stone doth lie / All of beauty that could die.

EPITHALAMION (*wedding song*)	And evermore they *Hymen Hymen* sing, That al the woods them answer and theyr eccho ring.
HYMN	Jerusalem, Jerusalem, Lift up your gates and sing, Hosanna in the highest . . .
INSCRIPTION	I the poet William Yeats . . . Restored this tower for my wife George: And may these characters remain When all is ruin once again.
LETTER	This is my letter to the world That never wrote to me.
LOVER'S COM-PLAINT	And wilt thou leave me thus?
LULLABY	Lullay, lullay, thou tiny child.
MUSE-POEM	"The Solitary Reaper" (Wordsworth)
NOCTURNE	'Tis the year's midnight, and it is the day's.
PASTORAL (*rustic poem*)	The shepherds' swains shall dance and sing For thy delight each May morning.
POLITICAL POEM	"Easter, 1916" (Yeats)
PRAISE-POEM	Shall I compare thee to a summer's day? Thou art more lovely and more temperate.
QUEST-POEM	"The Pilgrimage" (Herbert)
RELIGIOUS POEM	I saw eternity the other night.
ROMANCE (*fairy-tale poem*)	"The Eve of St. Agnes" (Keats)
SEASONAL POEM	Sumer is icumen in, Lhude sing cuccu!
SELF-REFLEXIVE POEM	I sing of brooks, of blossoms, birds, and bowers.
SHAPED POEM	"Easter Wings" (Herbert)
SONG	It was a lover and his lass, With a hey and a ho and a hey nonny no . . .
TWIN POEMS	"The Lamb" and "The Tyger" (Blake)
VALEDICTION	Adieu, farewell earth's bliss.

VARIATIONS ON	"Thirteen Ways of Looking at a Black-
A THEME	bird" (Stevens)

There are many other such that one could name: the *bird poem,* the *eclogue* (a dialogue of shepherds), the *georgic* (a poem on farming), the *testament* (a poem making a will), the *conversation poem* (a poem of a middle, or familiar, style recounting a conversation among friends), and so on. The essential thing is to realize that almost any poem is a repeat of a preceding genre, perhaps an answer to it, perhaps a revision of it. Thinking "What kind of a lyric is this?" makes you more aware of its place in a genre tradition, and of its response to that tradition.

Acknowledgments (*continued from p. iv*)

A. R. Ammons, "Easter Morning" from *A Coast of Trees* by A. R. Ammons. Copyright © 1981 by A. R. Ammons. Reprinted by permission of W. W. Norton & Company, Inc. "The City Limits" copyright © 1971 by A. R. Ammons, from *The Selected Poems, Expanded Edition* by A. R. Ammons. Reprinted by permission of W. W. Norton & Company, Inc.

John Ashbery, "Paradoxes and Oxymorons" from *Shadow Train* (New York: Viking, Penguin, 1981). Copyright © 1980, 1981 by John Ashbery. "Street Musicians" from *Houseboat Days* (New York: Viking Penguin, 1977.) Copyright © 1975, 1976, 1977 by John Ashbery. "The Painter" from *Some Trees* (New Haven: Yale University Press, 1956). Copyright © 1956 by John Ashbery. Reprinted by permission of Georges Borchardt, Inc. for the author.

W. H. Auden, "As I Walked Out One Evening" and "Musée des Beaux Arts" from *W. H. Auden: Collected Poems,* edited by Edward Mendelson. Copyright 1940 and renewed 1968 by W. H. Auden. Reprinted by permission of Faber and Faber Limited.

John Berryman, Dream Songs 4, 45, 384 and "Henry sats in de bar & was odd" from *The Dream Songs* © 1959, 1962, 1964, 1965, 1966, 1967, 1968, 1969 by John Berryman. Reprinted with permission of Farrar, Straus & Giroux, Inc.

Frank Bidart, "To My Father" and "Ellen West" from *In the Western Night: Collected Poems 1965–1990* (Farrar, Straus & Giroux, Inc., 1990). Reprinted with permission of Farrar, Straus & Giroux, Inc.

Elizabeth Bishop, "At the Fishhouses," "Brazil, January 1, 1502," "Crusoe in England," "One Art," "Poem," "Sestina," and "The Fish" from *Elizabeth Bishop: The Complete Poems 1927–1979* © 1979, 1983 by Alice Helen Methfessel. Reprinted with permission of Farrar, Straus & Giroux, Inc.

Michael Blumenthal, "A Marriage" from *Against Romance* by Michael Blumenthal. Copyright © 1987 by Michael Blumenthal. Used by permission of Viking Penguin, a division of Penguin Books USA, Inc. "Wishful Thinking" from *Days We Would Rather Know* (Viking Penguin, 1984). Reprinted by permission of the author.

Anne Bradstreet, "A Letter to Her Husband" from *Poems of Anne Bradstreet.* Copyright © 1969 by Dover Publications, Inc.

Lucie Brock-Broido, "Carrowmore" from *The Master Letters* by Lucie Brock-Broido. Copyright © 1995 by Lucie Brock-Broido. Reprinted by permission of Alfred A Knopf Inc. "Domestic Mysticism" from *A Hunger* by Lucie Brock-Broido. Copyright © 1988 by Lucie Brock-Broido. Reprinted by permission of Alfred A Knopf Inc.

Gwendolyn Brooks, "Kitchenette Building," "The Bean Eaters," "The Mother," and "We Real Cool" from *Blacks*. Copyright © 1991 by Gwendolyn Brooks. Reprinted by permission of the poet.

Lorna Dee Cervantes, "Refugee Ship," reprinted with permission from the publisher of *A Decade of Hispanic Literature: An Anniversery Anthology* (Arte Público Press-University of Houston, 1982). "Poem for the Young White Man Who Asked Me How I, An Intelligent Well-Read Person Could Believe in the War Between Races" and "Poema para los Californias Muertos" from *Emplumada*, by Lorna Dee Cervantes, © 1981. Reprinted by permission of the University of Pittsburgh Press.

Marilyn Chin, "Altar" and "Autumn Leaves," first published in *The Phoenix Gone, the Terrace Empty* by Marilyn Chin (Milkweed Editions, 1994). Copyright © 1994 by Marilyn Chin. Reprinted by permission from Milkweed Editions.

Amy Clampitt, "A Procession at Candlemas" from The *Kingfisher* by Amy Clampitt. Copyright © 1983 by Amy Clampitt. Reprinted by permission of Alfred A Knopf Inc.

Henri Cole, "40 Days and 40 Nights" from *The Look of Things* by Henri Cole. Copyright © 1994 by Henri Cole. Reprinted by permission of Alfred A Knopf Inc.

Hart Crane, "Proem: To Brooklyn Bridge" and "The Broken Tower" from *Complete Poems of Hart Crane* edited by Marc Simon. Copyright 1933, © 1958, 1966 by Liveright Publishing Corporation. Copyright © 1986 by Marc Simon. Reprinted by permission of Liveright Publishing Corporation.

Robert Creeley, "A Marriage" from *The Collected Poems of Robert Creeley*, University of California Press, 1982. Reprinted by permission of the University of California Press.

Countee Cullen, "Heritage" and "Incident" from *On These I Stand*, 1925. Reprinted by permission of the Amistad Research Center. Copyright © The Amistad Research Center, Tulane University, New Orleans, Louisiana. Administered by JJKR Associates, New York, New York.

E. E. Cummings, "Anyone lived in a pretty how town," "in Just-," "may I feel said he," and "r-p-o-p-h-e-s-s-a-g-r" are reprinted from *Complete Poems: 1904–1962* by E. E. Cummings, edited by George J. Firmage, by permission of Liveright Publishing Corporation. Copyright © 1923, 1935, 1940, 1951, 1963, 1968, 1991 by the Trustees for the E. E. Cummings Trust. Copyright © 1976, 1978 by George James Firmage.

Emily Dickinson, "A narrow fellow in the grass," "After great pain, a formal feeling comes," "Because I could not stop for death ," "I like a look of Agony," "My life had stood — a Loaded Gun — ," "Much Madness is divinest Sense — ," "Success is counted sweetest," "Wild Nights — Wild Nights!," "I heard a Fly buzz — when I died," "I'm Nobody! Who are you?," "Safe in their alabaster chambers" (1859 and 1861 versions), "The Heart asks Pleasure — first — ," "The Brain — is wider than the Sky — ," "The Soul selects her own Society," and "There's a certain Slant of Light" used by permission of the Publishers and Trustees of Amherst College from *The Poems of Emily Dickinson,* Thomas H. Johnson, ed., Cambridge, MA: The Belknap Press of Harvard University Press, Copyright © 1951, 1955, 1979, 1983 by the President and Fellows of Harvard College. All rights reserved. Also from *The Complete Poems of Emily Dickinson* edited by Thomas H. Johnson. Copyright 1929 by Martha Dickinson Bianchi; copyright © renewed 1957 by Mary L. Hampson. By permission of Little, Brown and Company.

Rita Dove, "Adolescence — II," "Dusting," "Parsley," and "Wingfoot Lake" from *Selected Poems* by Rita Dove (Random House), copyright © 1993 by Rita Dove. Reprinted by permission of the author. "Flash Cards" from *Grace Notes* by Rita Dove. Copyright © 1989 by Rita Dove. Reprinted by permission of the author and W. W. Norton & Company, Inc.

T. S. Eliot, "Marina," "Preludes," "Sweeney Among the Nightingales," and "The Love Song of J. Alfred Prufrock" from *Collected Poems 1909–1962* by T. S. Eliot, copyright © 1963. Reprinted by permission of Faber and Faber Limited.

Louise Erdrich, "The Strange People," "I Was Sleeping Where the Black Oaks Move," and "Windigo" from *Jacklight* by Louise Erdrich. Copyright © 1984 by Louise Erdrich. Reprinted by permission of Henry Holt and Co., Inc.

•

Robert Frost, "Birches," "Design," "Mending Wall," "Stopping by Woods on a Snowy Evening," "The Road Not Taken," and "The Gift Outright" from *The Poetry of Robert Frost,* edited by Edward Connery Lathem. Copyright 1936, 1942, 1951 by Robert Frost. Copyright © 1964, 1970 by Lesley Frost Ballantine. Copyright 1923 © 1969 by Henry Holt and Co., Inc. Reprinted by permission of Henry Holt and Co., Inc.

James Galvin, "Independence Day, 1956: A Fairy Tale" from *Lethal Frequencies* © 1995 by James Galvin. Reprinted by permission of Copper Canyon Press, PO Box 271, Port Townsend, WA 98368. Originally published in *The New Yorker.*

Allen Ginsberg, "America" and "Sunflower Sutra" from *Collected Poems 1947–1980* by Allen Ginsberg. Copyright © 1955 by Allen Ginsberg. Copyright renewed. Reprinted by permission of HarperCollins Publishers, Inc.

Louise Glück, "All Hallows" and "The School Children" from *The House on Marshland.* Copyright © 1975 by Louise Glück. First published by The Ecco Press in 1975. Contract requires additional contract for each reprint. "Mock Orange" from *The Triumph of Achilles.* Copyright © 1985 by Louise Glück. First published by The Ecco Press in 1985. "The White Lilies" from *The Wild Iris.* Copyright © 1992 by Louise Glück. First published by The Ecco Press in 1992.

Jorie Graham, "Of Forced Sightes and Trusty Ferefulness" and "San Sepolcro" from *Erosion* by Jorie Graham. Copyright © 1983 by Princeton University Press. Reprinted by permission of Princeton University Press. "Soul Says" from *Region of Unlikeness* by Jorie Graham. Copyright © 1991 by Jorie Graham. First published by The Ecco Press in 1991. "What the End Is For" from *The End of Beauty.* Copyright © 1987 by Jorie Graham. First published by The Ecco Press in 1987.

Thom Gunn, "My Sad Captains" from *My Sad Captains* (Faber and Faber, 1961). "The Man with Night Sweats" from *The Man with Night Sweats* (Faber and Faber, 1992). Reprinted with permission of Faber and Faber Limited.

H. D., "Helen" and "Oread" from *Collected Poems, 1912–1944.* Copyright © 1982 by The Estate of Hilda Doolitle. Reprinted by permission of New Directions Publishing Corp.

Thomas Hardy, "Afterwards," "Channel Firing," "The Convergence of the Twain," "The Darkling Thrush," and "The Ruined Maid." Reprinted with permission of Simon & Schuster from *The Complete Poems of Thomas Hardy,* edited by James Gibson. Copyright © 1976 by Macmillan London Ltd.

Joy Harjo, "Santa Fe" from *In Mad Love & War* © 1990 by Joy Harjo, Wesleyan University Press by permission of University Press of New England.

Michael S. Harper, "American History" from *Dear John, Dear Coltrane* © Michael S. Harper 1970, 1985. Reprinted by permission of the author. "Nightmare Begins Responsibility" copyright 1975 by Michael S. Harper. Used with permission of the University of Illinois Press.

Robert Hayden, "Frederick Douglass," copyright © 1966 by Robert Hayden, "Mourning Poem for the Queen of Sunday" copyright © 1975, 1972, 1966 by Robert Hayden, "Night, Death, Mississippi" copyright © 1975, 1972, 1966 by Robert Hayden, "Those Winter Sundays" copyright © 1966 by Robert Hayden, from *Angle of Ascent: New and Selected Poems* by Robert Hayden. Reprinted by permission of Liveright Publishing Corporation.

Seamus Heaney, "Bogland," "From the Frontier of Writing," "Mid-Term Break," "Punishment," and "Terminus" from *Seamus Heaney: Selected Poems 1966–*

1987. Copyright © 1990. Reprinted with permission of Farrar, Straus & Giroux, Inc.

Garrett Kaoru Hongo, "The Hongo Store" from *Yellow Light* ©1982 by Garrett Kaoru Hongo, Wesleyan University Press by permission of the University Press of New England.

A. E. Housman, "Loveliest of Trees" and "With Rue My Heart is Laden" from *The Collected Poems of A. E. Housman.* Copyright 1939, 1940 by Holt, Rinehart, and Winston, Inc. Copyright © 1967 by Robert E. Symons. Reprinted by permission of Henry Holt and Co., Inc.

Langston Hughes, "Genius Child," "Harlem," "High to Low," "I, Too," " Me and the Mule," " Suicide's Note," "The Weary Blues," "Theme for English B," and " World War II" from *Collected Poems* by Langston Hughes. Copyright © 1994 by the Estate of Langston Hughes. Reprinted by permission of Alfred A Knopf Inc.

Randall Jarrell, "The Death of the Ball Turret Gunner" from *The Complete Poems* by Randall Jarrell. Copyright © 1945 and renewal copyright by Mrs. Randall Jarrell. Reprinted with permission of Farrar, Straus & Giroux, Inc.

Robinson Jeffers, "Shine, Perishing Republic" from *Selected Poetry* by Robinson Jeffers. Copyright 1925 and renewed 1953 by Robinson Jeffers. Reprinted by permission of Alfred A Knopf Inc.

Etheridge Knight, "A Poem for Myself" from *Poems from Prison* (Broadside Press © 1966). Reprinted by permission of Broadside Press.

Kenneth Koch, "Variations on a Theme by William Carlos Williams" from *Thank You and Other Poems* © 1962. Reprinted by permission of the author.

Yusef Komunyakaa, "Boat People" and "Facing It" from *Dien Cai Dau* © 1988 by Yuself Komunyakaa, "My Father's Loveletters" from *Magic City* © 1992 by Yuself Komunyakaa, Wesleyan University Press by permission of the University Press of New England.

Philip Larkin, "High Windows," "Mr. Bleaney," "Talking in Bed," and "This Be the Verse" from *Philip Larkin: Collected Poems*, edited by Anthony Thwaite. Copyright © 1989. "Reasons for Attendance" by Philip Larkin is reprinted from *The Less Deceived* by permission of The Marvell Press, England.

D. H. Lawrence, "Bavarian Gentians" and "The English Are So Nice!" by D. H. Lawrence, from *The Complete Poems of D. H. Lawrence* by D. H. Lawrence, edited by V. de Sola Pinto & F. W. Roberts. Copyright © 1964, 1971 by Angelo Ravagli and C. M. Weekley, Executors of the Estate of Frieda Lawrence Ravagli. Used by permission of Viking Penguin, a division of Penguin Books USA, Inc.

Li-Young Lee, "The Interrogation" copyright © 1990 by Li-Young Lee. Reprinted from *The City in Which I Love You*, by Li-Young Lee, with the permission of BOA Editions, Ltd., 92 Park Ave., Brockport, NY, 14420.

Denise Levertov, "The Ache of Marriage" and "O Taste and See" from *Poems 1960–1967.* Copyright © 1966, 1964 by Denise Levertov. Reprinted by permission of New Directions Publishing Corp.

Audre Lorde, "Hanging Fire" from *The Black Unicorn* by Audre Lorde. Copyright © 1978 by Audre Lorde. Reprinted by permission of W. W. Norton & Company, Inc.

Robert Lowell, "Epilogue" from *Day by Day* (Farrar, Straus & Giroux, 1977). "For the Union Dead" from *For the Union Dead* (Farrar, Straus & Giroux, 1964)."The March 1" from *History* (Farrar, Straus & Giroux, 1973)."Sailing

Home from Rapallo" and "Skunk Hour" from *Life Studies*. Copyright © 1956, 1959 by Robert Lowell. Renewal copyright © 1987 by Harriet Lowell. Reprinted by permission of Farrar, Straus & Giroux Inc.

Archibald MacLeish, "Ars Poetica" from *Collected Poems 1917–1982* by Archibald MacLeish. Copyright © 1985 by The Estate of Archibald MacLeish. Reprinted by permission of Houghton Mifflin Co. All rights reserved.

James Merrill, "An Upward Look" from *A Scattering of Salts* by James Merrill. Copyright © 1995 by James Merrill. Reprinted by permission of Alfred A. Knopf Inc. "The Broken Home" from *Selected Poems: 1946–1985* by James Merrill. Copyright © 1995 by James Merrill. Reprinted by permission of Alfred A Knopf Inc.

W. S. Merwin, "For a Coming Extinction," "For the Anniversary of My Death" and "The Asians Dying" from *The Lice* © 1967 by W. S. Merwin. Reprinted by permission of Georges Borchardt, Inc.

Marianne Moore, "Poetry" "The Steeple-Jack" "To a Snail" and "To a Steam-roller." Reprinted with the permission of Simon & Schuster from *The Collected Poems of Marianne Moore*. Copyright © 1935 by Marianne Moore, renewed 1963 by Marianne Moore and T. S. Eliot.

Thylias Moss, "Lunch Counter Freedom" from *Small Congregations*. Copyright © 1983, 1990, 1991, 1993 by Thylias Moss. First published by The Ecco Press in 1993.

David Mura, "An Argument: On 1942" from *After We Lost Our Way* (E. P. Dutton) © 1989. Reprinted by permission of the author.

Frank O'Hara, "Ave Maria" from *The Selected Poems of Frank O'Hara* © 1974. Reprinted by permission of CityLights. "Why I Am Not a Painter" from *Collected Poems* by Frank O'Hara. Copyright © 1958 by Maureen Granville-Smith, Administratrix of the Estate of Frank O'Hara. Reprinted by permission of Alfred A Knopf Inc.

Simon J. Ortiz, "Bend in the River" from *Going for the Rain* © 1976. Reprinted by permission of the author.

Wilfred Owen, "Anthem for Doomed Youth," "Dulce Et Decorum Est," and "The Disabled" from *The Collected Poems of Wilfred Owen*. Copyright © 1963 by Chatto & Windus, Ltd. Reprinted by permission of New Directions Publishing Corp.

Carl Phillips, "Africa Says" and "Passing" from *In the Blood* by Carl Phillips. Copyright 1992 by Carl Phillips. Reprinted with the permission of Northeastern University Press.

Sylvia Plath, "Daddy," "Edge," "Lady Lazarus," "Morning Song," and "The Applicant" from *Ariel* by Sylvia Plath. Copyright © 1963 by Ted Hughes. Copyright renewed. Reprinted by permission of HarperCollins Publishers Inc. and Faber & Faber, Inc. "Blackberrying" from *Crossing the Water* by Sylvia Plath. Copyright © 1962 by Ted Hughes. Copyright renewed. This poem originally appeared in *Uncollected Poems,* Turret Books, London, and in the *Hudson Review*. Reprinted by permission of HarperCollins Publisher, Inc. and Faber & Faber Limited.

Ezra Pound, "In a Station of the Metro," "The Garden," and "The River Merchant's Wife: A Letter" from *Personae*. Copyright © 1926 by Ezra Pound. Reprinted by permission of New Direction Publishing Corp.

Henry Reed, "The Naming of Parts" is reprinted from *Henry Reed's Collected Poems,* edited by Jon Stallworthy (1991), by permission of Oxford University Press.

Adrienne Rich, "Diving into the Wreck," "Mother-in-Law," "Necessities of Life," "Prospective Immigrants Please Note," "Snapshots of a Daughter-in-Law," and "The Middle-Aged" reprinted from *Collected Early Poems: 1950–1970* by Adrienne Rich, by permission of the author and W. W. Norton & Company, Inc. Copyright © 1993 by Adrienne Rich. Copright © 1967, 1963, 1962, 1961, 1960, 1959, 1958, 1957, 1956, 1955, 1954, 1953, 1952, 1951 by Adrienne Rich. Copyright © 1984, 1975, 1971, 1969, 1966 by W. W. Norton & Company, Inc.

Alberto Ríos, "Teodoro Luna's Two Kisses" and "Mi Abuelo" from *Teodoro Luna's Two Kisses* by Alberto Rios. Copyright © 1990 by Alberto Rios. Reprinted by permission of W. W. Norton & Company, Inc.

Edwin Arlington Robinson, "Eros Turannos," "New England," and "Richard Cory." Reprinted with the permission of Simon & Schuster from *The Collected Poems of Edward Arlington Robinson*. Copyright © 1925 by Edward Arlington Robinson, renewed 1953 by Rugh Nivison and Barbara R. Holt.

Theodore Roethke, "My Papa's Waltz" copyright 1942 by Hearst Magazines Inc. "The Waking" copyright 1953 by Theodore Roethke. "Elegy for Jane," copyright 1950 by Theordore Roethke. Poems from *The Collected Poems of Theodore Roethke* by Theodore Roethke. Used by permission of Doubleday, a division of Bantam Doubleday Dell Publishing Group, Inc.

Carl Sandburg, "Grass" from *Cornhuskers* by Carl Sandburg, copyright 1918 by Holt, Rinehart & Winston, Inc. and renewed 1946 by Carl Sandburg. Reprinted by permission of Harcourt Brace & Company.

Anne Sexton, "Her Kind" from *To Bedlam and Part Way Back*. Copyright © 1960 by Anne Sexton, renewed 1988 by Linda G. Sexton. Reprinted by permission of Houghton Mifflin Co. All rights reserved. "Snow White and the Seven Dwarfs" from *Transformations*. Copyright © 1971 by Anne Sexton. Reprinted by permission of Houghton Mifflin Co. All rights reserved.

Leslie Marmon Silko, "Prayer to the Pacific." Copyright © 1981 by Leslie Marmon Silko, published by Seaver Books, New York, New York.

Charles Simic, "Charon's Cosmology" from *Charon's Cosmology,* copyright © 1977 by Charles Simic. "Fork" from *Dismantling the Silence*, copyright © 1971 by Charles Simic. Reprinted by permission of George Braziller, Inc. "Old Couple" from *Weather Forecast for Utopia and the Vicinity* © 1983. Reprinted with the permission of Station Hill Press.

Dave Smith, "On a Field Trip at Fredericksburg" and "The Spring Poem" © 1971–76 by Dave Smith. Used with the permission of the author and of the University of Illinois Press.

Stevie Smith, "Not Waving but Drowning" and "Pretty" from *Collected Poems of Stevie Smith*. Copyright © 1972 by Stevie Smith. Reprinted by permission of New Directions Publishing Corp.

Gary Snyder, "Axe Handles," "How Poetry Comes to Me," and "Riprap" from *No Nature: New and Selected Poems* by Gary Snyder. Copyright © 1992 by Gary Snyder. Reprinted by permission of Pantheon Books, a division of Random House, Inc.

Wallace Stevens, "Anecdote of the Jar," "Sunday Morning," "The Emperor of Ice Cream," " The Idea of Order at Key West," "The Planet on the Table," "The Snow Man," and "Thirteen Ways of Looking at a Blackbird" from *Collected Poems* by Wallace Stevens. Copyright 1923 and renewed 1951 by Wallace Stevens. Reprinted by permission of Alfred A. Knopf, Inc.

Mark Strand, "Courtship" and "Keeping Things Whole" from *Selected Poems* by Mark Strand. Copyright © 1979, 1980 by Mark Strand. Reprinted by permission of Alfred A. Knopf, Inc.

Dylan Thomas, "Do Not Go Gentle Into That Good Night" and "Fern Hill" from *The Poems of Dylan Thomas*. Copyright © 1952 by Dylan Thomas. Reprinted by permission of New Directions Publishing Corp. "In My Craft or Sullen Art" from *The Poems of Dylan Thomas*. Copyright © 1946 by New Directions Publishing Corp. Reprinted by permission of New Directions Publishing Corp.

Derek Walcott, "Ruins of a Great House," "The Season of Phantasmal Peace," and "The Gulf" from *Collected Poems 1948–1984* (Farrar, Straus & Giroux, 1986). Reprinted with permission of Farrar, Straus & Giroux, Inc.

Rosanna Warren, "In Creve Coeur, Missouri" from *Stained Glass* by Rosanna Warren. Copyright © 1993 by Rosanna Warren. Reprinted by permission of W. W. Norton & Company, Inc.

Michael Weaver, "The Picnic, an Homage to Civil Rights." First published in *Callaloo Magazine*. Reprinted by permission of the Johns Hopkins University Press.

James Welch, "Harlem, Montana: Just Off the Reservation" and "The Man from Washington" are reprinted from *Riding the Earthboy 40* by James Welch, Copyright 1971, 1976, and 1990 by James Welch. Reprinted by permission of Confluence Press at Lewis-Clark State College, Lewiston, Idaho.

Richard Wilbur, "Cottage Street, 1953" from *The Mind-Reader,* copyright © 1972 by Richard Wilbur, reprinted by permission of Harcourt Brace & Company. "The Writer" from *The Mind-Reader,* copyright © 1971 by Richard Wilbur, reprinted by permission of Harcourt Brace & Company.

William Carlos Williams, "This Is Just To Say," "The Dance, "To Elsie," "Poem," "The Raper from Passenack," and "Spring and All" from *Collected Poems: 1909–1939*, Volume I. Copyright © 1938, 1944, 1945 by New Directions Publishing Corp. Reprinted by permission of New Directions Publishing Corp. "Landscape with the Fall of Icarus" from *Collected Poems: 1939–1962*, Volume II. Copyright © 1962 by William Carlos Williams. Reprinted by permission of New Directions Publishing Corp

Charles Wright, "Laguna Blues" and "Self-Portrait" from *The World of the Ten Thousand Things: Poems 1980–1990* by Charles Wright. Copyright © 1990. Reprinted with permission of Farrar, Straus & Giroux, Inc.

James Wright, "A Blessing" and "Small Frogs Killed on the Highway" from *Collected Poems* by James Wright © 1969. Reprinted by permission of Farrar, Straus & Giroux, Inc.

William Butler Yeats, "Among School Children," "An Irish Airman Foresees His Death," " Crazy Jane Talks with the Bishop," "Down by the Salley Gardens," "Easter 1916," "Leda and the Swan," "Meru," "Sailing to Byzantium," "The Lake Isle of Innisfree," "The Second Coming," and "The Wild Swans at Coole" reprinted by permission of Simon & Schuster from *The Poems of W. B. Yeats: A New Edition*, edited by Richard J. Finneran. Copyright 1934 by Macmillan Publishing Company, renewed 1962 by Bertha Georgie Yeats.

Index of Terms

627

Index of First Lines

Index of Authors & Titles

Chronological Index